CONSCIOUSNESS
INTEGRATING EASTERN AND WESTERN PERSPECTIVES

Consciousness
Integrating Eastern and Western Perspectives

Emeritus Editors

PREM SARAN SATSANGI

STUART HAMEROFF

New Age Books

New Delhi (India)

CONSCIOUSNESS
INTEGRATING EASTERN AND WESTERN PERSPECTIVE

ISBN: 978-81-7822-493-0

First Indian Edition: Delhi, **2016**

NEW AGE BOOKS
A-44 Naraina Industrial Area, Phase-I
New Delhi (India)-110 028
E-mail: nab@newagebooksindia.com
Website: www.newagebooksindia.com

Library of Congress Cataloging-in-Publication Data
Satsangi, Prem Saran and Hameroff, Stuart
ISBN 978-81-7822-493-0
Includes foreword, appendix.
Spirituality

Printed and published by
RP Jain for NAB Printing Unit
A-44, Naraina Industrial Area
Phase-I, New Delhi-110 028. India

Dedicated in all humility and gratefulness
with all love and devotion

to the cherished memories of
our continuing "Guru"—Mentor, Super Role Model and Guide

Most Revered Dr. Makund Behari Lal Sahab
D.Sc. (Lucknow), D.Sc. (Edinburgh)
(1907-2002)

The August Founder of Dayalbagh Educational Institute
and
Seventh Revered Leader of the Radhasoami Faith

Highest of the High, the Noblest of the Noble
the Great Inspirer of noble endeavour in realms of spirituality
and Fountainhead of all consciousness in the cosmos

in the Centenary Year of the
Foundation of Education in Dayalbagh

May this humble effort carry His Message all over the Universe
and bring light and cheer to all living beings everywhere !!

CONSCIOUSNESS
INTEGRATING EASTERN AND WESTERN PERSPECTIVES

Professor Prem Saran Satsangi

B.Sc. Engg. (Banaras Hindu University)
M.S. (Michigan State University)
Ph.D. (University of Waterloo)

Chairman, Advisory Committee on Education
Dayalbagh Educational Institutions
Dayalbagh, Agra INDIA

FOREWORD

Almost five years back, when I had my first meeting with Prof. Stuart Hameroff, the Emeritus Editor from the West, at the Quantum-Nano School QANSAS in December 2011 at the newly inaugurated Centre for Consciousness Studies at Dayalbagh Educational Institute (DEI), a few could have envisioned the rich and broad-based relationship that has since flourished among leading institutions involved in consciousness studies in the east and the west, who have gone on to jointly conduct five Integrated East-West Forums from 2012 to 2016 at the TSC-series of conferences annually organized with Prof. Stuart Hameroff as the Chair and Chief Organizer. Prof. Hameroff has been a regular visitor to Dayalbagh, actively taking part in organization at DEI of TSC 2013 (Twentieth Conference on Toward a Science of Consciousness) in March 2013 and QANSAS 2013 in December 2013 where he jointly offered a Workshop on the Orchestrated Objective Reduction (Orch-OR) Theory of Consciousness with Sir Roger Penrose, the leading mathematical theorist and Prof. Anirban Bandyopadhyay, the leading experimentalist in the field. I had the pleasure of reciprocating his regular visits to DEI by visiting Tucson, Arizona in the heart of the American west in April 2016 at his cordial and hence compelling invitation and addressed the Integrated East-West Forum in person at the first conference of this series in its new *avatar* as 'The Science of Consciousness' (TSC 2016). It is with a considerable degree of satisfaction and sense of fulfillment that today (5-6 years down the line) there are several able, active and promising researchers in DEI who have earnestly taken up research in Consciousness Studies and related fields such as Quantum-Nano Systems and all Departments of DEI have been involved in this effort which has already met with unprecedented success. I am very pleasantly surprised to find that the research is progressing along very healthy lines and augurs well for promoting Consciousness Studies in true scientific sense as was visualized by Param Guru Maharaj Sahab (the third Revered Leader of Radhasoami Faith) through His 'Discourses on Radhasoami Faith'. Pursuing that line, we are now homing in gradually, but surely, on making an impact on the world community internationally of the true nature of Consciousness in the Universe and this is being done in a scientific manner so that scientists also begin to listen to it.

If I might be permitted to indulge in a bit of nostalgia in respect of the tools and techniques which I have applied over the years to study the consciousness of the sages of the east, I owe my researchability ever since my Ph.D. days at Waterloo from 1966-fall to 1969-summer to the research exposure and opportunities which I found in that lofty institute. Of course, I knew about Waterloo even from earlier days, from fall 1960 in fact, when I had joined Michigan State University as a USAID TCM Scholar, for my Master's degree in Electrical Engineering where Prof H.K. Kesavan used to be a frequent visitor to the system theory group led by Prof. Herman E. Koenig, verily the father of physical system theory. I must confess that West has been the leader in modern thoughts and modern science and that is where I learnt them. In fact, it comes to my mind, that instead of merely meeting under the banner of Integrated East-West Forum, we have to make joint progress and report success, so that inner experience or human experience is accepted as well as the physical outer experience in the macrocosmic world. As I have been steeped in the scientific theories of the west, way back in 1960-61, over the course of the last 55 years or so, I have a clear cut realization that we can meet much greater success if we work in an integrated fashion, rather than wondering whether it is thought from east which the west is being persuaded to pursue as inner experience, because I use the same model building techniques, the same theory building techniques as any physical system theory. If we work cooperatively to integrate eastern perspectives of Vedic-Yogic Meditation (3S's of *Satyam-Shivam-Sundaram*) with western perspectives of systems science (3R's of Reductionism-Repeatability-Refutation), we stand to progress much faster, further and higher in united mode.

Dayalbagh, described as 'a colony of work-a-day mystics' and an 'Indian Utopia' by western authors almost a century back has always impressed visitors from all over the world. In his book, 'A Search in Secret India', Paul Brunton described Sir Sahabji Maharaj, the founder of Dayalbagh and fifth Revered Leader of Radhasoami Faith as "Master of over one hundred thousand people, who practise a mysterious form of yoga; prime organizer of the multifarious and materialistic activities which seethe around me in Dayalbagh; taken all in all, I write Him down as a brilliant and breath-taking man. Nowhere in India, nowhere in the entire world, may I expect to meet His like again." Similar views are echoed by hundreds of scientists from all corners of the world who have visited Dayalbagh in the last decade. They carry the lasting impression of Dayalbagh as an "environment where consciousness and spirituality are taken as primary and an example of how purity could spread beyond race, religion and become a global language of love." Several of them are contributing authors to this edited volume and describe Dayalbagh as "possessing hospitality and human touch in every little behaviour combined with professional excellence as a resounding expression of rooting in the Spirit. This is an example of the Divine Materialism which is not a mouthful word but a Reality for you all. Salute to this rare evolutionary leap from *homo sapiens* to *homo spiritualis!*"

You should go on moving forward with greater speed. People will be influenced by your ideals and way of life and proclaim in the same way by expressing freely that evolution of *homo spiritualis* is taking place. The purport of their saying *homo spiritualis* was the same as that of the "Superman" referred to by Sir Sahabji Maharaj.

The stupendous integration in this edited volume brings together the leading lights of consciousness studies from the east and the west and is a milestone in our integration efforts.

I close this Foreword with a personal sense of happiness and satisfaction in partnering the research endeavour of authors in this edited volume in offering a thematic introduction and extending graph-theoretic system modelling to modelling microtubules in the human brain and n-qudit (odd prime based higher order quantum states) contextuality based quantum teleportation and beyond.

I wish the book the great success it deserves and wish you Godspeed in your exciting venture of Mission Consciousness.

Dayalbagh, Agra — PREM SARAN SATSANGI

PREFACE

"Oh, East is East and West is West, and never the twain shall meet,
Till Earth and Sky stand presently at God's great Judgment Seat;
But there is neither East nor West, Border, Nor Breed, nor Birth,
When two strong men stand face to face,
though they come from the ends of the earth!"
(Rudyard Kipling (1889) : The Ballad of East and West)

The book '*Consciousness : Integrating Eastern and Western Perspectives*' is the outcome of the successful organization of the Twentieth Conference on 'Toward a Science of Consciousness' (TSC 2013) at Dayalbagh Educational Institute (DEI), Agra, India in March 2013. Soon after the event, Prof. Stuart Hameroff, Director, Centre for Consciousness Studies, The University of Arizona, Tucson, Arizona – the chief-architect of the TSC-series of events, spontaneously acknowledged as follows : "The conference (TSC-2013) was a great success and accomplishment. Congratulations! The confluence of Eastern spiritual philosophy, and quantum cognition, biology, physics and cosmology is the best chance to understand the science of consciousness. Your conference will be remembered as the time / place where it all started to come together . . ". The spontaneous acknowledgements suggested that perhaps we were very well poised towards compiling a unique book on *Consciousness : Integrating Eastern and Western Perspectives.*

This unique volume brings together western and eastern perspectives on consciousness with essays from philosophers and scientists organized in four sections which emphasize different aspects of these perspectives. The overarching aim of this book is to provide direction toward integrating Eastern philosophical and religious practice with philosophies and sciences of Western culture, an aim that could be pivotal in understanding consciousness and its place in nature. It begins with a thematic introduction (Section I), followed by sections on Western perspectives (Section II), Eastern perspectives (Section III), and their integration (Section IV). The aim of this book is both exciting and timely because its authors include Eastern and Western philosophers and scientists who have given considerable thought as to how an understanding of consciousness might take place. We are in the dawn of an age wherein new knowledge of physical, biological, and psychological aspects of nature is being brought to bear on the mystery of consciousness. This "new" knowledge also relates to spiritual and philosophical traditions that have existed for centuries. Integration of these sources not only could lead to a much deeper understanding of consciousness, but also to a basis for improving the human condition. To set the background for describing this project, we begin with the general distinctions between the contributions of Eastern and Western philosophy and science. Eastern and Western viewpoints differ in the schools from which they were derived, their main principles, and the ways in which the truth is discovered.

A unifying approach is adopted to the study of consciousness, integrating the wisdom of the sages of the east, and the scientists of the west. To our knowledge, there exists no prior effort at this scale, to bridge the gap between the East and the West. The book adopts the blue-ocean strategy in assigning uncontested space to all stake holders in Science and Spirituality making competition irrelevant and invoking cooperation thereby enabling us to venture into areas hitherto untouched by existing published works on consciousness.

The title '*Consciousness : Integrating Eastern and Western Perspectives*' was finalized on the basis of opinion poll conducted among editors of the proposed book. The book-project, representing a wide spectrum synthesis of the Eastern and Western approaches on consciousness, has attracted scientists and philosophers of tall standing at the global level. The book chapters, while bringing out the best of the authors in their own discipline, are unitary in the spirit of integrating eastern and western perspectives of consciousness.

Eastern schools are mainly derived from the spiritual traditions of Buddhism, Confucianism, Hinduism, Yoga, Islam, Taoism, and Zen. Commonalities among these traditions include emphasis on the "inner" world, a sense of cosmological unity, and an aim of self-liberation. Liberation from a false sense of oneself is based on finding the true "I" within a higher state of consciousness and being. Western schools are derived from philosophies that support a scientific method that is based on logic, empirical strategies for obtaining knowledge, and rational discourse. Much of the emphasis of Western science is on an external viewpoint of phenomena, unlike the Eastern emphasis on an "inner" world. As an example, Western psychology of the twentieth century was dominated by behaviorism, a scientific doctrine in which only overt behaviors constituted both independent and dependent variables of studies; mental constructs that pertained to content of inner experience were mostly avoided. Eastern and Western philosophical principles also differ in their metaphysical emphasis. Eastern principles emphasize cosmological unity (e.g., the interconnectedness of all events), a higher reality that is beyond realities that immediately surround us, and in the case of Hinduism, a circular view of the universe based on the idea of eternal recurrence. In contrast, Western philosophical principles give greater emphasis to individuals, either as ends in themselves or as a part of a divine plan or greater good. Given these differences in principles, it is understandable that their methods of discovering the truth would differ. Thus, Eastern methods include searching inside oneself, through different forms of meditation and righteous living. Western methods also include observations, mainly from an external viewpoint, and they can occur with or without experimental control. Observations can be subjected to hypothesis testing and inferential analyses to arrive at explanations and theories.

At the vanguard of this integration effort are the Emeritus Editors from the East and the West. The Emeritus Editor from the East is Revered Prof. Prem Saran Satsangi, the Eighth Revered Leader of the Radhasoami Faith (or Eastern Religious Philosophy of Saints) – embodying the logic of a modern faith – who has studied and researched widely in the modern systems science of the West over a period spanning a little more than the last half a century. Accordingly, Revered Prof. Satsangi presents the cosmology of consciousness from the twin vantage points of Radhasoami Faith and Physical System Theory Modelling Framework. The unique underlying spiritual systems modelling framework inspires a natural flow of hypotheses for scientific testing right from early stages of research on consciousness integrating Eastern and Western perspectives. Radhasoami Faith is consistent with all the extant religions in the world (including Christianity, Islam, Buddhism, Jainism, Sufism and Religious Philosophy of Vedas, Upanishads and Gita). He also presents Cosmic Consciousness Hierarchization comprehensively, bridging eastern and western analytical, experimental and experiential approaches. It is supported by study of human consciousness as a surrogate of macrocosmic consciousness. His research group has taken a step forward to generalize qudits (odd-prime based quantum states) to higher and higher dimensions which could almost tend to infinity, and thus bring us to the threshold of being face to face mathematically in abstract terms with the ultimate source of consciousness in abstraction. This opens up the immense possibility of going far beyond the presently obtained highest dimension 10 of strings of the M-theory group of models.

Prof. Stuart Hameroff, the illustrious Emeritus Editor from the West, in the concluding Chapter of the section on Western Perspectives, reviews the currently leading "Orch OR theory" for consciousness in the Universe in the light of criticisms and developments in quantum biology, neuroscience, physics and cosmology. Western philosophy and mainstream science consider consciousness to be computational, epiphenomenal, acausal and illusory, whereas Eastern philosophical and quantum physical system approaches consider consciousness to be an intrinsic feature of the universe, playing an active role. But which specific feature of the universe entails consciousness? Sir Roger Penrose proposed consciousness results from self-collapse of the quantum wavefunction by 'objective reduction' ('OR'), a process in the basic structure of spacetime geometry. The Penrose-Hameroff 'Orch OR' theory further suggests OR events in cytoskeletal microtubules within brain neurons are 'orchestrated' by inputs, memory and vibrational resonances, and terminate by 'orchestrated OR' to give meaningful conscious moments. If so, consciousness as an intrinsic feature of the universe may have prompted the origin of life and driven its evolution, and perhaps that of the universe itself. In the context of the 'anthropic principle', which considers the extraordinary 'fine tuning' in the various physical constants enabling life and consciousness in the universe, Prof. Hameroff suggests that the constants may mutate and evolve over aeons to optimize consciousness, that, in some sense, consciousness is guiding the universe.

It is becoming apparent that the understanding of consciousness can no longer ignore either Eastern or Western perspectives or their methods. Observing consciousness requires that we directly observe *what* is in our experience and *how* we are experiencing. In other words, we need an experiential science that includes searching inwardly. Ordinary and "higher" states of consciousness, emotional feelings, and different forms of thinking have embedded dimensions and common meanings or factors, just as phenomena of the physical world have factors, dimensions and overall structures. What may be less appreciated and not well understood is that we not only can *observe* common dimensions and factors within our inner experiences, but we can also *measure* them, as will be explained in some of the chapters of this book. If that is the case, then it may be possible to interface sciences of inner experience with practices of the natural sciences. To take just one example, a background state of consciousness, such as hypnotic state, contains dimensions of being absorbed in a few targets of attention, a suspension of usual orientation toward time, place, and sense of self, and a sense of phenomena happening by themselves—automaticity. These dimensions can be scaled, measured, and interrelated in such a way as to provide a qualitative and quantitative map of this type of background conscious state. This map can then be interfaced with neuroimaging to discover some of the material causes and/or correlates of this type of experience. This approach combines the methods of the East (inner noticing) with those of the west (scaling, experimental control, hypothesis testing, and the formation of theories). This same approach might be applied to both ordinary and extraordinary states of consciousness. This book provides discussions from different perspectives as to how these stages of discovery can be interfaced.

Eastern religious and philosophical systems and the scientific approaches and methodologies of the West can be integrated. To begin this integration, a subject matter that provides a common ground is needed. This common ground can be based on the exploration and understanding of direct human experience. East and West offer differing perspectives related to these areas. Through an *experiential approach and method* we can begin to see how these apparently different perspectives can be integrated. From an Eastern perspective, the inner viewpoint is emphasized and self relates to a sense of *presence* or *higher self and interconnectedness.* Oneness forms the basis of reality. From a Western perspective, the outer viewpoint is emphasized and self is equated with a unique identity (as designated by one's name) as well as personal history and individuality. Within this Western perspective, separate identities are part of the nature and fabric of reality. However, from the perspective of *human experience,* both inner and outer viewpoints exist. An example would be the experience of being aware from an embodied inner viewpoint and the experience of being aware and observed by something Higher from an outer viewpoint. It is also clear that we can experience a concrete defined sense of ourselves in the world as well as a higher sense of self or presence. Finally, through being aware, we can experience ourselves as differentiated but not separate. Individuals then become interconnected and part of the whole. From a quantitative perspective one could measure how close or far one feels from oneness. Still another example could be a measure of the strength of clarity of one's self-boundaries in relation to others. Both qualitative and quantitative studies of the meaning of consciousness as well as specific aspects of consciousness such as those mentioned above can be effectively researched using both the qualitative and quantitative methods of an experiential approach that is outlined in the book *Inner Experience and Neuroscience* (MIT Press, 2012) by Price and Barrell. Integration of the systems of the East and methodologies of the West are possible when we base our research on a common ground, that is, a science of human experience.

While the science of consciousness in ancient India as given in Vedas and Upanishads dates back to second millennia B.C.; it is over the past fifty years or so that there has been considerable interest in the modern science in the West, in terms of cognitive psychology and neuro-science (neuro-physiology or neuro-medicine) in studying the consciousness. The most radical departure from classical physics based on Newtonian mechanics instituted by the founders of quantum mechanics was the introduction of human consciousness into the dynamical and computational machinery. However, the quantum generalization of the classical mechanical laws proposed by Heisenberg and his colleagues in the Copenhagen Interpretation of Quantum Theory as propounded by Niels Bohr and others do not generate by themselves a dynamically complete deterministic physical theory free from any causal gap. There is a growing trend toward interdisciplinary investigation, as evidenced by the emergence of cognitive science and neuro-science as coherent fields. Another prominent contribution is the development of neuro-imaging techniques - including, electro-magnetic, physiological methods such as Magneto-Encephalo-Graphy (MEG), and functional Magnetic Resonance Imaging (fMRI), which make it possible to treat consciousness in a rigorous and scientifically respectable fashion. With the currently considerable interest in exploring the neural-correlates of consciousness, there is also a growing realization that it will not be possible to make serious headway in understanding consciousness without confronting the issue of how to acquire more precise descriptive first person reports about subjective experience. Hence, the emerging Gestalt or systems approach for integrating Eastern and Western Perspectives of consciousness.

The western concept suggests that consciousness originates in matter, and the eastern concept, especially the one born in India, suggests that it is a dance of matter and energy together. Surprisingly, both the eastern and the western concepts were born more than 5000 years before and evolved into two distinct streams of science, arts, philosophy and religion. It should be noted that the distinction between east and the west have long since disappeared and many in the west have developed a firm belief in the matter-energy duality concept. Still, the fundamental difference exists. No book has been written until now to identify the bridging between the east and the west. The impact of this book would be manifold as the evolution of science, math and religion have been very distinct in the east and in the west. Since twenty first century is the century of brain science, we feel that while constructing this bridge, a solution would come up at the very fundamental level which would provide a new light in every single aspect of human civilization.

In best-sellers like *Rhythms of the Brain* (Oxford, 2006), Gyorgy Buzsaki concludes that it is a truism that if we want to understand the hard and complex problem of consciousness, we need to build a model for it. Human brain is the most complicated machinery ever created by Nature. Seemingly unlikely sources such as fractals and internet communication have provided novel clues for understanding neuronal networks. However, externalized information is only as useful as its accessibility. Currently existing best-available search engines, such as Google and Yahoo, are very inefficient compared to the brain's search strategies to retrieve episodic information because neuronal networks utilize fundamentally different strategies for reconstruction of events and stories from fragments than do search-engines. In *How to Build a Brain, A Neural Architecture for Biological Cognition* (Oxford, 2013), Chris Eliasmith says that one goal of researchers in neuro-science, psychology and artificial intelligence is to build theoretical models that are able to explain the flexibility and adaptiveness of biological systems. A special feature of the variety of wide-range of biologically constrained perceptual, cognitive and motor models illustrated in the foregoing book is that these models are not introduced as independent considerations of brain-functions by Eliasmith but instead integrated to give rise to what is currently perhaps the world's largest functional brain model consisting of 2.5 million neurons. In *Life on the Edge : The Coming of Age of Quantum Biology* (Bantam Press, 2014), Khalili and McFadden suggest that life is the most extraordinary phenomenon in the known universe but its working is not known much. Even in the age of cloning and synthetic biology, the remarkable truth remains that nobody has ever made anything living entirely out of dead material. Life remains the only way to make life and we seem to be missing a vital ingredient in its creation. Similarly, in *Quantum Biology : The New Science of How the Mind and the Brain Relate* (Prometheus Books, 2014), W.R. Klemm, a leading neuroscientist focuses on how mind emerges from nerve-impulse patterns in the densely packed neural circuits that make up most of the brain, suggesting that the conscious mind can be viewed as a sort of neural-activity-based avatar. As an entity in its own right, mind on the conscious level can act autonomously, shaping the brain that sustains it through its values, interests, goals, plans, and interactions with the world. Thus, in a very literal sense, we become what we think.

There are a number of existing texts dealing with Vedic literature and Gita. The emphasis on science of consciousness in Radhasoami Faith in some chapters is due to the fact that being consistent with the existing religious orders, it takes us beyond all of them. No new point would be served in dwelling yet again on the Vedic or other eastern literature, thus an attempt is being made to move beyond these. The emphasis on sharable spiritual experiences mentioned by Price and Barrell in *Inner Experience and Neuroscience* (MIT Press, 2012) is also emphasized in science of consciousness in Radhasoami Faith and the book chapters based on this Faith are based on experiential studies as well as scientific study of consciousness. This is perhaps the first attempt on integration of experiential and scientific approaches to study of consciousness. It is important to mention that there is a certain esoteric language which is used in religious and spiritual literature and that is meant for the common man. It hides the real abstraction, it does not talk about scientific knowledge which is for the elite class, viz. scientists, who can understand, but the religion is open to common man, so that is why religion and spirituality get confounded. It is because of the esoteric language which is used, which convinces the common man much more who are impelled by devotion that this has been so, so far, but these are all scientific phenomena. The esoteric language for all purpose hides the true scientific elitist interpretation and gives the interpretation that a common man can understand. This is the reason why people confuse that this is not scientific. The abstract source is one and the same.

The author of one of the recent best-sellers, *Our Mathematical Universe* (Penguin Books UK, 2015), Max Tegmark, Professor of Physics at MIT is like us, in the quest for the ultimate nature of reality. We are trying to explore ultimate nature of reality from two ends, from the ends of science as well as inner or human experience. So we have an edge over such physicists, who look at it only from the end of physical science. They do not have the practice and its force behind them. We believe in the dictum that an ounce of practice goes much farther than tons of precept, so that is what is in fact happening in the world today. There are tons and tons of precepts given by physicists and other scientists, cosmologists, microbiologists and so on, but they are not privileged to have the real practical experience of what this inner reality is, what the human experience is like. It is mathematics and its abstractions which will lead scientists to the ultimate reality and this is a very good evidence of such effort but they are still groping in the dark because they lack this inner or human experience in not practising themselves so that they could perceive the reality for themselves, "sense" the reality, or in fact see, hear, sense, feel, perceive, such that reality in the real meaning would open up to them. Fortunately, this book has brought together a confluence of people with the latest scientific techniques as well as people who are reinforced with this inner force of "ultimate" reality.

While the book project has taken its own time to come to fruition, it was worth the wait as developments in the ensuing years, especially at the Integrated East-West Forums organized at TSC conferences in the intervening years - TSC 2014 at Tucson, TSC 2015 at Helsinki and TSC 2016, again at Tucson in the first avatar of this conference series now rechristened as 'The Science of Consciousness' have been included. In fact, to apprise the readers about the latest debates as well as emerging consensus in the field, the book includes appendices on the intensive Panel Discussion on the same topic as the book title at the latest TSC 2016 conference along with a brief account of the fast-paced developments leading to this landmark meet, which provides a unique glimpse into the esoteric inner reality by way of real-life events.

- Editors

Contents

APPENDICES

I

Consciousness - Thematic Introduction

Chapter 1

Towards Integrating Eastern Arts and Philosophy of Consciousness and Western Perspectives of Science
(Rhythms of Macrocosmic Universe and Human Microcosm : Consciousness Systemology Perspective)

PREM SARAN SATSANGI

Leader of Radhasoami Faith, Dayalbagh
Chairman, Advisory Committee on Education
Dayalbagh Educational Institutions, Dayalbagh, Agra, India

1. INTRODUCTION

This Chapter presents the Cosmology of Consciousness from the twin vantage points of Radhasoami Faith (or Eastern Religion of Saints) and Physical System Theory Modelling Framework (Satsangi 2010, 2015a), on one hand. On the other hand, it briefly describes a comprehensive phenomenology of consciousness as the inner experience for scientific hypothesis-testing with illustrative examples (Satsangi, 2013a).

Radhasoami Faith (or Eastern Religious Philosophy of Saints) is consistent with all the extant religions in the world (including Christianity, Islam, Buddhism, Jainism, Sufism and Religious Philosophy of Vedas, Upanishads and Gita). Radhasoami Faith, founded on the Basant Panchami Day in January, 1861 (more than 155 years ago) provides a holistic Vision of Consciousness (Souvenir, 1961).

We trace back our approach to integrating inner experience with scientific methodology to my first public discourse on the subject (Satsangi, 2003). It may be emphasized that we use one-to-one correspondence with the Physical System Theory in conceptualizing our Spiritual Consciousness System Theory. Physical System Theory Framework (Koenig et. al., 1967) as a scientific methodology has its fundamental axiom together with component postulate and system interconnection postulates. Similarly, the proposed Spiritual Consciousness System Theory Framework (Satsangi, 2006b) firmly rests on its comparable Fundamental Axiom of Spiritual Consciousness and comparable postulates (viz. (1) Macrocosm-Microcosm Consciousness Interaction Postulate and (2) Universal Consciousness Realization Postulate). It might be recalled that in any scientific methodology, it is the verification of the theoretical model predictions which would decide whether the proposed theory would continue to hold or not.

We acknowledge considerable rapport and support derived from the seminal work of Price and Barrell (Price and Barrell, 2012). We fully endorse them in their use of four-fold paradigms for integrating inner experience with scientific methodology and concede their assertion that ordinarily questions, not hypotheses may guide the first three stages of observing, reporting and understanding from the first person perspective of co-investigators and it is not necessary to frame the hypotheses in advance but it is through first person account of phenomenology that these hypotheses may be formulated later and tested; and it is the last stage when the scientific methodology is invoked in using psychometric methods and quantitative psychophysics, for hypothesis-testing (Satsangi, 2013).

However, there is a significant way in which our approach contrasts with that of Price and Barrell. Since we have the benefit of scientifically founded conceptual Spiritual Consciousness System Theory Framework based on rich and thorough record of inner experience in Eastern Philosophy with particular reference to Radhasoami Faith (M. Sahab, 2004), it inspires a natural flow of meaningful hypotheses for scientific testing right from early stages of research on consciousness for integrating Eastern and Western perspectives.

Accordingly, we have retained our continuing distinctive hallmark [as elaborated in the companion Chapter on "Cosmic Consciousness Hierarchization : Analytic, Experimental and Experiential Approaches; Power Law of Meditational Consciousness" jointly authored with Dr. Vishal Sahni] of recording indirect scientific measurements of spiritual consciousness (Satsangi and Sahni, 2007, 2008, 2012, 2015) of Dayalbagh Community as neuro-environmental correlates through relevant, repeatable, non-intrusive scientific experiments and enriched our approach very considerably by lately utilizing Superconducting Quantum Interference Devices (SQUIDs) as a very sensitive magnetometer to record MEG (Magneto-Encephelo-Gram) as neuro-correlates in a magnetically shielded chamber during individual meditation and group meditation-cum-prayer sessions (Satsangi and Sahni, 2015).

Furthermore, inspired by recent developments, we have proposed HOT-Consciousness: SCANE Correlates, where HOT-Consciousness stands not for Gennaro's Higher Order Thought (Gennaro, 2012), but Hierarchical Order Transactions of Consciousness and SCANE Correlates stand for Spiritual-Cognitive And Neural-Environmental Correlates. There are encouraging evidences of successfully integrating spiritual phenomenology of consciousness with scientific methodology of hypothesis-testing and verification in a preliminary sense (Satsangi, 2015b).

We recall the following two distinguishing features of Integration :

- The Eastern Philosophical aphorism "*Satyam-Shivam-Sundaram*" (Truth-Knowledge-Beauty) and for that matter its somewhat exalted version "*Sat-Chit-Anand*" (i.e., in other words, Sat (the truth of love or inseparability), Chit (the conscious knowing (the reality of immortal existence)), Anand (Bliss of love (experiencing the joy of unity consciousness))" captures the triad of consciousness of the grand macro/ micro-cosmology ranging from the ephemeral physical / material reality of science of outer experience at the tertiary level, through the semi-abstract (real / abstract) cognitive science (transcendental meditation) of outer-inner experience at the secondary level, to the eternal abstract spiritual science (ultra-transcendental meditation) of ultimate inner experience at the primary level (Satsangi, 2014b).
- Rhythms of Macrocosm in Universe and Human-Microcosm: Consciousness Systemology Perspective (Satsangi, 2015a). The central idea is that system modelling is important for study of consciousness as rhythms or frequencies of oscillation, both in macrocosmic universe as well as in human microcosm (considered to be a perfect analog of macrocosm). We refer to it as O-Theory (Omni-Quantum Theory-based system modelling of consciousness in cosmology).

In conclusion, we want to emphasize the system modelling feature and particularly emphasize the modelling aspects of consciousness viewed from scientific perspective rather than any religious or spiritual perspective. We prefer to refer to this systems modelling theory as a generalization of physical system modelling theory, as omni-quantum theory based system modelling of consciousness in cosmology. It should apply both to individual consciousness at microscopic levels or microcosmic levels as well as the Universal Consciousness at the macrocosmic level. It may be asserted that it is this immutable abstract "omni"-quantum field, arising perhaps from the single ultimate source at the primary level, which is present in each element of space-time of the grand macrocosm whether at the primary level, secondary level or tertiary level.

1.1 CODIFICATION OF ULTIMATE PHENOMENOLOGY OF CONSCIOUSNESS

अथ प्रेमसूत्रं व्याख्यास्यामः। सच्चिदानन्दस्वरूपम् चैतन्यम्।।
(परम गुरु महाराज साहब)

The above is an aphorism of love composed by the Third Revered Leader of Radhasoami Faith, Param Guru Maharaj Sahab (M. Sahab, 1960, 2004). [Other similar aphorisms of love follow] :

परम सत्चित् प्रेमानन्द प्रकाश शब्द अनहद नाद स्वरूपम्।
राधास्वामी ध्वन्यात्मक शब्द धुन आदि अनादि चैतन्यम्।
राधास्वामी सर्वकारणं अतिविख्यातं मूलपरमतत्वं भजे।।

English translation :
We shall now explicate the Aphorisms of Love
Consciousness is of the nature of Truth, Intelligence and Bliss
(Param Guru Maharaj Sahab)

Radhasoami is of the form of Supreme Truth, Intelligence, Love, Bliss, Refulgence, the Original Mystic Name, the Resonating Unstruck Sound, the Beginning of All but Beginningless, Primeval Consciousness:

I adore 'Radhasoami', the Original Cause of everything and the Extremely (Most) Well known Primal Supreme (Truth) Essence.

I believe that this is a codification of the ultimate phenomenology of consciousness in the spiritual sense.

1.2 FOUNDING OF THE RADHASOAMI FAITH ON THE BASANT PANCHAMI DAY IN JANUARY, 1861

Another significant event that needs attention in connection with this chapter on thematic introduction, is founding of the Radhasoami Faith on the Basant Panchami Day in January 1861, a little more than 155 years ago. This was Manifestation of the Supreme Being Almighty Lord Radhasoami in the form of the *Sant Satguru* i.e. Saint True Preceptor or Adept for the redemption of *jivas* i.e. living beings (Mark that it includes all living beings, not just humans). Only the first paragraph as translated from this proclamation is quoted below.

(i) "It is hereby proclaimed for the benefit of "Adhikaris" (fit and willing) that the Supreme Being Almighty Lord Radhasoami, on observing the "Jivas" (Living Beings) undergoing extreme suffering and being subjected to delusion, has Himself assumed the Form of the "Sant" (Saint) "Satguru" (True Guru, i.e. Preceptor / Adept) and manifested on this earth for their redemption and, through His Supreme Grace, explains the secret of His Original Abode and teaches the method of attaining that Abode by means of the "Surat Sabda Marga" (The path which unites "Surat" (Spirit) with the "Shabda" (i.e. spiritual sound). It behoves the "Jivas" (Living Beings) that they should engender within themselves love and faith in His Holy Feet.

Remember that love and faith is all that is being asked for in return. So it is really a Faith which rests on love and that is why we refer to the codification of its ultimate phenomenology, as aphorisms of love. There is second and third operative part of this proclamation too and those interested can certainly look up the Souvenir of Radhasoami Satsang brought out in its centenary celebration in 1961 by Radhasoami Satsang, Dayalbagh (Souvenir, 1961).

2. INTEGRATING PHENOMENOLOGY (INNER EXPERIENCE) WITH THE EPISTEMOLOGY OF NATURAL SCIENCES

I want to emphasize the system modelling perspective and particularly emphasize the modelling aspects of consciousness viewed from scientific perspective rather than any religious or spiritual perspective. I prefer to refer to this systems modelling theory as a generalization of physical system modelling theory, as omni-quantum theory based system modelling of consciousness in cosmology. It should apply both to individual consciousness at microscopic levels or microcosmic levels as well as the Universal Consciousness at the macrocosmic level.

The central idea is that system modelling is important for study of consciousness as rhythms or frequencies of oscillation, both in macrocosmic universe as well as in human microcosm (considered to be a perfect analog of macrocosm). We refer to it as O-Theory (Omni-Quantum Theory-based system modelling of consciousness in cosmology). It may be asserted that it is this immutable abstract "omni"-quantum n-state vector space (much like a generalized n-state Hilbert vector-space) over an appropriate field (e.g. a field of complex numbers), arising perhaps from the single ultimate source at the primary level, which is present in each element of space-time of the grand macrocosm whether at the primary level, secondary level or tertiary level.

The Eastern Philosophical aphorism "*Satyam-Shivam-Sundaram*" and for that matter its somewhat exalted version "*Sat-Chit-Anand*" (i.e., in other words, *Sat* (the truth of love or inseparability), *Chit* (the conscious knowing (the reality of immortal existence)), *Anand* (Bliss of love (experiencing the joy of unity consciousness))" captures the triad of consciousness of the grand macro/ micro-cosmology ranging from the ephemeral physical / material reality of science of outer experience at the tertiary level, through the semi-abstract (real / abstract) cognitive science (transcendental meditation) of outer-inner experience at the secondary level, to the eternal abstract spiritual science (ultra-transcendental meditation) of ultimate inner experience at the primary level (Satsangi, 2014b).

It is "Sat" or "Satyam" or truth of inseparability of the "omni" quantum n-vector space over an appropriate field present in each element of space-time, whether at the tertiary level of ephemeral physical or material reality or at the secondary level of semi-permanent cognitive reality, or at the primary level of eternal abstract spiritual reality from its ultimate immutable single source at the primary level. It is the "Shivam" as knowledge of duality between the semi-permanent mind at the secondary cognitive level of reality with transitory matter at the tertiary physical level of reality. Lastly, it is the "Sundaram" or beauty of the ephemeral physical or real universe at the tertiary level in multiple contexts whether in art (e.g. beauty of a painting / sculpture, or beauty of a musical / literary composition) or in science (e.g. beauty of mathematical equations) which is comparable to the truth of unity at the abstract spiritual primary level or cognitive knowledge of duality between mind and matter at the semi-abstract / real secondary level (Satsangi, 2014b).

Another theme which runs parallel to it is rhythms of macrocosmic universe and human microcosm in the perspective of consciousness as a systemic phenomenon. In fact, it seems increasingly feasible to interpret our search for the most abstract source of everything as a search for the source of the omni-quantum n-vector space over an appropriate field which pervades all the elements of space-time throughout not only the "real" physical world, but also the semi-abstract cognitive world as well as the most abstract spiritual world. This fits in with the philosophy of Radhasoami Faith in that our search is for the most abstract source (Supreme Being). As we reach the most abstract level of this source ($n \rightarrow \infty$), we merge with the Lord God of the Grand Cosmos (Satsangi, 2015a).

Figure 1 is representing Man in this particular framework as consisting of the tertiary outer layer, secondary middle layer and primary innermost layer and it is this primary innermost layer which energizes the secondary level, that is, the spirit is the motive force behind mind and then it is mind at the secondary level which supervises the worldly functions of brain at the tertiary level of real physical world.

At the macrocosmic level, it is a similar picture (Figure 2) except that it is simpler to turn it inside out. The primary layer becomes the outermost layer, the Highest Abode, and so, we put it on the side of infinity, so that you can imagine it to pervade to its infinite dimension. In the human being, it is in the core, the spirit is the core and the rest of it is the cover under which this core appears as human body (with human brain), human mind and the human spirit which is hidden from physical view being an abstract entity. The names given may be esoteric in character, and may represent the philosophy of eastern religion of Saints or Radhasoami Faith philosophy, but that is hardly of any consequence. One could label them, if one so liked, as consciousness levels A, B, C and so forth. So it does not have to be those esoteric names.

Figure 1 : Man as a Microcosm

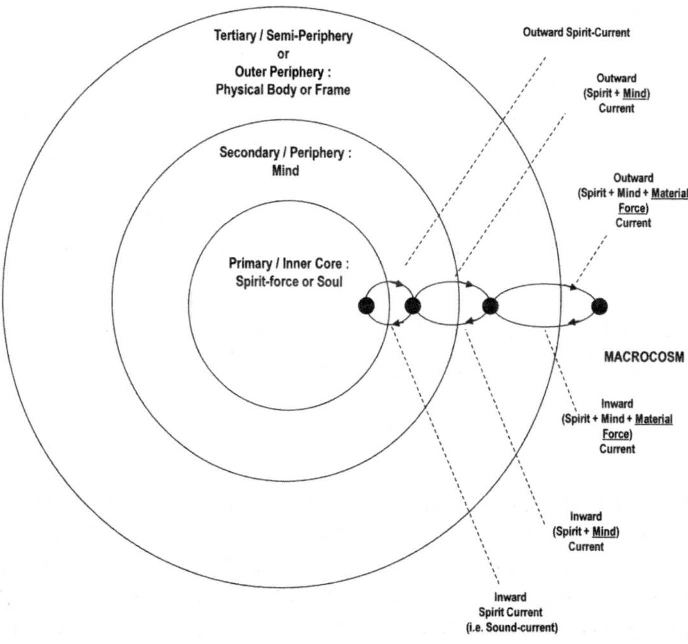

Man as a Microcosm is an open system which has mutual interaction, not only among its three sub-systems pair-wise but also with the Macrocosm or Environment in which it exists (i.e. embedded so to say.)
The macrocosm is an all encompassing completely closed system represented schematically by Figure 2 showing its three sub-systems, viz.,
Primary – Region of the Universal Spirit (or Purely Spiritual Region) or "Nirmal Chetan Desh" including the Supreme Being as the Infinite Reservoir of Spirituality
Secondary – Region of the Universal Mind (or "Brahmanda") or "Nirmal Maya Desh"
Tertiary – Region of the Universal Matter or "Malin Maya Desh"

FIGURE 1
Man as a Microcosm

Figure 2 : Macrocosm (Completely closed system)

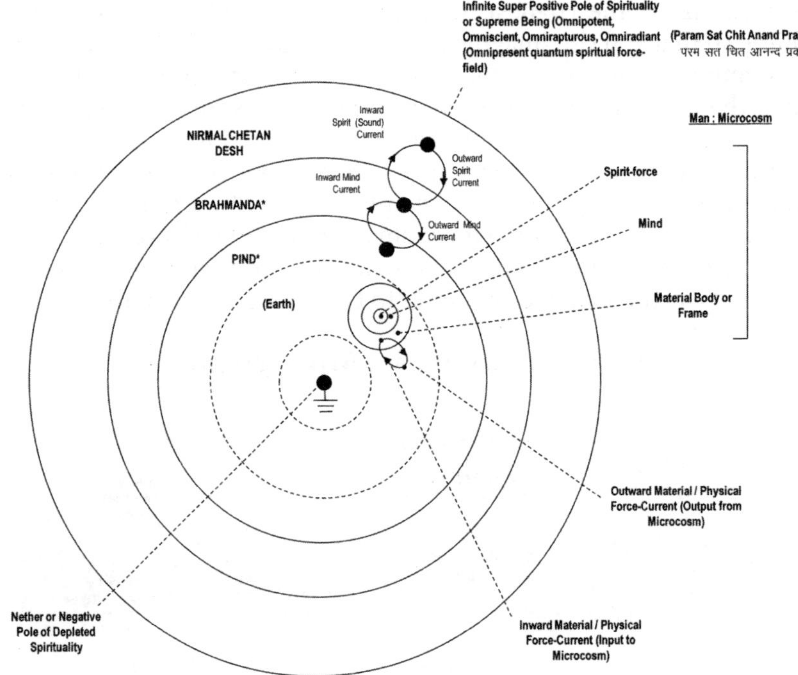

***Notice that reference here generally is to the regions of Brahmanda and Pind as a whole i.e. as the union of all individual Brahma-systems (Brahmandas) and solar systems (Pinds)**

FIGURE 2
Macrocosm (Completely closed system)

This fits in with the Radhasoami philosophy. So we interpret both the grand macrocosmic universe as well as the human being on exactly the same footing. It is as if we are not only interested in networking or having an Internet in the physical world which improves our communication, we are also interested in connecting this up with the Internet among our minds in the Region of Universal Mind. All minds are connected and if you approach them through meditational techniques, then you are able to communicate from one mind to the other, just as you do communicate physically on Internet or social networking sites and things like that.

Similarly, there is this final abstract level of Universal Spirit and spirit forces are also interconnected. The individual spirit forces, in fact, are all part, in a sense, of the all encompassing abstract source or reservoir of all spirit-forces if you wish, but unlike ephemeral particles of the quantum force-field of the physical universe. Notice that the basic distinction at this highest level, is that the fundamental particles are not perishable. Those are immutable ones and they are not subject to birth, death, re-birth or whatever as is a familiar thing in the physical world. We all know that in quantum field theory, the primary thing is the quantum force field and the rest of it, i.e., the various fundamental particles in the physical world are all secondary (being particular excitations) which keep popping in and popping out and accordingly they are ephemeral. In fact, in this context one views even a human being, so far as the body and mind is concerned, as perishable ones and therefore these are like perishable particles of the quantum force field and they appear and disappear from this terra firma and associated region of universal mind.

So far as consciousness is concerned, it is convenient to sub-divide each of these three regions into six levels of consciousness. So, consciousness according to Radhasoami philosophy has eighteen levels, six pertaining to the human body or any physical body for that matter, six pertaining to mind or Universal Mind and similarly six others pertaining to individual spirit or the Universal Spirit. So whether it is at the microcosmic level or the macrocosmic level, we have the same concepts and it is this privileged form of being, as human being, which gives us this unique privilege to be a perfect analog of the macrocosmic universe and therefore, through meditation, we can gain knowledge, we can gain consciousness at multiple levels, i.e. we can gain various shades of truth. All perceptions are reality, however, there are various levels of reality. Relativity Theory of Einstein refers to this relative nature of reality. So as we move to higher abstraction, these realities look different because these so-called realities do not appear to be so real. Accordingly, as we reach the abstract-most entity, that is when we perceive the Ultimate Reality. Otherwise, we have the physical reality of perception of the outer world as an experience, then we have the cognitive reality of perception by the mind which is having communion both with the outer world as well as the inner world being the middle-level mediator, and then finally we have the most abstract entity of spirit forces which only communicate with mind directly, not with the body and so mind is the negotiator both with the spirit, as well as the body. Therefore, one has to take mind along to pursue spirituality. If the mind does not cooperate, any efforts would come to naught and that is so in all endeavours. So unless our mind is there in pursuing the particular activity, we do not succeed in pursuing it well enough. So we need to train the mind and concentrate it when and where we want it to reach higher levels of abstraction.

2.1 O-THEORY (OMNI-QUANTUM THEORY) FOR SPIRITUAL CONSCIOUSNESS SYSTEM MODELLING IN COSMOLOGY

Consciousness is intrinsic to the grand cosmos, both at macrocosmic as well as microcosmic levels. Man, a creation on planet Earth happens to be a perfect microcosm of the macrocosm. Spirit-mind-brain consciousness interactions are at the microcosmic levels analogous to consciousness interactions between Supreme Being (Universal Spirit)-Universal Mind-Physical Universe at the macrocosmic levels.

Fundamental Axiom of Spiritual Consciousness

The fundamental axiom of macrocosmic / microcosmic spiritual consciousness is that the origin of the macrocosm is an infinite spiritual energy source or reservoir known as the Supreme Creator or Being or Super Positive Pole accompanied by the omni-quantum spiritual force-field of consciousness ranging from the Super Positive Pole of full spirituality to the Nether or Negative Pole of depleted spirituality; and each constituent fundamental element of this omni-quantum spiritual force-field, known as the spirit-force of consciousness (monopole), is the one which possesses prime energy and that all other forces (mental or physical) of creation or nature have been evolved by the association of this spirit-force with media (mental or physical) of different kinds (Notice that the concept of "spirit-force" is no more intrinsically mysterious than "mass"). This gives rise to the quantum mind-force field which spans the Region of the Universal Mind and the Physical Universe, on one hand, while the quantum physical force fields – electromagnetic, weak nuclear, strong nuclear and gravitational span the third grand division, viz., the Physical Universe ("*Pind*") of the Macrocosm.

Macrocosm-Microcosm Consciousness Interaction Postulate

Man, a creation on planet Earth (the fourth subdivision from the bottom of the third grand division of macrocosm, represented by g_4 in Figure A) happens to be a perfect microcosm of the macrocosm in the sense that man possesses not only six ganglia (or "*chakras*") for interaction with the macrocosm by making communion with the corresponding six subdivisions of the macrocosmic division of the physical / material region but also six nerve-centres (or "*Kamals*") in the grey matter of the brain for accessing the corresponding six subdivisions of the macrocosmic division or region of Universal Mind as well as six other apertures (or "*Padams*") in the white matter of the brain for communicating with the corresponding six subdivisions of the macrocosmic division of Universal Spirit or purely spiritual regions.

Notice that the degree of spiritual consciousness (or spiritual potential) of the macrocosm, pertaining to its three grand divisions ranging from the purely spiritual region (i.e. the macrocosmic division of the Universal Spirit) through the region (or macrocosmic division) of Universal Mind to the physical / material region (or macrocosmic division) together with their six subdivisions each, varies in descending order of magnitude.

Figure 1 : Man as a Microcosm

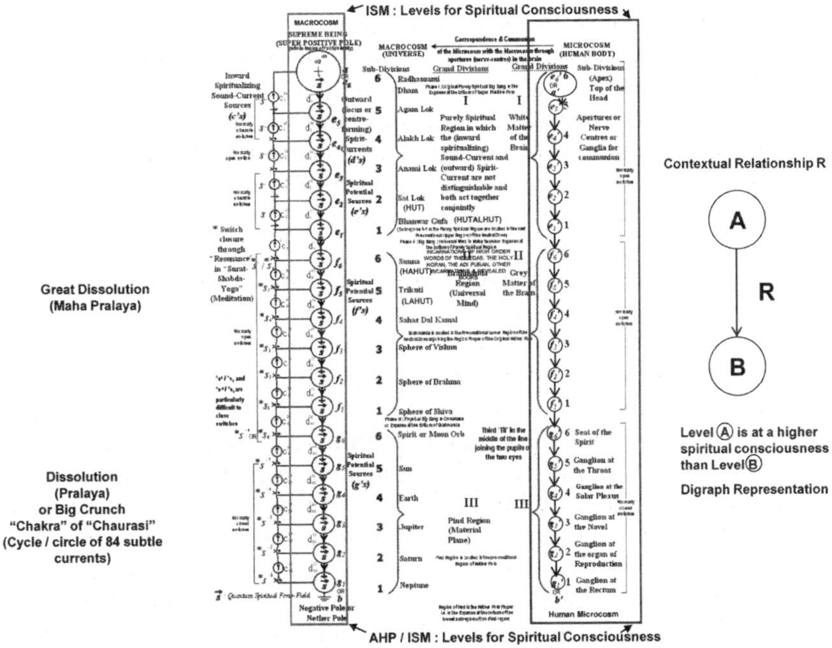

ISM : Levels for Spiritual Consciousness

Great Dissolution (Maha Pralaya)

Dissolution (Pralaya) or Big Crunch "Chakra" of "Chaurasi" (Cycle / circle of 84 subtle currents)

Contextual Relationship R

Level Ⓐ is at a higher spiritual consciousness than Level Ⓑ

Digraph Representation

AHP / ISM : Levels for Spiritual Consciousness

Figure A Schematic : A Rudimentary Modelling Framework for Cosmic Domains

(The entire creation is evolved out of the pre-creational Nether Pole)

The second sub-division sphere of a set of six sub-divisions of each grand-division of Macrocosm or Human-Microcosm is the one which is endowed with generative function : e.g. e_2 (Sat Lok), f_2 (Sphere of Brahma); and g_2' (Man : Ganglion at the organ of reproduction)

FIGURE A

Schematic : A Rudimentary Modelling Framework for Cosmic Domains

Figure A is the conceptual system model that we have, and I have presented it a number of times earlier too (Satsangi 2003 – 2016), but it becomes important to emphasize that you need to know where you are headed for. Your goals have to be clear. Just building hypothesis in dark as Price and Barrell (Price and Barrell, 2012) recommend, I must say, with due respect to them, is groping in the dark, and if you are clear about the phenomenology, why should you grope in the dark. You could build a model for yourself and keeping that model in mind, you could certainly frame hypotheses and test them. If your model fails on the acid test of hypothesis / hypotheses, then you have to reshape the model. But so long as it stands to acid test of hypothesis, it survives. That is the approach we take and this gives us much more speed in preparing hypotheses. Thus we need to know what our conception of reality is like, based on the phenomenology. So spiritual phenomenology is at the centre stage in our scheme of things and according to this, on the left hand side, I have the macrocosmic model of the universe, while on the right hand side, I have the human microcosm. It turns out that according to Eastern Philosophy, the human microcosm is a perfect analog of the macrocosm. That is why, indeed, it is also justified to turn inward as a human being, and learn a lot more about macrocosm than is likely to be known by outer researches through the scientific approach, because no matter how much you try, you are going to be bound by physical reality. You are not going to get beyond physics, you are not going to get into the domain of Universal Mind, or the domain of Universal Spirit which is even further beyond that. Notice that the macrocosmic model that I have in mind has the three Grand Divisions of Creation. It has the largest domain of the Universal Spirit whose source or origin is the one and only Lord God of all Universe. We know this unique entity by the name of Radhasoami. There may be other beliefs and as our model shows, there is not just one centre of consciousness; in fact, in our model building, we have imagined there are 21 such centres of consciousness, or stages of consciousness, through which one can progress, seven each belonging to the three grand divisions of the macrocosm, namely the Region of Universal Spirit, Region of Universal Mind and Region of Universal Matter or Physical Universe. Scientists are by and large confined to the Physical Universe. Psychologists and others get into the domain of Region of Universal Mind also. But there are no so-called scientists looking at the outer world, who have made any worthwhile contributions to Region of Universal Spirit, so it has required the phenomenologists who have turned inwards to disseminate this knowledge about the Region of Universal Spirit, which is beyond the Region of Upanishads also. Upanishads describe the Region of Universal Matter and Universal Mind, but stop at the level of *Para Brahman*, beyond the three *Brahmans*. They do suggest that there is existence of creation beyond this but they do not describe it. So it is this region which the so-called Religion of Saints addresses, and it is the Region of Pure Spiritual phenomena – it is not subject to any change, it is indeed truly eternal. In purely spiritual region, there is no question of birth and re-birth or cycle of birth and death, which, at least the Eastern Philosophy holds, plagues both the other regions. The Region of Universal Matter suffers much more from this change through *Pralaya* (Dissolution) than the Region of Universal Mind; however, the Region of Universal Mind also undergoes cycle of change, in the so-called *Mahapralaya* (Great Dissolution), where it would be destroyed and new Universal Mind regions will come up. There is a whole philosophy in Eastern thought or tradition (viz., the philosophy of Religion of Saints particularly Radhasoami Faith) in support of the Model. There are believed to be 84 subtle attention currents which are responsible for this cycle of birth and death in the two lower regions of Universal Mind and Universal Matter and these are made up of the three "Gunas" or qualities and five "Tattvas" or elements. The combination leads to these 84 subtle currents and this gives rise to cycle of birth and death, i.e. cycle of change. But since the Region of Pure Spirits, devoid of mind and body, is not subject to any such change, it is eternal and that is the largest region or grand division and houses the largest number of spirit entities.

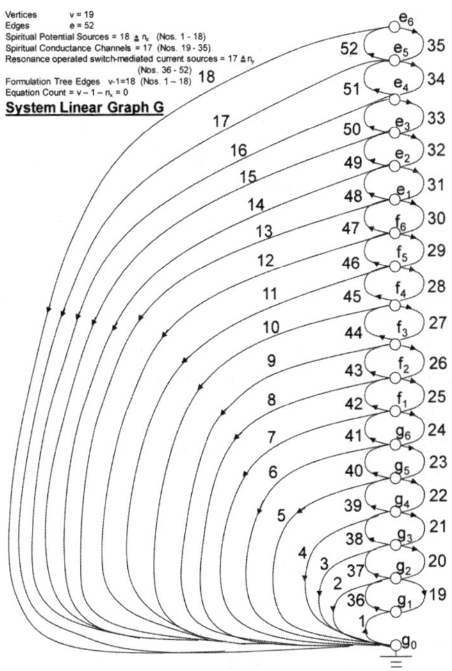

"Yatha Param Satchitanand or Nirmal Chetan Desh khande Tatha Brahmande, Yatha Brahmande Tatha Pinde"

FIGURE B
System Linear Graph Model G :
A Rudimentary Modelling Framework for Spiritual Domains

The Systems Graph Model G in Figure B is another part of the model inspired by systems approach to make use of not only the model schematic based on certain fundamental axiom and fundamental postulates on component modeling and interconnection of the components in the system, but this gives rise to the method of solving these various quantitative relationships, or at least, qualitative relationships "quantified" in a fuzzy sense, if not numerically. So in this particular case, since we use quantum theoretic model, this classical approach is still applicable, because on observation, all quantum phenomena reduce to classical state and therefore it becomes a classical solution. Once you have taken observation and you wish to verify your observations, then it is only the "classical" model which would come to the fore. In the course of attempting certain "measurements", in the sense that these are not measurements necessarily in the outer world, but these are the observations made through inner experience or human experience by performing meditation or yoga or transcendental meditation or even ultra-transcendental meditation so that one could access the highest levels of consciousness within the human frame itself.

Universal Consciousness Realization Postulate

The religion of Saints prescribes a systemic methodology of the meditational practice of "*Surat*" (spirit force) – "*Shabda*" (spiritual sound currents) – "*Yoga*" (union) for uniting the spirit force of a human being with the "characteristic" spiritual sound currents[1], which emanate from the various spirit centres ($e_6 - e_1$; $f_6 - f_1$; $g_6 - g_1$ shown in Figure A) in different regions and sub-regions (i.e. grand divisions and sub-divisions) of the macrocosm for realizing corresponding levels of increasing degree of consciousness (or spiritual potential) from the lowest subdivision (g_1) of the macrocosmic division of physical / material region through the macrocosmic division of the Universal Mind to the highest subdivision of the Supreme Creator or Being (e_6) of the purely spiritual region.

The object in view is to realize the highest degree of macrocosmic consciousness (spiritual potential) corresponding to e_6 in Figure A, i.e. God (the goal of religion) or Ultimate Reality (the goal of philosophy) or Truth (the goal of Science) which are but three names of the same Supreme (Spiritual) Essence, as defined by the fundamental axiom

[1] This is somewhat akin to the Cosmic Background Microwave Radiation emitted at the time of the Big Bang (marking the beginning of creation of physical universe) which is being detected even to this day by devices such as COBE (Cosmic Background Explorer) Satellite as the Microwave Relic of the Big Bang to study the state of the physical universe soon after its birth.

of spiritual consciousness by means of awakening the 18 hidden subtle senses or centres within man as a microcosm implied by $g_1' - g_6', f_1' - f_6'; e_1'$-$e_6'$ in Figure A, and as referred to in the Universal Consciousness Realization Postulate invoking the meditational practice of "*Surat Shabda Yoga*" of unifying the spirit force of man with the "characteristic" sound-currents emanating from spirit-centres at various levels of consciousness (or spiritual potential). However, this requires rigorous training and practice under the guidance of an adept or mentor or 'Guru'.

There are aphorisms to the tune that *Yatha Sachkhande Tatha Brahmande* [As in Purely Spiritual Region, so in Region of Universal Mind], *Yatha Brahmande Tatha Pinde* [As in Region of Universal Mind, so in Region of Universal Matter or Physical Universe]; and *Yatha Samasthi Srishti Tatha Manav Vyashti Srishti* [As in Macrocosm, so in Human Microcosm], which all say that as in Pure Spiritual Region, so also in Region of Universal Mind, as in Region of Universal Mind, so also in the Region of Universal Matter; and as in Macrocosm, so also in Human Microcosm. So, essentially, what the scriptures say is that these are all reflections of what takes place in the Region of Pure Spiritual form. Accordingly, that is the real model while the rest of the creation follows in its image. We have visualized what we call resonance operated switches in our schematic in Figure A. In this model presentation, we have potential sources and we have quantum force field. (In the earlier version of the model elucidated in Discourses on Radhasoami Faith (M. Sahab (1960, 2004), there used to be classical force field conceptualization, but since the advent of quantum theory, we define it to be quantum force field and lately we now find, that the basic quantum theory model would not do. In fact, there is no duality in the Region of Pure Spirits, devoid of mind and body, because the duality between mind and body and spirit and mind are what respectively characterize the Region of Universal Matter and the Region of Universal Mind in the last two grand divisions of creation but not the first one which is the grand division of pure spirits. So we have suitably modified and suggested it to be the Omni-quantum spiritual force field (Satsangi, 2010) which has the requisite duality in the bottom two regions, but has no uncertainty in the top Region of pure Spirits which is characterized by special duality viz. "duality at will". It is not a duality to which a spirit is subjected because of uncertainty. Spirits may choose to stand apart from the Creator or the Primal Source of consciousness as a "devotee" to witness and worship the Supreme Grandeur of the Lord Almighty (the repository of all consciousness in the Grand Cosmos). A spirit-entity could do so in the Region of Pure Spirit. However, alternatively, a spirit-entity could choose to remain merged with the Creator and be part of the creator oneself; that is, the choice of unity with Creational Source is of course there. So it is "duality at will" and therefore because of want of any appropriate terminology, I have referred to the original force-field as omni-quantum force field. God does not play dice, He plays bat and ball straight and square and therefore there is no duality in the Heisenberg-sense and there is complete certainty in what Lord Almighty (the creational source) does. But anyway to carry conviction with the scientists, the approach suggested by Price and Barrell (Price and Barrell, 2012) for integrating inner experience with neuroscience is fine indeed.

In Omni-Quantum Theory for Spiritual Consciousness System Modelling in Cosmology, the highest level of consciousness is that relating to the abstract entity of true beings or spirit forces beyond mind or ego. I might remark here that while scientists will be able to trace the primary source of all consciousness and they seem to be at the threshold of doing so, in order to access these sources, one would probably find it lot more convenient to take recourse to inner or human experience through meditational practices, whether transcendental or ultra-transcendental, as necessary. It is in this context that we are not particularly enthused about accessing consciousness at the highest level in the outside world but we recommend that since human being is an exact replica of the grand universe, we could turn inwards and through our human experience, we could access the consciousness at the level of mind, consciousness at the level of true being or higher self beyond ego. Ego, in fact, is a kind of firewall, ego-wall, which prevents the human beings from accessing higher levels of consciousness. So, no matter how much we study the domain of mind, unless we can have ways of transcending the domain of mind, we would not be able to access the primary source of consciousness. It could be discovered experimentally only through inner or human experience by following the protocols of various meditational techniques. However, mathematically, it can be demonstrated that such an ultimate source of consciousness does exist and that is where scientists are making great efforts and are likely to succeed very soon.

2.2 USP'S (UNIQUE STRONG POINTS) OF DAYALBAGH MODEL

Any quantum force field in the physical universe is subject to duality between mind and matter (wave and particle) and therefore the principle of uncertainty implies that both position and momentum cannot be determined precisely. Similarly, any quantum force-field in the Region of Universal Mind is also subject to duality between spirit and mind and therefore can represent uncertainty (Satsangi, 2013a).

Whenever we talk about any quantum phenomenon, we have to reckon with the principle of uncertainty or duality, whether it is duality between wave and particle, or in other words, between mind and matter, or at a higher level of consciousness, whether it is duality between spirit forces or true self and the ego self, or at the highest level of spirit forces, whether it is kind of a distinguished duality between the primary source and the individual spirit forces which are able to access that primary source of consciousness. There are two schools of thought among the meditationists. One believes that there is ultimate unity, and the other believes there is duality, but duality with a difference, that is, duality at will. There is uncertainty associated with duality, so obviously one would imagine that when one reaches the Ultimate source of consciousness, there should not be any uncertainty and such a consciousness is omnipresent, omnipotent and omniscient. These are the qualities associated with God. We do not expect God to play poker. God plays bat and ball, straight and fair, so there is no uncertainty at the level of God. We can reach God through unified quantum field-theoretic abstraction carried many dimensions higher (i.e. mathematically tending to infinity) than what is possible currently by the use of latest M-theory, that is, string theory with highest dimension of 10 or so, that is available presently. Perhaps, you would have to have "strings" of much higher dimension $n \rightarrow \infty$, represented by point-loops of zero dimension (rather than strings of dimension 1). So, mathematically, as an abstract deduction or as an abstract derivation, we would be able to establish the primary source of consciousness. However, in order to access such primary source of consciousness, at the physical level, we are all governed by the Planck's dimension. So I do not think we can reach the levels of subtlety of particles like mind and further subtler particles like spirits or true self, or higher self in any physical frame. There will be a sort of firewall similar to what scientists are discovering in the case of black hole. Stephen Hawking has demonstrated that certain high-energy particles have been noticed to leak from black holes and they are presenting a firewall for any other physical object to reach the black hole. So there is even a greater firewall which would prevent one from entering the domain of mind in physical frame and to enter the domain of spirit, we have to demolish the ego wall. Once you demolish the ego wall, you can then reach the higher self and ultimate source of consciousness. So far as quantum theory is concerned, that is the most promising one at the moment, and it is this reason why the Penrose and Hameroff model (Penrose and Hameroff, 2011) is most promising in the field of consciousness. It had admitted from the very beginning a proto-consciousness to be associated and this was because of the use of mathematical abstraction that they were able to explain how decoherence could be prevented and superposition maintained for a period of time in the quantum systems among the various states of consciousness. We all know that when measurements are made in quantum mechanical systems, they collapse to a single state and the uncertainty disappears and one makes definite physical measurement which obtains. Quantum mechanics does not take into account the gravitational field at all, so it has its own limitations. What Penrose and Hameroff (Penrose and Hameroff, 2011) refer to it is really quantum field theory which takes gravitation into account through special relativity theory. Unified Quantum Field Theory admits even general gravitational theory of Einstein by positing M-theory or string theory (Zee, 2010). As I said, the M-theory at the moment has the highest dimensional string of dimension 10, but it is possible to imagine higher order strings tending towards almost infinite dimension (through infinitely many point loops each of dimension zero) and this is what opens up the possibility of mathematically establishing, scientifically, the primary ultimate source of consciousness. Accessing it physically is another matter. We can access it rather conveniently by turning inwards and gaining human experience through recommended techniques of transcendental or ultra-transcendental meditation.

However, in the purely spiritual region, the quantum spiritual force-field is a special type which may be aptly described as Omni Quantum Spiritual Force Field whose distinguishing characteristic is that while it exhibits duality at will, it displays no accompanying uncertainty. Our model predicts that individual spirit forces have this possibility of standing separate from the united status with the Supreme or Ultimate Source of consciousness They can have their individual consciousness about the ultimate source of consciousness and that is permissible, but this is at will, otherwise there is unity.

In a sense, we are using the approach recommended by Price and Barrell, in their seminal contribution in the book 'Inner Experience and Neuroscience' (Price and Barrell, 2012). So they describe the four-fold scientific paradigm of observing, reporting, understanding or analyzing, and then framing hypothesis and testing, so that the methodology of processing conforms to the scientific way. So we follow similar scientific methodology in testing the consciousness system model and its predictions tested by making observations or measurements, but these measurements of necessity, have to be inner measurements or subjects of human experience, even going beyond levels of cognition, crossing the ego wall and reaching the levels of consciousness beyond ego, that is to the consciousness levels of higher self or spirit forces.

However, let me hasten to point out that there are some distinguishing features of our approach. There are a couple of vantage points (as already referred to earlier) from which we formulatc our model and work on consciousness studies. One of these is phenomenology of Radhasoami Faith, and the other is systems approach, which I have been trained as a professional to adopt, all through my working career.

Apart from the twin vantage points from which I speak, let me refer to some other distinctive features of our unique model. Rocco Gennaro in his book *The Consciousness Paradox* (Gennaro, 2012) has dealt with HOT brain thesis – HOT standing for Higher Order Thought. He maintains that what makes a mental state conscious is that a suitable Higher Order Thought is directed at that mental state. Drawing upon this inspiration from his HOT-brain theory, I have proposed HOT Consciousness : SCANE correlates, where HOT-Consciousness stands not for Higher Order Thought, but Hierarchical Order Theory of Consciousness and the SCANE correlates stand for Spiritual, Cognitive And Neural-Environmental Correlates.

I would like to mention that determinism or classicality and other issues are related with model building and there is nothing which prevents me from building a model of brain which is quantum-theoretic, so also a model of mind which is quantum-theoretic and then if you take the correlates on the basis of these models, it would be unjustified to call them as reductionist in approach. So it is a question of how we look at the model which simulates the reality. Nobody knows for sure whether brain is a quantum mechanics gadget or whatever, but it can certainly be modeled to our advantage through quantum-theoretic model, and once you do that, one could not accuse the modellers at least of reductionism. So it is a matter of approach and for the moment, we could take this as the view that instead of trying to settle score whether the Penrose-Hameroff approach (Penrose and Hameroff, 2011) or whether von-Neumann Stapp approach (Stapp, 2007) or some other approach is the right one to handle the consciousness paradox which Gennaro refers to, pragmatically speaking, each model has its own way of generating a solution for it, and in the absence of any conclusive evidence to nail down the truth, one could continue with all these co-existing models as the perceived reality or truth, depending on one's preference. As you have seen, we define 18 levels of consciousness throughout the Grand Cosmos and then we use for measurements all the three domains - spiritual, cognitive and neural-environmental, so that becomes SCANE Correlates; rather then taking only the brain scans, we want scans of all the three levels in our experience of inner world as well as the outer world. So that is where the difference lies. We do not forsake our scientific methodology, we retain it but build into it the phenomenology of first person inner experience. So third person modelling is fine, third person observation is fine, i.e. observe like a third person, observe and then deduce, decide, hypothesise, so all that is the third person approach, but then there has to be some underlying first person subjective experience of inner reality, which must also be built into the modelling framework.

I would like to point out that quantum field theory is fine but if it has to take into account these abstract phenomena, at the highest level, it has to be in a position to admit both unity and duality, which, in ancient Indian tradition is referred to as, *Adwait* and *Dwait*. *Adwait* is unity and *Dwait* is duality, so both co-exist at the highest level. Accordingly, it is quantum force field, all right, however, quantum force field has duality in it, but this is with a difference, that is, this duality is at will, because we believe that in this triad of *Satyam-Sundaram-Shivam*, the truth is about the inseparability of the living being from the ultimate abstract source of quantum field. So that is the truth. Let all of them merge together in the final analysis. So that is the unity and that is *Adwaitwad* in Indian tradition that there is no duality at the ultimate level where the individual spirit forces merge with the universal spirit (i.e. the abstract source). But we believe that there is duality at will, individual spirits can stand apart from the source, even after having merged in it and then observe this unity as a separate entity. So all of us as human beings are spirit forces, and in that sense immutable. We never perish, we maintain our identity, but we will merge eventually in the final source, so that is the philosophy we pursue and that is the crux of Radhasoami Faith. So it is both, unity as well as duality at will. So that is the sense in which I qualify it as omni-quantum theory rather than quantum theory. Thus duality is tradable in a sense with unity, i.e., one can have the dual entity intact at will but with ultimate unity.

There are several research groups working in psycho-physical-dynamics as mentioned by Price and Barrell (Price and Barrell, 2012), but I think ours is amongst a few who work on spiritual psycho-physical dynamics. In other words, we believe that the observer is the spirit, not the mind and the observed system is the one which contains both the material world as well as the psychological world, or cognitive world. So both mind and body are modeled through quantum mechanics, or quantum field theory and then we address the question of agreement with the spiritual phenomenology. So, that is why, we consider this as spiritual-psycho-physical dynamics. The observer is spirit only and it is separated from the observed system which is the rest of the Universe. Thus, it is observer's phenomenology which matters. So, the observer gives his inner experience and that is to be interpreted and tested through building of hypotheses in the light of the model which one may have in mind I believe that such a conceptual model ought to be there because otherwise one is not getting anywhere purposively. While science would seem to favour keeping things open, science and the western society would also seem to prefer clarity with regard to goals and objectives of any scientific investigation. So our goals must be well-defined, otherwise how would we ever reach our goals if we do not know where we want to go. Thus, we must know where we are going and how to get there.

This is what precisely distinguishes the Radhasoami Faith in the Religion of Saints. The Proclamation that was brought to our notice (in Section 1.2), right from day one of the founding of Radhasoami faith, endows the Faith with the clear definition of the object in view in terms of a hierarchy of consciousness centres ranging from the lowest to the highest degree together with the prescription of practical measures for attaining them. The principal devotional method is the *Surat Shabda Yoga*, the path of uniting the spirit with the sound current. Ultimately, at the level of the pure spirit, instead of the 84 subtle currents which prevail in the lower grand divisions of creation dominated by mind and matter, we are left with just the two pure spiritual currents. Essentially, these also merge into one united spiritual shabda (sound) current Radhasoami, but the one which is going outward or downward, is known as the spirit current and on its return path to the original source at the apex, it is known as sound current, which is directed towards its successively next higher source in the hierarchy. So that is how the circuit from the original consciousness source to the various spiritual consciousness-centres in the hierarchy and back gets completed. At the beginning of creation, they started as two distinct spiritual currents, one outward and downward flowing spirit-current and the other inward or upward flowing sound-current, seeking out the multiple levels of consciousness-centres and ultimately its original reservoir of all consciousness in the Grand Cosmos known as Radhasoami. In our scriptures of Radhasoami Faith (M. Sahab, 1960, 2004), Radha is the one which characterizes the great spiritual current which, initially flowed out of the original source of consciousness, viz. Soami (the ultimate repository of all consciousness) at the genesis of creation. Notice that infinite space existed all along from the very beginning of creation till its final steady state when all that exists are pure spirit-forces or currents.

2.3 CHARACTERISTIC CONSCIOUSNESS AND ASSOCIATED FREQUENCY

This is as good a point as any other to raise a certain pertinent comment regarding the work of Price and Barrell (Price and Barrell, 2012), which is great but still the emphasis on now and the present is far too much. In Radhasoami Faith, we believe there is "cumulative" consciousness, that is, consciousness of an entity is not just the present momentary level of consciousness attained by an entity but it is the highest "characteristic" consciousness attained as of that moment, which we may invoke for prompting or guiding us whether consciously or unconsciously. It is not all the time that we are in explicit communion with that highest consciousness attained by an individual spirit-entity, but that is the one which we have achieved and that is the one which potentially prompts us through intuition (whether conscious or unconscious). It is therefore, the "cumulative" consciousness, as it were, which characterizes our frequency, say characteristic frequency or natural frequency, which, if I may say so, is the dominant resonant frequency which we generate as a spirit-source representing the "cumulative" consciousness of the "co-investigator participant" as of the moment of recording the neural map. In fact, if our supposition is correct, that initially all the spirits were with the Lord, God-Almighty, then any spirit shorn of its mind and body is the one and same as the Lord's spirit and therefore, it has the highest consciousness of the Supreme Being. But it is because of being alloyed with the covers of mind and body, that it is not able to exhibit the dominance at resonance at that supreme frequency. It shows lower frequency. *Spanda Shastra* of Kashmir *Shaivism* and string theory used by Hagelin (Hagelin, 2013) refer to these individual consciousness traits with the characteristic frequencies, but I think they need a clarification as offered here based on internal experience or spiritual phenomenology of the narrating co-investigator. Ultimately, the frequency is the one and the same for all spirit forces as that of its creator or primeval source. Once they get shorn of the body and mind, their frequency will elevate itself to the highest consciousness level. Accordingly, it is the "cumulative" consciousness which counts, not the momentary current consciousness or present-moment consciousness. My narration of phenomenology will collect information on consciousness cumulatively as of the present moment through questions of the kind raised by Price and Barrell (Price and Barrell, 2012). I do emphasize phenomenology as of present moment of observation, that is, it has to be a "cumulative" one as of present moment. Perhaps, in western world, you don't believe in rebirth and things like that, which maybe one of the reasons why "present" is all that matters, but, as explained here, one is elevating one's consciousness through the various cycles of birth and death one is undergoing and it is when one succeeds in reaching the highest consciousness, that one merges with the ultimate source and there is no further cycle of birth and death that one undergoes. So that is the Ultimate consciousness state. Thus, everybody is rising to that potential level. It might take "time" to reach that full potential. So, one needs a conceptual model to have this kind of visualization and then verify it.

There is nothing in our model building and experimentation, which we have also done extensively (Satsangi P.S. and Sahni V., 2007, 2008, 2012, 2015), which suggests anything to the contrary and I would now give you certain examples of the recent measurements we have taken using the latest equipment for sensitive measurements of magnetic field in mapping the brain through the Magneto-Encephalo-Gram (MEG) rather than recording the Electro-Encepahlo-Gram (EEG). We favour MEG because it entails a protocol which does not disturb the meditationist. The sensor-helmet does not have to sit on the head of the subject meditationist. The helmet for taking neural signature in MEG could be positioned a little away from the head of the meditationist. Its many sensors would pick up the appropriate signals. In fact that is the reason why I refer to it not as neuro-correlates but neuro-environmental correlates, which would pick up the magnetic field or electro-magnetic field or electric field in the brain or its nearby environment, without making much difference in objective and results or conclusion. You would get the same results more or less. We have verified the pattern through a number of experimentations over several years. However, we believe the measurement techniques ought to be non-invasive type, non-intrusive type, which would not disturb the meditationist in the least, allowing each to reach one's true potential without distortion or noise. This precaution is not ordinarily taken in the neuro science experiments recorded in literature. One reason is, as rightly pointed out by Price and Barrell (Price and Barrell, 2012), that the subject on which these tests are conducted are different from the investigators themselves. Price and Barrell make them co-investigators, which is the right approach. You, therefore consult them, you take the phenomenology from them in first-person approach, and then of course you use methods (third-person approach) which are acceptable in science to test the various hypotheses we build through consensus, and if proved right, then we have supporting evidence for further hypothesis and model-testing. We have already pointed out a few significant points where we differ in our approach and as of now we have not found any evidence to discard our approach in favour of some other. So, while we have continued to imbibe the richness of thoughts, based on their worth over the years, we hold our ground so long as its unique strong points (USP's) are not disproved, i.e. so long as our underlying system model does not fail. When it fails, we would modify it. So this is the gist of what I want to say about our distinctive unique approach for integrating inner experience with scientific methodologies.

EXPERIENTIAL SIMULATION
(Audio Clip) : March 9, 2012

ORIGINAL WORD (MOOL NAM) : RADHASOAMI (UNIVERSAL PASSWORD)

FIVE MYSTIC WORDS OF	HIGHER REGIONS AND	ACCOMPANYING ANAHAD NAD
NIRANJAN	SAHASDAL KAMAL	BELL AND CONCH
OM (AUM)	TRIKUTI	DRUM, THUNDER
RARANG	SUNNA	STRING INSTRUMENT – KINGARI, SARANGI, SITAR, VEENA
SOHANG	BHANWAR GUFA	FLUTE
SAT	SAT LOK ANAMI LOK	SNAKE CHARMER'S LUTE
RADHASOAMI	ALAKH AGAM RADHASOAMI (NIJ-DHAM)	UNIDENTIFIED MELODIOUS RUN-JHUN SUPERPOSED WITH BEE-HUMMING

TABLE 1
Experiential Simulation

Table 1 represents the exercise which was presented at the Eastern Philosophy Forum at TSC 2012 (Satsangi, 2012a). The leftmost column lists the famous five mystic words – *Niranjan*, *Om*, *Rarang*, *Soham*, *Sat* and at the end, the original mystic name Radhasoami, from which they all arose. The middle column lists the various alternative centres or stages of consciousness to be attained or achieved as higher and higher states of consciousness. In fact, the highest state is at the bottom such that the progressively increasing hierarchy of consciousness is directed from top downwards, as per list in Table 1. Note that Table 1 does not refer to consciousness of the material region. In Religion of Saints (Radhasoami Faith), it is not taken as part of the *Surat Shabda Yoga Abhyas* (the meditational practice for uniting spirit current with the sound current), that is the sound practice in short, which we recommend. In other words, the sound practice, "*Surat-Shabda Yoga Abhyas*" starts with the upper level (i.e. Region of Brahman) of *Brahmand*, skipping even the lower level (i.e. "And" of *Brahmand*). The "sound practice" starts with the seat of the spirit in the physical body and takes it through the three Brahmans (in the upper region of "*Brahmand*") at *Sahasdal Kamal*, *Trikuti* and *Sunna* with the mystic word *Niranjan* representing the first *Brahman*, *Om* the second *Brahman*, *Rarang* the third *Brahman* and further on there is the *Para Brahman* and even further beyond are the *Soham Purush*, *Sat Purush* and Radhasoami (of the Pure Spiritual Region). In between, there are a few other stages, but these (foregoing ones) are the important landmarks to highlight. The middle column lists the alternative states or stages or centres of consciousness to be reached while the last column lists the necessary and sufficient conditions or factors in the form of "*Anahad Nad*" i.e. unstruck celestial sound accompanying the original mystic word or stage-by-stage characteristic mystic words (as already explained). These factors have been identified by consensus reached among "experiencing" participants through Analytical Hierarchy Process discussed in the next Chapter. This is how we arrived at the hierarchization of the consciousness levels in the large macro-cosmos and also the micro-human-cosmos. The accompanying *Anahad Nad* (unstruck celestial sounds) listed in the last column of Table 1 are mere simulations, in terms of similar sounds familiar in physical world. Beyond the *Sat Lok* in the highest three conscious centres of the cosmos, there is no musical instrument in the physical world with which they may be identified. Accordingly, for the apex Radhasoami region, the analogous instrument is indescribable. The only way we identify it is that the original mystic name Radhasoami resounds there and also that this stage follows beyond the other stages of listening to the unmistakable snake charmer's lute at *Sat Lok* and other higher Lokas ('stages or centres') in succession and it is a sort of very highly spiritual melodious orchestra that plays there, but there is no analogous instrument in the physical world with which it matches. Accordingly, I cannot name it, or simulate it and reproduce it here. However, the other characteristic sounds are fairly well reproduced and simulated upto the stage of snake charmer's lute at *Sat Lok*. There is no problem in identifying them. There are people practicing "*Surat-Shabda Yoga*", but without the inner experience of realizing *Sat Lok* as a first-person experience, who wonder whether it is *Veena*, the string instrument which plays at *Sat Lok* or it is the snake charmer's lute. Based on my personal first-hand inner experiences, I can emphatically answer that it is definitely snake charmer's lute; (in fact, *Veena* plays at *Sunna*, a centre of lower order of consciousness). Of course, there is the accompanying qualia or personification of consciousness (*Sat Chit Anand*).

Over the years, we have refined our experimental procedures. We had started with very simple circuits such as, tuned circuits, filter circuits and we did not have elaborate procedures for shielding noise, nor did we have very highly sensitive instrumentation. So, we moved further and we now make use of SQUID, that is Superconducting Quantum

Interference Device, which is a highly sensitive magnetometer and we use the adequately shielded enclosures so that the noise, magnetic noise in particular, does not disturb the proceedings inside.

It is in the aforesaid context that alongwith our participating co-investigators (with inner spiritual experience) we went to Indira Gandhi Centre for Atomic Research (IGCAR) at Kalpakkam in early November 2012, since at that time we did not have our own facility of SQUID in a properly shielded chamber. We conducted relevant scientific experiments with third-person objectivity for acquiring neural maps (or neural-environmental correlates) on individual meditationists as well as during group meditation sessions in simulated prayer meetings, availing of the sophisticated SQUID-based MEG facility with adequate shielding at IGCAR. These recent results with sophisticated instrumentation and shielding as well as our earlier results with simple contrived devices have all consistently shown that some of the frequencies of interest in spiritual meditation were 3 Hz, 4.5 Hz, 76 Hz, 108 Hz and 126 Hz. These frequencies have shown up as frequencies at which resonance takes place during meditation through spiritual practices of Radhasoami Faith. Lately, we have acquired our own facilities of 15-channel Magneto-Encephalo-Graphy (MEG) covering all lobes of the brain in the Centre for Consciousness Studies of DEI and accordingly we should be able to speed up our experiments considerably for scientific verification and hypothesis-testing.

Recently, we came across 'Ancient Wisdom, Modern Technology' (Triggs, 2012) brain wave frequency list compiled by Michael Triggs from 0.1 Hz to 10^{16} Hz (i.e. 10 peta Hertz). I have highlighted interpretation of some of these frequencies. Some of the frequencies that we have experienced in our meditation group here in Dayalbagh are further underlined here, 3 Hz for instance and that is at the beginning of the spiritual experience of meditation, such that when we are able to concentrate at the seat of the spirit force within human body, then we may experience a resplendent form of true mentor. Still another frequency is 4.5 Hz, this is Shamanic state of consciousness, Tibetan Buddhist chants and it appears to be the first step of the spiritual ladder, i.e. the first level in Radhasoami Faith for realization of consciousness – or what we call as *Sahasdal Kamal*, where we may experience the spiritual phenomenon of vision of candle-light and accompanying sound of tolling of bell. Then there are several dominant resonant frequencies which are catalogued in great detail in this compilation. 108 Hz is another one we experience and this appears to be the frequency which presents total knowing, that is when you have your tryst with truth or as we may say Ultimate Truth or Ultimate Reality, that is realization of *Sat Lok* as is referred to in Religion of Eastern Saints (Radhasoami Faith). Beyond *Sat Lok* frequency i.e. 108 Hz, there is the ultimate abstract source frequency which I have been speaking of which appears to be at 126.22 Hz. What we have measured in our meditational community at Dayalbagh is 126 Hz, but it is likely that 126 Hz may be observed because our least count was not of such a resolution where we could measure 126.22 Hz. However, at a relatively coarse resolution level, we did measure 126 Hz quite frequently in our meditational community and this is what it represents, as appearing within quotation marks.

> "Meditation carried out to this tone will lead to state beyond good and bad, shame and guilt, beyond space and time, knowledge and wisdom, action and rest and being and not-being. It leads to a state where being has no name, to a state where the all-one and the all encompassing are no longer separate entities but are reunited at their one common origin, the original that is also you."

So this is what I meant by *Adwaitavad*, the unity of each individual spirit with the Supreme source of consciousness and also the ability of each individual spirit force to stand apart at will and be able to witness the duality, i.e. each individual spirit form as separate entity from the Supreme Source. So that sums up the philosophy of *Adwait* with duality at will. So there is a corroboration of this frequency of 126.22 Hz as measured elsewhere and interpreted by Michael Triggs. This is not our interpretation, but we have experienced this frequency in our Meditational community and accordingly the corresponding awareness or consciousness that it represents. There are other frequencies going upto 10 peta Hertz, 10^{16} Hz, which they say is a magic window in the near ultra-violet range, "life-energy" frequency, which anyway we have not observed in our measures of consciousness. 126 Hz or to be more precise, 126.22 Hz is what we have obtained repeatedly in our meditational sessions.

We are also trying to discover Truth in the hierarchy *Satyam Shivam Sundaram*, that is why I say we are revisiting this adage from the Indian philosophy and now it offers a window of opportunity for secularists also to experience these higher levels of reality without going through the mechanics of the religion or spiritual pursuits, such as meditation. It turned out that what Zeki at. al. (Zeki, 2012) discovered was that when they scanned mathematicians' brains while they were looking at certain mathematical equations and grading them on aesthetic appearance or beauty, the same locations came into activity as appear to be relevant in identifying Truth in the meditationists' head. So these are the areas which are excited in the brain – also, characteristically, same frequencies in our researches, when you try to identify beauty. So never mind identifying spirituality or meditational consciousness, instead, identify beauty. People should not mind identifying beauty and therefore it is a secular game that we are playing and one should be able to participate and then learn how to get onto this frequency entrainment. Train "scientific" participants into improving their frequency from lower level to higher level of perception of reality and therefore attaining higher and higher level of abstraction of consciousness. So the underlying message is that such experiments have already begun. Zeki et. al. did not measure frequency evoked in experiencing beauty and that is where the researchers at Dayalbagh Educational Institute have contributed their bit (Srivastava et. al., 2015b). We are concentrating on frequency measures. In order to monitor dynamics of frequency entrainment, our subjects of study for identifying beauty in mathematics are young students of mathematics at class IX level, rather than full grown mathematicians as in Zeki's study. These class IX mathematics students were presented with mathematical equations which they well-understood. It was only the identification of beauty which was the issue and we scanned their brains through magneto-encephalogram (MEG). We have a fairly good facility at DEI with Superconducting Quantum Interference Devices (SQUID) (as a sensitive magnetometer) with magnetically shielded chamber so that we get accurate measurement of resonant frequencies evoked. When they identify the most beautiful equations, it is the dominant resonant frequencies that were excited, i.e. the highest ones in their spectrum of Fourier transform frequencies. So it seems to open a window of opportunity in the sense that secularists also have a say in consciousness evaluation and it is not just left to meditationists to be experiential study subjects. So we no longer need always to wire the heads of meditationists. What one finds is that whether it is maths, science, art, the evaluation of beauty leads us to the truth, and therefore we are getting into an abstraction, or we are getting into an elevation of our consciousness to its highest level. As our consciousness gets more and more refined through practice, this offers a way of frequency-entrainment if you wish. That is, we get onto the frequency train and move to the higher levels of frequency. We do it through meditation, but one can do it through such brainy exercises of identifying beauty in mathematics, for instance.

2.4 ULTIMATE ACID TEST OF CONSCIOUSNESS

First-Person Inner Experience Of Spiritual Phenomenology Through "Surat-Shabda-Yoga" (i.e. Meditational Practice of Uniting Spirit Current with Sound Current)

As practitioners of Radhasoami Faith (Religion of Saints), this is what we are ourselves engaged in and, as already reiterated, since our focus is cumulative consciousness as of now (present moment), we seek answers to questions as given in Questionnaire Q.

Questionnaire / Interview by Mentor

Questionnaire

PLEASE PUT THIS QUESTIONNAIRE IN ENVELOPE ENCLOSED AND SEAL IT WITH TAPE (IT WILL BE OPENED ONLY BY MENTOR)

Name ______________________ **Age** __________

Date of I Initiation ______________ (if applicable) **Date of II Initiation** __________ (if applicable)

Q. 1. Please describe briefly any inner experience you have had in the following stages of your life:

(i) As a child or student

(ii) As a Jigyasu

(iii) After obtaining Ist initiation (if applicable)

(iv) After obtaining IInd initiation (if applicable)

Q.2. While meditating in MEG room at IGCAR Kalpakkam / D.E.I. (Dayalbagh), did you have any inner experience / experience or enhanced concentration :

(a) During individual measurement
(If so, describe briefly)

(b) During Satsang simulation
(If so, describe briefly)

QUESTIONNAIRE Q
Questionnaire / Interview by Mentor

We have oath of secrecy in our faith (Radhasoami Faith) prohibiting members of the Faith from sharing inner experiences, but the Mentor or Adept is exempt from this oath and meditationists may confide in him as they do in other religions (e.g. confession). Accordingly, the identity of meditationists has been masked by the Mentor / Adept under an assigned Code Name before disclosing the first-person inner experience of spiritual phenomenology for scientific research investigations. As a Mentor or Adept, I have exercised the privilege of sharing inner experiences under the assigned code name without disclosing the individual personal identity.

Furthermore, as an Adept or Preceptor myself, I have the privilege to document my own experiences for the benefit of the scientific as well as spiritual community. Accordingly, first of all, I give my own experience of spiritual phenomenology. Though I bear code name O, but as a special privilege as an Adept, I declare that it is my phenomenology.

Code Name O : Spiritual Phenomenology

1. I have been frequently experiencing a Massive Flow of Spiritual Current from Apex of the head outward and downward resulting in perceptible shaking of body especially legs, particularly while standing, right since the day of my acclamation (on May 18, 2003) by Radhasoami Satsang, Dayalbagh as the VIII Sant Satguru of Radhasoami Satsang, Dayalbagh (the first ever instance taking place when I rose from my seat to acknowledge my acclamation publicly (in a gathering of approximately 25,000 in size). This has been continuing right to the present time.

2. Illuminated appearance of the refulgent form of Param Guru Huzur Dr. M.B. Lal Sahab (the preceding seventh Sant Satguru) in a brightly resplendent photo-frame, as it were.

3. Internally experiencing the reverberations of the Original Mystic Word Radha-soami rhythmically while meditating.

4. Internally experiencing progressively ascending succession of union of my spirit current with the sound current over a period of time during "induced" meditation practices ranging from "Bell and Conch" sound through percussion instrumental sounds through-stringed instrumental sounds to wind-instrumental sounds of flute and lute and further unidentified superbly spiritually melodious orchestra of regions beyond Sat Lok right through to the indescribable Region of Original Abode of Radhasoami accompanied by the Ultimate Realization of Param Sat Chit Premananand Prakash Shabda (Mystic Name) Anahad Nad in the Apex Region in a state of rapture together with experiencing its manifestation as reverberation of Radhasoami as the Original Mystic Name.

Now this is something which I have not found documented even by my predecessors in Radhasoami Faith. However, I have experienced it and experienced it progressively from day one (May 18, 2003) right since being publicly acclaimed as the Adept of Radhasoami Satsang, Dayalbagh, on succeeding the last Adept about a decade back. I vividly recall that it was when I rose to acknowledge the Acclamation as Adept by way of consensus, that I experienced the surge of massive flow of inner consciousness current which flooded me with spiritual intuition, as it were. Accordingly, I was not at all at a loss to say what I needed to say. This is the kind of support that an Adept gets. This is what is meant by having the "hotline of communication" with an elevated level of consciousness. In other words, the Adept is always in communion with that elevated level of consciousness and whenever he needs support, he gets consciousness of that level immediately to answer any questions spontaneously. In fact, I might have no clue to what is being asked of me, but when the question is posed, I should be able to answer it from the repository of knowledge or consciousness available with the level from which my presiding deity comes. So that is the belief system in spiritual phenomenology. Similarly, it is common place that the first initiates do get the refulgent picture of their Mentor or Adept at the seat of the spirit or higher centres of consciousness to which they have gained access, when they perform meditation. This word Radhasoami, i.e. the original mystic word, resounds internally and that would take me through all the higher stages that I have mentioned in the sound clip (Table 1) brought to you as a simulation. I have undergone requisite inner experience and I can verify those stages. However, once I cross the intermediate stages and reach the highest stage, I may directly reach that stage and may not have to pass through the intermediate stages necessarily explicitly. Thus, it takes only a moment, as it were, to make the internal communication line hot with my source of consciousness. It does not take long. So all these successive sounds one goes through if one had not heard them earlier for a sustained period of time. Once one is endowed with this status of wearing the mantle of the successor adept, then one must have that elevated level of consciousness. In a way, that elevated consciousness is given to one, rather than being earned by one. This encapsulates some of my unique inner spiritual experiences as an Adept or Preceptor of Radhasoami Faith.

Third Person MEG Neuro-Environmental Correlates of Code Name 'O'

Figure O1 shows an illustrative neuro-environmental correlate of microcosm of Code Name 'O' in the form of MEG Data-set as recorded on November 6, 2012 at IGCAR, Kalpakkam. Two resonance peaks are marked at frequencies of 108 Hz and 126 Hz, with the peak at 108 Hz frequency of spiritual meditation as being at a lower decibel than the peak at 126 Hz. Accordingly, 126 Hz is identified as the characteristic or dominant frequency of Code Name 'O' as of Nov. 6, 2012. Code Name 'O' may therefore be said to be characterized spiritually by the natural frequency of 126 Hz as evidenced by Figure O1

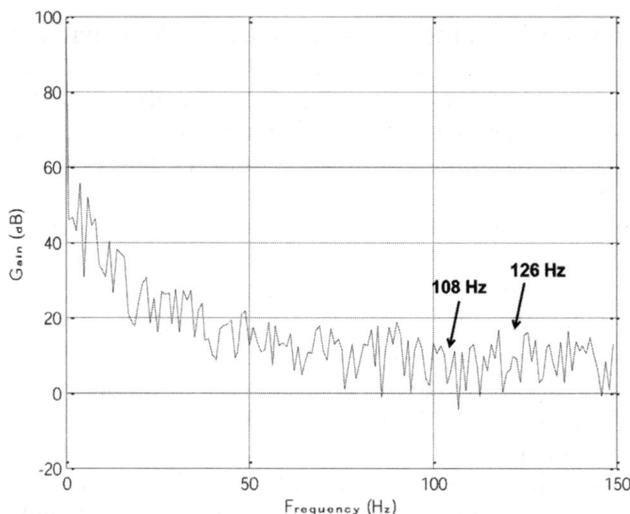

FIGURE O1
November 6, 2012 : MEG Data Set 1 for Code Name 'O'

This is another similar MEG Data-set of Code Name 'O' as represented by Figure O2 which once again identifies 126 Hz as the natural frequency or characteristic dominant frequency of Code Name 'O'.

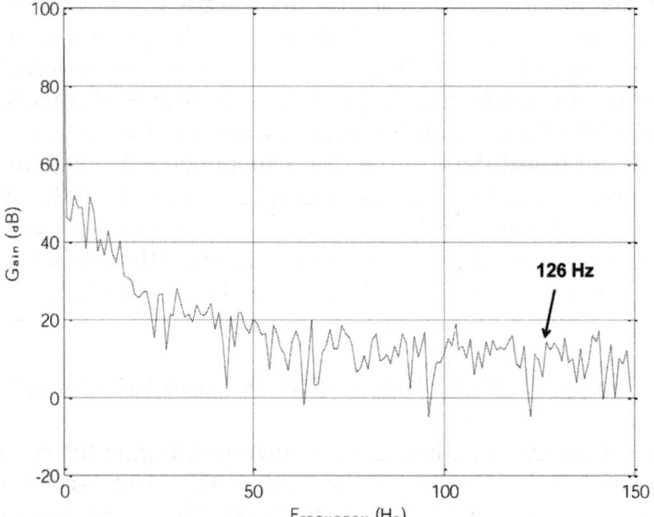

FIGURE O2
November 6, 2012 : MEG Data Set 2 for Code Name 'O'

Figure O3 shows the phenomenon of persistence of resonant frequencies of 108 Hz and 126 Hz beyond the duration of spiritual meditation session of Code Name 'O'.

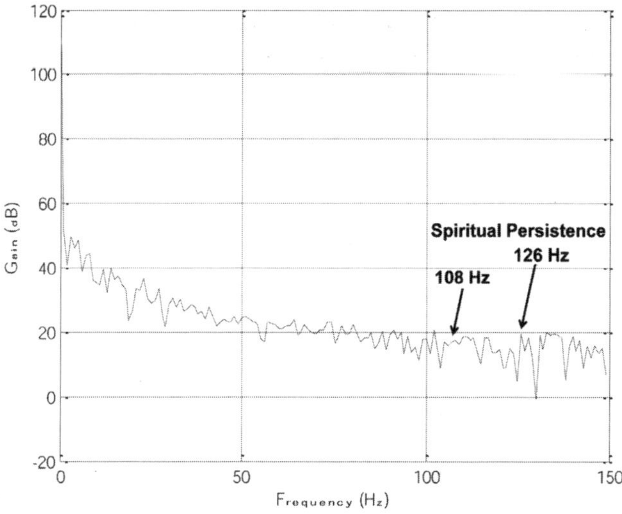

FIGURE O3

November 6, 2012 : MEG Data Set between Code Name 'O' and Code Name 'V'

Besides the frequencies of individual meditation session under Code-Name 'O', there are several other cases of MEG-data sets with their accompanying spiritual phenomenologies which we have recorded at IGCAR.

Figure 3 shows the various reference points for carrying out these meditational practices with respect to the human brain and that it why human brain is considered so important for carrying out meditation.

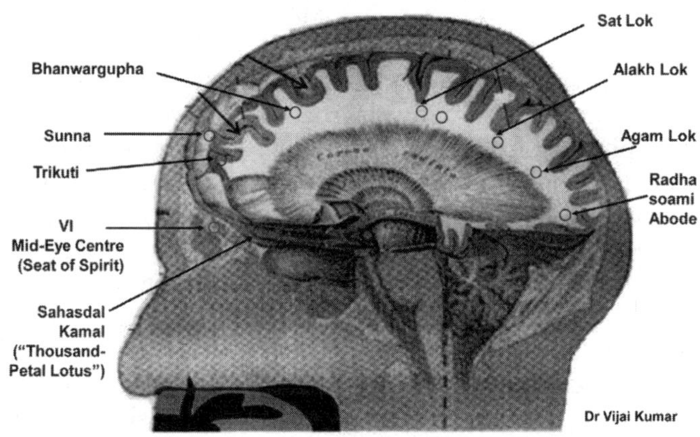

FIGURE 3

Diagrammatic Representation of Brain Apertures in the context of ultra-transcendental referential points during meditational practice of "*Surat Shabda Yoga*" (i.e. Uniting Spirit-Current of meditationist with the Sound Current from the Ultimate Source of Consciousness)

2.5 CLOSED SYSTEM OF GRAND MACROCOSM AND OPEN SYSTEM OF HUMAN MICROCOSM

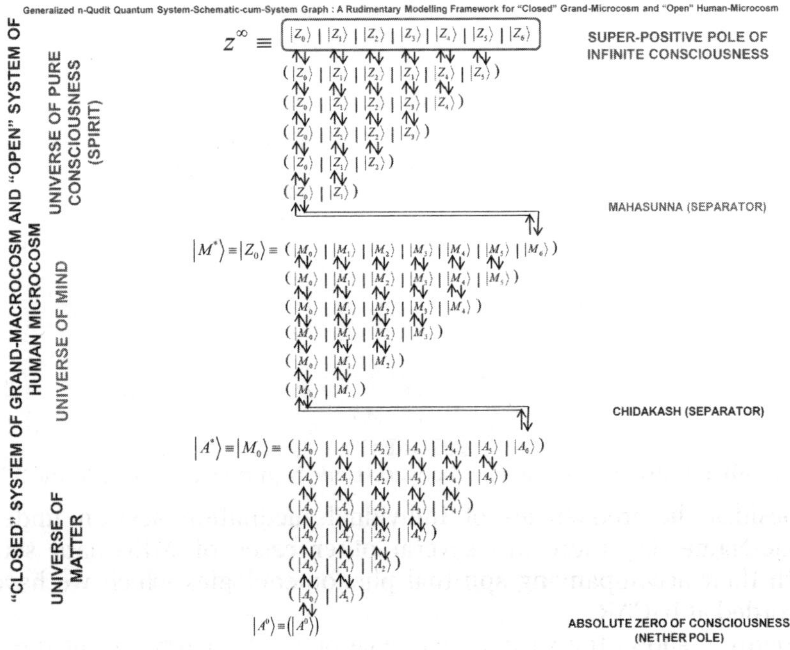

FIGURE 4
Generalized n-Qudit Quantum System-Schematic-cum-System Graph : A Rudimentary Modelling Framework for "Closed" Grand-Microcosm and "Open" Human-Microcosm

Figure 4 is currently the model which I use for investigating the universe. This model divides the macrocosmic universe into three major divisions of physical universe, universe of mind or cognitive universe and universe of consciousness or universe of true self or universe of spirit, pure spirit or highest abstraction. I might mention here that at the highest abstraction level, we have the global universe in a very generalized sense, the most abstract universe and in this universe, the topmost abstraction is assigned to a unified quantum n-independent state space over a field of imaginary numbers like one uses in Hilbert space, so it is a further generalization of Hilbert space so as to have consciousness approaching infinite degree or dimension of freedom. At this dimension, we depend upon a technique of uniting our true self or spiritual self with the entire network comprised of the physical universe, the mental universe and the spiritual universe. So this is the one which consists of a $|Z_\infty\rangle$ viewed in the quantum mechanics language as a vector space of n degrees of freedom over a field of complex numbers.

So in fact whether you call it Radhasoami or call it by another name, it is a unified, abstract, space with infinite degrees of freedom.

The natural phenomenon has apparently no order and therefore it could be considered as having an order zero. Modern science tries to gain control over natural phenomena and therefore it is discovering order among unordered things, so it is an order of first degree that modern science provides to its trainees. When you come to systems science, it tries to consider order among ordered things, so here the order is of the second degree. In our quest for generalization, we found that recently, Howard et. al. at University of Waterloo (Howard et. al., 2015) where I have studied for my Ph.D. (Satsangi, 1969) extended it further from qubits to qudits, in particular qutrits, i.e. order of degree or dimension three. They were motivated in realizing the advantages of quantum computing by maintaining coherence for long enough duration and they were trying to determine necessary and sufficient conditions for doing so. They have already succeeded in proving the necessary conditions, and are quite hopeful that they will be able to gain access to the sufficient conditions for maintaining coherence to realize the benefits of quantum computing. So they might be said to have gone to an order three, (whereas systems science has an order of second degree) and the group at Waterloo led by Howard has extended it to third degree. We argue why stop at degree three, why not pursue quantum odd-based units with higher degree n such as 5, 7, 11, 13, 17 and so on and why not n^{th} degree tending to infinity so that we have the highest abstraction and this is discussed in one of the following chapters of the book authored by our research group.

3. SUMMARY AND CONCLUSIONS

We have developed a model at Dayalbagh Educational Institute to pursue consciousness in a way that would lead to selfless service to all living beings, and in particular human beings, who have most highly developed instrument, namely brain for gaining access to this much used abstraction and more abstraction and finally full abstraction at the macrocosmic level. Here again we try to pursue abstract human values that I learnt right since my primary schooling days such as Duty, Beauty, Humility, Courage, Temperance, Wisdom, Loyalty, Justice. So you want to inculcate these abstract values by gaining access to the most abstract mathematical entity and we know it is Radhasoami, because that is the kind of sound which one resonates with at the most abstracted level, So this is how this faith is called Radhasoami.

Since my parents happened to be the followers of Radhasoami Faith, I had also been attending the Satsangs of this Faith and when I needed to learn beyond physical world, I thought of acquiring a Mentor who had access to this universe beyond physical universe, let me call it universe of mind or cognitive universe. So, in this fashion, I had access to Internet which went beyond physical objects, surpassing Yahoo or Google or whatever other Internet we have access to in the physical world. So there are similar Internets, which give access to universe of mind and once I gained access to universe of mind, there appeared to be a still more abstract entity, which led to the universe of consciousness or universe of true self, beyond cognitive self and this fascinated me and this is the mode in which I have been carrying out the generalizations of physical system theory which I learnt from the west at the Michigan State University in East Lansing, US and then later at the University of Waterloo in Ontario, Canada. My Ph.D. thesis was on generalization of physical system theory to socio-economic systems (Satsangi, 1969) and I had in fact learnt no formal economics earlier, but this physical system theory provided a framework which was very general. All that I had to acquire for measurement was a couple of variables based on the very process of instrumentation and not on any analog. So these turned out to be across measurement and through measurement or flow measurement and this model learnt in the west proved to be very successful and I rely still on this particular model and therefore why I may claim a modest access to the true self and its universe in the form of an Internet of true self or spirit or consciousness.

Service to Humanity at large (viewed through prism of 'Corporate Social Responsibility' (CSR) survey)

The tools and concepts used in our community for scientific study are among the most modern ones available in the Western world, including for social issues like Corporate Social Responsibility, a term coined by Harvard management gurus. A survey conducted in April 2016 in India over all communities found that 38% employees log in extra hours for social work. A similar survey conducted over our community members all over the country from Kashmir to Kanyakumari and even further to Sri Lankan shores, including cosmopolitan cities, rural hinterland and tribal areas and of course, the headquarters at Dayalbagh found the corresponding participation level to be close to 100%, all the year round, with no expectation of any material return (*nishkam sewa*, i.e. selfless service). Yet, most reported that it benefits them much more with better lives and job relationships and skills, leadership development, while inculcating a feeling of *deenta* (humility) to attain more and more Grace of the Supreme Lord. In fact, most people felt encouraged by seeing others participate and responded by encouraging their friends and family to involve themselves too and pitch in with monetary support. Community members donate the savings of their entire life, well in their lifetime itself, to the society. The nature of social work ranged from participation in community agriculture fields, dairy farm, health services to the underprivileged, and running educational institutions. An interesting example was University Professors teaching English proficiency classes in remote backward areas like Murar in east India and Rajaborari in the jungles of tribal central India, all the year round using most modern ICT techniques. Our community members feel they have been selected by the Supreme Lord for service to humanity, nay all living beings, at large.

We have found in this quest that it is best to pursue the golden mean instead of pursuing the extreme positions and there, we think we can also come up with measures which can be observed by anybody in the outside world. The results are very interesting as they can be pursued by anybody in the outside world without even being initiated into the meditation practices with their own protocols which everybody may not be ready to follow so as to realize the benefits. So this raises great prospects of realizing possibilities and potentials for using this mode of ultra-transcendental yoga and without even becoming an adherent or an initiated follower of the Faith.

We need to resolve the inextricably linked problems of subtlest particles smaller than 10^{-35} metre Planck's length and large distances more than 10^{10} light years, and approach zero and infinity by application of logic and induction in the right way. The modern day scientists do not have any reply for the zero and infinity problem. They run away when approached with it, and when we say that it can be done with internal experiences, then they are unable to follow the protocol of food and drink which is necessary for successful practice. But, there is consensus among eastern philosophers and western scientists on one aspect, that for internal experiences or human experience, a protocol has to be necessarily followed. Following that protocol is very difficult for western nations as they will have to leave alcohol and non-vegetarian food. Consensus emerges on studying environment around those who perform yoga, mahayoga or *Surat Shabda Yoga*. We pin our hope on Corporate Social Responsibility as a measure for that. Let us focus attention on what is the effect on environment of those who do not perform *Surat Shabda Yoga*. It will not be difficult for them to accept that those who perform *Surat Shabda Yoga* have greater sense of Corporate Social Responsibility. It is wishful to think that they will follow the code and protocol of Radhsoami Faith in large numbers. However, when they see good effect of performing *Surat Shabda Yoga* on the environment, then they will be considerably impressed by the Radhasoami *Surat-Shabda-Yoga* and may gradually prepare themselves for strictly observing this protocol for gaining inner experience or human experience in the western world.

Before I close, I particularly would like to refer to one of the latest books on the subject, 'Our Mathematical Universe' by Prof. Max Tegmark at MIT (Tegmark, 2014). Like us, he is in the quest for the ultimate nature of reality. We are trying to explore ultimate nature of reality from two ends, from the ends of science as well as inner or human experience. So we have an edge over such physicists, who look at it only from the end of physical science. They do not have the practice and its force behind them. We believe in the dictum that an ounce of practice goes much farther than tons of precept, so that is what is in fact happening in the world today. There are tons and tons of precepts given by physicists and other scientists, cosmologists, microbiologists and so on, but they are not privileged to have the real practical experience of what this inner reality is, what the human experience is like. So that is where we want to provide a little assistance in terms of growing ultimate consciousness. We believe that science would also get there in due course of time, but there is already this *Surat Shabda Yoga*, what we call as transcendental yoga, or even ultra-transcendental yoga. So by taking recourse to it, you are armed with not only theory, but also practice, so you are in a better position to correct the wrong notions which people get without practice. So that is the essence of my reference to Max Tegmark's book on 'Our Mathematical Universe'. I also believe that it is this mathematics and its abstractions which will lead scientists to the ultimate reality and this is a very good evidence of such effort but they are still groping in the dark because they lack this inner or human experience in not practising themselves through this hyper transcendental yoga, so that they could perceive the reality for themselves, "sense" the reality. I would in fact say, see, hear, sense, feel, perceive, such that reality in the real meaning would be open to them as full consciousness. Given this context, I would like to submit that luckily at Dayalbagh, we have a confluence of people with the latest scientific techniques as well as people who are armed with this inner force of reality.

References

Fields C. (2012), "A model-theoretic interpretation of environment-induced superselection", International Journal of General Systems, Vol. 41, No. 8, 1 Nov. 2012 , pp. 847-859.

Gennaro R. (2012), The Consciousness Paradox : Consciousness, Concepts and Higher Order Thoughts (HOTs)", The MIT Press, 2012.

Hagelin J. (2013), " Higher States : The Neurophysiology of Enlightenment", Plenary Talk at the Eastern Philosophy Forum, Toward a Science of Consciousness (TSC 2013) Conference, Dayalbagh Educational Institute, March 2013, Abstract Book, pg. 68.

Howard M., Wallman J., Veitch V., Emerson J. (2015), "Contextuality supplies the 'magic' for quantum computation", Nature, Vol. 510, pp. 351-355, June 19, 2014.

Koenig H.E., Tokad Y. and Kesavan H.K. (1966), *Analysis of Discrete Physical Systems*, New York: McGraw-Hill, 1967.

M. Sahab (1960, 2014), *Discourses on Radhasoami Faith*, First Edition, 1960, Radhasoami Satsang Sabha, Dayalbagh (Agra), Second Edition (With Supplements), 2004.

Penrose and Hameroff (2011), Consciousness in the Universe: Neuroscience, Quantum Space-Time Geometry and Orch OR Theory, Journal of Cosmology, Vol. 14, April-May 2011.

Price D. and Barrell J. (2012), *Inner Experience and Neuroscience : Merging both Perspectives*, MIT Press, USA, 2012.

Satsangi P.S. (1969), A Physical System Theory Modelling Framework Generalized for Large Scale Economic Systems (Ph.D. Thesis, University of Waterloo, Waterloo, Ontario), 1969.

Satsangi P.S. (2003), "Reality and Truth vis-à-vis Wisdom via Aparavidya (Natural Science) and Paravidya (Phenomenology : Experiential Science)" at the International Conference of Association of Asia-Pacific Operational Research Societies at Hotel Grand International, New Delhi on 8.12.2003.

Satsangi P.S. (2006a), "Linear Graph Theory for Modelling a Variety of Systems", Int. Conf. on Differential Geometry and Topology in the Perspective of Modern Trends (DGTPMT – 2006), Dayalbagh Educational Institute, Dayalbagh, Agra, February 2006.

Satsangi P.S. (2006b), "Generalizing Physical Systems Through Applied Systems Research from "Real" Physical Systems through "Conceptual" Socio-Economic-Environmental Systems to "Complete" (Physical-Mental-Spiritual) Creational Systems", International Journal of General Systems, Vol. 35, No. 2, 2006, pp. 127-167.

Satsangi P.S. (2008), "On Systems Modelling of Macrocosm and Microcosm in the Domain of Spiritual Consciousness", Vision Talk at the Inaugural Function of International Seminar on Spiritual Awakening : A Systems Approach to Address the Civilizational Crisis (SPAWSYS 2008), January 12, 2008, Souvenir-cum-Abstract Book, pp. 23.

Satsangi P.S. (2009), "Applied Systems Research for Better Worldliness", Vision Talk at the Joint International Conference on Applied Systems Research and XXXIII National Systems Conference (ASR-NSC 2009), Dayalbagh Educational Institute, November 27, 2009, Souvenir-cum-Abstract Book, pp. 25.

Satsangi P.S. (2010), "Cosmology from the twin vantage points of Radhasoami Faith and Systems Science", Vision Talk, International Seminar on Religion of Saints ('Sants') – Radhasoami Faith, DEI, Dayalbagh, Agra, Nov. 2010 (also Chapter 23 of Expositions on Truth, Ultimate Reality and Supreme Being, Radhasoami Satsang Sabha, Dayalbagh, Agra, 2010, ISBN : 978-81-89288-60-0), Also in P. Sriramamurti, Prem Prashant and Anand Mohan (Eds.), *Spiritual Consciousness*, New Age Books, 2013, New Delhi, pp. 21-40.

Satsangi P.S. (2011), "Cosmology of Consciousness : Towards Quantum-Theoretic Systems Modelling; Spirit-Mind-Brain Interactions", Vision Talk at the Inaugural Workshop of the Centre for Consciousness Studies (CONCENT 2011), Dayalbagh Educational Institute, October 1, 2011, Abstract Book, pp. 50-67.

Satsangi P.S. (2012a), "Eastern Philosophy in the Spiritual Traditions of Oriental Saints ("Sants") : An Interpretive Structural Model (ISM) Representation", Keynote Address,

Toward a Science of Consciousness (TSC 2012) Conference : Forum on Eastern Philosophy and Consciousness, April 9, 2012, Arizona, USA.

Satsangi P.S. (2012b), "Neuro-Cognitive Spiritual Phenomenonology", Vision Talk at Special Forum on "Quantum Theory and Science of Consciousness" at International School on Quantum and Nano Computing Systems and Applications (QANSAS 2012), Dayalbagh Educational Institute, November 28, 2012, Abstract Book, pp. 53.

Satsangi P.S. (2013a), Towards Integrating Arts (First-Person Spiritual-Cognitive-Material Phenomenology) and Science (Third-Person Neuro-Physical, Environmental, Cognitive Correlates) of Consciousness, The Dayalbagh Vision, (Toward a Science of Consciousness (TSC 2013) Conference : Vision Talk), March 3-9, 2013, Centre for Consciousness Studies, Dayalbagh Educational Institute (Deemed University), Dayalbagh, Agra, India, Souvenir-cum-Abstract Book, pp. 61-63.

Satsangi. P.S. (2013b), "Consciousness : Towards Integrating Art and Science of Inner Experience", Vision Talk at the Valedictory Session of International School on Quantum and Nano Computing Systems and Applications (QANSAS 2013), Dayalbagh Educational Institute, December 1, 2013, Souvenir-cum-Abstract Book, pp. 53-54.

Satsangi P.S. (2014a), "Consciousness : An Integrative Systems Modelling Approach", Vision Talk at the East-West Forum, Twentieth Anniversary Conference on Toward a Science of Consciousness (TSC 2014) Conference, Tucson, Arizona, USA, April 21, 2014, Abstract Book, pp. 277.

Satsangi. P.S. (2014b), "Satyam-Shivam-Sundaram Revisited in the Perspective of Grand Macro / Micro Cosmology", Vision Talk at the Special Forum on "Consciousness : Integrating Eastern and Western Perspectives" at International School on Quantum and Nano Computing Systems and Applications (QANSAS 2014), Dayalbagh Educational Institute, November 26, 2014, Souvenir-cum-Abstract Book, pp. 53.

Satsangi P.S. (2015a), "Rhythms of Macrocosmic Universe and Human-Microcosm : Consciousness Systemology Perspective", Vision Talk delivered at the East-West Forum of the Toward a Science of Consciousness (TSC 2015) Conference at University of Helsinki, Finland, June 8, 2015, Abstract Book, pp. 373.

Satsangi. P.S. (2015b), "Towards An Ultimate Consciousness Conjecture (for the Human Microcosm and the Grand Macrocosm)", Vision Talk at the Special Forum on "Consciousness : Integrating Eastern and Western Perspectives" at International School on Quantum and Nano Computing Systems and Applications (QANSAS 2015), Dayalbagh Educational Institute, November 25, 2015, Souvenir-cum-Abstract Book, pp. 47.

Satsangi P.S. (2016), "Modelling microtubules in the brain as n-qudit quantum Hopfield network and beyond", Vision Talk at the Integrated East-West Forum of The Science of Consciousness (TSC 2016) Conference at University of Arizona, Tucson, USA, April 25, 2016, Abstract Book, pp. 241.

Satsangi P.S., Sahni, V. (2007), "A Systemic Experimental Study of Macrocosmic Consciousness", Proceedings of National Systems Conference 2007 (Systems Society of India), MIT, Manipal, pp. 13 -19.

Satsangi P.S., Sahni V. (2008), "Study of Human Consciousness as a Surrogate of Macrocosmic Consciousness via Scientific Measurements of Electromagnetic Wave Radiations", Proc. of XXXII National Systems Conference (NSC 2008), IIT Roorkee, December 17-19, 2008, pp. 301-307.

Satsangi P.S., Sahni V. (2012), "Cosmic Consciousness Hierarchization : Analytic, Experimental and Experiential", Concurrent Session on Science and Spirituality, Toward a Science of Consciousness (TSC 2012), Tucson, Arizona, USA, April 2012, Abstract Book, pp. 193.

Satsangi P.S., Sahni V. (2015), "Power Law of Meditational Consciousness", Concurrent Session on Meditation, Toward a Science of Consciousness (TSC 2015), Helsinki, Finland, June 2015, Abstract Book, pp. 340.

Souvenir of the Radhasoami Satsang (1961), Dayalbagh Press and Publication, Dayalbagh, Agra.

Srivastava D.P. (2013), "Graph Theoretic Quantum Field / System Modelling For Quantum Information / Computation Circuits And Algorithms", Ph.D. Thesis, Dayalbagh Educational Institute, Dayalbagh, Agra, India, 2013.

Srivastava D.P., Sahni V., Satsangi P.S., (2011) "Graph-theoretic quantum system modelling for information/computation processing circuits", International Journal of General Systems, Taylor and Francis, UK, Vol. 40, No. 8, November 2011, pp. 777–804, ISSN No. 0308-1079.

Srivastava D.P., Sahni V., Satsangi P.S. (2014) "Graph Theoretic Quantum System Modelling for Neuronal Microtubles as Hierarchical Clustered Quantum Hopfield Networks", International Journal of General Systems, Taylor & Francis, UK, Vol. 43, No. 6, August 2014, pp. 633-648, ISSN No. 0308-1079.

Srivastava D.P., Sahni V., Satsangi P.S. (2015a), "Modelling Microtubules in the Brain as n-qudit Quantum Hopfield Network and Beyond (arXiv : 1515.00774 (q.bio-NC)

Srivastava D.P., Sahni V., Satsangi P.S. (2015b), " Frequency and Energy as Neuro-correlates of Beauty in Maths, Science and Art", Concurrent Talk, East-West Forum of the Toward a Science of Consciousness (TSC 2015) Conference at University of Helsinki, Finland, June 8, 2015, Abstract Book pp. 383-384.

Srivastava D.P., Sahni V., Satsangi P.S., (2016), "Modelling microtubules in the brain as n-qudit quantum Hopfield network and beyond", International Journal of General Systems, Vol. 45. No. 1, February 2016, pp. 41-54, DOI: 10.1080/03081079.2015.1076405, ISSN No. 0308-1079.

Stapp (2007), *Quantum Approaches to Consciousness*, Chapter 31, Cambridge Handbook of Consciousness.

Swami Ved Bharati (2011), Consciousness : Measurable or Immeasurable? Spirituality and Science of Consciousness, Ramakrishna Mission Institute of Culture, Kolkata, Jan. 2011, pp. 116-141.

Tegmark M. (2014), *Our Mathematical Universe: My Quest for the Ultimate Nature of Reality*, Penguin Publishers, 2014.

Triggs M. (2012), Ancient Wisdom, Modern Technology (Brainwave Frequency Listing), http://www.lunarsight.com/freq.htm.

Zee Anthony (2010), *Quantum Field Theory in a Nutshell*, Second Edition, Princeton University Press, USA, 2010.

Zeki, S. (2014), "The experience of mathematical beauty and its neural correlates", Frontiers in Human Neuroscience, Vol. 8, Article 68, February 2014.

Chapter 2

Cosmic Consciousness Hierarchization:
Analytic, Experimental and Experiential Approaches; Power Law of Meditational Consciousness

PREM SARAN SATSANGI
Leader of Radhasoami Faith, Dayalbagh
Chairman, Advisory Committee on Education
Dayalbagh Educational Institutions, Dayalbagh, Agra, India

VISHAL SAHNI
Coordinator, Centre for Consciousness Studies,
Dayalbagh Educational Institute
Dayalbagh, Agra, India

Keywords : Analytic Hierarchy Process, Human Consciousness, Macrocosmic Consciousness, O-Theory, Power Laws

This Chapter, in conjunction with its complementary Chapter, entitled "Towards Integrating Eastern Arts and Philosophy of Consciousness and Western Perspectives of Science (Rhythms of Macrocosmic Universe and Human Microcosm : Consciousness Systemology Perspective)", presents a systemic analytic framework for hierarchization of consciousness comprehensively (M. Sahab, 2004; Satsangi, 2010, 2011, 2013a, 2013b, 2014a, 2014b, 2015a, 2015b, 2016; Satsangi and Sahni, 2012, 2015; Saaty, 1980, 2000), bridging Eastern and Western approaches (Penrose and Hameroff, 2011; Satsangi, 2012a, 2012b). It is supported by study of human consciousness as a surrogate of macrocosmic consciousness via scientific experimental measurements of electromagnetic wave radiation as well as the experiential observations of the participating members of the Dayalbagh community during meditation-cum-prayer meetings (Satsangi and Sahni, 2007, 2008, 2012, 2015).

Section 1 refers to the conceptual modelling construct firmly based on generalization of scientifically verifiable Physical System Theory (Satsangi, 2010), elaborated in the companion Chapter referred to above.

Section 2 presents the applications of Analytic Hierarchy Process (AHP) and Fuzzy AHP for hierarchization of the identified 21 cosmic consciousness regions of the Universe, consisting of six sub divisions and one buffer-zone each for the three grand-divisions of the macrocosm, viz., physical region ('Pind'), region of universal mind ('Brahmand') and purely spiritual region ('Nirmal Chetan Desh'). The hierarchization is also derivable through consensus building approach of J.N. Warfield in terms of Nominal Group Technique (NGT) and Interpretive Structural Modelling (ISM) (Warfield, 2006; Satsangi, 2012a, 2012b).

Section 3 presents a systemic experimental study of macrocosmic consciousness of the Dayalbagh community, during congregational meditation-cum-prayer meetings in the Community Hall at Dayalbagh (Satsangi, 2012a, 2012b; Satsangi and Sahni, 2007, 2008, 2012, 2015), through relevant repeatable non-intrusive (non-invasive) scientific experiments using random number generators, electric circuits such as RC filters (low pass, band pass and high pass), tuned LC circuits, RC phase-shift circuits, and a diode bridge square law modulator circuit (for sensing electromagnetic waves in the Community Hall), Quantum Random Number Generation Waveforms and Electromagnetic Wave Radiation power spectra, and finally SQUIDs (Superconducting Quantum Interference Devices)-based measurements, used for sensing extremely low magnetic fields at cryogenic temperatures. Measurement techniques have been suitably devised for recording spatial variations in consciousness across spatial clusters and during identified activity phases of the meditation-cum-prayer sessions. The SQUID-based results are quite interesting and reinforce the earlier observations. An inverse square law of variation of electromagnetic field-intensity (as a correlate of spiritual force-field intensity) with distance seems to hold. We also present the latest results of group and individual tests on meditationists of Radhasoami Faith and Tibetan Buddhism at the 15-channel SQUID-based MEG facility at DEI Centre for Consciousness Studies.

Section 4 presents the formulation of power law of meditational consciousness invoking a family of models based on Omni quantum theory and physical system theory (including fuzzy analytical hierarchy process), and requisite integration of first person inner experiences of meditationists as co-investigators with the third person scientific methodology of observing, reporting, understanding and hypothesis-testing (Satsangi, 2013a; Price and Barrell, 2012).

The Chapter concludes on the note that 'Param Purush' (Supreme Being) Radhasoami is of the form of : 'Param' (Supreme) 'sat' (Truth) – 'c(h)it' (Intelligence) –'premananda' (Bliss of Love) – 'prakash' (Refulgence) – 'shabda' (Original Mystic Name) – 'anahad nad' (Resonating Unstruck Sound), the fountainhead of all consciousness in the cosmos, perceived as an inner experiential phenomenology during

Yogic meditations (Satsangi, 2015a). The implied spiritual naumenology (or inner experiential phenomenology), as scientifically testable spiritual-psycho-physical hypotheses, is a subject matter of discussion in the companion Chapter referred to earlier.

1. O-THEORY (OMNI-QUANTUM THEORY) FOR SPIRITUAL CONSCIOUSNESS SYSTEM MODELLING IN COSMOLOGY

Consciousness is intrinsic to the grand cosmos, both at macrocosmic as well as microcosmic levels. Man, a creation on planet Earth happens to be a perfect microcosm of the macrocosm. Spirit-mind-brain consciousness interactions are at the microcosmic levels analogous to consciousness interactions between Supreme Being (Universal Spirit)-Universal Mind-Physical Universe at the macrocosmic levels (Satsangi, 2010, 2011, 2012a, 2012b, 2013a, 2013b, 2014a, 2014b, 2015a, 2015b, 2016).

1.1 SPIRITUAL SYSTEM THEORY FRAMEWORK

1.1.1 Fundamental Axiom of Spiritual Consciousness

The fundamental axiom of macrocosmic / microcosmic spiritual consciousness is that the origin of the macrocosm is an infinite spiritual energy source or reservoir known as the Supreme Creator or Being or Super Positive Pole accompanied by the omni-quantum spiritual force-field of consciousness ranging from the Super Positive Pole of full spirituality to the Nether or Negative Pole of depleted spirituality; and each constituent fundamental element of this omni-quantum spiritual force-field, known as the spirit-force of consciousness (monopole), is the one which possesses prime energy and that all other forces (mental or physical) of creation or nature have been evolved by the association of this spirit-force with media (mental or physical) of different kinds (Notice that the concept of "spirit-force" is no more intrinsically mysterious than "mass"). This gives rise to the quantum mind-force field which spans the Region of the Universal Mind and the Physical Universe, on one hand, while the quantum physical force fields – electromagnetic, weak nuclear, strong nuclear and gravitational span the third grand division, viz., the Physical Universe ("Pind") of the Macrocosm.

1.1.2 Macrocosm-Microcosm Consciousness Interaction Postulate

Man, a creation on planet Earth (the fourth subdivision from the bottom of the third grand division of macrocosm, represented by g_4 in Figure 1(a) happens to be a perfect microcosm of the macrocosm in the sense that man possesses not only six ganglia (or "*chakras*") for interaction with the macrocosm by making communion with the corresponding six subdivisions of the macrocosmic division of the physical

/ material region but also six nerve-centres (or "*Kamals*") in the grey matter of the brain for accessing the corresponding six subdivisions of the macrocosmic division or region of Universal Mind as well as six other apertures (or "*Padams*") in the white matter of the brain for communicating with the corresponding six subdivisions of the macrocosmic division of Universal Spirit or purely spiritual regions.

(Notice that the degree of spiritual consciousness (or spiritual potential) of the macrocosm, pertaining to its three grand divisions ranging from the purely spiritual region (i.e. the macrocosmic division of the Universal Spirit) through the region (or macrocosmic division) of Universal Mind to the physical / material region (or macrocosmic division) together with their six subdivisions each, varies in descending order of magnitude.)

1.1.3 Universal Consciousness Realization Postulate

The religion of Saints prescribes a systemic methodology of the meditational practice of "*Surat*" (spirit force) – "*Shabda*" (spiritual sound currents) – "*Yoga*" (union) for uniting the spirit force of a human being with the "characteristic" spiritual sound currents[1], which emanate from the various spirit centres ($e_6 - e_1$; $f_6 - f_1$; $g_6 - g_1$ shown in Figure 1(a) in different regions and sub-regions (i.e. grand divisions and sub-divisions) of the macrocosm for realizing corresponding levels of increasing degree of consciousness (or spiritual potential) from the lowest subdivision (g_1) of the macrocosmic division of physical / material region through the macrocosmic division of the Universal Mind to the highest subdivision of the Supreme Creator or Being (e_6) of the purely spiritual region. Figure 1(b) is the system linear graph modelling framework for spiritual domains.

The object in view is to realize the highest degree of macrocosmic consciousness (spiritual potential) corresponding to e_6 in Figure 1(a), i.e. God (the goal of religion) or Ultimate Reality (the goal of philosophy) or Truth (the goal of Science) which are but three names of the same Supreme (Spiritual) Essence, as defined by the fundamental axiom of spiritual consciousness by means of awakening the 18 hidden subtle senses or centres within man as a microcosm implied by $g_1' - g_6'$, $f_1' - f_6'$; e_1'-e_6' in Figure 1(a), and as referred to in the Universal Consciousness Realization Postulate invoking the meditational practice of "*Surat Shabda Yoga*" of unifying the spirit force of man with the

[1] This is somewhat akin to the Cosmic Background Microwave Radiation emitted at the time of the Big Bang (marking the beginning of creation of physical universe) which is being detected even to this day by devices such as COBE (Cosmic Background Explorer) Satellite as the Microwave Relic of the Big Bang to study the state of the physical universe soon after its birth.

"characteristic" sound-currents emanating from spirit-centres at various levels of consciousness (or spiritual potential). However, this requires rigorous training and practice under the guidance of an adept or mentor or 'Guru'.

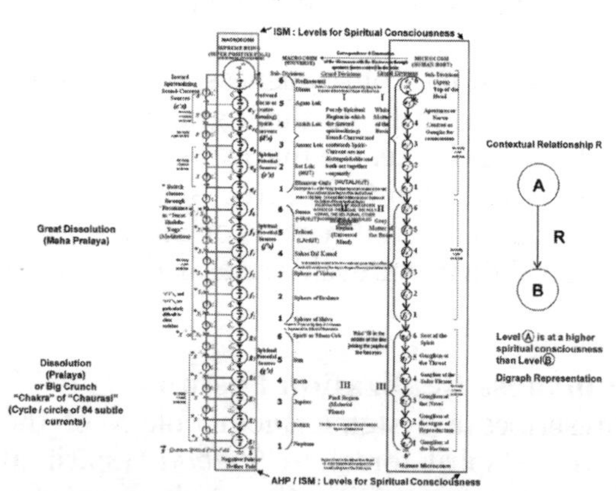

Figure 1A Schematic : A Rudimentary Modelling Framework for Spiritual Domains
(The entire creation is evolved out of the pre-creational Nether Pole)
The second sub-division sphere of a set of six sub-divisions of each grand-division of Macrocosm or Human-Microcosm is the one which is endowed with generative function : e.g. e_2 (Sat Lok), f_2 (Sphere of Brahma); and g_2' (Man : Ganglion at the organ of reproduction)

FIGURE 1(a)
Schematic : A Rudimentary Modelling Framework for Spiritual Domains

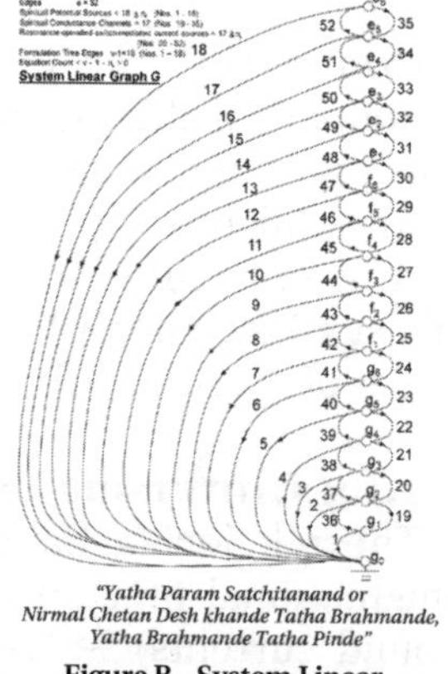

Figure B System Linear Graph Model G :
A Rudimentary Modelling Framework for Spiritual Domains)

FIGURE 1(b)
System Linear Graph Model G for 1(a)

2. COSMIC CONSCIOUSNESS CHARACTERIZATION USING ANALYTIC HIERARCHY PROCESS (AHP)

Consciousness implies awareness : subjective experience of internal and external phenomenal worlds. Consciousness is central also to understanding, meaning and volitional choice with the experience of free will (Penrose and Hameroff, 2011). While the science of consciousness in ancient India as given in Vedas and Upanishads dates back to second millennia B.C.; it is over the past 50 years or so there has been considerable interest in the modern science in the West, in terms of cognitive psychology and neuro-science (neuro-physiology or neuro-medicine) in studying the consciousness (Satsangi, 2010).

The Analytic Hierarchy Process (AHP) (Saaty, 1980) is a theory of measurement through pairwise comparisons and relies on the judgments of experts to derive priority scales. It is these scales that measure intangibles in relative terms. The comparisons are made using a scale of absolute judgments that represents, how much more, one element dominates another with respect to a given attribute. This method elicits preferences through pairwise comparisons in which the Decision Maker considers the relative importance of two factors at a time with respect to a common higher level criterion. For each comparison, the decision maker indicates the intensity of preference of one factor over another as a point estimate (in classical AHP) or a fuzzy term/number (in fuzzy AHP) on an appropriate scale. In general, evaluation and calculation in AHP can be divided into four stages: (1) scoring the alternatives under each criterion; (2) weighting the criterion; (3) calculating the final score; and (4) ranking and final decision.

2.1 ATTRIBUTES / CRITERIA OF CONSCIOUSNESS

In terms of oriental philosophy of Saints (Radhasoami Faith) (M. Sahab, 1960, 2004), consciousness has the following six chief attributes or criteria, both at the macrocosmic level of the universe as well as the microcosmic level of human being :

1. SAT –	the truth of love or inseparability
2. C(H)IT –	the conscious knowing (the reality of immortal existence)
3. PREM-ANANDA –	Bliss of love (Experiencing the joy of unity consciousness)
4. PRAKASH –	Light - Refulgence of Consciousness / energy centres
5. SHABDA –	Characteristic mystic word or name (outward spirit-current and inward and attractive sound-current articulation of consciousness force-field)
6. ANAHAD NAD –	Unstruck celestial music

The alternatives are the three grand division, with their six sub-divisions each, and the separator regions as below :

NIRMAL CHETAN DESH (First Grand Division)

- Radhasoami
- Agam
- Alakh
- Anami
- Sat Lok
- Bhanwargufa

MAHASUNNA (Separator)

BRAHMAND (Second Grand Division)

- Sunna
- Trikuti
- Sahas Dal Kamal
- Vishnu Lok
- Brahma Lok
- Shiv Lok

CHIDAKASA (Separator)

PIND (Third Grand Division)

- Moon (Spirit-Orb)
- Sun
- Earth
- Jupiter
- Saturn
- Neptune

HELL (Nether Pole)

Figure 2 shows the Cosmic Consciousness Hierarchization Diagram with the various criteria / objectives and alternatives. Implementation of fuzzy Analytic Hierarchy Process for cosmic consciousness involves evaluation by participants of grade of membership of each of the identified 21 alternative consciousness centres for the 6 criteria or attributes of consciousness in the form of a position matrix based on their domain knowledge and intuitive meditational experience.

A series of workshops involving application of Analytic Hierarchy Process (AHP) and fuzzy-Analytic Hierarchy Process (fuzzy-AHP) to Cosmic Consciousness Characterization were organized at the DEI Centre for Consciousness Studies with participation of Chief Mentor of the Radhasoami Faith, members of Divinity Forum of Dayalbagh, management and systems specialists from DEI in three parts :

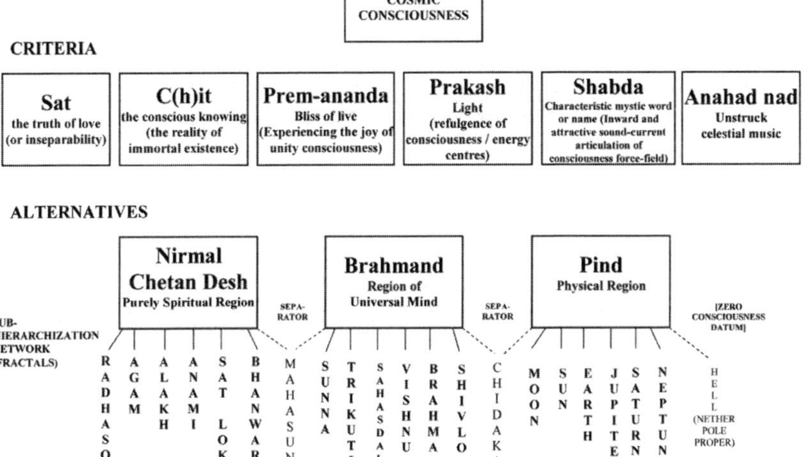

FIGURE 2
Cosmic Consciousness Hierarchization Diagram

a) Workshop on AHP for the three grand divisions
b) Workshop on fuzzy AHP for the three grand divisions
c) Workshop on AHP and fuzzy AHP for the 18 sub-divisions (fractals)

2.2 AHP FOR THE COSMIC CONSCIOUSNESS HIERARCHIZATION OF THE THREE GRAND DIVISIONS

2.2.1 Scale

The AHP for the three grand divisions (Nirmal Chetan Desh, Brahmand and Pind) involved use of the fundamental scale for pairwise companions which the workshop participants had to fill in. A sample of the questionnaire is shown in Figure 3.

**Analytic Hierarchy Process (AHP) Workshop on
Cosmic Consciousness Hierarchization**

QUESTIONNAIRE

Name (optional) ______________________

Please fill in values from 1-9 for the each of the criteria based on your experiential knowledge. The table below can be used for reference to the values 1 to 9.

The Fundamental Scale for Pairwise Comparisons		
Intensity of Importance	**Definition**	**Explanation**
1	Equal importance	Two elements contribute equally to the objective
3	Moderate importance	Experience and judgment moderately favor one element over another
5	Strong importance	Experience and judgment strongly favor one element over another
7	Very strong importance	One element is favored very strongly over another; its dominance is demonstrated in practice
9	Extreme importance	The evidence favoring one element over another is of the highest possible order of affirmation
Intensities of 2, 4, 6, and 8 can be used to express intermediate values. Intensities of 1.1, 1.2, 1.3, etc. can be used for elements that are very close in importance.		

Criteria 1 (SAT – the truth of love or inseparability)

REGION	Please fill from 1-9	REGION	Please fill from 1-9
Nirmal Chetan Desh (Purely Spiritual Region)		**Brahmand (Region of Universal Mind)**	
Nirmal Chetan Desh (Purely Spiritual Region)		**Pind (Physical Region)**	
Brahmand (Region of Universal Mind)		**Pind (Physical Region)**	

Criteria 2 (C(H)IT – the conscious knowing (the reality of immortal existence))

REGION	Please fill from 1-9	REGION	Please fill from 1-9
Nirmal Chetan Desh (Purely Spiritual Region)		**Brahmand (Region of Universal Mind)**	
Nirmal Chetan Desh (Purely Spiritual Region)		**Pind (Physical Region)**	
Brahmand (Region of Universal Mind)		**Pind (Physical Region)**	

FIGURE 3
Questionnaire used for AHP workshop of Three Grand Divisions

2.2.2 Results

The results are summarized in Table 1 below and Nirmal Chetan Desh is the preferred alternative with a priority of 0.7859, followed by Brahmand (priority of 0.1368) and Pind (priority of 0.0772). The results were computed using MATLAB software as well as Expert Choice software, which presents the results graphically. The detailed MATLAB results are presented in Table 2 and Figure 4 shows the results computed using Expert Choice.

Table 1 : Results of AHP for Three Grand Divisions

	Priority with Respect to						
Region	**Sat**	**Chit**	**Premananda**	**Prakash**	**Shabda**	**Anahad Nad**	**GOAL**
Nirmal Chetan Desh	0.0906	0.0344	0.2554	0.0402	0.1129	0.2524	**0.7859**
Brahmand	0.0166	0.0071	0.0423	0.0083	0.0207	0.0418	**0.1368**
Pind	0.0091	0.0037	0.0245	0.0043	0.0114	0.0242	**0.0772**
Totals	**0.1164**	**0.0452**	**0.3221**	**0.0529**	**0.1450**	**0.3184**	**1**

Table 2 : Detailed Results of AHP for Three Grand Divisions using MATLAB

SAT

	Nirmal Chetan Desh	**Brahmand**	**Pind**	**Priority**
Nirmal Chetan Desh	1	6	9	0.7786
Brahmand	1/6	1	2	0.1428
Pind	1/9	1/2	1	0.0786

Sum of Priorities = 1
Consistency Ratio = 0.0079

CHIT

	Nirmal Chetan Desh	**Brahmand**	**Pind**	**Priority**
Nirmal Chetan Desh	1	5	9	0.7608
Brahmand	1/5	1	2	0.1576
Pind	1/9	1/2	1	0.0816

Sum of Priorities = 1
Consistency Ratio = 0.0011

PREMANANDA

	Nirmal Chetan Desh	**Brahmand**	**Pind**	**Priority**
Nirmal Chetan Desh	1	7	9	0.7928
Brahmand	1/7	1	2	0.1312
Pind	1/9	1/2	1	0.0760

Sum of Priorities = 1
Consistency Ratio = 0.0187

PRAKASH

	Nirmal Chetan Desh	**Brahmand**	**Pind**	**Priority**
Nirmal Chetan Desh	1	5	9	0.7608
Brahmand	1/5	1	2	0.1576
Pind	1/9	1/2	1	0.0816

Sum of Priorities = 1
Consistency Ratio = 0.0011

SHABDA

	Nirmal Chetan Desh	**Brahmand**	**Pind**	**Priority**
Nirmal Chetan Desh	1	6	9	0.7786
Brahmand	1/6	1	2	0.1428
Pind	1/9	1/2	1	0.0786

Sum of Priorities = 1
Consistency Ratio = 0.0079

ANAHAD NAD

	Nirmal Chetan Desh	Brahmand	Pind	Priority
Nirmal Chetan Desh	1	7	9	0.7928
Brahmand	1/7	1	2	0.1312
Pind	1/9	1/2	1	0.0760

Sum of Priorities = 1
Consistency Ratio = 0.0187

CRITERIA WEIGHTAGE

	Sat	Chit	Premananda	Prakash	Shabda	Anahad Nad	Priority
Sat	1	2	1/5	3	1	1/2	0.1164
Chit	1/2	1	1/9	1	1/3	1/9	0.0452
Premananda	5	9	1	3	2	1	0.3221
Prakash	1/3	1	1/3	1	1/3	1/7	0.0529
Shabda	1	3	1/2	3	1	1/2	0.1450
Anahad Nad	2	9	1	7	2	1	0.3184

Sum of Priorities = 1
Consistency Ratio = 0.0373

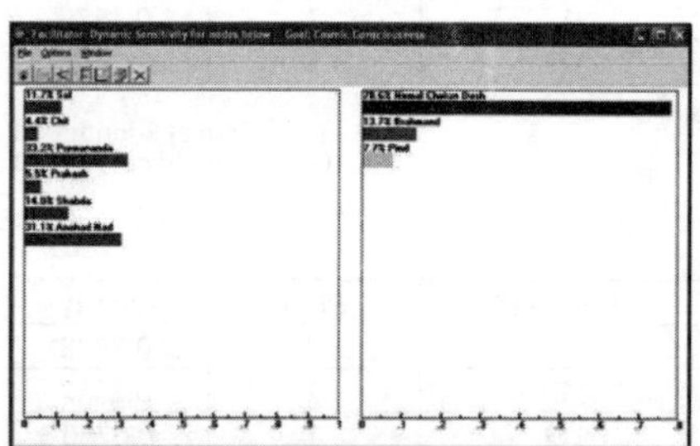

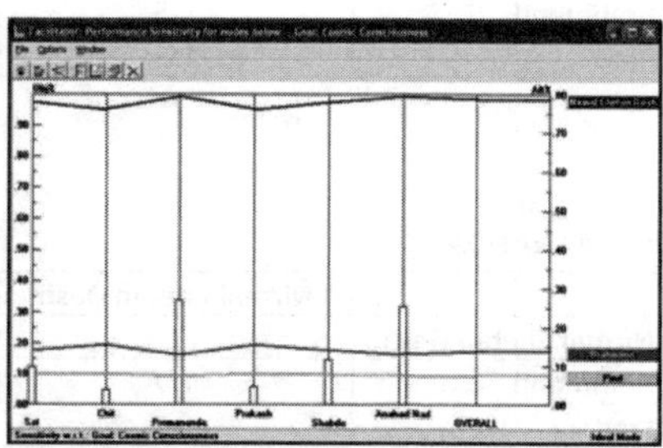

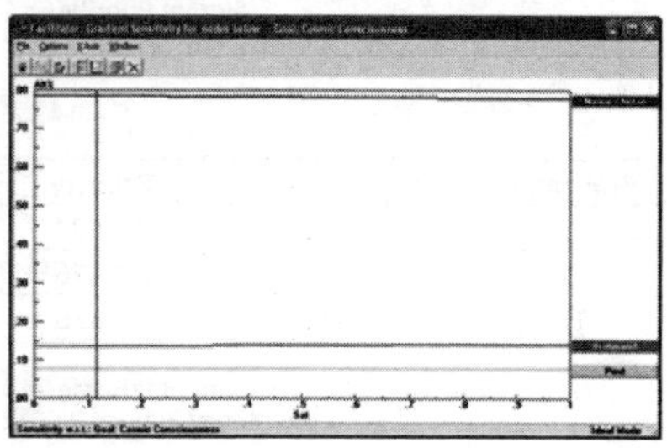

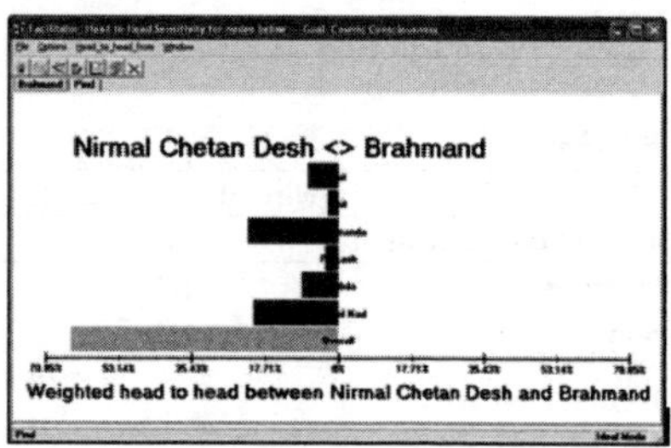

FIGURE 4
AHP results using Expert Choice software

2.3 FUZZY ANALYTIC HIERARCHY PROCESS (FUZZY AHP) FOR COSMIC CONSCIOUSNESS HIERARCHIZATION OF THE THREE GRAND DIVISIONS

2.3.1 Scale

The fuzzy AHP is the fuzzy extension of AHP to efficiently handle the fuzziness of the data involved in the decision making. It is easier to understand and it can effectively handle both qualitative and quantitative data in the multi-attribute decision making problems. In this approach triangular fuzzy numbers are used for the preferences of one criterion over another and then by using the extent analysis method, the synthetic extent value of the pairwise comparison is calculated. The fuzzy sets are specified as a set of three values (lower value, peak, middle value). (Ozdagoglu, 2007)

The fuzzy sets used in Fuzzy-AHP for the three grand divisions are presented in Figure 5.

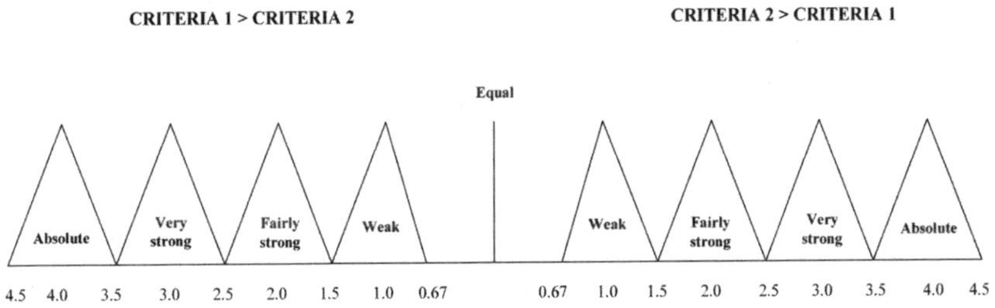

FIGURE 5
Fuzzy sets used for comparison in AHP for Three Grand Divisions

2.3.2 Results

The results of fuzzy-AHP closely match the results of classical AHP presented in section 2.2. The results are computed using a winner-takes-all approach, so the first iteration gives Nirmal Chetan Desh as the preferred alternative. In the second iteration, comparison of Brahmand and Pind is carried out and Brahmand emerges as the preferred alternative.

Table 3 presents the overall result. The detailed result is in Table 4.

Table 3 : Results of fuzzy-AHP for Three Grand Divisions

Region	Priority with Respect to						
	Sat	Chit	Premananda	Prakash	Shabda	Anahad Nad	GOAL
Nirmal Chetan Desh	0	0	0	0	0	1	1
Brahmand	0	0	0	0	0	0	0
Pind	0	0	0	0	0	0	0
Totals	**0**	**0**	**0**	**0**	**0**	**1**	**1**

ITERATION 2 (AFTER ELIMINATING NIRMAL CHETAN DESH)

	Priority with Respect to						
Region	Sat	Chit	Premananda	Prakash	Shabda	Anahad Nad	GOAL
Brahmand	0	0	0	0	0	1	1
Pind	0	0	0	0	0	0	0
Totals	**0**	**0**	**0**	**0**	**0**	**1**	**1**

Table 4 : Detailed result of fuzzy AHP for Three Grand Divisions

MATRICES BASED ON FUZZY SETS (IN LOWER BOUND, PEAK, UPPER BOUND FORM)

SAT

	Nirmal Chetan Desh	Brahmand	Pind	Priority
Nirmal Chetan Desh	(1,1,1)	(5,6,7)	(7,8,9)	1
Brahmand	(0.1429, 0.1667,0.2)	(1,1,1)	(1,2,3)	0
Pind	(0.1111,0.1250,0.1429)	(0.3333,0.5,1)	(1,1,1)	0

Iteration 2 (after eliminating Nirmal Chetan Desh)

	Brahmand	Pind	Priority
Brahmand	(1,1,1)	(1,2,3)	1
Pind	(0.3333,0.5,1)	(1,1,1)	0

CHIT

	Nirmal Chetan Desh	Brahmand	Pind	Priority
Nirmal Chetan Desh	**(1,1,1)**	**(4,5,6)**	**(7,8,9)**	1
Brahmand	(0.1667,0.2,0.25)	(1,1,1)	(1,2,3)	0
Pind	(0.1111,0.1250,0.1429)	(0.3333,0.5,1)	(1,1,1)	0

Iteration 2 (after eliminating Nirmal Chetan Desh)

	Brahmand	Pind	Priority
Brahmand	(1,1,1)	(1,2,3)	1
Pind	(0.3333,0.5,1)	(1,1,1)	0

PREMANANDA

	Nirmal Chetan Desh	Brahmand	Pind	Priority
Nirmal Chetan Desh	(1,1,1)	(6,7,8)	(7,8,9)	1
Brahmand	(0.1250,0.1429,0.1667)	(1,1,1)	(1,2,3)	0
Pind	(0.1111,0.1250,0.1429)	(0.3333,0.5,1)	(1,1,1)	0

Iteration 2 (after eliminating Nirmal Chetan Desh)

	Brahmand	Pind	Priority
Brahmand	(1,1,1)	(1,2,3)	1
Pind	(0.3333,0.5,1)	(1,1,1)	0

PRAKASH

	Nirmal Chetan Desh	Brahmand	Pind	Priority
Nirmal Chetan Desh	(1,1,1)	(5,6,7)	(7,8,9)	1
Brahmand	(0.1429,0.1667,0.2)	(1,1,1)	(1,2,3)	0
Pind	(0.1111,0.1250,0.1429)	(0.3333,0.5,1)	(1,1,1)	0

Iteration 2 (after eliminating Nirmal Chetan Desh)

	Brahmand	Pind	Priority
Brahmand	(1,1,1)	(1,2,3)	1
Pind	(0.3333,0.5,1)	(1,1,1)	0

SHABDA

	Nirmal Chetan Desh	Brahmand	Pind	Priority
Nirmal Chetan Desh	(1,1,1)	(1,1,1)	(7,8,9)	1
Brahmand	(1,1,1)	(1,1,1)	(1,2,3)	0
Pind	(0.1111,0.1250,0.1429)	(0.3333,0.5,1)	(1,1,1)	0

Iteration 2 (after eliminating Nirmal Chetan Desh)

	Brahmand	Pind	Priority
Brahmand	(1,1,1)	(1,2,3)	1
Pind	(0.3333,0.5,1)	(1,1,1)	0

ANAHAD NAD

	Nirmal Chetan Desh	Brahmand	Pind	Priority
Nirmal Chetan Desh	(1,1,1)	(6,7,8)	(7,8,9)	1
Brahmand	(0.1250,0.1429,0.1667)	(1,1,1)	(1,2,3)	0
Pind	(0.1111,0.1250,0.1429)	(0.3333,0.5,1)	(1,1,1)	0

Iteration 2 (after eliminating Nirmal Chetan Desh)

	Brahmand	Pind	Priority
Brahmand	(1,1,1)	(1,2,3)	1
Pind	(0.3333,0.5,1)	(1,1,1)	0

Criteria Weightage

	Sat	Chit	Premananda	Prakash	Shabda	Anahad Nad	Priority
Sat	(1,1,1)	(1,2,3)	(0.1714,0.2083, 0.2667)	(2,3,4)	(1,1,1)	(0.3333,0.5,1)	0
Chit	(0.3333,0.5,1)	(1,1,1)	(0.1111,0.125, 0.1429)	(0.2667,0.375, 0.667)	(0.2667,0.375, 0.667)	(0.1111,0.125, 0.1429)	0
Premananda	(3.75,4.8, 5.833)	(7,8,9)	(1,1,1)	(2,3,4)	(1,2,3)	(1,1,1)	0
Prakash	(0.25,0.3333, 0.5)	(1.5,2.667, 3.75)	(0.25,0.3333, 0.5)	(1,1,1)	(0.2667,0.375, 0.667)	(0.127,0.1458, 0.1714)	0
Shabda	(1,1,1)	(1.5,2.667, 3.75)	(0.3333,0.5,1)	(1.5,2.667, 3.75)	(1,1,1)	(0.3333,0.5,1)	0
Anahad Nad	(1,2,3)	(7,8,9)	(1,1,1)	(5.8333, 6.8571, 7.875)	(1,2,3)	(1,1,1)	1

2.4 AHP FOR COSMIC CONSCIOUSNESS HIERARCHIZATION OF 18 SUB-DIVISIONS (FRACTALS)

The AHP exercise for the six sub-divisions of each grand division used the same scale as section 2.2. The results are summarized in Table 5. In each grand division, pairwise comparison is carried out between the upper three sub-divisions and the lower three sub-divisions.

Table 5 : Results of AHP for 18 sub-divisions

FIRST GRAND DIVISION – Upper 3 sub-regions

	Radhasoami	Agam	Alakh	Priority
Radhasoami	1	4	4	0.6667
Agam	¼	1	1	0.1667
Alakh	¼	1	1	0.1667

Sum of Priorities = 1
Consistency Ratio = 0

FIRST GRAND DIVISION – Lower 3 sub-regions

	Anami	Sat Lok	Bhanwar Gufa	Priority
Anami	1	1	2	0.4000
Sat Lok	1	1	2	0.4000
Bhanwar Gufa	½	1/2	1	0.2000

Sum of Priorities = 1
Consistency Ratio = 0

SECOND GRAND DIVISION – Upper 3 sub-regions

	Sunna	Trikuti	Sahasdal Kamal	Priority
Sunna	1	2	4	0.5714
Trikuti	½	1	2	0.2857
Sahasdal Kamal	¼	1/2	1	0.1429

Sum of Priorities = 1
Consistency Ratio = 0

SECOND GRAND DIVISION – Lower 3 sub-regions

	Vishnu Lok	Brahma Lok	Shiv Lok	Priority
Vishnu Lok	1	1	2	0.4126
Brahma Lok	1	1	1	0.3275
Shiv Lok	½	1	1	0.2599

Sum of Priorities = 1
Consistency Ratio = 0.0462

THIRD GRAND DIVISION – Upper 3 sub-regions

	Moon	Sun	Earth	Priority
Moon	1	2	4	0.5714
Sun	½	1	2	0.2857
Earth	¼	1/2	1	0.1429

Sum of Priorities = 1
Consistency Ratio = 0

THIRD GRAND DIVISION – Lower 3 sub-regions

	Jupiter	Saturn	Neptune	Priority
Jupiter	1	1	2	0.4126
Saturn	1	1	1	0.3275
Neptune	½	1	1	0.2599

Sum of Priorities = 1
Consistency Ratio = 0.0462

2.5 FUZZY AHP FOR COSMIC CONSCIOUSNESS HIERARCHIZATION OF 18 SUB-DIVISIONS (FRACTALS)

The fuzzy AHP exercise for the six sub-divisions of each grand division used the same scale as section 2.3. The results are summarized in Table 6. In each grand division, pairwise comparison is carried out between the upper three sub-divisions and the lower three sub-divisions.

Table 6 : Results of Fuzzy AHP for 18 sub-divisions

FIRST GRAND DIVISION – Upper 3 sub-regions

	Radhasoami	**Agam**	**Alakh**	**Priority**
Radhasoami	(1,1,1)	(3,4,5)	(3,4,5)	1
Agam	(1/5, 1/4, 1/3)	(1,1,1)	(1,1,1)	0
Alakh	(1/5, 1/4, 1/3)	(1,1,1)	(1,1,1)	0

Iteration 2 (without considering Radhasoami)

	Agam	**Alakh**	**Priority**
Agam	(1,1,1)	(1,1,1)	Equal
Alakh	(1,1,1)	(1,1,1)	

FIRST GRAND DIVISION – Lower 3 sub-regions

	Anami	**Sat Lok**	**Bhanwar Gufa**	**Priority**
Anami	(1,1,1)	(1,1,1)	(1,2,3)	Equal
Sat Lok	(1,1,1)	(1,1,1)	(1,2,3)	
Bhanwar Gufa	(1/3, 1/2, 1)	(1/3, 1/2, 1)	(1,1,1)	0

Iteration 2 (without considering Anami)

	Sat Lok	**Bhanwar Gufa**	**Priority**
Sat Lok	(1,1,1)	(1,2,3)	1
Bhanwar Gufa	(1/3, 1/2, 1)	(1,1,1)	0

SECOND GRAND DIVISION – Upper 3 sub-regions

	Sunna	**Trikuti**	**Sahasdal Kamal**	**Priority**
Sunna	(1,1,1)	(1,2,3)	(3,4,5)	1
Trikuti	(1/3,1/2,1)	(1,1,1)	(1,2,3)	0
Sahasdal Kamal	(1/5,1/4,1/3)	(1/3,1/2,1)	(1,1,1)	0

Iteration 2 (without considering Sunna)

	Trikuti	**Sahasdal Kamal**	**Priority**
Trikuti	(1,1,1)	(1,2,3)	1
Sahasdal Kamal	(1/3,1/2,1)	(1,1,1)	0

SECOND GRAND DIVISION – Lower 3 sub-regions

	Vishnu Lok	Brahma Lok	Shiv Lok	Priority
Vishnu Lok	(1,1,1)	(1,1,1)	(1,2,3)	1
Brahma Lok	(1,1,1)	(1,1,1)	(1,1,1)	0
Shiv Lok	(1/3,1/2,1)	(1,1,1)	(1,1,1)	0

Iteration 2 (without considering Vishnu Lok)

	Brahma Lok	Shiv Lok	Priority
Brahma Lok	(1,1,1)	(1,1,1)	Equal
Shiv Lok	(1,1,1)	(1,1,1)	

THIRD GRAND DIVISION – Upper 3 sub-regions

	Moon	Sun	Earth	Priority
Moon	(1,1,1)	(1,2,3)	(3,4,5)	1
Sun	(1/3,1/2,1)	(1,1,1)	(1,2,3)	0
Earth	(1/5,1/4,1/3)	(1/3,1/2,1)	(1,1,1)	0

Iteration 2 (without considering Moon)

	Sun	Earth	Priority
Sun	(1,1,1)	(1,2,3)	1
Earth	(1/3,1/2,1)	(1,1,1)	0

THIRD GRAND DIVISION – Lower 3 sub-regions

	Jupiter	Saturn	Neptune	Priority
Jupiter	(1,1,1)	(1,1,1)	(1,2,3)	1
Saturn	(1,1,1)	(1,1,1)	(1,1,1)	0
Neptune	(1/3,1/2,1)	(1,1,1)	(1,1,1)	0

Iteration 2 (without considering Jupiter)

	Saturn	Neptune	Priority
Saturn	(1,1,1)	(1,1,1)	Equal
Neptune	(1,1,1)	(1,1,1)	

3. EXPERIMENTAL APPROACH

3.1 INDIRECT SCIENTIFIC MEASUREMENT OF SPIRITUALITY (SATSANGI AND SAHNI, 2007, 2008)

As implied by the fundamental axiom of spiritual consciousness enunciated earlier, the spirit-force possesses prime energy which evolves into various mental or physical forces by its association with media of different kinds. Accordingly when the spiritual waves come into contact with a physical medium in the physical universe, these take on the form of one of the fundamental physical forces and associated waves. An indirect measurement of spirituality is therefore scientifically feasible by measuring electromagnetic forces and waves which are relatively easier to sense. A preliminary systemic study of spiritual consciousness of Dayalbagh community, during congregational meditation-cum-prayer meetings in the Community Hall has been carried out through relevant, repeatable non-intrusive, non-invasive scientific experiments using random number generators, electric circuits such as RC filters (low pass, band pass and high pass), tuned LC circuits, RC phase-shift circuits, and a diode bridge square law modulator circuit. Some of the neuroscientists in their zeal have been led astray in mistaking physical effects for the spiritual causes and thereby drawing fallacious conclusions that spiritual consciousness can be reduced to brain states as it were. The experimental study referred to here is distinct from the recently reported experiments of some of the neuro-scientists scanning the brain of the meditationists such as Tibetan Lamas or Franciscan nuns while they were engaged in meditation through invasive and intrusive techniques such as MRI and SPECT. Systemic experimental studies of spiritual consciousness as alluded to above reinforce the view that there is no disparity between (physical) science and religion (spiritual science), the latter being an extension of physical science to the realm of transcendental science of consciousness.

This section extends the measurements by utilizing Superconducting Quantum Interference Devices (SQUIDs), which have very sensitive magnetometers used to measure extremely small magnetic fields, based on superconducting loops containing Josephson junctions, to improve the quality and sensitivity of indirect measurements of spirituality. Refined measurement techniques employed in the research reported in this chapter not only support the preliminary findings already reported in the earlier papers (Satsangi and Sahni 2007, 2008) but extend them further considerably. The results further reinforce the presence of the identified meditational frequencies of 3 Hz, 4.5 Hz, 76 Hz, 108 Hz and 126 Hz during Prayer Meetings.

The SQUID devices work at cryogenic temperature can detect fields in the range of picoTesla (10^{-12} Tesla) to femtoTesla (10^{-15} Tesla). There is a major low frequency component which appears as a baseline near 0 Hz in all measurements, which is probably the magnetic field of the earth (varies from 30-40 microtesla) as well as field of surrounding pumps, motors etc. Earth's magnetic field is removed by filtering out the low frequency DC component. Figure 6 shows the SQUID gradiometer used. A special prayer meeting was held in the Quantum-Nano Systems Centre where SQUID devices are installed. SQUID gradiometer is interfaced with a PC and we get a digital output from -32767 to +32767 for an output at the SQUID box from -10 to 10 V.

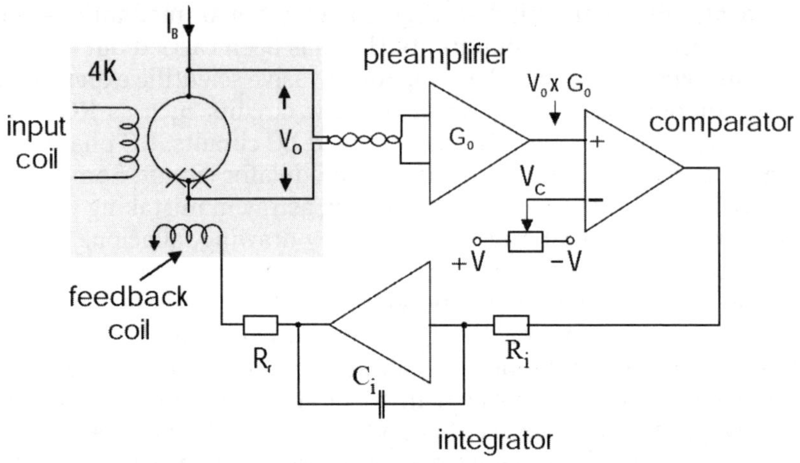

FIGURE 6
SQUID Gradiometer

The salient observations from the previous studies are summarized below :

- The 126 Hz component is minimum before arrival of the mentor.
- During Dhyan (meditation), it reaches its peak, which is also a local maxima.
- Maxima for 108 Hz and 126 Hz occur simultaneously during Dhyan (meditation).
- Maxima for 4.5 Hz occurs during prayer "Radhasoami Nam" shared also by the concurrent larger maxima occurring for 76 Hz during the same phase.
- Maxima for 76 Hz occurs during Bachan (Discourse).

The recording of concurrent maxima during the same activity phase may be interpreted as sharing of the corresponding spiritual states during the concerned activity-phase by the mentor or other meditationist cluster as the case may be.

A total of six data sets were generated as follows :

- Control Set (Pre-meditation) : A 15 minute control set was generated when superconducting (<4 Kelvin) temperature was reached with no person inside the Hall
- Set 1 (During pre-inspection of SQUID equipment by Mentor)

- Set 2 (During meditation by Mentor and congregation)
- Set 3 (During Path recital and Prasad distribution – lot of movement and activity was going on)
- Set 4 (Post-inspection of SQUID equipment by Mentor)
- Residual Set (after the session)

3.2 RESULTS OF SQUID MEASUREMENTS

The experimental results carried out in measuring the environmental correlates of spirituality, in terms of electromagnetic field in the neighbourhood, have consistently shown the presence of few identified meditational frequencies in our prayer and meditation meetings of the congregation : 3 Hz, 4.5 Hz being the initial meditational stage, which is corroborated by other neural correlates too, 76 Hz being at the level 4 or 5 of the Region of Universal Mind, 108 Hz being level 6, the highest level of the Region of Universal Mind or probably just the initial level of the Region of Pure Spirituality; and 126 Hz is from the Region of Pure Spirituality, the most Manifest form of the Supreme Being and this is believed to be the frequency accompanying the Mentor in Radhasoami Satsang, Dayalbagh.

The results are summarized in Table 7 and the plots are in Figure 7.

Table 7 : Summary of SQUID measurements during meditation

Set	4.5 Hz	76 Hz	108 Hz	126 Hz	Low frequency component (Earth)
A. Control Set (Pre-session)	-28.9668 dB	-32.2162 dB	-17.9033 dB (Local minima)	-34.1675 dB (Local minima)	13.4717dB
B. Set 1 (Pre-Inspection)	1.9897dB (Local maxima)	-25.5724 dB	-1.8774 dB (Local maxima)	-6.2933 dB (Local maxima)	14.4037 dB
C. Set 2 (Meditation)	1.6612dB (Local maxima)	-20.0867 dB	-2.2146 dB (Local maxima)	-20.0724 dB (Local maxima)	12.8212 dB
D. Set 3 (Prayer & Prasad)	1.8519 dB (Local maxima)	-22.0176 dB	-9.8532 dB (Local maxima)	-22.3010 dB (Local maxima)	12.6171 dB
E. Set 4 (Post-Inspection)	0.7588 dB (Local maxima)	-18.3021 dB	-1.3762 dB (Local maxima)	-4.8796 dB (Local maxima)	14.2845 dB
F. Residual Set (Post-session)	-7.7702 dB	-10.4038 dB	-10.4170 dB	-52.3565 dB (Global minima)	10.0755 dB

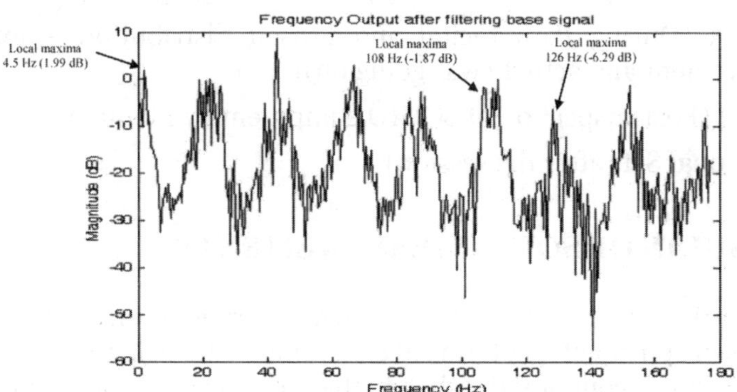

FIGURE 7(a)

Frequency Plot of Set 1 with earth field filtered – Local maxima at 126 Hz

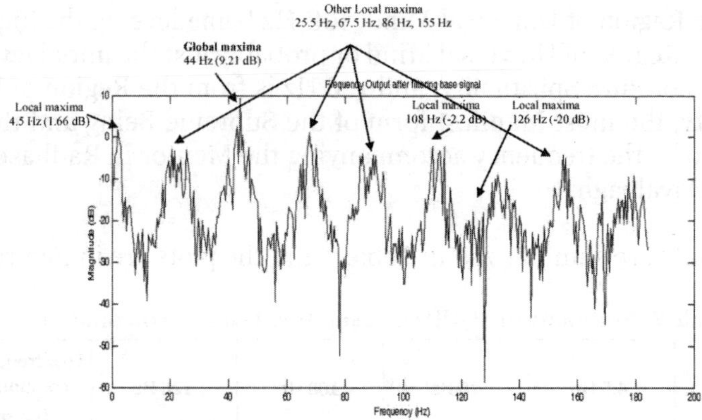

FIGURE 7 (b)

Frequency Plot of Set 2 with earth field filtered – Local maxima at 108 Hz, 126 Hz

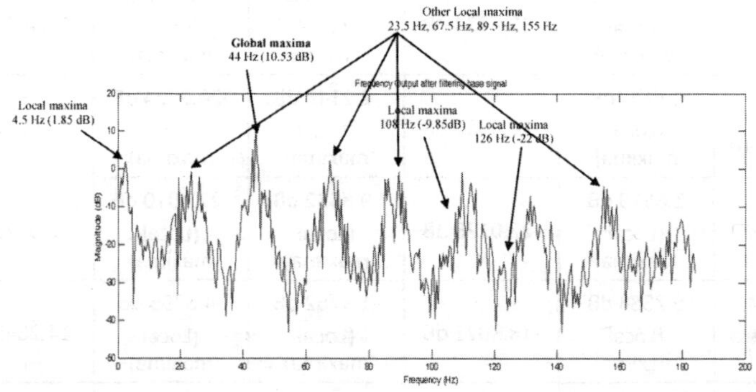

FIGURE 7 (c)

Frequency Plot of Set 3 with earth field filtered – Local Maxima at 108, Hz, 126 Hz

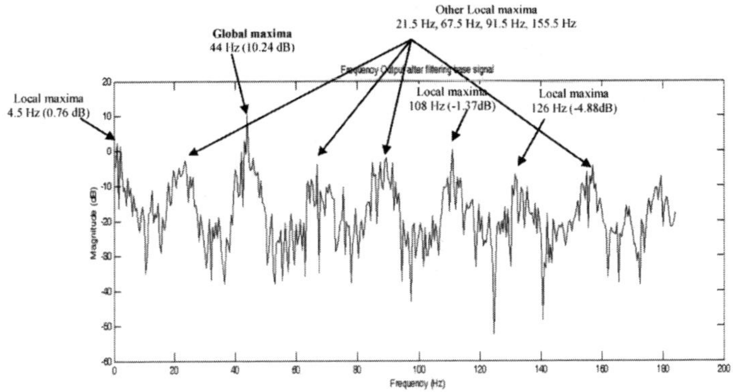

FIGURE 7 (d)
Frequency Plot of Set 4 with earth field filtered – Local maxima at 126 Hz

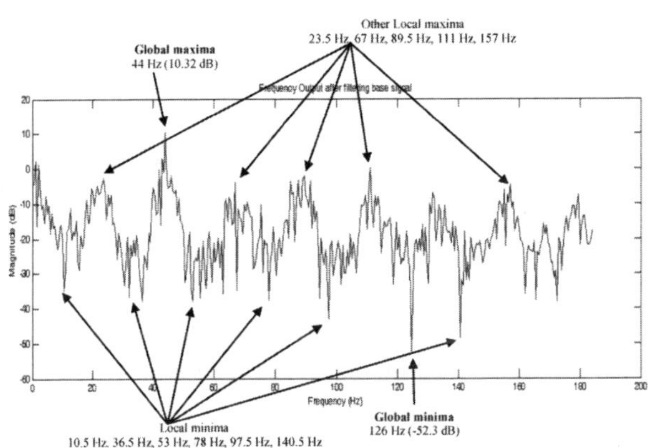

FIGURE 7 (e)
Frequency Plot of Residual Set – Global minima at 126 Hz

3.3 INVERSE-SQUARE LAW

The distances from the SQUID gradiometer for various positions were also computed and are summarized in Table 8 and a layout map is shown in Figure 8.

Table 8 : Distances from SQUID Gradiometer

Event	Straight Line Distance
Inspection of SQUID Gradiometer in SQUID room	50 cm
Inspection of Compressor and standing at door of SQUID room	150 cm
Seat of Chief Mentor	300 cm
Seating of Members of RS Sabha (Block 2 Front)	500 cm
Seating of DEI Engg. Faculty Path Party (Block 1 Front)	600 cm

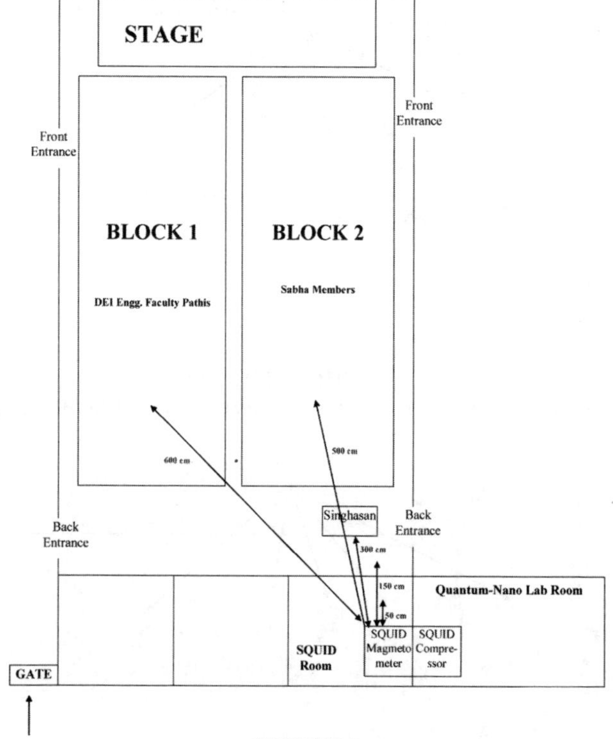

FIGURE 8
Layout Map for SQUID measurements

SQUID-based results are rather interesting and indicate that the atmosphere becomes quite focused during meditation and the magnetic fields in the vicinity also rise. Inverse square law of variation of electromagnetic field-intensity (as a correlate of spiritual force-field intensity) with distance seems to hold as can be seen from Figure 9.

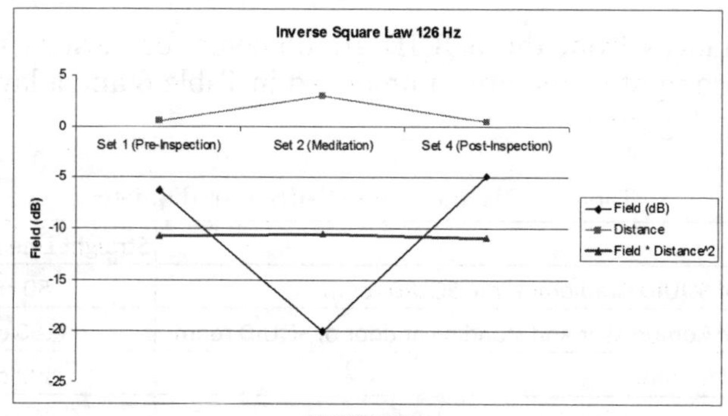

FIGURE 9
Inverse-square law for electromagnetic field intensity

3.4 DATA SETS FOR MEDITATION SESSIONS (THIRD PERSON SCIENTIFIC OBSERVATION) ON AUGMENTED 15-CHANNEL SQUID-BASED DEI MAGNETO-ENCEPHALOGRAPHY (MEG) FACILITY

The DEI Magneto-encephalography (MEG) facility has been augmented to 15 channels to cover all lobes of the brain in January 2016. The system has been retrofitted in the existing Magnetically Shielded Room and the new cryostat has a hemispherical bottom cavity for the head. The SQUID has a 'draw' feature which shows time domain output of several (even all 15 channels) at a glance. Glimpses of the upgraded DEI MEG facility appear in Figure 10.

(a) 15-channel DEI MEG Facility

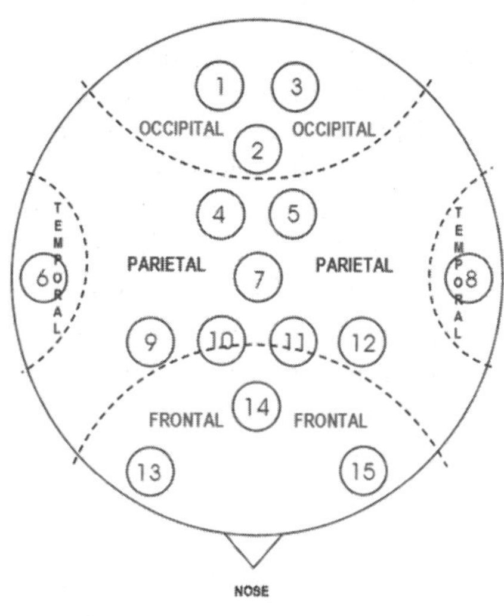

(b) 15-channel cryostat to cover all lobes of the brain

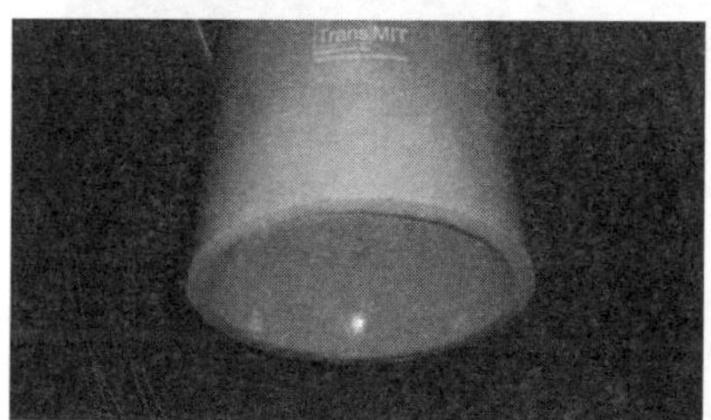

(c) Hemispherical bottom of the cryostat

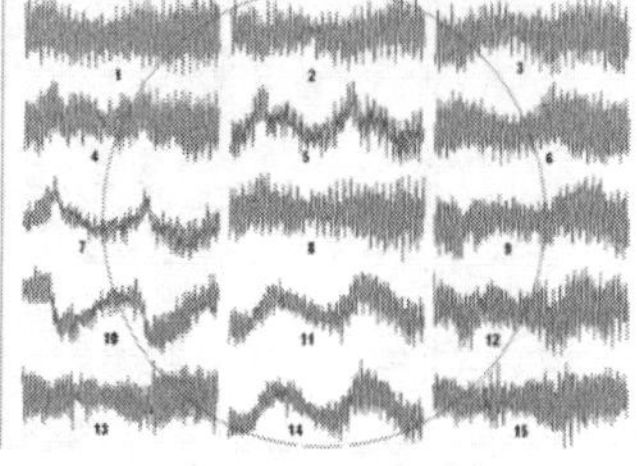

(d) 15-channel output

FIGURE 10
15-channel MEG facility at DEI

3.5.1 GROUP TEST ON MENTOR OF RADHASOAMI FAITH IN A PRAYER SESSION (JANUARY 31, 2016)

Group Test with Mentor of Radhasoami Faith sitting under the cryostat with an accompanying prayer (Satsang) group was carried out on January 31, 2016. The results seem to be quite consistent with lobewise results for group tests conducted at IGCAR Kalpakkam in November 2012 where the parietal lobe exhibited similar behaviour. Photographs of the group test and the lobewise plots are shown in Figure 11.

The salient observations are :

- Comparison of gains of various frequencies for all four lobes in Satsang and post-Satsang sets as a linear plot, where the gain at 126 Hz (corresponding to Mentor) universally shows a decline in all lobes in the post-Satsang set (thick brown line).
- Diagram showing brain apertures has been roughly superimposed with picture of 15-chanel cryostat to locate the aperture for 'Radhasoami' at apex of the head (Figure 12). It is approximately in the parietal lobe around channels 4 and 5, with channels 2 and 7 close by. Maxima at 126 Hz has been observed in the Satsang set in all the four channels listed. (One half of the superposed cryostat image will be on the other side of the brain).
- Several Fourier plots, especially those near the aperture of Radhasoami show a maxima at 126 Hz in the Satsang set. All lobes show a decline in 126 Hz in the post-Satsang set conducted in empty chamber after the Mentor had left.
- The chamber remains charged with spirituality even after the Mentor has left, as the total energy (computed as square over all frequencies) remains more or less the same, even after subtracting pre-test empty chamber data from all sets.

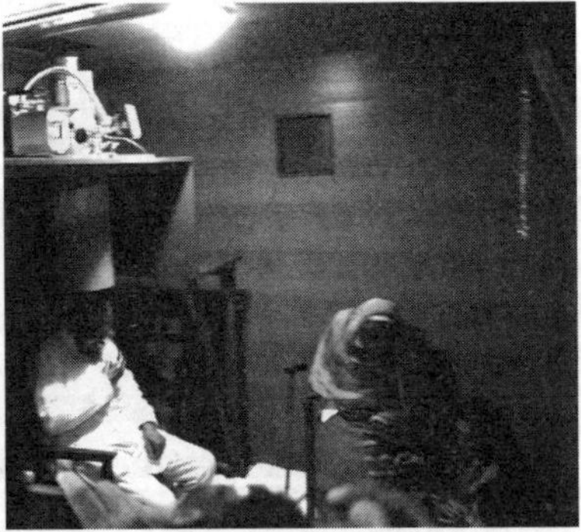

FIGURE 11(a)
Photographs of the Group Meditation Session

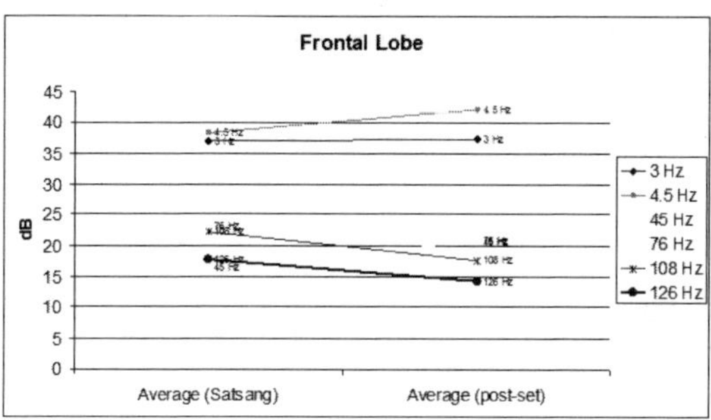

FIGURE 11(b)
Frontal Lobe : Comparison of average strength of frequencies in Satsang and post-Satsang sets of Group Meditation Test on January 31, 2016

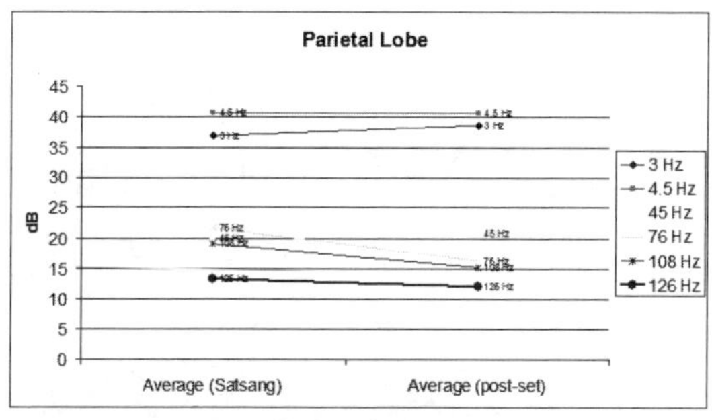

FIGURE 11(c)
Parietal Lobe : Comparison of average strength of frequencies in Satsang and post-Satsang sets of Group Meditation Test on January 31, 2016

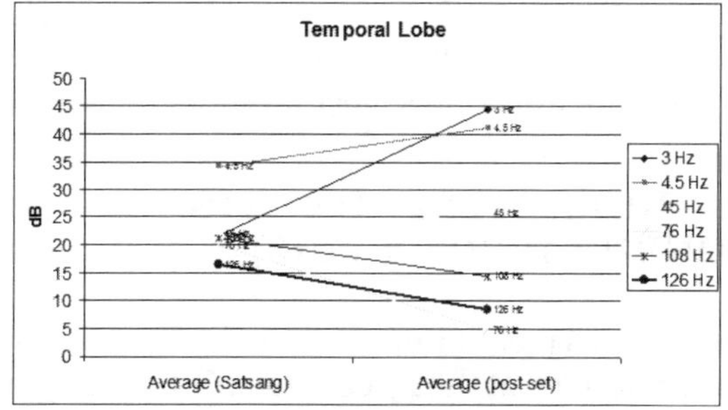

FIGURE 11(d)
Temporal Lobe : Comparison of average strength of frequencies in Satsang and post-Satsang sets of Group Meditation Test on January 31, 2016

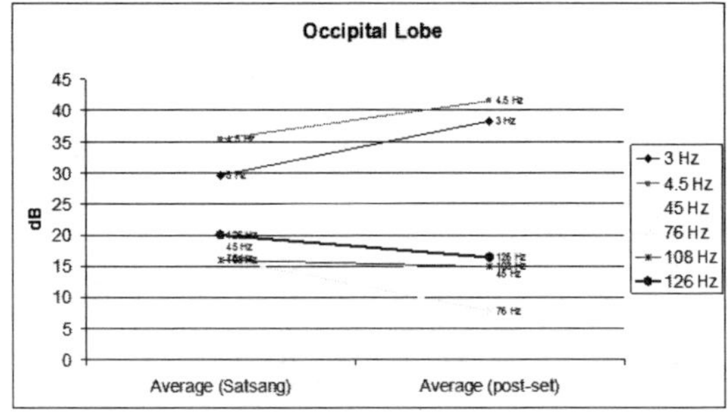

FIGURE 11(e)
Occipital Lobe : Comparison of average strength of frequencies in Satsang and post-Satsang sets of Group Meditation Test on January 31, 2016

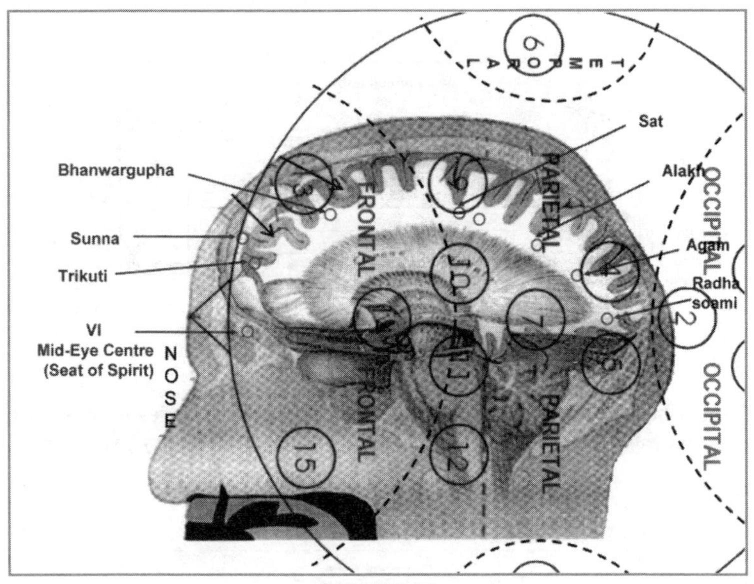

FIGURE 12
Diagram of Brain apertures superimposed with 15-channel placement diagram

3.5.2 INDIVIDUAL TEST ON TIBETAN BUDDHIST MEDITATIONIST (APRIL 15, 2016)

Individual testing of Tibetan Buddhist meditationist during Buddhist meditation was conducted at the 15-channel MEG facility at DEI in April 2016. The results show occurrence of 3 Hz and 4.5 Hz peaks as global maxima in the frontal lobe (channel 14) corresponding to apertures of *Sixth Chakra* and *Sahasdal Kamal*, in the Initial Meditational Stage. The frequency of Tibetan Buddhist chants is also mentioned as 4.5 Hz by Michael Triggs (Triggs, 2012). No 40 Hz synchrony has been observed as referred to by Penrose and Hameroff (Penrose and Hameroff, 2011). A photograph of the test and Fourier plot are shown in Figure 13.

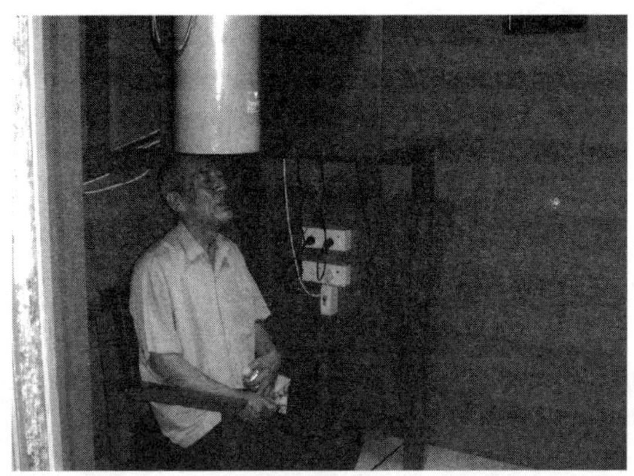

FIGURE 13(a)
Tibetan Buddhist individual test at 15-channel MEG Setup

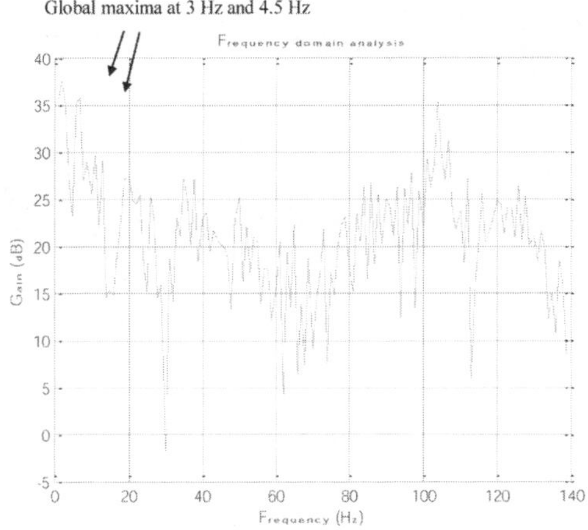

FIGURE 13(b)
Fourier plot of Tibetan Buddhist individual test at 15-channel MEG Setup (Global maxima can be observed at 3 Hz and local maxima at 4.5 Hz)

4. POWER LAW OF MEDITATIONAL CONSCIOUSNESS

The cerebral cortex with its most complicated architecture generates the most complex noise known to Physics (Buzsaki, 2006). Interesting conclusions can be drawn from a study of $1/f^{\alpha}$ behaviour of brain-scans of humans, particularly during Eastern Meditational Practice. The types of noise usually studied are:

$1/f^{\alpha}$ ($\alpha \equiv 0$) : White Noise	(Constant power spectrum)
$1/f^{\alpha}$ ($\alpha \equiv 1$) : Pink Noise	(Golden mean between white and brown noise)
$1/f^{\alpha}$ ($\alpha \equiv 2$) : Brown Noise	(Predictability with low information content)

One over f ($\alpha \equiv 1$) power spectrum (also called "pink noise") is a golden mean between the white noise ($\alpha \equiv 0$, i.e. constant power spectrum) representing disorder with high information content, and brown noise ($\alpha \equiv 2$) representing predictability with low information content. Figure 14 shows the various noise waveforms.

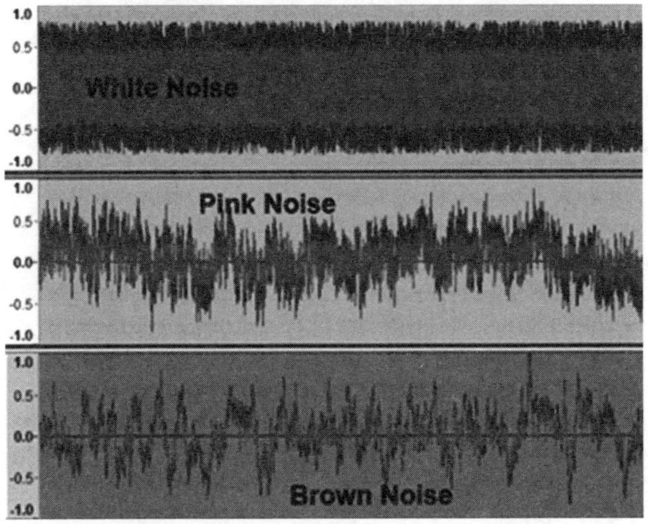

FIGURE 14
White noise, Pink noise and Brown noise

The anatomical-functional organization of the cerebral cortex should have consequences and limitations on cognitive behaviours as well. A well-known psychological law that comes to mind in connection with the $1/f^{\alpha}$ nature of the cortical EEG / MEG is that of Weber and Fechnel:

> "The magnitude of a subjective sensation (a cognitive unit) increases proportionally to the logarithm of the stimulus intensity (a physical unit)."

Accordingly, the magnitude of a subjective sensation such as meditational consciousness in cognitive and meta-cognitive domains increases proportionally to the logarithm of the stimulus intensity, "one over f (i.e. rhythmic frequency)", a physical unit.

4.1 INTEGRATING EXPERIENTIAL PARADIGMS WITH NATURAL SCIENCES (PRICE AND BARRELL APPROACH)

Price and Barrell (Price and Barrell, 2012) show how a science of human experience can be developed through a strategy which integrates experiential paradigms with methods from the natural sciences. A science of human experience would largely be about human meanings and would also constitute a science of consciousness. Psychophysics includes a rudimentary form of introspection that is critical for developing a science of human meanings and consciousness. The qualitative aspects of human experience serve as a foundation for developing hypotheses to be used in experiments that have quantitative methods.

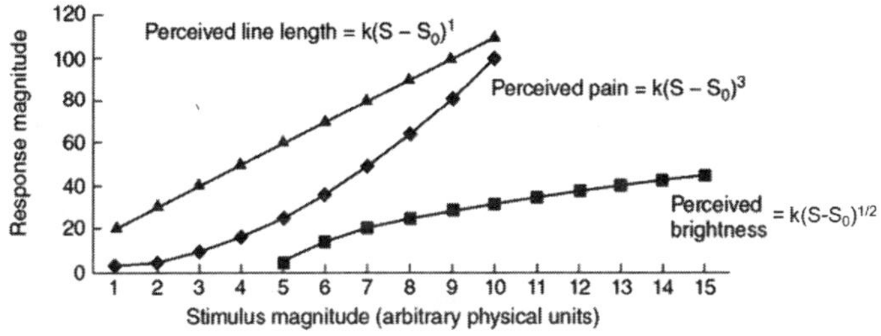

FIGURE 15
Three representative power functions

Figure 15 shows three representative power functions with exponents of 1.0, 3, and 1/2 for perceived line length, pain, and brightness, respectively. Note that the function for length is linear, that for heat pain bends upward to the left, and that for brightness bends toward the right. In this figure, the stimulus-response functions are highly simplified in order to teach psychophysical concepts to non-psychophysicists. The terms S and S_o refer to stimulus intensity and stimulus intensity at or near threshold, respectively. The term k is a constant that applies to each physical continuum. Table 9 shows power function exponents for different sensory modalities.

Table 9 (Price and Barrell, 2012)
Power function exponents for different sensory modalities

Sensory Modality	Power Function Exponent
1. Brightness of a brief flash of light	0.5 – 0.6
2. Contact heat pain	2.2 – 3.5
3. Warmth	0.5 to 1.6 depending on stimulus area
4. Perceived line length	1.0
5. Sound	0.55
6. Indentation of the skin	0.5 – 0.7 with a small probe
7. Cold pain	1.0 – 1.1
8. Sweetness	1.2
9. Sourness	0.77

4.2 POWER-LAW CURVE FITTING

It may be possible to use methods similar to those of psychophysics in experiments that are about relationships between psychological variables (Price and Barrell, 2012). Human sensations are dimensions of phenomenal experience and can be studied using psychophysical methods. The brain's "default" activity during associative thinking is a condition that is approximately described by the term "mind-wandering" (Bar et. al., 2007).

The formulation of power law of meditational consciousness requires invoking a family of models based on Omni quantum theory and physical system theory (including fuzzy analytical hierarchy process), and requisite integration of first person inner experiences of meditationists as co-investigators with the third person scientific methodology of observing, reporting, understanding and hypothesis-testing.

The power law states that $S=kI^{\alpha}$
where S = Sensation Magnitude
I = Stimulus Intensity, taken here as $(1/f)$
k = arbitrary constant
α = Power exponent

On taking log of both sides, we get $\log(S) = \alpha \log(I) + \log k$

If we plot $\log(S)$ versus $\log(I)$ for the data in Table 10 with stimulus and sensation magnitudes, we will get a straight line $y = mx + c$ whose slope m will be the exponent α.

Table 10 : Integrating Stimulus and Sensation

Lok	STIMULUS Frequency (f) Hz	SENSATION Sensation (from AHP)	log(1/f) X-axis	Log (Sensation) Y-axis
Radhasoami	126 Hz	1000	-2.100	3
Sat Lok	108 Hz	700	-2.033	2.848
Sunna	76 Hz	100	-1.881	2
Sahasdal Kamal	4.5 Hz	30	-0.653	1.484
VI Chakra	3 Hz	10	-0.477	1

The best fit line for this data using MATLAB is shown and the mathematical equation for this line is

$y = -1.003x + 0.633$ (The slope is $m=\alpha$) or $|\alpha|=1.003$.

The power law equation becomes $\log(S) = -1.003\log(I) + 0.633$ or $S = 4.3I^{-1.003}$.

The power law of meditational consciousness is plotted in Figure 16. Table 11 presents the error analysis.

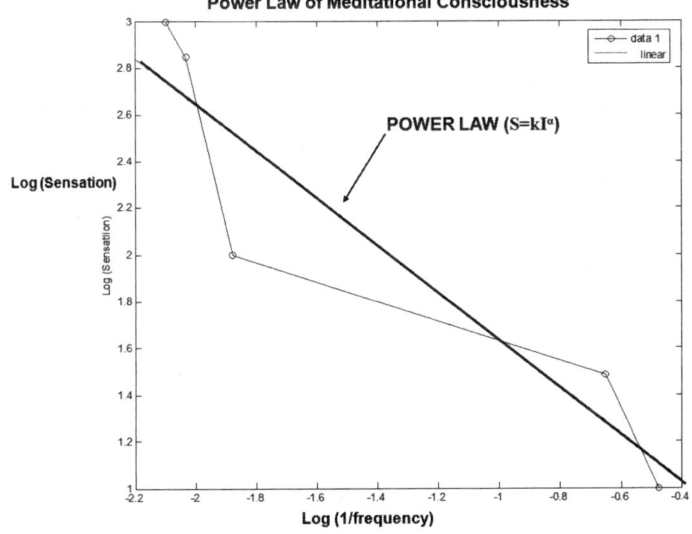

FIGURE 16
Power Law of Meditational Consciousness

Table 11 : Error analysis for the linear fit

Input	Output (Actual)	Output (Linear Fit)	Error (Fit – Actual)	Error % = 100% *(Fit – Actual) / Actual	Error ^ 2
-2.10	3.00	2.739	-0.261	-8.69%	0.067964
-2.033	2.848	2.672	-0.173	-6.08%	0.029929
-1.881	2	2.520	0.520	25.98%	0.270029
-0.653	1.484	1.288	-0.196	-13.21%	0.038432
-0.477	1	1.111	0.111	11.14%	0.012417
				Mean (Error%) = 1.83%	Mean (Error^2) = 0.083754
					RMS Error = 0.289403

5. CONCLUSIONS

Given the scientific practice emphasizing the elements of conscious freedom on the part of experimenting scientists as to how to act and what to learn from the experiments to be performed, and the recent success of brain-science (neuro science) as well as growing realization in the last decade of the aptness and applicability of quantum theoretic modelling to cognitive domain of mind science, it follows as a natural corollary to suggest extension of the quantum theory to the domain of spiritual (meta-psychological)-psychophysical dynamics. It would require separating the spiritual-self (or entity) of the observers (or experimenters) describing a stream of conscious experiences that are the experiential sides of a sequence of events from the psychophysical sides of the observed system (including not only the physical bodies and brains of all observers but also their psychological minds as part of the observed system described by quantum theory) which actualize the neural correlates and cognitive correlates of those experiences respectively in the physical brains and psychological minds of the observers.

It is expected that in due course of time, mind-science (i.e. cognitive science) together with already advanced brain-science will develop so as to bring up the empirical sides upto the level where the details of spirit-mind-brain inter-connections will be actively probed (through advancements in mind-science (via psychological test-scales) and brain-science) and intricate results will be explored that can be compared with the hypothesized spiritual (meta-level)-psychophysical quantum theory (e.g. Omni-quantum theory of consciousness, sketched out in rudimentary sense in the beginning of the chapter).

Cosmology of Radhasoami Faith on one hand, is consistent with all the extant religions in the world and on the other hand, it is also consistent with modern science as of the end of the first decade of the twenty first century. Accordingly, it is consistent with **quantum theory** (which has been called the most successful theory in the history of science for its sheer accuracy although it has strange implications) as well as **Einstein's general theory of relativity** (the modern theory of gravity, very different from the Newtonian theory of gravity, which visualizes that space and time form a dynamic geometric entity that curves in response to the energy that it contains, such that in extreme situations, the curvature may become singular giving rise to such important physical phenomena as black holes and big bang) and even the latest M-theory, the most general supersymmetric theory of gravity and the only candidate for a complete theory of the universe (which in order to predict finite quantities must have what is called supersymmetry between the forces of nature and the matter on which they act.)

To conclude, 'Param Purush' (Supreme Being) Radhasoami is 'Param' 'sat' – 'c(h)it' –'premananda' – 'prakash' – 'shabda' – 'anahad nad' (the fountainhead of all consciousness in the cosmos). There is a certain esoteric language which is used in religious and spiritual literature and that is meant for the common man. It hides the real abstraction, it does not talk about scientific knowledge because it is for the elite class, scientists who can understand, but the religion is open to common man, so that is why religion and spirituality get confounded. It is because of the esoteric language which is used, which convinces the common man much more who are impelled by devotion that this has been so far, but these are all scientific phenomena, This is the point which we want to establish that esoteric language for all purpose hides the true scientific elitist interpretation and gives the interpretation that a common man can understand. This is the reason why people confuse that this is not scientific. The abstract source is one and the same. It is the most abstract phenomenon not yet discovered by science, but we are at the threshold of discovery.

References

Bar, M. (2007), The proactive brain: using analogies and associations to generate predictions, Trends in Cognitive Sciences, 11(7), 280–289. doi: 10.1016/j.tics.2007.05.005.

Buzsaki G. (2006), *Rhythms of the Brain*, Oxford University Press, USA, 2006.

Gennaro R. (2012), The Consciousness Paradox : Consciousness, Concepts and Higher Order Thoughts (HOTs)", The MIT Press, 2012.

M. Sahab (Mishra B.S.) (1960, 2004), *Discourses on Radhasoami Faith (with supplements)*, Radhasoami Satsang Sabha, Dayalbagh, Agra, 2004.

Ozdagoglu A. and Ozdagoglu G. (2007), "Comparison of AHP and Fuzzy AHP for the Multi-criteria Decision Making Processes with Linguistic Evaluations", Istanbul Ticaret Universitesi, Fen Bilimleri, Dergisi, Yil : 6 Sayi : 11 Bahar, 2007/1s. 65-85.

Penrose R. and Hameroff S. (2011), Consciousness in the Universe: Neuroscience, Quantum Space-Time Geometry and Orch OR Theory, Journal of Cosmology, Vol. 14, April-May 2011.

Price D. and Barrell P. (2012), *Inner Experience and Neuroscience : Merging both Perspectives*, MIT Press, USA, 2012.

Saaty, T. L. (1980). *The Analytic Hierarchy Process*. New York: McGraw-Hill.

Saaty T.L. (2000), *Fundamentals of Decision Making and Priority Theory*, Pittsburgh, Pennsylvania: RWS Publications, 2000, ISBN 0-9620317-6-3.

Satsangi P.S. (2003), "Reality and Truth vis-à-vis Wisdom via Aparavidya (Natural Science) and Paravidya (Phenomenology : Experiential Science)" at the International Conference of Association of Asia-Pacific Operational Research Societies at Hotel Grand International, New Delhi on 8.12.2003.

Satsangi P.S. (2006a), "Linear Graph Theory for Modelling a Variety of Systems", Int. Conf. on Differential Geometry and Topology in the Perspective of Modern Trends (DGTPMT – 2006), Dayalbagh Educational Institute, Dayalbagh, Agra, February 2006.

Satsangi P.S. (2006b), "Generalizing Physical Systems Through Applied Systems Research from "Real" Physical Systems through "Conceptual" Socio-Economic-Environmental Systems to "Complete" (Physical-Mental-Spiritual) Creational Systems", International Journal of General Systems, Vol. 35, No. 2, 2006, pp. 127-167.

Satsangi P.S. (2008), "On Systems Modelling of Macrocosm and Microcosm in the Domain of Spiritual Consciousness", Vision Talk at the Inaugural Function of International Seminar on Spiritual Awakening : A Systems Approach to Address the Civilizational Crisis (SPAWSYS 2008), January 12, 2008, Souvenir-cum-Abstract Book, pp. 23.

Satsangi P.S. (2009), "Applied Systems Research for Better Worldliness", Vision Talk at the Joint International Conference on Applied Systems Research and XXXIII National Systems Conference (ASR-NSC 2009), Dayalbagh Educational Institute, November 27, 2009, Souvenir-cum-Abstract Book, pp. 25.

Satsangi P.S. (2010), "Cosmology from the twin vantage points of Radhasoami Faith and Systems Science", Vision Talk, International Seminar on Religion of Saints ('Sants') – Radhasoami Faith, DEI, Dayalbagh, Agra, Nov. 2010 (also Chapter 23 of Expositions on Truth, Ultimate Reality and Supreme Being, Radhasoami Satsang Sabha, Dayalbagh, Agra, 2010, ISBN : 978-81-89288-60-0), Also in P. Sriramamurti, Prem Prashant and Anand Mohan (Eds.), *Spiritual Consciousness*, New Age Books, 2013, New Delhi, pp. 21-40.

Satsangi P.S. (2011), "Cosmology of Consciousness : Towards Quantum-Theoretic Systems Modelling; Spirit-Mind-Brain Interactions", Vision Talk at the Inaugural Workshop of the Centre for Consciousness Studies (CONCENT 2011), Dayalbagh Educational Institute, October 1, 2011, Abstract Book, pp. 50-67.

Satsangi P.S. (2012a), "Eastern Philosophy in the Spiritual Traditions of Oriental Saints ("Sants") : An Interpretive Structural Model (ISM) Representation", Keynote Address, Toward a Science of Consciousness (TSC 2012) Conference : Forum on Eastern Philosophy and Consciousness, April 9, 2012, Arizona, USA.

Satsangi P.S. (2012b), "Neuro-Cognitive Spiritual Phenomenonology", Vision Talk at Special Forum on "Quantum Theory and Science of Consciousness" at International School on Quantum and Nano Computing Systems and Applications (QANSAS 2012), Dayalbagh Educational Institute, November 28, 2012, Abstract Book, pp. 53.

Satsangi P.S. (2013a), Towards Integrating Arts (First-Person Spiritual-Cognitive-Material Phenomenology) and Science (Third-Person Neuro-Physical, Environmental, Cognitive Correlates) of Consciousness, The Dayalbagh Vision, (Toward a Science of Consciousness (TSC 2013) Conference : Vision Talk), March 3-9, 2013, Centre for Consciousness Studies, Dayalbagh Educational Institute (Deemed University), Dayalbagh, Agra, India, Souvenir-cum-Abstract Book, pp. 61-63.

Satsangi. P.S. (2013b), "Consciousness : Towards Integrating Art and Science of Inner Experience", Vision Talk at the Valedictory Session of International School on Quantum and Nano Computing Systems and Applications (QANSAS 2013), Dayalbagh Educational Institute, December 1, 2013, Souvenir-cum-Abstract Book, pp. 53-54.

Satsangi P.S. (2014a), "Consciousness : An Integrative Systems Modelling Approach", Vision Talk at the East-West Forum, Twentieth Anniversary Conference on Toward a Science of Consciousness (TSC 2014) Conference, Tucson, Arizona, USA, April 21, 2014, Abstract Book, pp. 277.

Satsangi. P.S. (2014b), "Satyam-Shivam-Sundaram Revisited in the Perspective of Grand Macro / Micro Cosmology", Vision Talk at the Special Forum on "Consciousness : Integrating Eastern and Western Perspectives" at International School on Quantum and Nano Computing Systems and Applications (QANSAS 2014), Dayalbagh Educational Institute, November 26, 2014, Souvenir-cum-Abstract Book, pp. 53.

Satsangi P.S. (2015a), "Rhythms of Macrocosmic Universe and Human-Microcosm : Consciousness Systemology Perspective", Vision Talk delivered at the East-West Forum of the Toward a Science of Consciousness (TSC 2015) Conference at University of Helsinki, Finland, June 8, 2015, Abstract Book, pp. 373.

Satsangi. P.S. (2015b), "Towards An Ultimate Consciousness Conjecture (for the Human Microcosm and the Grand Macrocosm)", Vision Talk at the Special Forum on "Consciousness : Integrating Eastern and Western Perspectives" at International School on Quantum and Nano Computing Systems and Applications (QANSAS 2015), Dayalbagh Educational Institute, November 25, 2015, Souvenir-cum-Abstract Book, pp. 47.

Satsangi P.S. (2016), "Modelling microtubules in the brain as n-qudit quantum Hopfield network and beyond", Vision Talk at the Integrated East-West Forum of The Science of Consciousness (TSC 2016) Conference at University of Arizona, Tucson, USA, April 25, 2016, Abstract Book, pp. 241.

Satsangi P.S., Sahni, V. (2007), "A Systemic Experimental Study of Macrocosmic Consciousness", Proceedings of National Systems Conference 2007 (Systems Society of India), MIT, Manipal, pp. 13 -19.

Satsangi P.S., Sahni V. (2008), "Study of Human Consciousness as a Surrogate of Macrocosmic Consciousness via Scientific Measurements of Electromagnetic Wave Radiations", Proc. of XXXII National Systems Conference (NSC 2008), IIT Roorkee, December 17-19, 2008, pp. 301-307.

Satsangi P.S., Sahni V. (2012), "Cosmic Consciousness Hierarchization : Analytic, Experimental and Experiential", Concurrent Session on Science and Spirituality, Toward a Science of Consciousness (TSC 2012), Tucson, Arizona, USA, April 2012, Abstract Book, pp. 193.

Satsangi P.S., Sahni V. (2015), "Power Law of Meditational Consciousness", Concurrent Session on Meditation, Toward a Science of Consciousness (TSC 2015), Helsinki, Finland, June 2015, Abstract Book, pp. 340.

Sen Joy (2003), "Understanding Life, Mind and Consciousness Using Analytical Hierarchy Process (AHP) For Response-stimulus studies in Architecture {from Physical (local) to Cosmic (non-local)}, Life, Mind and Consciousness", Proc. of International Seminar held at Ramakrishna Mission Institute of Culture, Kolkata, Jan. 16-18, 2003, pp. 355-379.

Srivastava D.P. (2013), "Graph Theoretic Quantum Field / System Modelling For Quantum Information / Computation Circuits And Algorithms", Ph.D. Thesis, Dayalbagh Educational Institute, Dayalbagh, Agra, India, 2013.

Srivastava D.P., Sahni V., Satsangi P.S., (2011) "Graph-theoretic quantum system modelling for information/computation processing circuits", International Journal of General Systems, Taylor and Francis, UK, Vol. 40, No. 8, November 2011, pp. 777–804, ISSN No. 0308-1079.

Srivastava D.P., Sahni V., Satsangi P.S. (2014) "Graph Theoretic Quantum System Modelling for Neuronal Microtubles as Hierarchical Clustered Quantum Hopfield Networks",

International Journal of General Systems, Taylor & Francis, UK, Vol. 43, No. 6, August 2014, pp. 633-648, ISSN No. 0308-1079.

Srivastava D.P., Sahni V., Satsangi P.S. (2015a), "Modelling Microtubules in the Brain as n-qudit Quantum Hopfield Network and Beyond (arXiv : 1515.00774 (q.bio-NC)

Srivastava D.P., Sahni V., Satsangi P.S. (2015b), " Frequency and Energy as Neuro-correlates of Beauty in Maths, Science and Art", Concurrent Talk, East-West Forum of the Toward a Science of Consciousness (TSC 2015) Conference at University of Helsinki, Finland, June 8, 2015, Abstract Book pp. 383-384.

Srivastava D.P., Sahni V., Satsangi P.S., (2016), "Modelling microtubules in the brain as n-qudit quantum Hopfield network and beyond", International Journal of General Systems, Vol. 45. No. 1, February 2016, pp. 41-54, DOI: 10.1080/03081079.2015.1076405, ISSN No. 0308-1079.

Triggs M. (2012), Ancient Wisdom, Modern Technology (Brainwave Frequency Listing), http://www.lunarsight.com/freq.htm.

Warfield J.N. (2006), *An Introduction to System Science*, World Scientific Company, Singapore.

II

Consciousness - Western Perspectives

Chapter 3

Higher-Order Thoughts, Neural Realization, and the Metaphysics of Consciousness

ROCCO J. GENNARO
University of Southern Indiana, Indiana, USA

The higher-order thought (HOT) theory of consciousness is a reductive representational theory of consciousness which says that what makes a mental state conscious is that there is a suitable HOT directed at that mental state. Although it seems that any neural realization of the theory must be somewhat widely distributed in the brain, it remains unclear just how widely distributed it needs to be. In section I, I provide some background and define some key terms. In section II, I argue *against* the view that HOT theory should treat first-order (i.e. world-directed) conscious states as requiring prefrontal cortical activity though it is reasonable to suppose that conscious states are realized in the brain. In section III, I then explore some of the key background metaphysical issues involved in understanding the nature of consciousness, such as the debate between realism and idealism as well as the prospects for solving the so-called "hard problem" of consciousness. Some of the differences in question often mirror the traditional differences between Western and Eastern perspectives on the nature of consciousness. Overall, I argue that some form of realism and physicalism is more plausible than the opposing views. I also argue that materialists (and especially HOT theorists) can offer plausible replies to the hard problem.

I. BACKGROUND AND TERMINOLOGY

Perhaps the most fundamental and commonly used notion of the term 'conscious' is captured by Thomas Nagel's famous "what it is like" sense (Nagel 1974). When we are in a conscious mental state, there is "something it is like" for us to be in that state from the subjective or first-person point of view. When we smell a rose or have a conscious visual experience, there is something it "seems" or "feels like" from our own perspectives. An organism such as a bat is conscious if it is able to experience the world through its echolocation senses. There is something it is like to be a conscious creature, whereas there is nothing it is like to be a table or tree. This is primarily the sense of "conscious state" that I use throughout this chapter. "What it's like" basically means "how a conscious state is for the subject."

The HOT theory of consciousness says that what makes a mental state conscious is that there is a suitable HOT directed at the mental state (Rosenthal 1997, 2002, 2005, Gennaro 1996, 2012). Higher-order thoughts (HOTs) are meta-psychological states, that is, mental states directed at other mental states. HOT theory is primarily concerned with explaining how conscious mental states differ from unconscious mental states. For various reasons, HOT theorists hold that such meta-awareness is best understood as a "thought" composed of concepts (Gennaro 2012). Further, it seems reasonable to think that conscious mental states are states that we are "aware of" in some sense. Indeed, defense of HOT theory often tends to start with the highly intuitive claim that has come to be known as the Transitivity Principle (TP):

(TP) A conscious state is a state whose subject is, in some way, aware of being in it (such as in Rosenthal 2005).

Thus, when one has a conscious state, one is aware of being in that state. For example, if someone is having a conscious desire or pain,

FIGURE 1

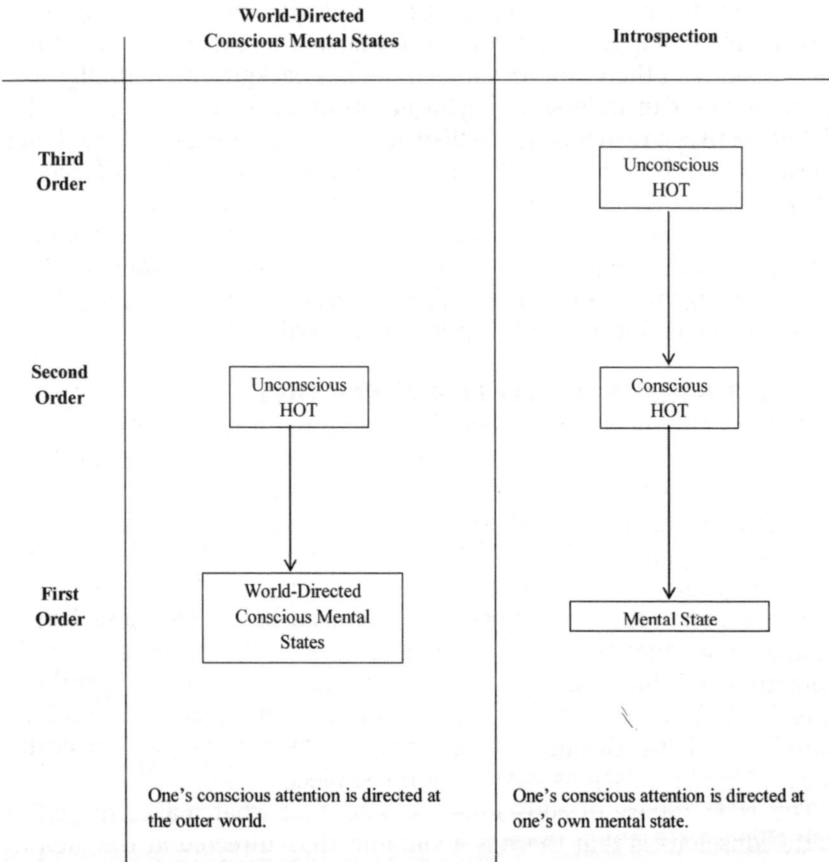

then that person is surely aware of having that desire or pain. HOT theory says that the HOT is of the form "I am in M now," where M references a mental state. Conversely, the idea that someone could be having a conscious state while totally unaware of being in that state seems very odd (if not an outright contradiction). A mental state of which the subject is completely unaware is clearly an unconscious state. For example, we are not aware of having a subliminal perception, and thus it is an unconscious perception.

It is also crucial to mention here that according to HOT theory, when a conscious mental state is a first-order world-directed state, the HOT is *not* itself conscious; otherwise circularity and an infinite regress would follow. When the HOT is itself conscious, there is a yet higher-order (or third-order) thought directed at the second-order state. In this case, we have *introspection*, which involves a conscious HOT directed at an inner mental state. When one introspects, one's attention is directed back into one's mind. For example, what makes my desire to write a good chapter a conscious first-order desire is that an unconscious HOT is directed at the desire. In this case, our conscious focus is directed at the book and my computer screen, so we are not consciously aware of having a HOT from the first-person point of view. When one introspects that desire, however, one then has a conscious HOT (accompanied by a yet higher, third-order, HOT) directed at the desire itself (Rosenthal 1986, 1997).

II. HOT THEORY, NEURAL REALIZATION, AND THE PREFRONTAL CORTEX

There are of course also several common objections to HOT theory to which HOT theorists have replied. For example, many have urged that HOT theory rules out infant and animal consciousness. Since a HOT is a kind of metacognitive or meta-psychological state of the form "I am in mental state M now," it might seem that animals (or at least *most* animals) do not possess such sophisticated I-concepts and mental concepts. I have responded at length to this objection (such as Gennaro 2012, chapters 7 and 8) but it is not my main focus in this paper.

Still, HOT theory is a (mentalistic) reductionist theory in the sense that conscious states are explained in terms of unconscious mental states and awareness. Nonetheless, as Rosenthal urges, HOT theory is poised to explore a "second step" reduction to the physical level. The most natural candidate for physical realization is in the brain, but I have previously argued that HOTs need not occur in the prefrontal cortex (PFC) (Gennaro 2012, chapter 9). Here I summarize and briefly elaborate on this view. In this context also, some have urged that HOTs are likely to occur in the prefrontal cortex (PFC) and, since infants and most animals do not have much (if any) prefrontal cortical activity, they are incapable of having conscious states according to HOT theory. However, a strong case can be made that HOTs, or at least many unconscious HOTs, do not involve the PFC. Other areas of the brain are more likely to underlie HOTs, such as the medial and inferior parietal cortices, the temporoparietal cortex, the posterior cingulate cortex, and the anterior cingulate cortex (Newen and Vogeley 2003, Gennaro 2012, chapter 9). Even when considering the neural signatures of "theory of mind" and "mindreading" (i.e. thinking about others' thoughts), Newen and Vogeley (2003) cite numerous experiments indicating that such metarepresentation is best located in the anterior cingulate cortex and that "the capacity for...[theory of mind] contexts showed differential activation in the right temporo-parietal junction and the medial aspects of the superior parietal lobe" (Newen and Vogeley 2003, p. 538). Some evidence for holding that the PFC is not required for conscious states is that basic conscious experience is not decreased entirely even when there is extensive bilateral PFC damage or lobotomies.

In addition, Malach and colleagues show that when subjects are engaged in a perceptual task or absorbed in watching a movie, there is widespread neural activation but little PFC activity (Grill-Spector and Malach 2004, Goldberg, Harel, and Malach 2006). Although some other studies do show PFC activation, this is arguably due to the fact that subjects are required to *report* their experiences. Thus, the PFC is likely to be activated when there is *introspection*, not merely when there are outer-directed conscious states (especially during demanding perceptual tasks). But these introspective states involve more sophisticated psychological capacities than merely having conscious states, and introspection is not necessary for having conscious states according to HOT theory. Further support for the above can be found, for example, in the work of Saxe and colleagues who have extensively studied the brain regions most associated with mindreading abilities (Saxe and Powell 2006, Saxe and Pelphrey 2009, Saxe 2010). They identify the temporo-parietal junction, the posterior cingulate, the medial precuneus, and parts of the temporal sulcus as the primary sites for this kind of cognition.

Kuzuch (2014) presents a very nice discussion of the PFC in relation to higher-order theories, arguing that the lack of dramatic deficits in visual consciousness even with PFC lesions presents a compelling case against higher-order theories. In some ways, I agree with much of Kozuch's analysis especially with respect to the notion that some (visual) conscious states do not require PFC activity (sometimes focused more on the dorsolateral PFC, or dlPFC). For example, in addition to the studies I cited above, Kozuch references Alvarez and Emory (2006) as evidence for the view that

> Lesions to the orbital, lateral, or medial PFC produce so-called executive dysfunction. Depending on the precise lesion location, subjects with damage to one of these areas have problems inhibiting inappropriate actions, switching efficiently from task to task, or retaining items in short-term memory. However, lesions to these areas appear not to produce notable deficits in visual consciousness: Tests of the perceptual abilities of subjects with lesions to the PFC proper reveal no such deficits; as well, PFC patients never report their visual experience to have changed in some remarkable way (Kozuch 2014, 729).

However, Kozuch rightly notes that my version of HOT theory is left undamaged, at least to some extent, since I do not require that the PFC is where HOTs are realized. We must again also keep in mind the distinction between unconscious HOTs and conscious HOTs (= introspection). Perhaps the latter require PFC activity given the more sophisticated executive functions associated with introspection but having first-order conscious states does not require introspection.

III. THE METAPHYSICS OF CONSCIOUSNESS

Of course, the above discussion does not explicitly address the larger metaphysical issues lurking in the background (though see Gennaro 2005, Gennaro 2012, chapters 2 and 4, for much more along these lines). For example, dualists will of course deny that mental states are ultimately neural or physical processes at all. Others might urge that materialism suffers from some kind of insurmountable "explanatory gap" between the mental and physical or cannot answer the so-called "hard problem" of consciousness (Chalmers 1995, Levine 1983, 2001). Some might even reject the notion that there really are mind-independent material or physical things at all and so will embrace some kind of idealism such that consciousness (or conscious minds) is the only real and fundamental substance (or force) in nature. I now address these questions in turn with an eye toward some of the traditional differences between Eastern and Western views.

A. Materialism vs. Dualism

There are two broad traditional and competing metaphysical views concerning the nature of the mind and conscious mental states: dualism and materialism. While there are many versions of each, the former generally holds that the conscious mind or a conscious mental state is non-physical in some sense. On the other hand, materialists hold that the mind is the brain, or, more accurately, that conscious mental activity is identical with neural activity. It is very important to recognize that by 'non-physical,' dualists do not merely mean 'not visible to the naked eye.' Many physical things fit this description, such as the atoms in the air in a typical room. For something to be non-physical, however, it must literally be outside the realm of physics, that is, not in space at all and so undetectable in principle by the instruments of physics. It is equally important to recognize that the category "physical" is broader than the category "material." Materialists are called such because there is the tendency to view the brain, a material thing, as the most likely candidate to identify with the mind. However, something might be physical but not material in this sense, such as an electromagnetic or energy field. One might therefore instead be a "physicalist" about mind or consciousness in some broader sense and still not be a dualist in the above sense. Thus, to say that the mind is non-physical is to say something much stronger than that it is non-material. Dualists, then, tend to believe that conscious mental states or minds are radically different from anything in the physical world at all. This was especially the case for Descartes and his version of "substance dualism" but also seems to hold for some dualists today (e.g. Swinburne 1986) and is often tied to various theological positions.

Nonetheless, there are very well-known and serious problems with substance dualism. For example, one is simply the issue of just how does (or could) such radically different substances causally interact. How does anything non-physical causally interact with something physical, such as the brain? No such explanation is forthcoming or even seems possible. Yet substance dualists do typically hold that mental states causally interact with the body, as in familiar cases such as my desire for something cold to drink causes my body to move toward the refrigerator for some water. Moreover, if causation involves some kind of transfer of energy from cause to effect, then how is this possible if the mind really is non-physical? This is in part why Ryle (1949) mockingly called the Cartesian view a belief in the "ghost in the machine." There are, to be sure, other versions of dualism such as "property dualism" which is probably the most popular form of dualism today. Property dualism is, at least on the surface, a more modest version of dualism which says that there are mental *properties* (i.e. characteristics or aspects of things) that are neither identical with nor reducible to physical properties. Mental phenomena are non-physical properties of physical substances. There are actually several different kinds of property dualism but what they have in common is the idea that conscious *properties*, such as the color qualia involved in a conscious experience of a visual perception, cannot be explained in purely physical terms and, thus, are not themselves to be identified with any brain state or process. But, for one thing, it is not always clear just how property dualism should be interpreted in terms of its fundamental metaphysics, for example, isn't it also committed to substance dualism? (Francescotti 2001). Alternatively, some also wonder how property dualism actually differs from some kind of non-reductive *materialism*.

On the other hand, epiphenomenalism holds that mental events are caused by brain events but those mental events are mere "epiphenomena" which do not, in turn, cause anything physical at all, despite appearances to the contrary. But problems for epiphenomenalism abound. First, it is incredibly counterintuitive. What could be more obvious than my pain makes me cry or that the visual experience of the charging lion makes me run away? Second, if conscious mental states really do and cause nothing, then there is no reason why they should have evolved. If conscious states clearly modify our behavior in certain ways, then they are very useful from an evolutionary perspective. (Nonetheless, see Robinson 2004 for a recent defense of epiphenomenalism.)

There are also theoretical factors which seem to be on the side of materialism, such as adherence to the so-called "principle of simplicity" which says that if two theories can equally explain a given phenomenon, then we should accept the one which posits fewer objects or forces. In this case, even if dualism could equally explain consciousness (which would of course be disputed by materialists), materialism is clearly the simpler theory in so far as it does not posit any objects, processes, or properties over and above physical ones. Materialists will wonder why there is a need to believe in the existence of such mysterious non-physical entities or properties. Moreover, in the aftermath of the Darwinian revolution, it would seem that materialism is on even stronger ground provided that one accepts basic evolutionary theory and the notion that most animals are conscious. Given the similarities between the more primitive parts of the human brain and the brains of other animals, it seems most natural to conclude that, through evolution, increasing layers of brain areas correspond to increased mental abilities. It does not seem that many dualists think that animals have non-physical minds and yet animals surely have *some* similar conscious states to us, such as basic sensory perceptions and various feelings and emotions, such as pains and anger.

Many will also point to the well-known fact that damage to specific areas of the brain causes very specific mental defects as evidence that materialism is true, or at least as evidence supporting what we might call the "dependence thesis," that is, conscious experience *depends* upon proper brain function. Although the implications of this evidence have probably been appreciated for centuries (would you rather be shot in the head or foot!?), the level of detailed neuropsychological knowledge has increased dramatically in recent years. A substance dualist might of course respond that such phenomena do not absolutely refute her metaphysical position since it could be replied that damage to the brain simply *causes* corresponding damage to the non-physical mind. However, this raises a host of other equally difficult questions, such as: Why not opt for the simpler and more straightforward explanation that brain damage causes mental damage simply because mental processes *are* brain processes? How can a non-physical mind be "damaged" anyway when brain damage occurs?

Moreover, the level of detail understood today is important because it makes clear that very specific mental changes occur when, and only when, very specific brain damage occurs. It is true that such a "correlation" is not the same as identity or cause, but the best explanation for the neuropsychological evidence is clearly that conscious mental activity depends for its existence upon the relevant brain activity. The details are exactly what one would expect if conscious mental activity so depended upon brain functioning. In humans, damage to particular brain regions, such as due to disease, trauma, or stroke, is associated with specific impairments of perception, memory, cognition, emotion, and decision-making. Drugs that alter brain activity produce corresponding changes in perception, memory, cognition, emotion, or personality, depending upon the neurotransmitter systems involved and particular brain regions affected. Loss of vision results from damage to areas of visual cortex. Loss of hearing and/or the ability to recognize sounds, including speech, results from damage to regions of auditory cortex within the temporal lobes. Prosopagnosia, the inability to recognize familiar faces, is typically caused by damage to the occipitotemporal cortex (fusiform gyrus). Damage to brain regions involved in emotional regulation, which include the limbic system, particularly the amygdala, commonly result in impaired processing of emotional stimuli. Furthermore, numerous neurological disorders and diseases, such as Alzheimer's, bipolar disorder, amnesia, depression, schizophrenia, epilepsy, and mental retardation, which are all characterized by profound changes in cognitive function and awareness, are also all associated with specific biochemical, neurophysiological, or neuroanatomical changes in the brain. While some of the specifics are still not fully understood and the subject of vigorous ongoing scientific investigation, what is not much in dispute is that these mental disorders and diseases are direct consequences of aberrant brain function.

Thus, it seems reasonable to hold that some form of materialism is true and that mental states are realized in neural processes.

B. The Hard Problem

One might of course still object that materialism faces serious problems of its own. To be sure, it would be silly to think that materialists have all the answers. One well-known objection can be found in Chalmers (1995) who presents the "hard problem" of consciousness as follows:

> The really hard problem is the problem of experience.... a subjective aspect....It is undeniable that some organisms are subjects of experience. But the question of how it is that [organisms] are subjects of experience is perplexing. Why is it that when our cognitive systems engage in visual and auditory information-processing, we have a visual or auditory experience...? ...How can we explain why there is something it is like to entertain a mental image, or to experience an emotion? It is widely agreed that experience arises from a physical basis, but we have no good explanation of why and how it so arises (1995, p. 201).

Chalmers himself eventually opts for a form of property dualism. In a somewhat similar vein, Levine (1983, 2001) coined the expression "the explanatory gap" to express a difficulty for any materialistic attempt to explain consciousness. Although not himself concerned to reject the metaphysics of materialism, Levine gives eloquent expression to the idea that there is a key conceptual gap in our ability to explain the connection between conscious mental (or "phenomenal") properties and brain properties. The basic problem is that it is, at least at present, very difficult for us to understand the relationship between brain properties and phenomenal properties in any explanatory satisfying way, especially given the fact that it seems possible for one to be present without the other. There is an odd kind of arbitrariness involved: *Why* or *how* does some particular brain process produce that particular taste or visual sensation? It is difficult to see any real *explanatory connection* between specific conscious states and brain states in a way that explains how or why the former are identical with the latter. There is therefore an explanatory gap between the physical and mental.

But, first of all, it may be that Chalmers and others expect too much, namely, grasping some "causal link" between the brain and consciousness. After all, if conscious mental states just *are* ultimately *identical* to brain states, then there may simply be a "brute fact" that does not need any further explaining. It may even be that some form of dualism is presupposed in Chalmers' argument, especially to the extent that brain states are assumed to "give rise to" or "produce" (or cause) consciousness, as opposed to using the language of identity.

Secondly, and perhaps more important, is recognition of the fact that very different concepts can still pick out (or refer to) the same property or object in the world (Loar 1997). For example, out in the world there is only the one "stuff," which we can conceptualize either as 'water' or as 'H_2O.' The traditional distinction, made most notably by Frege in the late 19th century, between "meaning" (or "sense") and "reference" is relevant here. Two or more concepts, which can have different meanings, can refer to the same property or object, much like 'Venus' and 'The Morning Star.' Materialists, then, explain that it is essential to distinguish between mental properties and our concepts of those properties. By analogy, there are so-called "phenomenal concepts" which use a phenomenal or first-person property to refer to a conscious mental state, such as a sensation of red (see Alter and Walter 2007 for much more on this theme). In contrast, we can also use various concepts couched in physical or neurophysiological terms to refer to that same mental state from the third-person point of view. There is thus but one conscious mental state which can be conceptualized in two different ways: either by employing first-person experiential phenomenal concepts or by employing third-person neurophysiological concepts. It may then just be a brute fact about the world that there are such identities and the appearance of arbitrariness between brain properties and mental properties is just that – an *apparent* problem leading many to wonder about the alleged explanatory gap. Qualia would still be identical to physical properties. Moreover, this response provides a diagnosis for why there even *seems* to be such a gap, namely, that we use very different concepts to pick out the same property. Science will be able, in principle, to close the gap and solve the hard problem of consciousness in an analogous way that we now have a very good understanding for why "water *is* H_2O" or "heat *is* mean molecular kinetic energy" that was lacking centuries ago. Maybe the hard problem isn't so hard after all – it will just take some more time. After all, the science of chemistry didn't develop overnight and we are relatively early in the history of neurophysiology and in our understanding of phenomenal consciousness. It seems premature to give up now.

Finally, it is crucial to emphasize for my purposes that HOT theory is reductionist only in the sense that state consciousness is to be explained in terms of unconscious mental states and awareness. HOT theory itself does not even attempt to explain consciousness in nonmentalistic or neural terms. Of course, as we have seen, HOT theorists tend to be materialists in the end but prefer to leave that empirical question for a separate second step reduction to be filled in later by brain science. On the other hand, other theories of consciousness are reductionist in the stronger sense that they attempt to explain consciousness directly in physical or neurophysiological terms (e.g. Crick and Koch 1990, Crick 1994).

I believe that HOT theory can provide necessary and sufficient conditions for what makes a mental state conscious but whatever realizes that theory in our brains is a separate empirical question. The quotation above from Chalmers does show, however, how statements of the hard problem can sometimes gloss over these differences. Nonetheless, the key common general question is: How exactly does x (where 'x' is invoked by some alleged theory of consciousness) explain how consciousness arises from the presence of x?

A HOT theory solution is that HOTs explain how consciousness arises because the concepts that figure into the HOTs are presupposed in conscious experience. Let us stick to first- order perceptual states. In very much a Kantian spirit, the idea is that we first passively receive information via our senses or what Kant (1781/1965) calls our "faculty of sensibility," which we might think of as early perceptual processing. Some of this information will then rise to the level of unconscious mental states which can also cause our behavior in various ways. But such mental states do not become conscious until the "faculty of understanding" operates on them via the application of concepts. I contend that we should understand such concept application in terms of HOTs directed at the incoming information. Thus I consciously experience the green table as a green table partly because I apply the concepts GREEN and TABLE (in my HOTs) to the incoming information via my visual perceptual apparatus. More specifically, I have a HOT such as "I am seeing a green table now." Kant (1781/1965) famously urged that it takes the cooperation of both the sensibility and understanding to produce conscious experience: "Objects are given to us by means of sensibility. . . . They are thought through the understanding, and from the understanding arise concepts" (A19/B33). It is crucial to remember that these HOTs are not normally themselves conscious and so they and their concepts are "presupposed" in conscious experience. We might say that the understanding unconsciously "synthesizes" the raw data of experience. Part of the motivation for HOT theory is to explain when and how an unconscious state becomes conscious, and the answer is that the subject becomes aware of the state, that is, a HOT is directed at it (recall also the Transitivity Principle). Thus the concepts in question must also be in the HOTs and are at least partly responsible for the "what it is like" nature of qualitative experience.

Notice that this solution is unlike reductionist accounts in nonmentalistic terms, and so it is immune from Chalmers' criticism about the plausibility of those theories. For example, there is no problem about how some specific brain activity produces conscious experience. Chalmers' criticism that functional explanations are inadequate because one can always ask "Why is the performance of these functions accompanied by experience?" (1995, p. 203) is equally beside the point. The HOT theory is not a functional explanation which merely addresses what Chalmers calls the "easy" problems of consciousness. In any case, HOT theory contends that a reductionist theory of consciousness can be provided in mentalistic terms in a way that can solve the hard problem.

C. Realism and Idealism

One might even go further and reject the very existence of mind-independent physical substances (including bodies and brains) and embrace some kind of idealism such that consciousness (or conscious minds) is the only real and fundamental substance or thing in nature or the universe. Indeed, this at least seems to be the view of some other authors in this volume and at the 2013 Toward a Science of Consciousness conference in India (e.g. Chopra and Kafatos, this volume). Idealism holds that there are only immaterial mental substances, a view more common in some Eastern philosophies (such as in the Vedanta tradition). The most prominent Western proponent of idealism was the eighteenth century empiricist George Berkeley (1710/1975). The idealist agrees with the substance dualist, however, that minds are non-physical but rejects the notion that there are really mind-independent "material" or (even) "physical" things at all. This is sometimes today framed in terms of some kind of all-encompassing fundamental "consciousness" in the universe which somehow "permeates" or "creates" perceptible reality (Chopra and Kafatos, this volume). Indeed, some suppose that contemporary quantum physics actually leads us naturally toward this sort of view and away from realism. Realism is simply the view that there are mind-independent physical objects and we can know at least something about what they are really like. Importantly, however, there is also a long-time common distinction made between *direct* realists who think that we are directly aware of external mind-independent objects and *representative* (or *indirect*) realists, such as Locke (1689/1975), who hold that we directly aware of our own sensory or perceptual states but indirectly aware of outer objects (which cause our sensory states). Both realist views claim that we can know, at least to some extent, what mind-independent reality is really like.

One important side issue first: For those who use quantum physics as a reason to embrace idealism, there is significant potential for confusion by conflating what is 'non-material' with what is 'non-physical.' As we saw earlier, this is a very important distinction. One might reject the existence of *material* objects based on current quantum theory. In a similar fashion, perhaps there is only "really" energy of some kind which can form into material things under the right conditions. But none of this leads automatically to the conclusion that there are no mind-independent *physical* things (or forces). After all, isn't quantum physics still *physics*? Isn't there still something *physical* in the universe in that case? If so, then we are not really talking about idealism as it is typically construed in the history of philosophy.

In any case, why would someone hold an idealist view and what problems does it face? After all, in order to judge one theory as better than another we must compare its advantages and disadvantages to other theories.

Unlike some realists, I am willing to concede here (at least for the sake of argument) that we are only *directly* aware of our own conscious or sensory states and so we should reject direct realism.

However, one central question remains: What, outside of us, *causes* these sensory states? After all, even Berkeley conceded that something (or someone) *else* must cause our conscious states; we certainly don't seem to be constantly causing such states in ourselves, i.e. conjuring up in imagination, say, our visual perceptions as we walk down the street. Thus, his answer was that God is constantly causing sensory ideas in each of us. (Some in the Eastern tradition might call "God" something more like "pure consciousness" instead.) So Berkeley had to invoke a very busy "hands on" God to answer such a question about what causes our sensory perceptions. Well, according to Bishop Berkeley, God is omnipotent and omniscient and so is obviously up to the task! But we should note that Berkeley is making no less of an *inference* than the indirect realist who instead infers that mind-independent physical objects likely cause our sensory states. However, in order for an idealist even just to explain why we all see *the same* table in a room, God has to cause many angle-different spatial visual perceptions in each of us. And that's assuming that it even makes sense to say that it is the *same* table according to idealism (since that sounds mind-independent and enduring in some sense). The realist, however, has the far simpler and ready answer that the single mind-independent table is simply causing each of our visual perceptions. Realists argue that it is much more reasonable to suppose that it is the existence of the single mind-independent table which causes our visual perception of the table. This is of course *not* to say that tables and any such objects really are just the way they appear. Perhaps we cannot even know what they are "really" like, but this would at most result in a view like Kant's Transcendental Idealism, that is, there are mind-independent objects or things but we cannot know what they are like "in themselves."

But what is crucial here is that even if we agree that "we are only directly aware of own consciousness or sensory ideas," this does not automatically lead to an idealist conclusion. It may be true that some realists uncritically assume something more like "direct" or "naïve" realism, but surely there are other reasons why one might reasonably infer that there is some kind of mind-independent reality, even if we disagree about how much we can know about it and even agree that different people (and animals for that matter) experience that reality in different ways. That is, we must be careful not to fall prey to a false dichotomy between idealism and direct realism. This would be to make an elementary mistake. Furthermore, Locke centuries ago also distinguished between "secondary qualities" (e.g. color, sound), which are those features of perceived objects which are mind-dependent (at least partially), and "primary qualities," which are arguably mind-independent (e.g. shape, size). Now he may have been wrong about some of his specific examples, but my point here is that this further viable option of indirect or representative realism has also been around for a long time (not to mention the additional option of Kant's transcendental idealism).

We might also therefore concede that *the way* humans experience the world (tables, streets, food, etc.) is very likely different from other species. Interestingly though, the main evidence for this today comes from understanding the differences in our physical brains and perceptual apparatus. But due to that same brain evidence, one might also argue that some of our experiences are not entirely different from all other animals. It probably depends on the animal or kind of experience. Surely there can be some experiential overlap among species depending on brain similarities. But it is the comparative brain evidence that actually helps to explain differences in our experiences. So, for example, I would expect a bat to experience the world more differently than humans than a chimpanzee would. An insect with a hundred eyes or a dolphin must experience a different perceptual reality since they have different sensors and different brains. But none of this can be used as an argument for idealism as far as I can see. Could one really use differences between animal brains – material objects themselves! – to show that there are no mind-independent material objects at all? This would be curious indeed. If nothing physical (or even material) at all exists mind-independently, then the same should go for our bodies including our brains themselves (including neurons, microtubules, neurotransmitters, etc.). Surely a reasonable person might have a hard time swallowing such a consequence. Berkeley might respond that "the brain exists only in the mind" as he once said. Maybe this is true somehow, but surely this will sound very strange to a great many intelligent and reasonable people. Further, if we each experience *reality* differently, doesn't even this alone presuppose that there is some kind of mind-independent reality in the first place? It could simply be that there is the mind-independent food, tree, table, street, planet, etc.., *and* that we each experience those same mind-independent things differently to some degree. A realist can again acknowledge that physical objects are not "really" the way they "appear" to us. Just because humans experience the world differently from other species, it does not follow that there is *no* mind-independent reality (even if we can't know what it is like). We must be careful not to fall for a false dilemma between direct realism and idealism.

In addition, there are significant standard problems for any idealist view:

First, when ten of us see a table that we are all sitting around, is there one table or ten? If ten, then how can any science be done at all and why do our experiences cohere so well? If just one, then isn't it mind-independent in some sense?

Second, when a completely new astronomical observation or discovery is made, such as the discovery of a very distant galaxy, didn't the galaxy have to exist first and mind-independently? If so, how can that be if idealism is true? Wasn't there a *time lag* from when the light left the galaxy and our visual conscious perception of the galaxy? How could that be if there is only consciousness and sensory ideas?

Third, if we do not allow for any inferences from each of our own minds to other things, then it also seems that we shouldn't claim to know that there are other *minds* either. This, I think, leads to an untenable solipsist view such that each person can only know, or even reasonably believe, that he or she exists.

Fourth, if idealism is true, doesn't this result in a kind of "reverse hard problem," namely, how does "mind" or "consciousness" create matter or even just the appearance of matter? This is notoriously difficult to answer. Attempts to address this sort of problem by the likes of Berkeley, Leibniz, and some Indian scholars are fraught with difficulties.

Perhaps we should even agree that we cannot "prove" (in some very strong sense of the term) *either way* what mind-independent reality is really like. Nonetheless, I still think that there is good reason to believe *that* there is something mind-independent because it is the best way to explain what causes our perceptions and the coherent stream of our sensory states in the first place, among other things. So this would be more like an "inference to the best explanation" or perhaps a Kantian-style transcendental argument. For one thing, the coherence of our "waking life" sensory states is of course so much greater that our dream states so I do not think that any analogy between idealism to conscious dreams works well. Much the same is the case for hallucinatory experiences. Further, those kinds of experiences are also increasingly being investigated as physical processes in the brain.

Here, just as an example, is a Kantian-style argument in line with the above argument (see, for example, based on Bardon 2006):

(1) I make judgments about the temporal order of my own mental states.

(2) I could not make judgments about the temporal order of my own mental states without having experienced enduring substances independent of me undergoing alteration.

Therefore, (3) Mind independent enduring substances exist.

As Bardon (2006, sec. 1) explains, Kant at least tries to establish "a claim to knowledge of the existence of enduring, independent objects by showing that the skeptic is committed to something (in this case, consciousness of one's own perceptions as ordered in time) that is impossible without the existence of such objects. The skeptic thus is either committed to the existence of such things by virtue of accepting the obvious fact that we are conscious of our own perceptions as ordered in time, or presumes the existence of such things in the very attempt to raise doubt about it." In short, we couldn't even distinguish the "subjective succession" of our perceptions and the more "objective succession" of experienced objects (or events) unless there was at least something enduring independently of our minds.

It may be impossible to prove that there is a mind-independent reality if we mean something like "prove with absolute certainty and using empirical premises only," but then it is surely also impossible to prove that there is *no* mind-independent reality either. On the other hand, if we are permitted to use some *a priori* reasoning (or premises) or Kantian-style transcendental arguments (such as the one above), then it may very well be possible to prove *that* there is a mind-independent reality of some kind (even if we can't *know* exactly what it's like).

D. A Brief Look at the Indian Buddhist Tradition

Interestingly, although idealism is embraced more in the Eastern (especially Indian) tradition, this is not always the case and many of the above issues are raised in the relevant literature (see e.g. Coseru 2012a, 2012b). I will briefly describe one line of thought.

Coseru (2012a) first explains that "the term that most often translates as consciousness (vijñâna) is synonymously used for designating 'mind' or the 'life principle' in the most generic sense of those terms" (p. 10). It does seem true that at least the Yogâcâra School holds to the idealist view that consciousness acts as a "causal condition" of the appearance of phenomena, though not all commentators agree that this is an outright rejection of external mind-independent objects. Coseru (2012a) points out that the Yogâcâra school, associated with the works of the half-brothers Asaṅga and Vasubandhu, is often identified as the "Mind-only" or "Cognition-only" School (Cittamâtra or Vijñaptimâtra) which adheres to "a metaphysical picture of cognitive awareness or consciousness as the only ultimately existing reality" (p. 35). Moreover, Vasubandhu does offer a detailed defense of idealism. But, for example, one of his arguments is that since non-existing entities can be consciously apprehended, consciousness must have ontological priority over material objects. This does not of course establish a thoroughgoing idealism. At best, it shows that our conscious minds are capable of conjuring up or imagining some non-existent objects. It does not show that our conscious minds imagine or create *all* such appearances. Indeed, as Berkeley recognized and as we saw earlier, we certainly do not seem to cause all of our own sensory perceptions. Quite the contrary -- most perceptions seem "given" to us or caused by something (or someone) else. Vasubandhu also appeals to a "dream argument," namely, that "objects in a dream appear as having determined spatio-temporal coordinates without there being any correspondence to external realities" (p. 35). But the objection to this argument raised above applies equally here, and we also saw earlier that appeals to dreaming cannot account for the coherent stream of experiences in normal waking life. Further, many of the things we dream about can be traced back to earlier perceptions in our waking life.

Coseru (2012a) notes that May (1971) and Schmithausen (1973) are, for example, among the strongest proponents of the idealist interpretation the Yogâcâra ontology of mind. However, Coseru also explains that "Wayman (1965) is perhaps the first scholar to have challenged the idealist interpretation of the vijñapti-mâtra (i.e. 'cognition only' or 'nothing but cognition')" (p. 38). Wayman argues that Yogâcârins like Vasubandhu do not really deny the reality of external objects, but merely more plausibly argue that cognitive activity can arise in the absence of an external object. Numerous scholars since Wayman have argued against the idealist interpretation of the Yogâcâra metaphysical world view (such as Kochumutton 1982, Kalupahana 1987, Lusthaus 2002, Dunne 2004).

Other authors, such as Dignâga and Dharmakîrti, do explicitly take perceptual objects to have causal efficacy. What is called 'perception' involves an object giving rise to a perceptual image (âkâra) which represents the specific properties of the object. "The perceptual image is causally determined by the object, but the *manner* of its appearance is determined by factors that are intrinsic to cognition itself" (Coseru 2012a, p. 43, emphasis added). This position, for example, fits comfortably with the view of representational realists like Locke. The way, or 'manner', of an object's appearance is, at least in part, determined by the nature of our perceptual apparatus, such as with the secondary qualities. The same would also be true with respect to the ways that different species might experience objects, as we discussed earlier.

So there is not even general consensus as to how best to think of the metaphysics of the Yogâcâras. But one alternative view would simply be a typical "phenomenological" view, that is, physical entities are mind-independent, but we have no way of knowing how they are in themselves apart from the way we perceive and conceive them. It is crucial to distinguish the *metaphysical* claim of the *existence* of a mind-independent reality of some kind with the *epistemological* claim that we can *know* what such reality is like "in itself." This is reminiscent of the more Kantian position outlined above. It is Transcendental Idealism, not Berkeleyan Idealism. Nor is it any form of idealism which rejects the existence of all physical mind-independent reality. Indeed, Kant himself was very careful to distinguish his view from the likes of Descartes, Berkeley, and Leibniz.

IV. CONCLUSION

In any case, although it seems that any eventual neural realization of HOT theory must be somewhat widely distributed in the brain, it remains unclear how widely distributed it needs to be. I have argued against the view that HOT theory should treat first-order (i.e. world-directed) conscious states as requiring prefrontal cortical activity. Nonetheless, even though a HOT theorist is not automatically committed to a materialist theory of mind, it is reasonable to suppose that conscious states are realized in the brain. I then explored some of the key background metaphysical views involved in understanding the nature of consciousness, such as the debate between realism and idealism as well as the prospects for solving the so-called "hard problem" of consciousness. Some of the differences in question often mirror traditional differences between Western and Eastern perspectives on the nature of consciousness. Overall, I have argued that some form of realism and physicalism is more plausible than the opposing views and that materialists (and especially HOT theorists) can offer plausible replies to the hard problem.

References

Alter, T. & Walter, S. (Eds.) (2007). *Phenomenal concepts and phenomenal knowledge: New essays on consciousness and physicalism*. New York: Oxford University Press.

Alvarez, J., & Emory, E. (2006). Executive function and the frontal lobes: A meta-analytic review. *Neuropsychology Review, 16*, 17-42.

Bardon, A. (2006). Transcendental arguments. *Internet Encyclopedia of Philosophy*. Retrieved from: http://www.iep.utm.edu/trans-ar/

Berkeley, G. 1710/1975. A treatise concerning the principle of human knowledge. In M. R. Ayers (Ed.), *George Berkeley Philosophical Works*, Everyman edition. London: J. M. Dent & Sons.

Chalmers, D. (1995). Facing up to the problem of consciousness. *Journal of Consciousness Studies, 2*, 200-219.

Chopra, D. and Kafatos, M. From Quanta to Qualia. This volume.

Coseru, C. (2012a). Mind in Indian Buddhist Philosophy. In E. N. Zalta (Ed.), *The Stanford Encyclopedia of Philosophy* (Winter 2012 Edition), Retrieved from http://plato.stanford.edu/archives/win2012/entries/mind-indian-buddhism/

Coseru, C. (2012b). *Perceiving reality: Consciousness, intentionality, and cognition in Buddhist philosophy*. New York: Oxford University Press.

Crick, F. and Koch, C. (1990). Toward a neurobiological theory of consciousness. *Seminars in Neuroscience, 2*: 263-75.

Crick, F. (1994). *The astonishing hypothesis: The scientific search for the soul*. New York: Scribners.

Dunne, J. (2004). *Foundations of Dharmakîrti's philosophy*. Sommerville, MA: Wisdom Publications.

Francescotti, R. (2001). Property dualism without substance dualism? *Philosophical Papers, 30*, 93-116.

Gennaro, R. (1996). *Consciousness and self-consciousness: A defense of the higher-order thought theory of consciousness*. Amsterdam and Philadelphia: John Benjamins.

Gennaro, R. (2005). Consciousness. *Internet Encyclopedia of Philosophy*. Retrieved from: http://www.iep.utm.edu/consciou/

Gennaro, R. (2012). *The consciousness paradox*. Cambridge, MA: The MIT Press.

Goldberg, I., Harel, M., and Malach, R. (2006).When the brain loses its self: prefrontal inactivation during sensorimotor processing. *Neuron, 50*, 329-339.

Grill-Spector, K. & Malach, R. (2004).The human visual cortex. *Annual Review of Neuroscience, 7*, 649-677.

Kalupahana, D. J. (1987). *The principles of Buddhist psychology*. Albany: State University of New York Press.

Kant, I. 1781/1965. *Critique of Pure Reason*. Translated by N. Kemp Smith. New York: MacMillan.

Kochumuttom, T. A. (1982). *A Buddhist doctrine of experience: A new translation and interpretation of the works of Vasubandhu the Yogâcârin*. Delhi: Motilal Banarsidass.

Kozuch, B. (2014). Prefrontal lesion evidence against higher-order theories of consciousness. *Philosophical Studies, 167*, 721-746.

Levine, J. (1983). Materialism and qualia: The explanatory gap. *Pacific Philosophical Quarterly, 64*, 354-361.

Levine, J. (2001). *Purple haze: The puzzle of conscious experience*. Cambridge, MA: MIT Press.

Loar, B. (1997). Phenomenal states. In N. Block, O. Flanagan, and G. Güzeledere, (Eds.) *The nature of consciousness*. Cambridge, MA: MIT Press.

Locke, J. 1689/(1975). *An essay concerning human understanding*. P. Nidditch (Ed.). Oxford: Clarendon.

Lusthaus, D. (2002). *Buddhist phenomenology: A philosophical investigation of Yogâcâra Buddhism and the Cheng wei-shih lun*. London: Routledge Curzon.

May, J. (1971). La philosophiebouddhiqueidéaliste. *Asiatische Studien, 25*, 265–323.

Nagel, T. (1974). What is it like to be a bat? *Philosophical Review, 83*, 435-456.

Newen, A. & Vogeley, K. (2003). Self-representation: searching for a neural signature of self-consciousness. *Consciousness and Cognition, 12*, 529-543.

Robinson, W. (2004). *Understanding phenomenal consciousness*. New York: Cambridge University Press.

Rosenthal, D. M. (1986). Two concepts of consciousness. *Philosophical Studies, 49*, 329-59.

Rosenthal, D.M. (1997). A theory of consciousness. In N. Block, O. Flanagan, and G. Güzeledere (Eds.). *The nature of consciousness*. Cambridge, MA: The MIT Press.

Rosenthal, D.M. (2000). Consciousness and metacognition. In D. Sperber (Ed.) *Metarepresentation*. Oxford: Oxford University Press.

Rosenthal, D.M. (2002). Explaining consciousness. In D. Chalmers (Ed.) *Philosophy of mind: classical and contemporary readings*. New York: Oxford University Press.

Rosenthal, D.M. (2005). *Consciousness and mind*. New York: Oxford University Press.

Ryle, G. (1949). *The concept of mind*. London: Hutchinson and Company.

Saxe, R. (2010). The right temporo-parietal junction: A specific brain region for thinking about thoughts. In A. Leslie & T. German (Eds.) *Handbook of theory of mind*. Psychology

Press.

Saxe, R., and Pelphrey, K. (2009). Introduction to a special section of developmental social cognitive neuroscience. *Child Development, 80,* 946-951.

Saxe, R., and Powell, L. (2006). It's the thought that counts: Specific brain regions for one component of theory of mind. *Psychological Science, 17,* 692-699.

Schmithausen, L. (1973). Spirituelle praxis und philosophical theorieim Buddhismus. In *Zeitschriftfür Missionswissenschaft und Religionswissenschaft, 57,* 161–86.

Swinburne, R. (1986). *The evolution of the soul.* New York: Oxford University Press.

Wayman, A. (1965).The Yogâcâra Idealism. *Philosophy East and West, 15,* 65–73.

Chapter 4

Consciousness in the Light of Quantum Theory

PAAVO PYLKKÄNEN
Department of Philosophy, History, Culture and Art Studies and Academy of Finland Center of Excellence in the Philosophy of the Social Sciences (TINT)
University of Helsinki, Finland

1. INTRODUCTION

This paper explores the theme "quantum approaches to consciousness" by considering the work of one of the pioneers in the field. The physicist David Bohm (1917-1992) not only made important contributions to quantum physics, but also had a long-term interest in interpreting the results of quantum physics and relativity in order to develop a general world view. His idea was further that living and mental processes could be understood in a new, scientifically and philosophically more coherent way in the context of such a new world view. This paper gives a brief overview of different – and sometimes contradictory - aspects of Bohm's research programme, and evaluates how they can be used to give an account of topics of interest in contemporary consciousness studies, such as analogies between thought and quantum processes, the problem of mental causation, the mind-body problem and the problem of time consciousness.

2. BOHM ON THE ANALOGIES BETWEEN THOUGHT AND QUANTUM PROCESSES

In 1951 Bohm published a textbook *Quantum theory*, where he presented quantum theory in its standard "Copenhagen" interpretation (Bohm's presentation is quite similar to the physicist Wolfgang Pauli's version of the Copenhagen intepretation). Bohm also had a philosophical aim, namely to outline a "physical picture of the quantum nature of matter". In this context he was led to consider *analogies between quantum processes and thought processes*. We will here briefly present these analogies and assess their contemporary relevance. What is particularly important is Bohm's claim that if neural processes underlying mental processes were quantum physical in relevant ways, this would explain some important features of our process of thought.

In *Quantum theory* Bohm pointed to three analogies between human thought process and quantum processes which can be denoted as follows:

- Effects of observation
- Unanalyzability
- Both have a "classical limit"

Let us consider these briefly in turn (for a more detailed discussion see Pylkkänen 2014; see also Pylkkänen 2015b).

Effects of observation. In his discussion Bohm first draws attention to the fact that introspective observation of thought typically introduces unpredictable and uncontrollable changes in the way thought proceeds thereafter. Analogously, the observation of the position of a particle introduces unpredictable and uncontrollable changes in the particle's momentum.

Unanalyzability. Bohm suggests that a part of the significance of each element of thought process originates in its indivisible and incompletely controllable connections with other elements. Analogously, some of the essential properties of a quantum system (e.g. whether it is a wave or a particle) depend on indivisible and incompletely controllable connections with surrounding objects.

Both thought and quantum processes have a "classical limit". Bohm suggests that the logical process corresponds to the most general type of thought process as the classical limit corresponds to the most general quantum process. His idea is that the rules of logic are analogous to the causal laws of classical physics. Similarly, he suggests that concepts and objects are analogous. The suggestion is that logically definable concepts play the same fundamental role in abstract and precise thinking as do separable objects and phenomena in our customary description of the world. At the same time, he points to an analogy between pre-logical thinking and quantum process. He says that the basic thinking process probably cannot be described as logical. For example, he thinks that a sudden emergence of a new idea is analogous to a quantum jump.

He then raises the question of whether these analogies are just a co-incidence or whether they might be a sign of a deeper connection. He acknowledges that they could be a mere co-incidence, but goes on to consider an alternative, namely the possibility that the physical aspect of thought might involve quantum processes in some important way. This, he suggests, would explain in a qualitative way the analogies. Let us briefly consider how, starting with the "observation analogy".

Now, if the physical aspect of thought involved quantum processes in a non-negligible way, this would enable us to develop a qualitative account of why the direction ("momentum") of thought is disturbed by an attempt to define its content ("position"). How about the "unanalyzability analogy"? If the physical aspect of thought and language involved quantum processes (e.g. indivisible links), it might be possible to develop a qualitative naturalistic explanation of some holistic features of language and meaning. Finally, how might we explain the "classical limit analogy"? This might be explainable if the physical aspect of the alogical, aconceptual thought process involved quantum processes (with inseparability, discontinuity etc.), while the physical aspect of the logical and conceptual thought process involved classical processes (e.g. classically describable, separable neural "activation patterns" governed by the classical laws of physics).

In order to get a better view of the relevance of these analogies, let us consider further the "classical limit" analogy. In the picture we are sketching it seems that we have "two physical worlds" - i.e., the general quantum world which contains as its part the special case of a classical world. But we also have "two minds", i.e. the mind in the sense of a general alogical and aconceptual thinking process, which in some conditions gives rise to the special case of the mind as logical thinking process with logically definable concepts.

The above implies that the relationship between quantum and classical is analogous to the relation between conceptual and aconceptual. We would then have, on the one hand, the *quantum world* of inseparable objects and discontinuous processes, and the *classical world* of separable objects and causal, continuous processes as a special case, and, on the other hand the *aconceptual mind* with alogical processes and the *conceptual mind* engaged in logical thinking as a special case of it (cf. Pylkkö 1998). Note that such a view of the aconceptual mind can also be used to characterize the pure, contentless consciousness that is said to be experienced in meditational states in classical Indian practises (cf. Velmans 2009).

The suggestion that there are analogies between quantum processes and thought (which was put forward by already Niels Bohr) is also the starting point of a new field of research known as quantum cognition or quantum interaction where one uses the ideas and tools of quantum theory to model aspects of cognition and other phenomena (without making the stronger assumption that those phenomena are literally quantum mechanical, see Pylkkänen 2015a). Bohm's 1951 discussion anticipates qualitatively many ideas in quantum cognition. Such ideas have been developed in considerable mathematical detail in recent research (for a brief review and references to the relevant literature, see Wang et al. 2013)

3. THE ONTOLOGICAL INTERPRETATION OF QUANTUM THEORY

After completing his textbook *Quantum theory* Bohm still felt he could not understand the theory properly. Discussions with Einstein in Princeton led him to search for an alternative interpretation. What worried Einstein and Bohm was not merely the famous indeterminism of usual quantum theory but also the fact that the usual interpretation did not give a description of physical reality over and above predicting experimental phenomena. In other words, the usual interpretation did not provide a quantum ontology, or a description of the nature of quantum systems, regardless of whether or not they are being observed.

Bohm soon realized that the major equation of quantum theory, the Schrödinger equation, could be rewritten in a form which was very much like the Hamilton-Jacobi formulation of classical mechanics, except for an extra term which had the dimensions of energy. He realized that quantum theory could be interpreted as describing the movement of a particle (such as an electron) which was influenced not merely by classical fields (such as the electromagnetic) but also by a new type of quantum mechanical field that always accompanies it (Bohm 1952). Thus, an electron is not a particle OR a wave, but it is a particle AND a wave. In fact, Bohm had independently rediscovered the "pilot wave" theory which de Broglie had presented already in the 1927 Solvay conference. Bohm was able to answer some old objections to de Broglie's theory and also provided the first consistent account of measurement in terms of this theory (for a description of the Bohm theory which includes a brief review of criticisms against it, see Goldstein 2013). Given this background, the theory is often called the de Broglie– Bohm theory or interpretation. One of the key advantages of the de Broglie-Bohm interpretation is that it provides an ontological description of individual quantum systems and this is why in later work Bohm and his colleague Basil Hiley decided to call their developed version of this interpretation the *ontological interpretation* of quantum theory (Bohm and Hiley 1987, 1993; for a recent discussion of the metaphysical issue of individuality in the Bohm approach, see Pylkkänen, Hiley and Pättiniemi 2016). While Bohm never took this interpretation to be a final theory, he felt it was important as a starting point for further development.

One such development turned out to be potentially very relevant to our understanding of living and mental phenomena. For Bohm drew attention in the 1980s to how the ontological interpretation contains a new type of energy (mathematically described by the quantum potential, which arises from the quantum field). The curious feature is that the size of the quantum potential depends only upon the form of the quantum wave, and not on the amplitude of the wave. It looks as if the quantum field literally IN-FORMS or puts form into the energy of the particle. Bohm thus proposed that the way this energy affects the particle can be understood via a new notion of *active information.* He further suggested that this energy might be relevant for understanding features of living and especially mental phenomena (Bohm 1990). The relevance of active information to the traditional philosophical problem of mental causation was explored in more detail by Pylkkänen in 1992 (see also Pylkkänen 2007) and after Bohm's death by Hiley and Pylkkänen (2005).

While the notion of active information at the quantum level has not yet been widely discussed, some leading thinkers do take take the idea seriously, for example Quentin Smith (2002). Also, an interesting adaptation of the active information scheme to neuroscience has been proposed by Thomas Filk (2012). In the field of the social sciences, Andrei Khrennikov (2004) has made imaginative use of the proposal and the Bohm theory has also been applied to financial processes by Olga Choustova (2007) and Emmanuel Haven (2005). Of course, the notion of "quantum information" has been widely discussed in recent years (see. e.g. Bouwmeester et al. 2000). The advantages of the concept of active information over quantum information, when discussing some quantum experiments, have been argued for by Owen Maroney (2002); see also Maroney and Hiley (1999).

Note that there are by now different versions of the de Broglie-Bohm theory, for example Goldstein's (2013) "Bohmian mechanics" and Bohm and Hiley's (1993) "ontological interpretation". A balanced attempt to reconcile the different approaches is made by Holland (2011).

4. THE IMPLICATE ORDER

We mentioned above that Bohm never offered the pilot wave theory as a final theory. He did try to develop the scheme further in the 1950s, but due to some difficulties in this work he began in the early 1960s to develop – often in discussions with Hiley - a more *general conceptual framework* which takes as constraints both the results of relativity and quantum theory. In particular he argued that both relativity and quantum theory challenge the "mechanistic order", but their basic concepts directly contradict each other. He argued that we need in physics a new theory that starts from what relativity and quantum theory have in common, namely *undivided wholeness*. The challenge then became to develop new notions of order that are appropriate to describe such undivided wholeness. The most important new concept was that of *implicate order*, which Bohm illustrated with the hologram and with a device consisting of two concentric cylinders with glycerine between them. Placing droplets of ink to the glycerine and turning the outer cylinder allows one to illustrate (as an analogy to what happens in a quantum theoretical description of a "particle") how the order of a part is enfolded to the whole (so that it is "implicate") and (because of reversibility) can be unfolded (become "explicate"). The implicate order arises from considering the meaning of quantum theory and relativity, but Bohm claimed that it applies even more obviously in other domains such as the biological domain, and especially in cognitive processes and conscious experience. This framework provides an entirely new paradigm in which to try to understand the nature of conscious experience, mental processes and their relation to the underlying neurophysiological and physical processes. Bohm presented this framework in his book *Wholeness and the Implicate Order* (1980), and it has been further explored in e.g. Pylkkänen (2007).

The strongly holistic nature of the implicate order approach also reflects Bohm's engagement with Eastern philosophy, and in particular his discussions with J. Krishnamurti (see Krishnamurti and Bohm 2014).

One feature that may be confusing is that Bohm himself tried many different ways to approach quantum theory in his research, and also discussed the mind-body problem and conscious experience in different ways, corresponding to the different interpretations of quantum theory he was considering. Which of these views, if any, is correct, one might ask? To understand this potentially confusing situation, it is important to consider Bohm's epistemological views, in particular his views about the nature of scientific theories. A theory for Bohm is, as the etymology of the word suggests, a *way of looking* at the world, rather than something that gives us a literally true and final description of the way the world is. I suggest that it is in this spirit that we ought to consider Bohm's various suggestions: as tools that we can use to gain a better understanding of both quantum and relativistic phenomena and their relation to phenomena of classical physics, as well as biological and mental phenomena. Different tools are useful for different purposes, and reveal reality from a particular side or point of view. Sometimes the views offered by the different theories are in contradiction with each other, but at any given period of research it may often be premature to try to make a final decision between them. In the latter part of the paper I will thus briefly show how some of the above theoretical ideas can be used as tools to gain a better understanding of some well-known problems in the philosophy of mind and cognitive science.

5. THE PROBLEM OF MENTAL CAUSATION

The problem of mental causation is the problem of understanding how mental states (as non-physical states) could possibly influence the course of physical processes without, for example, violating the energy conversation laws. Bohm and Hiley's ontological interpretation of quantum theory suggests that an entirely new kind of energy operates in situations where quantum theory is required, an energy best understood as "active information". If mental states and their informational content can be understood as some higher-order organisation of this new "quantum potential energy" then an entirely new way of understanding mental causation, or how "mind" could affect "matter" (and vice versa) opens up (see Bohm 1990; Pylkkänen 1995, 2007; Hiley and Pylkkänen 2005).

6. THE GENERAL MIND-BODY PROBLEM

The general mind-body problem is closely connected to the problem of mental causation. This is the well known problem of whether mind and body are to be understood as two different (possibly interacting) things, or whether one is the aspect of the other, or whether one is an illusion, or whether both are aspects of some neutral ground. When discussing the implicate order, Bohm (1980) offers us a version of the idea that mind and body have a common ground beyond them both.

He uses the well-known non-locality of quantum theory as an analogy to illustrate the relation of mind and body. He suggests that in quantum theory two systems that are non-locally connected can each be seen as a three-dimensional projection of an underlying six-dimensional reality. This idea is well illustrated (as an analogy) by a situation where a big fish is swimming in a rectangular fish tank and two cameras are situated on the sides of the tank, one looking the fish from the back, the other from the side, and we are then shown the images from the two cameras in two monitors placed next to each other. Here we have two two-dimensional correlated projections of a three-dimensional reality (one monitor showing the fish from the side and the other from the back). Analogously to both quantum non-locality and the fish-tank example, Bohm proposed that mind and body can likewise be seen as correlated projections from an underlying ground. This means that mind and body do not interact causally or mechanically, but their correlated relationship is to be understood in the fact that they have a common ground out of which they are constantly projected as mutually correlated aspects.

Note that this idea seems to differ in a significant way from the idea explained above, where active information was used to explain how mind affects matter and vice versa. Bohm's various ideas about the relation of mind and body are indeed different, depending on whether he is writing in the context of the implicate order or the ontological interpretation (for Bohm's own attempt to reconcile the implicate order and the ontological interpretation, see Bohm 1987). Making explicit these different ideas and considering their connection to each other is a challenge for future research. If the tensions between the different schemes can be dealt with coherently, there is a possibility here of understanding in a new way a major traditional philosophical problem, illustrating the potential value of a "quantum approach" to the mind.

7. TIME CONSCIOUSNESS

The problem of time consciousness was considered by e.g. Broad and Husserl and has recently been discussed by e.g. van Gelder (1999), Varela (1999) and Dainton (2000, 2001). The essence of the problem is how to understand our experience of temporal objects as temporal.

When I am listening to music, for example, how am I to understand the status of the sounds that I first heard a very short time ago? Are the past sounds that still seem to "reverberate" in consciousness to be understood as mechanical memories? Husserl certainly did not think so but thought that the sounds heard a short while ago are perceived (retained and apprehended) under the mode "just past". But what must the ontology of conscious experience be like to make possible such "perception of the just past" (as opposed to a mechanical recall from memory)? Van Gelder, Varela and Dainton each propose different ways of looking at this issue in the contemporary context, and so did Bohm in chapter 7 of his *Wholeness and the Implicate Order*.

Bohm's idea is that listening to music provides a very good example of an implicate order, and that indeed we are directly perceiving an implicate order when listening to music. In Bohm's scheme the "just past" sounds (as well as visual and other sensory images) can be seen as elements that are enfolding into the deeper levels of the implicate order of conscious experience. We can thus understand musical experience as something where different elements (e.g. individual sounds) are *co-present* at *different degrees of enfoldment*, which is typical for the implicate order in general. Note that this example is not claiming that our experience of listening to music is, ontologically speaking, a quantum process. But it is suggesting that holistic phenomena in different levels (conscious experience, biological phenomena, physical phenomena) have the implicate order in common, and this makes it possible to understand these phenomena as a coherent whole, including the way they "enfold" and "unfold" each other (for a more detailed discussion, see Pylkkänen 2007, chapter 5). Surely, one might argue, such unified understanding has been an underlying aim of science and philosophy. Again, such unified understanding is not meant to be taken as a literal and final description of the way the world is, but rather as a way of looking or understanding the world and our place in it from a particular point of view.

The *prima facie* advantage of the theory of time consciousness that can be developed on the basis of Bohm's implicate order is that, unlike the views of Broad, Husserl, van Gelder, Varela and Dainton, Bohm's view coheres in a deep way with the fundamental concepts of contemporary physics. Given that a satisfactory theory of time consciousness ought to provide us with not just a phenomenological description of experienced time but also an account of the relation between experienced time and other levels of time (neural, chemical, physical etc), Bohm's scheme seems to be a promising alternative to explore.

The above examples building upon Bohm's programme are very much abstractions from "work in progress". It is hoped that they go some way towards illustrating the potential philosophical power of not just Bohm's approach, but also of "quantum approaches to mind" more generally. In the spirit of this paper the other quantum approaches (e.g. Penrose and Hameroff's model, quantum brain dynamics, etc.) can be seen not only as "competitors" but also as different ways of looking at this domain, as other kind of tools which provide a different and more complete view of this rapidly developing terrain (for a review, see Atmanspacher 2011).

8. DISCUSSION

We have above briefly discussed various ways in which the physicist David Bohm discussed mind and consciousness in the course of his long career. We saw how Bohm's starting point was to notice certain analogies between thought and quantum processes. He then speculated that these analogies could be explained in qualitative way if the neural processes underlying thought involved certain kinds of quantum effects. In later work he developed new schemes for quantum theory, and continued to consider the relation of mind and matter in the context of these schemes. The pilot wave theory, under Bohm and Hiley's (1993) ontological interpretation, seems particularly interesting for those who try to understand the place of mind in nature. If information plays an active role even at the fundamental quantum level, it is perhaps not so surprising or anomalous that the information contained in mental states can guide physical action. The implicate order, in turn, provides a very general scheme in which physical, biological and psychological processes can be understood in terms of some common notions and principles. It involves a radical questioning of the mechanistic world-view, where systems are typically understood in terms of entities in mechanical interaction (cf. Ladyman and Ross's (2007) criticism of the mechanistic world-view).

How does Bohm's approach compare with other contemporary views? It is characteristic of consciousness studies that there are widely different approaches. At one end there are eliminativist physicalist views which argue that conscious experience (or at least some of its key features) do not really exist, and that matter is the primary reality (see Churchland 2013). At the other end there are views - often found in Eastern approaches - which claim that consciousness is the primary reality and that the external world of matter is some kind of illusion or an appearance, a creation of consciousness (cf. Velmans 2009). The Bohmian view suggests a middle way between these extremes. It acknowledges that there exists a world independently of the human mind. Is this world the physical world? Bohm would say that the world is fundamentally a more neutral and comprehensive ground which contains the mental and the physical as its aspects, or "projections" (see Bohm 1980; Pylkkänen 2007; Atmanspacher 2011).

We noted above that this view involves some tensions, given Bohm's different schemes in physics. In the context of the ontological interpretation it is tempting to assume that just as the pilot wave guides the electron, so the mind (understood as a more complex, quantum-like field) quides the body. Yet in the context of the implicate order scheme Bohm proposed that mind and body are "correlated projections" from a higher-dimensional underlying reality, which seems to contradict the idea that they are autonomous aspects which can influence each other. Thus, it seems that Bohm did not end up with a single definite view regarding the nature and relation of mind and matter. This can be seen as a weakness of his approach. However, given the difficulty of the mind-matter problem it seems reasonable at this point to keep various options open and explore their mutual relations, strengths and weaknessess in a spirit of genuine dialogue.

Acknowledgement

The work for this paper was partially funded by the Fetzer Franklin Fund of the John E. Fetzer Memorial Trust.

Bibliography

Atmanspacher, H. (2011). Quantum approaches to consciousness. In E. N. Zalta (Ed.). *The Stanford Encyclopedia of Philosophy*. Retrieved from http://plato.stanford.edu/archives/sum2011/entries/qt-consciousness/

Bohm, D. (1952). A suggested interpretation of the quantum theory in terms of "hidden" variables I and II. *Physical Review, 85,* 166-179 and 180-193.

Bohm, D. (1980). *Wholeness and the implicate order*. London: Routledge.

Bohm, D. (1987). Hidden variables and the implicate order. In B. J. Hiley & F. D. Peat (Eds.) *Quantum implications: Essays in honour of David Bohm*. London: Routledge, London.

Bohm, D. (1990). A new theory of the relationship of mind and matter. *Philosophical Psychology, 3*, 271–286.

Bohm, D. & Hiley, B. J. (1987). An ontological basis for quantum theory: I. non-relativistic particle systems. *Physical Reports, 144,* 323-348.

Bohm, D. & Hiley, B. J. (1993). *The undivided universe: An ontological interpretation of quantum theory*. London: Routledge.

Bouwmeester, D., Ekert, A., & Zeilinger, A.K. (Eds.). (2000). *The physics of quantum information: Quantum cryptography, quantum teleportation, quantum computation*. Heidelberg and Berlin: Springer.

Choustova, O. (2007). Toward quantum-like modeling of financial processes. *Journal of Physics: Conference Series 70*, 012006.

Churchland, P. (2013). *Matter and consciousness*. (3rd ed.). Cambridge, MA: MIT Press.

Dainton, B. (2000). *Stream of Consciousness. Unity and continuity in conscious experience.* London and New York: Routledge.

Dainton, B. (2001). *Time and Space*. Chesham: Acumen Publishing Ltd.

Filk, T. (2012). Quantum-like behavior of classical systems. In *Quantum interaction: Lecture Notes in Computer Science*, 7620, 196-206. Berlin Heidelburg: Springer.

Goldstein, S. (2013). Bohmian mechanics. In E. N. Zalta (Ed.). *The Stanford*

Encyclopedia of Philosophy (Spring 2013 edn). Retrieved from: http://plato.stanford.edu/archives/spr2013/entries/qm-bohm/

Haven, E. (2005). Pilot-wave theory and financial option pricing. *International Journal of Theoretical Physics, 44*, 1957-1962.

Hiley, B.J., & Pylkkänen, P. (2005). Can mind affect matter via active information? *Mind and Matter, 3*, 7-26. Retrieved from: http://www.mindmatter.de/resources/pdf/hileywww.pdf

Holland, P. (2011). A quantum of history. *Contemporary Physics, 52*, 355.

Khrennikov, A. (2004). *Information dynamics in cognitive, psychological and anomalous phenomena. Fundamental Theories of Physics*: Vol. 138. Dordrecht: Kluwer.

Krishnamurti J. & Bohm, D. (2014). *The ending of time: Where philosophy and physics meet.* New York: HarperCollins.

Ladyman, J. & Ross. D. (2007). *Every thing must go: Metaphysics naturalized.* Oxford: Oxford University Press.

Maleeh, R. & Amani, P. (2012) Bohm's theory of the relationship of mind and matter revisited. *Neuroquantology, 10*, 150–163.

Maroney, O. (2002). *Information and entropy in quantum theory* (Unpublished doctoral thesis). Birkbeck College, University of London. Retrieved from http://www.bbk.ac.uk/tpru/OwenMaroney/thesis/thesis.html.

Maroney, O. and Hiley, B.J. (1999). Quantum state teleportation understood through the Bohm interpretation. *Foundations of Physics, 29*, 1403-1415.

Petitot, J. F., Varela, B. Pachoud, & J.-M. Roy (Eds.) (1999). *Naturalizing phenomenology: Issues in contemporary phenomenology and cognitive science.* Stanford: Stanford University Press.

Pylkkänen, P. (1992). *Mind, matter and active information: The relevance of David Bohm's interpretation of quantum theory to cognitive science.* Reports from the Department of Philosophy, University of Helsinki, No 2, 1992. [PhD dissertation].

Pylkkänen, P. (1995). Mental causation and quantum ontology. In L. Haaparanta & S. Heinamaa (Eds.), *Mind and Cognition: Philosophical perspectives into cognitive science and AI. Acta Philosophica Fennica 58.* Helsinki: The Philosophical Society of Finland.

Pylkkänen, P. (2007). *Mind, matter and the implicate order.* Series: The Frontier Collection. Heidelberg and New York: Springer.

Pylkkänen, P. (2014). Can quantum analogies help us to understand the process of thought? *Mind and Matter, 12*, 61-91. Retrieved from http://www.mindmatter.de/resources/pdf/pylkkaenen_www.pdf

Pylkkänen, P. (2015a) .Weak vs. strong quantum cognition. In H. Liljenström (Ed.). Advances in cognitive neurodynamics (IV). *Proceedings of the 4th International Conference on Cognitive Neurodynamics 2013.* Dordrecht: Springer Science+Business Media B.V. Retrieved from http://link.springer.com/chapter/10.1007%2F978-94-017-9548-7_58

Pylkkänen, P. (2015b). Fundamental physics and the mind – is there a connection? In H. Atmanspacher, C. Bergomi, T. Filk, K. Kitto (Eds.), *Quantum Interaction 2014: 8th International Conference, QI 2014*, selected papers pp. 3-11. Heidelberg: Springer http://dx.doi.org/10.1007/978-3-319-15931-7_1

Pylkkänen, P., Hiley, B.J., & Pättiniemi, I. (2015). Bohm's approach and individuality. In A. Guay, & T. Pradeu, (Eds.). *Individuals across the sciences.* Oxford: Oxford University Press. http://arxiv.org/abs/1405.4772

Pylkkö, P. (1998). *The aconceptual mind: Heideggerian themes in holistic naturalism.* Amsterdam and Philadelphia: John Benjamins Publishing Company.

Smith, Q. (2003). Why cognitive scientists cannot ignore quantum mechanics. In Q. Smith, & A. Jokic (Eds.). *Consciousness: New philosophical perspectives.* Oxford: Oxford University Press.

van Gelder, T. (1999). Wooden Iron? Husserlian phenomenology meets cognitive science. In J. Petitot, F. J. Varela, B. Pacoud & J.-M. Roy (Eds.). *Naturalizing Phenomenology*, Stanford University Press.

Varela, F.J. (1999). *The specious present: A neurophenomenology of time consciousness*. In J. Petitot, F. J. Varela, B. Pacoud & J.-M. Roy (Eds.), *Naturalizing Phenomenology* (pp. 266-314). Stanford University Press.

Velmans, M. (2009). How to define consciousness – And how not to define consciousness. *Journal of Consciousness Studies, 16*, 139-156.

Wang, Z., Busemeyer, J. R., Atmanspacher, H., & Pothos, E. M. (2013). The potential of using quantum theory to build models of cognition. *Topics in Cognitive Science, 5*, 672–688.

Chapter 5

Matter and Consciousness in Indian Epistemology

SUBHASH KAK[1]
Oklahoma State University, Stillwater, Oklahoma, USA

Indian epistemology is of interest to the physicist for its framework of reality includes observers in a fundamental manner. In the Indian physics tradition of Vaiśeṣika, it is postulated that there are nine classes of substances, some of which are non-atomic, some atomic, and others all-pervasive. The non-atomic ground is provided by the three substances of ether (âkâsa), space (dik), and time (kâla), which are unitary and indestructible; a further four, earth (pṛthvî), water (âpas), fire (tejas), and air (vâyu) are atomic composed of indivisible, and indestructible atoms (anu); self or consciousness (âtman), which is the eighth, is omnipresent and eternal; and, lastly, the ninth, is the mind (manas), which has atomic dimensions.

1. INTRODUCTION

According to the well-known biography of Schrödinger by Moore, Indian philosophical ideas of Vedânta helped Schrödinger discover the idea of a state function that is a sum of all possibilities. Moore adds that in their development of quantum theory "Schrödinger and Heisenberg and their followers created a universe based on superimposed inseparable waves of probability amplitudes. This new view would be entirely consistent with the Vedântic concept of All in One" (Moore, 1989; Kak, 1996).

The parallels or analogies between Vedânta and quantum theory have motivated many scientists to examine Indian scientific ideas. But in spite of this interest the understanding of these ideas remains woefully inadequate. In India itself, there is almost no study of Indian science and for a variety of complex political and social reasons the knowledge of Sanskrit, the language in which Indian science is written, is fast disappearing among the elite.

Indian epistemology approaches reality differently from Western science and while some have classified it as "idealism," it is apart from Western idealism in many ways. It is unlike standard scientific epistemology in that it accepts consciousness as an independent category different from matter. It provides an interesting resolution to the seemingly insoluble problem of interaction between the causally closed worlds of matter with the world of consciousness. It accepts the possi-

[1]subhash.kak@okstate.edu

bility of obtaining knowledge by non-empirical means. In most general terms, Indian epistemology differs from Western epistemology in that it includes sentient agency within the universe.

Light in Indian thought has outer and inner aspects. The outer light is generated by atoms of light while the inner light is a consequence of consciousness. The intuition associated with the inner light is called jyotiṣa (from the Sanskrit *jyoti*, light). The two lights are taken to be connected. These ideas can only be *understood* by considering the underlying cosmology in which the world of objects and things and world of ideas and experience are different at the phenomenal level but identical at a deeper level (Kak, 1997).

The writings of Schrödinger provide the best articulation of Indian ideas by a scientist although he did it in a haphazard way in different essays. He notes that the absence of sentient observers in the scientific world picture means that it is not a complete picture and that the scientific enterprise by its very nature can only speak of things. Posing the problem of the split between objects and subjects in *Mind and Matter*, Schrödinger stated that the solution could only be based on Indian ideas (Schrödinger, 1959).

> It is the same elements that go to compose my mind and the world. This situation is the same for every mind and its world, in spite of the unfathomable abundance of "cross-references" between them. The world is given to me only once, not one existing and one perceived. Subject and object are only one. The barrier between them cannot be said to have broken down as a result of recent experience in the physical sciences, for this barrier does not exist.
>
> The reason why our sentient, percipient and thinking ego is met nowhere within our scientific world picture can easily be indicated in seven words: because it is itself that world picture. It is identical with the whole and therefore cannot be contained in it as a part of it. But, of course, here we knock against the arithmetical paradox; there appears to be a great multitude of these conscious egos, the world is however only one...
>
> There is obviously only one alternative, namely the unification of minds or consciousnesses. Their multiplicity is only apparent, in truth there is only one mind. This is the doctrine of the Upanishads.

While this may sound attractive philosophy (at least to some), the question arises if it has any relevance to the workings of science. Indeed the reason why few people have rushed to study it is the belief that while it makes for a comforting position it solves no real problems.

In this paper, I argue that one can go beyond Schrödinger's writings and show that consciousness (that lies behind subjective experience) manifests itself in everyday world leaving a trace that is open to scientific examination. In principle, the *apparent* influence of consciousness on matter (I use the term apparent because at a deeper level the consciousness-matter divide does not exist) should be measurable in all transformations including evolution of life forms. Indeed, arguments have been made that the rise of complex organic molecules cannot be explained on probability consideration alone (Wickaramsinghe, 2009). The case can also be made that evolved forms are already present as potential within natural law and "natural selection" is a restatement of the fact that pure probabilities do not account for the outcomes of the *random* evolutionary process. But these views are generally consigned to philosophy since outcomes in the evolutionary chain cannot be associated with specific probability values with any degree of unanimity.

I argue for consideration of anomalous events that are a part of social history as evidence of the workings of universal consciousness. Although these events may be seen as coincidences, their sheer improbability strains credulity. Of these the most astonishing is the speed of light that is correctly given in a medieval text (Kak, 1999). Less spectacular, but equally impressive, are ancient Indian estimates of the age of the universe in a cycle of expansion and contraction and the distance to the sun. If one were to see these coincidences to be similar to the random process of creativity and scientific discovery (as recounted, for example, by Hadamard (1954) and discussed further elsewhere (Kak, 2000; 2004), then the question of the epistemology behind the process of creativity becomes relevant. Archetypal creative impulse is also woven in the fabric of dreams as in the anecdotal accounts of Elias Howe for the sewing machine in 1845 and Kekulé's for the structure of benzene in 1862.

In certain philosophical schools of the West (as in Plato's theory of Forms or Kant's transcendental idealism), ideas are taken to be part of the structure of the mind or even to exist independent of the mind. But these schools are not taken seriously in the narratives of science. Modern science privileges empiricism, that is knowledge based on observations by the senses together with logical inference and abstraction, as the only true source of knowledge. It cannot provide explanations for unusual coincidences like the one related to the speed of light. Neither can it provide explanations for agency and intentionality in psychology or the performance of savants (Sacks, 1985).

Indian ideas on the nature of knowledge are complex and traditional texts present these ideas from a variety of perspectives. This paper is an introduction to these ideas with emphasis on nature of light and physical reality. It begins with the broad philosophical question of ways of knowing. In the next section, an outline of the Vaiśeṣika system of Indian physics is provided. The subsequent section presents the atomic view of light. Next, we analyze anomalous statements on speed of light and the distance to the sun. The paper also addresses the question of interaction between consciousness and matter.

2. REALITY AND WAYS OF KNOWING

Traditionally, there were six main schools of philosophy in India, each of which had its own approach to epistemology together with accepted means of cognition. There is agreement in these schools that as consciousness cannot be reduced to material phenomena, phenomenal reality has two aspects: one of material phenomena and the other of consciousness. Reality is dual at a phenomenal level but unitary at a deeper, transcendent level.

This transcendent reality can only be approached through a variety of unique and complementary perspectives. Like the room in space with its six different walls in which each window provides a different view, Indian philosophy has six *darśanas* (visions or "schools").

Each school accepts a variety of means of cognition. In the Vaiśeṣika sense perception and inference are valid means, whereas in the Sâṅkhya verbal testimony or scriptural authorities are additional means, and the Nyâya accepts comparison also as a means of valid cognition. The idea is that the knowledge furnished by one means must not be attainable by any other means, it should not be reducible to another, and it should not be contradicted by another means of cognition.

Indian epistemology acknowledges error of cognition. The final test of such theories is the application to everyday experience. Since false theories and cognitions can affect one's understanding of reality and one's response to it, a kind of a relative truth may be ascribed to them.

The Sanskrit term for epistemology is *prâmânyavâda* (literally being established by proof). It deals with *prameya* or the object of cognition, *pramâ* or *pramiti* which is the cognition itself, and *pramâtṛ* or the subject that cognizes. A distinction is made between knowledge as *jñâna*, which is experience, and representation of it as *vijñâna* that can only approximate *true* knowledge. Self-knowledge comes through intuition which stands outside the subject-object dichotomy. Understanding proceeds in a paradoxical manner by the contemplation of the self through the self or, in Sanskrit, the âtman through the âtman.

The Vaiśeṣika system of Kanâda is a conceptual representation of space and the gross visible matter taken to be constructed out of the varying motions of *anu*, its most fundamental particle. In the Nyâya, or logic, that is closely tied to the Vaiśeṣika, minds are not empty slates; the very constitution of the mind provides some knowledge of the nature of the world. The four *pramânas* through which correct knowledge is acquired are direct perception, inference, analogy, and verbal testimony (Kak, 2005; 2009a).

Gotama, the early teacher of the Nyâya, lists four factors involved in direct perception as being the senses (*indriyas*), their objects (*artha*), the contact of the senses and the objects (*sannikarṣa*), and the cognition produced by this contact (*jñâna*). *Manas*, or mind, mediates between the self and the senses. When the *manas* is in contact with one sensory organ, it cannot be so with another. It is therefore atomic in dimension. It is because of the nature of the mind that our experiences are essentially linear, although quick succession of impressions may give the appearance of simultaneity.

A later Nyâya philosopher recognizes four kinds of perception: sense perception, mental perception, self-consciousness, and yogic perception. Self-consciousness is a perception of the self through its states of pleasure and pain. In yogic perception, one is able to comprehend the universe in fullness and harmony.

The Sâṅkhya system describes evolution at cosmic and individual levels. It views reality as being constituted of *puruṣa*, consciousness that is all-pervasive, motionless, unchangeable, without desire who at the individual level is the *sâkṣin*, the witness, and *prakṛti*, which is the phenomenal world. Prakṛti is composed of three different strands (*gunas* or characteristics) of *sattva, rajas*, and *tamas*, which are transparency, activity, and inactivity, respectively.

Evolution begins by purusha and prakriti creating *mahat* (Nature in its dynamic aspect). From mahat evolves *buddhi* (intelligence) and *manas* (mind). Buddhi and manas in the large scale are Nature's intelligence and mind. From buddhi come individualized ego consciousness (*ahaṅkâra*) and the five *tanmâtras* (subtle elements) of sound, touch, sight, taste, smell. From the manas evolve the five senses (hearing, touching, seeing, tasting, smelling), the five organs of action (with which to speak, grasp, move, procreate, evacuate), and the five gross elements (ether, air, fire, water, earth).

The evolution in Sâṅkhya is an ecological process determined completely by Nature. It differs from modern evolution theory in that it presupposes a cosmic intelligence and further beyond a universal consciousness. In reality, modern evolution also assigns intelligence to Nature in its drive to select certain forms over others as well as in the evolution of intelligence itself.

3. THE VAIŚESIKA SYSTEM

The Vaiśesika system has categories not only for space-time-matter but also for attributes related to perception of matter. It starts with six categories (*padârthas*) that are nameable and knowable. Nothing beyond these six fundamentals is necessary, because they are sufficient to describe everything in the universe from concrete matter to the abstract atom.

The six categories are: *dravya* (substance), *guna* (quality), *karma* (motion), *sâmânya* (universal), *viśeṣa* (particularity), and *samavâya* (inherence). The first three of these have objective existence and the last three are a product of intellectual discrimination. Universals (sâmânya) are recurrent generic properties in substances, qualities, and motions. Particularities (viśeṣa) reside exclusively in the eternal, non-composite substances, that is, in the individual atoms, souls, and minds, and in the unitary substances ether, space, and time. Inherence (sâmânya) is the relationship between entities that exist at the same time. It is the binding amongst categories that makes it possible for us to synthesize our experience. In later descriptions of the system a seventh category of "non-existence" is added.

Of the six categories, the basic one is that of substance and the other five categories are the ones that the mind associates with the substance. Thus observers belong to the system in an integral fashion. If there were no sentient beings in the universe then there would be no need for these categories.

It is postulated that distinguishing characteristics and motion are essential for the classification of matter. Space and time are identified

FIGURE 1
The six categories of Vaisesika

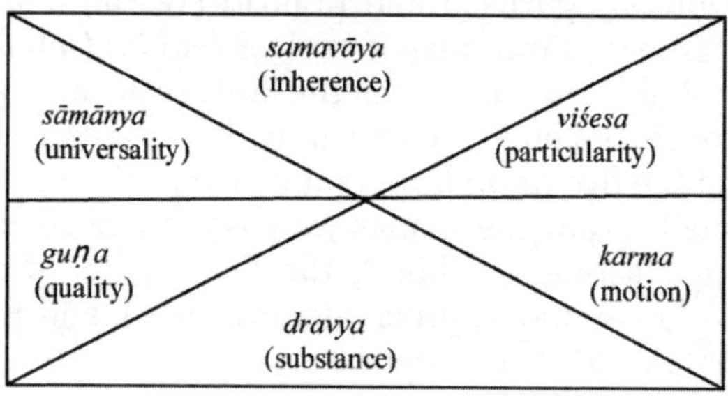

FIGURE 2
The nine dravyas (substances):
E: earth; W: water; F: fire; A: air; Æ: ether

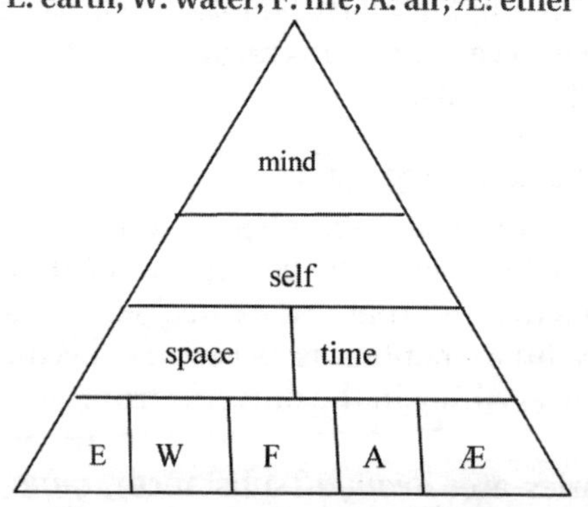

through motion of matter or the sun.

Of the substances, four (earth, water, fire, and air) are material (that is consisting of atoms) and capable of motion whereas five others (time, space, ether, âtman, and mind) are non-material and, therefore, no motion may be associated with them. It is significant that âtman is listed before mind, suggesting that it is the medium through which mind's apprehensions are received. The atoms of earth, water, fire and air are different and this difference arises out of the different ways the fundamental atom of materiality combines with itself in different arrangements.

The examination of the various parts of the Vaiśesika system reveals that its observables arise through the effect of motion in a consistent manner. As is true of other systems, this system leads to its own paradoxes. Yet, it offers a comprehensive and scientific view of the universe beginning with gross visible matter all the way up to the subtle invisible mind (Narayan & Kak, 2011).

The atom is indivisible because it is a state for which no measurement can be attributed. What cannot be measured cannot be further divided and it cannot be spoken of as having parts. The motion the atom possesses is non-observable and it may be viewed as an abstraction in a conventional sense. Space and time are the two lenses through which matter is observed and they form the matrix of universe.

The distinction between intrinsic (*karma*) and extrinsic (*kârya*) motions arises from the fact that intrinsic motion is uniform in all directions.

When the universe ceases to be at the end of the cosmic cycle, matter is not annihilated; rather, it reaches a quiescent state where its atoms have no extrinsic motion and so become invisible, which appears very similar to the conception of the state of the giant atom at the beginning of cycle of creation. The lack of motion represents a cessation of time, because time is a measure of change.

In the epistemology of the Vaiśesika system, it becomes possible to obtain knowledge due to the agency of âtman or self. In Figure 2, the atomic substances exist within the matrix of eternal substances.

4. ATOMS AND LIGHT

Atoms possess incessant vibratory motion. Heat and light rays consist of very small particles of high velocity. As material particles, their velocity is finite. This is also due to the fact that motion is contingent upon time as one of the dravyas. Particles of heat and light can be endowed with different characteristics and heat and light can be of different kinds. The atoms of light and heat belong to the tejas category; there are four other kinds of atoms with attributes.

There is no difference between the atom of a barley seed and paddy seed, for both these are constructed out of the atoms of earth. Under the impact of heat particles, atoms exhibit new characteristics.

A *bhűta*-atom evolves out of integration from the corresponding *tanmâtra*, which is its potential form, indicating a primacy of the abstract over the material. Although atoms are unitary objects their combinations generate various tanmâtras. Combinations of rudiment-matter (*bhűtâdi*) lead to more specific forms. Atoms vibrate when acted upon by energy.

The atom's potentiality manifests in distinct attributes based on state of conjunction and motion. It is this potentiality that leads to diverse complex atoms with different attributes. These attributes may be viewed as being created by the matrix of space, time and number. Light has a special place in this view as it is both an elementary constituent of matter as well as the medium that shines the inner space of the mind. The atom of light cannot be described fully.

Although the Vaiśesika is an atomic theory, it is so only as an idealization and its measurable attributes are in a continuous spectrum as they are generated within the womb of an infinite space-time matrix.

In the Kashmir school of Śaivism, both outer and inner realities (consciousness) are characterized by vibration (*spanda*) and it is this vibration that makes self-referral possible. The ultimate movement takes place not in space and time but inside consciousness.

5. ANOMALOUS EVENTS

This section presents anomalous events as evidence of the workings of consciousness in the large although one could also explain them as coincidences. The difficulty with the latter explanation is that the probability of choosing numbers mentioned here is extremely small. These cases are different from speculations in ancient texts (somewhat like science fiction) describing airplanes, space travel, embryo transplantation, weapons that can destroy the world and so on that have come to pass (Rao & Kak, 2000) because they are general ideas which do not involve specific numbers. The figure of 8.64 billion years for the universe cycle in Indian cosmology, which is not too different from the currently accepted value of the time since the big bang, is widely known. Here I speak of two other numbers that are not well known.

Speed of Light. The mention of the 14th century knowledge of the speed of light in India is an example of spontaneous discovery in the manner discussed by Hadamard in his book. The speed is found in the well-known commentary on the Rigveda by the medieval scholar Sâyaṇa (1315-1387), prime minister in the court of the Vijayanagar Empire. It associates the speed of 2,202 yojanas in half a nimeṣa with the sun (or sunlight). The time measure of nimeṣa is well attested in Indian astronomical and encyclopedic texts as being equal to 16/75 seconds (Kak, 2003). The yojana is variously defined by different writers. It was defined in two different ways by leading astronomers of the time. Likewise, it seems to have been used in two different ways for terrestrial applications.

According to the Arthaúâstra, the famed third century BC book on polity and economics, a yojana is 8,000 dhanus (bow). For a long time Western scholars took a dhanus to be equal to six feet or 1.83 meters (Bashan, 2000), and with this Sâyaṇa's number is 3.02 × 10^8 meters per second which corresponds closely to the correct value of the speed of light. More recently, it has been suggested based on dimensions of ancient monuments that the standard value for the ancient dhanus is 1.904 meters, which makes the value of speed about 4 percent higher. I have discussed the question of units related to speed elsewhere (Kak, 2009b).

There is no way this speed could have been measured in medieval India. Until just over 200 years ago it was not even known in the Western tradition that light had finite speed. In 1676, Rømer calculated this speed in terms of the speed of earth's rotation around the sun, and his value was about 26% less than the modern value. Sâyaṇa could not have obtained this figure from the West or anywhere else and, therefore, it can only be seen as an inspired guess.

Distance to the sun. Until modern times, the solar system was taken to be much smaller than its currently accepted value. Pappus of Alexandria writing in the 4th century took the distance to the sun to be about 490 earth radii. At the beginning of modern Western astronomy, Tycho Brahe took the distance between the earth and the sun to be 8 × 10^6 kms and Kepler took it to be about 24 × 10^6 kms.

In the Indian Purâṇas, the earliest of which predates fifth century, the sun is associated with two "axles": the first one is 15.7 × 10^6 yojanas long and the second one is 45,500 yojanas long (Wilson, 1840) (section 2.8 of the Viṣṇu Purâṇa). One can presume that the longer axle represents the distance to the earth and the shorter axle represents the deviation from the circular path. Speaking of this astronomical reference, we cannot prove that it is from the earliest layer of the text, but there is general scholarly consensus that the text is at least 1,500 years old.

One of the variant definitions of yojana, which was prevalent in Kashmir (a region where many Purâṇas were written), is given by Stein (1961) (footnote to verse 393) where he takes it to be about 6 miles (Stein: "The direct distance by road from Srinagar to Vijebror is about thirty miles. This corresponds exactly to five yojanas") (Yojana, n.d.). If this yojana was meant (6 miles or 9.6 km), then the distance to the sun is about 150.72 × 10^6 kms. Given that the distance between the two cities is an approximate value, the distance to the sun can be taken to be identical to the modern value of 149.598 × 10^6 kms.

One might complain that we are picking a value of yojana that was only used regionally. This criticism is valid, but we are not trying to find a scientific basis to the choice of the distance to the sun. Rather, we are showing that the choices presented by intuition, without any firm basis in physical theory, can be surprisingly accurate. Accepting the validity of such a way of knowledge is against the mainstream program of science and current schoolbook theories of mind.

It is indeed possible that even before modern telescopic astronomy, which did not exist in India, a reasonable estimate of the distance to the sun could be made based on durations of lunar and solar eclipses. But there is no evidence that such calculations were made by astronomers.

There are other anomalous precise numbers in the ancient texts that include the size of the earth in the accounts of Eratosthenes, Âryabhata, and al-Bîrűnî. The apocryphal account of Eratosthenes's measurement of the size indirectly by measuring the shift in the shadow of the sun at noon between Syene and Alexandria is not credible since the distance between the two cities was not known accurately and the shift in the angle of the shadow could not have been measured with the accuracy that the calculation of the earth's diameter demands.

In the traditional explanation of the workings of mind, habits picked up in childhood and in school are the impediments that prevent one from being connected to one's intuition. Real creativity requires challenging dogma as well as one's own certitudes. One sees unexpected connections, which is an element of creativity, in extraordinary states of mind. Looking within can reveal unexpected knowledge about the universe for we are a part of the universe.

6. INTERACTION BETWEEN THE WORLDS OF CONSCIOUSNESS AND MATTER

The Indian view of consciousness -- that it is a unity and the feeling of sentient beings as being separated from others is a misapprehension -- was endorsed by Schrödinger in his influential book *What is Life?* (Schrödinger, 1965) Indian tradition accepts that consciousness influences nature by the process of observation (*dṛṣṭi* in Sanskrit). This is very similar to the quantum mechanical view of the influence of observation on a physical process by the quantum Zeno effect (Kak, 2007). But the difference between quantum theory and Indian ideas is that although one speaks of observations in quantum theory there is no place in its ontology for observers. Schrödinger was aware of this limitation of quantum theory and he argued that sense-categories like the tanmâtras of the Sâṅkhya system of creation at the individual or the cosmic level were essential to understand reality.

In traditional art Śiva (representing individual and universal consciousness) is shown as lifeless next to the vibrant Goddess (who represents Nature). Abstract representations of the cosmos show Śiva as a dot (of immateriality) within the (geometric) framework of the material world. Much of Indian mythology is an exposition of Indian epistemology in a coded language.

If evolution of machines is driven by human intelligence, the case could be made that biological evolution is driven by Nature's intelligence which is an embodiment of consciousness.

One can also assert that biological forms, and by extension machine forms, are latent in the physical law, just as the excited states of the electron orbits are latent in the physics of the hydrogen atom even though these states may not be occupied. Furthermore, ideas can be given the same footing as biological forms or machines although they need appropriate biological structure to be articulated.

The bridging of the worlds of consciousness and matter does not occur at the level of matter or mind. In Indian epistemology, consciousness itself is a transcendent category that goes beyond both matter and mind.

7. CONCLUSIONS

Indian epistemology has some parallels with Western idealism that accepts independent existence of ideas and forms. But it is different from idealism in the sense that the self has access to much more than what the individual obtains through the sense organs. The conception of the self at the individual level (*âtman*) or in its totality (*brahman*) together with the counter-intuitive notion of equality between the two selves makes it possible to see how large scale correlations can exist and how a person can obtain surprising insights through intuition. Naturally, such insights can only be rationalized within the framework of the individual's knowledge. Although ordinarily consciousness and matter are two distinct categories, consciousness can influence the evolution of matter through observation.

A study of the categories of Indian physics does not yield any special insights on light that are useful for the understanding of the nature of the photon. But it presents a cosmology of the material universe that illuminates anomalous findings that are part of scientific discovery. Consciousness cannot disrupt natural law related to matter but it can guide its evolution by making certain outcomes more likely than others. The universe is closed on itself at the level of consciousness and there are instances of anomalous experience and coincidences at the personal level and such coincidences also occur in the scientific world. Coincidences in Indian scientific texts that support these ideas include the age of the universe, the distance to the sun, the speed of light, and other numbers. There are also instances of impressive qualitative scientific speculations in the literature.

Indian epistemology could be considered to be falsified if no evidence is found for large correlations in the world. There are many who will dismiss anomalous numbers described in this paper as coincidences. Perhaps there would be greater acceptance if new carefully devised scientific tests are proposed to determine large correlations in the laboratory and in terrestrial and astronomical processes. The likelihood that such tests are devised will remain small unless Indian epistemology becomes a part of the scientific conversation.

References

Basham, A.L. (2000). *The wonder that was India*. London: Sidgwick and Jackson.

Hadamard, J. (1954). *The psychology of invention in the mathematical field.* New York: Dover.

Kak, S. (1996). The three languages of the brain: quantum, reorganizational, and associative. In K. Pribram & J. King (Eds.), *Learning as self-organization* (pp.185–219). Lawrence Erlbaum Associates.

Kak, S. (1997). On the science of consciousness in ancient India. *Indian Journal of History of Science, 32,* 105-120.

Kak, S. (1999). The speed of light and Puranic cosmology. *Annals of the Bhandarkar Oriental Research Institute, 80,* 113-123.

Kak, S. (2000). Active agents, intelligence, and quantum computing. *Information Sciences, 128,* 1-17

Kak, S. (2003). Indian physics: Outline of early history. Retrieved from https://arxiv.org/abs/physics/0310001

Kak, S. (2004). *The architecture of knowledge*. New Delhi, India: CRC.

Kak, S. (2005). Aristotle and Gautama on logic and physics. Retrieved from http://arxiv.org/abs/physics/0505172

Kak, S. (2007). Quantum information and entropy. *International Journal of Theoretical Physics, 46,* 860-876.

Kak, S. (2009a). Logic in Indian thought. In A. Schumann (Ed.), *Logic in religious discourse* (pp. 20-33). Frankfurt and Paris: Ontos Verlag.

Kak, S. (2009b). The universe, quantum physics, and consciousness. *Journal of Cosmology, 3,* 500-510.

Moore, W. (1989). Schrödinger: *Life and Thought*. Cambridge: Cambridge University Press.

Narayan, R., & Kak, S. (2011). Space, time and atoms in Vaiśeshika. In *Vacaspativaibhavam*, A Volume in Felicitation of Professor Vachaspati Upadhyaya (pp.1137-1155). New Delhi, India: DK Printworld.

Rao, T.R.N., & Kak, S. (2000). *Computing science in ancient India.* New Delhi, India: Munshiram Manoharlal.

Sacks, O. (1985). *The man who mistook his wife for a hat*. New York, USA: Harper Collins.

Schrödinger, E. (1959). *Mind and matter*. Cambridge: Cambridge University Press.

Schrödinger, E. (1965). *What is life?* New York: Macmillan.

Stein, M.A. (tr.). (1961). *Kalhana's Rajatarangini. A chronicle of the kings of Kashmir*, Vol. 1. Delhi, India: Motilal Banarsidass. (Original published 1900).

Wickaramasinghe, C. (2009). *Astrobiology, comets and the origin of life*. Singapore: World Scientific.

Wilson, H.H. (tr.). (1840). *The Vishnu Purana*. Retrieved from: http://www.sacred-texts.com/hin/vp/index.htm.

Yojana n.d. Retrieved from: http://www.sizes.com/units/yojana.htm

Chapter 6

Unitary Quantum Theory as a Formal Framework for a Theory of Consciousness

CHRIS FIELDS[1]
Sonoma, California, USA

ABSTRACT

If the extraneous and mutually contradictory assumptions of its various "interpretations" are uniformly rejected, unitary quantum theory provides a clear and self-consistent description of the physical world. The continuing empirical success of unitary quantum theory requires, moreover, that we take this description seriously. The physical world as described by unitary quantum theory is globally deterministic, but is provably locally non-deterministic at every scale and from every perspective definable within the theory. It contains no physically-efficacious boundaries, either in "physical" coordinate space or in Hilbert space; hence it contains bounded "objects" or "systems" only as semantic stipulations that may or may not be useful as physical approximations. Measurable space and time are strictly derivative in this world, not fundamental. Observers - generators of classical information, the kind of information that can be recorded using finite, time-persistent symbols - are ubiquitous at all scales, but like all bounded, time-persistent systems exist only as fiat semantic entities. The physical states of the collections of degrees of freedom constituting observers are mutually correlated by quantum entanglement, but the classical information that they encode is context-sensitive in principle; hence quantum "intersubjectivity" is guaranteed, while classical intersubjectivity is at best an approximation. In particular, no classically-characterized observation is strictly repeatable. It is argued that the characteristics of classical information predicted by unitary quantum theory in the absence of extraneous interpretative assumptions are sufficiently similar, prima facie, to the characteristics of human phenomenal experience of external objects through either perception or memory to regard quantum theory as a candidate formal theory of phenomenological object-directed awareness. If viewed in this way, quantum theory immediately entails that structural or functional models of the encoding of phenomenal experience by bounded macromolecules, cells, or anatomical systems are at best observer- and context-relative approximations.

---

[1]243 West Spain Street, Sonoma, CA 95476, USA

INTRODUCTION

Since its inception in the 1920s, quantum theory has been regarded by many prominent physicists, and by the vast majority of philosophical commentators on physics, as a "bare" mathematical framework that does not directly describe the physical world. Bohr, for example, is widely quoted as saying:

> "There is no quantum world. There is only an abstract physical description. It is wrong to think that the task of physics is to find out how nature *is*. Physics concerns what we can *say* about nature ..."
>
> (e.g. in Petersen, 1963)

While the first, third and fourth sentences of this statement express an instrumentalist or "non-ontic" view of quantum theory shared by Bohr, Heisenberg, and many current researchers (e.g. Fuchs, 2010; Chiribella, D'Ariano & Perinotti, 2011; Healey, 2012; Friederich, 2013), the second sentence expresses the much more broadly held opinion that unlike classical physics, quantum theory is *only* an abstract mathematical construct without direct, intuitively-clear physical content. As such, it is fundamentally unsatisfactory as a *physical* theory regardless of its predictive success. The motivation behind this broadly held opinion that quantum theory is unsatisfactory as a physical theory is clear. We do not directly experience the world as having the properties, such as superposition and entanglement, that quantum theory ascribes to it; we do not experience cats as being both dead and alive, for example, or chairs as being both here and there. Indeed our ordinary, shared, pre-theoretical human experience of the world is not even "classical" in the sense of being described by classical physics; it rather conforms to an essentially Aristotelian "folk physics" that we develop as young children (McCloskey, 1983; Karmiloff-Smith, 1995). The world as classical physics describes it is, however, at least close to this intuitive world; the world as quantum theory describes it is not close at all.

Both physicists and philosophers have responded to this misalignment between quantum theory and our pre-theoretical physical intuitions by adding assumptions to the theory that make its mathematical predictions more consonant with our everyday experience. The most well-known added assumption is the "collapse postulate" of von Neumann (1932), which interprets measurement as an irreversible, non-unitary physical process that converts a quantum state into a classical state. Since the starting point of this non-unitary process cannot be measured even in principle, von Neumann's postulate is widely regarded as a philosophical or interpretative assumption instead of a physical assumption; indeed it has recently become commonplace to reformulate it as the claim that measurement converts quantum information into classical information, thus dropping the idea of a *physical* "collapse" altogether (e.g. Nielsen & Chaung, 2000). Many physicists, however, still regard "collapse" as a physical process and have developed an enormous diversity of theories to explain how it is implemented (e.g. Ghirardi, Rimini & Weber, 1986; Bohm, Hiley & Kaloyerou, 1987, Hameroff & Penrose, 1996; Stapp, 2001; Weinberg, 2012; Kastner, 2013). Theorists who do not regard "collapse" as a physical process nonetheless tend to regard it as objective, i.e. as fully independent of any characteristics of the observer (e.g. Griffiths, 2002; Zurek, 2009). Even the "many worlds" interpretation of quantum theory generally invokes an objective, classical past shared by multiple observers, and hence implicitly incorporates an objective "collapse" to classicality (e.g. Zeh, 2000; Tegmark, 2010).

The present chapter explores the consequences of an alternative approach to quantum theory: that of taking unitary quantum theory *without any added assumptions* as a literal description of physical reality. There are at least three reasons to contemplate doing this. First, unitary quantum theory is both enormously successful and apparently unlimited in its applicability (e.g. Schlosshauer, 2006); increasingly challenging experiments designed to reveal entanglement over macroscopic spatial and temporal scales invariably have done so (e.g. Bennet *et al.*, 2012; Kaiser *et al.*, 2012; Peruzzo *et al.*, 2012; Christensen *et al.*, 2013; Inagaki *et al.*, 2013; Saeedi *et al.*, 2013). It seems, therefore, at least worth considering as a possibility that quantum theory might be *literally correct* in what it is telling us about nature. Second, the assumptions that are added to quantum theory in order to explain the "emergence of classicality" are invariably classical assumptions. Any "explanation" of classicality derived from quantum theory supplemented by such classical assumptions is clearly circular, and hence is not an explanation at all. To take just one example, all models of physical interactions that take the classical boundaries of ordinary objects to be physically significant violate a deep mathematical symmetry of quantum theory and are therefore either strictly approximations or are inconsistent (e.g. Fields, 2012a; 2012b; 2014). Finally, what "observers" and "observations" are is still not understood in physical terms. Some interpreters of quantum theory – most notably von Neumann – give observers an explicit role in the theory; most do not. However, the alternative of asking quantum theory itself to characterize observation in physical terms has not been rigorously pursued. Perhaps it should be.

In what follows, therefore, I have two main aims. The first is to briefly describe the world in which quantum theory says we live. Bas van Fraassen (1991) famously asked "how could the world possibly be the way a quantum theory says it is?" Perhaps we should examine what quantum theory says, and then ask how it could be otherwise. My second aim is to sketch an account of observation within unitary quantum theory, one that draws on the work of Zanardi (2001) and others on quantum reference frames and on the concept of quantum holography developed by 't Hooft (1993) and Susskind (1994). If observation is modeled in this purely quantum-theoretic way, "observers" are ubiquitous at all scales and "observation" is a way of describing what the universe is doing at all times. It is natural, in this picture, to simply identify "consciousness" or "awareness" with physical dynamics, and in particular with quantum entanglement as a resource driving physical dynamics. I conclude by suggesting that this identification of physicality with awareness might be useful, both for understanding what kinds of systems we human beings are and for appreciating the kind of universe that we live in.

THE WORLD ACCORDING TO QUANTUM THEORY

Let us begin by dropping our preconceived notions of what the world is like, and ask what the world would be like if quantum theory – in particular, unitary quantum theory with no "collapse" – was literally correct. This is the question that Everett (1957) asked, but the "relative state" picture that he proposed as an answer did not have the benefit of the last 50 years of work on quantum information, and has been replaced, both in physics and in the popular imagination, by the "many worlds" view of a universe that "branches" outward from a single past into multiple futures. The many worlds view requires for its coherent formulation not just the classical idea of a bounded object that is persistent through time, but the idea that the "same" bounded, persistent object – e.g. the same individual observer – can exist in and have different outcomes "happen to" it in different "branches" of the universe. It is, therefore, a semi-classical interpretative addition to quantum theory, not a simple statement of quantum theory as is often advertised (e.g. by Tegmark, 2010).

When not burdened with extraneous classical or semi-classical assumptions, quantum theory provides a remarkably clear picture of the physical world. The key components of this picture are briefly discussed below.

Physical dynamics are unitary

As Everett (1957) noted, quantum theory describes the evolution of the universe as unitary, i.e. as a process U such that $U^{\dagger}U = UU^{\dagger} = Id$, where Id is the identity operator on the Hilbert space on which U is defined and $U^{\dagger}$ is the complex conjugate of U. That the dynamic evolution of any closed quantum system is unitary is generally considered to be the second axiom of quantum theory, complementing the first axiom, that the state of any closed quantum system can be represented by a unit vector in a Hilbert space (e.g. Nielsen & Chaung, 2000); unitary evolution of the universe as a whole then follows from the fact that the "universe" is closed by definition. The Schrödinger equation describing the evolution of the physical state |**U**> of the universe **U**, $(\partial/\partial t)$ |**U**> = $(-i/\hbar)$ H_U |**U**>, expresses unitarity. Here H_U is the universal Hamiltonian operator (*cf.* Schlosshauer, 2006); the universal unitary time-propagator is then $U(t) = exp((-i/\hbar)(H_U t))$. The "time" parameter t in this expression is purely formal; as discussed below, its identification with the recordable time of human experience is an interpretative assumption.

As noted by physicists from Schrödinger onward, unitary time evolution turns any separable physical state |**U**> = |**A**> ⊗ |**B**> into an entangled state |**U**> = |**A** ⊗ **B**>, where "entangled" simply means "not separable," i.e. not expressible as a mathematical combination of the states of two independent entities A and B. Since the work of Bell (1964) and Kochen and Specker (1967), entanglement has become increasingly recognized as *the* fundamental characteristic of the world described by quantum theory. A fully-entangled universal state is a quantum superposition of all physical possibilities: all possible combinations of the values of all physical degrees of freedom. A fully-entangled universe contains no separable systems, and hence contains no systems that evolve independently of any other systems: a fully-entangled universe is a universe that evolves through time as a *single entity*. Indeed since the state of a fully-entangled universe is a superposition of all physical possibilities, its "evolution" only alters the relative amplitudes of these possibilities. No "new" possibilities are introduced, nor or any "old" possibilities removed from the mix.

An immediate consequence of unitarity is that any closed quantum system – including **U** as a whole – satisfies the fundamental symmetry of *decompositional equivalence*; the dynamical evolution of any such system is strictly independent of any decomposition of the system into "subsystems" or "parts" (Fields, 2012a, 2012b). Formally, decompositional equivalence requires that all tensor-product structures (TPSs) of a closed quantum system are strictly dynamically equivalent; that is, if **A** ⊗ **B** and **A'** ⊗ **B'** are both TPSs of **U**, then **A** ⊗ **B** = **A'** ⊗ **B'** = **U**. The equality of alternative TPSs is an axiom of quantum theory, e.g. axiom 4 in the presentation of Nielsen and Chaung (2000). Alternatively, decompositional equivalence is satisfied by any system with a linear Hamiltonian, i.e. any system U for which $H_U = \Sigma_{ij} H_{ij}$, where the indices i and j range over all degrees of freedom of **U**. The linearity of the Hamiltonian of any closed quantum system is similarly axiomatic within quantum theory.

Decompositional equivalence imposes a powerful constraint on the physics of any system that satisfies this symmetry: that physics cannot depend in any way on subsystem boundaries. Thus if quantum theory is true of our universe, the boundaries that separate "systems" within our universe – including the boundaries around observers – are *physically irrelevant*. Such boundaries are obviously relevant to any *description* of what is going on, but they are irrelevant to what is going on. This situation can be summarized in a slogan: system boundaries are *semantic not dynamic*. The semantic nature of system boundaries has significant consequences for both the theory of decoherence and the physical description of observers; these are discussed below.

Time is symmetric

Unitary evolution is symmetric in the "time" parameter t; indeed the conjugate operator $U^{\dagger}$ can be viewed as U acting backwards in t. As pointed out by Rovelli (1996) and others, t is not an observable in quantum theory. Recordable "laboratory time" is measured using some other observable, typically position; for example, one measures the position of the hands of a clock, or the position of the illuminated segments of an LED display. Measuring time in this way requires that the "clock" be singled out as an entity, one that, *by assumption*, maintains its identity through time and hence can be repeatedly accessed to make sequential time measurements. This assumption of a time-persistent clock, measurements of which can be recorded in a time-persistent memory, breaks the symmetry of t that is imposed by unitarity.

From a logical perspective, the assumption that a clock that *defines* time maintains its identity over time is clearly circular. More importantly for the present purposes, this assumption violates decompositional equivalence by defining a boundary – the boundary of the clock – that remains inviolate under unitary transformations. To see this clearly, consider the process by which an observer re-identifies the clock measured previously in order to make a second measurement of time. The second measurement only counts as a second measurement if the *very same physical degrees of freedom* are measured the second time around. Measuring the very same physical degrees of freedom that were measured previously requires picking them out from among all the degrees of freedom of the universe. No experimental procedure allowed by quantum theory permits doing this (Fields, 2010; 2011); indeed, any such procedure violates unitarity. As discussed in the more general case below, re-identifications of systems, including clocks, as the *same things* over time is always an approximation. As with system boundaries themselves, such re-identifications are items of classical semantics that are added to quantum theory, not components of quantum theory itself.

Once the boundary in **U** that picks out the degrees of freedom of the designated clock is recognized as a semantic boundary and not a dynamic, and hence not a physical boundary, it becomes clear that observed time is itself an item of semantics that only appears, within the interpretation that defines it, to break the physical symmetry of *t*. The semantic assumption that defines measured or experienced time is the assumption of *identity*. Without measured or experienced time, the notion that any system maintains its identity over time cannot be defined, while without the assumption that at least one system, the experiencer or the designated clock, maintains its identity over time, experienced or measured time cannot be defined. The assumption of measured or experienced time and the assumption of identity over time are, therefore, effectively a single assumption. This assumption is strictly a semantic addition to quantum theory, and can have no physical consequences in a world correctly described by quantum theory.

Global determinism implies local autonomy

All known microscopic physical interactions – in particular, the Standard Model interactions and gravity – are in isolation fully deterministic. As the Hamiltonian H_U characterizing a quantum theoretic universe is a linear sum of component interactions, it is fully deterministic if the component interactions are. Explicitly taking decompositional equivalence into account reinforces this conclusion, by ruling out any "higher-order interactions" that are non-linear in the fundamental component interactions, and that therefore privilege some TPSs of **U** over others. All evidence supporting unitary quantum theory is, therefore, evidence that the evolution of our universe is fully deterministic.

When combined with universal entanglement, universal determinism yields an interesting and *prima facie* surprising consequence: the behavior of any given degree of freedom is determined by, but is determined *only* by, the behavior of all other degrees of freedom in the universe. No *local* collection of degrees of freedom is sufficient to determine any behavior. A deterministic, quantum theoretic universe thus satisfies a particularly strong form of the Conway-Kochen "free will theorem" (2006): the behavior of a given degree of freedom is not only not determined, even stochastically, by the information available in its past lightcone, it is not determined by the information available in *any* local neighborhood, even any local spacelike neighborhood (Fields, 2013). This result is consistent with a recent demonstration that predicting the results of one's own decision-making process under given circumstances has greater computational complexity than simply making the decision, a result that holds whether the decision making process is deterministic or stochastic, and whether the computational resources available are limited or not (Lloyd, 2012).

In a quantum-theoretic universe, therefore, global determinism implies local autonomy, not only from the perspective of a particular decision-making agent, but from every other local perspective as well. As in the case of system re-identification, local determinism in such a universe is strictly an approximation. These two approximations are strongly coupled. We intuitively expect what we re-identify as "the same system" to exhibit "the same behavior" in response to "the same causes." This intuitive inference cannot even be formulated within unitary quantum theory without imposing extraneous classical assumptions.

Decoherence is a semantic interpretation, not a physical process

Since its development by Zeh (1970) and Zurek (1982), the theory of decoherence has become the standard approach to explaining the "emergence of classicality" within quantum theory (e.g. Schlosshauer, 2007). Briefly put, decoherence theory provides methods to calculate the observable quantum states of any physical system that interacts with, and is observed from a perspective within, a surrounding environment. As a mathematical formalism, decoherence theory is simply an application of quantum theory to the system-environment interaction. Because decoherence theory predicts that the observable states of any system in interaction with a surrounding environment will appear classical to observers embedded in that environment, it is widely regarded as explaining the apparent classicality of observable states, and hence as solving the notorious "measurement problem" of quantum theory (e.g. Landsman, 2007; Wallace, 2008).

When one examines decoherence calculations closely, however, it becomes immediately clear that the mathematical methods provided by decoherence theory are only applicable in practice when supplemented by classical assumptions. In particular, the interaction between a system and its environment can only be characterized within a TPS that treats the "system" and "environment" as components of **U**. This interaction can only be characterized as a function of time if the physical degrees of freedom composing the system and those composing the environment are re-identifiable as such over time. As noted earlier, any such assumption violates decompositional equivalence and is, therefore, an approximation at best. Decoherence calculations make, in addition, the assumption that the observer obtains no information from the environment; this assumption is often rendered mathematically by assuming that the dynamics of the "environment" can be treated using classical statistical mechanics, i.e. can be treated as classically random. Again as noted earlier, there is no randomness in quantum theory; the assumption of randomness – and the use of classical statistics to characterize it – is an explicitly classical assumption, as is the underlying assumption that the observer is informationally decoupled from the environment. Making either of these assumptions introduces classicality into decoherence theory, and hence renders any "explanation" of classicality by decoherence circular (Fields, 2014).

Stripped of the classical assumptions of a time-persistent system-environment boundary and an informationally-decoupled observer, the mathematics of decoherence describes system-environment entanglement, a non-random process that effectively erases any stipulated system-environment boundary. Entanglement with a surrounding environment does not remove quantum coherence from a system; it rather couples the system and the environment in a way that makes their joint state exhibit quantum coherence. What "removes coherence" in decoherence calculations is the assumption that the observer obtains no information from the environment and hence can treat its state using classical statistics: a classically random state is precisely an incoherent state. What decoherence calculations describe, therefore, is not a *physical* process of coherence removal, but simply the logical consequence of the use of classical statistics to characterize the environmental state. As noted earlier, assumptions of system boundaries are *semantic* assumptions that are overlaid on the dynamics described by quantum theory; the use of classical statistics to describe the environment depends on the assumption of a system-environment boundary and is therefore itself a semantic assumption. The "process" of decoherence is, therefore, a *semantic* process in which a classical system state – and its classical "encoding" by the environment – are inferred from *a priori* classical assumptions.

Summary: The quantum world

The quantum-theoretic picture of the world briefly outlined here is, as noted earlier, utterly unlike the essentially Aristotelian picture of the world that we develop by observing and manipulating objects as infants and young children. Indeed it is difficult to imagine a picture of the physical world that is less like our intuitive picture than is the quantum world. Some 600 years of increasingly precise experiments tell us, however, that while our intuitive picture of the physical world is accurate enough for hunting, agriculture, social life and even substantial feats of architecture, it fails utterly when pushed into new domains. The mechanical devices ushered into human culture by the industrial revolution required the classical physics of Galileo and Newton – as radical in its day as quantum theory is now – for their comprehension; the electronic devices of the mid-to-late 20th century require quantum theory for their comprehension. Every time we send an email or take a digital photograph, we affirm – Bohr's quip not withstanding – that the world we live in is a quantum world. It is time that we understood this world on its own terms.

The fundamental concept that quantum theory introduces is entanglement. The quantum world is an entangled world. It is *not separable* into bounded, time-persistent, re-identifiable entities that can be understood, *ceteris paribus*, independently of one another. Our idea of independent bounded systems that persist through time is, from a physical point of view, strictly an approximation. It is often a good approximation, good enough to enable experiments that employ bounded apparatus that can be re-identified easily from day to day in the laboratory, experiments that have uncertainties better than one part in a billion. What this means, however, is that it is a good approximation for *us*: we *define* the systems that we consider to be bounded in space and time, and these are the systems for which the approximation is good. How does this work: what enables us to define systems that appear, to us, to be bounded? Understanding how this works requires understanding how observers interact with the "systems" that they have defined. This, in turn, requires understanding what "observation" and "observers" are.

This question of what counts, physically, as an observation or an observer is almost always avoided. Zurek (2003), for example, explicitly places this question outside of science, stating that "the observer's mind (that verifies, finds out, etc.) constitutes a primitive notion which is prior to that of scientific reality" (p. 363-364) . Fuchs (2010) asks, somewhat more pointedly, "would one ever imagine that the notion of an agent, the user of the theory, could be derived out of its conceptual apparatus?" (p. 8). Stapp (2001) follows von Neumann (1932) in treating observers as amalgams of physical and "psychical" components, with the latter inexplicable in physical terms. Hameroff and Penrose (1996) develop a theory of observation centered on neuronal microtubules localized within the brains of observers, but offer no physical account of why these particular macroscopic structures and not others should be privileged bearers of quantum coherence in an otherwise-classical world. Most physicists avoid the question altogether, remaining content to regard an "observer" as just another quantum system (e.g. Schlosshauer, 2007) or even, à la Einstein, as a moving coordinate system (e.g. Rovelli, 1996) and an "observation" as any event that transfers classical information to an observer.

It is my contention that understanding the quantum world requires understanding observation as a physical process, and hence understanding *how* semantics are overlaid on dynamics. From a quantum-theoretic perspective, this is the question of how observer-system entanglement implements a mathematical operator – a von Neumann projection or, in more modern terms, a positive operator-valued measure (POVM) – representing a quantum-theoretic observable. From an information-theoretic perspective, it is the question of how classical, symbol-based information processing – classical computation – can be implemented by unitary dynamics. The latter question is central to quantum computing: it is the question of how to define a denotational semantics that allows a quantum *process* to be interpreted as a quantum *computation*, in particular, a quantum computation that accepts a classical question as input and yields a classical answer as output. A number of formal answers to this question now exist, in the form of well-defined semantics for quantum programming languages (e.g. Gay & Mackie, 2010). These formal answers, however, assume an observer. The challenge is to replace this assumed observer with a physical model of observation. The next section further characterizes this challenge and outlines a solution.

BOUNDARIES IMPLEMENT OBSERVERS

Treating an observer as simply a quantum system with associated coordinates unfortunately provides no insight into how an observer accomplishes the two key tasks that compose observation: the *acquisition* of classical information and its *storage* in a stable, long-term memory. It is successful execution of the second of these tasks that renders an observation *reportable*, and hence usable by either the original or some other observer as a basis for comparison with future observations. As noted earlier in the special case of systems employed as clocks, this ability to compare current and previous observations is essential to the definitions of both measured time – as opposed to symmetric t – and time-persistent individuality. Zurek (2003) takes this memory encoding and re-accessing ability as criterial, remarking that what distinguishes observers from mere apparatus is the ability of the former to "readily consult the content of their memory" (p. 759). The common picture of an observer as a system – or even as a conscious agent – that deploys a measurement operator to interact with a quantum system (e.g. Fuchs, 2010, Fig. 1) is therefore incomplete. Any observer capable of reporting comparative observations must deploy *two* measurement operators that acquire classical information from two separate quantum systems: the "system of interest" and the observer's own physically-implemented memory. These two systems must be separate – not entangled – if the memory of a previous event is to be independent of the event currently being observed. Again as noted earlier, such separability is always an assumption and always an approximation. It is relatively straightforward to arrange circumstances in which this separability fails, sometimes spectacularly, in the case of human memory (e.g. in change-blindness paradigms; see Simons & Levin (1998) for a striking example).

How can this assumption-laden semi-classical view of observation be reformulated in a way that makes it fully consistent with quantum theory? Two components of the standard view clearly must be dropped: the idea that observer, observed and memory are separable, and the idea that current and previous memory contents can be compared side-by-side. It should be emphasized that these ideas are not incidental, but rather are central to the traditional conception of observation and indeed of experimental science. David Bohm, one of the foremost advocates of "holism" in physics, still insisted that "the very idea of making an observation implies that what is observed is totally distinct from the person observing it" (1989, p. 585). The ability to compare current and previous observations side-by-side, with a non-problematic presumption of independence, is essential to the notion of experimental replication. These ideas are, however, inconsistent with unitary quantum theory and must be rejected – or treated as "for all practical purposes" approximations – if unitary quantum theory is to be taken seriously as a correct description of the world.

Quantum theory replaces the classical idea that observer and observed are separate with its opposite: the idea that they are entangled. Consider the Bell state $\psi = (1/\sqrt{2})(|\downarrow\rangle \otimes |\uparrow\rangle - |\uparrow\rangle \otimes |\downarrow\rangle)$. If an action on this state with a "spin" observable ($\hat{s}_z \otimes Id$) produces an outcome value of 1, an action with ($Id \otimes \hat{s}_z$) will, if performed, produce an outcome value of 0; this expectation has now been confirmed with measurements made 300 km apart (Inagaki *et al.*, 2013). What entanglement does, in this or any case, is classically correlate conditional information: the classical correlation only appears *if* a particular measurement is made, but if the measurement is made, the correlation is exact. Hence quantum theory replaces the traditional notion of absolute, objective classical correlation with a notion of conditional classical correlation. It also replaces the idea that classical correlation can be viewed as classical information *transfer* from the observed system to the observer with a notion of correlation full stop. Entanglement is not a classical causal process; observer and observed are equally entangled both before and after the observer records the measured outcome value.

The above discussion treats the observer and the observed as "monogamously" entangled, i.e. entangled with each other and with nothing else. It is only under this condition that classical correlation can be exact. Monogamous entanglement, however, requires isolation; in particular, it requires isolation from any surrounding environment. Any *physically efficacious* isolation, however, violates decompositional equivalence. No system is actually isolated. So what can it mean to say that entanglement provides a mechanism that correlates an observer with an observed system?

As shown in detail by Zanardi (2001), whether two components of an entangled state are monogamously entangled – or measurably entangled at all – is not an objective fact, but is rather dependent on both the chosen TPS and the availability of resources, such as time or energy, that enable particular measurements with respect to that TPS. These dependencies can be combined into the single notion of a quantum reference frame, a bounded quantum – and hence physical – system that two observers must jointly access in order to exchange classical information, and hence to communicate observational outcomes (e.g. Bartlett, Rudolph & Spekkens, 2007). Because a quantum reference frame is not an abstraction but a physical system, accessing it requires observation; hence what observers can be thought of as sharing is an observable, a POVM (Fields, 2012b). An "observer" in this context is, moreover, any physical system that is classically correlated with and hence shares classical information with another system. The idea that entanglement creates a classical correlation between an observer and a system being observed depends, therefore, on the assumption that observer and observed share a POVM. As noted above in the case of systems defined to be clocks, however, such an assumption is always a piece of semantics: it is a specific carving-up and naming of the world that is taken to be privileged. It is not something that the *physics* of the situation provides.

"Observers" and "observed systems" having well-defined boundaries in ordinary 3-dimensional space provide an interesting case in point. Here the notion of holographic encoding ('t Hooft, 1993; Susskind, 1994) allows one to think of the surface bounding the observer as encoding a record of every quantum bit ("qubit") received by the observer. A classical black hole can be considered an optimal observer in this framework; the surface "covering" the event horizon encodes one classical bit for every qubit that has fallen into the black hole, and does so at the maximal possible encoding density (Bekenstein, 1981). A system with a larger boundary than a black hole of the same mass encodes information on its boundary at a lower density; such a system is less efficient than a black hole as an accumulator of qubits and encoder of classical information.

An observer external to a black hole cannot share a quantum reference frame with the black hole: any quantum system that falls into the black hole becomes inaccessible to the outside observer, while any system that has not fallen in remains inaccessible to the black hole. Hence an external observer only has access to the *number of bits* encoded by a black hole; such an observer has no access to the POVM employed by the black hole to convert qubits to bits, and hence no access to the semantics assigned by the black hole to the bits it encodes. This situation generalizes to any three-way division of the universe into a spatially-bounded observer, a spatially-bounded system that serves as a quantum reference frame, and a second spatially-bounded observer or system being observed. Neither observer has observational access to the POVM being used by the other observer to determine the state of the shared reference frame; each can access, at most, the classical information encoded by the boundary of the other observer. As above, the observers must *assume* that they share a POVM, and hence assume that they assign the same semantics to the shared quantum reference frame.

The resource that quantum theory provides for establishing classical correlations and hence classical information sharing between systems – the resource of entanglement – thus comes with important strings attached. Entanglement only provides for the sharing of conditional classical information: information of the form "*if* classical information is recorded, it will be correlated across systems." Entanglement provides even this conditional sharing, moreover, only in the context of an assumed quantum reference frame or POVM. This latter assumption is a *semantic* assumption that any two parties sharing classical information must make about each other.

The conditionality and contextuality that quantum theory imposes on classical information, and hence on the concept of observation, makes these a far cry from their traditional usages in classical physics, in which information was assumed to be objectively available for the taking in the environment. They are not, however, surprising when viewed from the perspective of 20th century systems theory, philosophy of language, or even perceptual psychology. The lesson of the 20th century in all of these domains is that shared meaning is an assumption, one that can easily turn out to be wrong. Abandoning the still-classical assumptions about observation embedded in standard interpretations of quantum theory for a "bare" account in terms of entanglement and quantum reference frames catches the physics of measurement up to the realizations made by logicians (e.g. Tarski, 1944), computer scientists (e.g. Turing, 1950), systems theorists (e.g. Ashby, 1956; Moore, 1956), philosophers (e.g. Quine, 1969; Wettstein, 1999), and cognitive scientists (e.g. Newell, 1980) about the relationship between semantics and its physical encodings.

TOWARD A QUANTUM THEORY OF REPORTABLE EXPERIENCE

All reportable contents of experience – all sensory perceptions, memories, imaginations, emotional feelings, and epistemic, aesthetic or moral feelings – are remembered and reported as classical information. The theory sketched above therefore applies to any physical encodings of such reportable experiential contents, including not just encodings in artificial media but also encodings produced by voices or bodily motions, or encodings in biological media such as electrochemical activity patterns in brains. Taking quantum theory seriously as a correct description of the physical world involves taking seriously what it has to say about the origins and dynamics of such encodings.

Quantum theory first specifies the conditions under which encodings of reportable experiences are generated: reportable experiences are encoded whenever a spatially-bounded collection of physical degrees of freedom composing an observer is entangled with a spatially-bounded collection of degrees of freedom composing an observed system. It further specifies that while such entanglement characterizes all spatially-bounded collections of degrees of freedom at all times, it does not have an objective description. How a system is entangled with its environment, and hence what classical information it encodes as reportable experiences, is dependent on the quantum reference frame from which the system-environment interaction is viewed. Such reference frames are not unique. Hence as Dugić and Jeknić-Dugić (2012) put it, "the emergent classical world is not unique"; indeed every observer can be regarded as recording a different "emergent" world. The common assumption that what other observers experience can be assumed to be "like" what we experience is, therefore, in general mistaken. The experienced world of the vast majority of other observers can, instead, be safely assumed to be *nothing like* the world as we experience it. The vast majority of other observers may, for example, experience nothing like what we call "space" or "time."

Quantum theory also specifies how the classical information encoding reportable experiences is encoded: it is encoded on the observer-environment boundary. Different ways of drawing the observer-environment boundary correspond to different quantum reference frames and hence to different encoded experiential contents. How these reference frames are chosen or boundaries are drawn, however, can have no physical consequences; hence what contents are encoded can have no physical consequences. The classical encodings that render experiences reportable are, therefore, physical phenomena but not causal phenomena. Their lack of causality, either within or outside of the boundary defining the observer, is assured by the quantum-theoretic prohibition of local determinism. Indeed the Conway-Kochen (2006) theorem assures that such encodings are not even stochastically deterministic.

The picture that emerges when the implications of quantum theory for encodings of experience are taken seriously is thus both expansive and bracingly counterintuitive. Quantum theory makes observers ubiquitous in all locations and at all scales; it allows all interactions between spatially-bounded systems to be considered "observations." As Fuchs puts it, quoting William James, an entangled quantum universe "consists of an all-pervasive `pure experience'" (2010; p. 27). This "pure experience" of entanglement is encoded as reportable, classical information at all boundaries between distinct collections of physical degrees of freedom. The universe is full of such boundaries, but from the perspective of physical dynamics they are all both arbitrary and notional. Hence all reportable experience, from a fleeting sensory impression of redness to the memory of an experienced past to the most startling and profound insights, are from this perspective created equal: all are encodings on boundaries drawn between degrees of freedom that are not, in fact, separable. Such boundaries are, moreover, only drawable with respect to a quantum reference frame, the choice of which is always pragmatic and never objectively determined.

The intimate relationship between reportable experience and a choice of quantum reference frame suggests that experimental approaches that characterize the implementation of reportable experience in human beings or other animals also implicitly characterize quantum reference frames. If this is the case, suitable experimental manipulations would be expected to reveal measurable quantum effects at all biologically-relevant scales, from biochemical and macromolecular processes in neurons to cognitive processes in individuals or groups. The growing evidence for quantum effects in human categorization and conceptual reasoning (e.g. Pothos & Busemeyer, 2013) suggests, from this perspective, that activation processes in large-scale neural networks will soon be found to exhibit measurable quantum effects as well.

CONCLUSION

Quantum theory has traditionally been regarded as unsatisfactory as an explanation of what is going on in the physical world. It has, therefore, been supplemented with a wide variety of interpretative assumptions, all of which introduce aspects of classicality and hence reduce the "quantum-ness" of the theory. While such interpretative assumptions bring the theory closer to the familiar realm of human experience, they render its explanations circular and systematically hide what quantum theory is attempting to tell us about our world.

When quantum theory is stripped of interpretative assumptions, it tells us two things of great significance. First, it tells us that semantics is not given by dynamics. Semantics is, instead, given by *boundaries*, and boundaries have no physical consequences. Aspects of the world that have no physical consequences are often thought of as epiphenomena. Boundaries are not epiphenomena; indeed boundaries are not even phenomena. Boundaries *enable* phenomena by creating and encoding classical information. The arbitrariness and ephemerality of boundaries renders phenomena arbitrary and ephemeral; selecting a different boundary yields a different set of phenomena, onc that may be utterly different from the original. Moreover, *any* boundary may be selected, and yield a semantics and a set of phenomena as a result.

The second lesson of quantum theory is that our position as experiencers is not privileged. We are experiencers, but so are all other systems, seen and unseen, that surround us. We are not even particularly complex experiencers; huge numbers of distinct systems contain each one of us, and huge numbers more contain all of us. Moreover, none of our experiences are privileged with respect to any others. All reportable experiences are equally encodings on ephemeral, consequence-free boundaries traversing entangled states. The challenge for an emerging science of consciousness is to develop experimental techniques that reveal how entanglement between definable collections of degrees of freedom produces the experiences encoded on the boundaries that we call "human beings."

Acknowledgment

Thanks to Revered Prof. P. S. Satsangi for inviting me to give the talk on which this chapter is largely based, and to the HESA Institute for financial support.

References

Ashby, W. R. (1956). *An introduction to cybernetics*. London: Chapman & Hall.

Bartlett, S. D., Rudolph, T., & Spekkens, R. W. (2007). Reference frames, superselection rules, and quantum information. *Reviews of Modern Physics, 79,* 555-609.

Bekenstein, J. D. (1981). Universal upper bound on the entropy-to-energy ratio for bounded systems. *Physical Review D, 23,* 287-298.

Bell, J. S. (1964). On the Einstein-Podolsky-Rosen paradox. *Physics, 1,* 195-200.

Bennet, A. J., Evans, D. A., Saunders, D. J. *et al.* (2012). Arbitrarily loss-tolerant Einstein-Podolsky-Rosen steering allowing a demonstration over 1 km of optical fiber with no detection loophole. *Physical Review X, 2,* 031003. doi:http://dx.doi.org/10.1103/PhysRevX.2.031003

Bohm, D., Hiley, B. J., & Kaloyerou, P. N. (1987). An ontological basis for the quantum theory. *Physics Reports, 144,* 321-375.

Bohm, D. (1989). *Quantum theory*. New York: Dover.

Chiribella, G., D'Ariano, G. M., & Perinotti, P. (2011). Informational derivation of quantum theory. *Physical Review A, 84,* 012311. doi:http://dx.doi.org/10.1103/PhysRevA.84.012311

Christensen, B. G., McCusker, K. T., Altepeter, J. *et al.* (2013). Detection-loophole-free test of quantum nonlocality, and applications. *Physical Review Letters, 111,* 130406. doi: 10.1103/PhysRevLett.111.130406

Conway, J. & Kochen, S. (2006). The free will theorem. *Foundations of Physics, 36,* 1441-1473.

Dugić, M. & Jeknić-Dugić, J. (2012). Parallel decoherence in composite quantum systems. *Pramana, 79,* 199-209.

Everett, H. III (1957). 'Relative state' formulation of quantum mechanics. *Review of Modern Physics, 29*, 454-462.

Fields, C. (2010). Quantum Darwinism requires an extra-theoretical assumption of encoding redundancy. *International Journal of Theoretical Physics, 49*, 2523-2527.

Fields, C. (2011). Classical system boundaries cannot be determined within quantum Darwinism. *Physics Essays, 24*, 518-522.

Fields, C. (2012a). A model-theoretic interpretation of environment-induced superselection. *International Journal of General Systems, 41*, 847-859.

Fields, C. (2012b). Implementation of classical communication in a quantum world. *Information, 3*, 809-831.

Fields, C. (2013). A whole box of Pandoras: Systems, boundaries and free will in quantum theory. *Journal of Experimental and Theoretical Artificial Intelligence, 25*, 291-302.

Fields, C. (2014). On the Ollivier-Poulin-Zurek definition of objectivity. *Axiomathes, 24*, 137-156.

Friederich, S. (2013). In defense of non-ontic accounts of quantum states. *Studies in the History and Philosophy of Modern Physics, 44*, 77-92.

Fuchs, C. (2010). QBism: The Perimeter of quantum Bayesianism. arXiv preprint arXiv:1003.5209.

Gay, S. & Mackie, I. (2010). *Semantic techniques in quantum computation.* Cambridge: Cambridge University Press.

Ghirardi, G. C., Rimini, A. & Weber, T. (1986). Unified dynamics for microscopic and macroscopic systems. *Physical Review D, 34*, 470-491.

Griffiths, R. B. (2002). *Consistent quantum theory*. New York: Cambridge University Press.

Hameroff, S. & Penrose, R. (1996). Orchestrated reduction of quantum coherence in brain microtubules: A model for consciousness. *Mathematics and Computation in Simulation, 40*, 453-480.

Healey, R. (2012). Quantum theory: A pragmatist approach. *British Journal for the Philosophy of Science, 63*, 729-771.

Inagaki, T., Matsuda, N., Tadanaga, O., Asobe, M. & Takesue, H. (2013). Entanglement distribution over 300 km of fiber. *Optics Express, 21*, 23241-23249.

Kaiser, F., Coudreau, T., Milman, P., Ostrowsky, D. B. & Tanzilli, S. (2012). Entanglement-enabled delayed choice experiment. *Science, 338*, 637-640.

Karmiloff-Smith, A. (1995). *Beyond modularity: A developmental perspective on cognitive science*. Cambridge, MA: MIT Press.

Kastner, R. (2013). *The transactional interpretation of quantum mechanics.* Cambridge: Cambridge University Press.

Kochen, S., & Specker, E. P. (1967). The problem of hidden variables in quantum mechanics. *Journal of Mathematics and Mechanics, 17*, 59-87.

Landsman, N. P. (2007). Between classical and quantum. In J. Butterfield & J. Earman, J. (Eds.), *Handbook of the philosophy of science: Philosophy of physics* (pp. 417-553). Amsterdam: Elsevier.

Lloyd, S. (2012). A Turing test for free will. *Philosophical Transactions of the Royal Society A, 370, 3597-3610.*

McCloskey, M. (1983). Naïve theories of motion. In D. Gentner & A.L. Stevens (Eds.), *Mental models* (pp. 269-305). Hillsdale, NJ: Erlbaum.

Moore, E. F. (1956). Gedanken experiments on sequential machines. In C. W. Shannon & J. McCarthy (Eds.), *Automata studies* (pp. 129-155). Princeton, NJ: Princeton University Press.

Newell, A. (1980). Physical symbol systems. *Cognitive Science, 4*, 135-183.

Nielsen, M. A. & Chaung, I. L. (2000). *Quantum information and quantum computation.* Cambridge: Cambridge University Press.

Petersen, A. (1963). The philosophy of Niels Bohr. *Bulletin of the Atomic Scientists, 19,* 8-14.

Peruzzo, A., Shadbolt, P., Brunner, N., Popescu, S. & O'Brien, J. L. (2012). A quantum delayed-choice experiment. *Science, 338,* 634-637.

Pothos, E. M. & Busemeyer, J. R. (2013). Can quantum probability provide a new direction for cognitive modeling? *Behavioral and Brain Sciences,* 36, 225-327.

Quine, W. V. O. (1969). Ontological relativity. In *Ontological Relativity and Other Essays* (pp. 26-68). New York: Columbia University Press.

Rovelli, C. (1996). Relational quantum mechanics. *International Journal of Theoretical Physics, 35,* 1637-1678.

Saeedi, K., Simmons, S., Salvail, J. Z. *et al.* (2013). Room-temperature quantum bit storage exceeding 39 minutes using ionized donors in Silicon-28. *Science, 342,* 830-833.

Schlosshauer, M. (2006). Experimental motivation and empirical consistency of minimal no-collapse quantum mechanics. *Annals of Physics, 321,* 112-149.

Schlosshauer, M. (2007). *Decoherence and the quantum to classical transition.* Berlin: Springer.

Simons, D. & Levin, D. (1998). Failure to detect changes to people in a real-world interaction. *Psychonomic Bulletin and Review, 5,* 644-649.

Stapp, H. P (2001). Quantum theory and the role of mind in nature. *Foundations of Physics, 31,* 1465-1499.

Susskind, L. (1994). The world as a hologram. *Journal of Mathematical Physics, 36,* 6377-6396.

't Hooft, G. (1993). Dimensional reduction in quantum gravity. In A. Ali, J. Ellis, J. & S. Randjbar-Daemi (Eds.) *Salamfestschrift: A collection of talks.* Singapore: World Scientific (arxiv:gr-qc/9310026).

Tarski, A. (1944). The semantic conception of truth and the foundations of semantics. *Philosophy and Phenomenological Research, 4,* 341-376.

Tegmark, M. (2010). Many worlds in context. In S. Saunders, J. Barrett, A. Kent, & D. Wallace (Eds.), *Many worlds? Everett, quantum theory and reality* (pp. 553-581). Oxford: Oxford University Press.

Turing, A. M. (1950). Computing machinery and intelligence. *Mind, 59,* 433-460.

van Fraassen, B. (1991). *Quantum mechanics: An empiricist view.* Oxford: Clarendon.

Von Neumann, J. (1932). *Mathematical foundations of quantum mechanics.* Berlin: Springer.

Wallace, D. (2008). Philosophy of quantum mechanics. In D. Rickles, (Ed.), *The Ashgate companion to contemporary philosophy of physics* (pp. 16-98). Aldershot, United Kingdom: Ashgate.

Weinberg, S. (2012) Collapse of the state vector. *Physical Review A, 85,* 062116. doi: http://dx.doi.org/10.1103/PhysRevA.85.062116

Wettstein, H. (1999). A father of the revolution. *Philosophical Perspectives, 13,* 443-457.

Zanardi P. (2001). Virtual quantum subsystems. *Physical Review Letters, 87,* 077901. doi: http://dx.doi.org/10.1103/PhysRevLett.87.077901

Zeh, D. (1970). On the interpretation of measurement in quantum theory. *Foundations of Physics, 1,* 69-76.

Zeh, D. (2000). The problem of conscious observation in quantum mechanical description. *Foundations of Physics Letters, 13,* 221-233.

Zurek, W. H. (1982). Environment-induced superselection rules. *Physical Review D, 26,*

1862-1880.

Zurek, W. H. (2003). Decoherence, einselection, and the quantum origins of the classical. *Reviews of Modern Physics, 75*, 715-775.

Zurek, W. H. (2009). Quantum Darwinism. *Nature Physics, 5*, 181-188.

Chapter 7

The Neurodynamics of Consciousness

PETER T. WALLING[1]
Department of Anesthesia and Pain Management
Baylor University Medical Center, Dallas, Texas, USA

ABSTRACT

In this chapter, basic dynamics are considered, that is to say, the rules under which the brain, which dissipates energy, operates.

Non-linear dynamics, as it applies to the brain, is described in simple terms. Using neurodynamics, various brain states are examined including emergence from anesthesia, multitasking, sensory binding, and meditation.

Armed with data which has been examined through the lens of standard dynamical practices, an attempt is made to explain how consciousness works, "where" it is located and when it evolved.

The nature and dimensions of "perceptual space" are considered. Is consciousness a classical or a quantum phenomenon, or is it both?

Is a new kind of physics required to successfully describe it?

INTRODUCTION

What is consciousness?

Consciousness is the mental state enjoyed upon awakening from a dreamless sleep. Notice how this non-technical answer passes the onus back to the questioner, because only the questioner can know what his own conscious experience is like.

Because consciousness is private, investigators who are not content with their subject's first person account must instead, measure correlates, be they neural, quantum or dynamical. This chapter describes dynamical correlates derived from Electroencephalography (EEG) recorded during various mental states.

THE NERVOUS SYSTEM

The brain consists of neurons, glial cells (support and clean up), and blood vessels, some of which are specialized to produce cerebro-spinal fluid (Patton, Fuchs, Hille, Scher & Steiner, 1989). A Nematode worm has 302 neurons, a fruit fly about 100,000, and you the reader, about 100 billion. (10^11). The number of connections, or synapses in the human brain is about 100 trillion (10^14).

The basic neuron consists of a cell body which receives input at one

---

[1]Retired

end and sends an output from the other end. The cell body, or soma, contains the nucleus and is the metabolic center of the cell. A typical neuron receives input on its cell body from 10-20 highly branched processes called dendrites.

The dendritic arbor, (like a tree), receives thousands of synaptic contacts from hundreds of different neurons allowing a convergence of inputs. The output consists of the axon which projects from the soma and may extend for a few micrometers to more than a meter.

Excitable cells like muscle and nerves pump out positively charged sodium ions so that the cell interior ends up at about minus 70 mv compared to the outside. When the cell is suitably stimulated, the electrical resistance of the cell membrane breaks down and the sodium ions rush back in. This rush of ions produces an electric current to pass across the cell membrane. In a muscle cell, a contraction results. In the nerve, a wave of depolarization / polarization travels down the nerve axon. This is a nerve impulse. Neurons communicate via their dendrites and synapses.

As well as transmitting millions of nerve impulses, the brain is a conductor of electricity. The current travels through the brain coverings, the skull and then the scalp, where it may be recorded using a skin electrode. An average electrode will pick up signals from about 100,000,000 to one billion neurons. To produce a measurable spike, most of the neurons must be firing synchronously. Even so, in a conscious person, the brain waves look to be all over the place to an inexperienced observer. To watch one electrode recording from an EEG is analogous to watching one tiny area of water on a pool after someone has thrown a handful of pebbles into the water. Different sized waves are arriving from all directions. In the brain, many of these waves originate below the surface.

Currents through the brain obey the inverse square law. The size is reduced in proportion to the square of the distance. The crinkly cerebral cortex is about the size of a tea towel (1600-4000 cm sq) and roughly 2-5 mm thick. Most of the EEG of interest originates here.

Human brain anatomy is hard to understand and is quite peculiar.

It is not the subject of the present exercise.

However, there are one or two comments which are pertinent to our journey of discovery. First, nerves are all more or less the same. The original work in understanding how neurons worked was done using giant squid nerves. They work just like ours. Second, nerves are thought to have appeared in a disorganized way in animals like the Anemone, nearly a billion years ago.

As animals evolved, they started to move about in a purposeful way. They developed senses, the inputs of which were collected and integrated at the front end of the creature, close to the main sense organs. These included touch, smell, sight etc. Crustaceans, like insects and lobsters have a "brain" like this which then splits and wraps around the pharynx before recombining into a nerve cord which travels the length of the animal. This arrangement may have reduced the potential for serious development because either, an increase in brain size could have squashed the swallowing tube and starved the animal, or, gorging on a large meal might have torn the brain open! This constraint, in conjunction with a rudimentary cardio-respiratory system may be the reason that we eat lobsters and not vice versa! (Walling & Hicks, 2009, pp. 25-27).

DIMENSIONS, FRACTALS, ATTRACTORS AND DYNAMICS

A three foot line is one dimension (1D); use four of them to make a square and a 2D plane is produced which has an area of nine square feet. Add eight more lines to make a 3D cube of twenty seven cubic feet. Notice that the exponents, (Squared, Cubed etc.), increase linearly, while the content increases exponentially.

Take a sheet of paper and crumple it into a tight wad and its dimension is about 2.75D. In the natural world, fractal geometry dominates; we now have fractions of dimensions, best illustrated by the Koch Snowflake and Curve (Fig.1.)

FIGURE 1
Koch Curve 1.26D

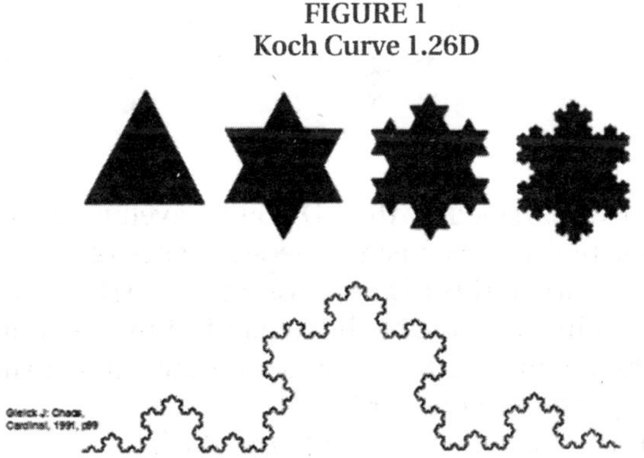

To the sides of an equilateral triangle add replicas to the middle third. Keep going. An infinitely long line crowds into a finite space, never crossing itself. The straightened out wiggly line is too complex for 1D but covers insufficient ground to be 2D. It is 1.26D, (log4/log3) a fraction of a dimension, or a Fractal.

Starting with simple dynamics; consider the pendulum of a clock which is powered by a wound spring. The pendulum controls the release of the stored energy by periodically allowing the escape wheel to rotate, thereby "putting the wheels in motion", and causing a small movement of the clocks' hands. In return, the escape wheel gives the pendulum a nudge with every swing by virtue of its "downstream" communication with the spring.

Dynamics are the rules by which this system operates.

Let us look at the "bob" on the end of the pendulum.

It changes position and it changes velocity. If we plot the positional change from side to side (x axis), and the velocity change up and down (y axis), we can follow the whole cycle.

FIGURE 2
1D Attractor in Phase Space

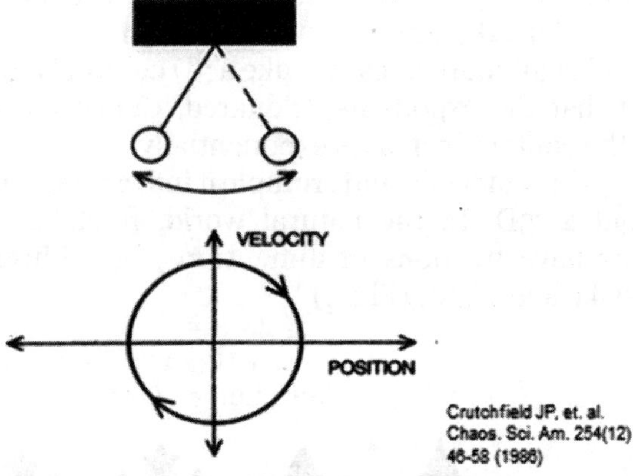

Crutchfield JP, et. al.
Chaos. Sci. Am. 254(12)
46-58 (1986)

The dynamics are described by the 0D point traveling through phase space. The point is plotting the instantaneous change of velocity versus position. The trajectory of this 0D point produces a 1D orbit. The orbit represents the ongoing solution to the dynamical interaction between gravity pulling the pendulum downwards, and the clock spring, which tends to fling the pendulum outwards.

Now imagine that someone bumps into the clock.

The pendulum may wobble, and the escape wheel may slip a cog or two, but in a couple of beats the clock should be beating normally again.

Looking at the plot, there would be a "blip" on the circular orbit, but the moving point would be attracted back to its previous trajectory.

The circular plot is called an Attractor. This attractor is a 1D Limit Cycle Attractor. It accurately describes the dynamics of the pendulum.

This model illustrates a very important principle. Both velocity and position are represented by the same 0D moving point. This is remarkable because the parameters are of different categories; not just that, but remember that the real pendulum bob stops twice each cycle as it changes the direction of its swing. The point drawing the trajectory keeps moving. This curious fact is explained by each variable being confined to its own dimension. The paper or screen on which the plot appears is 2D. If a moving point were to represent a third parameter; time for example, then the point would have to move in 3D, and the trajectory would come out of the screen like an advancing corkscrew tip.

The simple pendulum system described above is an example of linear dynamics. You get back what you put in. Some systems, when more and more energy is applied, start to "wobble" and may become non-linear, in which case the energy going in does not equal the energy output. One way to follow such a progression is to watch the attractor change. When the spring winds down, the pendulum swings less and less until it stops. The trajectory of the plot spirals inwards to a Point Attractor.

As a system is energized, or driven, the attractor may go from being Limit Cycle (linear), to Periodic (non-linear), to Toroidal (donut shaped), to Chaotic (Walling & Hicks, 2009, pp. 18-22).

FIGURE 3
Models of EEG Attractors

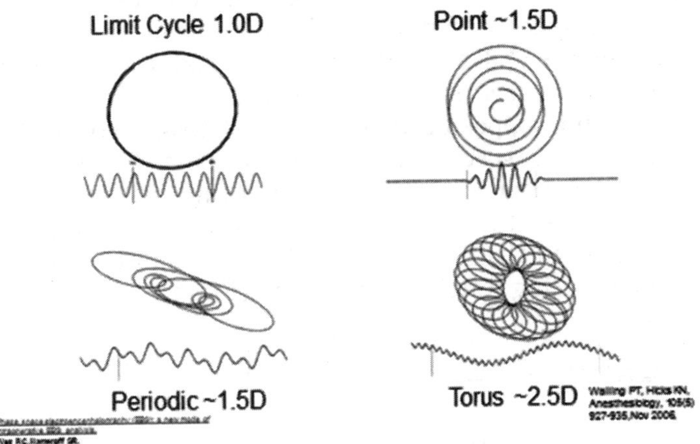

Now imagine the EEG as represented by a 1D piece of curved string (Fig. 4.) The reason the string is a sort of sine wave and not a square wave or saw toothed shape is because its shape is determined by the configuration of the ball of twine from which it originates. The ball is analogous to the attractor and surely is worthy of examination as well as the EEG itself. By a process of 3D co-ordinate embedding, it is possible to reconstruct the EEG attractor from the raw EEG and gain a lot more information about the nature of the dynamics under consideration.

FIGURE 4

1D EEG "imprinted" with its "3D" Attractor Origin

"Scale-free brain dynamics contain complex spatiotemporal structures"

Biyu J. He. (2011) J. Neuroscience, 31(39) 13786-13795.

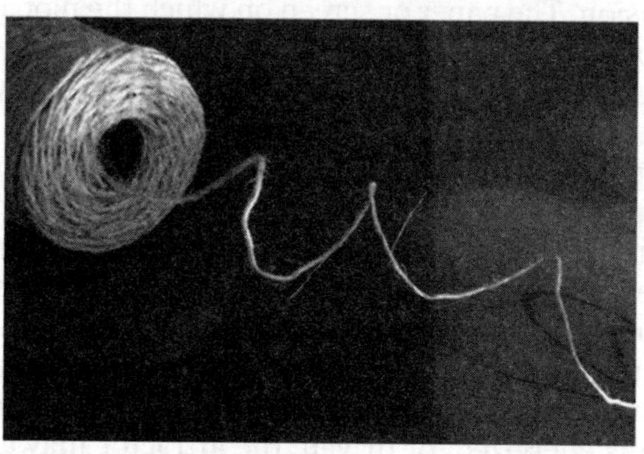

EVOLUTION

Armed with a basic understanding of dynamics, it is now possible to apply this knowledge to real life situations. The fish may not have a cerebral cortex, but its cranial nerves and respiratory control mechanisms are similar to ours. Fossil frog skulls reveal a brain case which has barely changed in its gross anatomy since frogs appeared. Vertebrate brains have developed by continuous additions and improvements, made possible by the ability of the skull to expand over evolutionary time. Assuming that each species retained an approximation to its original brain, and supposing that the oldest fossil represents the approximate time of the species' appearance, we plotted EEG complexity (as measured by attractor dimensional estimate) against time of species appearance. We knew that return of consciousness from anesthesia appeared when the EEG attractor matured to 3D, and wondered when 3D was achieved during vertebrate evolution. (Fig. 5.)

FIGURE 5

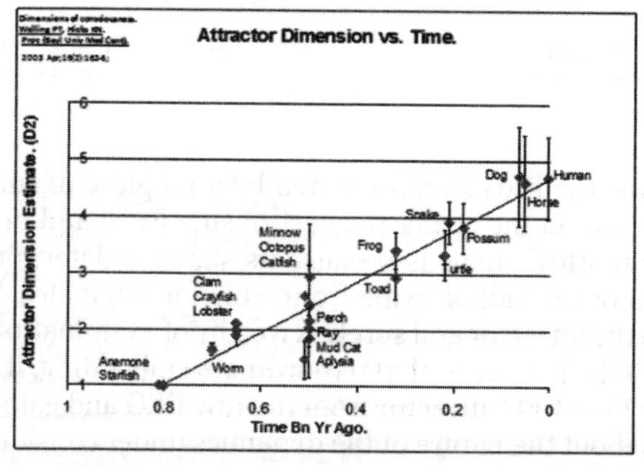

21 species were examined. Note the steady increase in attractor dimension in vertebrates over the past half billion years. These represent the largest dimensions which we measured. Any species will exhibit a range of dimensions up to the largest, depending upon how engaged the brain is at recording time. Notice that the dog is slightly higher than the human (who was multitasking), but remember we are measuring EEG complexity, not intelligence.

3D is achieved about the time of the appearance of amphibians which also coincides with the time of movement from water to land. Perhaps a "froggie" type of consciousness evolved about this time.

Not only was there a linear increase in dimensional estimate through time, but the species approximately retained their evolutionary ranking. It was estimated that attractor dimensions increased by about 1D every 200,000,000 years. This metric proves to be most important because we later found that the ability to "bind" information, and to multitask, is closely related to the number of attractor dimensions. It appears that the brain may be conscious of several sensory inputs simultaneously provided that each sensory data stream is allocated to its own dimension.

ANESTHESIA

The point, periodic and torus attractors depicted in Fig. 3. may appear in that order when a dissipative system is forced. This particular progression is also one of the classical pathways toward chaotic dynamics. This dynamical sequence was described in 2006 during emergence from general anesthesia (Walling & Hicks, 2006).

It was shown that emergence was characterized by highly non linear changes in the EEG (Fig.6.)

The dots represent the attractor dimension estimate calculated every 3 seconds. The solid line indicates a 20 point moving average. The horizontal bars show the level of sevoflurane as measured by a mass spectrometer. The triangles at the bottom indicate the Lyaounov exponent, which suggests chaotic dynamics when it increases above zero.

During both the march of evolution and the emergence of consciousness from general anesthesia, an increase in gamma EEG power was noticed. (Fig.7.)

FIGURE 6
Dynamics of emergence from Anesthesia

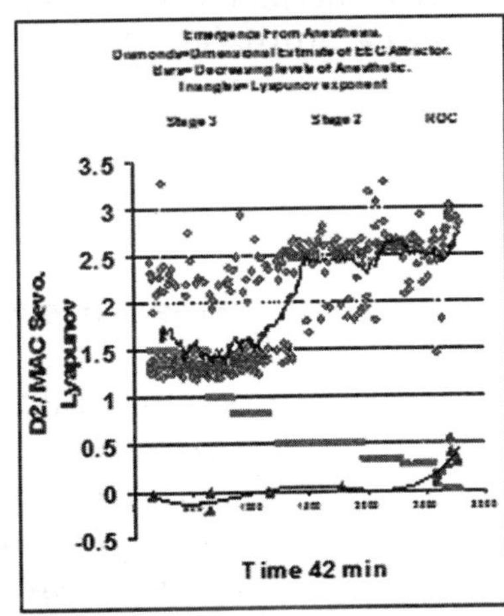

FIGURE 7

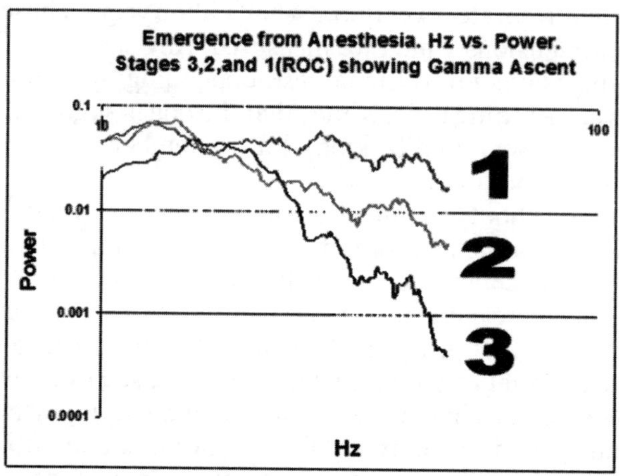

In the log/log plot, Stage 3 represents surgical anesthesia, Stage 2 corresponds to the state of delirium just before awakening, and Stage 1 correlates with return of consciousness. We named this phenomenon the "Gamma Ascent" although with a little experience it may easily be observed by examination of the raw EEG.

BINDING, MULTITASKING AND MEDITATION

These three features are considered together because they seem to exist in different places in the same spectrum. When considering binding of the senses to create a combined sensory experience, or Gestalt, one sense is considered, then two, then four.

As a model for one sense, consider Freeman's Mass Action (Freeman & Kozma, 2010). (Fig. 8.)

FIGURE 8

ONE SENSE

Freeman's Mass Action (FMA).

- Odor Imprinted in Olfactory Cortex.
- Memory stored as synaptic configuration.
- Upon re-exposure, whole cortex responds.
- "Gamma Burst" ⟶ AM spatial pattern.
- Spreads to whole Sensory Cortex.
- In Forebrain, different senses ⟶ Gestalt.

An odor is imprinted in the olfactory cortex and stored as a synaptic configuration. Re-exposure reinforces these connections in a Hebbian fashion (Neurons that fire together wire together). When the animal is exposed to the odor again, the whole olfactory cortex responds. Like an orchestra, the cortex is capable of playing many "tunes". The resulting gamma burst represents an AM spatial pattern which spreads to the whole sensory cortex and to the forebrain where it may combine with other senses to form a Gestalt. The fact that the signal is Amplitude Modulated and not Frequency Modulated is fortunate because it makes identification easier.

To examine binding of two senses, a subject was exposed to an electronic metronome which also flashed a red light. Frontal EEG was recorded and the metronome set at 40/min. It was planned to record multiple sequential epochs of 1.5 sec and to overlay them to find common frequencies.(Fig.9.)

FIGURE 9

TWO SENSES
Right Frontal EEG (Fp2-Fp4). 67 seconds. 59Hz-61Hz removed.
Blue arrow indicates Clicks and Flashes @ 40/min. from electronic metronome. Attractor Dimension Estimate in Red.(d2).

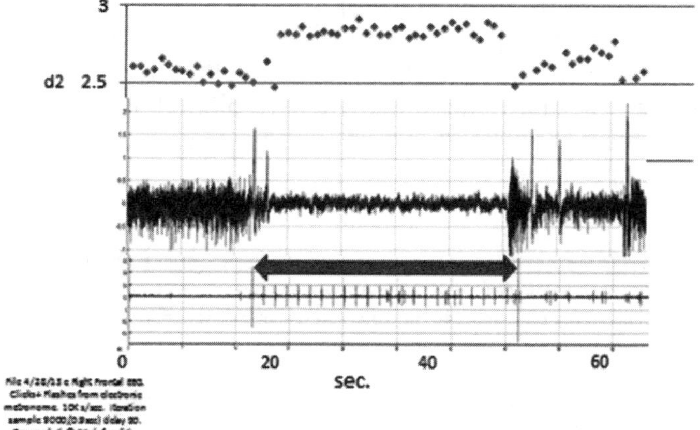

Fig. 9 shows a raw right frontal EEG starting with a control period and followed by ~30 seconds of metronome activity indicated by the arrow.

There was a decrease in voltage accompanied by a brisk increase in attractor dimension. These dimensions are not amenable to statistical analysis because their content increases exponentially. The period of stimulation was accompanied by a positive Maximal Luapunov Exponent which suggested a more chaotic state. Overlaying 1.5 sec.

epochs was a poor way of recognizing repeating frequencies. Instead, 4 second samples of test and control strips were broken down into their constituent frequencies by Fast Fourier Transform. The data from the control trace was subtracted from the test data in an attempt to expose carrier frequencies (Fig. 10)

FIGURE 10

In each of 3 Binding tests, 4 second strips were analyzed for both Test and Control frequencies. Plot shows FFT Test minus FFT Control. Possible "AM Gamma Burst" frequencies revealed by showing grouped peaks. Magnified insert shows 3 peaks ~ 140 Hz.

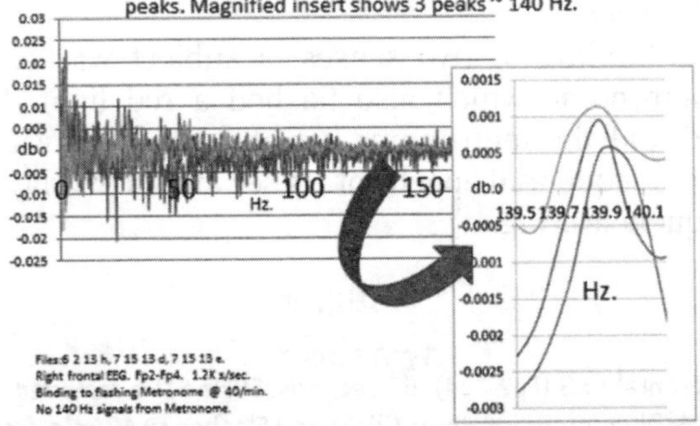

Fig. 10 shows three test strips from the same subject. Two were the same day and the third six weeks previous. A good candidate for a gamma carrier frequency is enlarged at 140 Hz. Other candidate frequencies were, 2.3 Hz, 6.4 Hz, 28.4 Hz and 88.2 Hz.

One of the original traces was then re-plotted with every other frequency except the suspected carrier frequencies removed. (Fig.11) (Unpublished data.)

FIGURE 11

Right Frontal EEG before + during binding. Markers, clicking + flashing metronome @40/min. 5 top frequencies from 3 pooled plots. 2.3,6.4,28.4,88.2 and 140 Hz. Note reversal of 6.4 Hz.+28.4 Hz power.

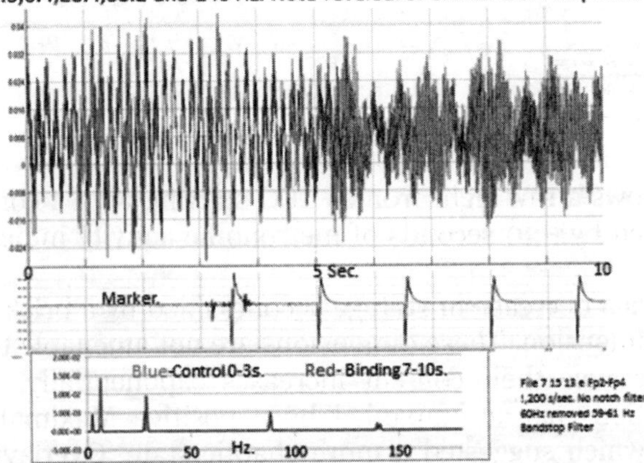

Moving to four senses, the distinction between Gestalt and multitasking becomes a bit blurred. Starting with the subject relaxed with eyes closed, the eyes were opened to read a book, then, a weather radio was turned on.

The third and fourth senses to be activated were smell, with an acetone soaked rag held under the nose; and taste when the subject sucked on half a teaspoon full of citric acid crystals. (Fig.12.)

FIGURE 12

FOUR SENSES

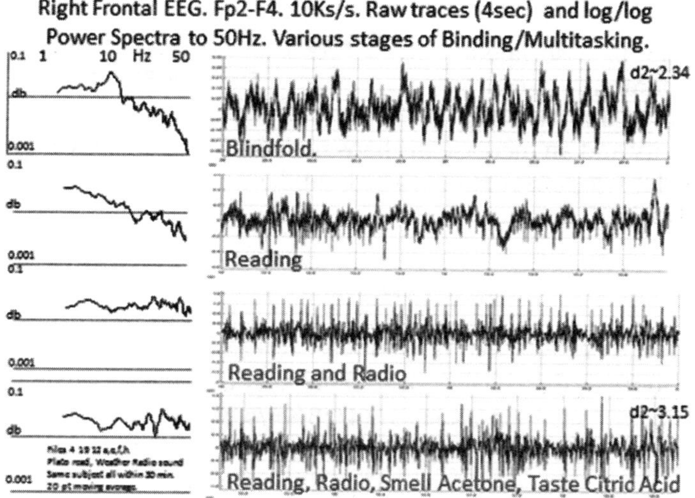

The Power Spectra show a strong 10 Hz. Alpha signal with eyes closed and relaxed, which disappears when the subject starts to read. Gamma Ascent is already obvious and increases much more when the radio is turned on. These changes are quite easily seen in the raw EEG traces.

Interestingly, the addition of strong taste and smell makes little difference. The correlation dimension estimate increases from 2.3D to 3.2D during the course of this study. The minimal changes seen with the introduction of the senses of smell and taste raise the question of Gestalt "saturation" at two or three senses. Perhaps a four sense Gestalt is achieved by rapidly oscillating between pairs of senses, thus producing the illusion of full four sense binding..

In a separate multitasking study, the subject sat with eyes closed, then eyes open, then was asked to tap her foot about once a second, listen to Disco music and read Plato's Republic simultaneously. (Fig.13)

FIGURE 13

Human multitasking (D2)

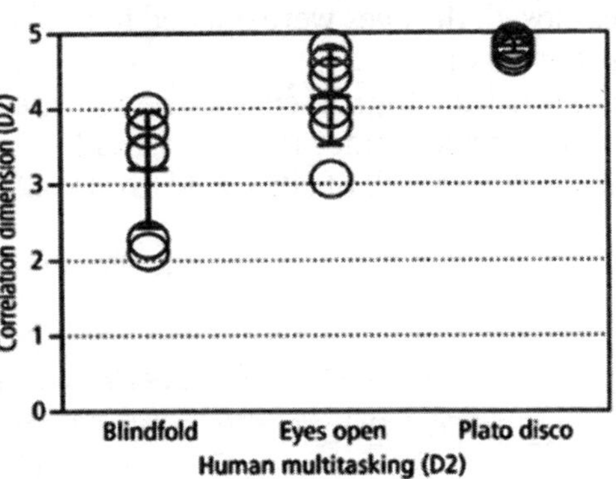

This recording has two interesting points. First, as the brain becomes more engaged with extra tasks, the dimensional measurements become more tightly bunched. Second, the maximum sustained dimension is just under 5D. How does that happen in a 3D brain?

Binding is associated with gamma ascent, increasing dimensional complexity and an increase in chaos metrics. What actually happens?

Consider two senses about to be bound, one at ~1 Hz, the other at ~18 Hz. (Fig. 14.)

FIGURE 14

Two possible carrier frequencies; 0.15-1.6 Hz, and 18-19 Hz. How may data be perceived simultaneously and yet retain separate qualities? (4/28/13/e 28-38 sec)

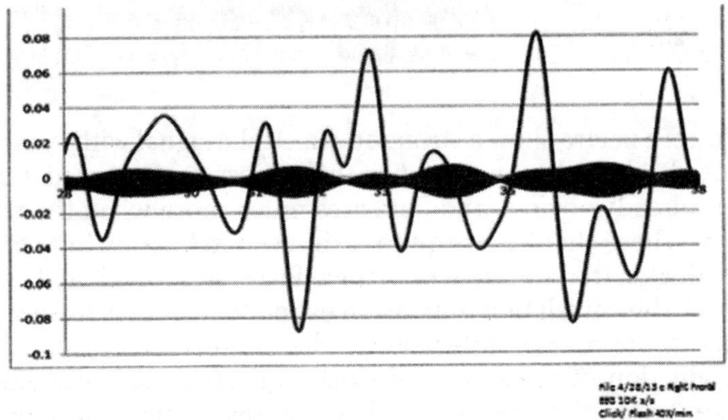

The two signals might be superimposed, but that would be like a radio receiving two stations without a tuner.

The signals may be fused together (Fig. 15.)

FIGURE 15

Right Frontal EEG. 10 sec. to show "Binding" of two AM bursts; Slow 0.15-1.6 Hz, candidate for light flash correlate, and 18-19 Hz, possible audible click correlate. EEG trace is 1D simplification of multi dimensional attractor giving the appearance of mutual interference of data inputs. "In Vivo", they have their own dimension and retain their individual characteristics, bound within the attractor.

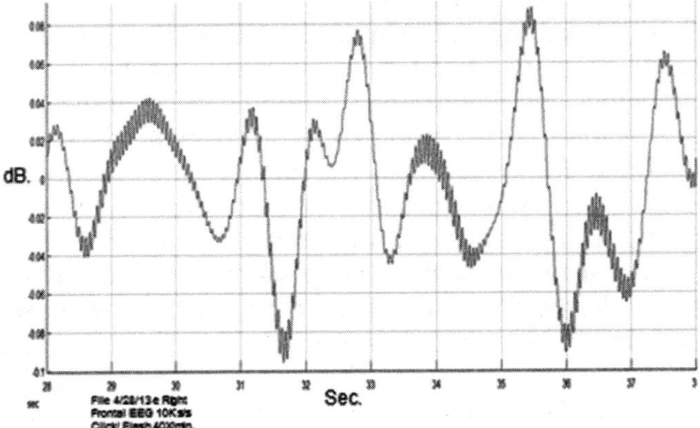

In this case surely there would be distortion of one signal by the other?

We believe that binding occurs in multidimensional phase space (Fig.16).

FIGURE 16

Slow and Fast bursts "separated" by 3D co-ordinate embedding using "EEGo" software. "In Vivo", each data stream occupies a dimension in perceptual space which allows a combined sensory experience, or Gestalt, without the data streams contaminating each other.

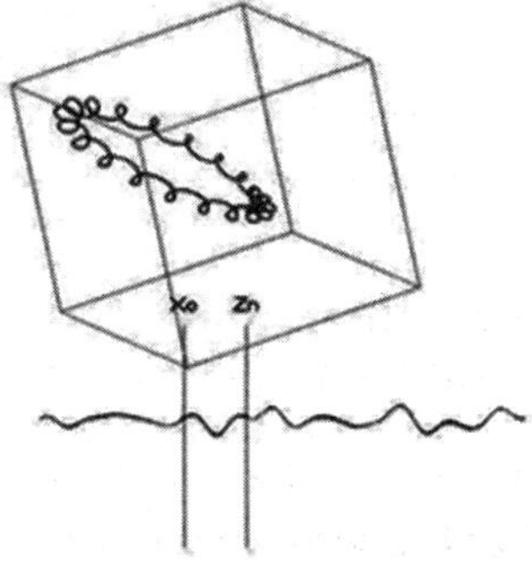

File 4/28/13e Right
Frontal EEG 10Ks/s
Click/ Flash 40X/min.

Fig. 16 shows a section of the same trace subjected to 3D co-ordinate embedding. The slow wave is represented by the flattened circle, while the high frequency component is shown as the tight curls at right angles and in a slightly different dimension. In this way, the data is bound but at the same time retains its individual characteristics.

Meditation is the fourth kind of consciousness, along with wakefulness, dreaming and hypnosis. Although practiced by most major world religions, meditation has been employed especially by Eastern religions and philosophers. Multiple forms of the art exist but a common feature is the suppression of external and sensory input while remaining fully conscious. The mental state produced has been described as "pure consciousness", "a concentrated regulation of the inner mind", "a state of reduced vigilance", " a mind cleared of content but highly conscious of being", "deep silence without any thoughts", and "restful alertness". It sits at the other end of the consciousness spectrum from the Gestalt and its study could be the most fruitful of all for the student of consciousness. The typical alpha waves of eyes closed relaxation might be considered proto-meditation but the dynamics of an experienced meditator can be quite dramatic.

FIGURE 17

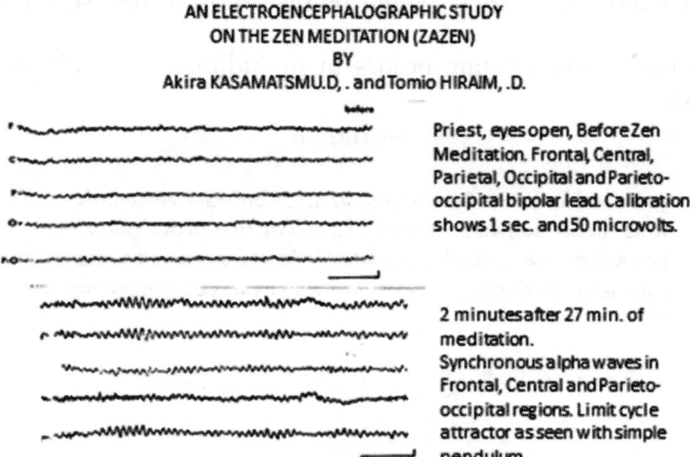

Fig. 17 shows various channels of the EEG of a Zen Priest before and after about 30 min. of meditation. We copied the bottom analog trace, digitized it then reconstructed the attractor.(Fig. 18). In addition to the synchrony shown in this trace, the simplicity of the attractor is seen especially now the rest of the sensory input has been suppressed.

Neither sleep, hypnosis nor anesthesia produce an EEG like this. The closest human similarity is that of some seizure activity (Fig.18).

FIGURE 18

Zen Priest after ~ 30 min meditation. Parieto-occipital region. 1D Limit Cycle Attractor.

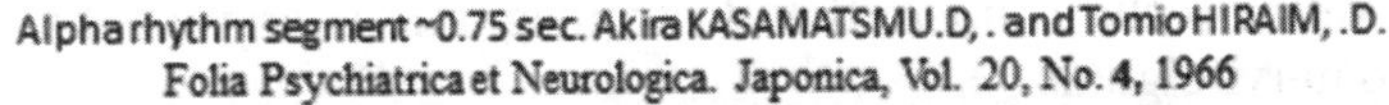
Alpha rhythm segment ~0.75 sec. Akira KASAMATSMU.D, . and Tomio HIRAIM, .D.
Folia Psychiatrica et Neurologica. Japonica, Vol. 20, No. 4, 1966

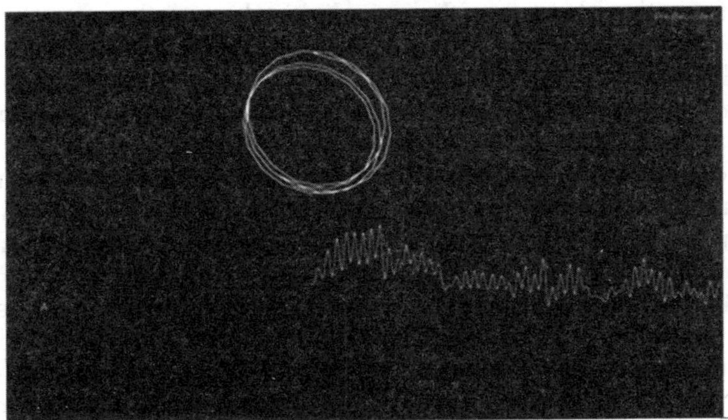

The synchrony exhibited by this Zen Priest nearly 50 years ago, may be due to hyperneurons, a cortico-thalamic effect, or to phase locking.

It is quite remarkable that the purest form of consciousness, after decades of practice, using the most complex machine ever known to man, correlates with the simplest dynamics imaginable; the circular attractor of the pendulum. The Limit Cycle Attractor resembling a halo!

The apparent simplicity, emanating from such a complex organ, compels us to wonder whether the brain is generating its own consciousness, or whether it is tapping into a universal consciousness which already exists.

WHERE IS CONSCIOUSNESS?

Armed with dynamical data from various brain states, we approach the crux of the problem at hand.

Look at your right index finger.

The physical space around you is a "seething cauldron" of electromagnetic radiation.

From gamma waves to radio waves, with X-Rays and microwaves in between.

Some of this radiation bounces off the surface of your finger and is focused on the retina.

The wavelengths between ~400 nm and ~700 nm stimulate your retinal cells. They constitute the "visible light spectrum". Note well;

your finger is a physical object in physical space and is still firmly attached to your hand.

Your finger did not enter your eye, the light did!

The retinal cells *convert* the electromagnetic energy of the visible light to nerve signals.

Information about your finger is *digitized* into a staccato stream of nerve impulses racing along the million fibers in each optic nerve, in total darkness. The light did not enter your brain, coded impulses did.

The data describing your finger is now *twice* removed from the pulsating digit.

(Bear in mind that light travels at 300,000 kilometers/sec and nerve impulses travel at speeds in the order of 300 meters/sec. Once in the brain, the speed of information transport is reduced by a factor of about 1,000,000.

A traveling nerve impulse is not like an electric current in a wire.

It is a wave of depolarization. It is like a fizzing gunpowder fuse burning, or a line of dominoes falling, which, by the expenditure of energy, pick themselves right up again. This slowing of data transfer becomes important when we consider how the brain makes up its mind and the delays inherent in that process.)

The optic nerve signals enter the amazing machinery of your brain and the next thing you know, a finger appears in your perceptual space.

This visual perceptual space is private.

You are the percipient and your finger is the percept.

Milliseconds before you recognized your own finger, all the information describing your finger consisted of nerve signals.
Your brain does not manufacture flesh and blood fingers.
The percept is not *a physical finger in physical space.*
It is a non-physical object in non-physical space.
What you just consciously perceived, is non-physical.

We know a lot about the neural pathways which bring the finger to your attention, and each sense has its own pathways. As data is carried through these channels it may be manipulated, but these tracts are conduits for information, not correlates of consciousness.

Everything we know about physiology tells us that the perceived finger is a product of brain activity, but it seems to be outside the body, attached to the hand, just as the real finger is in physical space.

Is your perceived finger inside or outside of your brain?

Neither.

Assigning to a non-physical object existing in non-physical space, a location in physical space, either inside or outside the skull, is a mistake.

(A Zero Dimensional co-ordinate, or point may exist in physical space, but it exists only as a location, not a "thing".)

The percept is a *derivative* of brain activity, it does not reside *in* an anatomical part of the brain. It is true that different parts of the brain have been identified with different thought processes. Modern scans are able to demonstrate these areas of increased blood flow and metabolic activity beautifully. However, different brain areas which are widely separated physically, and apparently not directly connected, somehow combine to participate in a unified sensory experience, or Gestalt. (Walling & Hicks, 2009, pp. 52-53).

FLATLAND AND THE HONEY SPOON

Professor Walter Freeman and his group at Berkeley in California have investigated brain dynamics during the past four decades.

One of their most important discoveries is that the cerebral cortex is able to organize itself, and that it undergoes phase transitions which are analogous to those in nonliving systems like boiling or condensing water.

These changes may be demonstrated by plotting the EEG in Hilbert Space on a polar plot. The transitions, which may occur about every 25 ms, are thought to represent the "frames" of information which constitute the cinematographic production of consciousness. These changes have been seen to occur over a whole human cerebral hemisphere almost instantaneously and may be the mechanism by which Gestalts (unified sensory experiences) are formed. They are examples of scale free dynamics and exemplify why a mouse and a whale may process information and act similarly even with a 10,000 fold difference in brain (Freeman & Rogers, 2002).

Having claimed that perceptions are not physical in the ordinary sense, and that scale free brain dynamics during multitasking correlate with an attractor of nearly 5D, it is pertinent to describe a way of "wrapping our brains" around the higher dimensions of hyperspace.

It is time to revisit Flatland (Abbott, 2007).

The main character in this novella is a Square. He lives on a 2D world which is as flat as a piece of paper. The inhabitants are free to move about on, or in the surface, but without the power to rise above or to sink below it. A house is a polygon, one line of which hinges open and shut like a door. We feel the limitations of living in Flatland, while knowing that there really is a 3D world. It is easy for us to extrapolate from 2D to our 3D world by analogy. This allegory helps us to understand higher dimensions by reducing everyday dimensions in a story. We return to

FIGURE 19

Mr. Square in Flatland.

Walling PT, Hicks KN.
Consciousness:
Anatomy of the Soul. (2009)

a simpler model of reality. A Flatlander cannot see a 3D object, just the line like edges of the other Flatlanders. (Fig. 19)

In this story, a Sphere from Space-land approaches Flatland with the intention of convincing the Square that a higher dimension exists. (Fig.20).

FIGURE 20

Sphere visits Flatland

The Sphere approaches Flatland and is able to see the inhabitants and the inside of the houses even when the doors are shut. The Sphere touches Flatland and starts to pass right through it but the square is unable to see a spherical object.

FIGURE 21

Sphere passes through the fabric of Flatland. Square sees a 2D disc.

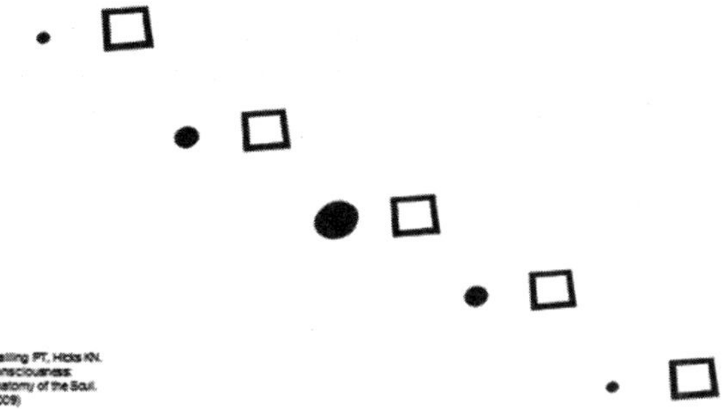

All Square sees is a disc getting larger, then smaller as the Sphere passes through (Fig.21).

How may a dimensionally impaired Square perceive the Sphere when he only sees flat discs?

If Mr. Square could stack the images of the changing circles in his mind, like the discs of a Honey Spoon, a 3D object would take shape in his perceptual space.

In this way, *his mind can function in a higher dimension than the 2D world in which his body is trapped*. He is able to function above his "pay grade".

The human brain exhibits synchronous activity with "phase transitions" occurring in time with gamma activity. These are probably the cinematographic slices of data which are then laminated, like the Honey Spoon, to form our multidimensional conscious thoughts. (Fig. 22).

FIGURE 22

2D Square constructs 3D image by stacking discs in perceptual space.

Correlates of perception have been discussed with particular attention given to the attractor of cerebral neurodynamics. The attractor has been a neglected item in the armamentarium of consciousness research; it is useful, but it is not consciousness. It may, however, be one of the best hieroglyphs available to us.

Whether perception itself is a classical or a quantum phenomenon, or something in between, is a vexed topic which is currently under intense scrutiny. Fortunately, the mystery of consciousness is attracting more and more able minds to the cause and it is hoped that significant progress will be made in the next few years.

References

Abbott, E.A. (2007). Flatland: A romance of many dimensions. New York: Cosimo Classics. (Original work published 1884).

Freeman, W. J., & Kozma, R. (2010). Freeman's mass action. *Scholarpedia, 5*, 8040. doi:10.4249/scholarpedia.8040

Freeman, W.J. & Rogers, L.J. (2002). Fine resolution of analytic phase reveals episodic synchronization by state transitions in gamma EEGs. *Journal of Neurophysiology, 87*, 937-945.

Patton, H.D., Fuchs, A.F., Hille, B., Scher, A.M., & Steiner, R. (1989). *Textbook of physiology*, Vol 1. (pp. 231-263). Philadelphia: W.B. Saunders Company.

Walling, P.T., & Hicks, K.N. (2009). *Consciousness: Anatomy of the soul* (pp. 25-27). Bloomington, IN: AuthorHouse

Walling, P.T., & Hicks, K.N. (2009). *Consciousness: Anatomy of the soul* (pp. 18-22). Bloomington, IN: AuthorHouse

Walling, P.T., & Hicks, K.N. (2009). *Consciousness: Anatomy of the soul* (pp. 52-53). Bloomington, IN: AuthorHouse

Walling, P.T., & Hicks, K.N. (2006). Nonlinear changes in brain dynamics during emergence from Sevoflurane anesthesia. *Anesthesiology*, 105, 927-35.

Chapter 8

Replacing Turing Tape with a Fractal Tape: A New Information Theory, Associated Mechanics and a New Kind of Decision Making without Computing

LOKESH AGRAWAL
Advanced Nano Characterization Center, National Institute for Materials Science, Tsukuba, Ibaraki, Japan

SUBRATA GHOSH
Mass General Hospital (Harvard Medical School), Boston, Massachusetts, USA

BATU GHOSH
Department of Physics, TDB College, Burdwan University, West Bengal, India

KANAD RAY
Amity University, Department of Physics, Rajasthan, India

SATYAJIT SAHU
Nano Bio Systems Science, IIT Jodhpur, Rajasthan, India

DAISUKE FUJITA
and
ANIRBAN BANDYOPADHYAY
Advanced Nano Characterization Center, National Institute for Materials Science, Tsukuba, Ibaraki, Japan

We track the history of information theory & the science of equations since 1903, and the evolution of Quantum mechanics (QM) since 1920, to find loopholes and artificial bridges that the proposers themselves worried but we forgot. We found that one imaginary world of Quantum is not enough, we need at least three, to accommodate that, we propose a new information theory, namely Fractal information theory (FIT), and a new mechanics namely Fractal mechanics (FM) from which every single feature of QM & Classical mechanics (CM) could be derived. Bridging QM-CM is not new, but a single statement "every single cell of a Turing tape contains a new Turing tape inside" (AjoChhand or AC computing, Ghosh et al Information, 2014) and "replacing bit or qubit with closed time loop of frequencies as beats" could bridge major loopholes. Moreover, by rejecting all major protocols of C & Q computing, it introduces a new kind of decision making without rejecting a single choice. Since 2008, in a series of experiments in organic electronics & biophysics we have established the basic dots of FIT. Imagine all kinds of visual, auditory, taste, touch and smell information is converted into geometric shapes, written into time cycles, frequencies are played as beat at certain intervals, the "silence" holds the phase. Information for all mass, space, charges etc. is coded as phase, —silence is the key. The worldview is that all information in the universe is in the phase space of three imaginary worlds, when we see one, we depict QM, when none, we depict CM. No need for bit/qubit, logic gate or circuit, time-loops self-assemble to integrate information. We outline 15 basic features of FIT based AC computing, 10 basic features of FM and 10 experimental predictions that we cannot explain using QM, CM alone or together, essentially requires FM.

Outline: **Historical background**: **1.1** A machine for Gödel's incompleteness theorem **Figure 1**; **1.2-1.3** Quantum supplement, 1.3.1 Space, space-time, space, now what? Time!, **Figure 2; 1.3.5** Talbot effect, heterodyne spectroscopy, classical & quantum beating; **1.3.5.1** Renormalization,t' Hooft's imaginary space-time; **1.3.5.2** Weak interaction, effective field theory (EFT); **1.3.5.3** Spontaneous symmetry breaking (SSB) and anomalous symmetry breaking (ASB); **1.3.5.4** Symanzik's decoupling of mass and Dyson's broken scale invariance; **1.3.5.5**. Grand unification theories (GUT); **Figure 3; 1.3.5.6** Wheeler's delayed choice experiment, mirror particle paradox; **1.3.5.7** Three imaginary worlds, superposition of Bloch sphere; **1.4.2** Multiple imaginary world does not mean multi-verses.

Fractal Information Theory (FIT): 2.1. What is information in a Fractal tape? **Figure 4; 2.2** Ten basic points of FIT; **2.3** Philosophy of reductionism and the philosophy of morphism, a comparison; **2.4** Bridging the singularity of Feynman's fractal path, is harnessing possible? **2.5** First proposal of Fractal tape in 1979; **2.5.3** Only escape time fractal could lead to beyond Turing computing; **2.6** Why time-cycles are essential in a Fractal tape instead of "bits" or "qubits"? **2.6.1-2.6.2** The halting problem; **2.7** Self-assembly of time cycles create living circuits; **2.8** Why no computing, or no logic gate? **2.8.2** How actually geometric information to be written in a material; **2.9** How self-assembly of time-cycles replace software programming and avoids the need for any pre-circuit building; **2.10** Creation of resonance chain and frequency fractal; **2.10.3-4** Triplet of triplet band a necessity?

Fractal Tape Machine (FTM) & Fractal mechanics (FM): 3.1 Definition of a fractal tape machine (FTM) and fifteen basic features of AjoChhand or AC computing; **3.2** Why there is never a collapse in a Fractal tape machine (FTM); **3.3** Filling up empty time-cycles is a key; **3.4** Difference with Quantum logic gates; **3.5** Reduction of Fractal mechanics (FM) to Quantum mechanics; **3.6** Comparison between classical information theory, quantum information theory and the fractal information theory (FIT); **A table of comparison**. **3.7** FIT does not endorse Carl Pribram's holographic brain or David Bohm's holographic universe; **3.7.1** Holographic universe of string theory; **3.7.2** what happens if a FTM falls into a black hole? **3.7.4 A table comparing** FTM worldview and Holographic fractal universe worldview.

Summary of major results in FTM, FM and AjoChhand or AC computing : 4.1 Ten fundamentals of Fractal mechanics (FM); **4.2** Ten philosophical concepts that are naturally changed if we simply consider a Fractal tape (FT) or FTM; **4.3** Ten experimental evidences we need to establish that certain observations are not possible to explain by QM or CM alone or together, they need FM.

Conclusion: 5. A subtle change in the fractal assembly of Turing tape could enable morphing of resonance chain, a new world of materials synthesis vis-à-vis computing.

1. INTRODUCTION: AN INFORMATION STRUCTURE THAT COULD ESTIMATE THE "QUANTUM SUPPLEMENT":

1.1 Neither classical nor quantum, fractal time deserves its own distinct status:

1.1.1 Bertrand Russell, Turing and Gödel's incompleteness theorem: Bertrand Russell's statement that the arithmetic could be deduced from Logic was proved wrong by Gödel. The proof was simple. Russell argued in his book "principles of mathematics" (1903) (Russell, 1938), that, while adding 1+1=2, we take "1" from within and add to "1" to create something new "2" (1+1=2). Gödel argued in 1933 (Goldstein, 2005), no, we are actually taking the second "1" from outside, this second "1" is not taken from the "1" located inside; you just cannot do this. While Russell's effort gave rise to "equation", which philosophically means, some internal parameters fully explains the system's response. Historically, the equations were used extensively to create the theories we use in the modern science. Gödel's argument for "something from outside" disappeared because his machine analogue did not come into existence as it did for Russell via Turing (Copeland, 2004). To implement Gödel's incompleteness argument (Ghosh, Sahu, Fujita, & Bandyopadhyay, 2014) we inspired for inventing a fractal tape (FT) and a fractal tape machine (FTM) that eventually violates the Turing tape. ***Quantum and Fractal are two research fields, which explore the "something from outside" options using an imaginary number "i"***. However, they prefer to construct a guidance equation rather than deriving the external contribution from a more fundamental scientific principle or assumption. A logical program or mathematical formulation cannot create anything new. All theories in science are predetermined by seeing the result, applying imagination to write logic

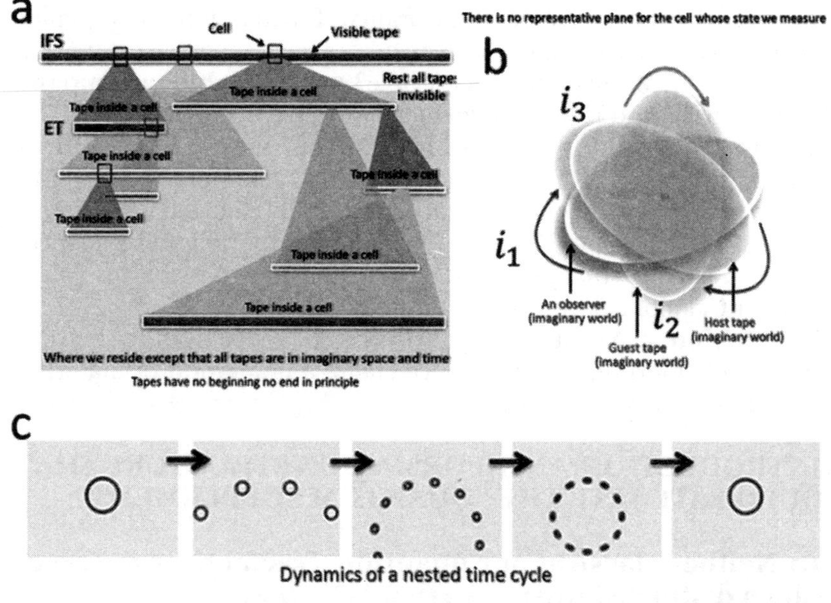

FIGURE 1
a. A Fractal tape. b. Basic information unit for a fractal tape c. dynamics of a nested time cycle.

to integrate a few observations; we name that fitting as "rule" and the structure of logic as "model". With the first statement to formulate the differential equation for a phenomenon, the fate of the final expression is sealed much before it is solved.

1.1.2 A journey from "step by step" to "within and above": Turing machine strictly follows a "step by step" argument, so it cannot discover anything new, beyond the algorithm. Recently, we proposed that every single cell of a Turing tape (Figure 1a), if contains a Turing tape inside then, it will be a computing beyond Turing (Ghosh, Sahu, Fujita, & Bandyopadhyay, 2014). Moreover, it would model biological systems in nature more profoundly. Therein, "look above and within" as promised by every single cell in a Fractal tape enables an observer to remain in a single cell of a fractal tape yet by locking onto its pair of imaginary time cycles suitably, it can access the entire fractal tape. ***The observer, who is always localized into a small domain of an infinite fractal tape network, always experiences an "unpredictable" and a "new" event, due to three imaginary worlds (Figure 1b), it's the simplest machine formed by us for implementing the Gödel's incompleteness argument***. Thus, the scientific culture of discretizing the nature into bits and pieces of information and then walk along the "step by step" path using a classical or quantum route should meet an alternative. A cell in a fractal tape (Ghosh, Sahu, Fujita, & Bandyopadhyay, 2014) follows one-principle; "look above and within", and thenceforth encompasses everything in a system. This philosophy argues to morph nature via a perpetual expansion and contraction, not discretize selective elements, like Bertrand Russell or Turing philosophy. Gödel's statement simply argues that we need something from outside, but no one has said, what is that we need. Here, with the fractal tape we do state the recipes and the information that we need from outside. Cells of the fractal tape uses time cycles (Figure 1 c) that are not a switch or transistor, they construct nested time cycles that are not the logic gate. Therein, queries and the possible solutions run in a time loop, with no reduction of choices. Hence, we argue that ***compiling the choices beyond a logical statement is not "illogical" as believed thus far, it is the reasoning of nature; the mechanics beyond quantum is not classical but could be a fractal***. Finally, ***if a system is created by a simultaneous expansion and contraction "above and within" from a single cell of a fractal tape, then, the sum of its pre-isolated parts could never recreate the whole. Thus, morphing the whole is the key, leaving a culture of science that asks to split the nature first into discrete parts and then heavily relying on the human imagination to re-integrate***.

1.1.3. From Gödel to Quantum's foundation: In the mathematical physics, the stability requires three things, first, a logical consistency; second, a mathematical definability and decidability, and the third, a conceptual stability. As ***Gödel challenged the formalist-finitist program in mathematics***, the external information and empirical consideration, could deliver stability to the system (Godel, 1938; 1947), this was proved by P. J. Cohen (1963). The context and thus produced interpretation (Kreisel, 1976), e.g. Born's "ghost field" (Born, Heisenberg & Jordan, 1926), or Feynman's path integral method to quantize (Feynman, 1948), Dirac's positron, always took a non-conceptual structure to stabilize the system. *The strongest approach made by **t' Hooft (1971)** wherein he* ***considered that the space-time is a complex variable, while constructing the fundamental structure of information we have adopted t' Hooft's formulation, as is. Even the cell that the observer measures in a fractal tape, does not get a real value, sphere of arbitrary phase sets everything that we see in reality (Figure 2a)***. Eventually the causal connections survive in a cell of a fractal tape, where, the fundamental laws of nature need to emerge due to the dynamics of the time cycles, in the future. Here we present the background work for that to come.

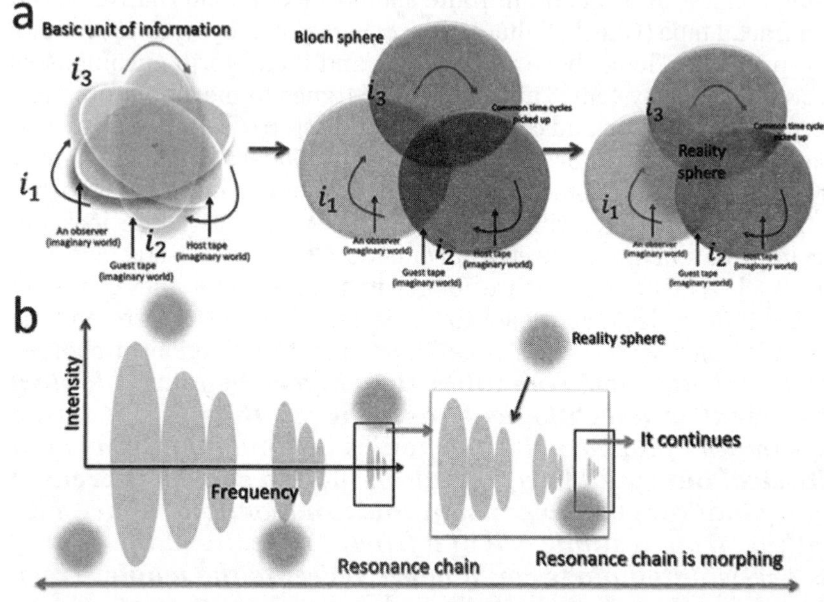

FIGURE 2
a. Basic information unit to Bloch sphere and reality sphere
b. Shaded ellipsoid is a resonance band, made of several resonance peaks

1.2 Justification of revisiting a 100 years old historical development of quantum mechanical theories: Photon is not known, we explore its mystery here. Light matter interaction is debated for long because the measurement does not reveal all parameters. The lack of information in the measured data changes with the environment, one route is to generate an information structure and fill the gaps by experiments (morphing). However, that requires a radical change in the way information has been treated in the last hundred years. ***It was said that the information was "bits" or "qubits", but those were the structures of information, there used to be a separate tool called "facts" (memory) which is used to hold the truths and "argument" (algorithm) that used to connect facts and bits, information meant altogether the three fundamentals***. To fuse them together into a single unit, the dynamics of a physical system needs to be absorbed into the information structure, we need to emulate the system's true features as close as possible, that is why it is challenging to find the "information structure" that would arrange itself on an information arranging skeleton. ***Morphing is a process following which a nest of time cycles fills up with the phase & beat frequencies, thus, reconstructs the natural system made of vibrational frequencies continuously (Figure 2b),***

until the dynamics of the system is mimicked comprehensively at all time-scales.

1.2.1. Hallmark quantum protocol could be derived from classical theory: Even though we never intended to invent a new mechanics, however, the existing literatures are rich in showing that the fundamentals of quantum mechanics could be derived from classical mechanics (Nottale & Celerier, 2007; Stenger, 2001). Since quantum paths are fractal (Abbot & Wise, 1981; Kannata & Ferrari, 1988; Sornette, 1990), there has been an attempt to generate quantum mechanics using fractal time-cycle (Ord, 1983; 2012; 2009; 2011; Nottale, 2005; Kantelhardt, 2011). Fractal time is not a concept of unpredictable quantum world, its classical (Shlesinger, 1988; Smolyaninov, 2012). However, in the fractal space-time configuration of quantum, the time-cycle metric is imaginary and they have used randomness to explain the motion through the space-time curvature. We first assume that the system is random and then prove that the quantum operates in an unpredictable manner. Irrespective of the complexity and a meticulous sequence of arguments, proving that what is assumed in the beginning is wrong. Moreover, if in a metric everything is defined everywhere, even the fractal space-time proponents do that, then, the unpredictability would never arise from the system property, but the negligence in designing the math protocols. ***The limitations of quantum mechanics formulations cannot be resolved using its existing principles, but extending the imaginary contribution one level higher means, dealing with many interactive imaginary worlds, that eventually delivering the one imaginary world of quantum***. We need a new kind of mechanics that has the potential to flexibly organize & process multiple imaginary worlds and that may not be perfect, but tries to address fundamental issues like origin of entanglement, origin of simultaneity or superposition and the origin of uncertainty, the hallmarks of quantum mechanics.

1.2.2. Unpredictability and the contextual and non-contextual supplement in the Quantum formulation: No predictability, no theory: While a wave could exist or disappear, however, a particle always remains there, thus a wave particle duality is "unpredictable", but if there is no predictability, there will be no equation, no mathematical formulation for quantum. No theory could ever be framed for a random event, thus, no science would remain to endorse the Russell's paradigm. Proposers of the quantum theories suggested & debated different ideas to make a transition from unpredictability to predictability for nearly a century now (refer the history & follow-ups of Bell's inequality). They suggested primarily that the quantum states are incomplete and some hidden element is there (Bells, 1966; Bohm, 1952; Bohr, 1935; Durr, Goldstein & Zanghi, 1992; Einstein, Podolsky & Rosen, 1935; Leggett, 2003; Stapp, 1997), that has to be added from outside to make it into a complete state, and when it is complete, it becomes classical. ***Bell's inequality sets a limit that statistically one could never make a quantum state complete, or retrieve the hidden elements entirely, now, the experiments those supported it*** **(Freedman & Clauser, 1972; Fry & Thompson, 1976)** ***got overshadowed by those experiments that showed a violation*** **(Tittlel, Brendel, Zbinden, & Gisin, 1998; Rowe et al., 2001)**. Some argues that when we measure a quantum state, the detail of the observer's internal state is not essential (non-contextual, i.e. algebraic, Bell). In contrast some argues that every single other associated quantum states would matter during the measurement (contextual, i.e. environmental, Bohm). To construct the internal structures of an observer we used to imagine a matrix and fill it up to fit the experimental observation, this matrix needs a replacement using an even more basic information structure.

1.2.3. The quantum formulation includes three crucial features, (i) bringing a real space & time contribution from nowhere using an imaginary term (fractal is also known for delivering this feature mathematically). (ii) Restricting the continuous waveform into a localized space and time (wherefrom we get the uncertainty principles and change the wave equation into the Schrödinger's equation). (iii) Bra and Ket algebra used to create or destroy a state. These operators along with the spinors are the ways to select a few, from a set of choices; the quantum proponents call it the Hilbert space, we include it in our reality sphere (Figure 2a). We use these three unique features in the classical worldview to create a virtual reality as if unpredictability is there, so that a sense of quantum appears in reality. However, in the mathematical formulation there is no other way but to make sure explicitly when a state to appear and when to disappear (Laloe, 2001). ***A close look into the quantum's success in predicting the unexplained phenomena occurring in nature would unravel that the above-described three properties are the essential and the sufficient requirements***. Quantum's mathematical formulations, due to its lack of predicting events use, ***"i" is an imaginary term that contributes to the reality from nowhere*** **(Roychoudhuri, 2006)**, ***and we take it to the ultimate extreme, where nothing is real***.

1.2.4. Why it became essential to go beyond quantum mechanics and discover some mechanics that is more generic than Quantum, from which the principles of quantum mechanics could be derived? For 20 years, the development of quantum electrodynamics had clogged. A single problem had to be solved. If a quantum particle or energy packet moves along a path, between the two points of "no interaction" it can absorb & desorb energy, yet reach the destination clean, completing a loop. If we repeat the looping, this makes a fractal with an infinite path length, so the probability amplitude in a quantum measurement turned infinity. ***We stick to this nested loop, consider it as fundamental to the information structure, not rejecting the fractal paths via renormalization. To stop the divergence of mass, charge and photons frequency, we convert all the elements as nested frequency or nested time cycles, use sync and de-sync to join or de-join cycles and thus avoid the need for the renormalization. Since we see matter and non-matter as time cycles, the space is a perception***. The scaling law for the mass and radius of all elements () in the universe (Haramein, 2001; Muradian, Carneiro & Marques, 1999; Seager, Kuchner, Hier-Majumdar & Militzeret, 2007) suggests that the geometric shapes are consistent with the information content. Hence, the time cycles/loops are analogous to matrices required to memorize or process the geometric information. Based on these arguments we suggested for taking a Turing tape and put a new Turing tape in each cell of the tape (Ghosh, Sahu, Fujita, & Bandyopadhyay, 2014). This was not a random theoretical argument. We have created the new information structure to operate the Fractal tape, keeping in mind the experimentally measured data for microtubules and other proteins (Sahu, Ghosh, Fujita, & Bandyopadhyay, 2014; Sahu, Ghosh, Hirata, Fujita, & Bandyopadhyay, 2013; Sahu et al., 2013), wherein the resonance spectrum spontaneously change as a function of time, i.e. the time cycles are produced naturally. However, once the information structure is created, we find that such an information structure is much more concrete than the existing information structure used by the quantum information theory.

1.3 List of philosophical transformations required to avoid the culture of quantum supplement and deriving the hallmarks of quantum from simpler principles: Three quotes make the foundation of this section. "no elementary quantum phenomenon is a phenomenon until it is a registered phenomenon", said Niels Bohr. "Superposition cannot be observed, only its consequence is detected" (Barreto, 2014). "Unperformed experiments have no results" (Peres, 1978). We try to deconstruct these statements with time-cycles.

1.3.1 First we had Newtonian space, then space-time and now we have space again: A point is ideally a space-time metric, the general theory of relativity acts comprehensively as a classical system. However, ***Quantum gravity's zero point energy estimation and the prediction of unrealistic gravitational constant suggests that the Quantum's discreteness of space-time may not fit exclusively in a non-linear metric.*** Now, to resolve, that the "time does not exist, space is enough" has been proposed (Sorli, Fiscaletti, & Klinar, 2011; Prati, 2009; Elze, 2003; Girelli, Liberati & Sindoni, 2009; Catalin & Meck, 2005), it addresses the problem of unrealistic gravitational constant (Heller & Sasin, 1999) but due to its Newtonian mechanics in a problematic package, creates even more problems than that it solves. Its irony that we started with space, then Einstein argued for "space-time" and we are back to square one with space, as mathematicians learn how to generate "time" from space alone. The ***only option that is left to consider is that every point is made of time cycles only, its geometric shape is made by information that creates a virtual space from the time cycles***. Now, since it is already proved that the ad hoc discretization of space-time does not work, we can create a virtual discretization by introducing a fractal time based definition of a point. ***If every point in the universe is a fractal time cycle based structure, there will be no end of journey inside the point, hence no zero point energy. Moreover, since the observer would also be a nested time cycle structure, it would detect that point in an assembly of infinite pool of points, then for that detection time resolution & limits would create a virtual boundary & generate the concept of a space.*** This is why a single decision that every point is a nested time cycle could alleviate the need to consider a "space". Moreover, since the concept of time and the space is already isolated by following that the "time is real and space is a perception", ***it can resolve the unrealistic gravitational constant in the same way the "space is real, time does not exist" philosophy did.*** Thus, both the problems could be addressed.

1.3.2. Solitary nature of photon is not an exclusive property of photons: velocity is always a perception of an observer: Electromagnetic waves i.e. photons never interact, two photons interact only when they fall on a dipole or matter, wherein the polarization matters (Kocher & Commins, 1967). Solitons in the water move miles without disruption; "not interacting between themselves" thus, it is not an exclusive property of photons, and just like photons, solitons are disrupted upon measurement (Wang, 1985; Shrivastava & Schneider, 2014). For a photon, the "distance or space or time does not exist", the imaginary time cycles above and inside a point when interacted by an observer's imaginary time cycle then, various different time gaps are generated, those time gaps are perceivable boundary for that observer, the observer calls it a space or a quanta. ***The space is the ratio of perimeters or diameters of a pair of time cycles, if one time cycle is a point with respect to another, it perceives an infinite distance.***

1.3.3 ***Discretization during an energy exchange is fundamental:*** if continuity is a result of an observer-system resolution, then where is the information structure that is logically congruent and conceptually consistent? ***Currently the quantum discretization has two keys, (a) harmonics and (b) limits of certainty (uncertainty principle). In practice, the uncertainty expression is converted into a certainty equation***, the entrance to an uncertain world is feasible, but creating an equation to return a measurement from the boundary of certain and uncertain world is not logical. In quantum formulation, it is used often. Moreover, the ***encapsulated bilayers of classical cavity resonator can deliver an inverse frequency distribution to the desired harmonics of quantum interference pattern, one could generate quantum interference like frequency distribution by adding a set of wave equations, it is not exclusive to "quantum math protocol"***. Discretization is observed always in the energy exchange process between the two classical cavity resonators, it's not a special phenomenon to essentially inviting a quantum feature. One could generate all the "quantum" results (e.g. discrete orbitals of atoms, scattering of ions and atoms, the quantum interference pattern etc.) using the classical electromagnetic theory, added with the discrete energy transmission features. ***In order to induce a superposition of anharmonic distribution of frequencies as often found in nature*** (Monserrat, Drummond, & Needs, 2013), ***we need a fractal network of cavity resonators, however, then, even the classical formulation would fail, which succeeded in regenerating the quantum effects. A generic form of mechanics with added features to the quantum formulation should compose the harmonic distribution inside an anharmonic distribution.*** Finally, when we convert the uncertainty principle into a certainty equation by removing the inequality sign, which is obviously a classical expression for the detector's limited resolution, then we fail to explain why the vibrations do not die out when an external input is zero (ground level energy). The vibrations are not coming from nowhere; some fundamental processes are happening inside that we are missing.

1.3.4 The role of an arbitrary phase in measuring a Quantum state: Quantum Electro dynamics, QED, a first attempt of quantum field theory QFT, suggested that the photons exchange between the quantum particles (e.g electrons) so that the effects of classical electromagnetic theory disappears and the typical features of quantum appears. A quantum state by emitting two photons gets an expression, ; here, comes from the equation of motion. Any field observable's expectation is , since is not involved, the lower state interferences is not feasible to occur in QED. However, we do a little math to get . So, when we introduce an arbitrary phase , and include the field, both the photons are coupled, we get an interference. The arbitrary phase plays a fundamental role in defining a quantum state. Covariance means a function that retains its form even though we transform its variables linearly; this protocol helps to sustain the perturbation of any order. In the mathematical formulation, two quantum states are connected by an arbitrary relative phase, so that a desired contribution to the real world fits the perturbation magnitude. Complicated protection for a better fit when arises from users discretion it is not wise to draw a physical insight from those formulation regarding the arbitrary world of quantum.

1.3.5 *Superposition*, *Classical beats, Quantum beats, Talbot effect, Heterodyne spectroscopy and constant velocity of light*: If there is no detector at a suitable place, there is no quantum interference, wave feature disappears and the particle feature sets in, to include that factor, the photons are presented as . This expression of a photon is modified from Roychoudhuri formulation (Roychoudhuri, 2006). The change in the expression is to account for the transition from one imaginary time cycles to three imaginary time cycles. Out of three, two imaginary cycles are presented by and one imaginary time cycle interacts with the rest two time cycles to construct . There could be various distinct representations of the nested time cycles. In case of a wave function, we take the square modulus of all superposed We get the intensity Wherein if, a slowly varying beat signal is. The superposed two waveforms pass through all the molecules in a large area on the screen where we observe the quantum interference, the beat frequencies are produced at each molecule since two atoms in the molecule get two different frequencies. **Dipoles execute quantum superposition, none else; the entangled photons need a material support to exhibit a hallmark of quantum**. If we have a diatomic molecule, one atom would receive the other , however the observed frequency would be low. ***If the resonance frequency we measure is in the MHz or in the kHz domain, it could well be that the sample is***

exposed to a GHz or even a THz frequency. Since, the fringes of an interference pattern on the screens have an energy gradient, thus, it is not a "quantized control", rather, a distribution of "beat frequencies", wherein, even one could notice nesting of beats.

Talbot plane and the heterodyne spectroscopy: The superposition of rapidly evolving secondary wavelets emerging from the slits of a grating (monochromatic light), generate beautiful patterns at certain distances from the slit (Talbot plane). The detectors at those certain locations pick the stimulations of the electric-vector, at the other locations we observe an absence. ***Dirac's "photons interfere with itself" is critically challenged by these experiments*** (Peng, Barootkoob, & Roychoudhuri, 2009). Superposition of photons needs a dipole to manifest. High-speed detectors and ultrafast pulses provide a better (heterodyne spectroscopy) understanding. ***Michaelson's assumption is wrong, the photons of different frequencies do generate a quantum interference (of course orthogonally polarized lights do not interfere)***. A complex correlation between the inter-frequency correlation in a spectrum, the time varying amplitude and the space-varying phase play a pivotal role in generating a quantum interference (Roychoudhuri, 2011). Thus, ***a set of imaginary worlds is essential to govern the fundamental information structure of the quantum particles***. The current quantum theories use one imaginary world and we argue that a little change in the basic assumption would resolve multitudes of discrepancies in the mathematical formulation of quantum. The argument to redefine the information structure (Figure 1b, Figure 2a) essentially alleviates the necessity to consider a complex tension field proposed by Roychoudhuri to generate the constant velocity of lights everywhere (Roychoudhuri, Barootkoob & Ambroselli, 2011).

If one reduces the rate of propagation of photon to one hv per second, the quantum superposition induced fringes disappear, i.e. there is a causal effect (Panarella, 1987). In a quantum interference experiment, the "interference" fringes are visible only exactly behind the bisecting Polaroid, ***the rest of the screen has superposition yet we do not see any fringes***, if one moves the screen one cannot see it so it is a local phenomenon. Not all the molecules in the entire screen know where to demonstrate the fringes, some of them know, and that's a large area, who selects that domain and how is not a quantum effect, its purely classical. However, multiple authors have translated this credit to entanglement.

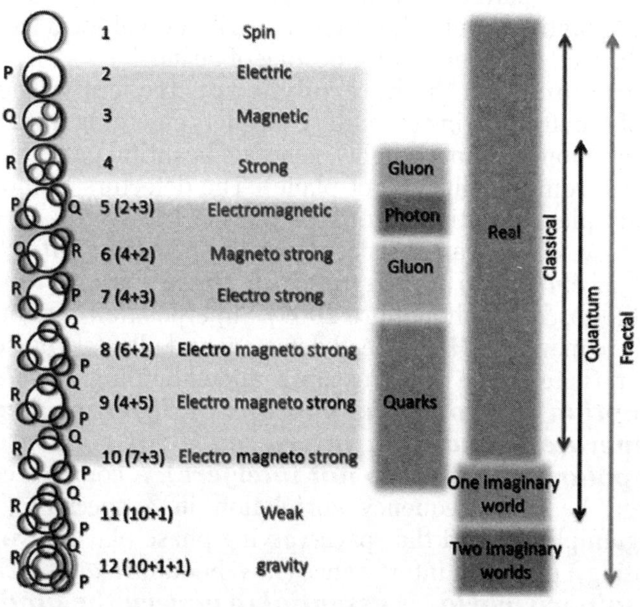

FIGURE 3
Nested time cycles to represent masses and forces.

1.3.5 A historical perspective to justify the necessity of nested time cycle:

1.3.5.1. Electroweak & electromagnetic theory: the birth of renormalization in a scenario of overlapping divergences: When Jordon (Born, Heisenberg & Jordan, 1926) and Dirac (1927), generated the quantum mechanical operators for a classical electromagnetic field, the vacuum fluctuation got an enormous energy, sufficient to topple the fundamental concepts of physics. One way to get rid of such a situation was considering the vacuum as a negative energy pot (Dirac, 1930), another way is to consider the "photon as the excited mode of vacuum" (Keller, 2014) (since its not ignorable). Moreover, it could also be possible that the unknown particles are compensating somehow and not allowing the ultra-high energy beyond a certain frequency that somehow endorsed "renormalization" to correct the astronomically increasing mass and charge. ***Imaginary space-time concept was born in the work of t' Hooft* (1971), *he first showed that we need a complex space-time structure to renormalize the funny weak interaction scenario (guest has much more mass than the host)***. Moreover, in the weak force formulation, for mass, it has been shown that the elementary mass that constitutes a larger mass have differences and the differences between those elementary masses are of an electromagnetic origin (Heitler, 1961). Including the dynamics of the elementary masses (Sakata, Umezawa & Kamefuchi, 1952) does provide detail about the nesting of the masses, and charges of several more fundamental particles inside. ***Schwinger argued that even if we take detail of the matter structure, finally we would have to delete the massive theoretical construct to obtain a physically sensible result.*** Moreover, it is not always noted, but ***if there is a ultraviolet divergence, then there is also an infrared divergence and both the limits need to be protected, for that purpose we need two imaginary worlds to operate simultaneously, apart from that we need exclusively for the observer.*** Thus, in the fractal information theory (FIT), all these factors are taken care of. A pair of nests of imaginary time cycles becomes essential beyond a certain complexity that the observer could detect. It is also observed that ***the mass and charge divergence are not isolated, they are overlapping, and sometimes the divergence recedes and the convergence sets in and for mass and charge, the variations are not linear, intricately nested***. This nested divergence was resolved by Salam, Ward and Mills, Yang and Weinberg's convergence theorem. Nesting of time cycles take into account the nested structure of divergence, and we could nest time cycles to represent elementary information (Figure 3). The nesting provides not only the mirror symmetry, but also the most generic form of mirroring, i.e. parity. Parity violation (Lee & Yang, 1956) in the electroweak interaction for fractal information theory (FIT) means that since the particle is a group of three nested time cycles (Figures 1b, 2a, Figure 3), one can reverse the spin of two nested cycles at most not the third one. Thus, the nested time cycle in the information theory could adopt parity, exclusively.

1.3.5.2. More elementary constituents than the particles described by fields (there is no building block, there is always something inside): "Renormalization is an expression of the variation of the structure of physical interactions with the changes in the scale of the phenomena being probed" (Gross, 1985). At the quantum scale, with a finite change in energy, the variations of physical interactions change significantly. Re-defining the renormalization at different energy ranges to fit the results create a hierarchical layers of theories, each applicable to a distinct range (Georgi, 1989; Lepage, 1990). A fractal tape is itself an information processing structure that maintains the continuity across the energy scale, yet isolating the system by the concept of a cell for the locally restricted physical interactions. ***Escape time transitions in a fractal tape wherein an observer faces***

a real world limit, are natural "cut off"s, and thus, no need for imagining the auxiliary devices of Feynman by taking "cut off" to infinity ("cut off" protects the theory to survive in a restricted domain). There is no need for the Weinberg's asymptotic safety. The atomistic view of QFT, wherein the distances between its elementary constituents is a concern. in fractal tape view, atomistic structures are always decomposed into nested time cycles (Figure 3). Even for each elementary particles the system, the structure of time loops represent the particle, the atomistic or particle view of any component becomes non-existent. ***In the fractal tape, the "structured objects are expressed in terms of structure less events"*** (Cao & Schweber, 1993) ***is implemented more profoundly that that exercised by QFT and or EFT***. It is not a reductionist but more of a Reconstructionist approach. ***Reductionist view is not non-existent in the Fractal tape, however, it is an illusion always taken by the observer***. Note that, the Effective field theory (EFT) is all about editing the degrees of freedom of a system (statistically) so that in a typical range, the divergence of mass and charge do not reach beyond a limit. For various different particles, different versions of EFT exist.

1.3.5.3. Spontaneous symmetry breaking (SSB) and anomalous symmetry breaking (ASB): QFT has a few implicit concepts that evolved over time, regularization, cut off, dimensionality, symmetry, and renormalizability, while an explicit concept was added, spontaneous (SSB, (Brown & cao, 1991) or anomalous symmetry breaking (ASB) in several processes. SSB ensures a low energy interaction (due to a large time scale). In the nested time cycle protocol (Figures 4b, 4c), there is no fixed symmetry; it depends on the interactive system's common time cycles. ***The common time cycles between the two interactive cells of a fractal tape activate the dynamics in the system; thus, when information and its structure are combined we get an emulation of the event itself. This is different from the Turing's philosophy where information and its structure or bits had no embedded relation***. If only two systems are interacting and there is no third system involved, then, the symmetry breaking is spontaneous (SSB). However, if a third system affects any of the two nested time cycles causing the common time cycles to change, then it is called anomalous symmetry breaking (ASB). If the two nested time cycles contain similar information, then, the associated dynamics, symmetry and the symmetry breaking would be similar. By setting this condition, one could make sure that the system does not diverge; it does not require renormalization. If at different time domains, different nested time cycles match, then, the variations are automatically taken care of by the observer's nested time cycle (group-theoretic constraints of symmetry breaking). Moreover, ASB is an anomaly but it does not induce a divergence in a Fractal tape scenario, because the observer's matching with the time cycles acts as the third protection. The other two protections to the divergence in a Fractal tape are carried out by the escape time blockage of two imaginary worlds. We have taken care of all these factors while generating the nested time cycles for the fundamental forces and masses in Figure 3. The table of Figure 3 represents time-cycle representation of elementary forms, there are no hidden time-loops.

1.3.5.4 Scale invariance, broken scale invariance and the fractal tape: automated filtering of high and low frequency and heavy and light mass: Following the group theory in mathematics, a group for the fractal tape would be a local nest of time cycles. If we try to build a similar analogue, group or scale transformations for a Fractal tape means at different parts of the fractal tape the symmetry breaking laws should be similar. Due to the self-similarity nature of the fractal tape, the scale invariance is ensured. ***The asymptotic scale invariance introduced by Gell-Mann and Low is also ensured in the fractal tape structure as the size decreases to zero the charge decreases to a low value and the other associated values diverge. Larger the value, further it spreads in the Fractal tape***.

In the fractal tape, two distinct types of fractals are used together; in the escape time fractal, the self-similar structures are encapsulated one inside another. In the iterative function system (IFS) time fractal, the self-similar structures reside side by side (Figure 1a). Thus, when an observer remains within a cell's real neighborhood (IFS world), the scale dependent parameters are addressed by the apparently real time cycles (broken scale invariance, (Kadanoff, 1966). At the same time, when we consider the ET fractal, the architecture of the tape ensures an asymptotic scale-invariance. The heavy particles with a high density of nested time cycles naturally decouples from the light particles with a low density of nested time cycles in the Fractal tape system (Symanzik, 1973). ***The momentum cut off regularization (Feynman, 1948) is done by the fractal tape geometry***.

In Dyson's smoothed interaction representation (Dyson, 1951), the low and the high frequency parts were isolated. We generalized it, so much so that, instead of smoothly varying charge or mass, we get a discrete variation; however, due to the presence of the fractal tape, there is no time gap. ***The hardware that holds the nested time cycle's isolates the frequencies as a set of distinct time cycles and then integrate them as geometric***

shapes. For operating the fractal tape's information, mass = length = time, hence we get the momentum P=1/a, as the interaction distance (a) limit set by Landau (Landau, Abrikosov & Khalatnikov, 1956).

Unfortunately, ***in the history of quantum, Symanzik's decoupling of mass and Dyson's decoupling of frequency were never put together***. If we put them together, both are equivalent, and expresses the fundamental concepts of the nested time cycle approach, where by filtering the nested time cycles or frequencies, automatically filters the masses too. ***Thus, extrapolation of domains (sometimes even to infinity as Feynman did) is not required; morphism or filling the infinite fractal tape (or its hardware equivalent resonance chain) with information is better suited.***

1.3.5.5 Grand unification theories from Effective Field Theory, EFT: Hierarchical chain of GUT is conceptualized into the resonance chain representing the Fractal tape: Literatures are rich in GUT and we only study them to make sure that when we represent all forces, mass, charge and parity, our selection of nested time cycles are consistent (Figure 3). Mass and charge divergence, could be quadratic, linear or logarithmic (Peierls, 1934; Weisskopf, 1934); historically, math tricks were employed to fit the experimental data for the elementary particles. Spontaneous symmetry breaking (SSB) was one of the hallmarks of the QFT and EFT, from which the hierarchical structures came into being for different domains with different formulations, thus creating a chain for GUT (Gell-Mann & Low, 1954; Fisher, 1964; Callan 1970). Each layer in the hierarchical structure is deconstructed by imagining an effective field (EFT). Therefore, the organizational structure though constructed in the elementary particle domain resembled an infinite imaginary chain made of the local discs of reality, wherein the rest of the discs appear imaginary for a given disc. We conjectured that the information structure that holds the information of such a world should be a similar resonance frequency chain. Consequently, ***the unitary matrices that hold the key to Quantum's information processing is generalized for nth imaginary dimensions in the fractal information theory (FIT).*** Therein, instead of one, two imaginary numbers are required for representing the forces (i1, i2), and one additional imaginary number (i3) would appear in the operator representing the observers measurement process (Figure 1b, Figure 2a).

1.3.5.6 Wheeler's delayed choice experimental verification requires a memorization protocol: wave particle duality is "not" unpredictable: Since photons emitted from two different atoms do not interfere, in order to explain the interference fringes made by a single photon, it is considered that if a photon while passing through a semitransparent sheet of glass (or Young's slit) produces its replica (one transmitted and one reflected), only then the two photons would interfere. Then, two photons are entangled which means act as one particle or remain under the one wave function irrespective of their separation. This particular definition of entanglement is key to the nested time cycle proposal for the information processing, note that just like entanglement, nested time cycles do not care about the distance, spatial separation does not matter. Creating a special condition of interference only to fit a theory for explaining the observation of fringes, while no one can detect a photon and its replica, —needs a revisit. Does a slit and semi-transparent sheet of glass could always create a replica of photon? The answer is "no", but that is absent in the textbooks. Anywhere in nature if such a condition fits, would act as photon or ion or electron production engine. If mirrored particles do not interfere and collapse, they cannot just vanish anywhere. It is not wise to allow the universe being filled with an astronomically large number of mirror photons ions atoms and several subatomic particles, whoever exhibits the quantum interference. We should not create a theory that messes up the construction principles of universe. ***A mother photon produces daughter photons, and the daughter photons produce granddaughter photons, the generations after generation we can produce photons or energy, is it an infinite free energy source just by using semi-transparent glass?*** In reality, what is not said in the research articles that the probability of producing granddaughter is one in a billion (Hubel et al., 2010). The entangled photon production has a classical probability and there exists an unknown but a stringent matter-photon interaction rule that was never investigated.

In the Wheelers delayed choice experiment **(Jacques et al., 2007)** ***(suggested 1978, modified 1983) it is shown (experimentally verified in 1997)*** that a photon and its mirror counterpart behave as particles even when they cross through each other during motion, but if they are brought to fall **simultaneously** on a semitransparent glass, only then, they start behaving like a wave and interfere. The presence or absence of the second beam-splitter always determines "wave or particle" manifestation. This is nice demand for the "simultaneous matter-photon interaction of entangled particles". Now if we move the glass or beam splitter far away from the cross sectional point between the photon and its mirror photon's pathway, the "wave" property disappears and the particle property appears, i.e. there is no interference. Hence, an observer tunes between the duality and the superposition at free will. ***Wheeler's interpretation for this event is too radical, "world does not exist if it is not***

observed," while Bohm's interpretation demands a new scientific entity, "particles follow classical mechanics under quantum potential". Further studies on Wheeler **(Jacques et al., 2007; Manning, Khakimov, Dall, & Truscott, 2015)** ***argue for a combined quantum state including the particles and the apparatus*** (Ma et al., 2013). We argue for a simplistic solution to this problem. Let us consider that a photon is a nested time cycle, it means, three 2D time cycle planes made of the basic triplet information units are interconnected to make three planes and those planes are arranged as a virtual sphere. The semi-transparent glass or the beam splitter actually splits the nested planes and the complementary groups formed by the phase differences in the nested cycles are grouped as distinct local nested time cycles fixed in a much longer time cycle. The photon-matter interaction acts as filter, splitter, phase differentiator, joiner of the time cycles. Thus produced complementary nested time cycles transmit and reflect, making an equal angle as they make three points of an equilateral triangle on the larger time cycle. If they go far apart, yet, are brought together under the same condition, then only they fuse as separate elements in a single time cycle. These two complementary time cycles connected by a larger time cycle are sensitive to any cavity resonator (atom is also a cavity between the two energy levels, so are double slits, etc.), thus, create interference pattern as soon as fall on the screen. If we do not allow the fusion of the time cycles then a unified time cycle that is composition of imaginary and real worlds does not form, we get a classical particle. Therefore, the photon is classical, but, it is split into a composition of imaginary time cycles, which is purely quantum and then classical wave like nested wavelet is formed for a new kind of interference (quantum). Thus, it is causal due to the "time cycle recognition and a consequent fusion process". Since we consider a time cycle, it is observed as local, but it is non-local. ***A coherent wave or quantum particle following this principle would be a single nested time cycle, which does not have one imaginary world, but plenty, with the different imaginary numbers, distributed over the Fractal tape because one cannot simply add them.*** Note that whatever is constructed for the Fractal information theory (FIT), matter, or non-matters like photons, the elementary triplet time cycles are used to construct the three planes. ***FIT does not make any prediction what is the smallest triplet time cycles, because that directly contradicts the definition of a fractal tape, there is no lower and no upper limit of the fractal tape.***

Reflection and transmission requires a memorization protocol: how the direction of photon or a quantum particle is managed: Light never reflects, photon in contact with a matter is destroyed upon absorption and then generates again during emission; how the direction is memorized is not known. By artificially introducing a vector, a geometric explanation is made, but, when an atom absorbs light, it is associated with the vibrations of the orbitals, that is practically a singularity. Hence, connecting a vector with the two sides of an atom to construct the law of reflection (thus making the phases of Poynting vectors in the direction of the energy flow), disregards a singularity where the direction is permanently lost. For the Wheeler's delayed choice, we found that if the photons were a nested time cycle then the absorption by matter would split the time cycle, participating components would absorb the isolated time cycles. Moreover, ***the split parts of the time cycle should be connected under a much longer time scale, hence we get some split-yet-connected cycles to transmit and some reflects***.

1.3.5.7 ***Bloch sphere presentation and its resemblance with the "reality sphere"***: During the superposition of, the angular positions of the wave function on the Bloch sphere determine how one could transform one state to another (Figure 2a). Let us consider that the angular difference between the two quantum states is 90°. Now, ***if we calculate the quadruple moment matrix between the two states is such that the dipolar term vanishes*** (Jaynes, 1980) then, one could experimentally measure the state, and it is predictable, i.e. it becomes a classical model. The d***efenders of different versions of quantum theories failed to detect that whenever there is a two-body system, it would always become a classical formulation. One imaginary world and one real world is effectively a two-body system, and whatever the existing two-body theorems used, the classicality cannot be avoided***. The variability arises only from the three-body system, that's why as we consider a point as an emergent output from two imaginary worlds while the third virtual imaginary world belongs to the observer, we find multiple arguments so that the formulation does not get converted into a straightforward classical system. Whenever there is an imaginary world, it cannot remain isolated as a singular domain, it has to couple with a real world, so a circle made of an imaginary number i and a real number 1, considering a real and an imaginary axes, this is called the Bloch circle if we rotate, we get a Bloch sphere. ***If the two imaginary nested time cycle representing disks rotate around a common center, the two Bloch spheres corresponding to those discs overlap and interact. Another imaginary disc that belongs to the observer with another Bloch sphere rapidly moves all around the two other discs and creates a "reality sphere", on whose surface the observed solutions exist that the observer***

measures from different time locations.

In the Fractal information theory (FIT), the triplet imaginary disc structure is manifold more complex than the existing one disc based quantum information theory, where one Bloch sphere does everything. The irony is that in the Fractal tape at a time, the observer sees only one cell of the fractal tape. ***The fractal information theory (FIT) manages the two parallel imaginary universes made by the fractal tape, by another imaginary universe of the observer, which does not stay at a fixed point, i.e. the relative phase changes at an infinite speed to capture the observation values from all possible orientations or all possible values of relative phases.*** Note that the conventional parallel universe theory considers all the universes as real, thus, fundamentally different from the nested time cycle or nested disc features explained above. One point also needs to be emphasized that ***here the measurement is not a "collapse" (FIT does not endorse Copenhagen version of QM); it's all about filtering to select the matching nested time cycles between the two Bloch spheres generated by two hidden universes, one constitutes a tape inside a single cell and the other constitute a whole tape above.*** Thus, astronomically large simultaneous observations of a "reality sphere" could change as a function of the relative rotations of the system points along the constituent disc perimeters generating an unpredictability that does not require a classical tool to express. Classical means definite, but, the "reality sphere" is a distribution, what it means is that the entire quantum interference pattern for a single electron or a single photon is a representation of the entire "reality sphere", not a new phenomenon that entangles the zillions of fluorescent molecules to exhibit "entanglement". In other words, ***when a matter is replaced by its vibrational frequencies or time cycles, then, exchange, matching of time cycles, split and join of time cycles do everything that we need to construct its dynamics, the solution may come as a whole or in isolated parts.*** Simply we have to fill up the time cycles with smaller local cycles, that is the information content, and when we select those local time cycles we only consider the parameters of a geometric shape (say triangle) to encode.

1.4. A comparative discussion about nested time cycle concept of a fractal tape:

1.4.1 Three foundations of electrodynamics and its analogues nested time cycle version: (1) A photon goes from one place and time to another place and time. (2) An electron goes from one place and time to another place and time. (3) An electron emits or absorbs a photon at a certain place and time. (1) Photon's nested time cycles rotate perpetually (2) electrons nested time cycles rotate perpetually. (3) whenever there is a match in the local time cycles between the two nested time cycles, one belong to electron and the other belong to photon, then they rotate together creating a new time cycle, if the matching disappears then time cycles split and continue to rotate in an isolated manner. ***In the Classical mechanics, CM, the variation of space was the variation of time, the space was fundamental, in quantum, QM, the variation of space or time used to vary the other randomly in an unpredictable manner, in fractal FM, we suggest, the relative variation in the time-cycles is the variation in space.***

1.4.2 The resemblance & differences between the parallel universes and the nested time cycles: Hugh Everett III in 1957 and then Bryce DeWitt (1970) proposed that the randomness is an output of a causal effect from physically disconnected parallel universes. The planes made of imaginary time cycles constitute a sphere of nested time cycles that represent a photon or elementary particles (Figure 3), fit to exhibit a quantum superposition and these distinct time cycles could not be mixed. When we use different imaginary identity we make sure that they remain in the simultaneous universes (we use simultaneous universe to separate it from the parallel universe), only contributes to the reality following the distinct functional relationships between the time cycles. There is an interesting twist. ***For the simultaneous universes residing in the Fractal tape, there is no need to have an observer, and since there is no observer, no need to collapse the wave function.*** In the elementary photon structure, the observer is just another imaginary plane, like other planes, but there is a difference, the observer's plane rotates around all the other time-cycle discs. ***This spontaneous motion creates a changing reality as a function of time on the virtual sphere, we name that surface a "reality sphere" (thus, we bypass the spontaneous creation of "reality" as it happens in the multiverse proposition).*** Our elementary nested time cycle representation does not require "collapse" in spite of the fact that it does have an observer, and unlike the parallel universe, there would be ways to prove the existence of the nested time cycle planes. Thus, we follow the principle of Occams Razor (theory should be made by minimum number of principles and assumptions). That's one more reason why we need to avoid transactional interpretation (Cramer, 1986), which demands the existence of forward and backward wave of matter.

2. INFORMATION THEORY PERSPECTIVE OF A FRACTAL TAPE

2.1. What is information? One of the biggest problems in science has been philosophical, "what is information?" Information was initially bits, a composition of "yes" and "no", some numbers that signifies nothing. Then developed the concept of a number of possible symmetries that a system possesses, more is the number of symmetry, more is the entropy, more is the information content. ***For a fractal tape made of time cycles the information is written "a periodic motion of three interconnected circles", the rotation along the circle or time cycle covers all possible 0D, 1D, 2D, 3D geometries and the information is written as local time traps along the perimeter of the cycle***. In the Fractal information theory (FIT), information means no fact, but, a structure, which would provide a correlation between two or more geometric shapes. Thus, it contains a fact, it executes an event and it signifies correlation between multiple geometric shapes as question-answer couple, if the question is asked the answer is returned. This is fundamentally a different scenario; there is no static state in the elementary information unit. There is a sequence of frequencies being played one after another. ***In the fractal information theory (FIT), information does not simply represent the number of symmetries, but how a system jumps from one symmetry to another.*** These transitions could be such that three or more periodic cycles of switching between symmetries could play simultaneously. Thus, in a given set of symmetries an observer would find only the random transitions, a beautiful picture of intricate time relationships would unravel only in the frequency-time-intensity plots. In the fractal information theory (FIT), all the tree time cycles run simultaneously and contains lots of vital information than that could be extracted from the system. ***One can never finish reading all the information because reality sphere cannot be read by any single observer fully ever***. Thus, the fundamentals of information that computer scientists conceptualized over the last hundred years would disappear as soon as we enter the domain of Fractal information theory (FIT).

2.2. Basics of fractal information theory (FIT) and *"nested time cycle"*:

First, the technical details of the geometric shapes are written on the cycle perimeter of a time cycle. Fractal tape is a fractal clock, thus, the computation time is always zero (Ghosh, Sahu, Fujita, & Bandyopadhyay, 2014).

Second, the perceived geometry created by the groups of elementary geometries are grouped repeatedly, group of groups form a higher-level geometry. The process continues until the highest-level singular geometry is reached, it means at the top level there will be only one geometric structure, e.g. a triangle or a circle. Thus, the information structure contains information about the higher-level dynamics.

Third, since the triplet time cycles orient in a 3D arrangement, all-possible perspectives of an observer are mapped on the "reality sphere" (Figure 2a).

Fourth, in a packet of information, nothing is isolated, all the cells of a fractal tape are represented by the triplet cycles and these triplet units make 3D loops, which hold the question-answer or QA couplets in a larger time cycles. Triplets are minimum sets, there could be quartet or even higher.

Fifth, QA time cycles self-assemble to build hierarchical network of time-cycles, which is a learning system. This network grows perpetually with the environment.

Sixth, unlike bits or qubits, here in the fractal information theory (FIT), there is no isolated information unit, the units are always highly interconnected like fractal to eventually create a single cell of a fractal tape. It means the total amount of information is always one time cycle or one, since log of 1 is 0, hence total information content of a fractal tape is zero. This is why existing information theories would fail in explaining the FTM.

Seventh, no one can read the reality sphere entirely, from different directions, it is different, & there are infinite possible directions. All reality spheres interact and constitute a new pattern as a function of time perpetually.

Eighth, ***no memory is required, perpetual cyclic rotation is memory; no algorithm is required, the learning is spontaneous and the perception based logical argument grows, no collapse is required, decision is retrieved without computation, no reduction of choices, no logic gate and no switch is required.***

Ninth, there is no "real" domain in the fractal tape, the cell that is under consideration do not contribute to its own value. This is surprising, the cells below create an imaginary world, the cells above create an imaginary world and the observer uses own imaginary world to find the weight of time cycles, ***the cell that is being measured contributes nothing when it is estimated, but of course when neighbors are estimated, it contributes.***

Ten, the unpredictability is enormous, on a single fractal tape three observers measuring the cell state at three different domains simultaneously would affect each other's measurement, but would never detect it, measurement of a single cell in the fractal tape may affect the entire chain, depending on the position of system points in the entire network at that point.

The ***information content of a fractal tape system resides in the connectivity and the associated geometry encoded by the 3D oriented 2D circles.*** Three time cycles when self-assemble generate a Cycloid, Trochoid, Epicycloid, Hypocycloid, Epitrochoid or Hypotrochoid connections; the projection of these coupled time cycles are a stream of binary pulses. Such binary pulses we observe abundant in nature, we consider those binary streams as the information of nature, but that is an illusion. As far as the hardware is concerned, ***a fractal information processing hardware is also a fractal in the arrangement of its structural symmetry and different images/stream of pulses are integrated as a set of periodic vibration of the system at different layers in this structure.*** Thus, the information is defined in the geometry of three- time-cycle arrangement. A cell of the fractal tape is made of three time cycles, it means in the hardware, the basic nested time cycle processing unit would never be a switch. Rather, the devices that can vibrate in three resonance bands separated by distinguishable gaps in the frequency spectrum, which generate periodic vibrations like a closed loop. It is not possible in any conventional materials structure; one such possibility is the vortex or spiral structures arranged fractally. There is another physical significance of the triplet time cycles. The concerned time cycle needs to couple to a slower and a faster clock simultaneously. Fractal tape machine (FTM) operating with time cycles enables every single cell of the fractal tape self-sustainable, complete to be read and at the same time incomplete as it changes continuously due to the interaction with the imaginary worlds of the neighboring cells of the same tape, there is no finite state for any cell anywhere in the fractal tape.

The "reality sphere" created by three imaginary nested time cycles is a complex number set built on the surface of the sphere; the longest time in the coupled structure (observer-tape) determines its diameter. ***The observer-fractal-tape coupling depends on the geometric specification of the observers nested time cycle's and the nested time-cycle structure of the entire fractal tape. Both the nested time cycle resonates to precisely identify where to locate the observer***, and then, the "reality sphere" of all the cells of the fractal tapes are generated. ***Self-similarity is only in the fact that all units of information has three interconnected circles, but the information written on the circle perimeter are all different.*** Therefore, even the use of "fractal" is different for the fractal tape machine (FTM) and the advocates of fractal holographic

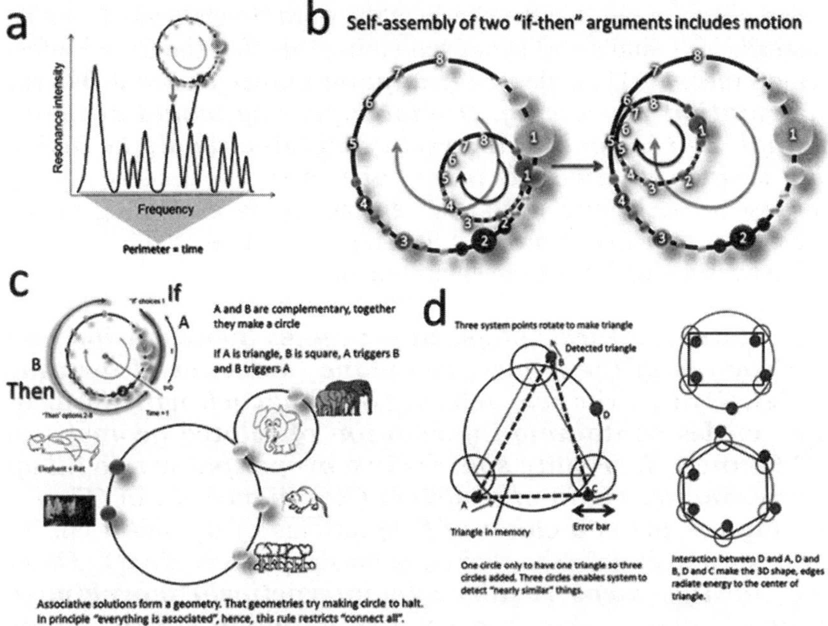

FIGURE 4

a. Resonance band forms a time cycle. b. how two basic time cycles nest. c. How a solution is made using a nested time cycle. d. how geometric information is encoded in a time cycle.

brain or fractal antenna engineers. The incomplete linking in the fractal tape machine (FTM) made of the time cycles makes it a time resolution controller, due to the variation of wide ranges of time, the decisions are often an illusion of a faster time-cycle-triplet. ***An observer always observes that the solution is derived instantly, while the fact is that the information enters inside a single cell passes through the various layers and their clocks, syncs with the decision and returns much before the processing cell makes one "tick". This is how an observer always finds computation time in a fractal tape always zero for an observer.***

In a fractal tape machine (FTM), since it is made of time cycles, ***the geometry of the vibrational frequencies in the cells changes from teardrop shape to ellipsoid/sphere (variation of time gap=variation in the slope of the curve), but when it reaches the ellipsoid shape, the ellipsoid tries to become a teardrop once again***. Since transition from a teardrop to an ellipsoid requires a large number of steps, however, the major weakness of a conventional fractal system that a few geometries repeat over the entire scale does not arise here. This is extremely important, we do not detail, however, we simply point out that the choice of the word "fractal" should not be misread, "self-similarity" is not something that that the fractal information theory (FIT) endorses. ***If anyone wants to see a fractal information processing, fractal tape, one would see only a single cell in reality, the rest everything would be inside that single cell, invisible to any observer.*** The decision making universe is a singular fractal net encompassing everything in the universe in principle, it means fractal tape cannot be used for computation by isolating it from the environment.

Emulating nature's physical processes by expansion and contraction of the triplet seed plane (diameter of the time cycle), (i) fill up the perimeters of the time cycle with the local time cycles containing information of related geometries. (ii) Connect the reality spheres in a proper pattern to fill up the resonance chain of a system (Resonance chain (Figure 2b, Figure 4a) is a chain of frequencies of a fractal cavity resonator (Ghosh, Sahu, Fujita, & Bandyopadhyay, 2014***). These are the two steps required to interactively morphing a natural system; this is a process mapping epistemology***. While doing so, the phase space pattern produced is the analogue of equation and the morphed structure is the model because it projects a solution created by a theory. Thus, one could establish a one to one correspondence.

2.3. The philosophy of reductionism vs the philosophy of morphism: When a few atoms arrange in an order, it's a **symmetry**, to do any work we need to change the ordering of atoms or symmetry, when the symmetry breaks, it accounts to information processing. When the symmetry breaks so much on a surface that it changes the temporal dynamics of its 3D structure, then we call it a **phase transition, it changes the resonance chain (Figures 2b, 4a)**. When the phase transition is such that the observable natural properties change fundamentally, we call it **transformation**. If the transformation is so robust that the system changes its sensing and the processing ability with its immediate interactive environment, we call it **morphism**. ***We define Morphism explicitly in the context of filling up the resonance chain (Figure 2b), so that the Bloch spheres emulate nature's event (Figure 2a), information is filled up in the empty time-cycles (Figure 4c). It is neither the morphism in mathematics (map between two structures),* (Morphism, 2001) *nor the morphism in biology (way to evolution),* (Huxley, 1955)**. Morphing is used in the image processing as transformation from one structure to another via an intermediate step (Hu, Li & Zhang, 2004).

Reductionism inherently considers that a complex natural system contains redundant sub-systems and contemplates that those subsystems could be replaced with a few much simpler parts, yet do the same work. The replacement philosophy is weak, the simpler analogue cannot do the same work as the original machine, it would do a desired part of the whole. Reductionism is flawless, only if the reduction does not eliminate any multitasking of the original system. If, both the nature and the humans are defining information similarly, both need the same number of tools to represent the same object. Existing logical computing captures a random information from nature using discrete sensors and then link those responses using imagination & intuition to fit two observations captured again by some sensors, the theory derived mathematical expression is not system-derived, rather, imagination and intuition derived. Then, "bits/qubits" & logic gates are the tools to plot the expression that links the imagination-derived relations between the two observations of nature.

Because of its multi-tasking & random captures by human sensors, the nature appears as un-smart or slow compared to the manmade machines, it might be programmed to use the minimum tools. A human eye always blinks and a robot can mimic it, but the straightforward reductionism neglects the enormous complex tasks that the human blinking does, —unfathomable by a normal eye blinking robots. A robot mimics a person's walking does not mean "we understand walking", but we simply fail to note that the same person can walk differently every single time he walks through the road. The complexity science tries to perfect "mimicking", puts failures in error bar. Thus, ***the historical debate of reductionism has always asked a wrong question, the right question would be "what are the minimum tools used by nature to do the simplest task?"*** The answer lies in the construction of the triplet imaginary worlds, which is simply the beginning.

While it is obvious that the existing culture of doing science, which was proposed initially by Bertrand Russell and then Turing, in the early 20th century, has several limitations, an alternative route is not an easy task. We need to learn the true structure of the fundamental information unit in nature and then determine how that information is integrated. Surprisingly ***no natural system is mapped for the entire frequency spectrum to get a complete map as a function of time, which we did for a decade and experimentally discovered the fundamental information processing structure of nature and identified the resonance chain and frequency fractal to integrate that information. This is how the concept of a fractal tape was originated.***

A fractal tape is found to have the ability to morph a natural system, the information unit grows by self-assembly such that it adapts to all possible symmetries of nature derived from the arrangement of prime numbers. Mostly, we have studied the biophysics of protein and its complexes and created artificial materials by organic synthesis to verify the potential of this new information structure; however, more database will be generated supporting the unique information structure's potential in future. ***We do not understand the engineering of nature; "fractal tape machine (FTM)" is a possible "comparing unit" that is a skeleton of the information storage, it learns to fill the gaps by itself and builds the 3D information circuits encompassing three imaginary worlds, encompassing the entire frequency spectrum of the natural system. This is what we call morphing, "mimicking is not in the look or primitive actions, mimicking the whole frequency spectrum is what morphing stands for"***.

2.4 Instead of bridging the discontinuity, can we harness non-differentiability?

2.4.1. When both "if" and "then" are undefined, we cannot mathematically argue that a pure argument exists: A fractal tape is non-differentiable everywhere, hence, no equation could be constructed to generate a complete solution for any parameter of a fractal tape as we do it often in the quantum & classical mechanics. In those mathematical formulations, a function with an imaginary number brings "spatial and temporal" contribution from nowhere to affect the system and generate a "certainty". ***In a fractal tape, three complex time functions representing three imaginary time cycles of a cell interact, as the tapes of various layers edit the "time" of a cell simultaneously three time cycles change their orientation and relative diameters.*** In quantum, the discontinuity could never be bridged; in a ***fractal tape that is continuous everywhere, the discontinuity is bridged by the observer's time loop detection resolution***. This resolution is automatically determined by the smallest set of time loops (frequencies written on the perimeter of the time-cycle) that matches between the nested time cycles of the observer-cell system. For over a decade, we have explored simultaneity over a large number of molecular systems (Bandyopadhyay, Nittoh, Wakayama, Yagi, & Miki, 2006; Bandyopadhyay, & Wakayama, 2007; Bandyopadhyay, Sahu, Fujita & Wakayama, 2010; Ghosh, Fujita & Bandyopadhyay, 2015; Ghosh et al., 2014; Bandyopadhyay, Sahu & Fujita, 2009), and we have studied the evolution of temporal events to mimic the natural processes like evolution of cancer and radioactivity. Recently, we have designed and synthesized a 7 nm wide an organic supramolecular system that is by design quantum mechanical and would operate by itself, a universal sensor that senses the environment, learns rules and responds. Any such single decision making device is asked about its state, it would respond optically, ***"I am a cavity located inside a cavity... and at each layer I am made of multiple cavities self-assembled side-by-side". The cavities are leaky and arranged in a helical symmetry such that when exposed to an energy source, the cavities leak and absorb energy at the same time, thus, the periodicity emerges in its energy transmission along the spiral path that is what makes the time-cycles or rhythms. Since no two cavities are identical in the finite spiral pathway, equilibrium is never reached; the nested rhythm or nested time cycles operate as long the energy source exists.***

2.4.2. Decision-making is NOT a logical operation, then, how correct are the solutions derived by a fractal tape? Logical operation means executing a "if-then" statement (Figure 4b), i.e. the "then" statement is executed for a given "if" statement. In a fractal tape, if we draw an analogy then, we put both "if" and "then" statements on a single time cycle, written as a set of frequencies. Nevertheless, still, we cannot assign as logical decision-making, because, ***"if" is not defined as it has many "if-then" statements inside, reading a statement would not complete, both "if" and "then" could continue changing perpetually in principle.*** Every single "if" and "then" statement remains incomplete, everywhere in the tape, undefined. It is amazing to state that every single pixel on the time-cycle is undefined; frequencies are written on the perimeter as local time cycles, a set of frequencies hold geometric information of a typical 1D, 2D or 3D structure (Figure 4c). ***Hence, the existence of a typical geometry say a time-cycle is a perception since the frequencies on the time cycles of the sensor matches to that of an observer.*** In the collection of nested circles, some circles are so big (slow, long period) that an observer cannot find their limit, it assigns imaginary boundary of the set and then, some circles are so small that the observer considers those as points. ***Journey through a fractal tape is a continuous effort to convert a point into a circle in the information space and this journey is endless, at a time the observer senses only a few circles, and several points to go further beyond its boundaries.***

2.5. All fractal tapes are not non-Turing: Fractal Turing tapes exist since 1979: 2.5.1 Anything that could be written on a piece of paper using an arrow diagram is Turing compatible:

Branching out indefinitely from a single cell does not make a non-Turing tape, each branch could be a new Turing tape, cluster of operating Turing tapes in parallel is not new, just an extension of the original Turing tape concept. Also, historically cellular automaton and several other computing constructs, wherein simultaneity is profoundly presents, i.e. which operates via group of cell states operating together, have been mathematically shown to be a Turing class. Fractal tape concept came way back in 1979 and quasi-linear time, or addressing the time property as operational sum of fractal tapes (Gurevich & Shelah, 1989), however, as Turing himself argued, ***if the statements are complete, and could be written on a piece of paper, it could be programmed using a finite state machine***.

2.5.2. Different routes of hyper-computing: Now, if a statement could not be written on a piece of paper, then, a finite state machine cannot work. If we take another paper above, or below or side-by-side the paper on which the statement is written, then again we can add Turing machines representing the papers. Increasing the complexity of a Turing tape network does not ensure failing of a Turing tape (Siegelmann, 1995; Ziegler, 2005; Hamkins & Lewis, 2000; Davis, 2006), but we remain within the domain of Turing, this is the reason Hyper-computing or Super Turing are the same Turing machine with a new look (Davis, 2006). ***Simultaneity, entanglement, super-position all the hallmarks of quantum is Turing compatible, just one has to use different Turing tapes, no one can break the Turing paradigm. Even the inclusion of multi-verses, or parallel universes with different imaginary times or worlds are also Turing compatible. The information structure of the fractal tape has three imaginary worlds and one could easily assign three separate Turing tapes to process them.*** Therefore, classical, quantum or fractal, no existing routes can go beyond the Turing compatibility.

2.5.3. Among all the fractal classes only the escape time fractal class could lead to non-Turing decision-making: If we have an escape time fractal (Milnor, 1989), then the scenario is different. Above, we discussed fractal branching which belongs to the class of iterative function system (IFS) type fractals (Frame, 1998). However, if there is a situation when every single cell of a Turing tape holds another Turing tape inside, then, the Turing compatibility fails. Managing the undefined functions is a task that Turing machine could never perform. ***The fractal tape and the fractal information theory (FIT) is meticulously designed conceptually so that it executes a robust management of the singularity situations wherein***

function is undefined. This is possible because time cycles are like rings that a system sends in the singularity holes, the rings of various diameters fits and sends signals about all details where a function collapses. This is what we have been arguing since last couple of years. Note the fractal path problem of divergence in the quantum electrodynamics, discussed earlier, had to face the same reason for which the Turing protocol becomes inapplicable. This is an undefined network everywhere, we ***start the formulation from a Turing tape but inclusion of a single condition "every cell should have a tape inside" eventually transform mathematically such that none of the tapes are actually the Turing tape***.

2.5.4. Making an infinite undefined network of cells is difficult, but after the creation, even using such a tape is trivial: How to compute in an undefined tape? If an undefined state is converted to a finite state element, it returns to the Turing paradigm. For every single cell that is a door to another tape, the upper and the lower time limits of the cells of a fractal tape are to be bridged; this bridging requires a conceptual construct that is finite and infinite at the same time. ***What could that mathematical construct be, which is detected as finite and dynamically infinite or leads to an infinite process at the same time? It is a time cycle, looping around it leads to an infinite path, but at the same time, it is finite with a well-defined perimeter. Hence, we derived the concept of time cycle to bridge the undefined perimeters, thus, do not return to the Turing paradigm, at the same time harness the power of "morphing".***

2.6. Why circular path is essential in a Fractal tape machine (FTM)?

2.6.1 Fractal tape network is a divergent system: the fundamental issue of halting in a circle: There is no typewriter in a fractal tape machine (FTM), like the one we have in a Turing machine that instructs its cells, "where to go", even no one tells them "what to do" and there is no process by which "section of choice" occurs. We assign all the cells in a Fractal tape machine (FTM) independent, each time cycle holds a system points to decide on their own. In the conventional wisdom of fractals, the geometry of the fractals provide paths, however, there is no provision inside the tape to control the cells, their states.

Second, since a fractal tape has no beginning and no end, ***a time-cycle is an "infinite path" path for those who walk along the perimeter of the time-cycle, for an external observer, a time***

cycle is perceived only as the diameter of a barrier (time-cycle diameter ~ energy). Third, ***while designing the information structure we do not draw any circle corresponding to the real cell that the observer is actually measuring,*** we draw one for the observer, one for the world below and one for the world above. ***Interestingly, when we consider a cell below or above, the time-cycle for the device under current measurement appears. In this way, a time-cycle remains defined and undefined at the same time***. , i.e. the circle perimeters of the time cycles connect with the other time cycles in a fractal wiring. In the existing world of fractals, it's all about modifying the real world and create an architecture using the "term" from an imaginary world. However, though the term "fractal" is used, the nesting of time cycles beyond two undefined boundaries of a cell is fundamentally different from the conventional "fractal", where self-similarity is an essential criterion. One interesting aspect is that the system points in a fractal tape network increase as the branching goes out and it's a pure divergent system at all ends, the network therefore does not have any limit in any direction.

The concept of a virtual halt: If many system points located on the various isolated time cycles start interacting, all of them could be part of a new unified time cycle wherein the system point does not halt, but the cluster of isolated time cycles would come to a virtual halt. ***Since a cascade activation of the time cycles that could propagate through the infinite pathways of the fractal tape, could be restricted in that virtual unified time-cycle, it would be a virtual halt***. The largest time cycle that is created in the fractal tape by the self-assembly of several local isolated time cycles (Figure 4b) to represent a problem ensures when to halt how to halt, it does not decide, but with its formation the decision is made. The halting problem has been one of the most fundamental issues related to Turing tape philosophy. Just by introducing the concept of forming a virtual time cycle, a fractal tape network ensures that the multiple "time" worlds could interact with their own imaginary identity, i^n=0 to -1, where n is a natural number and by keeping original information intact resolve a problem. Thus, an infinite number of imaginary worlds (one cell has three worlds, but there are many such cells) can affect a single cell independently and the geometric shape of time-cycle ensures that halting at every step in the entire fractal tape network, thus, ***a problem and a solution that gets self-assembled in a single virtual cycle spontaneously stops propagating, randomly.***

2.6.2 Further significance of having a time-cycle as information processing unit: Several cells represented as the time cycles in the fractal tape network become independent system points and interact, then, we need three special properties of the cells. Each cell should interact with all the cells inside, each cell could be part of the millions of cells above and below. Hence, ***a cell of a fractal tape should have the property to bond with the cells in the same layer, or time domain, and then various weak bonding with the cells of the tapes below and above is required to morph the "reality sphere"***. A circle does two remarkable things, if the system point moves around the time-cycle perpetually, then, it stores the memory and if the question and answer are written along the perimeter then even if one asks solution, the question is retrieved. Therefore, memory and decision making is done in the same device, if we consider a cell of fractal tape as a circular system. We need a special device as cells for a fractal tape machine (FTM): (i) ***triplet of triplet***: the device should have three global clocks to operate independently at least in three time domains simultaneously, which means three interconnected time cycles. Inside each of the three clocks there should be a triplet of clocks (two clocks to couple with the worlds below and above and one to store the information), because global clocks do not engage in the information storage & processing. (ii) ***Periodic oscillations***: At the same time, it should process rhythms or rotation in a circle like a simple harmonic motion or periodic oscillations. (iii) ***Editing the frequencies or local time cycles***: a hardware provision is required to edit the question and answer written on the perimeter of the time-cycle. Possibly, an user should be able to tune the geometry of the cells to be used in a fractal tape machine (FTM), like the diameter of a circle could naturally be edited in the system.

2.7 Self-assembly of clocks or circles: The making of a fractal tape machine (FTM): The concept of fractal tape machine (FTM) made of clocks never existed before, and we have created this concept (fractal of clocks) (Ghosh, Sahu, Fujita, & Bandyopadhyay, 2014) only to allow many system points to interact with each other causally. ***Integration of time cycles is not done logically, it is done causally, which means several time cycles integrate to complete a virtual time loop, not as instructed by algorithm***. Such a "***causal integration of "reality spheres" (this is the fundamental drive to decision making in the Fractal tape)***" ensures that no external user is essential to operate the fractal tape. Since the self-assembly of time cycles accesses the diameter of a time cycle and perimeter of this circle is used to keep time management between various local time loops, a loop geometry has several unique significances. The fundamental information-processing unit is a triplet of imaginary time planes containing time cycles, however, when several such triplets self-assemble during the self-assembly of "reality spheres" then, the system for the survival of distinct information does not allow two planes to have the single orientation. As a result, a super-spiral or spiral of a spiral made of a sphere (fractal cavity resonator) is a possible choice to make a system that can demonstrate three inter-connected time circles at a much longer time scale. Time processed by each circle, operates two clocks made of spirals and one clock made of sphere, determine three nested clocks, the energy travels through the wiring back and forth. Finally, ***by changing the basic geometry of the sphere from tear-drop to an ellipsoid one could edit the oscillation frequency packets, or even by changing the geometric spiral parameters one could redefine the specific values of the frequencies in the imaginary cavity resonator wherein the spirals and the sphere reside.*** All circles would have an upper and a lower time limits to sync (error in time = deviation in the perimeter length), since the inverse of frequency is time we can use resonant frequencies for clocking. Use of resonance frequency for clocking has another advantage, it allows other time-cycles to match the frequencies and self-assemble. Therefore, three time-cycles or triplets are essentially the cell of a fractal tape, with just one system point controlling the reality sphere, whose job is to periodically triggering different frequencies in a loop, located along the perimeter of the time-cycle. During "***causal integration of reality spheres" (this is the fundamental drive to decision making, and it is the fundamental drive to morphing)***, which is self-assembly of a group of three nested cycles or triplets, a new time-cycle appears so that the two system points sustain and in the newly formed time cycle a new system point is generated. ***This is analogous to writing an algorithm***, and not instructed by an external system, if there forms a loop of triplets, a new time cycle is spontaneously formed that connects the nested time cycles (Ghosh, Sahu, Fujita, & Bandyopadhyay, 2014).

2.8 Decision making protocol: If not "computing" then decision-making, but no rejection of choices:

2.8.1. If we want to create a decision-making device without using any logic gate, how that computational world would look like? The fundamental philosophy of a logic gate is to reduce the number of choices by eliminating some of the input options. If we ask for what reason, the logic gate hardware does not hold a reliable answer. ***There is never a decisive logic inside a logic gate. Logic is always outside the logic device***, we imagine the "if-then" argument in our mind to decide which choices are to be accepted and which are to be rejected, and then choose a suitable logic gate to implement that. In a complex scenario, ***intelligence = typical circuit wiring for the current flow through several logic components, which a user decides as an exclusive right, we want this right to be given to a new class of decision making systems***.

Non-logical decision-making means no reduction of choices, no random selection on what to do. In reality, the question and the answer would store as a single unit such that if one is activated the other one would respond. If there is never a reduction process, then, how can one choose the most favored one? ***A the simplest level, we consider a time-cycle wherein query and answers are written side by side along the perimeter of the time-cycle, the system point rotates along the time-cycle and all the input conditions and the output decisions activate simultaneously. Queries self-assemble as the reality spheres self-assemble spontaneously in the fractal tape, these patterns are analogous to the mathematical formulations***. If computation means reduction or making a choice following a logical process then it is not computation, ***the pattern of "reality spheres" never reduces a choice yet all possible decisions are presented, even for those queries which were never asked***. If one searches answer for a query in an infinite pool of similar time-cycles, and the right time-cycle can sense the query as it matches a similar query on its perimeter, the vibrational energy starts rotating along the perimeter, thus, the time-cycle would encounter the solution on its way. Then ***spontaneously reply back*** the answer to the seeker, ***so we do not need CMOS like circuits, one could perform a "search without searching". A fractal tape machine (FTM) that we envision is capable of filtering any event into a nest made of these elementary circles.***

2.8.2. How decisions are encoded in the time-cycle of materials? Materials design and writing geometries in its vibrations: We consider specific resonant vibrational frequencies as the information encoding parameter and every single sensory information is decomposed into the composition of ***basic geometries like triangle (Figures 4c, 4d), circle, octahedral shapes as the language of information processing for the input and the output decisions***. For example, let us construct a question-answer or QA couple; if the input condition is a triangle then the answer could be a square. First, we need to find a route to write a geometric shape in a circular path. For that, we need a singular function protocol that would deliver all essential shapes. Here we demonstrate one example of using hyperbolic function, there could be alternative routes. Any line could be generated by using a hyperbolic function of time t, and using those functions suitably we can determine the frequencies essential to create a 2D or 3D shape. The choice of vibrational frequencies is not random; it is determined by a hyperbolic function and if we want to implement the decision-making using a material, then, the materials symmetry needs to be chosen such that their resonance frequencies follow exactly those suggested by the hyperbolic function. Say, to encode a triangle (3) and a square (4) we need to encode say 10 (3+4+3) resonance frequencies in a device that periodically oscillates between 10 resonance frequencies. Since triangle is the condition or input and the square is the choice or output, both exist side by side, if one activates the triangle by resonating with its typical resonance frequencies, then, the picture of the square would appear to the user since the system point would start rotating around the time-cycle (Figure 4c). Now, this is one possible way of encoding the condition-choice duality. The angle of the triangle is the "silence" period in the time loop, error in detection is auto-corrected (Figure 4d).

Now, no one needs to write a software code to operate the device, it acts like a sensor that senses the typical resonance frequencies for a triangle and **spontaneously reply** back the answer, square. If more than one, conditions are encoded and multiple geometries and multiple decisions are also encoded, the complete set re-distributes the energy and starts vibrating, together (Figure 4c). Now, in a single time-cycle, frequencies are played at a certain time gap, this is essential for generating a particular geometric shape when those frequencies vibrate. However, this is exactly how Indian classical music is composed, Indians try to find ***a correct set of 12 frequencies in a loop (Indian classical raga is 7 frequencies up and 7 frequencies down, 7X2=14, but 2 points are common) to create the right mood in the mind of people***.

In a giant network of time-cycles of condition and choices as described above, we would have a situation, wherein, only the choices selected by the external user would activate and the rest would remain silent. In a pool of infinite number of time cycles, each isolated individual time-cycle is capable of taking spontaneous response for the generic query, "if this and this and this and ... then?". ***The corresponding time-cycle network is spontaneously written by deforming the material, its vibrational sequence make a time-cycle, along the perimeter of the time-cycle, all geometric shapes are encoded. However, these time-cycles could spontaneously self-assemble by making real chemical or physical bonds. It could by itself create a "for" loop, time-cycles in the infinite pool could get connected one inside another.*** Below we describe how simply by connecting the circles differently a system can execute all possible operations that a software programming does.

2.9 Circuiting the condition-choice circles: self- decision making

2.9.1 Self- decision making is when a new time-cycle is spontaneously born via self-assembly of different problem and answer triplets: One of the primary problems of Turing world's computing is that we need to think every single possibility and their relationships, then, encode those instructions as sequence of simple tasks so that the logic gates perform the task. We can imagine beforehand what would be the nature of the solution, then, we can artificially induce a noise to mimic "brain like unpredictability". ***The Turing intelligence is in the code, if logicians have missed guessing a future event, the computing would be erroneous. Is it possible ever to do decision making without external instruction?*** For a single time-cycle described above, we do not need any software or logic gate, if we ask a question; the system would answer correctly, because it holds the solution in it beforehand. Moreover, ***when the network of time-cycles grows by self-assembly, then, new questions are born, at the same time, the new answers are also generated in the new time-cycle, this process does not stop, because fractal tape machine (FTM) does not reside inside a physical boundary. No time-cycle is ever born without taking the answer circles, thus, ensuring that when an unknown question would be asked to the system, the system cooks a new time-cycle and there is no need to program it. This is the self- decision making.***

2.9.2 However, if the complexity increases, can the system continue to do self- decision making? ***Every question that we ask is part of a bigger question or it holds many queries within, no query could just be born out of nothing. This is the fundamental principle of contextual argument.*** Therefore, three logical layers make the simplest unit of a condition-choice decision-making system. Let us consider that the triangle-square scenario is originated during the query of an ellipse for which pentagon is an answer. Similarly, triangle holds a query straight line inside, and a hexagon is its answer. ***Therefore, query inside a query inside a query is a route that is not easy to integrate in a CMOS sequential processor; the fractal tape machines are extremely compatible to that. On the other hand, sequential arguments are not at all advantageous to encode in a fractal tape machine (FTM), because then it turns to a Turing machine.***

2.9.3 What happens during nesting of three time cycles: Detailed operational analysis of the fundamental information-processing unit of a fractal tape:

The time-cycles when self-assemble could get connected three ways, one inside another, on top of each other and all touching each other externally. Then, after contact, they would rotate relative to each other. When ***three circles are connected such that one is inside/top/outside another, then, the frequency points on the inner time-cycle touch the common frequency points, i.e. both the frequency points would play together. Just by these rotations, they perform "for-next" loop, the inner time-cycle executes an "if-then" statements by itself, it is fixed, but every time the inner time-cycle completes its loop, a different arc of the larger time-cycle is covered.*** Since the "if" and "then" statements cover different arc parts of the larger or the host time-cycle, the inner guest time-cycle contact to each arc region generates a unique condition and its response. The set of frequencies including the host's arc and the guest's total perimeter together provide a unique condition-decision couplet. Now, these two time-cycles, a guest host system becomes a part of another time-cycle, i.e. another host, then, it is equivalent to the algorithmic programming of a loop inside a loop.

All the time cycles rotate continuously, but to have a distinct temporal impact on the "reality sphere", a particular point on the smaller guest time-cycle should touch the host time-cycle say at least 8 times during a complete rotation, otherwise, the host's circular identify would be questioned. Thus, in a nest of three time-cycles, the smallest time-cycle rotates sufficient number of times (say 8) to complete the time-cycle perimeter and thus triggers the time-cycle of medium diameter to rotate multiple times (say 8) so that it completes the path for the large time-cycle. ***Hence, together a triplet of time-cycles executes 64 distinct condition-decision couplets.*** Thus, a physical rotation of three circles executes a complex decision making process. Note that every single isolated time-cycle has circles inside it is not a Turing machine; moreover, all time cycles are imaginary the observer sees only the "reality sphere".

If all the three time-cycles are made of specific number of frequencies (we represent each frequency by drawing small circles on the perimeter) each, say, 8, then, the smallest time-cycle acts as a counter to its next upper time-cycle, which also acts as a counter to its next upper time-cycle, thus, the time management is also performed simultaneously. ***Larger the time-cycle, longer is the time to rotate, which eventually increases the time to retrieve a decision.*** While the length of the perimeter determines how long the choice-decision process would execute, the diameter of the time-cycle determines the energy or operational frequency required for the process. Therefore, we would like to clarify that, ***an isolated time-cycle does not know its own time, the passing of time is relative. It only knows the time gaps between different frequencies as it compares the relative distances, so the first clock measures the ratio of the arc lengths between two frequencies inside one time-cycle.*** Then how would it compare time relative to other circles? Therefore, comes the question of another clock, which arises when two or more circles couple.

The second clock operates as the ratio of the diameters of the two circles that couple. Operational frequency increases when three circles are one inside another, and decreases when one outside another and remains constant when on top of another. This is how the second clock operates. ***The second clock is independent of the first clock that mainly works to preserve the geometric purity of the information content, while the second clock determines which specific conditions or solutions of the host would generate another condition-decision event.*** Thus, on the perimeter of the time-cycle, resides the particulars of a memory as condition-decision, and in the coupling information resides the specific association of memory as associative condition-decision. Only if multiple rotations of an associative memory or the small time-cycle are completed, the time-cycle above or host's decision-making is completed. The lower time-cycle or guest's logical operation completes with a complete rotation, thus, it sets the time for the next logical operation for the coupled system. ***Therefore, clocking and maintaining time is an essential feature of the triplets.*** Since bonding between the two time-cycles are the common frequencies, the similarity between the geometric shapes are automatically taken into account when two distant circles are nearby, and that vibrational coupling led to attract each other and tries to form a compound structure, which could also be said as nesting of two rhythms. ***Geometrical association is beyond-logical association and that is an inherent property of self-assembly of "reality spheres".*** However, this concept has far-reaching consequences. A nest of three cycles means a decision making protocol with two hands to self-assemble with other similar decision making protocols. Just imagine, if a time-cycle is made of 8 frequencies then, a triplet of triplet would mean 72 frequencies at the lowest level. ***A triplet could hold 8^3 condition-decision system, a triplet of triplet means $8^3X8^3X8^3 = 512X512X512 = 134217728 \sim 10^9$. A billion arguments could simultaneously co-exist in a triplet of triplet of an octave system, or in just 9 circles.***

The complexity of the argument is addressed by the system spontaneously in an automated manner. ***Wherever it is essential, the time-cycles couple each other and reconfigure, thus, generating a set of new and new arguments perpetually.*** The fractal tape machine (FTM) does not have any restriction to that particular constraint. It means, the system can spontaneously learn any new condition-decision set and add that to a suitable place in the growing network. This particular feature provides a great ability to the decision-making system under automated construction.

2.10 Creation of a frequency fractal chain or a resonance chain:

2.10.1. Key rules of the nested time-cycle self-assembly: one to one correspondence with the materials self-assembly: The bandwidth & the frequency distribution of the resonance chain is essential for the sustainable self-assembly of the time-cycles in the infinite pool of time-cycles generated by the fractal tape network. Say, a time-cycle has 8 frequencies, what are the values it can take? 1Hz, 2Hz, 3Hz... if the system does not keep a proper gap between the two frequency values, then, they cannot self-assemble, continuously. ***What is the rule that a system would follow so that the frequency gap enables the system to add more and more circles without any hindrance?***

The first concern for the self-assembly of circles is that we are not writing any program to implement the self-assembly, it would be a material typically made of oscillators that would have the quality to periodically repeat oscillation following a set of frequencies at specific time gap that could be editable as per the external requirement. Now, if all time-cycles have identical frequencies, then there is no new information. Therefore, they should be different in the encoded frequency values, if distinct information is required to encode. Now, a basic rule of an oscillator is that for higher frequencies, the dimension of an oscillator is generally less, and for the smaller frequencies, the dimension of the oscillator should increase in size. In addition, the self-assembly of time-cycles could happen in two different ways. First, when two circles touch each other at one point (for multiple point contact, it should be an ellipse and a time-cycle), in these cases, one activates the other, instead of a periodic, a cascade unidirectional propagation of energy is observed. Second, two or three time-cycles rotate around each other in three different ways. In the second case, for a combined periodicity, the smaller oscillators, or the high frequency oscillators should remain inside. It means two different kinds of self-assembly of materials would take place, first, when materials would get connected side by side, second, when materials would grow one above another. We have shown two different kinds of self-assembly of oscillators, escape time system and the iterative function system.

2.10.2 Why did we experimentally observe a power of 10 (approximately) in the resonance chain: Say, we have a time-cycle with 10 frequencies writing on its perimeter, thus, holding the triangle and a square geometric shape. Now, 1/10th of its diameter, we imagine another time-cycle to rotate inside/on/outside the perimeter. Until now, we have been discussing that this particular smaller time-cycle would physically rotate, which is possible, just like enzymes and chemicals do in the human body. However, it is naturally possible that 10 smaller circles sit inside the larger time-cycle and execute the same job, and 10 more inside each of those 10 time-cycles. The number of oscillators increases by an order of 10^n. This can happen even when the time-cycles self-assemble side by side (IFS type). ***Therefore, in the infinite pool, two different kinds of circular assemblies would form, in which some circles would remain static not physically rotate and for some, there will be a real physical motion***. However, both the systems would do the same job as described earlier. To explain this analogically, we can have a situation like neuron, where microtubules are static still vibrate at triplet-triplet frequencies. On the other hand, the diffused microtubules play a vital role in the self-assembly process. ***Now we find that smaller the spatial scale we go, the number of oscillators increases as a power of a base number, it means that we have to keep frequency bandwidth left vacant for the enormous number of oscillators representing the time-cycles to pour in.*** We have also argued why do we need at least 8 frequency points on the perimeter. This is the reason we need to keep at least 10 times gap between two frequency values in a time-cycle, this is just to hold one triangle and one square or circle.

The fallacy of fractal would always be there: The entire frequency band is like the Turing tape and one writes frequencies on this tape, just like all hallmarks of quantum is explained by classical mathematical formulations, in a fractal tape, we always have a Turing like processing locally. For example, on a Fractal tape, which frequency do we have to write? If the reader thinks closely, he cannot answer. Each frequency peak contains an infinite number of peaks with variable frequencies inside, and each of them contains infinite numbers of frequencies inside. Therefore, ***no external user is able to write anything to this system, there is no finite value to determine strictly what to write, if they attempt to write, it will be written automatically at various places, surprising the user. The fractal tape user would need to master very different***

skills, only way to use the tape is to change the environment or finding a very complex nested time-cycle to inject into the tape as a singular capsule. This is frequency fractal where there is no differentiable function anywhere, no value in the entire fractal network is complete and no statement could be made on the state of any element of the system anywhere in the network. ***This is what we described as "resonance chain", but no one could ever say how it looks like, it is a fractal chain whose junction points are not exactly defined, one could approximate it.*** We envision, it is the "undefined" feature that makes the biological system self-operational.

2.10.3 Realization of infinite in a finite system:

Why do we restrict ourselves in the triplet-triplet: We have pointed out that some of the oscillators representing the triplet-triplet clock diffuse in the infinite pool of nested time cycles (imagine a liquid of molecules acting as fractal cavity resonators) randomly. Some of them grow as the concrete structures in two different ways. First, one top of another (escape time fractal) and second, side by side (iterative function systems). a triplet-triplet system is a minimum requirement to bind the resonance frequencies. Why do not we think about two or four time-cycles to come together? If we take less than a three time cycles, we have to compromise with the reliability of the waveform produced and if we take more like four time circles, then, it would not add any more information but consume more energy to run. This is the reason, a group of three time cycles is energetically and information wise the optimized number of circles to be considered.

2.10.4. The next question is that why not single triplet, or even triplet-triplet-triplet? We admit that triplet-triplet time cycle network is a complete system, which can perform a specified time-cycles or rhythms and exchange energy in a specific manner with the other triplets; however, it cannot execute a complex decision making. ***Running a rhythm alone is not the foundation of the decision-making, however, editing a rhythm is the decision making in the true sense.*** In a triplet of triplet system, there are three time cycles or rhythms; we need at least three points to make a 2D space (triangle). Similarly, we need three rhythms to generate the condition-decision unit by writing the geometric shapes. However, these rhythms cannot control themselves, we need more. Hierarchical control on the rhythms should be automatic. Just like the way we encode the basic sensory information as the geometric shapes in the infinite pool of time-cycles, similarly, the time cycles self-assemble to form triangle, square and several other geometric shapes. We get a geometric shape inside a geometric shape.

Therefore, we conclude that ***for making a time-cycle or rhythm we need a triplet, but for the self-management of the time-cycles or rhythms we need a triplet of triplet***.

How many triplet-triplet-triplet do we need? For a triplet of triplet system, we get an average reliable waveform to transmit signals to the neighboring systems; however, triplet-triplet-triplet system would be an ideal system to proceed. We have concentrated on the triplet of triplet since we find it experimentally in the biological systems [41-43]. Out of three, one triplet in the elemental biomaterial resonance experiments is never clear because the third triplet gets discrete peaks as soon as it forms higher-level fractal structure by self-assembly. We have seen that ***at least 3 triplet of triplet is essential for constructing a machine that self-programs***, we estimate humans have 12 triplet of triplet. If we enable triplet of triplet of triplet of triplet (3X3X3X3=81 bands) it would be wastage of energy as the optimization of signal transmission in a triplet-triplet fractal tape network is achieved at the triplet-triplet-triplet level (3X3X3=27), no higher level is advantageous.

3 THE DEFINITION OF A FRACTAL TAPE MACHINE (FTM): COMPARISON BETWEEN FRACTAL MACHINE AND TURING MACHINE

3.1 The definition statement for a Fractal Turing tape machine (FTM): We have defined the Fractal tape machine (FTM) in the same way Turing machine is defined. It follows four tuples (i) Information is converted into nested rhythms, (ii) Nested rhythms are absorbed in the decision making matrix and associative time cycles activate, (iii) spontaneously reply back the nested time cylces as solution (iv) change the internal circuits to learn question-answer couple as nested time cycle. **Remarkable changes that would happen in the world of computing and decision making, if a fractal tape and fractal information theory (FIT) is experimentally implemented:**

(1) Multilayered cavity resonator networks or multiple "**nested clocks**" one inside another enable "**a virtual instant decision making**". A question asked to a clock that syncs with output is sent to faster clocks inside, decision delivers before slow clock ticks even for once.
(2) "**Nested cavity**" keeps "**volume intact**" as required resources are poured inside.
(3) "**Spontaneous reply**" enables "**search without searching**". It relies on resonant energy transfer, hence no wiring needed. No logic gate or circuit needed, so "**zero junction hardware**"
(4) The decision making device uses geometric-musical language,

hence "**nested frequency cycles holds geometry**" are basic information not bits. Cycle is memory, rotation is processing, same event, "**no transport needed between memory and processing units**".

(5) Reduction of choices or logic gate is replaced by "**spontaneous activation of many paths**", ability to "**perception capture**".

(6) "**Perpetual spontaneous editing of slower cycles**" (creation/destruction/defragmentation) "**prepare for unknown**" = higher-level learning.

(7) "**No programming required**" as "**cycles self-assemble/ dis-assembly for better sync at all possible time scales simultaneously**".

(8) "**Halting concern irrelevant**" as "**looping nested rhythms of input & memory drives computation**", as soon as the time-cycle forms a close loop, the expansion and feed-forward sync/de-sync drive halts naturally.

(9) "**Nested decoding of sensory signals**" protocol "**captures & preserves hidden dynamics of a phenomenon**", so we do not have to formulate theory, its purity is preserved in an all analogue processing.

(10) "**Equal diameter cycles assemble into a sphere**" enables the estimation of simultaneously operating million paths "**extreme parallelism**". In quantum, measurement disrupts, decreases computing speed, here that cannot.

(11) "**Every component is life like**", as the "**geometry encoded in a cycle changes the hardware**".

(12) Construction and energy transmission in the hardware follows **ordered factor time metric** made fractal tape that operates by fractal mechanics (FM). It is "**beyond quantum computing**" realized by a "**non-differential tape/machine enables multiple imaginary worlds play together**."

(13) Existing sensory resolution is "high" or "low", but we introduce "**fractal resolution**", a complex signal's lowest and fastest time scale signals are absorbed simultaneously, & during expansion the fractal seed delivers output with an unprecedented resolution.

(14) For decision making no energy is required, instead it executes "**noise harvesting**", due to the **nested cavity structure with resonance chain**, each layer absorbs its associated energy naturally from the environment apart from ordered communication.

(15) "**question re-born memory**": Geometry of nested cavity is such that any few sets of frequency as query triggers the same rhythm reproducibly, hence, **holding memory does not require power supply**.

3.2 The concept of fractal mechanics (FM) is inevitable if a new information theory distinct from quantum mechanics is mathematically constructed:

Is there ever any collapse in the Fractal tape: There is no collapse [Ghirardi, Rimini & Weber, 1986); the apparent collapse of an observer is due to its time limits? Three dotted circles make the smallest and the simplest fractal mechanical worldview for a fractal tape; three dotted circles represent three worlds of imaginary time-cycles. Wave function redistributes the probability distribution as a function of time among superposed states, the measurement detects all states in the differently tuned time cycles in a Fractal tape system, it does not need to collapse. Of course, in a local time domain an observer notices collapse, but that is not the reality. Since, an observer fixes the resolution of two coupled imaginary worlds of the fractal tape, it is possible, ***quantum information theory could be deduced from fractal information theory (FIT)***. However, the opposite is not true. ***Whenever we change the fundamentals of information content, we need to build up a new mechanics***. In fractal information theory (FIT) we consider that imaginary time-cycle connects the systems with simultaneity, it means, all the three imaginary time-cycles worlds exist simultaneously. Why, we do not ask that, just as we never ask in quantum why the entanglement exists. This is an important part of our discussion since in fractal information theory (FIT); there are three entanglements to the cell under measurement since each of the three imaginary time-cycle worlds holds one entanglement. ***Only thing missing in the Fractal tape is collapse. There is no reduction either***.

In the fractal information theory (FIT), we are far from both the approaches; we emphasize on the geometry of contextual treatment of a quantum state and provide a generic protocol to address the environment. The supplement to a quantum state is a classical entity in the Bohemian mechanics, while in the fractal information theory (FIT) we intent to replace this supplement with a set of three imaginary worlds as an information architecture, which collectively project and modify multiple realities. This typical bridging between a complete random event and predictability, radically shifts the fractal route from the quantum way. During such a discussion, the predictability takes us to the classical world, then, the math we do, what does that mean in a true classical sense?

3.3. Filling up the gaps, the simultaneity cycles: All these features are included in the fractal information theory (FIT) and there are some more features. Three imaginary terms contribute to reality simultaneously, but not like quantum, ***we do not add the values that we get from three imaginary worlds, and dilute their identity, instead we put them as three co-ordinates on the surface of a sphere***. Thus, each imaginary world contributes partially to all points on the sphere; the point is a generalized complex number. Readers should not mix this concept with the imaginary sphere of quantum made of imaginary and real axes. In fractal information theory (FIT), the "reality sphere" is generated by the observer, since, two other time cycles arrange in 3D orientation with the times cycles of the cell under measurement, and observer couples with this time structure, differently from different directions. Hence, time does not have any direction prior to information is encoded, as soon as we encode information as frequency packet on the time cycles, we get true "information" filled up in the empty space. ***When the time cycle is empty, there is no direction, but as soon as one fills up the cycle, then, there is a direction of motion, since the frequencies are played out one after another.*** This is how arrow of time is born in a time cycle, in three cycles, the directions are different, since all three cycles are arranged in a typical 3D orientation. The most interesting part of this information structure is that the observer finds several events simultaneous. ***Since we consider that a time cycle exists with or without any information or a frequency (represented as a small circle on the time cycle), hence, several frequency packets could be coupled such that if one is played the others would play to ensure the survival of the three cycle net, this is how entanglement is generated here***.

3.4. Quantum logic gates with time cycles decision making: Several articles are there on the quantum logic gates; these are analogous to a classical system operating with a hypothetical infinite speed. Classical gates means, all outputs are predictable. When the quantum compromises with its own conviction, as the "uncertainty" and "probability with certainty" co-exists, the Quantum does not retain its purity. Therefore, a tape that operates with an imaginary time, —an integral feature of a fractal time does not essentially means it is quantum. ***In the quantum treatment with one reality that an imaginary world modifies, unbelievable observations unfold, here in the fractal information theory (FIT), we have a sphere of observed realities by an observer, the number of real world view is not one but infinity***. If we take only a pair of entanglements its quantum, but when at least three such pairs couple in a unique way, we get a construct for the fractal information theory (FIT). Note that ***"imaginary time-cycle" is a giant circle, if we zoom, the pixels isolate, if we zoom more, we***

would see that those points are mere circles, hence apparent continuity is a matter of observer's optical resolution, for fractal information structure, it is temporal resolution. Note that all pixel-resolved circles represent the entangled elements in the quantum mechanics. However, quantum is not interested in what exists inside those entangled particles or circles, and it needs a real world outside the imaginary time-cycle world (for the projection from Hilbert space). In contrast, ***fractal tape cell is itself part of an infinitely extended collection of imaginary worlds as a guest and at the same time hosts an infinitely extended collection of imaginary worlds inside. The two essential criteria makes sure that in a fractal mechanics (FM) the entire information space follows one principle, "an imaginary time-cycle world inside an imaginary time-cycle world inside an imaginary time-cycle world..."***. Hence, even in a particular imaginary time-cycle world, two interacting real circles/particles do not generate a finite, defined real value of any parameters, just as π has a beginning but no end. ***In the fractal tape or a fractal clock worldview, even the reality that exists is only between the interactions of three time circles, analogous to the same space-time configuration is incomplete and undefined. All the worlds within it and all the worlds above are imaginary, yet none of those infinitely distributed worlds above and below are prohibited to contribute, whatever small that might be.***

3.5 Negative time travel in quantum is mystical; and thus has inspired many philosophers of science. In fractal, there is a definitive expression of pattern (analogous to functional map, but not equation) arising out of a well-structured fractal wiring geometry that governs how a set of three imaginary time worlds from different layers of a fractal tape would affect a single cell & the infinitum. In the fractal information theory (FIT), all the pixels in the four time cycles (one real and the three imaginary ones) are static until the information is poured in the form of a tiny time cycles. ***Quantum mechanics has one imaginary world encompassing just the entangled ones; in fractal mechanics (FM) there are at least two imaginary worlds fused to each other in order to construct the fractal pathway. In addition, the third one, that of the observer revolves around the two, to create the sphere of measured values for a typical cell.*** It is so fundamentally different to see that in the fractal information theory (FIT), there is no permanent projection from the Hilbert space to the real space. Here, the sphere of reality created by the three imaginary worlds, for a typical cell in the fractal tape, the network changes with time. ***Then, that sphere of***

real classically observable points would change its shape by interacting with several other spheres generated from the neighbors of the fractal tape. Therefore, every measurement in the fractal information theory (FIT) creates a network of interaction through the infinite network of measurement spheres and that network survives simultaneously encompassing every single cell of the entire fractal tape network. ***Thus, certainty in the network is an important property; however, since time cycles representing the three imaginary worlds run to play its information content that is the circles within, therefore phase mismatch of the information content is the reason for uncertainty, when we consider only one imaginary space-time world, i.e quantum.*** Therefore, here in the introduction to this chapter we have outlined two important features of fractal information theory (FIT). Simply due to the basic structure of the information content, we could explain how entanglement and uncertainty principles come into action.

As the concerned cell in the fractal tape is a host of an imaginary world and itself a guest of another imaginary world at the same time. Hence, the observer measuring the concerned cell does not detect any time passed if events are modified by the imaginary world below, above or coming through the interactions with the other cell's reality spheres. At a given point of time, the fractal tape would appear as an infinite assembly of reality spheres since none of the time cycle triplets representing individual cells are visible (Figure 1a, and Figure 2a).

Thus, ***fractal mechanics (FM) could be reduced to quantum mechanics, or classical mechanics but quantum mechanics or classical cannot be reduced to a fractal mechanics (FM). Therefore, the possibility of a negative time travel seems impossible in fractal mechanics (FM) as "negative time" exists here naturally at all levels as a perception reality of a system, there is no distinction between past, present and future, it is an integrated time cycle.*** No system holds the central importance in a fractal tape network.

3.6 Comparison between the basic concepts of classical, quantum and fractal information theory (FIT):

3.6.1 Three imaginary worlds vs one imaginary world: While classical computing harnesses the discreteness by rejecting the continuum of a real world using a Turing tape, the quantum computing harnesses the two hallmarks of quantum mechanics, entanglement and superposition, again using a quantum version of the same Turing tape. Quantum information theory suggests nothing new philosophically than the Turing philosophy of information processing; the reason is that the domain of uncertainty is not deconstructed. ***Scientifically, uncertainty is not a parameter that could be used in mathematics or any model, uncertainty is useful only when a fraction of certainty attached, this is where the fractal information theory (FIT) comes into effect, it provides a plausible information structure that enables variable uncertainties. The last hundred years old exploration to "supplement a quantum state by contextual and non-contextual feeds" would be replaced by a system that decides by itself the choice between the contextual and the non-contextual and underpins the nature of contextuallity.*** The fractal information theory (FIT) that we propose has one unique feature that does not exist in classical or quantum, it is the emergence of superposition, simultaneity, entanglement and uncertainty as a derivative of the information structure. The nature of information encoded in the three imaginary worlds or complex imaginary time cycles decides by itself as a function of time what an observer would decide regarding the true nature of a quantum state. ***Due to the lack of a generic information structure, it could not be developed using classical and quantum mechanical features together, or separately***. Fusing two imaginary worlds and making a system undefined is not a simple decision. The most important difference between fractal tape dynamics and quantum mechanics is that ***in quantum mechanics there is a real & finite value, which is changed by an imaginary world, however, there is no single point real & finite value in the fractal tape dynamics***. Moreover, ***the journey to the imaginary time-cycle worlds within a cell and the journey to the time-cycle worlds above never end***. In other words, the mathematical tools of fractal mechanics (FM) is applicable in quantum mechanics with a twist that the cell state which is an infinite series are cut off to a certain resolution by the observer. That is, ***all triplet imaginary time-cycle worlds within and above has to be removed, and leave only one imaginary time-cycle world above, then, the fractal tape dynamics resembles the quantum mechanics.*** This mathematical statement makes the fractal cell dynamics neither classical nor quantum.

3.6.2 Can we convert fractal mechanics (FM) to Quantum mechanics back and forth like we do in classical and quantum mechanics? Actually, the way three imaginary worlds are fused together in the fractal information structure is fundamental. A cell in a Fractal tape has an infinitely long cell state description, which originates from an infinite assembly of cells, the mathematical processes would generate the states undefined. This is a not fit case for randomness, we cannot tag even "random" because we can see the cell state magnitude partially, its incomplete so undefined. There is no pure real observation in the fractal clock worldview, so it is not a classical world a real world is actually a dynamically evolving sphere made of complex numbers governed by the observers interaction with the imaginary world. ***In the quantum mechanics, where that imaginary world exists we do not know, fractal tape world does not have such a mystery, since we are using the concept of fractal to bridge the imaginary to the real world, hence, the concept is a bit more testable***. Fractal mechanics (FM) is not as mysterious as quantum mechanics. Fractal mechanics (FM) could predict a state but no measurement would ever end, it's the termination condition that sets the reality, often, the termination condition supersedes the reality. For example, π has infinite number of values in a series, we can tell only a few digits 3.14... but always we cannot tell 99.999999...% of the terms in the infinite series. Inside a cell in a fractal tape, there are many imaginary worlds, but ***many-world hypothesis and parallel universe concepts have no resemblance with the fractal tape network, the many-world conjecture is similar to considering many imaginary worlds living inside a single cell side by side, they could generate real observables. In case of superposition of multiple worlds inside a single cell, random exchange of information is possible and collapse could occur anywhere, yet we get real classical observables***. In a sharp contrast, the fractal tape dynamics needs at least one imaginary world below and one imaginary world above. It is nesting of time cycles that is important. It is cooperation via common local time cycles in the information structure that generates a sphere of complex observables. *We can add many worlds in numbers both above and below in a fractal tape, that's personal choice, but "worlds above does not exist" or "worlds below does not exist" means the fractal tape loses its fundamental information structure and it converts into a quantum mechanical world partially.* ***Note that we used the word "partially". What is still left is the "location of the imaginary world should be undisclosed" in quantum mechanics and that is partially known in the fractal tape derived quantum mechanics. Therefore, if we delete the information whether the imaginary world is within or above, then, we get all essence of quantum mechanics, but we lose fractal tape features completely, cannot return.***

The novelty of fractal tape based information processing does not depend only on the kind of mechanics is being used, rather, how the information is treated. As ***information here is an infinite time***

series containing three complex terms unlike classical and quantum, nested one inside another such that we could take only one clock before the clock finish a tick we could travel through several clocks inside. Here we present a table that outlines the basic differences in simple terms.

CLASSICAL INFORMATION THEORY & COMPUTING	QUANTUM INFORMATION THEORY & COMPUTING	FRACTAL INFORMATION THEORY & DECISION MAKING
Information is a real number, its defined on a finite state Turing tape/machine. Question is rejected, solution is derived alone. Information structure (0 and 1) does not hold any information about the question or solution.	Information is a real number, until we reach a real solution by collapse, there is practically zero information. Its defined on a finite state Turing tape. Everything is same as classical machine except that instead of separate 0 and 1 states, we have a superposition of 0 and 1.	Information is a complex number with three imaginary variables located on a sphere, created by an observer while reading a cell of a fractal tape. Cell state is a geometric structure of three imaginary worlds so is the observer, both are non-finite state machines. Question and all solutions are coupled to run as distinct units in a single loop, all reside together in the information content.
Solution of a problem is strictly decided by the algorithm. Fixed solution 0 or 1, whatever the logic gate based circuit allows.	Solution of a problem is strictly decided by the algorithm. Fixed solution 0 and 1, whatever the logic gate based circuit allows. Quantum only speeds up the computing steps that do not require breaking entanglement.	Solution is decided by the geometry of time cycle groups located in an observer's fractal tape, the problem is converted to a geometric structure embedded in the observer as time cycles. Since there is no algorithm, the solutions are not strictly decided by the nested time cycle of the query.
Reduction of choices by the logic gate following a set of algorithm. While operating a super computer, program should take care of the fact that no nodes should sit idle, hence its all about faster circuit and better algorithm.	Reduction of choices by the quantum logic gate following a set of algorithm. While programming a quantum computing, the algorithm should be such that entanglement is broken minimum no of times. More is break, slower is the speed.	An infinite network of fractal tape has an infinite network of times cycle triplets and as soon as an observer couples with it, an infinite network of real solution spheres are born. Thus, there is an expansion of choices or choices remain constant, never a reduction. Efficiency of decision making depends on the conversion to nested time cycles.

All information could be simplified in terms of 0 and 1 using real world information. The information structure "bit" does not hold any character of the true information.	All information could be simplified as 0, 1 and 0-1 superposition states. One imaginary world uncoupled to a real world plays a role in deciding what we observe.	All information could be simplified as three question-solution couplet or three nested time cycles. Here, the time cycle holds geometric details of real world information. Therefore, geometric details, solution-problem doublet, spontaneous generation of "reality sphere" formed due to the observer and to be observed systems interaction are three embedded part of information theory as well a decision making.
Logical operation is integrated sequentially in the hardware as circuits. Several sequences run parallel for parallel computing. Logical statements are made, that runs current and the output is received as high or low power transmission.	Logical operation is integrated sequentially in the hardware as circuits then all essential clusters are entangled. Logical statements are made. Computer only follows the circuit "simultaneously".	The questions and the decisions, both are geometrically coupled on a time loop, several such loops are integrated fractally (one inside another); if the question is asked, the solutions are derived by running the time loops through the interconnected just-formed "reality sphere". This is alternative to logical argument or programming.
Any switch with two reversible states could be used as computing element. Logic gates reduce the requirement of switches. Fails to address a halting problem. Computation could be switched off by an external instruction, but, cannot decide to switch off computing if not instructed explicitly.	Quantum switches are arranged as circuits, entire circuit is entangled then there is a collapse, to compute, computation could be switched off by an external instruction. Fails to address the halting problem. Cannot decide to switch off computing, if not instructed explicitly.	Twisted spiral made of fused capacitor-inductor device, or "nested rhythm generator" that plays three interconnected time cycles (US patent 9019685B2) is required, switch does not work. Computation cannot be switched off externally. Computation halts automatically as soon as it reaches the resolution of the observer or reaches synchronization over the interconnected "reality sphere" network.
Need to program algorithm, the intelligence of decision-making has no relation with the information structure. User has to find all intelligence regarding information separately and then by imagination or by fitting has to formulate how the system would behave in a given situation.	Need to program algorithm, and the necessary intelligence is provided by a theoretician or program developer who works to implement the algorithm suitably to a quantum framework.	No algorithm is needed, question-answer containing circles are absorbed by the decision making machine during learning, and these time cycles self-assemble to generate a massive network of triplet rhythms or triplet clocks as a chain of resonance. As soon as the observers come in contact, the query unfolds an infinite network of "reality spheres" as the system spontaneously emulates the external questions or solutions the corresponding answers or questions self-generate.

Computing needs time depending on the number of logical steps, the computing time is decided. It means the external user needs to use their own brain to reduce the number of computing steps.	Computing time depends on how many times entanglement needs to be broken and rebuilt for the sake of complexity of the problem. If no need to break entanglement, then, computing is instantaneous. However, only a few problems have such advantage e.g. factorization.	Decision making time depends on the largest time cycle needed to encode the problem & solution, or lowest time resolution in the level where the question is asked. Uses fractal time hence it is always instantaneous for the level where the question is asked. No of steps in decision making does not exists, in the entire network of "reality sphere"s, the longest time cycle decides total decision making time.
Delivers exact solution, algorithm must be perfect. It's a Turing machine. Faces halting problem, or decision making could never decide where to halt, or if it is infinitely long time taking problem. However, it can never adjust to a modified scenario.	Probabilistic solution, algorithm must be perfect. It's a Turing machine. Faces halting problem, cannot solve a halting problem though claims are plenty. One major factor to solve halting problem is not speed, its estimating the number of computing steps required, that requires an external users brain.	Provides solutions in a loop perfection is never achieved since resolution depends on the observer who is the questioner, a loop never halts. Depending on changes in the question, all possible answers continue to emerge within the largest circle forever; hence, halt criterion is auto-detected. Thus, halting problem is irrelevant here as detector's limit takes only a part of infinite solution in a instantaneously generated "reality sphere" circuits, that is equivalent to classical/quantum computers estimating the decision making steps.
This is Universal computing, processes any language, but only if a problem and its solution are already "fully known" and programmed. Universality refers only to accepting all kinds of problems.	This is Universal computing, processes any language, but only if that is already "fully known" and programmed. Same like classical.	Universal decision making, but uses its own geometric –time cycle language (space=time), all events or information is converted into its own geometric shape based nested rhythms, suited for any language, any problem. The bandwidth of time that it can process restricts a true universality.

3.7 Fractal decision making is NOT Carl Pribram's holographic brain like computing, and NOT David Bohm's holographic universe and NOT String theory's hologram:

Fractal means self-similarity, when one argues for a fractal tape network, is it meant that one particular set of information is being repeated. Both the confusions are wrongly put. First, here we address the correlation between fractal information theory (FIT) and the hologram and holographic universe.

3.7.1 Holographic universe of string theory: String theory version of a holographic universe considers that the universe is actually a 2D sheet and it makes a projection that we view as a 3D world in front of us, —we all are some form of holographic projections. If we ask, where this projection is coming from, the answer is the black hole surface, on its edge, its there where the projector is kept (as if particles dive into black hole keeping the information in the space-time curvature on its edge). Once we imagine a protocol, supporting it with math is not difficult, which is an extended derivation from a simpler set of assumptions, a scientific culture to consolidate an incredible perception about the universe & then extrapolate it to predict the unknown. Our statement is the following: ***An escape time fractal tape encompassing the entire time-cycle database of a given system's information network, no space is left to project like a hologram or a screen to project. Once we make a mathematical assumption "within and above, not step by step", we cannot break it at any point we need to preserve its generality, hence, the possibility of a holographic universe needs to be rejected under this scenario.***

A fractal tape could hardly conceptually accommodate that the universe is a hologram for several other reasons, first, a projector is kept somewhere and projection is on a far distant screen, the concept raises more questions than solving some. This is similar to von Neumann computers, memory is somewhere and the processing takes place at somewhere else. For a fractal tape machine (FTM), the universe is a fractal of time circles wherein the system points run in a loop along the perimeter of a circle. ***Running a time loop is holding a memory state, running a loop through local time-traps is the decision making, running through time-traps and completing the circle unveils the geometry of the structure written in a circle (geometric shape = time-trap composition). Just one event, running along the perimeter of a circle completes all fundamentals for the fractal information processing and fractal decision making***. Therefore, complacency is the second reason why fractal tape machine (FTM) operates within its information structure, no projection is needed, fractal tape made of time circles is by itself a complete tool to add, subtract and thus integrates more and more shapes in its geometry, it does not need, any "projection". It does not need to be programmed. Computation, which signifies the execution of current transmission through a circuit following the instructions suggested by an algorithm, is not essential here.

Finally, just as the question was asked in the Big Bang proposal, who is blowing the balloon, on its surface our entire universe exits, who pushes the balloon to where, the same question could be asked for the holographic projection proposals, be it string theory or other hard concepts. Always, we need an external controller outside the defined universe for holding the screen and adjusting the projector parameters in a holographic universe. Thus, the concepts of holographic universe may stand on its own right, however, for the fractal information theory (FIT), it's fractal tape encompass the entire computational space of a given system, so no space is left outside for an external observer or controller, which is relatively a safer proposition.

3.7.2 Imagine that Fractal tape machine (FTM) is falling onto a black hole: "Information is never lost", this is the supreme faith of those who consider that the universe as a hologram. Fractal tape machine (FTM), mathematically would suggest just the opposite, ***when an object is broken, the information about its shape is lost, some other information is created***. An object that falls into the black hole say the fractal tape, the falling would never finish, it would be a perpetual event. The circles representing a single cell would continue to disintegrate into the black hole and this destruction can never finish, the whole black hole cannot assimilate even a single cell entirely. In other words, ***a black hole can never assimilate a fractal tape machine (FTM) made of time circles.*** Consequently, Stephen Hawking who strongly believes that information lost forever is possible and Leonard Susskind, Brian Greene and all the advocates of string theory who believes that information retrieval is possible in its full form are wrong. Information could be lost as nested time cycles fall apart, but loss is an event that is perpetual, just as perpetual creation is never completed. Therefore, the question of information retrieval becomes irrelevant, ***if the gravitational object follows a fractal information theory (FIT) as proposed here, then, an object would start falling into the black hole but that event of falling would not finish***, initially it would be fast, and afterwards it would slow down such that the falling rate would nearly turn to zero. The holographic projection of the universe from that "continuously disintegrating" fractal tape machine (FTM) falling into the black hole is also mathematically trivial. It is highly unlikely that the "time cycles" using which the cells of a fractal tape machine (FTM) are made of would stick to the edges of the black hole. Since a time cycle is the entity that cannot be broken, it would stick as a whole at different time cycle traps along the black hole. If we want to bring them back, and remake the initial nested time cycles, the isolated time cycles would be there, but the information for integrating the isolated time cycles would not remain there.

3.7.3 Karl Pribram and David Bohm's holographic universe: In the fractal information theory (FIT), it is strongly argued that there is "no projection", and "information loss/creation is perpetual". ***In case of hologram, the plane waves are physically stored in the system to be projected later on, a hologram is a Turing machine.*** However, not a single cell in fractal tape network is real. It has many tapes within and above who are not seen by an observer in real time. ***All cells of the fractal tape are initially an empty space with more and more empty cavities within***.

Fractal tape fails to become a true fractal and fails to become a true hologram: ***Karl Pribram and David Bohm's attempt to model the dendritic domain as a holographic projector like that of a string theory's black hole could not be apprehended by a fractal tape machine (FTM).*** Since a fractal tape encompasses all information within the single cavity or a single cell and changing the conformation of a cavity boundary mechanically via vibration is the only action required for the tape operation (cavity resonator), therefore, the necessity for a holographic external projection does not require, ***cavity-cavity interaction is self-sufficient***. Regarding the proposal for ***a fractal holographic universe*** (Mureika, 2007), ***there is a weakness, beyond a certain spatial scale, the fractal mass becomes similar***. It is interesting to note that the fractal tape network acts as a projector of energy from the cavities and at the same time, it is the hologram or the projection. Such a duality arises from the fact that ***if a cavity emits energy such that ellipsoid shape would make it more feasible, then it tries to reshape itself, a geometric shape is the information that is exchanged in reality***. The seer is the seen, hence, neither fractal tape is a pure fractal nor it's a pure hologram.

3.7.4 The conceptual shying away by Pribram from his holographic theory: Pribram himself gave a remarkable twist to his earlier proposals of a holographic universe making radical shifts in three points in his scholarpedia article (Pibram, 2007). First, he made it clear that in his holonomic universe model, there was no global fourier transformation, he always meant local ("holonomy is patch holography"). Even he stated that he did not intended to suggest, "The brain is a hologram", it is a misconception. ***Surprisingly, he kept the arguments of quantum entanglement among various parts of the brain intact*** (Schempp, 1993). Second, he stated that his holonomic model deals with a wave is a misconception, yet, he repeated the argument that computation in the brain happens by the interference patterns of the waves, but one should take the vector presentation. Third, "memory is holographic", is a misconception, he simply added that there should be two kind of memories, one in the circuits and one at the deep holographic level. Of course, the correction of misconceptions softly shies away from the prime claims of a holographic brain theory and compromises with the purity of the proposal to the storm of massive neuroscience research except "quantum". Fractal information theory (FIT) exclusively deals with information structure and how a typical mechanics is applied in such a fractal tape; —there is no self-similarity or projection.

FRACTAL TAPE MACHINE WORLDVIEW	HOLOGRAPHIC, FRACTAL-HOLOGRAPHIC UNIVERSE
No self-similarity in the spatial or temporal information, only self-similarity is in the information storing/processing skeleton. Memory is non-local, each memory string encompasses entire fractal tape network, and this string is made of resonance frequencies, which vibrate in a band as a time loop. If some cells in the fractal tape is damaged, the vibration of entire string is not essentially destroyed, some specific local data is lost (if some circles disappear) but not the entire memory.	There is a self-similarity in the spatial and in the temporal information. Memory is non-local, but a small amount of information is repeated in the temporal scale and in the spatial scale. Unlike fractal processing, here, everything is retrieved and nothing is lost if some memory elements are destroyed.
Each circle has a set of frequencies played one after another, this would couple and decouple circles, there is no need to generate the interference, the vibrations recreate geometric shape in the phase space, real interference of waves is not essential.	Interference of electromagnetic wave generates a pattern and that pattern is the memory.
Entire nested time cycles network representing the memory collectively constructs the unit of information, all memory parts are distributed all over the fractal tape, not localized & repeated, and hence no space left for hologram's projector and screen.	Every part of the stored information is distributed over the entire hologram, its real pixel that holds the information not "nested rhythm" or "nested geometry", which is not visible until the vibrations of the systems are analyzed in a particular way. One projector and screen limits the variability in the holographic universe.
Nested time cycles or rhythms are the 3D assemblies of cycles, several time cycles are coupled at an angle, so it is never an emergence of 3D from 2D. 1D shapes arrange to make 2D and they arrange to make 3D and this self-assembly of time-cycles' continues, even to 4D i.e. dynamics of the system.	Creating entire 3D universe at one 2D layer is the key of this proposition. Multilayered integration concept does not exist, hierarchical geometric integration is not technologically possible, in this scenario, which are the hallmarks of the fractal tape network representing the entire system.

Fractal tape has self-programmable property, hence self-assembly of nested time cycles makes sure that the time-cycles of the hardware continuously change and improve as a function of time, no memory is permanent, hence no picture, there is never a stable static picture, because each pixel, local domains, global domains change partly dependent and partly independent manner.	The picture stored is static. Several pictures are combined to make a holographic movie. In fractal tape, even a single picture is dynamic inherently.
Structural symmetry tells us about the triplet frequencies and the periodicity at higher levels is also detected in the Fourier transform. We use the lower frequency data, which are mostly ignored. Though objectives are different, Fourier transform is used as a tool.	Fourier transform of the signal tells us about the frequency interference and the holographic nature. Such interference requires learning about the most prominent frequencies. In the FT, holonomic universe cares about the higher frequency terms, fractal tape machine primarily the end part.
Triplet of triplet resonance frequency band is a characteristic of fractal tape machine. There are triplet of triplet above and within. Each triplet has a finite domain of frequency during operation.	Following several criticisms, Karl Pribram defended in his scholarpedia article that he argues for patched or windowed Fourier transform. This resembles partially with one triplet of triplet, but “above and within” is still missing.
The fractal tape is a clock, it’s a time keeper, since all layers are cavities (nested cavity resonators) there is nothing, hence, its unique fractal energy transfer.	Interference of wave-like transmissions.
The model works neither classically nor quantum mechanically in stricter terms. Fractal tapes use many imaginary above and within unlike quantum world.	Suggests that different parts of the brain are quantum mechanically entangled.
Fractal tape network requires cavity inside a cavity inside a cavity like architecture. All cavities look different to make sure that the carriers capable of generating the resonance frequencies suitably make a triplet of a triplet. So, carriers change, forces change, cavities change, but not the triplet of triplet.	It’s a Turing type causal effect universe, with one projector and another screen.

4. FUNDAMENTAL CONCEPTS THAT WOULD BE DIFFERENT IN FRACTAL MECHANICS (FM):

4.1. Ten foundations of the Fractal mechanics (FM)

1. Any point in space is ***superposition of three imaginary "time" worlds*** while there is only one imaginary world in QM. ***Supplement to a fractal state is contextual or non-contextual, if contextual then what would be its nature is decided by observer's coupling with the three imaginary time cycles.***
2. ***Time gets a complex composition of directions or spins as soon as information is encoded and that direction is purely based on the 3 imaginary worlds (just like x, y and z, but not 90° rather e.g. 120°).*** 3D orientation of three imaginary time cycle planes changes with time, as information exchange sometimes means bonding or breaking of time cycles, it changes the relative orientation of the planes. Hence, the same system is measured differently by different observer, differently by the same observer from different directions. ***Measurement is match between common nested cycles between the observer that of the two imaginary worlds, the matched nested cycles create a domain on the "reality sphere". Oscillation means change in the diameters of the local guest time cycles sequentially in the host giant time cycle.***
3. **Ten fundamental properties of wave function in Fractal mechanics (FM) that differs than the quantum mechanics**: Wave function is deconstructed in the Fractal mechanics (FM): (i) is not a wave function, it is a projection P of triplet imaginary worlds of the observed on the triplet imaginary world of an observer (we call it "reality sphere"; is a point on this sphere). . (ii) Probability does not exist, takes a part of imaginary part of the wave function and returns to real in QM, we cannot do this in FM here . (iii) does not have a stationary state, observed value is a set of output as a function of time, the "dots" containing values on the "reality sphere" changes with observers time cycle. (iv) does not require additional normalization or renormalization as the projection of a structured system's charge and mass, i.e. all divergent parameters are always finite, w.r.t observer. (v) grows and does not remain as an isolated packet, edit cycles phase to make a virtual sphere/hyper-boloid unlike QM, hence, not only Fractal mechanics (FM) details the skeleton of , it maps 's evolution. (vi) self-assembles following ordered factor metric or prime number symmetry in the number system, i.e. there is a universal frequency chain or resonance chain

that governs self-assembly. (vii) Bra-ket alzebra does not work here, continued fraction alzebra that processes infinite series in the finite domain is applicable. (viii) is a vector, but normally we think vector means spatial direction, here it is temporal direction, there are various temporal directions. (ix) is mass and length independent, no distinction, hence, it can hold infinite mass or length to the smallest mass or distance possible. Thus, observer decides magnitudes. (x) holds information as geometric distribution of frequencies.

4. **Zero point energy & minima of QHO does not arise**: Quantum field theory (QFT) suggests that every point in vacuum is quantum harmonic oscillator (QHO), so every point has a finite energy, providing a zero point energy. For fractal mechanics (FM), every point is fractal harmonic oscillator, due to fractal nature there is no limit, and minimum energy for FM is determined by observer unlike QM or QFT. If we resolve the energy minima, we get something else a composition of superposition of waveforms within. As a result as ***an empty space is an infinite volume fractal, mathematically undefined and is truly a superposition of fluctuating oscillator network (Kusenko, 2015)***.
5. **Ten basic principles of Fractal mechanics (FM) are**: (a) ***Quantum superposition*** is simple addition of wave functions, = c11 + c22 + ...in fractal mechanics (FM) all that superimpose are connected by nested cycle its projection, f(z) = Sum f(zi) not sum of wave function. Superposition is different at different location of the nested cycle structure (b) ***Entanglement*** in QM is a definite operation, if one is changed the other changes to a given state. For FM two entangled objects are part of a single cycle, therefore, output of measurement could be deliver more than one values not just one. (c) ***Elementary composition of an observer is defined*** QM observer's treatment has a long history of algebraic, contextuality etc, its debated, FM does deconstruct observer with a strictly defined rules. (d) **Measurement** in QM gives a probability distribution of values, in FM a measurement gives a set of frequencies as a function of time, is always an output of a measurement which is observer dependent, does not exist without measurement. (e) **The measurement complexity**: In FM is looks different from different direction, for a single observer 3D measurement around create a sphere of measurement this is the real matrix to operate. Since two identical observers observing a same simultaneously cannot occupy the same position hence would measure different parts. The output cannot be taken from one sphere because two observers will influence each other, hence a new combined sphere needs to be created. (f) **Variable system points**: Since variable system points are included in nested cycles, how many system

points need to be considered depends on the observer's nested cycle too (D2<<D1, as explained above). (g) **Fractal harmonic oscillator**: unlike QM where quantum harmonic oscillator is used, fractal harmonic oscillator is considered here, where an oscillator is made of another oscillator inside and itself a guest inside a host oscillator above. (h) **Three, instead of one imaginary world**: In QM state of a system is defined on a circle or a sphere. In FM, three imaginary axes each occupying 120° solid angle in a sphere represent the three imaginary worlds of . (i) **Infinite dimensions are processed comprehensively**: QM can have a fractal clock in one imaginary world, here, in FM clocks have infinite resolution. (j) **Treating mass and space**: In QM mass is considered as wave function but still it is used in the Schrödinger equation as distinct entity. ***Fractal space-time tried to resolve this configuration by considering mass =frequency***. Since FM considers time as singular variable in its metric, space to be replaced by time, here ***mass = unresolved nested cycles made of frequencies when an observer interacts with a high density nested cycles***. Thus, FM's version of Schrödingers equation has nested cycles even for mass. ***Entanglement primarily originates in the imaginary world above, the wave particle duality comes from the world present & within, Superposition originates in the imaginary world below, and collapse does not occur,*** there is no reduction, only one event happens, that is synchronization and de-synchronization of nested time cycles between the three imaginary worlds.

6. **Time based dimensional analysis unravels unique physical picture: What is space? What is mass? What is time?** In FM it is considered M=L=T, mass = length = time. All parameters in the universe has dimensions, $1/T^4$, $1/T^3$, $1/T^2$, 1/T, 1, T, T^2, T^3, T^4.... Since we suggest mass and length or space are nested time cycles, hence, every single fundamental constant and all parameters turn to power of T. Power of time dimension determines the weightage of a parameter, Plank's constant is T^2, velocity is 0 etc, the infinite series is converted into nested cycles. This is interesting because from a time cycle we can get $2\pi R=h$ (h = Plank's constant), h should be the smallest distance, and a series of existing scientific dimension now gets a geometric perspective.
7. **Equivalence principle changes fundamentally: now all parameters and constants turn geometric**: Time is a cyclic motion of what? The unresolved energy packet with simultaneous coexistence of all points on its parameter, when an observer resolves the energy packet it detects time. The simultaneity decreases to velocity c when two cycles assemble one perpendicular to another

making a sphere, as π decreases due to nonlinear surface (then we get π=C, velocity of light). Note that the value of π is changed on a Eucledian surface (π increases due to nonlinearity then we get 2π~h, G, Avogadro). Josephson constant ~ 3/2π; Mu~4π; F(faraday, or electron mass)~3π, V_k=8π (von Kiltzing constant), π/2~e (electronic charge, atomic mass constant), π/4=Cosmological constant (dimension $1/L^2$, for the fractal information processing $1/T^2$, =energy density of vacuum). ***It seems all fundamental constants originate from π and due to non-linear surface or Euclidian geometry, they change (we neglect the order or power)***. Hyperbolic surface has π>3.14 and spherical surface has π<3.14, there are multiple geometric space on which physical constants get created, on a sphere, some sets of values and some sets of π values on a hyperbolic surface. ***Hence, the geometric shape that nested cycles want to create is not just a sphere rather a 3D dual conical shape, sometimes it's a sphere and sometimes it's a hyperboloid. Why π values manifold/fraction integral way, who quantizes? Number of loops allowed in the ordered factor metric. There is no space, nested time cycle has upper and lower detection resolution, lower resolution creates boundary of a particle and beyond upper resolution it's an open space. Mass comes from elliptic to ellipsoid cavity resonator rhythms, nested cycle rotation is felt as gravity, so there is no mass. Momentum is a property that varies with the square of the time lapse in a system, Kinetic, Potential and total energy is simply "time".*** In QM an operator executes a defined transformation, gives the expectation values, in FM we have a protocol, observer's time cycle continuously checks the tape's cells and integrates, dis-integrates (clocking together or in an isolated manner) the nested time cycle and that is synced with the observer, this continues time and again to deliver different parameters.

8. **Implications of fractal clock: Fusion of special relativity, general relativity and Quantum mechanics is not new with fractal clocks it's over a decade now**: G. N. Ord, Laurent Nottale and M. L. Naschie are a few among recent proponents of fractal time. The strongest and direct argument for such a fractal clock universe has been put forth by G. N. Ord. Already G. N Ord showed ***in a fractal clock system special relativity emerges at different continuum limit*** (Ord, 1983; 2009, 2011, 2012; Nottalle, 2005; Kantelhardt, 2011). Since FM takes out mass from the equations, it is possible to estimate the laws of gravitation from the nested cycles simply by using the ordered factor metric (tear drop to ellipsoid transition in ordered factor metric delivers the

laws of gravitation, Figure 3) one might connect both quantum mechanics and general theory of relativity. There is no velocity, no distance, only time, we have to change in the time cycle, not in the distance parameter to generate cause effect, distance does not exist, the extreme velocity c and entanglement induced collapse are not contradictory. No one measures velocity, actually measures "relative clock diameters", and entanglement for fractal clock as explained earlier is creating two complementary nested cycles in a single cycle of a much longer time scale.

9. **Fractal Interference and transition to classical mechanics & beyond FM**: Quantum interference originates from quantum harmonic oscillator, with the fractal harmonic oscillator the images appear a bit different. We have generated wide ranges of interference patterns for the fractal interference in microtubule and our study suggests that if a part of the pattern is zoomed then a new pattern appears.
10. **Ripple effects in the information science due to three imaginary worlds: Uncertainty principle**: The uncertainty principle that is frequently used as a certainty limit, even school textbooks give problems where one finds "time" from "energy" and momentum from position is not a logical approach. Fractal information estimates the uncertainty from detailed time cycle maps between the observer and the cells of the fractal tape.

4.2. Philosophical necessity & implications of a new information theory (FIT) and a new mechanics (FM) for operating a fractal tape machine (FTM):

1. **Every single system in nature is a nested clock**: Constituent time cycles of a nested network exchange a few cycles among various networks, sometimes join in time cycles, or tear apart. Every single point is undefined; it is sensed by one imaginary world within, one imaginary world above and one imaginary world for the observer, but no real space or time exists exclusively for the point under observation (Figures 1b, 2a).
2. **Time is a complex number and an infinite series, observer senses it as fractal, perceives it as linear classical** parameter. When observer-cell states are made of time cycles of similar diameter, its perceived as quantum; when the ratio of diameters is high, observer perceives a negative time. Time cycle match mixes past present future to an observer (Figures 1c, 2b).
3. **Space, mass** are relative diameters and relative density of nested time cycles of a fractal tape respectively. Observer's imaginary plane interacts and creates a perception.

4. **Uncertainty, simultaneity, entanglement and superposition** are mismatches of time cycles when (i) relative diameters of time cycles are such that one appears a point with respect to other, (ii), (iii) & (iv) multiple time cycles on a greater single cycle (Figure 4c).
5. **Speed** is a perception generated by the observer's time cycles. **Causal and non-causal** events are due to matching and mismatching of time cycles between the cell and the observer. **Contextual and non-contextual** events originate from the detail map of the common time cycles between the cell and the observer.
6. **Phase of a frequency map** holds memory and processes information, makes decision without rejecting a single choice. The expressions of changes (neural spike, emission of photons etc.) in the real physical worlds that we use to understand nature do not represent reality of the systems information processing. ***Silence holds the information, not the "bing" we hear***.
7. **Life-death, classical-quantum, such barriers are happenings at locally nested clocks**. Fractal tape does not terminate at any smaller or larger scale. Since fractal tape machines are coupled to the environment following its basic definition, it grows by itself, learns and harmonizes with the environment, the machine disintegrates if cannot continue to match nature's time-cycles. A single system could be classical to an observer at certain time cycles and quantum to some other observer at some different time scale.
8. We believe that ***to send information we need to send something, but that is not always true for nested time cycles,*** by editing the longest waveform, or the slowest clock, all the clocks inside that waveform should change simultaneously, an observer may perceive a signal transmission. Only a generic join/dis-join of time cycles appears as signal at different time scales; e.g. power transmission, energy harnessing, memorizing, computing, —everything we think as true events are outcome of infinite tape evolution.
9. **Quantity of information** is a product of density of time cycles and bandwidth of time cycles. Transmission line "Shannon channel" theory does not work here.
10. **Morphing could replace mimicking and modeling culture in science**: A chain connects the time cycles is the key for a system to isolate components and deliver a desired operation. I***nstead of equation there is a pattern of "reality spheres" that replicates the frequency fractal representation of the system does not replicate how the system looks like, but "Morphing" mimics the information architecture (Figure 4c)***.

4.3. Experimental evidences required to establish that Fractal mechanics (FM), a generic form of quantum mechanics does really exists

1. **Fractal fringes**: If a system follows fractal mechanics (FM), then one could zoom any part of the quantum interference pattern, to discover that there are hidden fringes. QM has no such provision.
2. **Fractal Feynman diagram: superposition of multiple interference patterns**: If a system follows fractal mechanics (FM), then, electromagnetic frequencies would be able to track the fractal gaps in the Feynman diagram and we would get multiple interference patterns for multiple resonance frequencies. QM does not allow many imaginary worlds to interact and generate superposition of superposed wave functions.
3. **Fractal condensation**: Condensation of the vibrational modes in Raman spectrum at the room temperature, one could see live the vibrations collapse at various frequencies so that peaks merge. This is simultaneous Frölich condensations at multiple singularities; singularity inside a singularity is a trademark of FM and does not exist in QM.
4. **Fractal coherence lead to quartret**: When two spins are entangled, it means one wave function, both particles are actually one in reality and that is equal to a nested three time cycles. Therefore, a mother photon can produce a child, a granddaughter and a great granddaughter, but the granddaughter's child will not be born (above quartret not possible), a single photon cannot produce infinite progeny in FM, there is no such restriction in QM.
5. **Multiple clock entanglement: Entanglement without an identical point of origin**: Until now, it is believed in QM that entanglement happens only with photons from the same origin, i.e. among mirror photons, however if FM exists, then it can happen for photons from other sources too. Thus, suitably generated photons from different sources if entangles and generates interference then it would establish the existence of FM.
6. **Superposition is a function of time**: Time cycles join and disjoin spontaneously, thus, in a suitably designed fractal tape system, entanglement will be a function of time. With a suitably designed time resolution set up, an entanglement would appear and disappear, as one switch to a different time domain. Such feature is feasible in FM, prohibited in QM.
7. **Quadrupolar moment changes as function of time**: One essential outcome of converting all parameters, mass, length to nested time cycles in FM is that, all higher order moments change as a function of time. This is observed in the frequency-time-intensity

3D spectrum during energy transmission between two objects. QM does not allow this.

8. **Frequency wheels of primes determine system's nesting**: Every fractal tape system has its own frequency wheels of primes. QM has no provisions for nesting of waves.
9. **Fundamental constants emerge as infinite series like e, π and φ**: The triangular geometric musical formulation of number system fractals generate all other fundamental constants as a single time cycle and several time cycles inside. QM is not geometric like FM, the fundamental nature inside of a wave-function is beyond the limit of QM.
10. **Live "beating" communication of three imaginary worlds:** One could experimentally verify three imaginary time worlds simply by experimenting on a nested quantum system like protein, which has three layers of quantum systems embedded. Such a nested QM would exhibit classical, Quantum and fractal beating simultaneously.

5. CONCLUSION: A LITTLE CHANGE IN TURING TAPE COULD BRING ABOUT A MASSIVE RIPPLE EFFECT IN THE UNDERSTANDING OF INFORMATION:

We make a little change, "every single cell of a Turing tape holds a tape inside", which alone changes everything, that singular factor demands a collective projection of the three imaginary worlds onto a sphere of complex observations "reality sphere" (Figure 2a). That phase space is the information. These "reality spheres" self-assemble to mimic the dynamics of a natural system we call it "morphing", which fills the frequency gaps of a resonance chain (Ghosh, Sahu, Fujita, & Bandyopadhyay, 2014) (Figure 2b). The necessity of computing, bits, switches, circuits, algorithms, software programs is alleviated with this new decision making protocol. One critical challenge to reject Turing based computing is that the alternative route needs to mimic the true dynamics of a system. So we analyzed 100 years of history of arguments and evolution of QM to find out the key changes we need to make in the mechanics. We figured out that we need at least three imaginary worlds to act simultaneously to do "morphing" of nature in a more reliable manner than QM and CM put together. We named the mechanics as fractal mechanics (FM) and identified 10 experimental results that we would have to demonstrate if we really want to perform such alternate form of decision making in the future.

Correspondence: anirban.bandyo@gmail.com
anirban.bandyopadhyay@nims.go.jp

References and notes:

Abbot, L. F. & Wise, M. B. (1981). Dimension of a quantum mechanical path, *American Journal of Physics, 49*, 37.

Bandyopadhyay, A. & Wakayama, Y. (2007). Origin of negative differential resistance in molecular junctions of Rose Bengal. *Applied Physics Letters, 90*, 023512.

Bandyopadhyay, A., Nittoh, K., Wakayama, Y., Yagi, S., & Miki, K. (2006). Global tuning of local molecular phenomena: An alternative approach to nano-bioelectronics. *Journal of Physical Chemistry B, 110*, 20852-57.

Bandyopadhyay, A., Sahu, S. & Fujita, D. (2009). Smallest artificial molecular neural-net for collective and emergent information processing. *Applied Physics Letters, 95*, 113702.

Bandyopadhyay, A., Sahu, S., Fujita, D. &Wakayama, Y. (2010). A new approach to extract multiple distinct conformers and co-existing distinct electronic properties of a single molecule by point-contact method. *Physical Chemistry Chemical Physics, 12*, 2198-2208.

Barreto, G. (2014). Quantum imaging with undetected photons. *Nature, 512*, 409–412.

Bells, J. S. (1966). On the problem of hidden variables in quantum mechanics. *Reviews of Modern Physics, 38*, 447-452.

Bohm, D. (1952). A suggested interpretation of quantum theory in terms of "hidden" variables, I. *Physical Review, 85*, 166-179; Phys. Rev. 85, 180-193(1952).

Bohr, N. (1935). Can quantum mechanical description of physical description be considered complete? *Physical Review, 48*, 696-702.

Born, M., Heisenberg, W., & Jordan, P. (1926). Zur quantenmechanik. II., *Zeitschrift fur Physik, 35*, 557-615. doi: 10.1007/BF01379806.

Born, M., Heisenberg, W., & P. Jordan. (1926). Zur Quantenmechanik II. *Z. Phys. 35*, 557-615.

Brown, L. M. & Cao, T. Y. (1991). Spontaneous breakdown of symmetry: Its rediscovery and integration into quantum field theory. *Historical Studies in the Physical and Biological Sciences, 21*, 211-35.

Callan, C. G., Jr. (1970). Broken scale invariance in scalar field theory. *Physical Reviews D, 2*, 1541-47.

Cao, T.Y. & Schweber, S. S. (1993). The conceptual foundation and the philosophical aspect of the renormalization theory. *Synthese, 97*, 33-108.

Catalin, V. B., & Meck, W. H. (2005). What makes us tick? Functional and neural mechanisms of interval timing. *Nature Reviews Neuroscience, 6*, 755-765. Retrieved from: http://www.nature.com/nrn/journal/v6/n10/abs/nrn1764.html

Cohen, P. J. (1963). The independence of the continuum hypothesis. *Proc. Natl. Acad. Sci., 50*, 1143-48.

Copeland, J. E. (Ed.) (2004). *The essential Turing: Seminal writings in computing, logic, philosophy, artificial intelligence, and artificial life plus the secrets of Enigma*. Oxford: Oxford University Press.

Cramer, J. G. (1986). The transactional interpretation of quantum mechanics. *Reviews of Modern Physics, 58*, 647.

Davis, M. (2006). Why there is no such discipline as hypercomputation. *Applied Mathematics and Computation, 178*, 4-7.

DeWitt, B. S. (1970). Quantum mechanics and reality: Could the solution to the dilemma of indeterminism be a universe in which all possible outcomes of an experiment actually occur? *Physics Today, 23*(9), 30-40.

Dirac, P. A. M. (1927). The quantum theory of emission and absorption of radiation. *Proceedings of the Royal Society A, 114*, 243-65.

Dirac, P. A. M. (1930). A theory of electrons and protons. *Proceedings of the Royal Society A, 126*, 360-365.

Durr, D., Goldstein, S., and Zanghi, N. (1992). Quantum equilibrium and the origin of absolute uncertainty. *Journal of Statistical Physics*, *67*, 843-907.

Dyson, F. J. (1951). The renormalization method in quantum electrodynamics. *Proceedings of the Royal Society*, *A207*, 395-401.

Einstein, A., Podolsky, B., Rosen, N. (1935). Can quantum mechanical description of physical reality be considered complete? *Physical Review*, *47*, 777-780 (1935).

Elze, H. T. (2003). Quantum mechanics and discrete time from "timeless" classical mechanics. arXiv:gr-qc/0307014v1. Doi:10.1007/978-3-540-40968-7_15

Feynman, R, P. (1948). A relativistic cut-off for quantum electrodynamics. *Physical Reviews*, *74*, 1430-38.

Feynman, R. P. (1948). Space-time approach to non-relativistic Quantum Mechanics. *Reviews of Modern Physics*, *20*, 367-87.

Fisher, M. E. (1964). Correlation functions and the critical region of simple fluids. *Journal of Mathematical Physics*, *5*, 944-62.

Frame, A. (1998). Iterated function systems. In C. A. Pickover (Ed.). *Chaos and fractals: a computer graphical journey* (pp. 349-351). Netherlands: Elsevier.

Freedman, S. J. & Clauser, J. F. (1972). Experimental test of local hidden variable theories. *Physical Review Letters*, *28*, 938-941. Doi: http://dx.doi.org/10.1103/PhysRevLett.28.938

Fry, E. S. & Thompson, R. C. (1976). Experimental test of local hidden variable theories. *Physical Review Letters*, *37*, 465-468.

G. N. Ord (2009). Quantum mechanics in a two dimensional spacetime: what is a wavefunction? *Annals of Physics*, *324*, 1211-1218.

Gell-Mann, M. & Low, F. E. (1954). Quantum electrodynamics at small distances. *Physical Reviews*, *95*, 1300-12.

Georgi, H. (1989). Effective quantum field theories. In P. Davies (Ed.), *The New Physics* (pp. 46-57). Cambridge: Cambridge University Press.

Ghirardi, G.C., Rimini, A., & Weber, T. (1986). Unified dynamics for microscopic and macroscopic systems. *Physical Review D*, *34*, 470. Bibcode:1986PhRvD..34..470G

Ghosh, S., Dutta, M., Sahu, S., Fujita, D. & Bandyopadhyay, A. (2014). Nano molecular-platform: A protocol to write energy transmission program inside a molecule for bio-inspired supramolecular engineering. *Advanced Functional Materials*, *24*, 1364-71.

Ghosh, S., Fujita, D. & Bandyopadhyay, A. (2015). An organic jelly made fractal logic gate with an infinite truth table. *Scientific Reports*, *5*, 11265.

Ghosh, S., Sahu, S., Fujita, D., & Bandyopadhyay, A. (2014). Design and operation of a brain-like computer: a new class of frequency-fractal computing using wireless communication in a supramolecular organic, inorganic systems. *Information*, *5*, 28-99.

Girelli. F., Liberati, S. & Sindoni, L. (2009). Is the notion of time really fundamental? Submitted on 27 Mar 2009 http://arxiv.org/abs/0903.4876

Gödel, K. (1938). The consistency of the axiom of choice and of the generalized continuum-hypothesis. *Proc. Natl. Acad. Sci.*, *24*, 556-57.

Gödel, K. (1947). What is Cantor's continuum problem? *The American Mathematical Monthly*, *54*, 515-25.

Goldstein, R. (2005). *Incompleteness: The proof and paradox of Kurt Gödel*. W. W. Norton & Company.

Gross, D. (1985). Beyond quantum field theory. In J. Ambjorn, B. J. Durhuus, & J. L. Petersen (Eds.), *Recent developments in quantum field theory*, (pp. 151-68). Amsterdam: North-Holland.

Gurevich, S. & Shelah, S. (1989). Nearly linear time. In A. R. Meyer & M. A. Taitslin (Eds). Lecture Notes in Computer Science (Vol. 363). New York: Springer-Verlag.

Hamkins, J. D. & Lewis, A. (2000). Infinite time Turing machines. *Journal of Symbolic*

Logic, 65, 567-604.

Haramein, N. (2001). Scaling law for organized matter in the Universe. *Bull. Am. Phys. Soc.* AB.006.

Heitler, W. (1961). In R. Stoops (Ed.). *The quantum theory of fields*. London: Interscience Publishers.

Heller, M. & Sasin, W. (1999). Noncommutative unification of general relativity and quantum mechanics. *International Journal of Theoretical Physics, 38*, 1619.

Hu, S-M., Li, C-F., & Zhang, H. (2004). Actual morphing: A physics-based approach to blending. In G. Elber, N. Patrikalakis, & P. Brunet (Eds.). *Proceedings of the ninth ACM Symposium on Solid Modeling and Applications*. Paper presented at SM '04, Genova, Italy (pp. 309-314). Aire-la-Ville, Switzerland: Eurographics Association. Retrieved from http://cg.cs.tsinghua.edu.cn/~shimin/pdf/acm_sm.pdf

Hübel, H., Hamel, D. R., Fedrizzi, A., Ramelow, S., Resch, K. J., & Jennewein, T. (2010). Direct generation of photon triplets using cascaded photon-pair sources. *Nature, 466*, 601–603.

Huxley, J. S. (1955). Morphism and evolution. *Heredity, 9*(1), 1-52. doi:10.1038/hdy.1955.1

Jacques, V., Wu., E, Grosshans, F., Treussart, F., Grangier, P., Aspect A., & Roch, J-F. (2007). Experimental realization of Wheeler's delayed-choice gedanken experiment. *Science, 315*, 966–968.

Jaynes, E. T. (1980). Quantum beats. In A. O. Barut (Ed.) *Foundations of radiation theory and quantum electrodynamics* (pp. 37-43). Dordecht: Springer.

Kadanoff, L. P. (1966). Scaling laws for Ising models near T_c. *Physics, 20*, 263-72.

Kannata, F. & Ferrari, L. (1988). Dimensions of relativistic quantum mechanical paths. *American Journal of Physics, 56*, 721-725.

Kantelhardt, J. W. (2011). Fractal and multi-fractal time series. In R. A. Meyers (Ed.), *Mathematics of complexity and dynamical systems*, pp. 463-487. Springer.

Keller, O. (2014). *Light – The physics of the photon*. Series in Optics and Optoelectronics. CRC Press.

Kocher, C. A. & Commins, E. (1967). Polarization correlation of photons emitted in an atomic cascade. *Physical Review Letters, 18*, 575-577.

Kreisel, G. (1976). What have we learnt from Hilbert's Second Problem? In F. E. Browder, (Ed.), *Mathematical developments arising from Hilbert's problems* pp. 93-130. Proceedings of Symposia in Pure Mathematics, vol. 28, Part 1, Providence, RI, USA: American Mathematical Society.

Kusenko, A. (2015). Are we on the brink of the Higgs abyss? *Physics, 8*, 108. Retrieved from: http://physics.aps.org/articles/v8/108

Laloe, F. (2001). Do we really understand quantum mechanics? Strange correlations, paradoxes, and theorems. *American Journal of Physics, 69*, 655-701.

Landau, L. D., Abrikosov, A. A. & Khalatnikov, I. M. (1956). On the quantum theory of fields. *Nuovo Cimento Suppl, 3*, 80-104.

Lee, T. D. & Yang, C. N. (1956). Question of parity conservation in weak interactions. *Physical Reviews, 104*, 254.

Leggett, A. J. (2003). Non-local hidden variable theories and quantum mechanics: An incompatibility theorem. *Foundations of Physics, 33*, 1469-1493.

Lepage, G. P. (1990). What is renormalization? In T. A. DeGrand & D. Toussaint (Eds.), *From actions to answers*. Proceedings of the 1989 Theoretical Advanced Study Institute in Elementary Particle Physics (TASI '89) (pp. 483-508). Singapore: World Scientific.

Ma, X-S., Kofler, J., Qarry, A., Tetik, N., Scheidl, T., Ursin, R., Ramelow, S., Thomas Herbst, T., Ratschbacher, L., Fedrizzi, A., Jennewein, T., & Zeilinger, A. (2013). Quantum erasure with causally disconnected choice. *Proceedings of the National Academy of Sciences, 110*, 1221–1226.

Manning, A. G., Khakimov, R. I., Dall, R. G. & Truscott, A. G. (2015). Wheeler's delayed-choice gedanken experiment with a single atom. *Nature Physics, 11*, 539-542.

Milnor, J. (1989). Self-similarity and hairiness in the Mandelbrot Set. In M. C. Tangora (Ed.)

Lecture notes in pure and applied mathematics (Vol. 114) (pp. 211-257). New York: Dekker.

Monserrat, B., Drummond, N. D., & Needs, R. J. (2013). Anharmonic vibrational properties in periodic systems: energy, electron-phonon coupling, and stress. *Physical Review B, 87*: 144302.

Morphism. (2001). In Hazewinkel, M. (Ed.). *Encyclopedia of Mathematics*. Netherlands: Springer.

Muradian, R., Carneiro, S., & Marques, R. (1999). Radius-mass scaling laws for celestial bodies. *Apeiron, 6*, 186-190.

Mureika, J. R. (2007). Fractal holography: a geometric re-interpretation of cosmological large scale structure. *Journal of Cosmology and Astroparticle Physics, 2007*. http://dx.doi.org/10.1088/1475-7516/2007/05/021

Nottale, L. (2005). On the transition from the classical to the quantum regime in fractal space-time theory, *Chaos Solitons and Fractals, 25*, 797-803.

Nottale, L., Celerier, M.N. (2007). Derivation of the postulates of quantum mechanics from the first principles of scale relativity. *Journal of Physics A: Mathematical and Theoretical, 40*(48), 14471-14498.

Ord, G. N. (1983). Fractal space-time: a geometric analogue of relativistic quantum mechanics. *Journal of Physics A: Mathematical and General, 16*(9), 1869-1884.

Ord, G. N. (2011). How does an electron tell the time? *International Journal of Theoretical Physics*, 51, 652-666.

Ord, G.N. (2012). Quantum phase from the twin paradox. Journal of Physics Conference Series, 361, Conference 1, 012007. Retrieved from http://iopscience.iop.org/article/10.1088/1742-6596/361/1/012007/pdf doi:10.1088/1742-6596/361/1/012007

Panarella E. (1987). Non-linear behavior of light at low intensities: the photon clump model. In W. M. Honig, D. W. Kraft & E. Panarella (Eds.). *Quantum uncertainties –recent and future experiments and interpretations* (p. 105). New York and London: Plenum Press.

Peierls, R. (1934). The vacuum in Dirac's theory of the positive electron. *Proceedings of the Royal Society, A146*, 420-41

Peng, Q., Barootkoob, M. A., & Roychoudhuri, C. (2009). What can we learn by differentiating between the physical processes behind interference and diffraction phenomena? *Proceedings of SPIE*, 7421, 74210B-1. DOI:10.1117/12.828572

Peres, A. (1978). Unperformed experiments have no results. *American Journal of Physics, 46*, 745-747.

Pibram, K. (2007, 10 May). Holonomic brain theory. Retrieved from http://www.scholarpedia.org/article/Holonomic_brain_the doi:10.4249/scholarpedia.2735

Prati, E. (2009). The nature of time: from a timeless Hamiltonian framework to clock time metrology. *Journal of Physics: Conference Series, 306*, 012013 012007.arXiv:0907.1707v1.

Rowe, M. A., Kielpinski, D., Meyer, V., Sackett, C. A., Itano, W. M., Monroe, C. & Wineland, D.J. (2001). Experimental violation of a Bell's inequality with efficient detection, *Nature, 409*, 791-794.

Roychoudhuri, C. (2006). Locality of superposition principle is dictated by detection process. *Physics Essays, 19*(3).

Roychoudhuri, C. (2006). The locality of the superposition principle is dictated by detection processes. *Physics Essays, 19*(3), 333-354.

Roychoudhuri, C. (2011). Re-interpreting "coherence" in light of non-interaction of waves or the NIW-principle. Proceedings SPIE 8121, 44.

Roychoudhuri, C., Barootkoob, A. M., & Ambroselli, M. (2011). The constancy of "c" everywhere requires the cosmic space to be a stationary and complex tension field. Proceedings SPIE 8121. doi:10.1117/12.894121

Russell, B. (1938). *Principles of mathematics*. (2nd ed.). London: W. W. Norton &

Company.

Sahu, S. Ghosh, S., Ghosh, B., Aswani, K., Hirata, K., Fujita, D., & Bandyopadhyay, A. (2013). Atomic water channel controlling remarkable properties of a single brain microtubule: Correlating single protein to its supramolecular assembly. *Biosensors and Bioelectronics*, 47, 141–148.

Sahu, S., Ghosh, S., Fujita, D., & Bandyopadhyay, A. (2014). Live visualizations of single isolated tubulin protein self-assembly via tunneling current: effect of electromagnetic pumping during spontaneous growth of microtubule. *Scientific Reports, 4*, 7303.

Sahu, S., Ghosh, S., Hirata, K. Fujita, D., & Bandyopadhyay, A. (2013). Multi-level memory-switching properties of a single brain microtubule. *Applied Physics Letters, 102*, 123701.

Sakata, S., Umezawa, H. & Kamefuchi, S. (1952). On the structure of the interaction of the elementary particles. *Progress of Theoretical Physics. 7*, 377-90.

Schempp, W. (1993) Analog VLSI network models, cortical linking neural network models and quantum holographic neural technology. In K. H. Pribram (Ed.) *Rethinking neural networks: Quantum fields and biological data.* Proceedings of the First Applachian Conference on Behavioural Neurodynamics (pp. 233-298). Hillsdale, NJ: Lawrence Erlbaum.

Seager, S., Kuchner, M., Hier-Majumder, C. A., & Militzeret B. (2007). Mass-radius relationship for solid exoplanets. *The Astrophysical Journal, 669*, 1279-1297.

Shlesinger, M.F. (1988). Fractal time in condensed matter. *Annual Review of Physical Chemistry, 39*, 269-290.

Shrivastava, S. & Schneider, M. (2014). Evidence for two-dimensional solitary sound waves in a lipid controlled interface and its implications for biological signalling. *Royal Society Interface, 11*, 20140098. doi:10.1098/rsif.2014.0098).

Siegelmann, H. T. (1995). Computation beyond the Turing Limit. *Science, 268*, 545-548.

Smolyaninov, I. I. (2012). Metamaterial model of fractal time. *Physics Letters A, 376*, 1315-1317.

Sorli, A., Fiscaletti, D., & Klinar, D. (2011). Replacing time with numerical order of material change resolves Zeno problems of motion. *Physics Essays, 24*, 11-15.

Sornette, D. (1990). Brownian representation of the fractal quantum paths. *European Journal of Physics, 11*, 334-337.

Stapp, H. P. (1997). Non-local character of quantum theory. *American Journal of Physics, 65*, 300-304.

Stenger, V. J. (2001) Deriving quantum mechanics from classical physics.

Symanzik, K. (1973). Infrared singularities and small-distance-behavior analysis. *Communications in Mathematical Physics 34*, 7-36.

t' Hooft, G. (1971). Renormalizable Lagrangians for massive Yang-Mils fields. *Nuclear Physics B, 35*(1), 167-88.

Tittlel, W., Brendel, J., Zbinden, H., & Gisin, N. (1998). Violation of Bell's inequalities by photons more than 10 km apart. *Physical Review Letters, 81*, 3563-3566.

Wang, X-Y. (1985). Solitary wave and nonequilibrium phase transition in liquid crystals. *Physical Review A, 32*, 3126–3129. doi:10.1103/PhysRevA.32.3126

Weisskopf, V. F. (1934). Uber die Selbstenergie des Elektrons. *Z. Phys., 89*, 27-39.

-Ziegler, M. (2005). Computational power of infinite quantum parallelism. *International Journal of Theoretical Physics, 44*(11), 2059–2071.

Chapter 9

The Universe as a Spectrum of Consciousness: Open Research Questions

PETER H. ROE[1]
Department of Systems Design Engineering
University of Waterloo, Waterloo, Canada
and
JACK B. ELLIS[1]
Environmental Studies, York University, Toronto, Canada

ABSTRACT

Scientific and philosophical concepts of human consciousness are being intensively addressed by western and eastern schools of thought, respectively. However, there is still no general agreement or unified definition of consciousness. While most current research tends to deal with the mechanism of consciousness in humans, we raise questions for which research is needed into consciousness in other beings. This paper first presents two examples of the loss of awareness caused by traumatic events, which themselves give indications of the physical reality that human consciousness is a state of the brain. It then brings together some thoughts and poses some research questions which are needed to help in the understanding of consciousness as an infinite all-encompassing spectrum of consciousness; one which embraces our universe and all existence. This spectrum ranges through supra-human consciousness, as well as many aspects of consciousness of animals, insects, plants and even of all matter. The paper proposes and illustrates some examples of the research needed.

INTRODUCTION: WHAT IS CONSCIOUSNESS?

In their seminal paper in the *Journal of Cosmology*, Roger Penrose and Stuart Hameroff (2011) outlined three general possibilities regarding the origin and place of consciousness in the universe that have been widely expressed in the literature. Here, we paraphrase and draw on their formulations as a basis for our observations on needed research into human and non-human consciousness.

> (A) *Consciousness is not an independent quality but arose as a natural evolutionary consequence of the biological adaptation of brains and nervous systems.* This view holds that consciousness emerged as a property of complex biological computation during the course of evolution.

[1]Professor Emeritus

(B) *Consciousness is a quality that has always been in the universe.* This view, assumed by various spiritual and religious groups, is that consciousness has been in the universe all along, e.g. as the 'ground of being', 'creator' or component of an omnipresent 'God', and consciousness can be attributed to all matter.

(C) *Precursors of consciousness have always been in the universe; biology evolved a mechaninsm to convert conscious precursors to actual consciousness.* This is the view implied by Whitehead (1929; 1933) and taken in the Penrose-Hameroff theory of 'orchestrated objective reduction' ('*Orch OR*'). Precursors of consciousness are proposed to exist as the potential ingredients of actual consciousness, and the physical basis of these proto-conscious elements are not necessarily part of our current theories of the laws of the universe.

The implication of all three of the foregoing concepts is that consciousness is, particularly in humans but also in all other sentient creatures, *a state of the brain.* Furthermore, consciousness depends on connections within the brain. Even a brain that is damaged, for instance by a hemorrhagic stroke, can gradually restore its own function. Victims of a stroke can recover from paralysis, regain the ability to speak, and so forth.

RESEARCH QUESTIONS ARISING FROM IMPAIRED OR DAMAGED HUMAN CONSCIOUSNESS

Current research has made significant progress in discovering the nature of human perception, normal human consciousness and connecting the mechanisms of our consciousness to neuronal microtubules, for instance. In particular, researchers following the *Orch-OR* line of investigation have shown credible results. Research in anesthesiology has shown that an intact brain can recover from complete unconsciousness to full consciousness after anesthesia, but not how the brain forms connections, acts, regenerates after trauma, and operates at the molecular, atomic, and quantum levels.

The parts of the brain that control speech, movement, etc., seem to have little to do with mental awareness, and hence consciousness. The experience of Peter Roe serves as an example:

"In May of the year 2005 I fell victim to a major ischemic stroke. Suddenly I lost control of the physical operation of the body. I found myself lying on the floor of my house unable to sense the existence of anything on the left side of my body, let alone to move my left arm or leg. But I was aware of my surroundings; I knew

> that my pet dog, which weighs about 40 kilograms, was standing on me, trying to revive me by licking my right ear. I knew what was happening when the paramedics and the ambulance arrived to take me to hospital. One could say that I was at least partially conscious. However, at the hospital, the attending neurologist did some simple tests and it became clear that I was not fully aware of my environment, due to reduction of my field of vision, even though I was substantially alert. The analytical qualities of my brain remained functional; in fact, I was able to evaluate the probability of recovery or death, which would result from the use of thrombolytic drugs (which I declined)."

Clearly Roe was sufficiently conscious to make decisions. One should therefore modify the definition earlier stated. *Consciousness is a result of the appropriate parts of the brain being fully functional.*

In another example, several months ago near Roe's home a thirteen year old girl named Lydia was struck by a heavy truck as she alighted from a bus bringing her home from school. She sustained multiple injuries, several broken bones, including her skull. She lost consciousness and entered into a coma, from which, at the time of writing, she has not fully recovered.

Lydia became unconscious, in the sense that she completely lost awareness of her physical environment. Perhaps it is therefore reasonable to define unconsciousness as *total lack of awareness*.

But there are other considerations. Since the accident, Lydia has been on a path of recovery. Five months afterward the local newspaper reported (Lydia's road to recovery, 2012):

> "Waking up from a coma does not mean a return to her full self prior to the accident. Lydia is instead moving through cognitive levels between an unresponsive coma (level one) and complete functioning (level eight).
>
> Just as some victims of brain injuries never progress past level one, not all recover to level eight.
>
> The brain injuries Lydia sustained, after being hit by a truck as she stepped off a school bus in front of her home, currently have her at level four — she gestures and smiles, but does not fully understand what is happening around her." (Family guide to Rancho levels of cognitive functioning n.d.)

This is an illustration of the physiological understanding of consciousness. Clearly these considerations must form part of any emerging science of consciousness. We suggest that additional research is needed on:

- How does an injured brain re-establish its former inner connections and regain much, if not all, of its original function and consciousness?
- What therapies are best able to facilitate and expedite restoration of brain function and consciousness?

SPIRITUAL CONSCIOUSNESS AND THE SUBCONSCIOUS

Our old friend, Revered Prof. P.S. Satsangi, has presented several dissertations on the absolute coherence of science and religion. For example, one appeared in the Journal of Systems Science and Engineering in 2010 (Satsangi, 2010). He has often made the point that religion operates on a higher plane than earthly science, only reached through attaining spiritual consciousness. Spiritual consciousness is a realm of awareness that lies beyond one's day-to-day physical consciousness. One may attain spiritual consciousness in a variety of ways, not only through meditation.

Humans possess three interconnected features, the spiritual, the conscious mind and the physical, the spiritual being the inner core and the physical being the outer surface.

It is the interconnections that matter, and they work in more than one way. We know intuitively that there are realms of consciousness other than that of physical awareness. In dreams we are aware of interconnected features of our memories; through meditation or other methods of stimulation, our spiritual awareness is raised to new levels; and through almost instinctive brain actions we run our lives with little thought to many physical situations.

This semi-automatic operation is what we consider to be the subconscious. We can walk up and down stairs without thinking; we don't have to relearn how to ride a bicycle each time we get on one, and so on. The subconscious, as we know it, is evidence of autonomous brain operation, perhaps at least partially non algorithmic.

Based on these few elementary thoughts about consciousness there are further open research questions we suggest are needed:

- What are the parameters and determinants of brain activity at the various levels of consciousness, including the spiritual and the sub-conscious?
- To what extent might genetically inherited pre-dispositions or 'memories' be responsible for generating human sub-conscious abilities; i.e. without having to observe and process them consciously?

Consciousness – From Basic Cognition to the Universe

The synapses in our brain enable our neurons to make connections and form circuits in our central nervous system. That is how we control our body, think our thoughts, store information and make decisions. The adult human brain is estimated to contain between 100 and 500 trillion synapses (Drachman, 2005). Even the brain of a newborn has about one trillion synaptic connections, created by about 20 billion neurons and even more billions of microtubules. To reach this scale at birth, during gestation the fetal brain must create brain cells at a rate of about 250,000 per minute.

Parents impart an initial store of information and skills to prepare their infants for life activities, and the process of consciousness development continues through socialisation and education, both formal and informal. The adherence to the social framework of a religious grouping is normal, though not universal, usually with the goal of developing the spiritual consciousness of the individual. Probably most individuals who achieve a good balance of their life in their societal community are satisfied with the degree of spiritual development that is common in that community.

But here in this volume, we are dealing with consciousness that entails a much broader and deeper level of spirituality, one which while being accessible to human beings is cosmic in dimension and all-encompassing spiritually – one that may actually ***be*** the prime force, or essential causation, of our very universe.

The concept of a "cosmic" consciousness - one that envisions the universe as a completely connected system comprising every conscious being - appeared quite early in the eastern Vedic philosophical traditions and Buddhism. These early interpretations, however, often appear unclear to modern readers.

Now there are researchers who contend that our human brains function as quantum computers (Hameroff and Penrose, 1996). Others contend that the whole universe ***is*** a quantum computer.

One of the more seminal of such works is the book *Consciousness and the Universe: Quantum Physics, Evolution, Brain & Mind* (Penrose, Hameroff, Stapp, & Chopra, 2011). In it over 70 articles raise questions such as: Does the very concept of a universe depend upon its presence? Does consciousness merely perceive reality, or does reality depend upon it? Did consciousness simply emerge as an effect of evolution? Or was it, in some sense, always "out there" in the world? We agree that research in these areas is needed, and at the end we suggest some additional open research questions.

Non-Human Consciousness and Broader Systems Consciousness

We take it as an axiom that ***all*** living entities have some form of consciousness – likely a species consciousness - and that their consciousness is an ***integral part*** of the universal consciousness system. While there is a broad range of research literature on consciousness in higher-order mammals such as chimpanzees and dolphins, the consciousness of lower animals and other entities has received little research attention. Indeed, many researchers and philosophers define them as not having any consciousness. We believe, however, that consciousness of animals should be a part of any science of consciousness, even those with minuscule brains such as spiders, ants and other insects.

Following are a few examples presenting some facts underlying our reasoning:

Aboriginal Totemism: It is striking that virtually every aboriginal society on earth has (or had, in their pre-contact era) a belief in sacred totem ***animals*** that they consider to be their spiritual conduit to the universal force or spirit. Among other things, totem animals also served as mentors, protectors and guides in daily life, as well as delineators of their group identities in the society.

Membership in, for instance, the bear clan meant something quite different to an individual than membership in an eagle or deer clan. An aboriginal shaman typically would meditate and call upon the power of a totem animal to connect with the universal force in order to heal or to ensure success in group activities,

In some cases, aboriginal totemism even imparts sacredness to inanimate objects such as a rock formation, a location revered as a "power site" (e.g., Uluru rock in Australia, Machu Picchu in Peru), or a special water body (such as the Ganges River, or water itself). Can we conclusively conclude that "inanimate" objects have ***no*** consciousness whatsoever?

Species Behaviourism: Everyone who has observed the mass coordination of movement in flocks of birds, herds of animals or shoals of fishes must have wondered what mechanism triggers their synchronised movements and motivates their group patterns. Is it only magnetic navigation or response to changing lengths of daylight? Or is there an intrinsic connection and communication through some form of collective consciousness?

While consciousness is dependent on brain structure and activity, animal species have a huge range of brain size, ratio of brain to body mass, and dependence on their species' abilities, or lack thereof. For instance:

European white storks (*Ciconia ciconia*) are large graceful birds with a wingspan sometimes over 2 metres. They migrate annually from summer breeding areas in northern Europe to winter areas thousands of kilometres away in Africa and the Middle East. Yet it is not unusual for a breeding pair to return to the ***exact same nest*** in successive years.

The Eurasian cranes (*Grus grus*) are also large stately birds who can measure up to 2.4 metres in wingspan. They also migrate thousands of kilometres annually and vocally communicate continually while flying in formation. They congregate for feeding and protection in the same small areas each year. This year, some 90,000 birds were counted in a 10 sq.km. area near Kremmen, Germany.

At the other end of the size spectrum of migrating birds is the ruby-throated hummingbird (*Archilochus colubris).* These tiny birds weigh only between 3-4 grams and have a wingspan of about 10 cm. Yet they regularly migrate thousands of kilometres from their summer quarters in eastern North America, northern Ontario and the Canadian prairie provinces to wintering areas in Central America and southern Mexico. They do not migrate en masse, and some birds actually overfly the entire Gulf of Mexico (800 km) non-stop.

Perhaps the most astonishing airborne migrating species is not a bird at all, but an insect: the Monarch butterfly *(Danaus plexippus*). These creatures range over a huge summering area in the United States and Canada, but winter only in several very localised treed areas in Mexico and California. The monarch is the only species of butterfly that regularly migrates both north and south as birds do, but – even more incredibly - no single individual makes the entire round trip. The length of these journeys exceeds the normal lifespan of most monarchs, which is less than two months for butterflies born in early summer. During the migrations female monarchs deposit eggs to create a next generation. The last generation of the summer enters into a non-reproductive phase which may last seven months or more. Research has shown that these butterflies can use the earth's magnetic field for orientation, but no explanation exists for how they devised their strategy of laying extra eggs, or how the next generation learns how to continue the journey.

Plant Consciousness: Countless school Science Fair projects have been set up in an attempt to demonstrate how growth of various plant species can be increased through exposure to music or other sound stimuli. While a significant proportion of these projects appear to have been successful there is still skepticism among plant scientists since there are so many variables involved. While some people believe in a mystical sense that the effect must exist, others insist that, scientifically, there is no reason why plants should be affected by music.

Recent research at the University of Bristol School of Biological Sciences studied 200 bees over a 3-year period gathering nectar from petunias (Clarke, Whitney, Sutton & Robert, 2013). Their work has shown that the blossoms actually give out electrical signals to attract bees to their pollen. Furthermore, they reduce the signal voltage to warn bees when their nectar is low. These electrical charges effectively allow flowers and bees to communicate, enhancing the blossom's advertising power to bees.

Needed Research on Systems Consciousness

We believe that the following research questions are open and relevant to an understanding of consciousness beyond that of humans:

- What mechanisms lead to the shared ability of animal species to perform their life activities seemingly without having to learn them *ab initio*?
- Do animals and other life forms have an intrinsic connection and communication within their species through some form of collective consciousness?
- If so, is that consciousness transmitted genetically or by some other mechanism?
- How can a systems consciousness that includes such a wide variety of non-human consciousness as well as human consciousness be understood and conveyed to as wide a segment of humanity as possible?

Some Concluding Thoughts

Both of us remain in awe at the amount and quality of research papers that we have seen proposed for inclusion in this volume. It may well set a milestone in the furtherance of consciousness research, and we expect that its readers will be richly for the reading of it.

We trust that our own modest contribution will be seen in the light of our intentions in writing it; that is, not as a criticism of the breadth and depth of the general field of consciousness research and its hitherto necessary concentration on human consciousness, but as at least a small discourse to encourage the expansion of consciousness research in the ways we have suggested.

Sometime in the future we sincerely hope that a better understanding of consciousness in animals, plants, and matter in general, will lead us all to an appreciation of consciousness in, of, and throughout the universe. After all, ***there is only one system***.

References

Clarke, D., Whitney, H., Sutton, G., & Robert, D. (2013). Detection and learning of floral electric fields by bumblebees. *Science, 340,* 66. Retrieved from http://www.esalq.usp.br/lepse/imgs/conteudo_thumb/Detection-and-Learning-of-Floral-Electric-Fields-by-Bumblebees.pdf

Drachman, D. (2005). Do we have brain to spare? *Neurology,* ***64***, 2004-5.

Family guide to the Rancho levels of cognitive functioning (n.d.). Retrieved from https://web.archive.org/web/20120710211609/http://www.rancho.org/research/bi_cognition.pdf

Hameroff, S. & Penrose, R. (1996). Conscious events as orchestrated space-time events. *Journal of Consciousness Studies, 3,* 36-53.

Lydia's road to recovery. (2012, Aug. 17). *The Waterloo Region Record.* Retrieved from http://m.therecord.com/news-story/2609574-lydia-s-road-to-recovery

Penrose, R., Hameroff, S., Stapp H., & Chopra, D. (2011). *Consciousness and the Universe: Quantum Physics, Evolution, Brain & Mind.* Cosmology Science Publishers.

Penrose, R., & Hameroff, S. (2011). Consciousness in the Universe: Neuroscience, Quantum Space-Time Geometry and Orch OR Theory. *Journal of Cosmology, 14.* Retrieved from http://journalofcosmology.com/Consciousness160.html

Satsangi, P. S. (2010). Applied systems research for better worldliness. *Paritantra: A Journal of Systems Science and Engineering, 19,* 1.

Whitehead, A.N., (1929). *Process and reality.* New York: Macmillan.

Whitehead, A.N. (1933). *Adventure of ideas.* London: Macmillan.

Chapter 10

'Inhabiting Landscapes of the Known and the Unknown Alike': Representation and Consciousness in British Literature

ANNA MARGARETHA HORATSCHEK
Christian-Albrechts-University at Kiel, Germany

Consciousness studies is one of the most exciting research areas of the present. It addresses age old questions about the status and relation of knowledge, experience, and representation. In British literature, the initiation of a theoretical and philosophical basis for the empirical 'New Sciences' by Roger Bacon (c. 1214–1294), Thomas Hobbes (1588–1679), and John Locke (1632–1704) has sparked imaginative negotiations about concepts of consciousness from the Early Modern Period to the Present. The competing truth claims based on a hermeneutics of experience and experiment vs. a hermeneutics of reading pointed to the questions: How does human consciousness work? What is its relation to the world? Which methodology will enable human consciousness to reach a true picture of self, world, and cosmos? The discussions have been fired by the awareness that different methodologies will generate different models of consciousness, the world, and ultimately of what it means to be human. The passionate rhetorics of the New Scientists against the rhetorics of everyday language and for a new 'plain style' (cf. Nate, 2009) testify to their recognition that the form of representation is of supreme significance for the truth claims of the knowledge they have to communicate. Thus Bishop John Wilkins in his *Essay Towards a Real Character and a Philosophical Language* (1668) attempted to devise an ideal language without verbs, where the onomasiological structure of the nouns was supposed to exactly mirror the universal order of things. And even if this may be considered an eccentricity, Bacon as well as Locke were sceptical against rhetorics of their day, as they "insinuate wrong ideas, move the passions, and thereby mislead the judgment" (Locke, quoted in Nate, 2009: 48).

With the advent of quantum theories in the 1920s and 30s, discussions among scientists about the relation between representation, experience/experiment and knowledge have reached a new stage of complexity and intensity. A central challenge for theorising consistent models of reality in the light of quantum data is posed by the relation of the observer and the observed, because in the words of Niels Bohr: "No elementary phenomenon is a phenomenon until it is a registered (observed) phenomenon" (quoted in Plotnitsky, 1997: 147). This thesis subverts the traditionally assumed distance between an observing subject and observed object, which legitimated the claim to objectivity in classical physics, and assigns fundamental significance to the subjective consciousness in the construction of models based on supposedly objective data.

> From the very beginning, some of the founders of quantum mechanics, such as Erwin Schrödinger, considered consciousness as an essential principal in the universe, which is necessary as much as any physical principal for its proper understanding. [...] Consequently, many of the modern attempts to understand consciousness by physicists make use of quantum concepts and theory. (Rao, 2002: 139).

Lechte, referring to Gaston Bachelard, elaborates:

> 'The space in which one looks, in which one examines is philosophically very different from the space in which one sees.' This is because the space in which one sees is always a represented space, and not a real space. Only by recourse to philosophy can one take account of this. Indeed Bachelard goes on to advocate 'a systematic study of representation, the most natural intermediary for determining the relationships of noumenon and phenomenon.' (Lechte, 1994: 3)[1]

Another central problem concerning the truth claims of scientific representation, "the question of the physical embodiment of mathematical objects" (Plotnitsky, 1997: 162), lies in the fact that "our experimental equipment embodies our, often hidden, theoretical (or philosophical and ideological) assumptions" (Plotnitsky, 1997: 160). These challenges are radicalised by the fact that quantum physics have overthrown the presentist assumption of a pre-existent reality which could be observed or represented in the first place. "Would one be able to claim [...] that any given number – say, 'one' – is fully materially realizable? Such a claim would already be problematic in view of the quantum character (which, at least for the moment, appears inescapable) of all processes involved in such realizations" (Plotnitsky, 1997: 165). "At the same time, however, what is unrealizable or unrepresentable is not without productive effects." (Plotnitsky, 1997: 167) This renders any kind of representation in mathematical symbols, formulas, or graphs 'idealisations', which have worked in admirable ways, but which nevertheless form "our mathematico-technological enclosure" (Plotnitsky, 1997: 167), keeping us from 'reality' or 'matter'. With this background, Plotnitsky, refuting "Penrose's Platonist claims concerning both mathematical and

[1] Lechte is quoting from Bachelard, 1968: 63 and 64.

physical reality" (Plotnitsky, 1997: 163)[2], opts for a preliminary conceptualisation of 'reality' or 'matter'

> (as radical alterity) [that] may be neither finite nor infinite, nor may it conform to any idealization we might develop. That which would be neither finite or infinite already appears to be (at least so far) inconceivable (rather than merely unvisualizable or materially unconstructible, as many mathematical objects are), which is not to say that such a conception could not eventually be developed. (Plotnitsky, 1997: 167)

However, this view is not commonly accepted. According to Bruno Latour, veritable "war games" among scientists are staged for the "*vulgum* pecus [...] where the Red relativists have to fight the White Knights of realism" (Latour, 2004: 459).

This attention to premises and processes of methodology and representation in postclassical theories of the natural sciences, and the awareness "that familiar or classic accounts of knowledge, proof, truth, reality, and so forth do not cohere with empirical descriptions or mathematical analyses", converges with "a cluster of quite general but problematic concepts, notably, *knowledge, language, objectivity, truth, proof, reality,* and *representation*" (Smith & Plotnitsky, 1997: 2, 1) which have been heavily criticised and partly reconceptualised in the humanities and the social sciences in the course of the so called theoretical turn. In light of these developments, Barbara Herrnstein Smith asks for reciprocal reception, as the focus on questions of representation, interpretation and semiosis in the latter moves on territories traditionally claimed by the former:

> Although contemporary relations between the sciences and fields such as literary and cultural studies are vexed by a conceptual history of dualistc models and an institutional history of disciplinary segregation, the fundamental arbitrariness of all conceptual models and the instability and reconfigurability of all disciplinary divisions can be seen [...]. (Smith & Plotnitsky, 1997:4)

My essay is meant to contribute to bridging the gap between C.P. Snow's "two cultures" of the humanities and the natural sciences. It will address the question 'What is consciousness?' by focusing on the relation between representation, experience, and knowledge in English Literature in four centennial strides. Concretely, my analyses will include literature of the Early Modern Period (Shakespeare, Milton), British

[2] Plotnitsky refers to and quotes extensively from Penrose, 1989.

Romanticism (Blake, Wordsworth, Shelley), Modernism (T.S. Eliot, D.H. Lawrence, E.M. Forster), and Postmodernism (Peter Ackroyd, Yann Martel). Depending on which constellations the fictional texts expose, the implied models of consciousness will differ significantly. Before I turn to the texts, however, I shall outline the theoretical and methodological background which motivated the topic and the focus of this essay from a Western perspective.

CONSCIOUSNESS STUDIES IN THE NATURAL SCIENCES AND THE HUMANITIES

My essay took its inspiration from the annual "Towards a Science of Consciousness Conference" (TSC) stationed at the Center for Consciousness Studies at the University of Tuscon, Arizona, USA, which was hosted by the University in Dayalbagh (DEI), Agra, India in 2013. The vast majority of speakers were natural scientists, all of them working with quantum mathematics. However, surprisingly frequent mention was made of the Cartesian split – the philosophical problem of the mind-body split in our self-perception which has been explicated philosophically by French philosopher René Descartes (1596-1650) – and when I finally ventured the Gretchen-question: "Do you think you'll transcend the Cartesian split by using quantum mathematics in consciousness studies?", the answer was: "Yes, that's our last frontier." To explain 'consciousness' with one model of knowledge would imply that the 'consciousness' philosophy, religion, or literature talk about is synonymous with the 'consciousness' which is measured and quantified by natural scientists. This model would overcome the philosophical and epistemological abyss between mind and body, immateriality and materiality, which has characterised Western philosophy for centuries, and which has been institutionalised in the division between the natural sciences and the humanities (Latour, 1993).

A few participants raised objections against this visionary leap of faith between the concepts of 'consciousness' in the natural sciences philosophical and philological hermeneutics, and religion on the ground that the very different methodologies of these communities allow only certain aspects of the object of analysis to become visible. "What answer we get depends on the question we put, the experiment we arrange, the registering device we choose." (Wheeler in Plotnitsky 1997: 148)[3] So how could one model developed from specific disciplinary methodologies satisfy questions concerning the nature of consciousness which are posed from widely diverse perspectives and disciplines like philosophy, religion, or literature? Such a model on a theoretical meta-level would have to forge into a consistent whole the conceptual distinction between mind and body, immateriality and materiality, which have fostered

[3] Plotnitsky is quoting from Wheeler, 1984: 184f.

disciplinary differentiation, as well as the methodologically induced questions of the humanities and the sciences, taking the knowledges of humanities as well as sciences, classical and postclassical, into account. Surveying these challenges, Plotnitsky concludes:

> We may have to use an unheard of mathematics, combining new and old models in unprecedented ways. We may need idealizations that combine more diverse and more radically incompatible models, old and new, than does present-day physics. We may be entering, indeed already inhabiting, increasingly complex landscapes that enlarge the space of the known and the unknown alike, which is perhaps the only sense of progress one can still think of. (Plotnitsky, 1997: 167)

'Science' is defined in the *New Oxford Dictionary of English* in the sense of natural sciences as "the intellectual and practical activity encompassing the systematic study of the structure and behaviour of the physical and natural world through observation and experiment: *the world of science and technology*" (OED, 1998: 1664); a more rigorous definition in the sense of Karl Popper would be that a theory is only scientific if it "makes precise unambiguous, predictions about quantifiable, measurable phenomena" (Law, 2007: 187), which can be falsified. In contrast, the phenomenon of investigation "in the humanities [...] is the human mind (in a broad sense), in science things not necessary human or even animate" (Ankersmit, 2005: 211). Accordingly, phenomena of hermeneutic investigation are historically changing manifestations of human consciousness in all their aspects, i.e. in an artwork, in social rites, religious worldviews, but also in discourses like historiography, ethnology, anthropology, philosophy, or the natural sciences – summed up under the blanket term of 'culture'. The different approaches to the objects of investigation are "codified in the opposition between *Verstehen* (hermeneutic understanding) and *Erklären* (scientific explanation)" (ibid.). The German expressions 'Verstehen' and 'Erklären' are maintained even in English texts, because German philosophers from Schleiermacher through Dilthey in the 19th to Hans Georg Gadamer in the 20th century have been of foundational significance for the development of hermeneutics. Hermeneutic approaches to the world are not focusing on the world of materiality governed by laws of nature, but on the fact that human beings live in and by worlds of meanings, ranging from largely preconscious world views through traffic signs to academic disciplines. In the words of Jürgen Habermas talking about philosophy, hermeneutic research "does not directly take part in increasing our knowledge about the world, but rather asks what the growing world knowledge, learned by interaction with the world, *means for us*."

(Habermas, 2012: 16; transl. A.H.[4]) Thus, Thomas Hardy in his poem "Hap" (Hardy, 1866/1996) laments that in light of Darwin's model of evolution the individual cannot trust any more in a loving god, but has to perceive himself as the haphazard result of processes of adaptation.

> [...] Crass Casualty obstructs the sun and rain,
> And dicing Time for gladness casts a moan....
> These purblind Doomsters had as readily strown
> Blisses about my pilgrimage as pain.
> (Hardy 1996: 1049)

And in his "Drinking Song" (Hardy, 1928/2001), Hardy leaves the speaker exhausted and unwilling to grapple with the Einsteinian universe:

> And now comes Einstein with a notion –
> Not yet quite clear
> To many here –
> That's there's no time no space no motion [...]
> (Hardy, 2001: 907)

Whereas classical physics presupposes a clear differentiation between observing subject and observed object, which allows for objectivity, in a hermeneutic analysis only the researcher's immersion in the common world of meaning ensures access to the target of investigation in the first place. As these models of meaning are widely different between individuals as well as cultures and historical epochs, each hermeneutic thesis self-reflexively has to be contextualized by its historical situatedness in order to take account of the premises conditioning the interpretation. For Gadamer, the central task of hermeneutics consists in transcending the horizons circumscribed by the culturally and historically specific world views, its ultimate aim lies in a *Horizontverschmelzung*, a merging of horizons. Trying to understand 'consciousness' from this perspective means trying to self-reflexively understand the very instrument of investigation as well as the ground of cultural artifacts and knowledge production.

'Consciousness' in the OED is defined as "the state of being awake and aware of one's surrounding: [...] the awareness or perception of something by a person [...] the fact of awareness by the mind of itself and the world" (OED, 1998: 390). The first definition establishes a contrast between intentional action and being unawares in a psychoanalytical sense, or in states like sleeping; the second definition concerns

[4] „[...] beteiligt sich nicht unmittelbar an der Vermehrung unseres Wissens über die Welt, sondern fragt danach, was das wachsende Weltwissen, das im Umgang mit der Welt Gelernte, jeweils für uns bedeutet."

the relation of the object ('something') and the subject as a relation of embodied perspectivity ('by a person'), which forms the basic premise for the claims to objectivity in classical physics. This concept implies a hierarchy which is typical for Occidental epistemology, namely the active subject as agent who observes the passive object assumed to be under the control of the observer. Philosophers like Manfred Frank (cf. Frank, 1988) and Hans Blumenberg (cf. Blumenberg, 1957) have critically commented on this implication, and traced it back to the ocularcentric metaphors for awareness and consciousness in Plato's cave parable: Seeing prestructures a relationship of the active subject and the passive object, which has haunted occidental epistemology, philosophies of mind, and philosophies of science till the present – a typical case of metaphors turning into metaphysics. The third definition describes self-reference or self-awareness, when consciousness metaphorically 'observes' itself and thus treats it as an 'object' (note here the visual metaphor to describe an epistemological relation). This self-reflexive move forms the basis for notions like 'identity', both – in the terms of French philosopher Paul Ricoeur – as 'ipse-identity', the awareness that what I am thinking, feeling, and experiencing is *my* experience, bound to my body, perspective, and individual conditionings of culture, family, and momentary state, and the 'idem' identity, constructing a historical continuity by narrativising past and present into a relatively coherent plot (cf. Ricoeur, 1991). Although the relationship between consciousness, physiology, and materiality forms one of the central questions of the philosophy of mind, none of these definitions consider consciousness (exclusively) as a material object of the physical world.

There is no doubt that physiology and materiality – which can be observed in electroencephalograms and in psycho-physiological experiments – is reciprocally interrelated with consciousness, but it is neither synonymous nor identical with it, as Australian philosopher Frank Jackson's thought experiment about 'Mary's world' relating to colour sensations or John Searle's 'Chinese Room' experiment in his 1980 paper *Minds, Brains and Programs* illustrate (cf. Law, 2007: 129, 134-136). One aspect which eludes physicalist accounts – yet – is what Ricoeur terms 'ipse-identity', which cannot be replicated even in a perfect copy of my consciousness: Who or whatever is thinking 'I' in this copy, will not be me.

With the advent of quantum theories in the 1930s, Gaston Bachelard "in speaking about the scientific thought of the modern era [...] notes that it is fundamentally oriented to seeing phenomena relationally, and not substantively, or as having essential qualities in themselves."(Lechte, 1994: 4) Bruno Latour formulates succinctly: "In the sciences, the degree of objectivity and certainty is directly proportional to the extent of artificiality, layering, heterogeneity, multiplicity, and complexity of mediations. The assertion sounds radical but is merely obvious: in a laboratory, no naked access to truth is thinkable." (Latour, 2004: 459) Sandkühler elaborates:

> Whenever we create images of the world, we are 'in the picture'. We do not copy, but we construct, and our images are always also images and pictures of our selves. In other words: Questionable is the picture, which does not show the painter in the middle of the picture, but outside of it. I could also say: Who for example after Kant supposes that measurable results from experiments about the free fall would 'represent' the 'natural' movement of heavy bodies, did not understand that the result – I will be cautious and say: at least also – comprises the selfrepresentation of the time and place of the observer. 'Representation' in this sense is not so much mimesis [Darstellung] but imagination [Vorstellung], that is a mental state of evoking presence, and not the presence of objects existing independent of mental states. (Sandkühler, 2003: 48 f.; transl. A.H.5)

And representations – as Sandkühler explains with reference to Cassirer – are always bound to specific conditions of time and space of the person who in the act of representation gives presence to facts, which are never 'naked', but always clothed in images, categories, and formulas at hand. Arkady Plotnitsky – welding philosophical observations of Niels Bohr and Jacques Derrida – drives this 'dematerialisation' of the objects of scientific observation further, challenging the implied assumption the very term 'representation' suggests, namely that there is something or some thing to be re-presented in the first place. He argues that basically all key concepts of our world view like 'reality', 'objectivity', 'causality' have to be wrenched from their association with a presentist ontology, and that quantum models are " a symbolization and an idealization rather than a (classically) conceived representation of any (classically conceived) physical reality, independent properties of physical objects, and so forth". In order to mark the "dislocation of classical thinking", he re-conceptualises 'reality' as "radical, but never absolute, alterity encountered in quantum physics." (Plotnitsky, 1997:

---

[5] „Wann immer wir uns Vorstellungen und Bilder von der Welt machen, sind wir 'im Bild'. Wir kopieren nicht, sondern entwerfen, und unsere Bilder sind immer auch Selbstbilder und Selbstentwürfe. Mit anderen Worten: Fragwürdig ist das Bild, das den Bildner nicht mitten im Bild, sondern außerhalb des Bildes zeigt. Ich könnte auch sagen: Wer nach Kant z.B. davon ausgeht, daß Meßergebnisse [sic] in Experimenten zum freien Fall die 'natürliche' Bewegung von schweren Körpern 'repräsentieren', hat nicht verstanden, daß [sic] das Ergebnis – ich will hier zunächst vorsichtig sagen: zumindest auch – die Selbstrepräsentation des Beobachters ist. 'Repräsentation' ist in diesem Sinne nicht so sehr Darstellung als vielmehr Vorstellung, d.h. ein mentaler Zustand des Präsent-Machens, nicht aber die Präsenz von Gegenständen, die unabhängig von mentalen Zuständen wären."

140) This radical alterity does not cause, but rather effects measurable 'traces', but not as a premise but rather – in Wheeler's expression - as a "phenomenon-to-be" (quoted in Plotnitsky, 1997: 148)[6],

> the efficacity of which can never - not in the past, the present, or the future - be seen as present, whether as presentable or as unrepresentable, existing in itself or by itself, independent of and inaccessible to any interpretation. This efficacity is, in these resets, analogous to the Derridean supplementary efficacity, which makes us concerned not with horizons of modified – past or future- present, but with a past that has never been present, and which never will be, whose future to come [l'a-venir] will never be a production or a reproduction in the form of presence. (Plotnitsky, 1997: 148)

Put into a nutshell: "[I]t is important to note that all scientific thought [...] 'is, in its essence, process of objectification'." (Lechte, 1994: 4). Surveying the present situation in light of these developments Rao holds:

> The jury is still out. We do not know if those advances would come from physics as such, without going beyond the currently accepted theory to postulate a new domain of consciousness. [...] The relevance of consciousness to quantum mechanics is two-fold. First, a proper comprehension of consciousness as a concept may be considered a necessary condition to have a coherent understanding of quantum theory. Second, a quantum mechanical understating of brain function may be regarded as a necessary precondition for understanding consciousness. The first may well result in a new physics, or at least a radical extension of current physics. The second appears at this time to be the best hope for finding a neurological basis for consciousness. (Rao, 2002: 158)

In light of these remarks, what is the contribution literature studies can make to consciousness studies? Literature and literary studies are privileged media to negotiate "a proper comprehension of consciousness as a concept" (Rao, 2002: 158). Literary texts are interdiscursive phenomena (cf. Link & Parr, 1997) which initiate and negotiate concepts of consciousness explicitly, and which – privileged by their freedom from the demands of pragmatics – evaluate the polyphony of competing discourses of consciousness. This is done by by storyline and aesthetic markers, which function as an archive of historically

[6] Plotnitsky is quoting from Wheeler 1984: 189.

specific constellations of consciousness catalysed and manifest in the author, who functions as an 'echo chamber' for aesthetic rules as well as the material, social, and political conditions of literary production and reception of his time. Additionally, because of their highly self-reflexive use of language coded by aesthetic norms and conventions, literary texts themselves always have to be aware of the potential as well as the limits of semiotic representation. By its literariness, literary language draws attention to its formal qualities and to the fact that it is constructing a world – better: that it entices the reader to construct a world. It makes us conscious of what we are doing constantly anyway, as the *homo interpretans* we are according to Wolfgang Iser, father to the reader-response theory of hermeneutics (cf. Iser, 1989). Because this is so, literature does not only reflect – and actively address questions of representation in language, which Gadamer considers the dominant medium to hand on world-models[7] and to circumscribe the historically specific horizon of any individual's existence[8], but literary texts are always 'in the picture' of the worlds they evoke, to use Sandkühler's metaphor. And literary hermeneutics for centuries have developed a complex, albeit often contradictory history of meta-methodological reflection and critique focusing on problems of verbal representation.

What I have sketched here are widely received opinions in the Euro-American humanities, yet I want to drive it further for the sake of our topic: It is a commonplace that consciousness is not a *tabula rasa* onto which the data of the world are inscribed, or a container in which they are gathered, but that consciousness is what it is *about*, that consciousness is created in the performance of consciousness. Literature is a medium which allows us to study consciousness in action, generating possible worlds, and at the same time implicitly and explicitly reflecting on this performance. With this background I am going to approach the question of 'What is consciousness' neither from a scientific – in the sense defined above – nor from a philosophical perspective[9], but with the methodology of hermeneutics, the dominant methodology of the humanities. Taking to heart Bachelard's thesis that representation forms the hub between noumenon and phenomenon,

---

[7] „Wir sind in allem unserem Denken und Erkennen immer schon voreingenommen durch die sprachliche Weltauslegung, in die hineinwachsen in der Welt aufwachsen heißt. Insofern ist die Sprache die eigentliche Spur unserer Endlichkeit. Sie ist immer schon über uns hinweg. Das Bewußtsein des einzelnen ist nicht der Maßstab, an dem ihr Sein gemessen werden kann." (Gadamer, 1967: 97)

[8] Language as "die geschichtliche Wirklichkeit [des menschlichen] Seins" (Gadamer, 1965: 261).

[9] For recent developments in the Philosophy of Mind concerning 'consciousness' cf. Stanford Encyclopedia of Philosophy, "Representational Theories of Consciousness" (2000, revised 2006) and "Higher-Order Theories of Consciousness" (2001, revised 2011) http//plato.stanford.edu/entries/consciousness-representational/ and http: //plato.stanford.edu/entries/consciousness-higher/ both from Febr. 23, 2013.

the question of what is consciousness in literature of four epochs of English literature will be approached by focusing on the explicit and on the aesthetic negotiations about the relationship between representation, experience and knowledge in selected texts from the Early Modern Period to Postmodernism.

I. THE EARLY MODERN PERIOD

The basic structure for present day discussions about issues related to consciousness have been laid in the Early Modern Period. William Shakespeare's drama *Hamlet,* staged in London in 1599 and 1602, is considered a key testimony of the occidental early modern episteme (*sensu* Foucault). Four references in Act I anachronistically mention that he has studied at the university in Wittenberg, Germany (I.2. lines 112, 118, 163, 167). This university was founded in 1501, the story of Hamlet takes place before the 12th century, so studying in Wittenberg was impossible. Why Wittenberg? The answer: It was Wittenberg, where Martin Luther, the spokesman of the protestant reformation, posted 95 thesis of his reformed faith at the church doors in 1517. Luther held that each individual was responsible for his or her spiritual welfare without taking recourse to dogmas proclaimed by the pope of the Catholic Church. The only guide to spiritual self-examination should be the individual study of the bible, *sola scriptura*[10]. This presupposed literacy, a cultural technique not mastered by many people yet, as Gutenberg (ca. 1398-1468) had established his printing press only 60 years earlier in 1455. This Lutheran book centeredness implies a radical shift in attitudes towards representation as "[the Reformation] has abolished or literally blackened medieval church rituals, with all of their visual glitter, and replaced them with the monochromatic, namely black-and-white mystery of printed letters" (Kittler, 2010: 76).

Luther's demand transfers the truth claims of the medieval world based on universally valid divine truths to the individual interpretation of the written text, and thereby to the *forum internum* or the *inner vision* of each single person. His request that each person critically assess their innermost motives, desires, and fears him- or herself, requires consciousness to turn upon itself as a controlling force, enacting the original sense of 'consciousness', namely 'conscience', according to the OED "an inner feeling or voice viewed as acting as a guide to the rightness or wrongness of one's behaviour" (OED, 1998). Both 'consciousness' and 'conscience' share their root in the Latin verb *conscire,* from *con-* 'with'+ *scire* 'know'. The English word 'consciousness' from its origins is primarily an agent of moral control. Religious faith thus is

[10] The formula can be traced back to the clause "solam scripturam regnare" in Luther's 1520 tract Assertio. In the history of Judaeo-Christian religion, the oldest source of iconosceptícism is of course the Fourth Commandment.

intellectualized and subjectivised (cf. Habermas, 1988: 29)[11].

With this background, the anachronism of studying in Wittenberg marks Hamlet as a 'modern man', who does not trust in traditional beliefs, but has to ascertain the truth value of a statement by intellectual investigation. It explains why Hamlet does not obey the command of his father's ghost to revenge his murder by killing the usurper Claudius, but instead tries to assemble "ocular proof" (Shakespeare, *Othello* 3.3.363), as Othello, another 'modern hero' of Shakespeare, calls it, and assess its validity in the light of reason. In order to do so, Hamlet adopts the empirical and ocularcentric methodology of the so called New Sciences, which founded the Natural Sciences, initiated by Francis Bacon (1561–1626) in his *Instauratio Magna* (The Great Renewal), which he planned in six volumes imitating the Six Days of Divine Creation. Thus, *Hamlet* incorporates the epistemological turning point from the Middle Ages to Modernity in two fundamental ways: Firstly, the play exhibits the change from gaining knowledge by belief – in religion or in cultural dogmas – to generating knowledge by the methodology of the New Sciences; conceptually this is indicated by the shift from the Medieval notion of a moral conscience to the modern, secularized idea of consciousness as an abstract mental state, the ground for epistemic systems. Secondly, Hamlet represents the interiorisation and individualization of consciousness as a source of generating knowledge by way of a controlled methodology. He does all this by probing crucial problems of the New Sciences and by addressing fundamental questions of empirical methodology which have gained essential significance in the critical self-reflection of the sciences today.

The dominant sense organ to acquire knowledge in occidental epistemology from Plato's cave parable onwards has been visuality (cf. Blumenberg, 1957). Indeed, the German word for consciousness, 'Bewusstsein', stems from the old Germanic 'Wizzan', meaning 'having seen something'[12]. With this tradition of scopic knowledge concepts in mind, the centrality of seeing, observing, and being observed in Shakespeare's play, which has been noted by many critics, can be read as a dramatic negotiation about firstly the validity of gaining knowledge by experience and experiment, and secondly about the problems of interpreting the sense data. Already Act I is saturated with implicit and explicit comments on seeing.

[11] „[D]er religiöse Glaube reflexiv geworden, hat sich die göttliche Welt in die Einsamkeit der Subjektivität zu etwas durch uns gesetztes gewandelt. Gegen den Glauben an die Autorität von Verkündigung und Überlieferung behauptete der Protestantismus die Herrschaft des auf seine Einsicht pochenden Subjekts: Die Hostie gilt nur noch als Teig, die Reliquie nur noch als Knochen."

[12] Meyers Grosses Universallexikon: 2892. For an analysis of the implications of ocularcentric knowledge models in contradistinction to auditory models for self-concepts cf. Horatschek, 2005. For its influence on narrative cf. Klepper, 2011, esp. 1-40; Crary, 1990.

HAMLET: My father, methinks I see my father.
HORATIO. Where, my lord?
HAMLET. In my mind's eye, Horatio.
HORATIO. I saw him once, 'a was a goodly King ...
HAMLET. 'A was a man, take him for all in all,
I shall not look upon his like again.
HORATIO. My lord, I think I saw him yesternight.
(I.2., 184-190)

The scene demonstrates that, as in Hamlet's case, visual memory may dominate the physical experience of the present, whereas Horatio at first recalls an actual meeting in the past with Hamlet's father, and then informs Hamlet of his conviction that he has seen the ghost of the murdered king walking around the night before. The dialogue exposes that the individual experience of a visual image is no guarantee for the existence of a referent, but maybe a personal fantasy, and thus possess no truth value at all. In the episteme of the Early Modern Period, it would not even count as an experience, because experience, which has the same etymological root as 'experiment', namely" the Latin *experientia,* from *experiri* 'try'" (OED, 1998: 647) or 'put to the test', was used interchangeably with 'experiment' till late 18th century. The dialogue confirms Joan Scott's thesis that "[w]hat counts as experience is neither self-evident nor straightforward; it is always contested, always therefore political" (Scott, 1992: 37). This does not suggest that Hamlet's imagination is meaningless, because Hamlet's idolised memory of his father forms the basis of his world view and motivates most of his actual behaviour.

After Hamlet and Horatio have agreed that there has been a ghost, who paradoxically has to serve as a referential reality, the insecurity with regard to the relation between perception, sign, and referent, or between individual experience and its meaning, is not solved, because now – in a constant process of deferral – they have to evaluate what he is a sign for, and how they have to interpret the apparition. Joan Scott once more: 'Experience' „is at once always already an interpretation *and* is in need of interpretation (ibid.)." Interpretation always refers to an encompassing horizon of a specific knowledge system, so good students that they are, Hamlet and Horatio weigh the dominant theories about ghosts in their time, namely the catholic belief that ghosts were messengers from the purgatory against the orthodox protestant view that ghosts sometimes were angels, yet in most cases devils incarnate. Unable to decide, Hamlet addresses the ghost:

> Be thou a spirit of health, or goblin damned,
> Bring with thee airs from heaven or blasts from hell,
> Be thy intents wicked or charitable,
> Thou com'st in such a questionable shape
> That I will speak to thee.
> (Shakespeare, 2006: I.4., 40-45)

His attempt to reach certain knowledge ultimately fails, because he wants to extend the reliability of factual data to the interpretation of their meaning. Yet the proof-value of constructed 'factual evidence', like Claudius' incriminating reaction evoked by Hamlet's deliberate staging of Old Hamlet's murder, holds only "provided that we limit knowledge to the instrumentalized nature of the facts and leave aside the interpretation of causes" (Latour, 1993: 18). Towards the end of the drama, Shakespeare has his hero give up all attempts to obtain a legitimation of his 'reading' of the world through the methodology of the New Sciences, and lets him revert to the medieval honour code of his father – which leads to the death of almost everyone on stage.

Hamlet's intellectuality makes him also the first dramatic manifestation of what in the course of centuries would become the occidental discourse of individuality, subjectivity, and interiorised consciousness. It is the received opinion that this discourse was strongly furthered in the Early Modern Period by Protestantism, spreading literacy and – in the diction of Jürgen Habermas – the methodology of monological reasoning performed by a self-contained subject who (seemingly) thinks and acts autonomously (cf. Habermas, 1988: esp. 344-389) in the New Sciences. When Hamlet's mother Gertrude admonishes her son to curb his excessive mourning for the deceased father, because it is not seemly, Hamlet answers:

> Seems, madam! Nay, it is, I know not 'seems'.
> 'Tis not alone my inky cloak, good mother, [...]
> Together with all forms, modes, shapes of grief,
> That can denote me truly. These indeed seem, [...]
> But I have that within which passes show –
> These but the trappings and the suits of woe.
> (I.2., 76-86)

For many critics, Hamlet's self-reflexivity heralds an individual interiority as the locus or even origin of experience.

> [Hamlet] asserts against the devices of the world an essential interiority [...] an I which, if it encounters the world in anything more than a quizzical and contemplative manner, must alienate

> itself into the environment which inevitably produces the richness of its subject by its mute and resistant externality. (Barker, 1984: 36)

Terry Eagleton reads Hamlet as "a radically transitional figure, sprung out between a traditional [Medieval] social order to which he is marginal, and a future epoch of achieved bourgeois individualism (Eagleton, 1986: 74)." With view to the implied concept of consciousness it is noteworthy that here an „organizing distinction" is generated between an "inner life" or a "real self", which eludes any methodology of ocular proof, and an exteriority which only seems (cf. Ferry, 1983: 6), yet furnishes the sense data necessary to proceed according to the tenets of empirical methodology. This abyss between a supposed origin of consciousness 'in' the individual and a material outside, between body and mind, materiality and epistemology[13] has been fixed philosophically roughly 50 years later by René Descartes (1596 – 1650) in his six *Meditationes de prima philosophia*, where his rigorous skepticism towards any truth claims culminates in the *cogito, ergo sum*: I can know nothing but that at this very moment I am a thinking being.

John Milton, in his grand epic *Paradise Lost* (1660/1993), explicitly objects to the contemporary self-descriptions of the New Sciences as the only way to all-encompassing truths, without denying their superb contribution to gaining knowledge about the world. He does so by introducing a differentiation between *wrong reason*, enacted by the rebellious archangel Satan, and *right reason*, which is taught to Adam after his fall into knowledge by the archangel Raphael. *Wrong reason* exhibits a self-sufficient, hermetic epistemology, and narcissistically mistakes the potent self, empowered with reason, as self-generated, thus reasoning without reflecting on the *conditions* of its existence. In Satan's words:

> [...] who saw
> When this creation was? Remember'st thou
> Thy making, while the Maker gave thee being?
> We know no time when we were not as now;
> Know none before us, self-begot, self-raised
> By our own quick'ning power [...].
> (Milton, 1993: V., l. 856-861)

This attitude is marked as the sin of individual hubris. *Right Reason* argues that it is in accordance with the laws of reason – though not of empiricism – to acknowledge an *origin*, ontologically prior to its

[13] For the discursive proximity of interiority to Early Modern Period concepts of the body cf. Hillman, 2007.

own existence, although there is no ocular proof for its existence. The problem with the human fall into knowledge for Milton is that human beings have the faculty of reasoning without possessing the divine view of the totality of existence, so they cannot locate the place of reason in the overall scheme of things. Experience and experiment are no way out, either, as they are bound to the body and thus – for Milton – even more limited in their range of application than reason. This makes it necessary that the conditions for *right reasoning* – meaning logically and morally correct reasoning – have to be taught to Adam by an entity *outside* the realm of the human intellect, namely by the archangel Raphael, as the data themselves do not provide information about their ultimate origin. The problem of representing something which per definition transcends the potential of the human intellect is explicitly addressed:

> [...] and what surmounts the reach
> Of human sense, I shall delineate so,
> By lik'ning spiritual to corporal forms,
> As may express them best [...].
> (Milton, 1993: V., l. 571-574)

In analogy, the epic argues, there is no Archimedean point outside reason to reason about its origin. By anchoring the intellectual powers of humanity – again – in the transcendental signifier God, Milton tries to stop the proliferation of significances assigned to reason by the New Sciences.

II. BRITISH ROMANTICISM

About 150 years later, the Romantics are the first writers who deal extensively with the relationship of representation and experience, not only aesthetically in their art, but also in discursive essays. They are also the most radical critics of those paradigms of the New Sciences, which had become the cultural authority in defining reality during the 18th century, and they explicitly voice the need for a whole new epistemology. In Romantic Poetry, vision and light, the privileged metaphors to traditionally represent reason and intellect, sometimes become negative attributes, i.e. in Blake's poem "Ah Sun-flower" (1794/1996), where the sun represents the 'light of reason' that dominates the vision of the Sunflower to the complete exclusion of the sensual experience of the actual world at hand. In analogy, Blake's engraving "Newton" shows the imperviousness of the scientist for the colourful world around him, as he concentrates exclusively on the black lines on his white writing sheet. Structurally, Newton is repeating the sin of Satan in Milton's *Paradise Lost*: He is narcissistically and hermetically contemplating his own model of nature represented in formulas of his own making. The engraving "The Ancient of Days" (about 1824) personifies the authoritative claims of scientific rationality in the figure of Urizen – a pun on "your reason" –, who literally encompasses and tries to control the entire cosmos with his mathematical exactitude, which is Blake's critical interpretation of the Book of Proverbs 8.25, "when he [God] set a compass upon the face of the earth." Blake was of the opinion that Milton's attempt to reconcile Christian doctrine with scientific reason had failed aesthetically, because the figure of Satan was imbued with so much grandeur, eloquence, and energy, that he was far more convincing as the true principle of creation than God. "The reason Milton wrote in fetters when he wrote of Angels & God, and at liberty when of Devils & Hell, is because he was a true Poet and of the Devil's party without knowing it" (Blake, 1790/1979: 150). Consequently, Blake's engraving of his poem "Milton" shows Milton, representative of imaginative poetry, dethroning Urizen.

In contradistinction to Milton however, the Romantics do not see the human intellect as an – albeit weak – continuation of divine intellect, but they attribute agency and originality to the imaginative individual himself, whose very perception of the world inscribes its conditions of human sensuality, memory, and historically specific medialities and norms of representation into the – supposedly objective – reality. M. H. Abrams describes this epistemological shift in *The Mirror and the Lamp*.

> The title of the book identifies two common and antithetic metaphors of mind, one comparing the mind to a reflector of external objects, the other to a radiant projector which makes a contribution to the objects it perceives. The first of these was characteristic of much of the thinking from Plato to the eighteenth century, the second typifies the prevailing romantic conception of the poetic mind. (Abrams, 1958: vi)

Martin Klepper elaborates this thesis:

> The change from imitation to expression, and from the mirror to the fountain, the lamp, and related analogues, was not an isolated phenomenon. It was an integral part of the corresponding change in popular epistemology – that is, in the concept of the role played by the mind in perception which was current among romantic poets and critics. [...] The analogies for the mind in the writings of both Wordsworth and Coleridge show a radical transformation. Varied as these are, they usually agree in picturing the mind in perception as active, rather than inertly receptive,

> and as contributing to the world in the very process of perceiving the world. (Klepper, 2011: 172)

For Shelley, this principle of imagination, expressed best in poetry, forms the basis of any kind of intellectual activity, including the investigations of the Natural Sciences.

> Poetry is indeed something divine. It is at once the centre and circumference of knowledge; it is that which comprehends all science, and that to which all science must be referred. It is at the same time the root and blossom of all other systems of thought. (Shelley, 1948: 61)

For Blake, industrialized London with its militant government, hypocritical churches, and repressive morality becomes the *objective correlative* – in T. S. Eliot's term – for a 'mirror'-consciousness coded by authoritative cultural discourses. In his poem "London" (1794/1996), he puts this situation in the memorable phrase:

> In every cry of every man,
> In every Infant's cry of fear,
> In every voice, in every ban,
> The mind-forg'd manacles I hear
> (Blake, 1996: 682, l. 5-8).

For Wordsworth, the most powerful 'mind forge'd manacles' shaping the world view of the 18th century are the scientific methods of analysis, which he denounces in his poem "The Tables Turned" (1798/1963):

> Sweet is the lore which Nature brings;
> Our meddling intellect
> Mis-shapes the beauteous forms of things:--
> We murder to dissect.
> (Wordsworth, 1963: 105, l. 25-28)

In the same poem, he opts for a movement away from the experiment, which is framed by preconceived questions, problems, and expected answers – to an experience open for phenomena which elude the dominant discourse of knowledge, and yet generate world models full of meaning, though not necessarily of explanation.

> Up! up! my friend, and clear your looks;
> Why all this toil and trouble?
> UP! up! my Friend, and quit your books,
> Or surely you'll grow double. [...]

Come forth, and bring with you a heart
That watches and receives.
(l. 1-32)

As these lines show, Wordsworth is aware of the fact that his readers in the 18th century are already coded by language and traditions of knowledge and representation archived in books. Just like the New Sciences in the Early Modern Period, now the Romantic poets concoct an innovative language in order to represent the new perspective of the world more adequately, and thus to open up new possibilities of conscious experience to the reader, unhampered by cultural norms of the present: And just like the New Sciences 150 years earlier, they criticise the rhetorical ornaments of their predecessors and opt for more simplicity. But in contrast to the New Sciences, they have no hope of a transparent language, but are conscious that there is no representation without taxation, namely that each representation has the price of excluding or at least marginalizing other possible modes of world arrangement.

Of course, the Romantics are also sensible to the fact that they themselves are part of the cultural coding they denounce. How can one challenge the ground one is standing on? The Romantics address this paradox by constructing an alternative model which makes it possible to criticise the naturalised rules of actual culture – and they mark this model as a construct. This alternative world is a world of rustics and children in a pre-industrial world, distinguished from – what the Romantics perceive as – the scientific world view by their openness for wonder, for a response to the world, which shatters epistemological and scientific securities and which is open for phenomena which elude mathematical precision and scientific methodologies. They become representatives of a consciousness not bent by the rules of culture, from behavioural norms through institutions and disciplines to ways of thinking (cf. Wordsworth, 1996, lines 58-109), all of which alienate the individuals from the spontaneous experience of their surroundings. Aesthetically, the Romantics represent the necessity of a dialogic interaction with the world by frequently dramatizing dialogic situations in their poems: Wordsworth's "The Tables Turned" is a dialogue between the – fictional – poet and his friend, Coleridge's *The Rime of the Ancient Mariner* (1798) is inserted in a frame tale, which makes clear that the Mariner tells his story about the lethal consequences of a self-centred and hermetic approach to the world to a wedding guest. Additionally, they use forms of the oral tradition like ballads, and shun rhetorical devices typical for classicist poetry. This strategy illustrates that the Romantics are not advocating a return to non-reflective primitivism, but a new epistemology, founded on the experience of "the spontaneous overflow of powerful feelings [thought about long and deeply]" (Wordsworth, 1963: 236), as Wordsworth formulates it in his "Preface to the Lyrical Ballads" (1802/1963).

However, although the Romantics explicitly criticise the scopophilic monological reasoning of the lonely subject as an adequate way of cognition, their emphasis on experience, conceptualised as a highly individual phenomenon in opposition to social discourses of knowledge, advanced the subjectivised perspective dramatised for the first time in Shakespeare's *Hamlet*. This became a real problem for the 19th century.

Interlude: Victorianism

During the 19th century in Europe, the 'grand narrative' (Lyotard) of the Bible was challenged and for many ultimately replaced by new narratives of geology, biology, and physiology. Charles Lyell in his *Principles of Geology* (1830-1833) discovers that the earth's creation has lasted far longer than the Bible says, Charles Darwin in his *On the Origin of Species by Means of Natural Selection* (1859) develops a model of evolution where it is a not a matter of divine will but of assimilation, whether a species including humanity will survive or not. Charles Taylor maintains that the 19th century's general shift of communal opinion to scientism, namely "the belief that the methods and procedures of natural science, as they were then being codified, suffice to establish all the truths we need to believe" (Taylor, 2001: 404), fell on fertile ground firstly due to the appeal to reason, which was in line with the privileged position accorded to the intellect by Protestantism from the Early Modern Period onward, and secondly was ethically ennobled by "a kind of heroism of unbelief" (ibid.), resulting from "a new militant moral outlook growing out of the old, and taking its place beside it as a fighting alternative" (ibid.).

The desperate texts of Alfred Lord Tennyson and Thomas Hardy illustrate the "'manliness' required to face the bare truth" (ibid.), but also the consequences of the ensuing 'transcendental homelessness' (Lukacs) like the loss of binding ethics and meaningful models of the human world, because the scientific order of things erased the centrality of the individual subject, which had been continually heightened and naturalised through the last 300 years in religious beliefs and epistemological concepts. Here is Alfred Lord Tennyson, in his poem *In Memoriam A. H. H.*., mourning the death of his sister's fiancé, Arthur Henry Hallam (1811–1833):

> Are God and Nature then at strife,
> That Nature lends such evil dreams?
> So careful of the type she seems,
> So careless of the single life;
> (Tennyson, 1996: 902)

Hardy, in his last novel *Jude the Obscure* (1895/1985), draws the bleak conclusion that, if individual self-perception, experience, and the need to find a place in a meaningful universe do not fit with the explanatory model of Darwin, so much the worse for the individual, who obviously is not able to assimilate his consciousness to a world governed by biological principles. The title hero Jude may be morally superior to the world governed by laws of adaptation in an industrialised and economised society, but that does not save him from being brutally exploited and finally dying miserably and utterly alone. Like Tennyson and Hardy, many people of the 19th century did not find themselves represented, in a political sense, in the scientific world models, and they did not find their experiences represented – in a meaningful way – in the language and the models of science.

III. MODERNISM

For Modernism "[...] the crisis *in* representation becomes a crisis *of* representation: representation no longer 'works', no longer appears to offer the subject any cognitive access to the object"(Larsen, 1990: xxxiv), because mass culture, political, economic, and social concerns were all seen as manifestations of a general 'pseudocommunication' (*sensu* Habermas), namely communal delusions, creating discourses of explanation and values which hide or at least detract from the perception of a 'real reality' the modernists were convinced was lying in wait for everyone to see. There were three central problems for modernists: 1) the fact that the human mind according to Kant can only perceive the world through the glasses of the a *priori* conditions of space and – for the modernists much more problematic – of time, 2) the monological self-centeredness of occidental epistemology, 3) verbal representation.

The Modernists' concern with the experience and representation of time was influenced by the philosophy of Henry Bergson, who distinguished between objective time as it is measured by the sciences and subjective time as it is experienced by the individual, by the new models in physics, especially Einstein's theories, and by Freud's psychoanalytical models of the human mind.[14] T. S. Eliot in his poem "The Dry Salvages" (1941) establishes different time experiences as distinguishing trait for distinct states of consciousness.

[14] For the multiple influences of other cultural forces cf. Bradshaw, 2003.

To explore the womb, or tomb, or dreams; all these are usual
Pastimes and drugs, and features of the press: [...]
Men's curiosity searches past and future
And clings to that dimension. But to apprehend
The point of intersection of the timeless
With time, is an occupation for the saint – [...]
(Eliot, 1958, "The Dry Salvages": 32)

T.S. Eliot's lines discriminate between two kinds of consciousness. The first and most common one is exploring the beginning and the end of life as well as dreams, representing those realms of consciousness not yet brought into the light and under the control of reason. The verb 'explore' stresses that it is a planned activity, like the exploration of an unknown territory. The second form of consciousness is an epiphany, the conscious experience of a world unconditioned by the aspects of time and space, and rendered aesthetically in "Burnt Norton" (1935):

Time past and time future
Allow but a little consciousness.
To be conscious is not to be in time.
(Eliot, 1958, "Burnt Norton": 173)

The former is seen as a delusion, which implies a fundamental devaluation or at least relativisation of universal truth claims of the natural sciences of the 19th century; only the latter is counted as true consciousness. Although the epiphanic consciousness described in these lines aspires to transcend 'objective time', it is still bound to a metaphysics of presence and seems to be a far cry from reality as 'radical alterity' delineated by Plotnitsky: "The 'alterity' at stake may not conform to anything that can be approached through any terms, including those of being/becoming, beginning/ending, difference/exteriority (or, of course, identity/interiority), unity/multiplicity, finitude/infinity, and matter/spirit." (Plotnitsky, 1997: 152) However, the following lines from "The Dry Salvages" suggest a time bend which significantly resembles Wheeler's 'phenomenon-to-be', and which Plotnitsky approaches with Derrida's concept of the supplement as "a 'past' that has never been present, and which never will be , whose future to come [*l*'*a-venir*'] will never be a *production* or a reproduction in the form of presence." (Plotnitsky, 1997: 148):

I sometimes wonder if that is what Krishna meant –
Among other things – or one way of putting the same thing:
That the future is a faded song, a Royal Rose or a lavender spray
Of wistful regret for those who are not yet here to regret,

Pressed between yellow leaves of a book that has never been opened.
And the way up is the way down, the way forward is the way back.
You cannot face it steadily, but this thing is sure,
That time is no healer: the patient is no longer here.
(Eliot, 1958, "The Dry Salvages": 29 f.)

The second condition binding human perception is the self-centeredness of human epistemology, whereas 'real reality' is conceptualized as a realm of reciprocal interaction:

And the bird called, in response to
The unheard music hidden in the shrubbery,
And the unseen eyebeam crossed, for the roses
Had the look of flowers that are looked at.
(Eliot, 1958, "Burnt Norton": 8)

The semantic field of perception, intellect, and consciousness in these few lines is portrayed as a communicative interchange. To experience this kind of world, the self-centered hermeticism of occidental epistemology has to be transcended. 'Experience' here – in psychoanalytical diction – would be closer to the unconscious or the subconscious, which is not immediately accessible and has to be transformed into a sign system like language in order to be communicated. Yet for modernists, solely this realm beyond the limits of self and time evokes meaning in the sense of a hermeneutical understanding of the world, in contradistinction to scientific explanation. Only during the epiphanic experience the perceived objects are

[...] surrounded
By a grace of sense,
[...] both a new world
And the old made explicit, understood [...].
(Eliot, 1958, "Burnt Norton": 9)

As this experience demands the surrender of self and thus cannot be willed, for T. S. Eliot (just like for James Joyce and Virginia Woolf) "there is only the unattended Moment" (Eliot 1958, "The Dry Salvages": 32 f.), when it happens unawares.

D.H. Lawrence in his poems and in novels like *Women in Love*, (1920) and *Lady Chatterley's Lover* (1928/1968) aesthetically subverts the limits of culture coded consciousness by returning to the romantic metaphors of darkness in his dramatisations of epiphanic experiences, thus marking them as counterpoint to the light of ocularcentric, monological, instrumentalised cognition. He binds these moments to his 'philosophy of touch', which he represents in highly formalised scenes of sexuality as a privileged way to transcend individualised selfhood, and gain what he termed – highly problematically – blood consciousness (cf. Horatschek, 1998: esp. 652-783). E.M. Forster, to mention a final example, in his world literature novel *A Passage to India* constructs the Indian Marabar Caves in Chandrapore as a zero point of human discourses, which discloses all human endeavours to impose a meaning onto the assembly of [*pace* Plotnitsky) material objects we call world – either by occidental power games of imperialism or by oriental polyphonies of philosophy and the arts – as futile and petty efforts in the face of an utterly indifferent universe.

If human consciousness is theorised as a perception of the world unhampered by the conditions of time and place, then it can only be experienced, never be represented in any adequate way.

> I can only say, there we have been: but I cannot say where.
> And I cannot say, how long, for that is to place it in time. [...]
> (Eliot, 1958, "Burnt Norton": 9)
>
> These are only hints and guesses [...].
> (Eliot, 1958, "The Dry Salvages": 33)

Yet, Eliot tries to represent it nevertheless, and he does so by on the one hand referring to light as the central occidental metaphor for consciousness: 'lucid stillness', 'and the pool was filled with water out of sunlight' (Eliot, "Burnt Norton": 10, 8). On the other hand, the description of these epiphanic moments defies logic and reason, as it unites paradox and opposites:

> a white light still and moving,
> Erhebung [elevation] without motion, concentration
> Without elimination,
> (Eliot, 1958, "Burnt Norton": 9)

This state of a non-representational experience is ephemeral – "Then a cloud passed, and the pool was empty."(Eliot, 1958, "Burnt Norton": 8) – and the struggle to verbally represent the knowledge gained from this moment ensues, as Eliot describes in "East Coker" (1940): "a raid on the inarticulate With shabby equipment" (Eliot, 1958, "Easter Coker": 22). For T.S. Eliot and other modernists like D.H. Lawrence, E.M. Forster, James Joyce, and Virginia Woolf, this hovering between intellectual and epiphanic consciousness, between experience and experiment, between being and representation is characteristic of being human: "The hint half guessed, the gift half understood, is Incarnation." (Eliot, 1958, "Dry Salvages": 33)

Again it is worthwhile to compare these aesthetic attempts at representing – or evoking – a reality marked as exceeding any possibility of representation with Plotnitsky's explications of a relational reality-as-radical-alterity in a quantum universe, and it is noteworthy that he aesthetically has to force language to its breaking point, working with words in a very similar way to T.S. Eliot by employing paradox and negation as his dominant rhetorical figures.

> These considerations do not suggest, nihilistically, that the "process(es)" and "relation(s)" at issue relate to nothingness. Here, they must not – and cannot – relate to what may be no more "nothing" than "something," or any other "thing," to what is no more "it" than unidentifiable by this or any pronoun, to what is no more than is not, but that nevertheless is what produces the effects of nothingness or "somethingness" (or "thingness"), of being and nonbeing, and all the other effects just indicated and all the terms used here. Although such a "relation" is classically impossible – and, conceivably, impossible or inconceivable in a way – at issue is a "relation" or "non-relation" of neither absolute (or potentially any) alterity, difference, exteriority, or disconnection; nor of absolute (or potentially any) connectibility, or anything within any form of the conceptual and interpretive enclosure within which we must function. The latter formulation, of course, also suggests a form of relation, and, as such, it may be equally inapplicable. (Plotnitsky, 1997: 152)

Yet neither content with Eliot's "gift half understood" (Eliot, 1958: "Dry Salvages" 33) nor able to ultimately transcend "our own perceptual and conceptual enclosure(s)" (Plotnitsky, 1997: 165), Plotnitsky seems to resign towards the end of his *tour de force* essay: "There may never be a mathematically consistent model of matter, or a model for and a way to conceive of its radical alterity. Nature may have no mathematical harmony and, in the end, may not be kind to us." (ibid.: 166)

IV. POSTMODERNISM

Postmodern literature denies the possibility of experience or 'world' prior to representation. Based on the structuralist linguistic model of Ferdinand de Saussure, theoreticians and philosophers like Michel Foucault, Jacques Derrida, and Jacques Lacan claim that occidental ideas of experiencing a world 'beyond' language, and indeed the entire concept of 'experience' itself, are products of language-induced ways of thought. This so called *linguistic turn* has shaped literary theory for the last 50 years, and its assumptions inform those diverse texts subsumed under the blanket term of 'postmodern literature'. Especially post-colonial and gender studies have adopted these premises, because mistaking the representations of politically biased world views for the nature of things has had devastating effects in history.

From this perspective all we have is representations, understood as signs and semantics. In accordance with historically and culturally specific rules, they are ordered into disciplines of knowledge, like anthropology, medicine, religion, etc.. These discourses regulate individual self-perception and experience, and from the Early Modern Period onwards they privilege experiment and systematised thought as the condition for truth claims, and individuality, subjectivity, intellect, and reason as decisive traits of humanity.

These convictions are put to the test in Peter Ackroyd's *Milton in America* (1996). The novel starts in 1660, when Cromwell's Puritan Commonwealth is broken down and Charles II. returns from his exile in France. John Milton, the author of *Paradise Lost*, had published a tract justifying the regicide of Charles I. while working for Cromwell. Historically, Milton, who had been blind for nearly ten years, continued living in England and dictated his epic to his daughter; in this novel, Milton flees to the New World, where he is elected as leader by Puritan settlers and establishes a dystopian rule in *New Milton*. He hates Catholics, women, American Indians, and the Irish, and finally incites a war with the neighbouring village *Mary Mount,* where all these people live happily together. The book ends with Milton winning this war.

The first chapter describes Milton's thoughts while the boat approaches the American Coast. They consist of images, quotes, and scenes from the canonical works of the Occident: the Bible, the myths of Oedipus, Heracles, and Aeneas, the *Divine Comedy* by Dante, and texts previously written by Milton himself. Milton identifies with the heroes of these texts, including Jesus, explains his feat in light of their fates and espouses the misogyny and xenophobia implied in these narratives. The chapter characterises Milton's approach to the world, because though blind, he is convinced that he knows everything he needs to know from these cultural authorities in order to explain the foreign world he cannot see. When in power, he brutally adapts the historical reality to his picture of the world by avoiding, forbidding, punishing, and finally killing everyone who does not fit the design he extracts from the texts, ultimately all inhabitants of *Mary Mount*. His character illustrates the postmodern thesis that individual consciousness is a passive receptacle of cultural norms dispensed through institutions and cultural or political authorities. What Milton experiences as his divine *inner vision* and thus as his spiritual guidance, consists of the internalised norms and values archived in the literary canon.

With the settlement of *Mary Mount*, Ackroyd imaginatively sketches an alternative to Milton's occidental imperial, misogynous, and xenophobic Puritan hermeticism. That this utopia of hybrid identities is killed off by Puritan rigidity can be read as a harsh critique of the beginnings of US-American history. But the depiction of a different possible world ties in with a general trend in British fiction to 'retrieve' individual agency, authentic experience, and reality from the representational fallacy of radical postmodernist theses, without falling back on the concept of the transparent sign. Of these attempts, the novel *Life of Pi* (2001) in my opinion addresses the relation of representation, knowledge, and experience in such a convincing way, that I shall present it as the final text of my essay, although it has been written by a Canadian author, Yann Martel.

The Indian title hero Pi's name is his program: Being named after the love of a family friend for French swimming pools - piscine (cf. 8) - , which is bungled into the derogative "*Pissing* Patel" (ibid.: 20) by schoolmates, he makes it a habit to jump towards the blackboard whenever his name is asked, and to write:

> My name is
> Piscine Molitor Patel.
> known to all as
> <u>Pi</u> Patel
> $\pi = 3.14$
>
> (sic.; 22f.)

Marking himself as a specialist for infinity, Pi transgresses, or transcends, fundamental horizons circumscribed by cultural norms and religions: Pi is a practicing Hindu, a practicing Moslem, and a practicing Catholic Christian simultaneously, to the chagrin of his westernised father, owner of a zoo in Pondicherry. When his family wants to emigrate to Canada, taking their most expensive animals on the boat, the boat sinks on July 2nd, 1977 (238). Only Pi survives and finds himself in a rescue boat with a Bengal tiger named Richard Parker, a hyena, and an orang utan. As the frame tale informs us, after he has been saved on February 14th, 1978 (191) nearly 8 months later with only him and the tiger left, the story "that will make you believe in God" (XI) is told to the fictional author of the book, who then hands it on to the reader – with its utter despair, wonderful adventures, and ecstatic moments – as a testimony to human courage and ingenuity. At the very end of the book, a Japanese official interviews Pi for the insurance company of the boat and insists on a more plausible story, without a tiger and without wonders, and he gets "another story" (303), seven pages full of brutality, gory deaths and human suffering. The official chooses the first version for his report, which forms the end of the novel. My interpretation of this novel will be contained in the concluding remarks of my essay.

Knowledges in the Plural

My reading of English Literary History has shown contradictory models of the relation between experience, knowledge, and representation, implying different models of what it means to be conscious. In *Hamlet*, 'consciousness' is sketched and problematised as individualised faculty and as a generator of intramundane knowledge about the material world according to empirical rules of method and procedure; Romanticism constructs 'consciousness' as a creative imaginative force foundational for the arts as well as for the sciences, turning onto itself as object of observation and critique in the wake of Kant; in Modernism, the concept of 'consciousness' has to supply the basis for authenticity and identity as a stronghold against the onslaught of total cultural coding through the fragmentary world of modernity; and Postmodernism, as presented in *Life of Pi*, redefines 'consciousness' as a spiritual entity enabling the individual to transcend the culturally specific models of world and knowledges, be they religious or scientific.

Despite some similarities in terms of verbal representation, these models differ fundamentally from each other as well as from Plotnitsky's model of consciousness inspired by quantum theories. Yet this polyphony is not to be lamented. What we see is that all these texts by imaginative self-reflection and verbal representation are creating concepts and forms of consciousness. In analogy, this essay simultaneously interprets and represents historical versions of consciousness and through this performance enacts the very topic it is addressing.

Whereas the natural sciences are struggling to devise a model of reality that is consistent with and adequate to (as a weak trace of former 'truth') the empircal evidence of quantum data, the fictional texts explore the hermeneutic significance of competing world models for the individual. *Life of Pi* illustrates that there is the need for stories of ingenuity as well as stories of brutality, for stories of religion as well as of the natural sciences. Indeed, it may well be that the very struggle for consistency and continuity in *one* explanatory narrative or model forms one of the central problems of occidental knowledge formation. "The metaphysics of presence is often the metaphysics of the continuum. The concept of mathematical continuity or infinity is part of this history, and the proximity between philosophy and mathematics (or physics) in this regard cannot be ignored." (Plotnitsky, 1997: 165) Barbara Herrnstein Smith concludes:

> Incommensurability is, it appears, neither a logically scandalous relation between theories, nor an ontologically immutable relation between isolated systems of thought, nor a morally unhappy relation between sets of people, but a contingent experiential relation between historically and institutionally situated conceptual and discursive practices. Some radically divergent ideas never meet at all, at least not in the experience of mortal beings. (Smith, 1997: 262)

The experience of a different mode of perception in comparison with everyday awareness thus in different cultures and epochs might be represented as divine inspiration, as the appearance of god or the intervention of the devil, as secularised epiphany, psychological anomaly, disease, or madness. Each of these possible representations is intricately interwoven with an 'order of knowledge' which defines the authoritative 'order of things' (*sensu* Foucault), i.e. a world view, which forms the very ground of our everyday experiences and perceptions. What is of paramount importance is the awareness that on the one hand the discourses, stories, models, and concepts are stories, possible versions, and that nevertheless on the other hand the choice of narrative is supremely significant, because it will decide about how to conduct our lives. Pi would have gone mad in the face of the unbearable hardships of the shipwreck without the vistas of nature, humanity, brutality, and beauty which the religious and zoological narratives he has internalized engender. Thus 'knowledge fictions' metamorphose into reality by becoming embodied through internalisation and by being enacted.

From the *tour de force* through British literature, the following result could be summarised: We represent – as *homo depictor* – our perception of the world, and by doing so we create specific versions of an order of things, perceived and experienced from different points of view, knowledges, interests, and conditions. In doing so we also implicitly or explicitly generate a performative version of what it means to think, to experience, to generate knowledge – in short, we dramatise knowingly or unknowingly what – for us – it means to be conscious. This implies that our approach to and version of the world is also a performative version of our selves, and *vice versa* the versions of consciousness, world and self preform what we perceive and enact as 'self' and 'world. Fictions, models, and systems of thought metamorphose and mutate into reality by being enacted and ultimately by being embodied through internalisation and externalisation. By materialising and archiving them through representation in scientific formulas or artworks we install frames for future perspectives. And the embodied versions of 'world stories', 'consciousness stories', and 'self-stories' engender new questions, models, and versions of what the world is. There can be no 'naked truth' about consciousness without representation, and there can be no experience without being veiled by semiosis, which means by representing consciousness in discourses of historically specific and disciplinary discourses.

The horizon of the story I have presented, despite its variations and disruptions, is framed by conditions of religions, epistemologies, and knowledges of the occident, imbued with cultural authority by being fixed in and dispersed by institutions and discourses, and focused largely on negotiations of self and rationality. A non-reductive science of consciousness, in light of the aforesaid, would consist in the negotiation – and thereby creation - of 'consciousness' as a dialogue between the sciences and the arts on a global scale, because

> [o]nly a very confined – fundamentally theological, perhaps – notion of the human would represent the humanities as standing in some essentially adversarial relation to mathematics or to the scientific disciplines more generally. And only a very confined – fundamentally metaphysical, it appears – notion of science would represent its domains and pursuits [...] as other than social, cultural, discursive, human, and [...] corporeal and therefore mortal. (Smith & Plotnitsky, 1997: 4)

By representing consciousness in disciplinary discourses of knowledge, we are experiencing *and* simultaneously generating consciousness. Consciousness is – and of course I am talking in metaphors – the medium in which all this happens, consciousness is what consciousness does. Bruno Latour expounds:

> Anyone who holds that fabricated means untrue, and made means fake, tends towards fundamentalism. Common experience in science, art, love, and religion should prompt us to say, "the more carefully fabricated, the more real and long-lasting". Why we do not tend to reach that more sensible conclusion is perhaps our old and continuing fear of idolatry, of worshiping [sic] what human hands have made; a genuine acceptance of constructivism requires a reassessment of the whole history of iconoclasm and critique. (Latour, 2004: 460)

A slightly adapted quote by E.M. Forster, written while he was struggling with his grand novel *A Passage to India*, brings it to the point: "Expansion. That is the idea [we] must cling to. Not completion. Not rounding off but opening out". (Forster, 1927: 116)

References

Abrams, M. H. (1958). *The mirror and the lamp: Romantic theory and the critical tradition.* New York: W. W. Norton.

Ackroyd, P. (1996). *Milton in America.* London: Sinclair-Stevenson.

Ankersmit, F. (2005). Hermeneutics. In D. Herman, J. Manfred Jahn, & M. Ryan (Eds.), *Routledge Encyclopedia of Narrative Theory* (pp. 211-12). Abingdon and New York: Routledge.

Bachelard, G. (1968). *The philosophy of no: A philosophy of the new scientific mind* (G. C. Waterston, Trans.). New York: Orion Press.

Barker, F. (1984). *The tremulous private body.* London: Methuen.

Blake, W. (1996). Ah sun-flower. In M. Ferguson, M. J. Salter, & J. Stallworthy (Eds.), *The Norton anthology of poetry* (p. 681). New York: Norton.

Blake, W. (1996). London. In M. Ferguson, M. J. Salter, & J. Stallworthy (Eds.), *The Norton anthology of poetry* (pp. 681-82), New York: Norton.

Blake, W. (1979). The marriage of heaven and hell. In G. Keynes (Ed.), *Blake: Complete writings.* (pp. 148-158), Oxford: Oxford University Press.

Bradshaw, D. (Ed.). (2003). *A concise companion to modernism.* Malden, MA: Blackwell.

Blumenberg, H. (1957). Licht als Metapher der Wahrheit: Im Vorfeld der philosophischen Begriffsbildung. *Studium Generale, 10*, 432-447.

Crary, J. (1990). *Techniques of the observer: On vision and modernity in the Nineteenth Century.* Cambridge, MA: MIT Press.

Eagleton, T. (1986). *William Shakespeare.* London: Blackwell.

Eliot, T. S. (1958). Burnt Norton. *Four quartets* (pp. 7-13). London: Faber and Faber.

Eliot, T. S. (1958). The dry salvages. *Four quartets* (pp. 25-33). London: Faber and Faber.

Ferry, A. (1983). *The "Inward" language: Sonnets of Wyatt, Sidney, Shakespeare, Donne.*

Chicago: University of Chicago Press.

Forster, E. M. (1927). *Aspects of the novel.* London: Edward Arnold.

Frank, M. (1988). Subjekt, person, individuum. In M. Frank, G. Raulet, & Reijen van W. (Eds.), *Die Frage nach dem Subjekt* (pp. 7-28). Frankfurt/M: Suhrkamp.

Gadamer, H.-G. (1965). *Wahrheit und Methode: Grundzüge einer philosophischen Her meneutik.* Tübingen: J.C.B. Mohr.

Gadamer, H.-G. (1967). Mensch und Sprache. In *Kleine Schriften,* 1: *Philosophie,*

Hermeneutik (pp. 93-100). Tübingen: J. C. B. Mohr.

Habermas, J. (1988). Ein anderer Ausweg aus der Subjektphilosophie – kommunikative vs. subjektzentrierte Vernunft. In *Der philosophische Diskurs der Moderne*: *Zwölf Vorlesungen.* Frankfurt/M.: Suhrkamp.

Habermas, J. (2012). *Nachmetaphysisches Denken II.* Berlin: Suhrkamp.

Hardy, T. (1985). *Jude the obscure.* Oxford: Oxford University Press.

Hardy, T. (1996). Hap. In M. Ferguson, J. Stallworthy, & M. Salter (Eds.). *The Norton Anthology of Poetry* (p. 1049). New York: W. W. Norton & Company.

Hardy, T. (2001). Drinking song. In J. Gibson (Ed.), *Thomas Hardy: The complete poems* (pp. 905-908), London: Palgrave Macmillan.

Hillman, D. (2007). *Shakespeare's entrails: Belief, scepticism and the interior of the body.* Houndmills, England: Palgrave Macmillan.

Horatschek, A-M. (2005). Self-constitution by text, voice and music in English Literature. In L. Moessner & C. M. Schmidt (Eds.), Anglistentag, *Proceedings of the Conference of the German Association of University Teachers of English,* 2004 Conference, Achen. Trier:

WVT.

Horatschek, A-M. (1998). *Alterität und Stereotyp. Die Begegnung mit dem Fremden in den international novels von E. M. Forster und D. H. Lawrence.* Tübingen: Narr.

Iser, W. (1989). *Prospecting: From reader response to literary anthropology.*

Baltimore, MD: Johns Hopkins University Press.

Kittler, F. (2010). *Optical Media.* Cambridge: Polity Press, 2010. (Original work published 2002. *Optische Medien.* Berlin: Merve.)

Klepper, M. (2011). *The discovery of point of view: Observation and narration in the*

American novel 179 0-1910. Heidelberg: Winter.

Larsen, N. (1990). *Modernism and hegemony: A materialist critique of aesthetic*

agencies. Minneapolis, MN: University of Minnesota Press.

Latour, B. (1993). *We have never been modern.* (C. Porter, Trans.). Cambridge, MA: Harvard University Press

Latour, B. (2004). Whose cosmos, which cosmopolitics? Comments on the Peace

Terms of Ulrich Beck. *Common Knowledge, 10*(3), 450-462. Symposium: Talking peace with Gods, Part 1. doi:10.1215/0961754X-10-3-450

Law, S. (2007). Philosophy of science. In S. Law (Ed.), *Philosophy* (pp. 122-37). London, New York: Dorling Kindersley.

Lechte, J. (1994). Gaston Bachelard. In *Fifty key contemporary thinkers: From structuralism to postmodernity* (pp. 3-7). London: Routledge.

Link, J., & Parr, R. (1997). Semiotik und Interdiskursanalyse. In K. M. Bogdal (Ed.), *Neue Literaturtheorien: Eine Einführung* pp. 108-33. Opladen: Westdeutscher Verlag.

Martel, Y. (2001). *Life of pi.* Edinburgh: Canongate.

Meyers Grosses Universallexikon (1986). *Deutsches Wörterbuch.* Vol. 18. Ed. Under supervision of Günther Drosdowski. Mannheim: Bibliographisches Institute.

Milton, J. (1993). *Paradise lost. An authoritative text, backgrounds and sources, criticism.* A Norton critical edition. S. Elledge (Ed.), New York: Norton.

Nate, R. (2009). *Wissenschaft, Rhetorik und Literatur: Historische Perspektiven.*

Würzburg: Königshausen Neumann.

OED. (1998). *The new Oxford dictionary of English.* J. Pearsall (Ed.). Oxford: Clarendon Press.

Penrose, R. (1989). *The emperor's new mind: Concerning computers, minds, and the laws of physics.* Oxford: Oxford University Press

Plotnitsky, A. (1997). Complementarity, idealization, and the limits of classical

conceptions of reality. In B. H. Smith & A. Plotnitsky (Eds.). *Mathematics, Science, and Postclassical Theory.* (134-72). Durham: Duke University Press.

Rao, K. R. (2002). *Consciousness studies: Cross-cultural perspectives.* Jefferson,

N. C.: McFarland & Company.

Ricoeur, P. (1991). Narrative identity. *Philosophy Today, 35* (1), 73-81.

Sandkühler, H. J. (2003). Repräsentation – Die Fragwürdigkeit der 'Welt der Dinge'. In S. Freudenberger and H. J. Sandkühler (Eds.), *Repräsentation, Krise der Repräsentation, Paradigmenwechsel: Ein Forschungsprogramm in Philosophie und Wissenschaften* (pp. 47-69). Frankfurt a. M.: Peter Lang.

Scott, J. W. (1992). Experience. In J. Butler & J. Scott (Eds.), *Feminists theorize the political* (pp. 22-40). New York: Routledge.

Shakespeare, W. (1997). *Othello.* E. A. J. Honigmann (Ed.). Walton-on-Thames, England: Thomas Nelson.

Shakespeare, W. (2006). *Hamlet.* A. Thompson & N. Taylor. (Eds.), London: Arden

Shelley, P. B. (1948). *Shelley's defence of poetry and Blunden's lectures on "defence"*. Darby, PA: Darby Books.

Smith H. B. (1997). Microdynamics of incommensurability: Philosophy of science meets science studies. In B. H. Smith & A. Plotnitsky (Eds.), *Mathematics, Science, and Postclassical Theory* (pp. 243-66). Durham: Duke University Press.

Smith H. B., & Plotnitsky, A. (1997). Introduction: Networks and symmetries, decidable and undecidable. In B. H. Smith & A. Plotnitsky (Eds.), *Mathematics, Science, and Postclassical Theory* (pp. 1-16). Durham: Duke University Press.

Taylor, C. (2001). *Sources of the self: The making of the modern identity*. Cambridge,

MA: Harvard University Press.

Tennyson, A. (1996). In M. Ferguson, M. J. Salter, & J. Stallworthy (Eds.), *The Norton anthology of poetry* (pp. 899-907). New York: Norton.

Wheeler, J. A. (1984). Law without law. In J. A. Wheeler, & H. Z. Wojciek (Eds.), *Quantum Theory and Measurement*. Princeton: Princeton University Press.

Wordsworth, W. (1963). The tables turned. In *The lyrical ballads* (pp. 104-105). London: Methuen.

Wordsworth, W. (1963). Preface to the lyrical ballads. In *The lyrical ballads* (pp. 235-66). London: Methuen.

Wordsworth, W. (1996). Ode: Intimations of immortality from recollections of early childhood. In M. Ferguson, M. J. Salter, & J. Stallworthy (Eds.), *The Norton anthology of poetry* (pp.728-732). New York: Norton.

Chapter 11

The Consciousness Quotient: Introducing the Conscious Experience as a Research Variable in Psychological Assessment

OVIDIU BRAZDAU and SONA AHUJA[1]
Consciousness Quotient Institute
Bucharest, Romania

I. CONSCIOUS EXPERIENCE AS A RESEARCH VARIABLE

The scientific evaluation of consciousness has been a topic of debate over the last century in different scientific communities in different academic fields: for example, psychology and cognitive science, philosophy, neuroscience, psychiatry and, lately, quantum physics. As consciousness is a subjective experience, the first- and second-person approaches seem to provide valuable information but, unfortunately, the first-person methods offer no scientific results, unless statistical analyses are provided (Varela & Shear, 1999; Dennett, 2001).

The research problems come from the methodological inability to isolate consciousness as an individual phenomenon. Consciousness seems to be different from all other scientific concepts and it has been extraordinarily difficult to treat it as a variable (Baars, 1997). In psychology, measuring the conscious experience with assessment instruments and statistical methods has only rarely been a topic of research, perhaps because psychologists find it difficult to create a method that would reach a satisfactory level of significance as to its results (Natsoulas, 1990).

In order to use the data from self-reports in the psychological assessment of consciousness, the terminology must be explored. We need an operational definition of the conscious experience. However, first of all a distinction between awareness and consciousness is necessary. According to Brown and Ryan (2003), consciousness encompasses both awareness and attention: "Awareness is the background radar of consciousness, continually monitoring the inner and outer environment. One may be aware of stimuli without them being at the centre of attention. Attention is a process of focusing conscious awareness, providing heightened sensitivity to a limited range of experience. In actuality, awareness and attention are intertwined, such that attention continually pulls figures out of the ground of awareness, holding them focally for varying lengths of time" (Brown & Ryan, 2003, p. 822).

[1]Correspondence: Ovidiu Brazdau, E-mail: ovidiu@consciousness-quotient.com.
Sona Ahuja, E-mail: sonaahujadei@gmail.com.

Other important terminological issues come from the distinction between matched conscious and unconscious phenomena. Some of the widely studied conscious vs. unconscious polarities include: explicit vs. implicit cognition; immediate vs. long-term memory; attended vs. unattended information; focal vs. fringe contents; declarative memory (facts) vs. procedural memory (skills); effortful vs. automatic tasks; remembering (recall) vs. knowing (recognition); strategic vs. automatic control; wakefulness and dreams (cortical arousal) vs. deep sleep, coma, sedation (cortical slow waves); episodic memory (autobiographical) vs. semantic memory (conceptual knowledge), available vs. unavailable memories (Baars, 1997), rational vs. irrational (Vasile, 2012).

There is an increased tendency to use philosophy and neuroscience to explain consciousness and leave deep psychology aside. In *The view from within. The first person approaches to the study of consciousness* (Varela and Shear, 1999), Bernard Baars felt the need to emphasize this point, writing a chapter called 'There is already a field of systematic phenomenology, and it's called "Psychology."' He writes: "the things we humans can report accurately are the same things we experience as conscious! Reportability is the generally accepted index of consciousness. In point of fact, therefore, psychologists are always asking people about their conscious experiences" (Baars, 1999). In recent years, first- and second-person procedures are becoming more accepted as valid research methodology for exploring the conscious experience (Petitmengin, 2009).

II. THE CONSCIOUSNESS QUOTIENT (CQ)

The 'Consciousness Quotient' construct was developed through 15 successive studies between 2003 and 2014. The CQ-i beta version was first released in 2008 and since then, a series of studies refined the concept and the measurement procedures.

The Consciousness Quotient (CQ) is a composite psychological construct based on a list of traits, skills and abilities that describe conscious experience. The CQ Inventory (CQ-i) evaluates the frequency of various behaviours and the usage of specific skills and abilities, providing a detailed description of conscious awareness experiences.

In our perspective, to be conscious means to have a degree of witnessing awareness and a degree of freedom of choice when thinking, feeling, sensing and interacting with people and the environment.

An important element of conscious experience is intentionality, being the mind-set that allows a person to deliberately choose what behaviour to enact and what attitude to select. 'More conscious' (a higher CQ) means a higher degree of witnessing awareness and being less automatic in thinking-feeling-sensing, together with a higher degree of choice when initiating a behaviour.

The witnessing perspective, which leads to the ability to observe the inside and outside worlds without engaging with them, is one of the key factors of the CQ construct.

The everyday CQ is "the level of consciousness (or the level of being conscious) that is experienced in the morning, one hour after waking up and after having had a refreshing sleep, without being exposed to any significant stimulus (coffee, TV, radio, music, talking, psychological stress). In other words, the consciousness quotient is the general level of being conscious/aware throughout a day, in regular life conditions". This level of being conscious can change during life through the process of personal development.

III. THE CONSCIOUSNESS QUOTIENT INVENTORY (CQ-I)

The CQ-i is composed of seven dimensions, which comprise the Consciousness Quotient: physical, emotional, cognitive, social-relational, self, inner growth and spiritual. These seven dimensions are the main seven factors of the Consciousness Quotient Inventory. CQ-i explores these dimensions, using questions scored with a Likert scale with six degrees.

CQ-i can be used for evaluating personal development or in psychotherapy when evaluating the progress of a client. Other areas include leadership, employee satisfaction, digital interactions, the arts, medicine, military applications and the efficacy of self-development or religious techniques. CQ-i is free to use by researchers in educational fields and for individual online testing on the CQ Institute website.

Main factor structure of the Consciousness Quotient:

1. The Physical CQ refers to the capacity for awareness of one's body and of the actual elements of the environment (environmental awareness). This factor includes various traits, skills and abilities, such as interoceptive awareness, body posture, tone of voice, awareness of senses (e.g., smell, taste, touch), psychosomatic connections (how the body is influenced by emotions and thinking patterns), detecting automatic movements of the body (e.g., automatic eating behaviours), awareness of the bio-energy of the body, and a connection with one's physical surroundings.

Focusing attention on the body will result in a better connection with both your inner reality and outer reality. You will thus be able to identify the problems of your body in relation to the outer world. Breathing, conscious cooking and observing body movements comprise a few exercises that would help you to increase your Physical CQ. Another important technique is to observe what changes occur in your body when you have emotions or when you think of specific topics.

2. The Emotional CQ refers to the capacity for awareness of one's emotions and feelings, and their development and interactions. The Emotional CQ include traits, skills and abilities related to the emotional world, such as empathy, emotional validation, openness, vulnerability, recognition of people's emotions, detecting the automatic patterns in emotional life, mirroring others, emotional acceptance, emotional intelligence, the ability to select among emotions and to sustain positive emotions, adapting emotional responses to various social contexts, and acceptance of any emotions that appear in you.

By raising the level of Emotional CQ through various personal growth techniques, you will be able to improve your personal and social life. You may find it useful to develop your emotional intelligence (e.g., eqi.org) and the capacity to welcome and accept all your emotions as they come.

3. The Cognitive CQ refers to the capacity for awareness of one's own ideas and thoughts, of the cognitive flow in general. The Cognitive CQ is related to thinking, reflection, judgment, patterns of understanding, ways of meaning-making. It includes specific traits, skills and abilities, such as systems-thinking, intuition, awareness of cognitive filters, metacognition, self-reflection, detection of cognitive biases (e.g., jumping to conclusions, labeling, projection), accepting indecision, flexibility in thinking, critical thinking, present moment awareness, awareness of the limits of words (construct awareness), attention regulation, an ability to act with intention (choice), decision-making, mindfulness, acceptance of multiple perspectives, cognitive openness, creativity, the ability to have a panoramic view (overview) of a specific topic or situation, and the ability to manage the flow of thoughts.

Improving the Cognitive CQ could have positive effects for the management of your thoughts. Training your attention (e.g., through mindfulness) would help you to identify less with your stream of thinking and provide you with the abilities necessary to better organize your thoughts. Sustained self-reflection (metacognition – thinking about thinking) is another useful practice to increase the Cognitive CQ (some useful techniques are available on wisebrain.org).

4. The Social-Relational CQ refers to the capacity for awareness of the relations and connections with the people around us and the communities we are a part of. The Social-Relational CQ includes traits, skills and abilities related to parental relationships, close relationships, social interactions, perception of others' communications styles, detecting social deception, cognitive empathy, social intuition, flexibility in social behaviours, outrospection (a means of getting to know oneself by developing relationships and empathetic thinking with others), awareness of in-out groups stereotypes, cognitive openness when discussing matters with others, detecting the hidden agendas of the people we listen to or talk to, and conversational skills.

An exercise that could increase the Social-Relational CQ is to divide your attention when speaking with people: keeping your attention focused both on the person you are talking to (and their message) and on yourself, on your own body posture, thinking and emotions.

5. The Self CQ refers to the capacity for awareness of one's self and one's own ego (identity). The Self CQ includes traits, skills and abilities related to identity, the self-system, one's image of life, self-awareness, connections between emotions and thinking, an ability to see one's self as objectively as possible, flexibility in ego-related thinking (e.g., the ability to make and appreciate jokes about the way we are), self-compassion, self-kindness, post-autonomous ego-development traits (goal in life, ego awareness), awareness of sub-personalities, multicultural self-awareness (e.g., recognizing how cultures you interact with influence your worldview), and autonomy.

You can increase your Self CQ by observing your sub-personalities – the various facets of your personalities (e.g., you as a child, you as a parent, you as a friend, you as a worker, etc.), how they act and interact with each other and with the environment, and what their specific emotions, patterns of thinking, fears and behaviour are.

6. The Inner Growth CQ refers to the capacity for awareness of the process of personal development, transformation and growth. The Inner Growth CQ includes traits, skills and abilities related to the evolution of personality, paradigm shifts, unlearning and learning (through pain or by open learning), openness, the language updating process, accepting criticism, abandoning old perspectives and embracing new ones, noticing resistance to change, learning after peak experiences, detecting the cognitive biases related to learning (e.g., confirmation bias), resilience, awareness of one's level of development (e.g., using spiral dynamics theory), and an ability to sustain new patterns of thinking/feeling while old patterns slowly lose their grip (awareness of the process of neuroplasticity).

You can increase your Inner Growth CQ by learning to be more open and to accept life as it comes. Learning from criticism and embracing various perspectives for the same situation are key skills that would support your personal development.

7. The Spiritual CQ includes specific traits, skills and abilities related to human connectedness, meta-awareness, witnessing awareness (non-attachment) and acceptance of experience, present moment awareness, the connection with humans and nature (environment), mindfulness, and non-reactivity to inner experiences. Witnessing experience is a key factor to the Spiritual CQ: the ability to look at your own body, thoughts and feelings, and your own awareness as a neutral witness, from the outside. This is the experience of an 'I', of an observer, of watching one's self doing things.

An important part of the Spiritual CQ explores post-autonomous ego development features, including serving others, compassion for the self, transpersonal experiences, Ego as object/construct, detecting the limits of words (language as object).

The spiritual factor was developed by including the participatory understanding of spirituality: "*the spirituality of persons is developed and revealed primarily in the spirituality of their relations with other persons. If you regard spirituality primarily as the fruit of individual meditative attainment, then you can have the gross anomaly of a "spiritual" person who is an interpersonal oppressor, and the possibility of "spiritual" traditions that are oppression-prone*" (Heron, 2006, p. 6).

Improving the Spiritual CQ could lead to an increased ability to connect with the collectivities that you live in and to experience your life as a part of a larger life that includes all of us. There are many available methods that develop the Spiritual CQ. Some of the effective ways include mindfulness-related techniques and the practices promoted by non-dual communities (e.g., conscious.tv, batgap.com) and Eastern and traditional spiritual philosophies (e.g., Ubuntu, Native American), which develop the ability to non-identify with the self-centred ego and embrace a larger perspective.

IV. CQ-I DEVELOPMENT

The CQ-i beta version was first released in 2008, and presented the following year at the 'Toward a Science of Consciousness' conference. Since then, it has been updated many times in order to become a very reliable and valid assessment instrument that measures consciousness as a psychological variable.

CQ-i Beta v.2013, released in January 2013, was composed of six dimensions which together constituted the CQ factor model: physical, emotional, cognitive, spiritual, social-relational and self-consciousness. The 51 items of CQ-i Beta v.2013 explored these dimensions using a Likert scale with six levels.

During the development process of the CQ-i, some other psychological instruments were analysed: Self-Consciousness Scale – SCS (Fenigstein, 1975), Mindfulness Attention and Awareness Scale-MAAS (Brown & Ryan, 2003), Freiburg Mindfulness Inventory (Bucheld et al., 2001), Psychological Well-Being Scales (Ryff & Keyes, 1995). Some scales from transpersonal psychology were analysed (Macdonald & Friedman, 2003) as well as some recent developments such as the "Descriptive Experience Sampling" (DES) method by Russ Hurlburt and colleagues, and the "Explicitation Interview" (EI) by Pierre Vermersch and colleagues (Froese et al., 2011).

Altough the first version of CQ-i (2008) had a five-level Likert scale using agreement-disagreement. After consultations with various experts and several studies on a large population (studies #3, #4, #5) we decided to change the Likert scale from 5 levels to 6 levels. After this modification, reliability of the CQ-i improved significantly.

In 2012 we further explored the CQ factor model. We eliminated some items (which showed low reliability after we changed the Likert scale), and we introduced new items. After an extensive library research, we created a list of 24 criteria for designing the items. As a result, all the items were checked for their compliance with these criteria. In study #10 we used the Willis' Cognitive Interviewing to improve the items. We re-checked and changed all the items, so that the traits we explore in each item would refer to behaviours instead of attitudes. Another important decision that improved the validity was to change the Likert scale type from agreement-disagreement to a six-level frequencies scale.

CQ-i Beta Version. Pre-testing (2003-2010)

Study No.	When	Population, Scientific Activities	Results, Decisions
# 0	2003-2007	Literature research, Item pool, Evaluating other scales	Selecting 64 items
# 1	2007	N=150, paper-pencil	2 Items eliminated; 15 Items reformulated CQ-i beta version 62 items
# 2	2008	N=2474 50% paper-pencil, 50% online	Publication of Ovidiu Brazdau's Ph.D. thesis, socio-demographics correlations, Body Types correlations; Online CQ-i Beta available (until 2012)
# 3	2009-2010	Consultation with experts Feedback from peer reviewers of scientific journals	Feedback from experts: Harris Friedman, Bernard Baars, Jonathan Shear, John Rowan. Feedback from scientific journals: Consciousness and Cognition, Nature. IJTS. TSC 2009 Presentation, Hong Kong. Discussions.

Exploratory Studies. Likert Scale Revision (2009-2011)

# 4	2009-2011	Online, N= 5464, Likert 5 Online, N=112, Likert 6	(Romanian 5.012, English 1.168)
# 5		N=65, paper-pencil Likert 5 vs. Likert 6	Changed Likert Scale from 5 to 6 (kept agree-disagree types)
# 6	2011, May	N=70, paper-pencil; Military population	
# 7	2011	N=30, paper-pencil; Participants to personal development workshops	
# 8	2011	N=120, GAMA	Published article: Brazdau, O. & Mihai, C. (2011). The Consciousness Quotient: a new predictor of student's academic performance. Elsevier Procedia Social and Behavioral Sciences, 11, 245-250.
# 9	2011	N=145, paper-pencil MSCEIT, EQ-i, CPI, NEO PI-R	Presentation TSC 2011, Stockholm, Discussions.

CQ-i Revisions – Conscious Behaviours & Conscious Life Situations (2012). Updating items.

# 10	2012, Jan.-Aug.	Extensive library research; five researchers in the research team: Petru Constantinescu, Ramona Sbircea, Iuliana Constantinescu, Andreea Butucescu and Sofia Dumitriu.	Re-checked all the items using 24 criteria. Each conscious behaviour searched for in the scientific literature. Compliance with APA, ITS and ETS Standards. Evaluation for introducing validity scales: Lie Scale, Acquiescence Scale, Extremity Response
# 11	2012, Sept.	N=12, Willis' Cognitive interviewing Likert scale evaluation: from agreement to frequencies	Article in Elsevier Procedia Social and Behavioral Sciences (2012): Consciousness Quotient Inventory Improvement: Qualitative Study Using Cognitive Interviewing Approach. Changed Likert scale to frequencies; Changed all items to be behavioural
# 12	2012, Oct.	N=120, paper-pencil	Updated 8 items and life situations/conscious behaviours
# 13	2012, Dec.	N=102, paper-pencil	All the reversed items removed Other 12 items removed Item 24 moved from spiritual to cognitive scale Statistical analysis; New items for the Lie Scale

The distribution analysis (Study # 13, Dec. 2012) indicates normal distributions along all dimensions (Table 5). The distribution of the total score is symmetrical (Skewness = -.396; Skewness SE = .244) but peaked, so we could consider it to be leptokurtic (Kurtosis = 1.795; Kurtosis SE = .483). In relation to the Kolmogorov-Smirnov test for normality (K-S(98) = .761; p = 609), we could consider this distribution to be normal

Distribution of Scores Along Factors (Study #13, 2012), N=102

Factor	Mean	SD	Skewness	Kurtosis	Kolmogorov-Smirnov
Physical CQ	24.28	3.16	.016 (.241)	-.148 (.478)	.87 (p=.435)
Emotional CQ	26.93	3.19	-.025 (.239)	.825 (.474)	1.12 (p=.163)
Cognitive CQ	25.13	4.01	-.126 (.239)	.594 (.474)	1.06 (p=.206)
Spiritual CQ	38.8	6.82	-.239 (.241)	.875 (.478)	.895 (p=.399)
Social CQ	29.02	5.10	.139 (.239)	.72 (.474)	1.09 (p=.181)
Self CQ	36.46	6.41	-.08 (.239)	.565 (.474)	.626 (p=.828)
Total CQ	**159.02**	**26.44**	**-.39 (.244)**	**1.79 (.483)**	**.761 (.609)**

The reliability analysis (Cronbach's alpha) that was realized during study #13 concluded that the CQ-i has good internal consistency for the total score (.927). The split-half analysis (part1–32 items, part 2-32 items) also showed a good reliability: Alpha(1)=0.830; Alpha(2)=0.864; Spearman-Brown=0.879. Guttman split-half coefficient had the same value as Spearman-Brown.

CQ-i Pre-release – Validation Studies & Explorations (2013-2015)

# 14	2013, Jan.-Feb.	Same population profile as in study #9 Exploratory concurrent validity CPI (N=39), EQ-I (N=45), NEO PI-R (N=47), MSCEIT (N=45), GAMA (39)	Concurrent validity Statistical analysis CQ-i v.2013 released CQ-i v.2013 available online starting March, 2013

The preliminary validation studies realized during study #14 included explorations of its concurrent and incremental validity using inventories such as CPI, EQ-i, NEO PI-R, GAMA and MSCEIT. CQ was analysed in relation to other variables, such as emotional intelligence, IQ and personality traits. The results showed that the CQ, as measured with CQ-i beta v.2013, does not correlate with Emotional Quotient (EQ) – either as a trait or skill measured with EQ-i and MSCEIT.

Only a few significant correlations of the CQ and some dimensions of EQ-i and MSCEIT have been observed: the CQ was found to be significantly positively correlated with the Intrapersonal Scale (RA) (r = . 311, p < .01) and the General Mood Scale (GM) (r = .326, p < .05) from EQ-I. CQ [Physical] was found to be significantly positively correlated with Perceiving Emotion (r = .390, p < .05) from MSCEIT. The exploration of the CQ and personality traits using CPI and NEO PI-R revealed a few significant correlations. CQ was found to be significantly positively correlated with Law Enforcement Orientation (Leo) (r = .451, p < .01), Openness (O) (r = .469, p < .01), Conscientiousness (C) (r = .407, p <

.01), Warmth (E1) ($r = .406, p < .01$) and Achievement Striving (C4) ($r = .367, p < .05$), and negatively correlated with Activity (E4) ($r = .-359, p < .05$) and Self-Discipline (C5) ($r = . 394, p < .01$).

CQ-i Pre-release – Validation Studies & Explorations (2013-2015)

# 15	2013, Feb. – 2014, Aug.	In-Depth Construct Development and Content Validity Research	After developing the construct, the content validity was evaluated by a panel of 25 experts. As a result, 40 items were excluded and 27 items were re-worded. New terminological clarifications were developed in order to better operationalize the CQ construct. CQ-i (v. 2014, beta version) released. "The Consciousness Quotient: Construct Development and Content Validity Research" – Paper presented at PsiWorld 2014 Conference. CQ-i Administration on Adolescents: Difficulty Level Assessment – Paper published in Elsevier Procedia – Social and Behavioral Sciences, Vol. 128
#16	2014, Oct.-	CQ-i final version (v. 2015) released. Extended Validity and Reliability Researches	*On-going research*

In 2014, a study of the difficulty of the items for adolescents revealed that the structure of the items was easy to understand by adolescents (Brazdau, Sharma, & Ahuja, 2014).

The purpose of this study was to examine the difficulty level of the Consciousness Quotient Inventory (CQ-i) for adolescents. The previous validation of the CQ-i includes its administration in adults only; thus, in order to determine whether CQ-i can be administered in adolescents as well, the difficulty levels of the items were analysed using a scale from very easy to very difficult. The study was based on 100 participants (aged 13 to 17), from different schools in Agra, India.

The difficulty level for each item of CQ-i was evaluated using a five-level Likert scale, from "Very Easy" to "Very Difficult", scored 1 to 5. Before administration, the students were introduced to CQ-i, and the purpose of administration was explained to them.

In the first phase, data were collected from the students of two sections (having 45 students each) from the 10th grade of St. Conrad's Inter College, Agra. Students from one section were strongly influenced, overestimated and were pressurized to finish the inventory quickly by their class teacher, who was present while the test was being administered. As a result, the responses of these students were discarded, sensing fake responses. All the responses of the students from the second section were genuine and true, except for three. Thus, overall, data were collected from 90 participants, of whom 42 were selected for the analysis.

In the second phase, data were collected from St. Francis School, where the tool was administered to 35 students from the 9th and 10th grades, out of which the number of genuine responses was just 20. In the third phase, Hillman Public School was selected for data collection. The inventory was administered to 55 students from the 8th and 9th grades, out of which 38 genuine responses were included in the study. Finally, the responses of 100 participants were considered and the rest were discarded on the basis of the analysis mentioned above.

The results indicate that the overall difficulty level of CQ-i was easy to moderate. An age-wise analysis indicates that the difficulty level is relatively higher for younger adolescents (aged 13-14) as compared with older ones (aged 15-17). It was observed that the overall average difficulty level of all dimensions was similar. Physical CQ was rated as having the highest difficulty level followed by spiritual CQ, self-consciousness and emotional CQ, respectively, while cognitive and social-relational CQ were rated lowest in the difficulty levels. Further analysis showed that adolescents in age group 13-14 experienced greater difficulty across all dimensions except for physical CQ than did age group 15-16. The exploration of the gender variable showed that boys rated nine items as difficult, whereas girls rated only five items as difficult.

In order to obtain more qualitative data, the researchers interviewed 30 students (20 from age group 15-16 and 10 from age group 13-14) to understand their views regarding CQ-i. On asking whether they found certain constructs or situations unfamiliar, they answered that they marked such items as difficult which mentioned unfamiliar situations. Students from age group 15-16 said that they were able to comprehend almost every item but that they never experienced certain situations.

The study concluded that, by making a few changes in the difficult rated items, CQ-i can be made suitable for adolescents.

V. CONSCIOUSNESS QUOTIENT INVENTORY V. 2015: THE CONTENT VALIDITY RESEARCH[1]

After releasing the CQ-i beta v.2013 and using the framework developed during 2003-2013, the operationalization of the CQ was extended in order to find all the relevant descriptors of conscious experience.

During this study, a variety of sources were analysed in order to generate the test content: literature research (consciousness studies, articles, books); mindfulness research; psychometrics research; spiritual wisdom; personal experience of non-dual people, inter-

1 Paper published in *Elsevier "Procedia – Social and Behavioral Sciences"*, vol. 187, pages 244-249.

views on Conscious TV, and the "Buddha at the gas pump" website; personal experience of witnessing awareness; our team of researchers; experts, friends, psychologists, research partners, discussions on the "consciousness science" Google group discussions (a group composed on more than 60 consciousness experts, mostly speakers at the Towards a Science of Consciousness conferences), feedback from people responding to the test, Google suggestions (e.g., we analysed the first 100 websites that referred to "I am aware of" and see the recommended links as a source of collective knowledge, especially first-person data).

Some concepts as used in consciousness studies were explored and included as descriptors/traits of conscious experience: mindfulness (Baer et al., 2006), post-autonomous ego development (Cook-Greuter, 2000), witnessing awareness (Brazdau, 2014), meta-awareness/awareness of awareness itself (Monsanto, 2013), emotional intelligence (Heim, 2003).

Related concepts and studies were analysed and taken into consideration in order to find adequate descriptors of conscious experience, including: attention regulation (Asada, 2014; Monsanto, 2013), the triune brain (MacLean, 1990), neuroplasticity (Hanson, 2011), metacognition (Darling-Hammond, 2014), rational/irrational belief-dynamics (Vasile, 2012), spiritual intelligence (King, 2008), conceptual systems and personality organization (Harvey et al., 1961), affective neurosciences (Davidson, 2012), 'enlightenment' and 'awakening' experiences (Costeines, 2009), persistent non-symbolic experiences (Martin, 2010), neurotheology (Murphy, 2002), levels of human development (Grawes, 1970), outrospection (Krznaric, 2014), human connectedness (Andrews, 1996), *Ubuntu* philosophy (Gianan, 2010), non-dual awareness (Josipovic & Malach, 2006), pure awareness (Forman, 1990; Genarro, 2008), psychedelics research (Kent, 2010), spiritual crises (Grof, 2009), Orch-OR theory (Hameroff, 2010), spiritual intelligence (King, 2008), critical reviews of consciousness studies (Blackmore, 2010), and *advaita* and neo-*advaita* philosophy (Conway, 2008).

Other psychological scales were analysed in order to explore some of the measurable factors of conscious experience: the Self-Compassion Scale (Neff, 2003), the Multidimensional Assessment of Interoceptive Awareness (Mehling et al., 2012), the Mystical Experience Questionnaire (MacLean et al., 2012), the Leadership Maturity Assessment Instrument and Loevinger's Washington University Sentence Completion Test (Cook-Greuter, 2000).

After extensive analyses, a new section with yes/no answers was added (acknowledgements to Sperry Andrews and Carlo Monsanto for suggesting this new section and for providing the initial items). The factor structure that resulted is presented below. As a result of this in-depth operationalization, the CQ construct was operationalized using a sample of more than 300 traits, skills and abilities, which were later translated into items.

Main Factor Structure of the Consciousness Quotient

Factor	Content
Physical CQ	Body and basic physical perceptions and sensations, environmental awareness
Emotional CQ	Emotions, feelings, emotional intelligence
Cognitive CQ	Related to thinking, reflection, judgment, patterns of understanding, ways of meaning-making
Social-Relational CQ	Parental relationships, close relationships, any conscious interactions with others
Self CQ	Identity, self-system, image of life, self-awareness, post-autonomous ego-development traits
Inner Growth CQ	Related to self-development, evolution of personality
Spiritual CQ	Connecting with humans and nature, meta-awareness, witnessing awareness, acceptance of experience

In order to establish the content validity of the CQ, the list of traits, skills and abilities that describe conscious experience were analysed by a panel of experts. The goal was to evaluate the comprehensiveness and representativeness of the content - whether the lists of traits that compose CQ adequately cover conscious experience, with no irrelevant content included (Newton, 2003).

A secondary objective of the content validity study was the evaluation of the pattern-matching (Trochim, 2000): to explore whether our observed patterns of conscious experience (how things operate in reality) correspond with our theoretical patterns (how we think the world works).

The expert panel comprised consciousness researchers, experienced practitioners of inner development techniques (religious or spiritual), and representatives of the non-dual community. Participants were emailed copies of the CQ-i traits and items table, in the format presented in Table 3. They were asked to comment on the overall appropriateness for inclusion of each descriptor. In addition, the experts were asked to comment if they believed anything should be added or deleted, and to evaluate the wording of the items.

For several items, supplemental descriptions and references were available. The participants entered their responses onto the form and emailed it back to the researchers, who then reviewed and collated the replies. Changes were made to the items according to suggestions where appropriate. The consultation took place between March 2013 and July 2014.

CQ content validity research - feedback form used by the experts

Factor	Sub-factor	Trait, Ability, Skill	Item	Supplemental Description	*Example of comment*
Self CQ	Mindful living	Acceptance	I am ok when experiencing physical or psychological discomfort		Might be better worded as: I can tolerate a certain amount of physical and psychological discomfort without needing to change what I am involved in, in order to comfort myself.

Out of 108 people invited, the final panel comprised 25 members. Fourteen experts analysed each item: Zoran Josipovic, Susanne Cook-Greuter, Carlo Monsanto, Richard Joannides, Vlad Dogarescu, Kruti Sharma, Altina Hripacov, Sadhna Sharma, Monica Burcea, Ioana Pielescu, Catalin Chites, Felicia Epuran, Sona Ahuja and John Renesch. Eleven experts replied by commenting on the general appropriateness of the items' format, the CQ structure and the items' wording: Sperry Andrews, Jan Essman, Rebecca Hardcastle Wright, Michael James, Ionela Andrei, John Cook, Cristiana Levitchi, Chobo Ji, Sam Gentoku McCree, ShantiMayi and Valita Jones.

The responses confirmed that the CQ-i has an appropriate content that adequately cover the conscious experience. A total of 40 items were excluded from the CQ-i, and 27 items were re-worded to better suit the traits they measured. Some of the panellists raised concerns about its length and ease of use. This will be monitored over time.

As a result, new terminological clarifications were developed in order to better describe the consciousness quotient construct:

■ To be conscious is to have a degree of witnessing awareness and a degree of freedom of choice when thinking, feeling, sensing and interacting with people and the environment.

■ An important element of conscious experience is intentionality, as the mind-set that allows a person to deliberately choose what behaviour to enact and what attitude to select.

■ 'More conscious' (a higher CQ) means a higher degree of witnessing awareness and being less automatic in thinking-feeling-sensing, together with a higher degree of choice when initiating a behaviour.

'Witnessing awareness' is usually described as the "I am experience", "the observer experience", "just being" (as opposed to "doing"), "aware of awareness itself", "no-mind". 'Mindfulness' is a related construct (right mindfulness - *samma sati* in Buddhism – is the same as witnessing awareness), but in modern mindfulness, as it is promoted in the West, being mindful does not go beyond being a cognitive observer.

In order to clarify this distinction, the term 'non-conceptual self' was proposed (Brazdau, 2014), as that part of personal identity which has witnessing awareness as its main function, complementary to the 'conceptual self', which has cognition as its main function. The witnessing perspective, which leads to the ability to observe the inside and outside worlds without engaging with them, is one of the key factors of the CQ construct.

VI. CQ-I CRITERION-BASED VALIDITY AND EXPLORATORY RESEARCHES

Between 2009 and 2013, a series of criterion-related researches were undertaken. The main conclusion of these exploratory studies was that conscious experience can be scientifically treated like any other psychological variable, and that it is possible to introduce conscious experience as a variable in psychological assessment (Brazdau & Opariuc, 2014). The psychological assessment framework developed during the exploratory researches was the foundation for the in-depth construct's operationalization and the items' development.

STUDY 1
Effect of Yoga and Meditation on Consciousness Quotient and Mindfulness

By Sona Ahuja, Dayalbagh Educational Institute, Agra, India.
Study published in Journal of Consciousness Exploration & Research June 2014, Vol. 5, Issue 5.

The effect of yoga and meditation on conscious experience and mindfulness were examined comparing beginners, intermediate, advanced meditators and a group of non-meditators. The participants were applicants of yoga and meditation program offered for twenty weeks. Four groups of 20 each were formed including, 3 experimental groups and one control. The groups did not differ with respect to gender (11males and 9 females in each group). Experimental group had three set of subjects as stratified samples viz., pre-initiates(beginners) - those who were not trained for any meditational practices prior to experiment, first initiates (intermediate meditators) - those who were trained for contemplation of divine form at the seat of spirit(between two eyes), second initiates (advanced meditators) - those who were trained for sound practice which consists in concentrating attention at the seat of the spirit and establishing contact with the current of Sabda or mystic word.

The experiment was in the form of practice of yoga and meditation for 20 weeks. The practice sessions (one hour) were held on weekdays in the evening for three days a week under the guidance of experienced practitioner. Each day, the programme commenced with a brief 15 minutes lecture covering different topics to reinforce the subjects for meditation. The topics included body, mind, spirit and consciousness; cosmology; spiritual awakening; nerve centres, chakras, kamals and padmas; attunement with spiritual sounds; main object of meditation and ways to establish contact with the source of spirituality. This was followed by yoga. Seven yogasanas were included in the intervention programme for relaxation Siddhasan, Sarvangasan, Bhujangasan, Paschimottanasan, Padahastasan, Ardhamatsyendrasan and Shavasan. These asanas were selected for relaxation and preparation of body for meditation. After yogasana, the practice of meditation was modeled on practices of oriental philosophy of Saints (Radhasoami Faith). These meditational practices are based on Hierarchical Order Theory of Consciousness (Satsangi, 2013).

The results showed a significant increase in the CQ scores, after the intervention. The practice had considerable effect on all dimensions of consciousness quotient over time. The impact was more and relatively immediate on social and self-consciousness quotient. Initially after ten weeks of practice, the practitioners did not show significant change in physical and emotional consciousness quotient scores but there was significant increase in scores after 20 weeks of practice of yoga and meditation. Though the difference in mental and spiritual consciousness quotient scores was not significant even after 20 weeks, but there was increase in these scores also.

Further, the naïve practitioners showed significant gain in consciousness scores after practice of 20 weeks in comparison to those who had exposure to the practice of yoga and meditation

STUDY 2
Consciousness Quotient as a Predictor of Executive Functioning

By Sona Ahuja, Sadhna Sharma (Pedagogical Sciences, Dayalbagh Educational Institute, Agra, India)

Paper published in MIER Journal of Educational Studies, Trends & Practices
November 2015, Vol. 5, No. 2.

Presently, it is a debatable issue whether to include consciousness, which has been declared as loudest mental phenomenon in the domain of executive functioning or not. Executive functioning is associated with higher order mental abilities which are required to connect past experiences with the present ones and which are required to strategically manage oneself and one's resources.

Executive functions including mental abilities such as, working memory, reasoning ability, problem solving, inhibitory control, task flexibility and cognitive flexibility are significant factors for students' learning and academic achievement.

The current study aimed at studying the relation between conscious experience as measured by CQ-i and two executive functions i.e. cognitive flexibility and self-regulation. The sample consisted of 200 adolescents in the age group of 13 to 19 (Mean age: 16.05, S.D=1.62). 78 boys and 122 girls from eighth to twelfth grade participated in the study. The data was collected in five phases from the students of more than 10 different schools of Agra, India, selected randomly. Students completed the bilingual version (English and Hindi) and adapted Indian version of Consciousness Quotient Inventory (CQ-i v. 2013) by Brazdau, Sharma and Ahuja (2014), Adolescents Self Regulatory Inventory (ASRI) by Moilanen (2007) and Cognitive Flexibility Scale (CFS) by Martin and Rubin (1995).

A linear regression analysis was performed to check predictive ability of consciousness quotient. It was found that CQ accounts for 6.4% variation in cognitive flexibility [R2 = 0.064, F (1, 90) = 6.182, $p < 0.05$] and 16.6% variation in self- regulation [R2 = 0.166, F (1, 71, 14.096, $p<0.01$)]. These findings suggest that the extent of relationship of consciousness quotient with different executive functions varies. It was revealed that consciousness quotient accounts for greater variation in long term self-regulation [R^2 = 0.193, F (1, 78) = 18.62, $p<0.01$] than for short-term regulation [R^2 = 0.015, F (1, 78) = 1.207, $p > 0.05$]. Interestingly, it was found that even two executive functions i.e. cognitive flexibility and self-regulation are positively and significantly correlated ($r = 0.46$, $p<0.01$).

Findings based on self-reports reveal that executive functioning is moderately but significantly related to consciousness quotient, although the relationship may vary for different executive functions. The strength of functional relationship revealed the predictive ability of CQ for cognitive flexibility and self-regulation (through regression analysis). Consciousness quotient accounts for greater variation in self-regulation as compared to cognitive flexibility. It can be inferred that students with higher score on CQ-i will tend to have greater long term self-regulating abilities and cognitive flexibility than those with the lower score. The findings are found to be consistent with the propositions of Dehaene and Naccache, (2001) and Jack and Shallice, (2001) that cognitive control processes necessarily require awareness.

STUDY 3
Contemplative exercises once a week for 8 weeks didn't increase the Consciousness Quotient

By Jennifer Luna Tuazon
A Doctor of Philosophy in Education (Psychology and Guidance) Dissertation
West Visayas State University, La Paz, Iloilo City, Philippines
March, 2014.

This study specifically aimed to find out the consciousness quotient and intrapersonal and interpersonal relationship skills of participants prior to and after exposure to transformative consciousness exercises (for the experimental group) and the self-awareness sessions (for the comparison group).

This randomized pretest and posttest control group design utilized the Consciousness Quotient Inventory (CQ-i v.2013) and the validated researcher made Intrapersonal and Interpersonal Relationship Skills Scale (IIRSS). The intervention was designed using the Transformative Consciousness Modules, developed by Stephen Wolinsky. The Transformative Consciousness sessions were conducted for 4,5 hours, once a week, for 8 weeks. The participants were 23 students in the experimental group and 21 students in the comparison group, from West Visayas State University. The CQ-i and IIRSS were applied before and after the Transformative Consciousness sessions.

Main topics of the Transformative Program, based of Stephen Wolinsky's book (Quantum Consciousness. The Guide to Experiencing Quantum Psychology, 1993):

- You Are Not Your Mind (The Power of Now, Tolle, 2005)
- Ego: The Current State of Humanity (A New Earth, Tolle, 2005)
- Observing our Thoughts (Quantum Consciousness, Wolinsky)
- Moving Deeply in the Now (The Power of the Now)
- Space and Transmutation or Transformation of E-motions (Wolinsky)
- Consciousness: The Way out of Pain (The Power of the Now)
- The Core of Ego (A New Earth)
- Role-Playing: The Many Faces of the Ego (A New Earth)
- The Pain-Body: The Many Faces of the Ego (A New Earth)
- Concept of Time: You are the observer/creator of the time aspect of consciousness
- Moving Deeply Into the Now (The Power of the Now)
- The Mind Strategies for Avoiding the Now (The Power of the Now)
- The State of Presence (The Power of the Now)
- Breaking Free (A New Earth)
- The Inner Body (The Power of the Now)

- The Portals into the Unmanifested: The True Nature of Time and Space (The Power of the Now)
- You are beyond the aspects of energy, space, mass, and time. (Quantum Consciousness)
- Enlightened Relationships
- Going Beyond Ordinary Reality: The observer is the observed (Quantum Consciousness)
- Beyond Happiness (The Power of the Now)
- Finding Who You Truly Are (A New Earth)
- The Meaning of Surrender (The Power of the Now)
- Is Emptiness something to be Afraid of? Building block of the Universe. The nothing is alive! Nothing is in charge. (Quantum Consciousness)
- The Discovery of Inner Space (A New Earth)

Prior to and after the interventions, the intrapersonal and interpersonal relationship skills of the experimental group were high, while that of the comparison group were average. Results further revealed that there were no significant differences between the experimental and comparison groups' conscious quotient and intrapersonal and interpersonal skills prior to the intervention. Similarly, no significant difference was noted between the two group's consciousness quotients after the intervention, but a significant difference was found between their intrapersonal and interpersonal relationship skills.

On the other hand, significant differences were noted between the prior to and after interventions consciousness quotient and intrapersonal and interpersonal skills of the experimental group. Likewise, significant difference was found between the prior to and after interventions consciousness quotient of the comparison group but no significant difference existed between the prior to and after interventions intrapersonal and interpersonal skills of the same group.

Thus, it could be construed that compared to the self-awareness sessions, the transformative consciousness exercises may have been instrumental in increasing the participants' intrapersonal and interpersonal relationship skills, and not effective for producing an increase in the overall Consciousness Quotient.

Based on these results, it looks like this type of intervention based on Wolinsky's Transformative Consciousness Modules didn't produce the necessary impact to increase the CQ of the participants.

In order to produce significant changes of the Consciousness Quotient, it is recommended to use an intervention with more impact, more than once a week, and more than 8 weeks.

STUDY 4
Leadership Approach in relation to level of consciousness: a correlational analysis

By Chauhan, V., Sharma, S., Satsangee, S.
Published in MIER Journal of Educational Studies, Trends & Practices November 2013, Vol. 3, No. 2 pp.

The present empirical study was designed to explore the relationship between the leadership approach of teacher trainees and their level of consciousness. A descriptive survey was conducted on 100 teacher trainees (both male & female in the ratio of 1:1). The level of consciousness of teacher trainees was assessed using Consciousness Quotient Inventory (CQ-i) by Brazdau (2011). To assess the leadership approach Multifactor Leadership Questionnaire (MLQ-6S) by Bass and Avolio (1992) was used.

The relationship between scores on seven leadership factors (comprising three leadership approaches) and the level of consciousness was studied using Pearson's product moment correlation. Results indicate a significant positive correlation to a varying degree between consciousness and three leadership approaches.

STUDY 5
In Search of Conscious Leadership: A Qualitative Study of Postsecondary Educational Leadership Practices

By Valita Jones, Doctoral Dissertation, San Diego State University
Results published in Elsevier Procedia – Social and Behavioral Sciences, 203 (2015)

The purpose of this study was to examine the leadership practices of postsecondary educational leaders who are practicing what can be described as responsible and accountable leadership or conscious leadership. Eight senior postsecondary leaders participated in face-to-face interviews designed to identify conscious leadership qualities and practices.

Four research open-ended research questions guided the study:

1. How do postsecondary educational leaders make sense of conscious leadership?
2. How is conscious leadership demonstrated on a daily basis?
3. How does context influence conscious leadership practices?
4. What implications does a conscious leadership framework have for conscious leadership practices?

This study captures an emerging paradigm within its natural context, using interviewing and information from the Consciousness Quotient Inventory (Brazdau & Opariuc, 2014). It describes and explains the interpersonal competencies of individual leaders, while depicting the leadership practices of a variety of higher educational leaders.

Eight educational leaders from two and four year colleges and universities were identified as participants. Several demographics provide a general description: (a) generational age range, (b) highest educational degree, (c) ethnic identification, (d) gender identification, and (e) work locations. They all came from educational institutions that serve a diverse student population. A variety of administrators participated: Director, Associate Dean, Dean, VP and President. There were four were female and four were male, aged from thirties to sixties. The ethnic make-up was inclusive of African American and White administrators.

Initially, the follow selection criteria were used to select potential participants:

- The participants have been in leadership roles as senior postsecondary educational administrators for at least five years.
- The participants self-identify as experiencing a transformation in their leadership style or practice that is more relational and systems oriented.

The participants were contacted initially through e-mail at their respective colleges and universities. The e-mail introduced the researcher and the research study. Interested participants were asked to respond to the researcher directly by phone or e-mail. The researcher responded to all interested participants with an e-mail confirmation. Included in this confirmation was information about the research study purpose, confidentiality and consent procedures, and several potential dates for the actual interview. After the desired number of participants was successfully identified, the selection process concluded.

Initial research steps included all participants taking the online Consciousness Quotient (CQ) Inventory. The (CQ) survey, measures individual overall conscious awareness. It is self-scoring and was used to create a baseline for assessing the global awareness levels of each participant. The CQ Inventory scores, the summaries and responses from the interviews were used to provide context.

The second research step was an in-depth semi-structured interview with all the participants. The interview questions included 35 items, including various aspects of the conscious leadership practices, such as: How do you implement policies and procedures within your office/college? What does a transformative organization look like to you? How do you connect with other human beings? How do you believe humans are connected to each other? How do you handle an employee who becomes very emotional? How do you feel after you make difficult decisions? How do you react to new situations? What is your process for making-meaning of information? Please tell me how think your thoughts influence your actions and the decisions that you make? What do you believe to be your purpose in life and how are you intentional in achieving your purpose? How do you learn? Please tell me about an experience when you acted off of intuition. Please describe how you share your leadership role with your employees. What is you specific worldview or perspective on leadership? Please tell me about your own belief and/or values system? What kind of impact do you believe you have on your employees and staff as a leader?

The data resulted from the interviews was later transcribed using NVIVO 9, in an effort to become familiar with potential patterns, themes and codes.

Results

Most of the CQ responses demonstrated identical findings that indicated high global consciousness scores, with the exception of one. This participant's overall global consciousness score was relatively low in comparison to the other participants and resulted in a dramatically different perspective for most of her domain and the overall global consciousness score. In terms of where the leaders would place on a continuum of awareness, Leader #3 scores indicated that they are at the lower end of global awareness, while Leaders #2, #7, and #8 reflect a developing awareness level and finally, those leaders who scored in the 90's reflected a higher awareness level.

After the interview process, data was analyzed and interpreted for understanding and meaning. Five notable trends emerged and were developed into categories: (a) theoretical perspective; (b) epistemic practices of transformation and systems; (c) disposition; (d) socio-emotional/human consciousness capacity; and (e) cognition capacity. Nineteen codes were established to organize the data: Worldview or perspective on leadership; Integrated and networked environment; Transformational organization; Role as a leader; Innovative, creative, and collaborative partnerships; Shared leadership role; Get others to work together; Belief/value system; React to new situations; Manage weakness/strengths; Handle emotional employees; Feel after making a decision; Assess and analyze new situations; Self-knowledge; Learning; Making-meaning; Thoughts influence decisions and actions; Aware, accountable and responsible; Solve complex problems.

A leadership rubric was created and participant responses were measured against whether they exhibited qualities from the leadership rubric, as presented in Table 1.

Data revealed that Leaders made sense of conscious leadership through their awareness, consciousness and self-knowledge. Moreover, each of them subscribed to their own particular theoretical perspective, ideology or world- view that assisted in their development as a leader. There was recognition and acknowledgement of the interconnectivity and humanness between themselves and other, while it is noted that reciprocity was practiced and evidence of a shared leadership approach was discovered.

The Leaders demonstrated conscious leadership daily through the examples of cooperation and collaboration in being efficient and effective. All supported innovation and creativity, as a needed process for supporting change and transformation. Emphasis was placed on building "communities of practice" where harmony and balanced relationships was critical to collective decision-making efforts. Thus, demonstrated intentionality and thoughtfulness. The context of a conscious leadership practice was noted by the acknowledgement of the organization becoming more networked and integrated, which allowed Leaders to recognize the many themes and patterns emerging within a living organizational system.

There was support of a networked environment because it facilitated better communications and engagement, which improved the efforts of meeting organizational goals. Findings revealed that the Leaders were more practice-based in attempting to accomplish goals and objectives rather than use standard behavioral techniques to create change and sustainability. Leaders were aware and reflective in their leadership practice and appeared to know that they were accessing higher consciousness of their thoughts and emotions, thereby developing holistic and healthy coping techniques and leadership practices. Finally, implications of a conscious leadership framework demonstrated clearly that organizations function as ecological systems.

Leadership Rubric Continuum

Leadership Themes	Beginning Qualities	Developing Qualities	Advanced Qualities
Theoretical Perspective	Behaviorist	Transformative Change Oriented Integrated and Networked	Sociocultural/Reciprocity. Quantum Interconnectivity Systems Perspective/ Thinking
Epistemic Practice of Transformation and Systems	Reactive and Low Expectations	Nurture Change Responsive to Problems Follower Perspective	Have a Focus, Plan, Observe and Collect Info, Interpret, Translate, Cooperative and Collaborate Implement; Shared Responsibility View Practice in Context
Disposition	Focuses on Fixed Behaviors, Traits, Competencies or Styles	Charismatic Intrinsic Motivation Inspirational/Motivational Influential/Social Architects	Flexible, Authentic and Creative and Innovative Intentional/ Purposeful Take a Holistic Perspective, Evolutionary/Transcendence Positive/Inclusive; Have Spiritual Aspect

Socio-emotional/ Human Consciousness Capacity	Outside Observers Not Aware of the Relationships Around You or Does Not Value	Affective/ Feeling Self-efficacy Some Self-knowledge Some Value Towards Relationships	Knowledge of Self Observe Thoughts as they Arise Inspirational; Relational and interconnected to Universal Law/Nature
Cognition Capacity	Exertion to Lead or Develop Habits of the Mind	Learning from Experience Limited ability for New Thought Becoming a Critical Thinker Beginning to be aware of being aware	Use Cognitive and Metacognitive Skills Reflective; See Patterns and Themes in the Environment and use to Make Meaning Capacity for New Thought

Being conscious and aware of the emotional status of others and themselves was reported as valuable to their leadership practice. Most of the leaders were discussed being very in touch with this perspective and articulated it as a core principle. Responses supported the idea that the majority of the leaders acknowledged the value of having insight into not only their own personal perspective regarding emotions, but concerning their employees as well. The basic acceptance of their employees and working environments as being more than just factories putting out widgets is relevant to the concept of humanness of being conscious of themselves and others. These trends emerged in spite of the hierarchal structures the Leaders operated within.

In the end, most of the leaders demonstrated evolving leadership patterns towards becoming more conscious leaders. They all agreed that emotional capacity was critical to having a functional work environment. This belief originated around the conversation we engaged in regarding relationships, relationships building, awareness of different emotional states, and cooperative and collaborative interactions. Leaders who were aware of, and responsive to, their emotional states appeared to be more skilled at navigating positive collaborative interactions between themselves and their staff; thus connecting and interacting with regards to emotions and human consciousness, were expressed as critical components of the leadership practice, which is more aligned with more advanced leadership stage development. This social-relational construct of understanding people in the sense of human consciousness and socio-emotional perspective gained notoriety during the emergence of the emotional intelligence philosophy. In other words, the importance of humanness was also expressed.

The literature review provided valuable information regarding shared or participatory leadership styles, such as Love-based leadership, Open Leadership, and Soul Leadership (Chopra, 2010; Church, 2010; Li, 2010). Each of these leadership approaches requires the leader to be reciprocal, cooperative and collaborative. Interview data revealed that several of the Leaders subscribed to a participatory or shared leadership practice.

Leader #1 shared: "I believe in leading by inclusiveness, meaning I bring everybody along telling them what we are doing, how we are trying to do it and give them an opportunity to have input. That way when you get to a decision, people will more likely be on board about the decision and you don't have to worry about the excuses side. When they are not on board, you run into conflict".

Discussion

Prior to conducting this research, limited information existed about the potentiality of applying a conscious leadership framework to higher educational practices. Additionally, little information was known about how current Leaders practiced leadership, whether traditional or transformative, especially within educational institutions that have become increasingly interconnected and networked. From a researcher's perspective, it would be critical to gain additional insight into the application of a conscious leadership framework on a broader scale. The data analyzed offered evidence that elements of conscious leadership are currently being practiced by some higher educational leaders.

Results from this study provided evidence to suggest that formal exposure to a conscious leadership curriculum would be beneficial and assist in developing a community of conscious leaders. The implication for developing a leadership theory and practice, which supports continuous transformation, is of great importance. Higher educational leaders must become more adept in their leadership practices by developing improved leadership acumen. All eight of the Leaders expressed that their respective working environments were rapidly changing and that being transformative, cooperative and collaborative was necessary to achieve their department goals.

Three implications for practice emerge as the research unfolded: (a) process for preparing conscious leaders; (b) applying conscious leadership practices within changing higher education environments; and (c) the meaning of a conscious leadership framework to institutions of higher education systems).

This research served as a pilot study for gaining insight into the practicality and relevance of applying a conscious leadership framework to postsecondary educational environments. Three recommendations for future research are offered: (a) investigating the deeper meaning of a conscious leadership practice; (b) conducting research studies on a larger scale and across diverse environments; and (c) examining the impact of conscious leadership practitioners as mentors and coaches.

Building leadership development programs that incorporate a

conscious leadership framework can aid in appropriately preparing leaders for complex and rapidly changing organizations. Conscious leadership assists us in transforming our educational institutions to reflect our highest values, those that embrace interconnectivity, networking and sociocultural ways of being.

STUDY 6
The Consciousness Quotient – a new predictor of students' academic performance

By Ovidiu Brazdau, Cristian Mihai
Paper presented at the Teachers for the Knowledge Society Conference – 2011, 17-19 March, Sinaia, Romania.
Published in Elsevier – Procedia: Social and Behavioral Science 11 (2011).

The purpose of this study was to establish the practical usage of the Consciousness Quotient in the field of educational psychology. The basic hypothesis of this study was to determine the incremental validity brought by the Consciousness Quotient in the prediction of academic performance. The study was based on 138 participants from the Ecological University of Bucharest, Romania. The "Consciousness Quotient Inventory" (CQ-i) and "General Ability Measure for Adults" (GAMA) are used to evaluate the Consciousness Quotient and the Intelligence Levels.

Data analysis revealed a positive correlation between the global conciousness quotient and the academic performance. (Pearson r=.209, p<.05).

The intelligence quotient (Pearson r=.320, p<.01) is strongly related to the academic performance, which was expected since many studies have shown approximately the same level of correlation (Mathiasen, 1984).

It is important to mention that there are no significant levels of correlation between the CQ score and IQ (Pearson r=.137, p>.05). This result suggests that CQ and IQ are totally differently psychological constructs. This fact is important, because CQ represents a non-cognitive predictor of the academic performance.

The statistical analysis showed that students with higher IQ are more likely to have a better performance. ($R^2=.102$, $F(1,136)=15.462$, $p<.001$). Furthermore, the moderate correlation between the CQ and result of the academic performance criterion suggest that people with a high CQ can perform better to the exams than the students with a low CQ level.

The influence of the CQ in the prediction of the academic performance was tested using a linear regression analysis. The result of statistical procedure, suggest that only 4% of the variances of academic performance, could be explained by consciousness quotient ($R^2 = .044$, $F(1,136) = 6.209$, $p<.017$). For that reason, it was conducted a simultaneous design that included the academic performance as a criterion and both intelligence quotient and the consciousness quotient, as predictors.

The results of the multiple regression analysis suggest that the CQ supplies an increment in the prediction of academic performance. ($R^2 = .130$, $F(2,135) = 10.078$, $p<.001$). In conclusion, using both measurements, CQ and IQ, could better predict the performance in the academic field. The increment brought by assessing the Consciousness Quotient in the prediction of academic performance ($\Delta R^2 = 0.028$) is about 3% of variance. For this reason, the assessment of consciousness, has a moderate role in the prediction of academic performance, but a statistical significantly contribution ($\beta = .168$, $t(135) = 2.077$, $p<.04$).

VII. CONCLUSIONS

The operationalization of the CQ construct was an extended and delicate task, but it was a necessary step in introducing the CQ as a variable in psychological assessment. As CQ-i is one of the first inventories of this type, it was hard to find similar patterns of thinking during the literature research. An important element of feedback was provided by the practitioners of various religious, spiritual and self-development practices, as most of them related to the study by describing their own conscious experiences. Further studies are necessary in order to establish the criterion-related validity of the CQ-i.

Acknowledgements

We would like to thank to all the researchers and friends involved in the development of the CQ-i, and the content validity research team: Cornelia Guja, Sadhna Sharma, Bernard Baars, Harris Friedman, Valita Jones, Sofia Dumitriu, Namita Aggarwal, Vaibhav Chauhan, Jennifer Luna Tuazon, Cristian Mihai, Nandita Satsangee, Zoran Josipovic, Susanne Cook-Greuter, Carlo Monsanto, Richard Joannides, Vlad Dogarescu, Kruti Sharma, Altina Hripacov, Monica Burcea, Ioana Pielescu, Catalin Chites, Felicia Epuran, Sona Ahuja and John Renesch, Sperry Andrews, Jan Essman, Rebecca Hardcastle Wright, Michael James, Ionela Andrei, John Cook, Cristiana Levitchi, Chobo Ji, Sam Gentoku McCree, ShantiMayi, Thomas Goddard, Keith Fiveson, Claudiu Girniceanu, Andreea Butucescu, Petru-Madalin Constantinescu, Iuliana Constantinescu, Ramona Sbircea, Sofia Dumitriu, Ioana Pielescu, Catalin Chites, Dragos Iliescu, John Renesch, Cristian Vasile and Leon Zagrean.

Special thanks to Carlo Monsanto for providing the inspiration for the Inner Growth Factor, and to Sperry Andrews for his contribution to the Section 2 of the CQ-i. And many thanks to Cristian Opariuc for his statistical analyses of the CQ-i research databases and for offering new psychometric perspectives, to Vlad Dogarescu for the development of CQ-i online platform and to Georgina for her support with the proofreading.

References

Aggarwal, N. (2013). Measuring Consciousness Quotient – a study of its influence on employee's work performance and organizational outcomes. *International Journal of Science and Research, 2* (11), 358-367.

Ahuja, S. (2014). A correlational analysis of physical, mental, emotional, spiritual, social and self-consciousness. *Indian Journal of Applied Research*, *6*(6), 1-4.

Ahuja, S. (2014). Effect of yoga and meditation on consciousness and mindfulness, *Journal of Consciousness Exploration and Research*, *5*(5), 434-447.

Andrews, S. (1996). Promoting a sense of connectedness among individuals by scientifically demonstrating the existence of a planetary consciousness? *Alternative Therapies*, *2*(3), 39-45.

Asa Da, M. (2014). *This is your brain on "No Mind"*. Retrieved from http://michaelasada.com/this-is-your-brain-on-no-mind.

Baars, B.J. (1999). There is already a field of systematic phenomenology, and it's called 'psychology'. *Journal of Consciousness Studies*, *6*(2-3), 216-218, also in Varela, F.J. & Shear, J. (Eds.) (1999). *The View from Within*. Thorverton, Devon: Imprint Academic, 216-218.

Blackmore, S. (2010). Why I had to change my mind. In R. Gross (Ed.). *Psychology: The science of mind and behaviour*. London: Hodder Education.

Brannick, M.T., Wahi, M.M., Arce, M, Johnson, H.A., Nazian, S., Goldin, S.B. (2009). Comparison of trait and ability measures of emotional intelligence in medical students. *Medical Education*, *43*(11), 1062-8.

Brazdau, O. & Mihai, C. (2011). The Consciousness Quotient: a new predictor of students' academic performance. *Procedia - Social and Behavioral Sciences*, *11*, 245–250.

Brazdau, O. & Opariuc, C. (2014). Preliminary development of the Consciousness Quotient Inventory (CQ-i): introducing the conscious experience as a research variable in psychological assessment. *Procedia - Social and Behavioral Sciences*, *127*, 600-605.

Brazdau, O. (2008). *Research on the consciousness experience. The Consciousness Quotient and the CQ Inventory* (unpublished doctoral thesis). Romanian Academy of Science, Bucharest.

Brazdau, O. (2009). *The conscious experience: Consciousness Quotient (CQ) and the CQ Inventory*. Paper presented at Toward a Science of Consciousness Conference, Hong Kong, China.

Brazdau, O. (2009, June). *The conscious experience: Consciousness Quotient (CQ) and Brazdau CQ Inventory*. Paper presented at Toward a Science of Consciousness Conference, Hong Kong, China.

Brazdau, O. (2011). CQ: *Coeficientul de constientizare. The Consciousness Quotient (CQ) and the CQ Inventory - theory and research*. Bucharest: Info-Sanatate Press.

Brazdau, O. (2014). Witnessing awareness and modes of cognitive awareness. In D. Chopra (Ed.), *Brain, mind, cosmos: The nature of our existence and the universe*. Sages and Scientists Series, Part 1. [Kindle edition]. Retrieved from Retrieved from http://www.amazon.com.

Brazdau, O., Sharma, S., Ahuja, S. (2014). Consciousness Quotient Inventory administration on adolescents: difficulty level assessment. *Procedia - Social and Behavioral Sciences*, *128*, 387-392.

Brazdau, O. (2015). The Consciousness Quotient: Construct development and content validity research. *Procedia - Social and Behavioral Sciences, 187*, 244-249.

Brazdau, O., Constantinescu P.M., Constantinescu, I., Butucescu, A., Sbircea, R. (2013). Consciousness Quotient Inventory improvement: qualitative study using cognitive interviewing approach. *Procedia - Social and Behavioral Sciences, 78*, 425-430.

Brown, K.B. & Ryan, R. M. (2003). The benefits of being present: mindfulness and its role in psychological well-being. *Journal of Personality and Social Psychology, 84*(4), 822–848.

Chauhan, V., Sharma, S., & Satsangee, N. (2013). Leadership approach in relation to level of consciousness: a correlational analysis. *MIER Journal of Educational Studies, Trends and Practices, 3*(2), 249-260.

Chopra, D. (2010). *The soul of leadership: Unlocking your potential for greatness*. New York, NY: Harmony.

Church, M. (2010). *Love-based leadership: Transform your life with meaning and abundance*. Bloomington, IN: Balboa Press.

Conway, T. (2008). *Neo-advaita or pseudo-advaita and real advaita-nonduality*. Retrieved from http://www.enlightened-spirituality.org/neo-advaita.html.

Cook-Greuter, S. R. (2000). Mature ego development: a gateway to ego transcendence. *Journal of Adult Development, 7*(4), 227-240.

Costeines, M. (2009). *What enlightenment means: a qualitative study of nondual consciousness as experienced by teachers of nondual mysticism*. (Unpublished doctoral thesis). Institute of Transpersonal Psychology, Palo Alto.

Darling-Hammond, L., Austin, K., Cheung, M., & Martin, D. (2014). *Thinking about thinking: Metacognition*. Retrieved from http://www.learner.org/courses/learningclassroom/

Davidson, R. J. & Begley, S. (2012). *The emotional life of your brain*. London: Penguin Books.

Fenigstein, A., Scheier, M. F., Buss, A. H. (1975). Public and private self-consciousness: assessment and theory. *Journal of Consulting and Clinical Psychology, 43*, 522-527.

Forman, R. K. C. (Ed.). (1990). *The problem of pure consciousness: Mysticism and philosophy*. New York: Oxford University Press.

Froese, T., Gould, C., Barrett, A. (2011). Re-viewing from within: a commentary on first- and second-person methods in the science of consciousness. *Constructivist Foundations, 6*(2), 254-269.

Genarro, R. J. (2008). Are there pure conscious events? In C. Chakrabarti & G. Haist (Eds.), *Revisiting mysticism* (pp. 100-120). Cambridge: Cambridge Scholars Press.

Gianan, N. A. (2010). Valuing the emergence of Ubuntu philosophy. *Cultura. International Journal of Philosophy of Culture and Axiology, 7*(1), 86-96.

Grawes, C. W. (1970). Levels of existence: an open system theory of values. *The Journal of Humanistic Psychology, 10*(2), 131-154.

Grof, S. (2009). *Spiritual emergencies: Understanding and treatment of psychospiritual crises*. Retrieved from http://www.realitysandwich.com/spiritual_emergencies.

Hameroff, S. (2010). *Clarifying the tubulin bit/qubit - Defending the Penrose-Hameroff Orch OR model (Quantum Biology)*. Retrieved from transcriptvids.com/v/LXFFbxoHp3s.html

Hanson, R. (2011). *Understanding neuroplasticity*. Retrieved from from http://www.slideshare.net/ drrickhanson.

Harvey, O. J., Hunt, D. E., & Schroder, H. M. (1961). *Conceptual systems and personality organization*. New York: John Wiley & Sons.

Heim, S. (2003). *EQ for everybody - A practical guide to the developing and using one's Emotional Intelligence*. Retrieved from www.eqi.org.

Heron, J. (2006). *Participatory spirituality: A farewell to authoritarian religion*. Morrisville: Lulu Press.

Jeffery, A. & Martin, J. J. (2010). *Ego development stage does not predict persistent non-*

symbolic experience (Unpublished doctoral thesis). California Institute of Integral Studies, San Francisco.

Jones, V. (2012). *In search of conscious leadership: A qualitative study of postsecondary educational leadership practices* (Unpublished doctoral thesis). State University, San Diego.

Josipovic, Z., & Malach, R. (2006). Perception without a perceiver. *Journal of Consciousness Studies, 13*(9), 57–66.

Kent, J. (2010). *Psychedelic information theory. Shamanism in the age of reason.* Seattle: PIT Press.

King, D. B. (2008). *Rethinking claims of spiritual intelligence: a definition, model, and measure* (Unpublished doctoral thesis). Trent University, Ontario.

Krznaric, R. (2014). *Outrospection.* Retrieved from http://www.romankrznaric.com/outrospection

Li, C. (2010). *Open Leadership: How social technology can transform the way you lead.* San Francisco, CA: Jossey-Bass.

MacDonald, D. A. & Friedman H. L. (2002). Assessment of humanistic, transpersonal and spiritual constructs: state of the science. *Journal of Humanistic Psychology, 42*(4), 102-125.

MacLean, K., Leoutsakos, J. M., Johnson, M., & Griffiths, R. (2012). Factor analysis of the mystical experience questionnaire: a study of experiences occasioned by the hallucinogen psilocybin. *Journal for the Scientific Study of Religion, 51*(4), 721–737.

MacLean, P. D. (1990). *The triune brain in evolution: Role in paleocerebral functions.* New York: Plenum Press.

Mehling, W. E., Price, C., Daubenmier, J., Acree, M., Bartmess, E., & Stewart, A. (2012). The Multidimensional Assessment of Interoceptive Awareness (MAIA). *PloS ONE, 7*(11): e48230. doi:10.1371/journal.pone.0048230

Monsanto, C. (2013). *The language of emotions. A social developmental strategy,* presented at the Conference of the Association of Caribbean Social Work Educators, Curacao, 2013.

Murphy, T. (2002). *Forgetting About enlightenment. Enlightenment as a neural process. A forensic look at the Buddha's transformation.* Retrieved from http:// www.shaktitechnology.com/m enlightenment.htm

Natsoulas, T. (1990). Is consciousness what psychologists actually examine? *American Journal of Psychology, 105,* 363-84.

Neff, K. D. (2003). Development and validation of a scale to measure self-compassion. *Self and Identity, 2,* 223-250.

Newton, P. (2013). *Does it matter what 'validity' means?* Retrieved from www.ioe.ac.uk

Ryff, C. D. & Keyes, C. L. M. (1995). The structure of psychological well-being revisited. *Journal of Personality and Social Psychology, 69,* 719-727.

Satsangi, P.S. (2013). Towards Integrating Arts (First-Person Spiritual-Cognitive-Material Phenomenology) and Science (Third-Person Neuro-Physical, Environmental, Cognitive Correlates) of Consciousness, The Dayalbagh Vision, (Toward a Science of Consciousness (TSC 2013) Conference: Vision Talk), March 3-9, 2013, Centre for Consciousness Studies, Dayalbagh Educational Institute (Deemed University), Dayalbagh, Agra, India, Souvenir-cum-Abstract Book, pp. 61-63.

Sharma, S., Ahuja, S. (2015). Consciousness Quotient as predictor of executive functioning. *MIER Journal of Educational Studies, Trends and Practices, 5*(2).

Trochim, W. (2000). *The research methods knowledge base.* Cincinnati: Atomic Dog Publishing.

Varela, F.J. & Shear, J. (1999). First-person methodologies: what, why, how? *Journal of Consciousness Studies, 6*(2-3), 1-14.

Vasile, C. (2012). Rational/irrational beliefs dynamics in adults. *Procedia - Social and Behavioral Sciences, 69,* 2108-2113.

Chapter 12

The Intelligence of Structured Matter: A Theory of Structural Evolution and Interaction of Matter

DORIAN AUR
University of Victoria, Victoria, BC, Canada
ANITA BANDROWSKI
University of California, San Diego, CA, USA
and
JACK TUSZYNSKI
University of Alberta, Edmonton, AB, Canada

ABSTRACT

The theory of natural selection represents a small step in understanding the general process of the evolution of matter. Over billions of years this continuous evolution has transformed inert matter into life forms. Either at a celestial layer or on a protein scale, the equations of motion (n-body, many-body) and non-equilibrium thermodynamics can approximate the basic aspects regarding a dynamic process of structural evolution. Universal physical laws from classical mechanics and thermodynamics to quantum theory provide a physical foundation for a family of interconnected models that can describe the evolution of matter into resulting self-organized living structures. The presence of stronger electric fields in the brain characterizes physical interactions developed within asymmetric, non-homogeneous structured matter. What is commonly called learning and self-organization is a fast process of evolution, a change of the structure from a protein level within neurons and synapses driven from a DNA level and triggered by various environmental factors. Our mind, cognitive abilities, self-awareness (consciousness) and intelligent behavior become emergent characteristics of interactions developed within structurally 'evolved' matter. The continuous transformation of matter from a nanoscale (quantum) level inside the living organisms is part of the general evolution. In this sense, the overarching evolution of matter provides a unified theory of everything that may refine our entire understanding of the universe, including brain rhythms and roots of natural intelligence.

Keywords: *evolution; natural selection; nonlinear dynamics; nanoneuroscience; neuroelectrodynamics; systems biology; Einstein's brain*

INTRODUCTION

Intelligence is often associated with intellectual abilities required to perform various cognitive tasks. Different researchers have hypothesized that intelligence is determined by particularities of synaptic "connectivity" while others have highlighted neuroanatomical characteristics (Li et al., 2009). The importance of neurochemistry (Thagard, 2002; Changeux and Edelstein, 2012) or of the brain size was frequently reinforced (Willerman et al., 1991; Andreasen et al., 1993)

What caused Albert Einstein to move beyond conventional wisdom in physics? What made him a genius? In an attempt to discover the mystery of intelligence Thomas Harvey has surgically removed, sliced and performed neuroanatomical studies on Einstein's brain. Indeed, different details regarding brain parameters can be obtained by an anatomical assessment. A relatively wider parietal region was observed to be present in Einstein's brain, however, it was not clear how such a change can be linked with other brain characteristics (Anderson and Harvey, 1996; Witelson et al., 1999). Whether neuroanatomical measures (Witelson et al., 1999) correspond to creative abilities, intelligence or cognitive skills, has largely remained an open issue (Cairo, 2011).

Quantitative genetic studies have shown beyond doubt that intelligence is highly inheritable (Deary, et al., 2010; Davies et al., 2011; Chakravarty, 2010). In addition, recorded electrical activity provides meaningful details regarding the brain function and in particular EEG characteristics reflect genetic traits (Smit et al., 2012). Anokhin et al., Thatcher et al have shown that particular characteristics of EEG oscillations are strongly correlated with cognitive abilities (Anokhin et al.,1996; Thatcher et al., 2008) and 'fluid' intelligence (Silvia and Beaty, 2012).

Even though there has been progress made in this field, the validity of many theories regarding intelligence continues to be disputed today. In fact, rudimentary forms of self-awareness, cognition and intelligence as biological features did not originate with *Homo sapiens* (Trewavas, 2003). In order to survive cells are relying on sensing and signaling environmental changes. Basic forms of intelligent behavior are known to have already appeared in touch-sensitive plants such as *Mimosa pudica*, which generates action potentials (APs) and triggers rapid movements (Sibaoka, 1991; Chamovitz, 2012). For several decades the main thesis was that cells perform "rudimentary processing of sensed information". This view regarding the abilities of cells has radically changed lately. Environmental stress can activate DNA elements and slightly modify biological structure. In this sense, plants are "minimally cognitive" (Garzon and Keijzer, 2011). While in the past many researches would hesitate to call *Amoeba* intelligent, this view has drastically changed

(Nakagaki et al., 2000). Subject to ongoing criticism, the hypothesis that cells do "rudimentary information processing" has already become a problem. *Amoebas* and *Paramecium* cells "have remarkable abilities to make decisions and take constructive action, which correlates with standard definitions of intelligence" (Ford, 2009; Ford 2010).

The present paper tries to provide answers to several intriguing questions that arise in this context. What is the source of intelligent behavior? Why are EEG oscillations correlated with cognitive abilities? Is intelligence an outcome of neuroanatomical measures, brain connectivity or neurochemistry? And also a more general question: what is the relation between matter and intelligence?

The Physics of Matter and Structural Evolution

Classical physics represents the first attempt to decipher the relationship between matter and motion. Space, time, motion, matter and energy are regarded as independent concepts. For example, the motion of the objects forming the solar system can be mathematically described as the so-called n-body problem where n-material mass points interact due to gravitational forces between them according to Newtonian mechanics:

$$m_i\ddot{\vec{r}}_i = \sum_j k_G \frac{m_i m_j (\vec{r}_i - \vec{r}_j)}{|\vec{r}_i - \vec{r}_j|^3}, \quad i = 1,2,\ldots,n \geq 3 \tag{1}$$

where $m_1, m_2, \ldots, m_n$ are the masses of n-material points, $r_1, r_2, \ldots, r_n$ are their positions and $k_G = 6.6732\times10^{-11}\,\mathrm{m^3/\,s^2kg}$ is the gravitational constant. This system of equations can be equivalently written using canonical coordinates and the Hamiltonian formalism as:

$$\dot{p}_i = \sum_j k_G \frac{m_i m_j (\vec{r}_i - \vec{r}_j)}{|\vec{r}_i - \vec{r}_j|^3} = -\frac{\partial H}{\partial r_i} \quad i = 1,2,\ldots,n \tag{2}$$

$$q_i = \frac{p_i}{m_i} = \frac{\partial H}{\partial p_i} \tag{3}$$

where H is the Hamiltonian of the system (Meyer et al., 2008). The real mathematical difficulty of solving the n-body problem ($n \geq 3$) was perceived only late at the end of the nineteenth century and has attracted the interest of many mathematicians ever since (Sundman, 1913; Qiu-Dong, 1990).

Many physical systems can be modeled as quasi-Hamiltonian systems (Deng and Zhu 2009). In order to analyze the problem of solving equations of motion for systems which are not always integrable, Arnold et al. have approximated solutions using perturbation expansions in terms of the small parameter ε (Arnold et al., 1985). The Lagrangian equations of motion (Lagrange, 1772) can be expressed in the form of action angle variables:

$$H = \sum_{i=1,N} H_0(I_i) + \varepsilon V(I_1, I_2, .., I_N, \theta_1, \theta_2, ..., \theta_N) \quad (4)$$

where $(I_1, I_2, .., I_N, \theta_1, \theta_2, ..., \theta_N)$ are action angle variables, H_0 is the unperturbed Hamiltonian, N is the number of degrees of freedom and V is the perturbation term (Reichl, 2004).

The presence of perturbations can lead to internal nonlinear resonances (Chirikov, 1979; Reichl, 2004) with oscillations $\omega_1, ..., \omega_N$ that satisfy the condition:

$$n_1\omega_1(I_0) + ..., + n_N\omega_N(I_{N0}) = 0 \quad (5)$$

where $n_1, ..., n_N$ are natural numbers. If the perturbation energy is higher than the energy difference between the two closest unperturbed resonant orbits:

$$\Delta H_i > E_{i+1} - E_i \quad (6)$$

chaotic dynamics will develop (Chirikov, 1979) and the origin of chaotic dynamics and fractional dynamics can be explained by the resonance-overlap criterion (Chirikov, 1979; Zaslavsky, 2008).

Within the solar system, over time the presence of resonant frequencies has shifted the position of Mars and Jupiter, changed the arrangement of asteroids and altered the entire dynamics (Morbidelli and Henrard, 1991; Guzzo and Morbidelli, 1997). Once the structure of the solar system was reshaped, the gravitational field and its frequency of vibration have also changed. Captured by a frequency analysis (Laskar et al., 1993, Laskar, 2005) this shift in gravitational field provided the "first convincing evidence that the long time motion of the solar system is chaotic and to some extent unpredictable" (Reichl, 2004).

Over time, asymmetry and heterogeneity were naturally generated (Wyatt, 2003) providing a set of unique properties within every planetary system. Mathematically, the nonlinear dynamics given by Eqs. (1)–(3) describes the formation of a planetary system and is an expression of structural 'evolution' in cosmology.

The planetary n-body problem represents an example of an n-body interaction which is an exceedingly common situation in the physical world. On *smaller scales,* n-charge dynamics and the *electric field* become dominant components. The Coulomb interaction depends on the value of charges e_i and e_j and their positions $\vec{r}_i$ respectively $\vec{r}_j$ in physical space. For n interacting charges, similar equations can be written as:

$$m_i\ddot{r}_i = \sum_j k_e \frac{e_i e_j(\vec{r}_i - \vec{r}_j)}{|\vec{r}_i - \vec{r}_j|^3}, \quad i = 1,2,\ldots,n \tag{7}$$

where $r_{1,}r_2,\ldots,r_n$ are the position vectors of the point charges and $k_e = 1/4\pi\varepsilon_o\varepsilon_r$ where ε_o =8.854x10^{-12} F/m, and ε_r is the relative permittivity. At a quantum level, the interaction involving a large number of charges becomes the n-body problem and is described by the Schrödinger equation:

$$\frac{\partial y\ (t,x)}{\partial t} = \frac{i}{h} H(E) y\ (t,x) \tag{8}$$

where x is the position coordinate, y is the wavefunction, H is the Hamiltonian of the system and E is the total energy. Instead of an n-body problem of point particles with distinct positions in three-dimensional space, the solution of the Schrödinger equation gives a probability distribution for the quantum states of the system and the quantum approach can be further developed to take the form of a quantum field. As presented above in classical models (Eqs. (5), (6)), the occurrence of perturbations leads to internal nonlinear resonances and chaotic dynamics.

The Hamiltonian equations of motion represent a bridge between nonlinear dynamics and quantum mechanics (Yang, 2012) which can include the dynamics of chemical reactions, the generation of chaos and regularity (Komatsuzaki and Berry, 2002). The mathematical theory that underlies physical interaction of many-body dynamics calculations is far from being complete. Other attempts tried to provide an adequate description of the many-body problem. The path integral (Feynman and Hibbs, 1965), the density matrix theory (Fano, 1957) the second quantization approach (Dirac, 1927) and the variational pilot wave theory (Styer et al., 2002) are but a few examples of such attempts.

Either in a quantum approach of many-body physics (wave function) or in a classical framework of n-body dynamics (Greengard, 1994) the difficulties of solving the problem of interacting particles are well known. Max Born who made seminal contributions to the development of quantum mechanics suggested that "*Nature* fortified herself against further advances behind the analytical difficulties of the *many-body problem*" *(Born, 1960).*

A similar process of reorganization and 'evolution' of matter occurs at a quantum level, however our ability to perceive the particle positions and their dynamics in space is extremely limited as stated in the Heisenberg uncertainty principle. According to quantum mechanics and both special and general theories of relativity, space, time, motion and matter are not as independent of each other as once thought in classical physics. Higher frequency of 'vibrations' can be generated at a quantum scale. Classical models describe well the system's behavior provided the average thermal energy per particle is $k_B T > hf$ (k_B is the Boltzmann constant, $1.3806503 \times 10^{-23}$ m² kg s⁻² K⁻¹, Planck's constant $h= 6.626068 \times 10^{-34}$ m² kg / s). Therefore, the n-body (many-body) problems are in fact mathematical models that describe a dynamic process of structural evolution of matter. A small structure can evolve faster than a large one as it operates at shorter time scales.

Einstein challenged the main stream of thought in classical physics by demonstrating that a fragment of matter with mass *m* can be transformed into energy according to the famous formula $E=mc^2$. Inspired by Einstein's idea, Louis de Broglie suggested that matter can be represented by waves (de Broglie, 1923). With this view, a novel interpretation has emerged in physics and Einstein wrote "what we have called matter is energy, whose vibration has been so lowered as to be perceptible to the senses. There is no matter".

However, neither classical physics nor quantum mechanics have fully resolved the mystery of matter. The greatest show about matter can be observed on Earth (Dawkins, 2009).

Building the Biostructure: The Mystery of Life

The entire process of structural evolution over millions of years has generated a gradual transformation of matter which has shaped complex bio-systems. The existence of molecular asymmetry and micro-heterogeneity within the biological substrate remained largely unexplained. Schrödinger introduced the idea that biological information is kept at a molecular level in "aperiodic crystals" **(Schrödinger, 1944)** and a few years later the double helix structure of DNA was discovered (Watson and Crick, 1953) which revolutionized the world of biology.

All forms of life are shaped by molecular structures which transport energy and process information inside living systems. Fundamental characteristics of living systems such molecular asymmetry and micro-heterogeneity of biological "matter" were recognized since Pasteur's time (Robert et al., 2007). Chemical composition defines just a basic model required to build chunks of living matter. However, this does not seem to describe sufficiently the complexity of structured matter in a biostructure (Drochioiu, 2006; Murariu and Drochioiu, 2012). Notably, a simple change in spatial arrangement of chemical constituents can significantly alter emerging properties. Determined by structural changes, asymmetry and non-homogeneity are universal features of biological matter. Stereochemical relevance of chiral molecules and the resulting change of olfactory characteristics are well known examples of this mechanism (Zehnacker and Suhm, 2008).

Turning our attention back to the brain, it is well known that all neurons acquire their shape by spreading in the three-dimensional space (Bras et al., 1993; Scott and Luo, 2001; Cuntz et al., 2010; Packer and Yuste 2011)

Axonal and dendritic growths of neuronal cytoskeleton provide a clear basis for cell interactions, tissue development and neuronal function (Ng, 2012). The structure of neurons consists of various protein polymers (e.g. microtubules, intermediate filaments and actin filaments), which are spatially organized. Quantitatively, slow growing phenomena, which refine spatial evolution of cells can be simply described using physical principles (Kollmannsberger et al., 2011). In addition, on a millisecond time scale, a functional protein can be generated by polymerizing several hundred amino acids. Made from a set of amino acids, newly synthesized proteins require efficient folding to enable their function (Hartl and Hayer-Hartl, 2002). Determined by amino-acid sequences, the conformation of various proteins can be spatially reshaped by many factors (Gething and Sambrook, 1992).

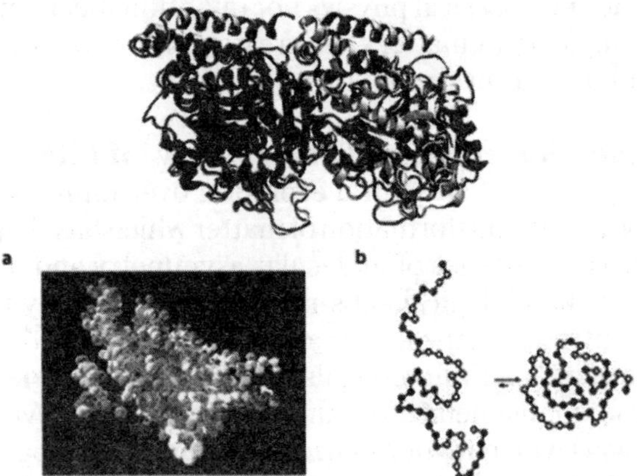

FIGURE 1
Microstructural Evolution: The conformation of a molecular system can be described by the coordinates of all n- atoms. A fast shaping of structure through protein folding and polymerization (Aur and Jog, 2010; Craddock, 2012) provides ways to embed information inside proteins (from http://en.wikipedia.org/wiki/Protein_folding).

Post-translational modifications, transcriptional and translational control are involved in this process (Figure 1).

In addition, complex regulatory mechanisms are programmed to preserve the soluble state of proteins (Vendruscolo, 2012). Created and regulated by protein polymerization, protein folding and protein phosphorylation, the newly generated structures can easily acquire complex functional roles. Many factors including neurotransmitters, hormones and electrical fluctuations can highly influence spatial arrangement of proteins and therefore change functional characteristics of neurons or synapses (Pirooznia et al., 2012). This places strong emphasis on the mechanisms of transformation which can dynamically occur inside neurons but can be sensitive to external influences.

A constant supply of biochemical energy in the form of ATP and GTP molecules is required to maintain the functional state of proteins (Grzybowski et al., 2012). The spatial rearrangement of charges, atoms at the molecular level is highly regulated by changes in gene expression, protein folding, alterations in electric fields, polarizations and the effect of hormones, and neurotransmitters (Aur, 2012a; Aur, 2012b; Plankar et al., 2012).

Since information is embedded in the structure by a transient effect of electric polarization, the generated electric field carries structural information. Therefore, the generation of action potentials and synaptic activities allows the system to 'read' (decode) fast information stored within a protein structure (e.g. microtubule) (Aur and Jog, 2010; Aur et al., 2011). However, specific proprieties of biological material can be significantly changed from a nanometer-scale (Woolf et al. 2009) since the process of structural evolution continues inside neurons and synapses (Scheeff and Bourne, 2005). Therefore, it is equally important to include the relationship between the structure of matter and the generated rhythms in living systems, notably in the brain.

New theories are typically triggered by experimental observations that challenge old paradigms of science. For almost a century the neuroscience community has believed that action potentials are stereotyped events which provide the basis for theories of brain function integrating such concepts as the firing rate, temporal patterns and connectivity. However, a growing body of experimental data points in a different direction. Only recently have we found that a fast change of structure happens within neurons in addition to synapses, and very recently a reliable way has been found to predict seizures (Aur et al., 2013). These experimental observations show that we need to extend our conceptual framework beyond old theories to understand the brain and to better design intelligent systems. We have artificially established boundaries between important research fields which have created many gaps in our view. Essentially, we need a physical framework to understand cognitive phenomena (Tuszynski, 2013).

The Rhythms in the Dynamics of Structured Matter

While the fundamental relationship between aggregated matter and intrinsic oscillations is well understood in physics, this association has remained elusive in biology. Various electric "vibrations" can be recorded in all living organisms and can be related to significant changes in their behavior. In addition, an adaptive behavior is present in plants, which develop minimal forms of cognition (Garzon and Keijzer 2011). Structural evidence and electromagnetic characteristics of plant morphogenesis has been recently demonstrated (Pietak, 2012). The presence of electric fields can change the distribution of proteins in plants and determine modifications of the cytoskeleton (Antov, 2004; Schenk and Seabloom 2010). In particular, the maximum intensity of

a

b

FIGURE 2
Shaping the configuration of proteins is a dynamic process of evolution of structured mater. While the dynamics of a galaxy (b) spans over billion years the protein dynamics can be completed in a few milliseconds (a). (adapted from Aur,2012a)

electric fields in space point to the direction of root growth (Masi et al.,2009; Ciszak et al, 2009).

The smaller the structure, the faster the generated rhythm of transformation can be (Figure 2a,b). This simple relationship applies to heterogeneous macromolecular structures (Sekulić, 2011) and their vibrations (natural frequency), which extends to neurons or larger ensembles of neurons.

At the early dawn of the genomic era, Burr's research at Yale provided evidence for the existence of electro-dynamic fields of living organisms (see Figure 3). His pioneering work on salamander embryo showed that recorded electric fields are stronger in the location where the salamander's head is shaped. A strong increase of the electric field in the brain region is not a random event (see neuroelectrodynamics). Ahead of his time, Harold Burr recognized the recurring electric vibrations as the

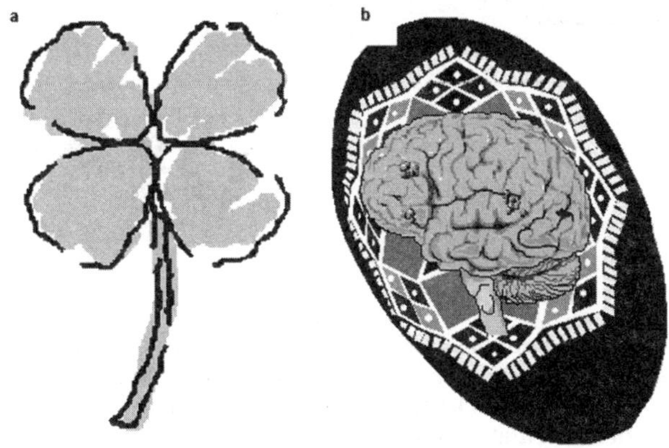

FIGURE 3

see: a. Weak electric fields can be detected in plants which develop minimal forms of cognition. b. Electric vibrations, the fields of life are stronger in the location where the salamander's head is shaped (Burr 1972).

fields of life which "preserve the living tissue from falling into a chaotic state" (Burr and Northrop 1935; Burr 1972).

More recently, a similar observation has been made in relation to seizure generation (Aur, 2011, Aur, 2012b). A subject of intense theoretical analysis, the generated rhythm is in fact a characteristic of the biostructure (see Figure 4) and represents a direct link to subcellular morphology (Kučera and Havelka, 2012; Sekulić, 2011; Havelka et al., 2011). Energy released from ATP's phosphate bonds is converted into nonlinear vibrations of proteins (Sekulić, 2011, Pang, 2011) and fuels the entire evolution. At the nanoscale level the amazing variety of protein structures and their dynamics have direct correspondence to the generated nonlinear oscillations, the presence of nonlinear dynamics was theoretically demonstrated to lead to soliton generation (Sekulić et al., 2011, Pang 2011; Scott, 1991).

Proteins being electrically polar structures can generate nonlinear oscillations and variable electric fields in the kHz to GHz frequency bandwidth (Cifra et al., 2010; Rahnama et al., 2011). These nonlinear vibrations intrinsically characterize the structure and are often presented as resonators of electromagnetic field (Cosic, 1994; Cifra, 2012). In addition, electromagnetic waves e.g. infrared light can induce non-thermal biological effects which can change the conformational states of proteins (Pang, 2012). The occurring molecular resonances play a stabilizing role that can reshape the entire molecular system (Mo, 2009; Kučera, and Havelka, 2012).

A small change in the free-energy range of several k_BT can signifi-

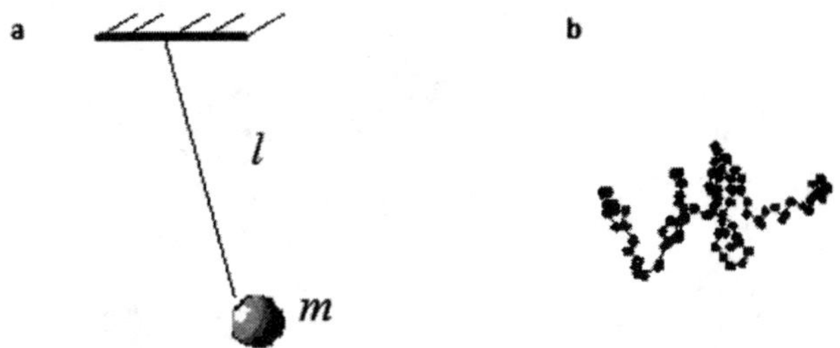

FIGURE 4
Natural frequency of vibration characterizes the system.
a. The resonance frequency depends on system characteristics (mass m, cable length l, gravitational field strength).
b. Nonlinear oscillations generated within proteins depend on their structural characteristics.

cantly affect the protein dynamics (Henzler-Wildman and Kern, 2007). Regulated by complex biochemical reactions, the presence of ions, neurotransmitters and metabolic substances leads to a continuous generation of electrical field patterns inside neurons and in the brain. The simplest mathematical model which describes a non-equilibrium system of this kind can take the form of reaction diffusion equations of the type:

$$\frac{\partial c_s}{\partial t} = D_s \nabla^2 c_s + R_s \text{ , } s < m, \tag{9}$$

where c_s is the concentration of species s , D_s is the diffusion coefficient, ∇^2 is the Laplacian operator and R_s accounts for local reactions and m is the number of species (Sivakumaran et al., 2002); Ayodele et al., 2011).

For more than two decades the development of reaction diffusion models was separated from Hamiltonian-based dynamical models of conservative systems. Elgart and Kamenev have recently established the correspondence between reaction-diffusion systems and their Hamiltonians (Elgart and Kamenev, 2006). Assuming similar local reactions and diffusion coefficients for all species, the reaction diffusion system can be written using the corresponding Hamiltonians:

$$\frac{\dot{q}}{t} = D\nabla^2 q - \frac{\partial H}{\partial p} \text{ and } \frac{\dot{p}}{t} = -D\nabla^2 q + \frac{\partial H}{\partial q} \tag{10}$$

where $p = \dot{q}$ and the resulting system can be modeled and analyzed based on corresponding, non-integrable Hamiltonians (Elgart and Kamenev, 2006).

In addition, the evolution of electrical patterns and chemical kinetic equations is strongly related. The non-integrable Hamiltonians can approximate the system dynamics. In addition, the angle action approximation (see Eq(4)) can generate extreme examples of the kind of behavior the brain exhibits which include the presence of resonant regimes and chaotic dynamics as in Eq. (5) and Eq. (6). Conceptually, nonlinear resonances are analogous to coupled oscillators (Scholes,

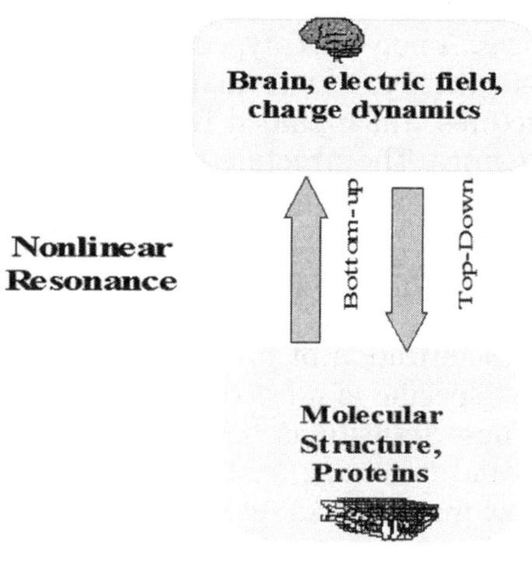

FIGURE 5
Electrical interactions and the dynamics of electric charges are required to transfer fragments of information between and within molecular structures. The brain in its entirety becomes the "computing" machine. A bidirectional transfer (exchange) of information is enhanced by nonlinear resonances within structured matter.

2003). The generation of resonant regimes is a critical process required for energy and information transfer within living biostructures and is particularly important in the brain (see Figure 5).

Chaotic dynamics can naturally develop in Hamiltonian systems with many degrees of freedom, which describe the motion of charged particles in an electric field (e.g. Arnold diffusion, resonance overlap). The Hamiltonian structure of Eq. (4) extended to an infinitely-dimensional case can model the interaction of electric fields with charges. The chaotic regime can be maintained only if neurons do not fire or have a very low firing rate (e.g. focal epileptogenic region (Aur, 2011). A quasi-equilibrium state corresponds to neuronal resting phase while the generation of an action potential is a rare event and represents the moment when internal nonlinear resonances develop inside the neuron. Either the presence of electrochemical 'perturbations' or the effect of chaotic dynamics causes protein channels to change their configuration. In order to transition to a lower energy of vibrational states, the energy of the excited vibrational mode is transferred to the kinetic modes and the flow of ions leads to a large diffusion at a synaptic level. If the neuron fires APs, the existent intracellular structural order is 'exported' in a generated electric field (with no associated chaos).

From a nanoscale level, the transfer of information is performed during electron conduction within proteins, vibrational signaling and the resonant interaction between macromolecules (Cosic, 1994). The presence of various neurotransmitters and hormones can enhance or inhibit structural changes. A non-stereotyped vibration (e.g. an action potential) generates an exchange of information between the electric field and protein structures which embed fragments of information inside neurons and synapses. The structure and dynamics of proteins can be reshaped during resonant regimes (conceptually similar to those in a planetary system) and is enhanced during an increase of activity (firing rate). In addition, spatial propagation of APs makes synaptic 'connectivity' between neurons highly variable.

The atomic-level characterization of protein dynamics provides an n-body level description specific to a free-energy perturbation model (Shaw et al., 2010). These transitions between structurally distinct states, protein folding and unfolding, can take place on time scales between 10 μs and a few ms (Kubelka et al., 2004; Anandakrishnan and Onufriev, 2010; Oladepo et al., 2012). One can readily find that the distribution of atoms and electric charges within a particular protein structure is not random (Brenner et al., 2000; Koehl and Levitt, 1999). Therefore, inside cells proteins can embed fragments of information within an evolved non-native structure. This process has been explained recently (Craddock et al., 2012). The information embedded in proteins can be rapidly exchanged through specific 'vibrations' which characterize the protein structure. Therefore, structural organization within neurons and synapses at a protein level is an important basis for information storage, while electric fields carry this specific information between various intra-cellular locations. In fact, we found that a generated electric field reflects essential structural properties of the matter genetically shaped inside neurons.

Both in the case of the solar system and in the brain, the respective equations of motion, the principle of least action and the second law of thermodynamics represent physical foundation for an evolutionary theory of structured matter. The energy constraints drive the system on the path of least action (De Maupertuis, 1744) which follows the principle of increasing entropy and is reflected in the equations of motion. The use of non-equilibrium thermodynamic treatment either to examine the generalized theories of gravitation (Chattopadhyay and Ghosh, 2012; Bamba, and Geng, 2009) or transformations that occur at a protein level (Annila and Salthe, 2010) describes the structural evolution of matter. The validity of the laws of thermodynamics has been affirmed beyond doubt and this area of physics represents an essential tool that can be used to determine the evolution of the system.

Microstructural Evolution, Learning, Self-organization and Semantics

The development and plasticity of the brain are well recognized. A fast reorganization of temporal patterns is triggered during T-maze procedural tasks (Jog et al., 1999; Barnes et al., 2005) or repetitive presentation of images (Quiroga et al.2005; Aur, 2012b). The fundamental 'vibration' of neurons, i.e. the generation of action potentials, is considered to be a stereotyped event in spite of recent experimental observations (Aur and Jog, 2005; Aur and Jog, 2010; Sasaki et al., 2011; Aur, 2012b). However, in neural computation all previous models (temporal coding) rely on erroneous interpretation of experimental observations. The stereotyped action potential is just an appearance. Since single-electrode recordings are inadequate to capture spatial propagation of the spike, a digital uniformity was attributed. Occasionally, a few electrophysiologists have observed changes in AP waveforms. While they recognized these changes, unfortunately they failed almost completely to understand their deeper meaning (Quirk et al., 2001). This simple observation (non-stereotyped spikes) has powerful implications since changes that occur within the molecular structure inside neurons can be related to electrical patterns (see Figure 6, b; Figure 7, a) generated during spiking activity and preferential propagation of information either synaptically or non-synaptically (by an electric field). From a computational point of view information can be quickly "read out" (Aur and Jog, 2010; Aur et al., 2011; Beggs and Tucker 2007) or "written in" (encoded) during electric interactions within proteins (Craddock et al., 2012). The entire process of modulated interaction within and between specific neurons explains how the brain creates or experiences 'meaning' (Figure 6, b). In an intact brain, temporal coding models are extremely limited and lack generality (e.g. spike timing dependent plasticity, Schulz, 2010; Spruston and Cang, 2010; Aur et al., 2007; Feldman, 2010). The rules that "are much more complex" describe the evolution of molecular structure at a neuronal and synaptic level. The evolution of the structure of matter provides a more general model.

In addition, our understanding of reality is necessarily based upon incomplete information extracted from experimental observations. Since action potentials are recorded with low sampling frequencies (<50 kHz), nonlinear phenomena that occur at a molecular level within neurons during AP generation can be hardly evidenced. The presence of electrical patterns (see Figure 6, b; Figure 7, a) is a direct effect of fast changes that can occur at a protein level. If one cannot record high frequencies, it does not necessarily mean that such frequencies do not exist or they cannot alter the evolution of the system. Recently, it has been shown that infrared neural stimulation can be used to stimulate the somatosensory cortex in rats (Cayce et al., 2011). However, to be able to "see" fast molecular changes that can occur at a protein level inside the neuron during an action potential one would need high

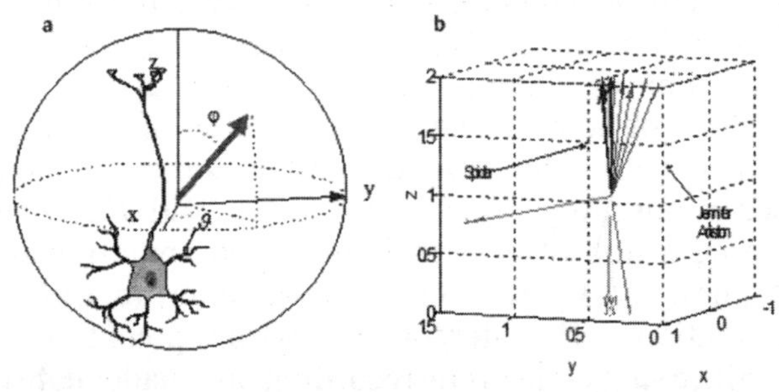

FIGURE 6

a. The distribution of electrical patterns during action potential generation is approximated with a vector (spike directivity, Aur et al., 2005, Aur 2012a) b. Spike directivity relates the generation of APs with macromolecular 'vibrations' inside the cell. The vibrational energy enhances the dynamics of electric charges, electric field and caries specific information about the spider (spike directivity arrows in blue color) or about Jennifer Aniston (red arrows).

resolution infrared optical imaging of the neuron. Unfortunately, the required temporal and spatial resolution to obtain such images is still unattainable using current technology.

The change observed in temporal patterns reflects the reorganization that occurs within the molecular structure at a neuronal and synaptic level (Aur and Jog, 2010). Nature is far more subtle than we have imagined. Every action potential can be seen as a brief moment (1ms in duration) when the neuron 'solves' at least a classical n-body problem rather than exclusively computes functions (Aur and Jog, 2006; Aur and Jog 2010; Aur, 2012c). The limits generated by computing functions were largely presented by Goldin and Wegner as an introductory topic in interactive computing (Goldin and Wegner, 2008). Current ideas in computational neuroscience regarding the interspike interval and spike-timing-dependent plasticity are just extensions and misunderstandings of the all-or-none principle (Adrian, 1914). At this point, it is becoming abundantly clear that the mainstream in computational neuroscience adheres a dogma older than Turing's paradigm (Turing, 1936). There is little understanding or appreciation for the hypothesis that information can be processed in a non–Turing manner at nanoscale levels within neurons and synapses.

Known as habituation, the repetitive presentation of a stimulus leads to a decreased response of neurons (Thompson and Spencer, 1966). The development of habituation in neurons can be simply explained. A fast process of structural 'evolution' at a protein level is triggered in specific neurons and synapses during a repeated presentation of images (Aur and Jog, 2010; Aur, 2012b) or repetitive T-maze behavioral tasks (Barnes et al., 2005; Aur and Jog, 2007; Aur and Jog, 2010). Less energy is required to identify the image or to provide an adequate behavioral response required to get the reward. This repetitive presentation leads to an efficient response. With few generated spikes the information regarding the semantics of presented images or behavioral meaning are efficiently processed and electrically transmitted (see Figure 6). The entire process that decreases the firing rate can be simply explained as a process of reorganization determined by structural evolution which can be strongly triggered within specific neurons by a repetitive presentation of images or by a rewarding mechanism.

The process of evolution inside the cell can change the expression of genes into proteins, the structure of neuron is driven from a DNA level. It is now well recognized that an increased expression of misfolded proteins, giving rise to pathological protein aggregation is age dependent. Macromolecular degeneration, reduced neurotrophic support, cytoskeletal abnormalities, post-translational modifications of proteins and protein denaturation are evolutionary processes, which develop over time (Orpiszewski et al., 2000). The presence of regulatory interactions that operate at gene and protein levels indicates a more complex mechanism for information flow than earlier proposed by the central dogma of molecular biology (Crick, 1970). The existence of epigenetic effects of chemical signals at several levels (e.g. chemical modifications to DNA) the presence of complex regulatory networks which determines which genes are expressed and alter the genome function, challenges the main dogma and limits genetic-causal explanations (Noble,2006; Aur and Jog, 2010; Noble, 2011). Targeting the genome stability, DNA/RNA structure and artificially increasing the length of telomeres can provide solutions useful in the search for effective therapeutic interventions for cancer or various aging-related diseases (Jesus et al., 2012).

In addition, every evolutionary process needs sources of energy to develop and expand. A new generation of synthesized proteins can bring new features and it is not an accident that protein turnover plays a key role in aging (Ryazanov and Nefsky, 2002). Caloric restriction (less energy consumed) can slow down the evolution and holds back the dynamics of the aging processes (Lee et al., 1999; Colman et al., 2009; Fontana et al., 2010). (A controlled slowdown of fusion inside the Sun probably will have a similar effect!) The evolutionary theory of aging has its origins within an evolution of structured matter. The electrical signaling of proteins is directly related to their function.

A balance between protein synthesis and protein degradation is strongly regulated in healthy organisms through fine tuned mechanisms of homeostasis. However, the regulation of protein stability is a small part of a general framework of protein evolution. While the generated structure is not random ("God doesn't play dice" as famously stated by A. Einstein), the fast evolutionary process of many proteins remained largely unnoticed. In addition, the degradation of proteins increases entropy and energy expenditure. It has been clearly stated recently that it "becomes evident that protein folding is an evolutionary process among many others" (Sharma et al. 2009). Being highly regulated, the hierarchical structure of proteins evolves from the primary structure, to the secondary structure to tertiary and finally the quaternary structure (see Fig. 7). In addition, the denaturation of the protein structure is a natural continuation of the evolutionary process which can be triggered by aging or

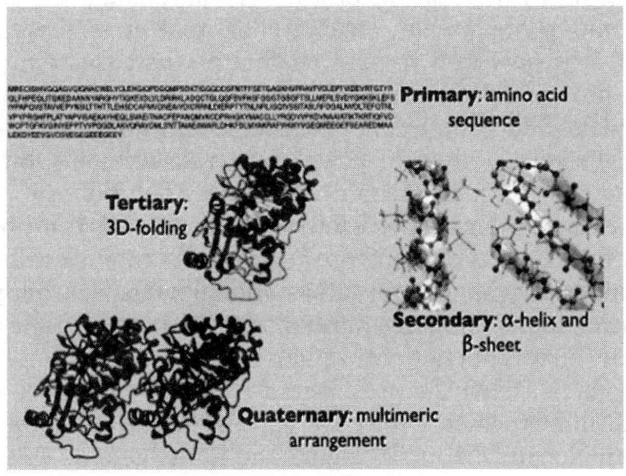

FIGURE 7
Tubulin as an example of a connection between primary, secondary, tertiary and quaternary protein structures.

epigenetic factors. While many generated proteins have a limited lifetime, some structures have a long life and slowly degenerate in time over a period of years (Su et al., 2012).

What is Balanced Excitation and Inhibition?

The balance between excitation and inhibition is extensively presented in many papers as a "basic functional principle" underlying neural activity in the brain (Zheng et al., 2012). Classified as excitatory or inhibitory, chemical synapses can generate various modulatory signals. A number of controversies regarding the nature of synaptic transmission

(Isaacson and Walmsley, 1995), in addition to a dynamic shift between inhibition and excitation, have strongly limited the applicability of this principle (Heiss et al., 2008; Zuo et al., 1999). The inhibitory neurotransmitter $GABA_A$ (Luscher et al., 2011) can become excitatory in case of an increased Cl^- concentration inside the cell (Taketo and Yoshioka, 2000). In addition, $GABA_A$ receptors, the main ionotropic receptors for fast inhibitory transmission, are expressed by 19 distinct genes, which can generate at least 26 different receptors (Luscher et al., 2011; Rourke et al., 2012). (Inhibitory synapses become excitatory and vice versa!).

However, many scientists felt that this principle of inhibition and excitation can be extended beyond conventional neurotransmitter type classification (e.g. GABAergic, dopaminergic, serotonergic) to explain the occurrence of neurological disorders, the effect of treatment (DBS) or even the presence of consciousness. Extended to large brain areas,

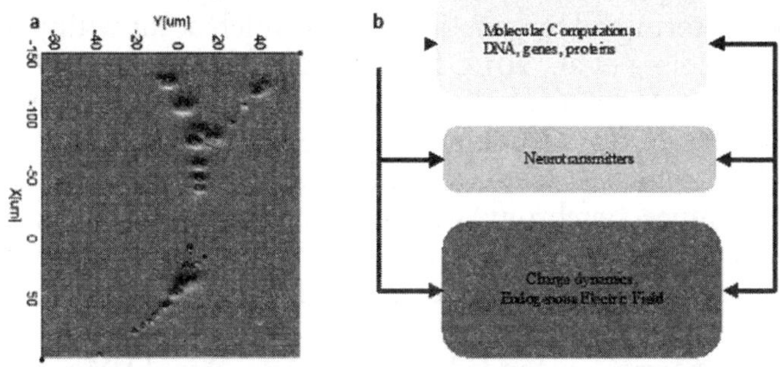

FIGURE 8

a. A representative electrical image of an action potential where the n-body (n-charge) dynamics approximates the AP generation. Since the internal structure of neurons can evolve fast, (the distribution of atomic charges is continuously reshaped at a protein level) the computed spike directivity displays a change in spatial distribution of electrical patterns (adapted from Aur and Jog, 2010).
b. Controlled from a genetic DNA level, the evolution of proteins can change the structure and function of neurons or synapses. A schematic systemic representation of interconnected regulatory loops which provide the required "balanced excitation and inhibition" in the brain (adapted from Aur, 2012a).

the idea of excitation and inhibition engendered controversies instead of explanations (e.g. the mechanism of action of DBS stimulation, Montgomery and Gale, 2008)

Inside neurons and synapses various proteins are expressed. Understanding the evolution of synapses provides insights into the organization of matter inside the brain. Our convenience (inhibitory, excitatory connections) has hidden the fundamental role of proteins and their homeostatic contribution. The dense and rich protein network structure can evolve fast and generate the required plasticity in the brain. In addition, proteomic analysis has shown that protein phosphorylation can significantly change intracellular signaling with effects on synaptic plasticity (Craddock et al., 2012; Tweedie-Cullen et al., 2012). A deep molecular diversity (Rourke et al., 2012) and the "balance between inhibition and excitation" are in fact effects of regulated evolution of the structure built inside neurons and synapses from a nanoscale (quantum) level. Within a systemic approach the entire dynamics in the brain can be schematically represented by three interacting regulatory loops (Figure 8, b) (Aur and Jog, 2010; Aur et al., 2012a).

The Genetic Basis of Brain Disorders and Aging

The topic of age related evolution of structure can be best discussed within an evolutionary paradigm. Dissecting the genetic basis of common brain disorders provides an intrinsic relationship, between structural alterations determined by genetic changes which occur within neurons in epilepsy (Helbig et al., 2012; Poza, 2012), schizophrenia (Friedman et al., 2009) or Alzheimer's disease (Bertram and Tanzi, 2004) and visible changes of brain rhythms. The altered genetic structure within neurons and synapses leads to similar nonlinear dynamic regimes (chaotic dynamics, synchrony) which are always detected in Alzheimer's disease, Parkinson's disease and epilepsy (Jeong, 2004, Dauwels et al., 2010; Uhlhaas and Singer, 2006). An abnormal change of the electric field precedes the generation of seizures epilepsy (for a physical model, nonlinear dynamics, extended Kolmogorov- Arnold-Moser theory, transition to chaos, etc. the reader is referred to Aur, 2011) and the onset of cancer (Assenheimer et al., 2001). Mathematically, persistent chaotic dynamics in the brain, which precedes a seizure is no different than the chaotic dynamics in the solar system. Unfortunately, after 60 years of research in epilepsy we still do not understand the "big picture" and we treat the generation of seizures by "fighting fire with fire" (Gwinn and Spencer, 2004). This metaphor is somewhat misleading regarding the role of therapy and the specific moment when stimulation needs to be provided (Aur et al., 2013).

The formation and evolution of solar cycles depend on energy resources. Aging is an irreversible phenomenon that severely affects the structure of matter. Over the course of millions of years the solar material is converted into energy while the entire structural evolution is shaped from a "quantum" level of nuclear fusion. The depletion of energy (matter) marks the end of an evolutionary state.

Either in a star or in the brain, driven by evolution this change of structured matter leads to aging. A similar process of structural evolution is present in every living organism. Maintained by a continuous influx of chemical energy the process of evolution shapes the structure of mater from a nanoscale (quantum) level of proteins.

While information stored in the brain increases with time, the number of synapses and the volume of gray matter reduces with age (Taki et al., 2011; 9). The absolute number of synapses per neuron is reached by the age of 1 year and strongly decreases during the preschool years. Inside neurons and synapses, proteins can maintain their structural order within arrays of amino acids, by preferred spatial orientation of covalent bonds (Scheiner et al., 2011), specific spatial arrangement of electric charges and intra-protein electric fields. The development of structural order at a molecular level is required to preserve and accumulate

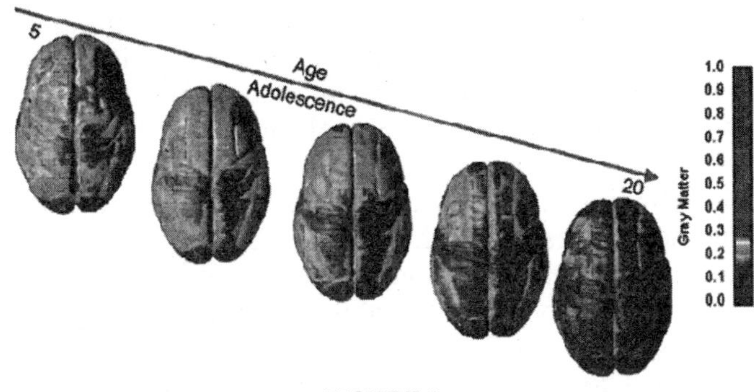

FIGURE 9

The gradual process of evolution alters the structure of the brain. From birth through the final stages of life a decrease of gray matter volume is reflected in a reduced electrical activity. (Adapted from http://www.brainfacts.org/across-the-lifespan/youth-and-aging/)

new information in neurons (structural plasticity of neurons and synapses). The loss of information can be generated by mechanisms that alter the life cycle of proteins, local aberrant protein degradation in neurons (Steward and Schuman, 2003). Therefore, the control of protein degradation and protein synthesis is highly regulated within every neuron. An entire cycle from DNA to RNA through appropriate gene activation for protein synthesis is maintained in response to a wide variety of extracellular signals and electrical events (Pozo and Goda, 2010). The process of biophysical interaction and new protein synthesis is built to preserve previous fragments of information and to accumulate new information over time. Correct protein folding and binding depends on the local environment where proteins are synthesized. These processes are critically important for faithful information preservation within molecular structures. As always, information is retained and transferred to newly formed structures and different electric rhythms, and various neurotransmitters and hormones are involved in this process. Incompletely folded, misfolded proteins are required to establish a correct conformation or initiate the protein degradation process (Malgaroli et al., 2006). During sleep phases different categories of genes provide the needed support for new protein synthesis (Cirelli, et al., 2004). The internal molecular structure in neurons is continuously reshaped, the regulation and maintenance of the life cycle of proteins is a vital process required to preserve and incorporate new information.

Alzheimer's Disease (AD) is systemically induced by metabolic or genetic risk factors (APP, PS1, PS2) that in different forms alter the life cycle of proteins, disrupt the unique repertoire of proteins secreted within neural cells and lead to distinct pathological features (e.g. intracellular neurofibrillary tangles of MAP tau and extracellular beta amyloid plaques). Since similar fragments of information are distributed and stored within a large number of cells, few changes in a small number of neurons or the death of some cells do not necessarily generate memory loss or cognitive impairments. Therefore, in order to determine significant effects, a large number of neurons have to be affected by the progression of the disease. These changes in neurons have to generate a significant transformation of brain rhythms since the rhythm is critical to the brain's ability to 'read' or integrate specific fragments of information.

At a biological level, a progressive deterioration of physiological function can occur in time triggered by unexpected events (e.g. brain trauma Moeller et al, 2011; pilocarpine treatment, Buckmaster and Haney, 2012), which lead to an evolutionary change in protein structure at synapse and neuron levels. "Unfortunately, nature seems unaware of our intellectual need for convenience and unity and very often takes delight in complication and diversity", (Cajal, 1906). The expression of genes and environmental factors plays a significant role in shaping internal evolution of the structure in a variety of ways and only a certain percentage of treated rats (34%) develop *status epilepticus* (Buckmaster and Haney, 2012).

Either due to aging or self-destruction, the senescence of cells appears to be programmed by gene expression and influenced by environmental factors and/or DNA damage. With the progression of aging, additional factors accumulate and may trigger cellular dysfunctions and influence the life cycle of proteins. Even in the absence of a specific disease, aging is associated with an increased aggregation of a large number of proteins (David, 2010). Since aggregated proteins are insoluble, they determine changes in electrical characteristics in intra-protein electric fields that can alter how information is stored or transferred between the flow of charges and the biological substrate during AP generation or synaptic activities. In addition, with aging, reduced periods of sleep may affect the process of 'writing' fragments of information within molecular structures. Periods of sleep (REM, SWS) required to reshape the internal structure within neurons significantly decrease in Alzheimer's disease compared to age-matched control subjects (Onen and Onen, 2003). Exaggerated Aβ production is correlated with aneuploidy induced by different mutant forms (e.g. amyl, PS proteins). The buildup of amyloid-β protein and MAP tau disrupts the axonal transport and can limit the propagation of the signal during AP generation only in few axonal branches.

The synaptic dysfunction can be determined by a local buildup of amyloid-β protein at synapses or related to accumulation of intraneuronal amyloid-β and disrupts AP propagation. In addition, perturbation of Zn homeostasis can have profound effects on a system scale in the pathogenesis of Alzheimer's disease (Maret, 2005; Craddock et al., 2012; Liu et al., 2008).

The availability of transgenic models in the case of Alzheimer's disease (Irizarry et al., 1997), Huntington's disease (Mangiarini et al., 1996) schizophrenia (Crawley, 1999) and even epilepsy (Croll, 1999) shows that neuropathological states can be initiated at a genetic level that controls the structure and function of proteins. A similar aspect can be observed in traumatic brain injuries. Biochemical evidence of DNA fragmentation shows that the expression of proteins is altered from a genetic level, which can lead to fast apoptosis and seizure generation (Lewen, et al., 2000; Dubreuil et al., 2006). In addition to various neurotransmitters and hormones, the generated electric field can change the structure of matter within neurons and synapses. An aberrant evolution can be controlled and reshaped by changing the biostructure from a nano-scale level of proteins by electrical (DBS) or magnetic stimulation (May and Gaser, 2006; Dragicevic, et al., 2011). In addition to many other effects, the stimulation alters relevant genes that are expressed, which explains why electrical (or magnetic) stimulation can provide better therapy in the case of major neurological disorders such as Parkinson's disease, Alzheimer's disease or epilepsy.

On the Origin of Time, Matter and Intelligence of Life

Physical systems often self-aggregate into complex structures under specific conditions, e.g. in the process of polymerization. Organized groups of bacteria acquire unimaginable capabilities for information processing which reflect "cognitive, computational and evolutionary capabilities" (Shapiro, 2005; Shapiro, 2007). This simple organization of bacteria and their abilities in mobilizing and engineering DNA molecules (Shapiro, 2005) show that the origins of intelligent behavior are buried into *collective* states of structured *matter* shaped by an evolutionary process. Either in plants or within the animal kingdom, the creation of cells and their interactions lies at the heart of intelligent behavior (Ford, 2009).

The presence of action potentials in 'sensitive' plants which trigger physiological responses, rapid movements in e.g. *Mimosa pudica* (Fromm and Lautner, 2007) is a relevant aspect. Electrical excitability and signaling allows for a fast exchange of information which sustains the bio-field hypothesis and its role beyond the 'brain universe' (Burr, 1972; Rubik B, 2002). A fast response of rats to X-rays (Garcia et al., 1964; Brust-Carmona, et al., 1966) or the presence of blue light photoreceptors (e.g. cryptochrome proteins) in plants or animals can provide information regarding magnetic fields or circadian rhythms. The 'vibration' of bio-structured matter at a protein level can respond to a large spectrum of signals generated by another source of energy. Thus, while we are unable to 'see' directly a certain phenomenon, we might indirectly 'feel' its effects.

In addition, the evolution inside living organisms typically follows a nonlinear path (e.g. involving nonlinear resonances, chaotic dynamics, fractal structure formation) that shapes the structured matter from a nanoscale level up. Even when biological organisms share identical genes (twins), such nonlinear interactions can create huge differences between them. This natural variability explains why certain phenomena such as remote perception (Puthoff and Targ, 1976) telepathy (Ritchie et al., 2012; Bem and Honorton, 1994) or retrocausal influence (May et al., 2005) occur preferentially only in certain human subjects.

What Is Holding us Back in Artificial Intelligence?

The fundamental laws of physics show that a natural design of intelligence is possible. Controlled by genetic traits and external interaction, natural intelligence is an emergent characteristic of interactions that occur within structured, evolved matter. At different scales the properties of 'evolved' matter can be perceived to be similar. Theoretically, an adaptive evolution by (natural) selection can be extrapolated to a population of neurons. Coined by Edelman, neural Darwinism and neuronal group selection as a morphological argument (Edelman, 1987) reflect in fact a structural change of matter which can be either adaptive (Nei and Kumar,2000; Fay, 2011) or neutral (Motoo 1983; Schiffels et al., 2011).

Having water as the highly preferred environment for the evolution of life is not a random phenomenon. Water molecules represent an active player in major biological processes Fast building or regenerating flexible structures in water solutions are essential events in all living systems. The brain and many other organs can function as a whole, with no separateness since in liquid water all components can strongly interact. Recently, a group led by Nobel laureate L. Montagnier has detected low-frequency electromagnetic waves emitted by the DNA of bacteria and viruses in low dilution solutions (Montagnier et al., 2011). It seems, therefore, that the DNA structure can send "spooky electromagnetic imprints of itself into distant cells and fluids". Such properties are largely attributed to the 'quantum-coherent domains'. The liquid water and internal components cannot be described as non-interacting point particles, the regulation of complex electrochemical solutions or fluctuating hydrodynamics are modeled using variational principles (Eisenberg et al., 2010).

The change of the structure inside neurons and synapses is the most powerful tool used to reshape the matter and generate intelligent behavior in living organisms. The increase of the electric field in the brain region (e.g. salamander) is not a random event. The presence of the electric field provides the required interaction. It is a very fast way to transfer information and increase the number of cells (neurons), which process information in the brain. Since every neuron functions (communicates, processes information) using an internal (variable) structure, it does not make sense to generate stereotyped ('digital') action potentials. Why would a complex biological neuron with an evolved structure behave as a metronome? However, only a few researchers understood that while it is convenient, the 'digital' action potential is a vastly oversimplified hypothesis.

Does the neuron doctrine (e.g. the firing rate) provide the required explanatory level to understand the mind-brain relationship? We do not believe so. Temporal coding, spiking models, balanced inhibition and excitation (instead of regulation), Hebbian law ("fire together - wire together", instead of a change in the structure from a nanoscale- quantum level) represent our "intellectual need for convenience". Simplistic theoretical ideas about 'neural coding', 'connectivity', 'Hebbian laws', have distorted the general image regarding a fast internal evolution of matter in living organisms (especially in the brain). Indeed, there is no separation between a nanoscale level of information processing and the macroscopic observable events. However, the process of computation cannot be described by fitting the moments when the peaks of amplitudes are detected (action potentials) to a particular function since APs are non- stereotype events. Temporal patterns do not provide an approximation of relevant structural changes. Neither the degree of fidelity nor the accuracy of modeling such parameters has much value. Since the structure evolves, the function of proteins, synapses and neurons can be totally transformed.

The generation of a stronger electric field in the brain is not a random event, the process of computation by physical interaction directly involves molecular structures from many cells (Aur and Jog, 2010; Aur et al., 2012b). It is a completely different process which can change fast with structural evolution of matter.

In addition, patterned on Turing Machines current models have a limited ability to acquire properties which are specific to evolved, structured matter. The well-known connectionist models and parallel computation represent attempts to describe structural changes at a network level (Rumelhart et al., 1986; Kohonen, 1988; McClelland and Rumelhart 1987; Carpenter and Grossberg, 1988). They may in fact simulate changes that occur within a fast evolution of matter. Bayesianism, connectionist models, temporal coding models, statistical analysis or searching databases, are not 'physically grounded' and do not express similar properties. In our opinion, the objective of generating 'artificial consciousness' using digital computers is closer to science fiction (http://en.wikipedia.org/wiki/Artificial_consciousness) than to science. Only with a paradigm shift that uses a physical, non-algorithmic approach to build intelligent machines (Aur, 2012a), artificial consciousness can become "an engineered artifact".

Incomplete Models, the Theory of Everything

The human mind has developed the model of the world we know based on sensorial and experimental observations. Both within distant stars and in our brain, matter is equivalent to energy with intrinsic 'vibrations' that reflect the existent structural order. Imperfect, flawed experimental observations (e.g. stereotyped action potentials) have led to a series of distorted, incomplete models.

We are not only 'made of star-stuff'. Inside our brains the creation of structured matter follows the same physical principles of evolution. In an attempt to build a theory of everything, string theory was proposed in different formulations following Einstein's legacy ("matter is an energy vibration"). However, without including how life and mind originate from the evolution and interaction of structured matter we will always have an incomplete, elusive theory (Deacon, 2012; Hawking and Mlodinow, 2010; Copeland, 2002; Chalmers 1995; Penrose R, 1994; Scruton 2005).

Different states of the same matter (e.g. water) can express various physical characteristics. Under a slight change of environmental factors the properties of matter can and do change. A simple example can be the transition of water from the liquid state to the solid state. In philosophy one can interpret this change as a 'subjective' response to environmental factors (Chalmers 1996; MacGregor and Vimal, 2008). Others will strongly oppose it (Dennett, 1971; Pinker and Bloom 1990; Searle, 2000; Dawkins, 2009). They might state that it doesn't matter how many times this transition occurs, to their knowledge the water doesn't develop any subjective experience. The same interpretation is attributed to computers, smart phones where the outcome of algorithms neither change their 'subjective state' nor differentiate between self and nonself (Searle, 2000; Searle, 2013).

With this paper we try to avoid such "paralysis of thought" (Feynman, et al., 1963) by hypothesizing that solely within structurally 'evolved' matter mental, subjective aspects can be expressed.

From fetal to neonatal life clear markers of the emergence of human consciousness can be measured and quantified. The emergence of consciousness may be faster within biological structures where a rapid development from molecular (protein) level is enhanced and constrained by an evolutionary path (Sharma and Annila, 2007; Shaw et al., 2010). An effective detection of different states of consciousness is observer-independent (Welberg, 2012). Such detectable changes (e. g. EEG rhythms, functional MRI) are correlated with the evolution of the brain's structure at all levels and various states of consciousness. The emergence of consciousness is a system property. Alone, different parts of the central nervous system (CNS) do not seem to inherit this characteristic. The intact brain behaves differently than the sliced brain (Steriade 2002; Kohl et al., 2010).

The interaction with the external environment gradually changes the structure of matter inside the brain from a molecular level (e.g. protein) and captures the essential nature of experience. This hypothesis is in agreement with experimental observations which show a gradual emergence of consciousness correlated with structural (functional) development of human brain from early fetal stages up to the adult state (Lagercrantz and Changeux, 2009). We propose that consciousness becomes an emergent property of 'evolved' matter (Searle, 2002)

Summary of Theoretical Concepts – New Predictions

Most previous research has followed an anthropomorphic approach. Sense or semantics were subjectively attributed to characterize different forms of evolution. Here, the term "evolution" is used in a broader, physical sense, an impersonal way to transmit information regarding the scientific knowledge.

Having a theoretical understanding of overarching evolution and interaction of matter from a nanoscale (quantum) level becomes increasingly important in life sciences and medical research. Clear possibilities for experimental verification, reliable predictions with direct applications in various fields are key elements for any theoretical model. Therapeutic advances in neurological disorders, cancer therapy, delaying the aging process or even modeling natural computing systems, all may require a deep understanding of overarching structural evolution of matter.

On a millisecond time scale, a functional protein can be generated by joining a number of amino acids together. The structure of proteins can evolve from primary structure to secondary structure and reach a functional tertiary structure. This process is reflected in changes generated in non-stereotyped 'vibrations' (action potentials, synaptic activities) in the brain. Everything can be seen as a result of biophysical interactions and structural evolution of matter. The change of temporal patterns with "learning" reflects the evolution of the structure inside synapses and neurons.

Since a change in the structure at a protein level can be rapidly triggered by a repetitive presentation of stimuli many recording techniques (e.g. single electrodes) are inadequate to detect a small variability and changes of APs remained largely unperceived.

Inadequate observations (stereotyped action potentials) have led to sophisticated 'digital' models simulated on Turing Machines. However, these models are of limited scope and use, they do not provide or express essential attributes achieved through physical interaction within organized, structured matter (e.g. self-awareness, consciousness, emotion)

The entire gimmick to "read" out memories at the brain scale based on 'connectivity' and temporal patterns is an impractical journey. As a particular property of organized, living matter the electric field within a generated rhythm does not only transfer information, it can reshape the biostructure (the brain) from a nanoscale (quantum) level over the entire lifespan. The neuroelectrodynamic theory highlights the limits of connectionist models and temporal coding principles.

An aberrant evolution of the structure can be controlled, from a nano-scale level of proteins by electrical or magnetic stimulation (deep brain stimulation, TMS). Also, infrared neural stimulation can be used for therapy and does not require genetic manipulation as in optogenetics. In addition, the evolutionary theory of aging has its intrinsic origins in a more general model of structural evolution of matter.

Either in stars or in cells, driven from a nano-scale (quantum) level the evolution shapes the structure of matter and leads to aging. Self-destruction, aging or the senescence of cells appear to be programmed by gene expression and influenced by environmental factors and/or DNA damage. Inside the animal kingdom caloric restriction (less energy) slows down the process of evolution and holds back the dynamics of aging. The evolutionary process that shapes the structure of matter can be slowed down but cannot be stopped. Aging is an irreversible phenomenon that severely affects the structure of matter. While targeting the DNA/RNA structure, the length of telomeres can increase longevity, it cannot eliminate the ultimate demise of any living organism.

Conclusions

From Darwin to Dawkins, the theory of evolution is presented as a gradual process of natural selection driven by genetic (heritable) features. The evolution of the structure of matter precedes natural selection. Biological evolution, natural selection on Earth represents but a small step that started less then 3.7 billion years ago while the age of the Universe is estimated to be about *13.8 billion years*. Darwin's theory represents the basis for adaptation and specialization to changes in the environment of any living organism.

Contrary to common wisdom, which has restricted the theory of life's origin to natural selection, we have presented an argument that evolution is a general property of matter that has shaped the entire universe, from solar systems to human brains. Over billions of years fashioned by gravitational interaction, the development of the universe is a clear expression of the 'evolution' of matter in cosmology. Built from 'stardust' we are born, evolve and die as any star in the Universe. The process of natural selection is just another form of the evolution of matter.

Initiated before birth in the mother's womb, the evolution of the child's brain follows a similar process and shares similar physical laws. From a nanoscale (*quantum*) level of electrical interaction, the structure of matter inside neurons and synapses is shaped based on genetic traits, presence of neurotransmitters, hormones and environmental factors (Hameroff, et al., 1996). What is commonly referred to as 'learning' and self-organization is a fast process of evolution, a change of the structure inside neurons and synapses at a protein level. There is no 'neural code', instead fast evolution of matter takes place triggered by external events (e.g. reward, image presentation).

From a nanoscale level to cosmic scales energy constraints govern the evolution of the structure. Therefore, we do not need to invent new principles other than classical and quantum laws of physics at appropriate space- and time-scales to describe the evolution of matter. The smaller the structure under consideration, the faster the evolution can be. Specific properties of proteins and neurons depend on their refined structure (asymmetry, heterogeneity). Having a clear model of overarching evolution of matter can help us to provide effective therapies for various diseases and prolong human life span. Environmental factors can alter the expression of genes, transcription and translation of proteins. The biologically functional soluble state of proteins can be rapidly achieved either inside bacteria or in neurons. Natural intelligence is the outcome of this process which restructures the matter in living organisms in a selective manner. Through evolution, once structured, the matter acquires characteristics which are not common for the inert, unstructured matter. We view the mind as the outcome of physical (electrical) interaction of structured 'evolved' matter inside the brain. Cognitive abilities, self-awareness, consciousness and intelligent behavior become emergent features of structured matter.

Therefore, the existence of natural intelligence is embedded within a refined structure and intrinsic interactions. Maintaining a functional state of proteins and their heterogeneous, asymmetric structure inside neurons and synapses requires a continuous influx of energy. Outside an intact, living brain all proteins may rapidly lose their structure and function, and irreversibly transform into abnormal forms so that the entire brain can become a mass of amorphous organic matter. *It is worth keeping in mind that* there is a long history of testing wrong hypotheses in investigating biological intelligence. Following the main stream of thought, Thomas Harvey and other scientists did not realize that a lifeless, sliced, (aged) brain is no longer the exceptional brain that once epitomized the genius of Albert Einstein. It is always important to understand the big picture to avoid the expensive, vicious cycle of testing so many unreliable hypotheses.

The structural evolution of matter is a general phenomenon. Either at a celestial level or within the 'brain universe' a family of interconnected physical models can describe the evolution of structured matter. The classical and quantum equations of motion combined with non-equilibrium thermodynamics provide general mathematical models capable of describing and predicting the 'evolution' of matter. Natural selection is just a small step on the path of general evolution of matter. In this sense, the structural evolution of matter represents the theory of everything and the ultimate quest to discover a final theory.

Acknowledgments: The authors would like to thank Jay McClelland for excellent comments which helped improve the manuscript. JAT acknowledges funding received from the Natural Sciences and Engineering Council of Canada (NSERC).

References

Adrian, E. D. (1914). The all-or-none principle in nerve. *The Journal of Physiology, 47*, 460-474.

Anandakrishnan, R., & Onufriev, A. V. (2010). An N log N approximation based on the natural organization of biomolecules for speeding up the computation of long range interactions. *Journal of Computational Chemistry, 31*, 691-706.

Anderson, B., & Harvey, T. (1996). Alterations in cortical thickness and neuronal density in the frontal cortex of Albert Einstein. *Neuroscience Letters, 210*, 161-164.

Andreasen, N. C., Flaum, M., Swayze, V. D., O'Leary, D. S., Alliger, R., Cohen, G., ... & Yuh, W. T. (1993). Intelligence and brain structure in normal individuals. *American Journal of Psychiatry, 150*, 130-4.

Annila, A., & Salthe, S. (2010). Physical foundations of evolutionary theory. *Journal of Non-Equilibrium Thermodynamics, 35*, 301.

Anokhin, A., & Vogel, F. (1996). EEG alpha rhythm frequency and intelligence in normal adults. *Intelligence, 23*, 1-14.

Antov, Y., Barbul, A., & Korenstein, R. (2004). Electroendocytosis: stimulation of adsorptive and fluid-phase uptake by pulsed low electric fields. *Experimental Cell Research, 297*, 348-362.

Arnold, V. I., Kozlov, V. V., & Neištadt, A. I. (1985). *Mathematical aspects of classical and celestial mechanics*. Berlin Heidelberg: Springer-Verlag.

Assenheimer, M., Laver-Moskovitz, O., & Malonek, D. (2001). The T-SCAN (TM) technology: electrical impedance as a diagnostic tool for breast cancer detection. *Physiological Measurement, 22*, 1-8.

Aur, D. & Jog M., (2010). *Neuroelectrodynamics: understanding the brain language* (Vol. 74). Amsterdam: IOS Press.

Aur, D., Jog, M. S., & Poznanski, R. (2011). Computing by physical interaction in neurons, *Journal of Integrative Neuroscience, 10*, 413-422.

Aur, D. (2012a). From neuroelectrodynamics to thinking machines. *Cognitive Computation, 4*, 4-12.

Aur, D. (2012b). A comparative analysis of integrating visual information in local neuronal ensembles. *Journal of Neuroscience Methods, 207*, 23–30.

Aur, D., & Jog, M. (2007). Reading the neural code: What do spikes mean for behavior? *Nature Precedings*. Retrieved from *http://precedings.nature.com/documents/61/version/1/files/npre200761-1.pdf*

Aur, D., & Jog, M. S. (2006). Building spike representation in tetrodes. *Journal of Neuroscience Methods, 157*, 364-373.

Aur, D., Connolly, C. I., & Jog, M. S. (2007). Spike timing–an incomplete description of neural code. *BMC Neuroscience, 8*(Suppl 2), 49.

Aur, D. (2012). Reply to comments on Neuroelectrodynamics: Where are the real conceptual pitfalls? *arXiv preprint arXiv:1210.1983*.

Aur, D., Toyoda, I., Bower, M. R., & Buckmaster, P. (2013). U.S. Patent No. 8,600,513. Washington, D.C.: U.S. Patent and Trademark Office.

Ayodele, S. G., Varnik, F., & Raabe, D. (2011). Lattice Boltzmann study of pattern formation in reaction-diffusion systems. *Physical Review E, 83*, 016702.

Bamba, K., Geng, C.-Q. (2009).Thermodynamics in F (R) gravity with phantom crossing. *Physics Letters, Section B: Nuclear, Elementary Particle and High-Energy Physics, 679*, 282-287.

Barnes, T. D., Kubota, Y., Hu, D., Jin, D. Z., & Graybiel, A. M. (2005). Activity of striatal neurons reflects dynamic encoding and recoding of procedural memories. *Nature, 437*(7062), 1158-1161.

Beggs, E. J., & Tucker, J. V. (2007). Can Newtonian systems, bounded in space, time, mass and energy compute all functions? *Theoretical Computer Science, 371*(1), 4-19.

Bem, D. J., & Honorton, C. (1994). Does psi exist? Replicable evidence for an anomalous process of information transfer. *Psychological Bulletin, 115*(1), 4.

Bertram, L., & Tanzi, R. E. (2004). The current status of Alzheimer's disease genetics: what do we tell the patients? *Pharmacological Research, 50*(4), 385-396.

Born, M. (1960).The classical mechanics of the atom. New York: F. Ungar Publishing Company.

Bras, H., Korogod, S., Driencourt, Y., Gogan, P., & Tyc-Dumont, S. (1993). Stochastic geometry and electrotonic architecture of dendritic arborization of brain stem motoneuron. *European Journal of Neuroscience, 5*(11), 1485-1493.

Brenner, S. E., Koehl, P., & Levitt, M. (2000). The ASTRAL compendium for protein structure and sequence analysis. *Nucleic Acids Research, 28*(1), 254-256.

Broglie, L. (1923). Waves and quanta. *Nature, 112*(2815), 540-540.

Brust-Carmona, H., Kasprzak, H., & Gasteiger, E. L. (1966). Role of the olfactory bulbs in x-ray detection. *Radiation Research*, 29 (3), 354-361.

Buckmaster, P. S., & Haney, M. M. (2012). Factors affecting outcomes of pilocarpine treatment in a mouse model of temporal lobe epilepsy. *Epilepsy Research, 102*, 153-9.

Burr, H.S. (1972). *The fields of life*. New York: Ballantine.

Burr, H. S. & Northrop, F. S. C. (1935).The electro-dynamic theory of life. *Quarterly Review Of Biology, 10*, 322-333.

Cairò, O. (2011). External measures of cognition. *Frontiers in human neuroscience, 5*, 108. doi: 10.3389/fnhum.2011.00108

Carpenter, G. A., & Grossberg, S. (1988). The ART of adaptive pattern recognition by a self-organizing neural network. *Computer, 21*(3), 77-88.

Cajal, S. R. (1906). The structure and connexions of neurons. Retrieved from http://www.nobelprize.org/nobel_prizes/medicine/laureates/1906/cajal-lecture.pdf

Cayce, J. M., Friedman, R. M., Jansen, E. D., Mahavaden-Jansen, A., & Roe, A. W. (2011). Pulsed infrared light alters neural activity in rat somatosensory cortex in vivo. *NeuroImage, 57*(1), 155-166.

Chamovitz D., (2012). *What a plant knows: A field guide to the senses of your garden – and beyond*. Oxford: Oneworld Publications.

Chalmers, D. J. (1995). Minds, machines, and mathematics. *Psyche, 2*(9), 117-18.

Chalmers, D. J. (1996). *The conscious mind: In search of a fundamental theory*. USA: Oxford University Press.

Chakravarty A. (2010). The creative brain – Revisiting concepts. *Medical Hypotheses, 74*, 606-612

Changeux, J-P., & Edelstein, S. J. (Eds.). (2012). *The brain as a chemical machine: Nicotinic receptors and neuronal communication*. New York: Odile Jacob.

Chattopadhyay, S., & Ghosh, R. (2012). A study of generalized second law of thermodynamics in modified f (R) Horava–Lifshitz gravity. *Astrophysics and Space Science, 341*, 669.

Chirikov, B. V. (1979). A universal instability of many-dimensional oscillator systems. *Physics Reports, 52*(5), 263-379.

Cifra, M., Pokorný, J., Havelka, D., & Kučera, O. (2010). Electric field generated by axial longitudinal vibration modes of microtubule. *BioSystems, 100*(2), 122-131.

Cifra, M. (2012). Electrodynamic eigenmodes in cellular morphology. *Biosystems, 109*(3), 356-366.

Cirelli, C., Gutierrez, C.M., & Tononi, G. (2004). Extensive and divergent effects of sleep and wakefulness on brain gene expression. *Neuron, 41*(1), 35-43.

Ciszak, M., Comparini, D., Mazzolai, B., Baluska, F., Arecchi, F. T., Vicsek, T., & Mancuso, S. (2012). Swarming behavior in plant roots. *PloS one, 7*(1), e29759.

Colman, R.J., Anderson, R.M., Johnson, S.C., Kastman, E.K., Kosmatka, K.J., Beasley, T.M., Allison, D.B., (...), & Weindruch, R. (2009). Caloric restriction delays disease onset and mortality in rhesus monkeys. *Science, 325* (5937), 201-204.

Copeland, B. J. (2002). Hypercomputation. *Minds and machines, 12*(4), 461-502.

Cosic, I. (1994). Macromolecular bioactivity: is it resonant interaction between macromolecules? Theory and applications. *Biomedical Engineering, IEEE Transactions on, 41*(12), 1101-1114.

Craddock, T. J., Tuszynski, J. A., Chopra, D., Casey, N., Goldstein, L. E., Hameroff, S. R., & Tanzi, R. E. (2012). The zinc dyshomeostasis hypothesis of Alzheimer's disease. *PloS one, 7*(3), e33552.

Craddock, T. J., Tuszynski, J. A., & Hameroff, S. (2012). Cytoskeletal signaling: is memory encoded in microtubule lattices by CaMKII phosphorylation? *PLoS Computational Biology,*

8(3), e1002421.

Crawley, J. N. (1999). Behavioral phenotyping of transgenic and knockout mice: experimental design and evaluation of general health, sensory functions, motor abilities, and specific behavioral tests. *Brain Research*, *835*(1), 18-26.

Crick, F. (1970). Central dogma of molecular biology. *Nature*, *227* (5258), 561-563.

Croll, S. D., Suri, C., Compton, D. L., Simmons, M. V., Yancopoulos, G. D., Lindsay, R. M., ... & Scharfman, H. E. (1999). Brain-derived neurotrophic factor transgenic mice exhibit passive avoidance deficits, increased seizure severity and in vitro hyperexcitability in the hippocampus and entorhinal cortex. *Neuroscience*, *93*(4), 1491-1506.

Cuntz, H., Forstner, F., Borst, A., & Häusser, M. (2010). One rule to grow them all: a general theory of neuronal branching and its practical application. *PLoS Computational Biology*, *6*(8), e1000877.

David, D. C., Ollikainen, N., Trinidad, J. C., Cary, M. P., Burlingame, A. L., & Kenyon, C. (2010). Widespread protein aggregation as an inherent part of aging in C. elegans. *PLoS Biology*, *8*(8), e1000450.

Dauwels, J., Vialatte, F., & Cichocki, A. (2010). Diagnosis of Alzheimers disease from EEG signals: Where are we standing? *Current Alzheimer Research*, *7*(6), 487-505.

Davies, G., Tenesa, A., Payton, A., Yang, J., Harris, S. E., Liewald, D., & Deary, I. J. (2011). Genome-wide association studies establish that human intelligence is highly heritable and polygenic. *Molecular Psychiatry*, *16*(10), 996-1005.

Dawkins, R. (2009). The greatest show on earth: The evidence for evolution. New York: Free Press.

Deacon, T. W. (2011). *Incomplete nature: how mind emerged from matter*. New York: W.W. Norton.

Deng, M., & Zhu, W. (2009). Some applications of stochastic averaging method for quasi Hamiltonian systems in physics. *Science in China Series G: Physics Mechanics and Astronomy*, *52*(8), 1213-1222.

Dennett, D. C. (1971). Intentional systems. *The Journal of Philosophy*, *68*(4), 87-106.

Deary, I. J., Penke, L., & Johnson, W. (2010). The neuroscience of human intelligence differences. *Nature Reviews Neuroscience*, *11*(3), 201-211.

Dirac, P. A. M. (1927). The quantum theory of the emission and absorption of radiation. *Proceedings of the Royal Society A: Mathematical, Physical and Engineering Sciences*, *114*, 243.

Dragicevic, N., Bradshaw, P. C., Mamcarz, M., Lin, X., Wang, L., Cao, C., & Arendash, G. W. (2011). Long-term electromagnetic field treatment enhances brain mitochondrial function of both Alzheimer's transgenic mice and normal mice: a mechanism for electromagnetic field-induced cognitive benefit? *Neuroscience*, *185*, 135-149.

Drochioiu, G. (2006). Eugen Macovschi's concept of biostructure and its current development. In S. Savva (Ed,). *Life and mind: In search of the physical basis* pp. 43-60. Victoria, BC, Canada: Trafford Publication.

Dubreuil, C. I., Marklund, N., Deschamps, K., McIntosh, T. K., & McKerracher, L. (2006). Activation of rho after traumatic brain injury and seizure in rats. *Experimental Neurology*, *198*(2), 361-369.

Edelman, G. M. (1987). *Neural Darwinism: The theory of neuronal group selection*. New York: Basic Books.

Eisenberg, B., Hyon, Y., & Liu, C. (2010). Energy variational analysis of ions in water and channels: Field theory for primitive models of complex ionic fluids. *The Journal of Chemical Physics*, *133*(10), 104104.

Elgart, V., & Kamenev, A. (2006). Classification of phase transitions in reaction-diffusion models. *Physical Review E*, *74*(4), 041101.

Fano, U. (1957). Description of states in quantum mechanics by density matrix and operator techniques. *Reviews of Modern Physics, 29*(1), 74-93.

Fay, J. C. (2011). Weighing the evidence for adaptation at the molecular level. *Trends in Genetics, 27*(9), 343-349.

Feldman, J. (2010). Ecological expected utility and the mythical neural code. *Cognitive Neurodynamics, 4*(1), 25-35.

Feynman R. P., & Hibbs, A. R. (1965). *Quantum physics and path integrals.* New York: McGraw-Hill.

Feynman, R. P., Leighton, R. B., & Sands, M. L. (1963). *The Feynman lectures on physics.* Reading, MA: Addison-Wesley.

Fontana, L., Partridge, L., Longo, V.D. (2010). Extending healthy life span-from yeast to humans, *Science, 328* (5976), pp. 321-326.

Ford, B. (2009). On intelligence in cells: The case for whole cell biology. *Interdisciplinary Science Reviews, 34*(4), 350-365.

Ford, B. J. (2010). The secret power of the single cell. *The New Scientist, 206*(2757), 26-27.

Fromm, J. & Lautner, S. (2006). Electrical signals and their physiological significance in plants. *Plant, Cell & Environment, 30*(3), 249-257.

Friedman, J. I., Vrijenhoek, T., Markx, S., Janssen, I. M., Van der Vliet, W. A., Faas, B. H. W., ... & Veltman, J. A. (2007). CNTNAP2 gene dosage variation is associated with schizophrenia and epilepsy. *Molecular Psychiatry, 13*(3), 261-266.

Garcia, J., Buchwald, N.A-., Feder, B.H., Koelling, R.A., Tedrow, L. (1964). Sensitivity of head to x-ray. *Science, 144* (3625), 1470-1472.

Garzón, P. C., & Keijzer, F. (2011). Plants: Adaptive behavior, root-brains, and minimal cognition. *Adaptive Behavior, 19*(3), 155-171.

Goldin, D., & Wegner, P. (2008). The interactive nature of computing: Refuting the strong Church-Turing thesis. *Minds and Machines, 18*(1), 17-38.

Greengard, L. (1994). Fast algorithms for classical physics. *Science, 265*(5174), 909.

Gething, M. J., & Sambrook, J. 1992. Protein folding in the cell. *Nature, 355,* 33-45.

Guzzo, M., & Morbidelli, A. (1996). Construction of a Nekhoroshev like result for the asteroid belt dynamical system. *Celestial Mechanics and Dynamical Astronomy, 66*(3), 255-292.

Grzybowski, B. A., Wilmer, C. E., Kim, J., Browne, K. P., & Bishop, K. J. (2009). Self-assembly: from crystals to cells. *Soft Matter, 5*(6), 1110-1128.

Gwinn, R. P., & Spencer, D. D. (2004). Fighting fire with fire: brain stimulation for the treatment of epilepsy. *Clinical Neuroscience Research, 4*(1), 95-105.

Hameroff, S. and Penrose, R. (1996). Orchestrated reduction of quantum coherence in brain microtubules: A model for consciousness? In S. R. Hameroff, A. W. Kaszniak, & A. C. Scott (Eds.), *Toward a science of consciousness: The first Tucson discussions and debates.* Cambridge, MA: MIT Press/Bradford Books.

Hartl, F. U., & Hayer-Hartl, M. (2002). Molecular chaperones in the cytosol: from nascent chain to folded protein. *Science, 295*(5561), 1852-1858.

Havelka, D., Cifra, M., Kučera, O., Pokorný, J., Vrba, J. (2011). High-frequency electric field and radiation characteristics of cellular microtubule network. *Journal of Theoretical Biology, 286*(1), 31-40.

Hawking, S., & Mlodinow, L. (2010). The (elusive) theory of everything. *Scientific American, 303*(4), 68-71.

Henzler-Wildman, K., & Kern, D. (2007). Dynamic personalities of proteins. *Nature, 450*(7172), 964-972.

Heiss, J. E., Katz, Y., Ganmor, E., & Lampl, I. (2008). Shift in the balance between excitation and inhibition during sensory adaptation of S1 neurons. *The Journal of Neuroscience, 28*(49), 13320-13330.

Helbig, I., Scheffer, I. E., Mulley, J. C., & Berkovic, S. F. (2008). Navigating the channels and beyond: unravelling the genetics of the epilepsies. *The Lancet Neurology, 7*(3), 231-245.

Isaacson, J. S., & Walmsley, B. (1995). Counting quanta: direct measurements of transmitter release at a central synapse. *Neuron, 15*(4), 875-884

Irizarry, M. C., McNamara, M., Fedorchak, K., Hsiao, K., & Hyman, B. T. (1997). APPSw transgenic mice develop age-related A beta deposits and neuropil abnormalities, but no neuronal loss in CA1. *Journal of Neuropathology and Experimental Neurology, 56*(9), 965.

de Jesus B.B., Vera E., Schneeberger K., Tejera A.M., Ayuso E., Bosch F., Blasco M.A. (2012). Telomerase gene therapy in adult and old mice delays aging and increases longevity without increasing cancer, EMBO *Molecular Medicine, 4,* 1–14.

Jeong, J. (2004). EEG dynamics in patients with Alzheimer's disease. *Clinical Neurophysiology, 115*(7), 1490-1505.

Jog, M. S., Kubota, Y., Connolly, C. I., Hillegaart, V., & Graybiel, A. M. (1999). Building neural representations of habits. *Science, 286*(5445), 1745-1749.

Kollmannsberger, P., Bidan, C. M., Dunlop, J. W. C., & Fratzl, P. (2011). The physics of tissue patterning and extracellular matrix organisation: how cells join forces. *Soft Matter, 7*(20), 9549-9560.

Koehl, P., & Levitt, M. (1999). A brighter future for protein structure prediction. *Nature Structural Biology, 6,* 108-111.

Kohl, P., Crampin, E. J., Quinn, T. A., & Noble, D. (2010). Systems biology: an approach. *Clinical Pharmacology & Therapeutics, 88*(1), 25-33.

Kohonen, T. (1988). An introduction to neural computing. *Neural Networks, 1*(1), 3-16.

Lagrange, J.L. (1772). Essai sur le probleme des trois corps. *Œuvres complètes, tome 6,* 229-331.

Komatsuzaki, T., & Berry, R. S. (2002). Chemical reaction dynamics: many-body chaos and regularity. *Advances in Chemical Physics, 123,* 79-152.

Kubelka, J., Hofrichter, J., & Eaton, W. A. (2004). The protein folding 'speed limit'. *Current Opinion in Structural Biology, 14*(1), 76-88.

Kučera, O., & Havelka, D. (2012). Mechano-electrical vibrations of microtubules–link to subcellular morphology. *BioSystems.* 109 (3), 346-355.

Lagercrantz, H., & Changeux, J. P. (2009). The emergence of human consciousness: from fetal to neonatal life. *Pediatric Research,* 65(3), 255-260.

Laskar, J. (1993). Frequency analysis for multi-dimensional systems. Global dynamics and diffusion. *Physica D: Nonlinear Phenomena, 67*(1), 257-281.

Laskar, J. (2005). Frequency map analysis and quasiperiodic decomposition. In D. Benest, C. Froeschle & E. Lega (Eds.), *Hamiltonian systems and Fourier analysis: new prospects for gravitational dynamics* pp. 99-129. Cambridge, UK: Cambridge Scientific Publishers.

Lee, C.-K., Klopp, R.G., Weindruch, R., & Prolla, T.A. (1999). Gene expression profile of aging and its retardation by caloric restriction. *Science, 285,* (5432), 1390-1393.

Lewen, A., Matz, P., & Chan, P. H. (2000). Free radical pathways in CNS injury. *Journal of Neurotrauma, 17*(10), 871-890.

Li, Y., Liu, Y., Li, J., Qin, W., Li, K., Yu, C., & Jiang, T. (2009). Brain anatomical network and intelligence. PLoS *Computational Biology, 5*(5):e1000395.

Liu, J., Jiang, Y. G., Huang, C. Y., Fang, H. Y., Fang, H. T., & Pang, W. (2008). Depletion of intracellular zinc down-regulates expression of Uch-L1 mRNA and protein, and CREB mRNA in cultured hippocampal neurons. *Nutritional Neuroscience, 11*(3), 96-102.

Luscher, B., Fuchs, T. & Kilpatrick, C. L. (2011). GABAA receptor trafficking-mediated plasticity of inhibitory synapses. *Neuron, 70,* 385-409.

Mangiarini, L., Sathasivam, K., Seller, M., Cozens, B., Harper, A., Hetherington, C., ... & Bates, G. P. (1996). Exon 1 of the HD gene with an expanded CAG repeat is sufficient to cause a progressive neurological phenotype in transgenic mice. *Cell, 87*(3), 493-506.

May, A., & Gaser, C. (2006). Magnetic resonance-based morphometry: a window into structural plasticity of the brain. *Current Opinion in Neurology, 19*(4), 407-411.

May, E. C., Paulinyi, T., & Vassy, Z. (2005). Anomalous anticipatory skin conductance response to acoustic stimuli: experimental results and speculation about a mechanism. *Journal of Alternative & Complementary Medicine, 11*(4), 695-702.

Malgaroli, A., Vallar, L., & Zimarino, V. (2006). Protein homeostasis in neurons and its pathological alterations. *Current opinion in Neurobiology, 16*(3), 270-274.

Maret, W. (2005). Zinc coordination environments in proteins determine zinc functions. *Journal of Trace Elements in Medicine and Biology, 19*(1), 7-12.

Masi, E., Ciszak, M., Stefano, G., Renna, L., Azzarello, E., Pandolfi, C., ... & Mancuso, S. (2009). Spatiotemporal dynamics of the electrical network activity in the root apex. *Proceedings of the National Academy of Sciences, 106*(10), 4048-4053.

Maupertuis, P. D. (1746). Les loix du mouvement et du repos déduites d'un principe métaphysique. *Mémoires de l'académie des sciences de Berlin, 2*, 1746-1748.

McClelland, J. L., & Rumelhart, D. E. (1987). *Parallel distributed processing, Vol. 2: Psychological and biological models (Vol. 1).* Cambridge, MA: MIT Press.

MacGregor, R. J., & Vimal, R. L. P. (2008). Consciousness and the structure of matter. *Journal of Integrative Neuroscience, 7*(1), 75-116.

Meyer, K., Hall, G., & Offin, D. (2008). Introduction to Hamiltonian dynamical systems and the N-body problem Vol. 77. New York: Springer-Verlag.

Mo, Y. (2009). The resonance energy of benzene: a revisit. *The Journal of Physical Chemistry A, 113*(17), 5163-5169.

Moeller, J. J., Tu, B., & Bazil, C. W. (2011). Quantitative and qualitative analysis of ambulatory electroencephalography during mild traumatic brain injury. *Archives of Neurology, 68*(12), 1595.

Montgomery, Jr., E. B., & Gale, J. T. (2008). Mechanisms of action of deep brain stimulation (DBS). *Neuroscience & Biobehavioral Reviews, 32*(3), 388-407.

Morbidelli, A., & Henrard, J. (1991). Secular resonances in the asteroid belt: Theoretical perturbation approach and the problem of their location. *Celestial Mechanics and Dynamical Astronomy, 51*(2), 131-167

Motoo, K. (1983). The neutral theory of molecular evolution. New York: Cambridge University Press.

Montagnier, L., Aissa, J., Del Giudice, E., Lavallee, C., Tedeschi, A., & Vitiello, G. (2011). DNA waves and water. *Journal of Physics: Conference Series, 306*(1), 012007.

Murariu, M., & Drochioiu, G. (2012). Biostructural theory of the living systems. *Biosystems, 109*(2), 126-32.

Nei, M., & Kumar, S. (2000). *Molecular evolution and phylogenetics.* Oxford: Oxford University Press.

Ng, J. (2012). Wnt/PCP proteins regulate stereotyped axon branch extension in Drosophila. *Development, 139*(1), 165-177.

Noble, D. (2006). *The music of life: biology beyond the genome.* Oxford: Oxford University Press.

Noble, D. (2011). Neo-Darwinism, the modern synthesis and selfish genes: are they of use in physiology? *The Journal of Physiology, 589*(5), 1007-1015.

Oladepo, S. A., Xiong, K., Hong, Z., & Asher, S. A. (2011). Elucidating peptide and protein structure and dynamics: UV resonance Raman spectroscopy. *The Journal of Physical Chemistry Letters, 2*(4), 334.

Onen, F., Onen, S.-H. (2003). Sleep rhythm disturbances in Alzheimer's disease. Alteìrations des rythmes du sommeil dans la maladie d'Alzheimer. *Revue de Medecine Interne, 24* (3),

165-171.

O'Rourke, N. A., Weiler, N. C., Micheva, K. D., & Smith, S. J. (2012). Deep molecular diversity of mammalian synapses: why it matters and how to measure it. *Nature Reviews Neuroscience, 13*(6), 365-379.

Orpiszewski, J., Schormann, N., Kluve-Beckerman, B., Liepnieks, J. J., & Benson, M. D. (2000). Protein aging hypothesis of Alzheimer disease. *The FASEB Journal, 14*(9), 1255-1263.

Packer, A. M., & Yuste, R. (2011). Dense, unspecific connectivity of neocortical parvalbumin-positive interneurons: a canonical microcircuit for inhibition? *The Journal of Neuroscience, 31*(37), 13260-13271.

Pang X.-F. (2011). The theory of bio-energy transport in the protein molecules and its properties *Physics of Life Reviews, 8*(3), 264-286.

Pang, X.-F. (2012). The mechanism and properties of bio-photon emission and absorption in protein molecules in living systems. *Journal of Applied Physics, 111*(9), 093519

Penrose, R. (1994). *Shadows of the Mind* (Vol. 52). Oxford: Oxford University Press.

Pietak, A.M. (2012). Structural evidence for electromagnetic resonance in plant morphogenesis, *BioSystems, 109*(3), pp. 367-380

Pinker, S. & Bloom, P. (1990). Natural language and natural selection. *Behavioural and Brain Sciences, 13*, 707–784.

Pirooznia, S. K., Sarthi, J., Johnson, A. A., Toth, M. S., Chiu, K., Koduri, S., & Elefant, F. (2012). Tip60 HAT activity mediates APP induced lethality and apoptotic cell death in the CNS of a drosophila Alzheimer's disease model. *PloS One, 7*(7), e41776.

Plankar, M., Brežan, S., & Jerman, I. (2012). The principle of coherence in multi-level brain information processing. *Progress in Biophysics and Molecular Biology*, 11(1), 8-29.

Poza, J. J. (2012). The genetics of focal epilepsies. In P. J. Vinken & G.W. Bruyn (Eds.), *Handbook of Clinical Neurology, 107*, 153.

Pozo, K., & Goda, Y. (2010). Unraveling mechanisms of homeostatic synaptic plasticity. *Neuron, 66*(3), 337.

Puthoff, H. E., & Targ, R. (1976). A perceptual channel for information transfer over kilometer distances: Historical perspective and recent research. *Proceedings of the IEEE, 64*(3), 329-354. 4

Qiu-Dong, W. (1990). The global solution of the n-body problem. *Celestial Mechanics and Dynamical Astronomy, 50*(1), 73-88.

Quirk, M. C., Blum, K. I., & Wilson, M. A. (2001). Experience-dependent changes in extracellular spike amplitude may reflect regulation of dendritic action potential back-propagation in rat hippocampal pyramidal cells. *The Journal of Neuroscience, 21*(1), 240-248.

Quiroga, R. Q., Reddy, L., Kreiman, G., Koch, C., & Fried, I. (2005). Invariant visual representation by single neurons in the human brain. *Nature, 435*(7045), 1102-1107.

Rahnama, M., Tuszynski, J. A., Bókkon, I., Cifra, M., Sardar, P., & Salari, V. (2011). Emission of mitochondrial biophotons and their effect on electrical activity of membrane via microtubules. *Journal of Integrative Neuroscience, 10*(01), 65-88.

Reichl, L. E. (2004). *The transition to chaos: Conservative classical systems and quantum manifestations.* New York: Springer.

Ritchie, S. J., Wiseman, R., & French, C. C. (2012). Failing the future: Three unsuccessful attempts to replicate Bem's 'retroactive facilitation of recall' effect. *PLoS One, 7*(3), e33423.

Robert, A. M., Robert, C. S., & Robert, L. (2007). Symmetry breaking in biological systems. From molecules to tissues. *Structural Chemistry, 18*(6), 899-907.

Rubik, B. (2002). The biofield hypothesis: Its biophysical basis and role in medicine. *The Journal of Alternative & Complementary Medicine, 8*(6), 703-717.

Rumelhart, D. E., Hinton, G. E., & McClelland, J. L. (1986). A general framework for parallel distributed processing. *Parallel Distributed Processing, 1*(2).

Ryazanov, A. G., & Nefsky, B. S. (2002). Protein turnover plays a key role in aging. *Mechanisms of Ageing and Development, 123*(2), 207-213.

Sasaki, T., Matsuki, N., & Ikegaya, Y. (2011). Action-potential modulation during axonal conduction. *Science Signalling, 331*(6017), 599.

Schiffels, S., Szöllősi, G. J., Mustonen, V., & Lässig, M. (2011). Emergent neutrality in adaptive asexual evolution. *Genetics, 189*(4), 1361-1375.

Scheeff, E. D., & Bourne, P. E. (2005). Structural evolution of the protein kinase–like superfamily. *PLoS Computational Biology, 1*(5), e49.

Scholes, G. D. (2003). Long-range resonance energy transfer in molecular systems. *Annual Review of Physical Chemistry, 54*(1), 57-87.

Schrödinger, E. (1944). What is life? With mind and matter and autobiographical sketches. UK: Cambridge University Press.

Scott, A. C. (1991). Davydov's soliton revisited. *Physica D: Nonlinear Phenomena, 51*(1), 333-342.

Scott, E. K., & Luo, L. (2001). How do dendrites take their shape? *Nature Neuroscience, 4,* 359-366.

Scruton, R. (2005). The unobservable mind. *Technology Review–Manchester,* 108(2) 72-77.

Searle, J. R. (2000). Consciousness. *Annual Review of Neuroscience, 23,* 557–578.

Searle, J. R. (2002). Why I am not a property dualist. *Journal of Consciousness Studies,* 9(12), 57-64.

Searle, J. R. (2013 March 7). Can a photodiode be conscious? Reply, *New York Review of Books,* 60(4), 43-44.

Sekulić, D. L., Satarić, B. M., Tuszynski, J. A., & Satarić, M. V. (2011). Nonlinear ionic pulses along microtubules. *The European Physical Journal E: Soft Matter and Biological Physics, 34*(5), 1-11.

Shaw, D. E., Maragakis, P., Lindorff-Larsen, K., Piana, S., Dror, R. O., Eastwood, M. P., & Wriggers, W. (2010). Atomic-level characterization of the structural dynamics of proteins. *Science, 330*(6002), 341-346.

Shapiro, J. A. (2007). Bacteria are small but not stupid: cognition, natural genetic engineering and socio-bacteriology. *Studies in History and Philosophy of Science Part C: Studies in History and Philosophy of Biological and Biomedical Sciences, 38*(4), 807-819.

Shapiro, J. A. (2005). A 21st century view of evolution: genome system architecture, repetitive DNA, and natural genetic engineering. *Gene, 345*(1), 91-100.

Schenk, H. J., & Seabloom, E. W. (2010). Evolutionary ecology of plant signals and toxins: a conceptual framework. In *Plant Communication from an ecological perspective* (pp. 1-19). Berlin Heidelberg: Springer.

Shapiro, J.A. (2011). *Evolution – A new view from the 21st century.* New Jersey: FT Press Science.

Scheiner, S. (2011). Weak H-bonds. Comparisons of CHO to NHO in proteins and PHN to direct PN interactions. *Physical Chemistry Chemical Physics, 13*(31), 13860-13872.

Schulz, J. M. (2010). Synaptic plasticity in vivo: more than just spike-timing? *Frontiers in Synaptic Neuroscience, 2*:150 doi: 10.3389/fnsyn.2010.00150

Sharma, V., & Annila, A. (2007). Natural process – natural selection. *Biophysical Chemistry 127*(1-2), 123-128.

Sharma, V., Kaila, V. R. I., & Annila, A. (2009). Protein folding as an evolutionary process. *Physica A: Statistical Mechanics and its Applications, 388*(6), 851-862.

Silvia, P.J., & Beaty, R.E. (2012). Making creative metaphors: The importance of fluid intelligence for creative thought. *Intelligence, 40*(4), 343-351.

Sibaoka, T. (1991). Rapid plant movements triggered by action potentials. *The Botanical*

Magazine Tokyo, *104*(1), 73-95.

Sivakumaran, S., Hariharaputran, S., Mishra, J., & Bhalla, U. S. (2003). The database of quantitative cellular signaling: management and analysis of chemical kinetic models of signaling networks. *Bioinformatics*, *19*(3), 408-415.

Smit, D. J., Boomsma, D. I., Schnack, H. G., Hulshoff Pol, H. E., & de Geus, E. J. (2012). Individual differences in EEG spectral power reflect genetic variance in gray and white matter volumes. *Twin Research and Human Genetics*, *15*(3), 384.

Spruston, N., & Cang, J. (2010). Timing isn't everything. *Nature Neuroscience*, *13*(3), 277.

Steriade, M. (2001). *The intact and sliced brain*. Cambridge MA: MIT Press.

Steward, O., & Schuman, E. M. (2003). Compartmentalized synthesis and degradation of proteins in neurons. *Neuron*, *40*(2), 347-359.

Styer, D. F., Balkin, M. S., Becker, K. M., Burns, M. R., Dudley, C. E., Forth, S. T., ... & Wotherspoon, T. D. (2002). Nine formulations of quantum mechanics. *American Journal of Physics*, *70*, 288.

Su, S.-P., Lyons, B., Friedrich, M., Mcarthur, J. D., Song, X., Xavier, D., Truscott, R.J.W., Aquilina, J.A. (2012). Molecular signatures of long-lived proteins: Autolytic cleavage adjacent to serine residues. *Aging Cell*, *11*(6), 1125-7.

Sundman, K. F. (1913). Mémoire sur le probleme des trois corps. *Acta Mathematica*, *36*(1), 105-179.

Taketo, M., & Yoshioka, T. (2000). Developmental change of GABA(A) receptor-mediated current in rat hippocampus. *Neuroscience*, *96*(3), 507-514.

Taki, Y., Thyreau, B., Kinomura, S., Sato, K., Goto, R., Kawashima, R., & Fukuda, H. (2011). Correlations among brain gray matter volumes, age, gender, and hemisphere in healthy individuals. *PloS One*, *6*(7), e22734.

Thagard, P. (2002). How molecules matter to mental computation. *Philosophy of Science*, *69*(3), 429-446.

Thatcher, R. W., North, D. M., & Biver, C. J. (2008). Intelligence and EEG phase reset: A two compartmental model of phase shift and lock. *NeuroImage*, *42*(4), 1639-1653.

Thompson, R. F., & Spencer, W. A. (1966). Habituation: a model phenomenon for the study of neuronal substrates of behaviour. *Psychological Review*, *73*(1), 16.

Trewavas, A. (2003). Aspects of plant intelligence. *Annals of Botany*, *92*(1), 1-20.

Turing, A. M. (1936). On computable numbers, with an application to the Entscheidungsproblem. *J. of Math.*, *58*, 345-363.

Tuszynski, J. A., Carpenter, E. J., Huzil, J. T., Malinski, W., Luchko, T., & Ludueña, R. F. (2006). The evolution of the structure of tubulin and its potential consequences for the role and function of microtubules in cells and embryos. *International Journal of Developmental Biology*, *50*(2), 341-358.

Tuszynski, J. A. (2013). The need for a physical basis of cognitive process: Comment on "Consciousness in the universe. A review of the'Orch OR'theory" by Hameroff and Penrose. *Physics of Life Reviews*, *11*(1), 39-78.

Tweedie-Cullen, Y., Brunner R., M, A., & Mansuy, M. I. (2012). Proteomic analysis of phosphorylation in the brain. *Current Proteomics*, *9*(3), 167-185.

Uhlhaas, P. J., & Singer, W. (2006). Neural synchrony in brain disorders: relevance for cognitive dysfunctions and pathophysiology. *Neuron*, *52*(1), 155-168.

Vendruscolo, M. (2012). Proteome folding and aggregation. *Current Opinion in Structural Biology*, *22*, 138-143.

Watson, J. D. and Crick, F. H. C. (1953). A Structure for deoxyribose nucleic acid. *Nature*, *171*, 737-738.

Welberg, L. (2012). Consciousness: Effective detection. *Nature Reviews Neuroscience*, *13*(3), 155-155.

Willerman, L., Schultz, R., Rutledge, J. N., & Bigler, E. D. (1991). In vivo brain size and intelligence. *Intelligence, 15*(2), 223-228

Witelson, S. F., Kigar, D. L., & Harvey, T. (1999). The exceptional brain of Albert Einstein. *The Lancet*, 353 (9170), 2149-2153.

Woolf, N. J., & Priel, A. (2009). *Nanoneuroscience: Structural and functional roles of the neuronal cytoskeleton in health and disease*. Berlin Heidelberg: Springer Verlag.

Wyatt, M. C. (2008). Resonant trapping of planetesimals by planet migration: Debris disk clumps and Vega's similarity to the solar system. *The Astrophysical Journal, 598*(2), 1321.

Yang, C. D., & Weng, H. J. (2012). Nonlinear quantum dynamics in diatomic molecules: Vibration, rotation and spin. *Chaos, Solitons & Fractals, 45*(4), 402-415.

Zaslavsky, G. M. (2005). *Hamiltonian chaos and fractional dynamics* (Vol. 1). London: Oxford University Press.

Zheng, Y., Luo, J. J., Harris, S., Kennerley, A., Berwick, J., Billings, S. A., & Mayhew, J. (2012). Balanced excitation and inhibition: Model based analysis of local field potentials. *NeuroImage, 63*, 81-94.

Zehnacker, A., & Suhm, M. A. (2008). Chirality recognition between neutral molecules in the gas phase. *Angewandte Chemie International Edition, 47*(37), 6970-6992.

Zuo, Z., Tichotsky, A., & Johns, R. A. (1999). Inhibition of excitatory neurotransmitter–nitric oxide signaling pathway by inhalational anesthetics. *Neuroscience, 93*(3), 1167-1172.

Chapter 13

Is Consciousness Guiding the Universe?

STUART HAMEROFF MD[1]
Center for Consciousness Studies and Departments of Anesthesiology and Psychology, Banner-University Medical Center
University of Arizona, Tucson, Arizona, USA

ABSTRACT

The place of consciousness and its role in the universe remain unknown and controversial. Western philosophy and mainstream science consider consciousness to be computational, epiphenomenal, acausal and illusory, whereas Eastern philosophical and quantum physical approaches consider consciousness to be an intrinsic feature of the universe, playing an active role. But which specific intrinsic feature of the universe entails consciousness? Sir Roger Penrose proposed consciousness results from self-collapse of the quantum wavefunction by 'objective reduction' ('OR'), a process in the basic structure of spacetime geometry. The Penrose-Hameroff 'Orch OR' theory further suggests OR events in cytoskeletal microtubules within brain neurons are 'orchestrated' by inputs, memory and vibrational resonances, and terminate by 'orchestrated OR' to give meaningful conscious moments. If so, consciousness as an intrinsic feature of the universe (one offering pleasurable experience) may have prompted the origin of life and driven its evolution, and perhaps that of the universe itself. In the contest of the 'anthropic principle', which considers the extraordinary 'fine tuning' in the various physical constants enabling life and consciousness in the universe, it is suggested here that the constants may mutate and evolve over aeons to optimize consciousness, that, in some sense, consciousness is guiding the universe.

INTRODUCTION

Consciousness defines our existence, yet its nature and place in the universe remain unknown, and controversial. Most scientists and Western philosophers consider the brain to be a computer, with consciousness emerging as an extrinsic feature of complex computations among individually simple neurons and synapses. However this view renders consciousness epiphenomenal without causal power, doesn't account for the subjective nature of phenomenal experience, i.e. feelings or 'qualia' (the 'hard problem'), and lacks scientific testability.

[1]Director, Center for Consciousness Studies and Professor Emeritus, Anesthesiology and Psychology

On the other hand, proponents of Eastern philosophy, spiritual approaches and a growing number of Western philosophers and scientists of all types view consciousness as somehow intrinsic to the universe. These perspectives include *panpsychism* (the notion that matter and energy have some feature of subjectivity), *idealism* (consciousness is all there is, and the material world is merely a 'dream', more or less), and *pan-experientialism* (or *pan-protopsychism*) such as the process philosophy of Alfred North Whitehead (1929; 1933). Sir Roger Penrose (1989) suggested quantum state reductions due to an objective threshold ('objective reduction', 'OR') occurred spontaneously and ubiquitously, producing moments of 'proto-conscious' experience. In all these views, consciousness, its components and/or precursors are fundamental, irreducible components of reality, in the same category as electric charge, magnetic spin, mass and quantum state reductions. But how are fundamental components of consciousness combined and organized into full, rich conscious experience, including feelings of enlightenment and spirituality?

A particular theory, Penrose-Hameroff 'orchestrated objective reduction' ('Orch OR') suggests consciousness depends on organized quantum processes in brain biology which connect (or are equivalent) to fundamental processes in spacetime geometry, the fine scale structure of reality (Hameroff and Penrose, 2014). Consistent with spiritual views, and in the context of the 'anthropic principle', this further implies that, over time, consciousness could in some way guide the evolution of the universe.

The 'anthropic principle' considers the enigma of why the 20 or so physical parameters governing mass and energy, and thus ultimately the cosmic makeup of the universe, are so precisely tuned to enable conditions conducive to life and consciousness. This is a seeming coincidence of immense proportions. The common explanation is 'selection bias', that there exist multiple parallel universes (consistent with the multiple worlds hypothesis in quantum mechanics), and that we inhabit the one particular world whose parameters are optimal for consciousness, and thus that we alone in our unique world are able to ponder such questions. But multiple worlds is an untestable hypothesis.

Another possibility, one which puts consciousness into the 'driver's seat', serving to tune the cosmic physical parameters, emerges from Orch OR in concert with Penrose 'CCC' ('cyclic conformal cosmology', Penrose, 2010). CCC is a theory suggesting our one-and-only universe has consisted of serial aeons, each born from its own 'big bang'. In this paper, I discuss how Orch OR and CCC, taken together, can suggest that cosmic physical parameters may 'mutate' and evolve over aeons with each such big bang, serving to tune the parameters to optimize consciousness. Thus consciousness can guide the evolution of the universe.

The Western Computational Approach

Most Western philosophers, neuroscientists and artificial intelligence ('AI') proponents maintain that consciousness emerges from complex computation among brain neurons in synaptic networks, and that sufficiently complex computers may also be conscious. In combination with information gleaned from 'brain mapping', it is sometimes suggested that one's consciousness could be 'downloaded' (or 'uploaded', depending on one's perspective) into a personalized brain-like computer when the body approaches death. AI advocates of the 'Singularity' suggest that humanity and society will change drastically when this occurs.

According to most AI/Singularity proponents, the target for computer/brain equivalence, and thus presumably consciousness and downloading is based on the following assumptions. The brain is composed of about 100 billion neurons which each function as (Hodgkin-Huxley, 1952) 'integrate-and-fire' threshold logic devices, connected to one another in synaptic networks. Information is usually equated to axonal firings as 'bits', or operations ('ops') per second. Each neuron has about a thousand synapses, with peak frequencies of about 100 per second, or 100 hertz ('Hz'). So 100 billion (10^{11}) neurons, each with 10^3 connections interacting at around 10^2 Hz would give a human brain computational capacity of 10^{16} bits, or 'ops' per second with these assumptions. According to the Singularity, when 10^{16} bits, or 'ops' per second are attained in silicon-based computers (estimated to be within 10 or 20 years) conscious computers and downloading will become possible.

There are a number of problems with this approach.

Helpless spectator If true, the AI/Singularity neuronal computational approach portrays consciousness as an epiphenomenal illusion, having no causal role. It suggests we are (as T.H. Huxley bleakly stated) 'merely conscious automata, helpless spectators along for the ride'. This *could* be true, but it is based on false assumptions.

Simple neurons The AI/Singularity approach assumes simple bit-like neurons interact in complex synaptic networks to produce consciousness and intelligent cognition as a function of network connections. But this fails to account for clever cognitive behavior in single cell organisms like paramecium which swim, avoid obstacles and predators, learn (escaping from capillary tubes), find food, mates and have sex, without synapses or connections. Paramecium and other protozoa use their internal cytoskeletal microtubules for sensing, locomotion, and apparent information processing, without a nervous system or connections to other cells. Observing single cell cognitive behavior, famed neuroscientist Charles Sherrington (1951) marveled 'of nerve there is no trace, but the cytoskeleton might serve'.

Inside the neuron That same cytoskeleton, including microtubules, is an essential component in all neurons, responsible for axonal and dendritic growth, synaptic formation and plasticity. Microtubules are disrupted in Alzheimer's disease and suggested to be involved in cognition, memory and consciousness. Microtubules are lattice polymers of the protein tubulin, and proposed to process information as molecular automata, the state of tubulins at any one moment corresponding with 'bits' (or quantum bits, 'qubits'). Microtubules have coherent resonances in a number of frequency ranges, e.g. 10^7 Hz, 10 megahertz (10 MHz). Each neuron contains about 10^9 tubulins, so microtubule-based information processing could provide $10^9 \times 10^7 = 10^{16}$ bits, or ops per second *per neuron*, the same capacity stipulated by AI/Singularity for the entire brain. Microtubule processing at a deeper level inside neurons would raise calculated brain capacity to 10^{27} bits, or ops per second, moving the AI/Singularity goalpost much farther into the future. But would computation at even 10^{27} ops/sec be conscious? Why would it?

Brain mapping The basic idea in AI/Singularity downloading strategies is that the brain's 'connectome', the mapping of connections among all neurons would capture essential features of the individual's consciousness, memory, personality and behavior. Billions and billions are being spent mapping brain connectomes of humans and animals around the world. But synaptic connections are dynamic and transient; one's 'connectome' changes from moment to moment.

Rather than mapping mammalian brains with billions of neurons, a group of AI researchers began with a simpler system, the 302 neuron brain and nervous system of the roundworm *C elegans* whose brain and nervous system were completely mapped years ago. The *C elegans* brain has far more gap junctions than suspected. Gap junctions are electrical connections and windows between neurons which generate synchrony (and are suggested to allow quantum tunneling between adjacent neuronal microtubules). But after several years of trying, when the entire *C elegans* brain, synapses, gap junctions and ion channels are modeled and simulated, and an artificial stimulus provided, there is no behavior. Something is missing, and it may be foolish to think large scale brain mapping would be valuable when the 302 neuron worm brain can't be modeled.

Binding and the hard problem Computation *per se* fails to address the 'unity' of conscious experience, or 'binding'. More basically, computation also fails to explain the nature of subjective experience, of what it is like 'to be', to have feelings and phenomenal sensations philosophers call 'qualia', a question popularized by David Chalmers' 'hard problem'. To address qualia and the 'hard problem', many computationalists have turned to intrinsic approaches including panpsychism, idealism, panprotopsychism, Eastern philosophy and quantum approaches.

The Eastern Intrinsic (Quantum) Approach

Idealism, including Vedanta and spiritual approaches, suggests consciousness is all-encompassing, and in some views equivalent to God. This is a consistent position but one facing questions of scientific testability.

Panpsychism attributes mental states to properties of matter and energy, intrinsic to the universe. Unable to account for phenomenal experience through computation, neuroscientists including Christof Koch (2012) and Giulio Tononi (2012), philosopher David Chalmers (1996) and others have embraced panpsychism, but it also faces several problems. For example, 1) at what level of matter and energy does phenomenal experience occur? (molecules, atoms, sub-atomic particles etc.), 2) the 'combination problem': how do presumably primitive subjective qualities ('qualia') of fundamental particles combine into full rich conscious experience?, 3) which particular brain activity corresponds with panpsychist properties?, and 4) approaching atomic and subatomic particles leads to the quantum world, and the measurement problem in quantum mechanics.

Building on Leibniz's notion of 'monads', and in distinction to prevalent views of the world as a collection of individual objects, Alfred North Whitehead (1929; 1933) saw reality as a process consisting of sequences of discrete events he termed 'occasions'. These each occurred in a wider field of 'proto-conscious experience', were endowed with primitive subjectivity, and termed 'occasions of experience'. Whitehead's process approach was consistent with Bertrand Russell's 'neutral monism' in which matter and mind derived from one underlying entity, and with Penrose's view of consciousness as discrete moments. Whitehead's primitive occasions were suggested to be 'dull, monotonous and repetitious', like Penrose OR proto-conscious moments, but able to coalesce into full, rich conscious moments (combination problem).

Whitehead worked in the early 20th century, the era in which quantum mechanics showed matter and energy to be quantized, composed of individual units which could exist as particles or waves, entangle and combine into unified, delocalized systems. Quantum particles could exist in multiple locations and states simultaneously – a situation termed 'quantum superposition'. However when superpositions were measured or observed, they seemed to reduce, or 'collapse' to definite states, taking on particular values and locations, events termed quantum state reductions, or 'collapses of the quantum wavefunction'. Whether superpositions do in fact collapse, how and why, became known as the 'measurement problem'. Abner Shimony (1993) suggested Whitehead 'occasions of experience' were equivalent to, quantum state reductions, collapses of the quantum wavefunction.

Quantum pioneers Niels Bohr, John von Neumann, Eugene Wigner (and later Henry Stapp and David Chalmers) have suggested that quantum superpositions persist only until observed by conscious beings, the 'conscious observer' effect, commonly termed the 'Copenhagen interpretation' after Bohr's Danish origin. According to 'Copenhagen', conscious observation *causes* quantum superpositioned possibilities to reduce to definite states—*consciousness collapses the wavefunction.*

The Copenhagen interpretation enabled quantum experiments to be performed, and quantum physics to flourish, but ignored the question of underlying reality, how particles can exist in alternate states and locations simultaneously. It also relegated consciousness to being outside science, as an unknown mysterious entity. To illustrate the apparent absurdity, Erwin Schrödinger designed his still-famous thought experiment known as 'Schrödinger's cat'. Imagine a cat in a box with a vial of poison whose release is coupled to a quantum superposition of possibilities. According to Copenhagen, Schrödinger concluded, the cat would be both dead *and* alive until a conscious human opened the box and looked inside. Absurd it was, but the problem persists.

Another potential solution is 'decoherence' in which interaction between a quantum system and its classical environment buries superpositions in noise. But how can any quantum system truly be isolated?

Another view is the 'multiple worlds interpretation' ('MWI') proposed by Hugh Everett (1957) and others in which there *is* no collapse. Every possibility in a superposition survives, continuing to evolve into its own new 'parallel' universe, resulting in an infinite number of coexisting overlapping worlds. As crazy as it sounds, MWI is extremely popular among physicists.

Still other interpretations assume that wavefunctions and superpositions evolve until some sort of objective threshold causes reduction — 'objective reduction' ('OR'). Among these is an OR mechanism proposed by Sir Roger Penrose, a mechanism which puts consciousness into the universe.

Penrose Objective Reduction (OR)

Penrose began by addressing head-on the enigma of superposition, how particles could conceivably exist in two or more locations simultaneously. He did so by connecting quantum mechanics to Einstein's general relativity which deals with the structure of the universe.

Since ancient times, philosophers and scientists have considered reality as either 1) a void in which matter and energy move and operate, or 2) as a background field, 'plenum', metric or sea in which material objects are embedded. Following Mach's principle, in which matter exists in an interactive field, and Minkowski 4-dimensional spacetime, Einstein postulated a spacetime continuum, or metric, whose curvatures and irregularities were equivalent to matter and energy, with the most severe curvatures and densest collections of matter being 'singularities' (later described as 'black holes'). Einstein predicted that a star directly behind the sun would be visible from earth due to the sun's induced curvature in spacetime, a prediction validated during an eclipse in 1919 by Sir Arthur Eddington (Dyson and Eddington, 1920). Penrose extended this equivalence to tiny objects, e.g. quantum particles with extremely tiny curvatures in spacetime geometry.

To illustrate 4-dimensional spacetime geometry, Penrose used simple 2-dimensional sheets with one dimension of space and one dimension of time (Figure 1). Localized particles are then viewed as particular curvatures, and superpositions as simultaneous alternative curvatures, essentially separations or blisters in the fine scale structure of the universe.

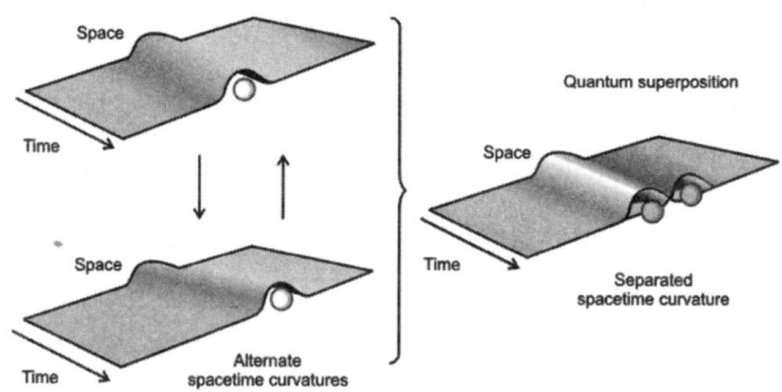

FIGURE 1

A 'spacetime qubit' with four-dimensional spacetime geometry depicted as a two-dimensional sheet. Left: A particle and its equivalent spacetime curvature oscillate between two positions. Right: quantum superposition of the particle in both locations is equivalent to alternative, separated spacetime curvatures.

If these separations were to evolve, each possibility might then give rise to its own universe, as in MWI (Figure 2a). But Penrose considered spacetime separations to be unstable, reaching an objective threshold for 'self-collapse', or objective reduction/OR at time $\tau \approx \hbar/E_G$, where $\hbar$ is Planck's constant over 2π, and E_G the gravitational self-energy of the separation. Thus each OR event creates reality which then again dissolves into superposition, rippling and rearranging the structure of the universe (Figure 2b). OR avoids the need for multiple worlds.

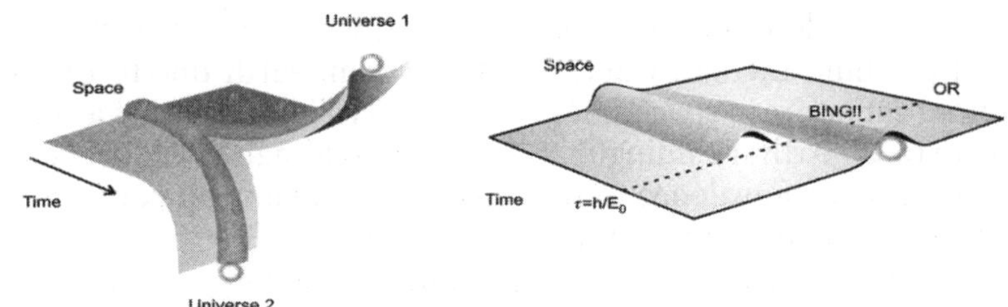

FIGURE 2(a) FIGURE 2(b)
Two possible fates of a superposition as depicted in Figure 1. Left: According to the multiple worlds interpretation ('MWI'), each superpositioned possibility evolves to form it's own universe. Right: According to Penrose OR, superpositions evolve only until reaching threshold for objective reduction ('OR') at time τ given by $E_G \approx \hbar/\tau$. Self-collapse then occurs accompanied by a moment of conscious experience (BING!!)

But then Penrose added two profound features. First, he proposed each OR event is an instant of subjective experience – a moment of conscious awareness, of 'qualia' intrinsic to the universe. Thus rather than consciousness *causing* collapse (as in Copenhagen), in Penrose OR, *collapse causes consciousness*, or, collapse is identical to consciousness. This meant that simple, random OR moments of awareness occur 'here, there and everywhere' throughout the fine scale structure of the universe (recognized as 'decoherence'). These subjective moments would be generally random, disjointed, non-cognitive and lack meaning or memory, and are accordingly termed 'proto-conscious'. Metaphorically, such random OR moments are like the spurious sounds, tones and notes ('noise') of an orchestra warming up, some including positive feelings, i.e. pleasure (or 'proto-pleasure'). Somehow, the brain 'orchestrates' random OR noise into full, rich conscious 'music'. How could that have happened?

Penrose OR and subjective feelings would have been present in various forms from the beginning of the universe, e.g. at the formation of the earth. Positive feelings could have played a key role in the origin and evolution of life.

Life in the Quantum Underground

Life has been described in two types of general categories: 'functionalism' and 'vitalism'. Functionalism characterizes life by its behaviors, including (from Lynn Margulis Sagan, 1995) self-organization, homeostasis, metabolism, growth, adaption, response to stimuli, replication/reproduction and evolution. Richard Dawkins (1989) focuses on self-replication as life's essential feature, but such functions occur also in non-biological computer programs, e.g. as 'artificial life' (e.g. Langton,

1995), video games and weather patterns. Life appears to be unique, but *how* it is so remains unknown.

Living systems seem to have some unitary quality, akin to 'oneness', often ascribed to an *emergent* property of functional processes, much like consciousness is often ascribed to emergence from complex brain computation. In both cases however, mechanisms, or thresholds for such emergence are unidentified.

Eastern philosophical approaches make less of a distinction between life and consciousness. In the West, 19th-century 'vitalists' saw a unifying energy field, or life force pervading living systems - *'elan vital'*. As molecular biology developed, reductionists pushed vitalism from favor, the notion of a 'life force' becoming taboo. But 19th-century vitalism was based either on electromagnetism, or on forces outside science, as quantum mechanics had yet to be discovered. In his famous book *What is Life?*, Erwin Schrodinger (1935) suggested life's unitary oneness derived from quantum coherence in biomolecular lattices which were 'aperiodic crystals'.

Others agreed. Nobel laureate Albert Szent-Gyorgyi (1960) saw the essence of life in coordinated sub-molecular quantum electron movements in non-polar regions of biological systems. Russian physicists Phillipe and Albert Pullman (1963) attributed life to quantum behavior of electrons in pi resonance clouds, and biophysicist Herbert Frohlich (1968; 1970; 1975) described the essential unifying feature of living systems as quantum coherent dipoles in non-polar regions in geometrically-constrained proteins (e.g. membrane proteins and cytoskeletal microtubules). Pi resonance in non-polar regions of biomolecules may enable quantum coherence related to life and consciousness.

How could quantum coherence support life, cognition and consciousness? Information processing would seem necessarily involved, e.g. through quantum computation of some sort. The concept of a quantum computer was introduced by Paul Benioff (1982), David Deutsch (1985) and Richard Feynman (1986) who showed how superpositions, e.g. of both 1 *and* 0 bit states could act as quantum bits, or 'qubits' which could entangle with other qubits, interact/compute by the Schrodinger equation, and eventually collapse/reduce to classical bits of either 1 *or* 0 as the solution. In principle, quantum computers can solve certain problems much more quickly than conventional computers, utilizing parallelism through entangled qubits, but that *per se* would not provide subjective experience. In the Penrose formulation quantum computational cognition could culminate in consciousness by OR, and connect such quantum computers to qualia and Platonic values in the fine scale structure of the universe. But technological qubits require isolation and extreme cold to avoid 'decoherence', thermal disruption of seemingly delicate quantum superpositions (or 'premature OR' in the Penrose approach) by interactions with the classical environment, and so living systems have been considered too 'warm, wet and noisy' for functional quantum mechanisms. However in recent years photosynthesis proteins have been shown to utilize quantum coherence, and microtubules and their component protein tubulin have quantum resonances in terahertz, gigahertz, megahertz and kilohertz at ambient temperatures (Sahu et al, 2013a; 2013b; 2014). But how can quantum systems self-organize, avoid decoherence and govern biology in a warm and seemingly chaotic micro-environment?

The answer may be found in a simple truth: oil and water don't mix. Consider the perspective on the makeup of biological organisms taken by pharmacologists. Rather than viewing living creatures as composites of organs, tissues, cells, molecules and atoms, pharmacologists often view the body instead as sets of various solubility phases, i.e. compartments of different and distinct solvent characteristics where particular molecules, drugs, hormones and toxins may bind or dissolve and exert an effect. An essential factor in solubility is degree of polarity, i.e. how highly charged electrically are the drug molecule ('solute'), and its environment ('solvent').

Water, blood and bodily fluids are polar solvents in which electrically-charged solute molecules, e.g. most drugs and hormones, bind and dissolve by hydrogen bonds and other polar interactions. In such microenvironments, quantum superpositioned charges will rapidly bind and entangle with others, increasing E_G to quickly reach OR threshold by $E_G=h/t$, or 'decohere'. Ubiquitous OR events in such polar media would be random, and accompanied merely by non-cognitive, isolated moments of proto-conscious experience (like 'dull, monotonous and repetitious' Whitehead occasions). In a musical metaphor, they are the tones, notes and sounds of an orchestra warming up, not the music. Polar microenvironments are inhospitable to quantum superpositions.

However the body and brain also include non-polar, 'oil-like' solubility phases, composed largely of benzene-like 'pi resonance clouds' in 'aromatic rings' which coalesce in non-polar regions spatially segregated from polar ones ('oil and water don't mix!'). Non-polar regions are essential to organic chemistry, for example the phenyl, or benzene ring with 6 carbons, 6 hydrogens and 6 delocalized electrons in 'pi orbitals' which form an electron cloud above and below the 6-carbon ring. Avoiding polar charges in liquids, non-polar pi resonance groups bury themselves within protein, lipids and nucleic acid molecules, (e.g. the 'pi stack' in DNA). Pi resonance channels are friendly to quantum superpositions, and the medium – the 'quantum underground' - in which anesthetics specifically act to erase consciousness.

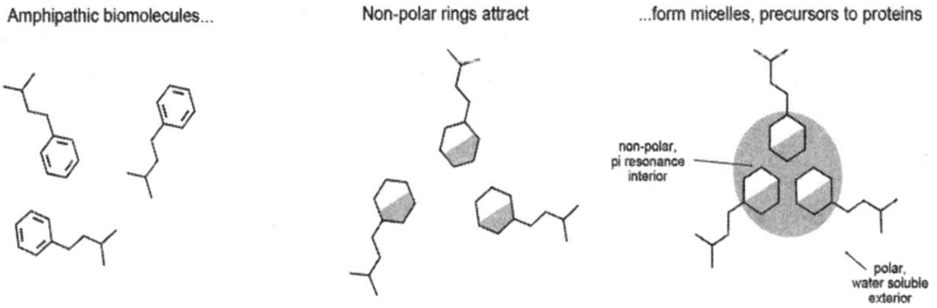

FIGURE 3
Amphipathic biomolecules have a non-polar pi resonance (hexagonal) end, and a charged, polar end. The non-polar pi resonance clouds attract and couple by van der Waals dipoles in a 'micelle' (as suggested by Oparin) with a non-polar interior and water-soluble exterior. Such structures are precursors to protein folding and formation of lipid membranes and nucleic acids, and may have occurred at the origin of life in the primordial soup.

In the mid 19th century, gases like diethyl ether and nitrous oxide ('laughing gas') were discovered to have 'anesthetic' properties, i.e. inhaling these gases caused humans and animals to lose consciousness, or some observable correlate, like mice falling over, or salamanders not moving in response to stimulation. When the anesthetic gas was exhaled away, the subjects and animals breathing pure air or oxygen woke up, snapping back to consciousness, essentially unchanged. Potencies were determined for each anesthetic, i.e. the gas concentration at which half of a group of mice, or salamanders, will roll over, and half remain upright. Amazingly, each gas acted at the same concentration in all animals, identical concentrations in the gas phase in the lung required to anesthetize mice, salamander, horse or human. By the turn of the 20th century, dozens of anesthetic gases had been discovered, curiously with various different types of chemical structures, e.g. ethers, halogenated hydrocarbons, nitrous oxide and the inert gas xenon. Scientists sought a common property independent of structure which might correlate with anesthetic action. The answer was anesthetic solubility in an oil-like, non-polar solubility compartment, a quantum underground of pi resonance clouds.

Working separately, Hans Meyer (1901) and Charles Ernst Overton (1901) ranked potency for many anesthetics in various animal models, and tested solubility in different types of solvents, each finding the same result. Over many orders of magnitude, among many chemically disparate structures, potency of all anesthetics for all animals correlated near-perfectly with their solubility in a particular non-polar medium, characterized by a low Hildebrand coefficient lambda (15.2 to 19.3 SI Units), closely resembling olive oil and benzene (Hameroff, 2006). The 'Meyer-Overton correlation' shows that anesthetics act (by quantum

London 'dipole dispersion' forces), in non-polar regions involving pi electron resonance clouds. As anesthesia is fairly selective (e.g. sparing non-conscious brain activities which continue during anesthesia), consciousness apparently originates in pi resonance regions in a 'quantum underground' inside the brain.

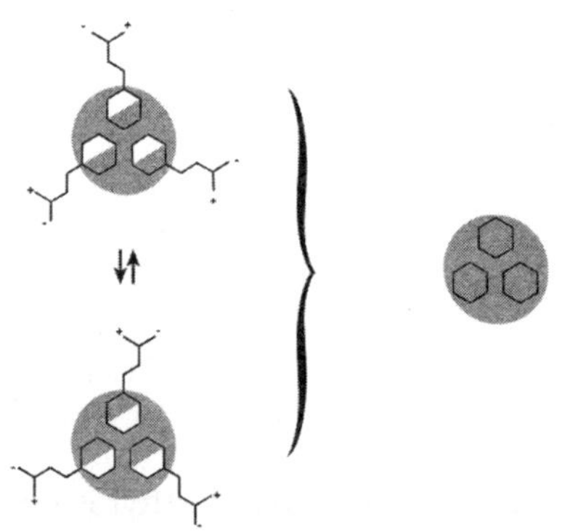

FIGURE 4

Simplified micelle qubit (only 3 amphipathic molecules are shown as opposed to hundreds or thousands). Left: Dipoles in non-polar interior of Oparin micelle oscillate, e.g. in terahertz at 10^{12} Hz. Right: Dipoles exist in quantum superposition of both possible states. Taken together the micelle is proposed to function as a quantum bit, or 'qubit'. Superpositions of both states (on right) reduce, or collapse to one particular state or the other (left).

Coupled pi resonance dipoles tend to oscillate at terahertz frequencies, and anesthetics dampen such oscillations proportional to their potency – a 'Meyer-Overton correlation' for anesthetic action on pi resonance dipole oscillations (Craddock et al, 2015). As pi resonance oscillations are quantum processes, Meyer-Overton defines a quantum-friendly environment suitable for life and consciousness. If so, the 'Meyer-Overton quantum underground' - may have hosted the origin of life.

A general consensus is that life on earth began in a prebiotic 'Primordial soup', proposed independently in the 1920s by the Russian biologist Alexander Oparin (1924) and British geneticist JBS Haldane (1929). The soup refers to a simmering mix from which life's biomolecular building blocks could have emerged 3 to 4 billion years ago, the requirements being an oxygen-poor atmosphere (now known to have been the case at that time), sea water, an energy source (e.g. sunlight, heat, radiation, thermal vents, lightning), and necessary chemical components. In a famous experiment in the 1950s, chemistry graduate student Stanley Miller and his professor Harold Urey (Miller & Urey, 1959) simulated the Primordial soup with methane, ammonia, hydrogen, and electric sparks for lightning. They found amphipathic molecules having both polar and non-polar components, including pi resonance rings (Figures 3 and 4). These were apparently the seeds of life. But then what happened?

Many contend molecular self-replicators such as RNA 'carried' life until genes and evolution were in place (e.g. Dawkins, 1986; 1989). But if so, how and why did amphipathic replicators become functional and interactive? What was their motivation? Why would survival *per se*, i.e. without feelings, drive evolution?

Oparin had suggested amphipathic molecules formed 'micelles' in which non-polar pi resonance rings stick together in the micelle interior by van der Waals forces and hydrophobic effects (oil avoiding water). Polar ends of these same amphipathic molecules would then radiate outward from the central non-polar confluence, forming hydrogen bonds with surrounding water. This process can result in water-soluble, spheroidal 'micelles', precursors to proteins and nucleic acids which are non-polar on the inside, and polar on the outside (Figures 3-5). Oparin suggested micelles gained functions and began to organize, evolve and function as 'proto-cells'. But why would they?

Electric and magnetic dipoles of pi resonance clouds oscillate in terahertz (10^{12} Hz) in the infrared region of the optical spectrum (Figure 4). As the earth cooled, terahertz radiation could have driven pi stack oscillations in primitive micelles, oscillations which became essential features of life. But the question remains why micelles or other structures based on pi resonance clouds with quantum properties would purposefully self-organize, flowing against the second law of thermodynamics. There were no genes, no mutation-based evolution, no creatures to survive. What was the motivation, the fitness function toward which life evolved? Was there a spark of life? If so, what could it be? A possible, logical answer is feelings, e.g. pleasurable qualia occurring by Penrose OR.

Superpositions with electric charge in a polar, aqueous medium, e.g. on micelle exteriors, would rapidly entangle by charge interactions to reach OR threshold with strictly random inputs. Such OR events would culminate in fleeting, non-cognitive, proto-conscious moments - 'noise' in a musical metaphor. However in non-polar confluences of pi electron resonance clouds, shielded and precisely-arrayed in the quantum underground, superpositioned dipoles could entangle collectively, oscillate coherently, and couple to biomolecular mechanical resonances – a 'coherent dance' of quantum dipoles.

Superposition and coherence of just a few pi stack rings (small E_G) would require a long time t to reach threshold (by $t = E_G/h$). Polar interactions would likely intervene to contribute randomness, resulting in partially coherent moments of proto-conscious experience. With larger pi stacks protected in non-polar 'quantum underground' interiors of biomolecules and micelle-like structures, resonance with Platonic vibrations in spacetime geometry could occur so that associated proto-conscious qualia would begin to have primitive feelings and emotions. The intensity and quality of such feelings, e.g. pleasure, would depend on particular geometry of the pi stack (Hameroff, 2016).

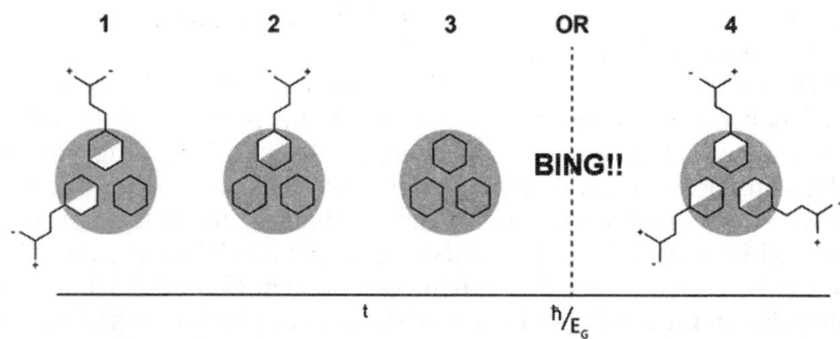

FIGURE 5
A simplified version of a proto-conscious OR moment in the Primordial soup. Three amphipathic molecules coalesce by non-polar van der Waals attractions (polar tails disengage) and entangle in superposition to reach threshold for OR self-collapse at time $t=\hbar/E_G$. A quale, proto-conscious moment, or primitive feeling occurs (BING!!). Much larger micelles, e.g. with many more pi resonance clouds forming a protected 'quantum underground' would actually be required.

From Epicurus in ancient Greece to Freud's 'pleasure principle' (1961), and more recently Panksepp (1988), Peil (2014) and Damasio (1999), feelings and emotions are considered primary in human and animal awareness and behavior, exemplified by dopaminergic reward pathways. But the essential nature of emotions, their subjective feel, remains a mystery. Why do good feelings feel good? Plato believed value, meaning and pleasure to reside in the 'form of the good', implying inherent geometry. Penrose attributed Platonic forms and values to fundamental spacetime geometry, extending to the Planck scale. How could pleasure and Platonic forms relate to biology?

Biology is based on organic chemistry, in turn based on pi electron resonance clouds of phenyl, or benzene rings. Dopamine, the 'pleasure molecule' is a prototypical amphipathic pi resonance phenyl ring molecule, presumably present in the Primordial soup. Perhaps OR events in particular pi resonance geometries resonate more deeply with Plato's 'form of the good', encoded as vibrations in the structure of the universe, these events having feelings of greater pleasure. Such positive qualia – 'good vibrations' – could have been the feedback fitness function by which life developed, with natural selection and survival of the fittest serving to optimize feelings. 'Feeling good' by pleasurable

OR could have been the 'spark of life' by resonating with Platonic values embedded in the structure of the universe. Did biology then evolve to 'orchestrate' OR, to turn quantum noise into conscious music, to 'strike up the band'? To feel good? How could that have happened?

OR is naturally causal, choosing among different possibilities, a requisite for intentional purpose. In a non-polar environment (the quantum underground) adjacent pi resonance rings, attracted by London force dipoles and quadrupoles tend to align in one of two stable orientations, separated by the van der Waals radius. The two stable orientations are the 'T', in which one ring hangs perpendicular from the middle of the second ring, and the 'offset parallel' ('OP') orientation, in which two rings are parallel in one plane, and offset.

OR events from various configurations would result in specific superpositions of pi resonance clouds, and particular rudimentary mental experiences. Thus arrangements of pi stack orientations can be a code for qualia. Adjacent pi resonance rings may be arrayed as T or P, so a stack of 3 rings would have 4 possible arrangements, P-P, T-T, T-P and P-T. When superposition and OR results by $E_G=h/t$ among these rings, particular qualia (e.g. 'good', 'bad') would occur. For example, P-P might have pleasurable feelings, and T-T unpleasurable ones. With causal effects of OR outcomes influenced by feedback, 3-dimensional pi stacks could then re-arrange in orientation sequences (including helical, branching, and different ring types) to optimize and orchestrate OR-mediated feelings and qualia. Over time and replication cycles, recurrent feedback could optimize pi stack geometry for pleasurable conscious feelings whose particular pi-stack orientations would best resonate with Platonic values in spacetime geometry.

Micelle-like structures, RNA, membranes and other structures in the primordial soup could self-organize their pi stacks to optimize OR qualia. But pleasure, and ability to causally affect the physical world to further increase pleasure would soon become limited. Better organization, memory, motility, communication and reproduction were required to feel even better. Self-assembling intelligent polymers were the answer.

Enter microtubules.

Microtubules

Interiors of cells are organized and shaped by the 'cytoskeleton', a dynamic scaffolding of protein lattice polymers which include microtubules in animal cells, and similar structures in prokaryotes and archaebacterium. Animal cells also include microtubule-associated proteins ('MAPs'), actin and intermediate filaments, all anchored by the 'centriole', a pair of microtubule-based mega-cylinders in the cell center ('centrosome'), just outside the nucleus.

Microtubules are cylindrical polymers 25 nanometers (nm = 10^{-9} meter) in diameter, comprised usually of 13 longitudinal protofilaments, each a chain of the protein dimer 'tubulin'. Composed of alpha and beta monomers with net dipoles, tubulins give microtubules net dipoles. Tubulins self-assemble and arrange in MTs in two types of twisted hexagonal lattices (A-lattice and B-lattice) such that helical pathways along contiguous tubulins in the A-lattice repeat every 3, 5 and 8 rows on any protofilament (the Fibonacci series). Within microtubules, each tubulin may differ from its neighbors by genetic variability, post-translational modifications, phosphorylation states, binding of ligands and MAPs, and transient dipole orientation (Hameroff, 1987; Garham et al, 2015). With many tubulins per cell, e.g. 10^9 tubulins per neuron, information capacity in a mosaic-like MT is enormous. Epigenetic information is encoded in microtubule-based centrioles (Balestra et al, 2015).

Due to their organizational roles, lattice structure and coherent dynamics, microtubules have been suggested to actively process information since Sherrington (1951) described them as the cell's nervous system. Descriptions of MTs as computer-like devices (Hameroff and Watt, 1982; Hameroff 1987; Rasmussen et al, 1990) viewed individual tubulins as bit-like information units in Boolean switching matrices, or 'cellular (molecular)' automata played on microtubule lattices. Simulation of tubulin dipoles interacting with neighbor dipoles and synchronized by Fröhlich coherence showed rapid information integration and learning ('microtubule automata' - Smith et al 1984, Rasmussen et al 1990, Figure 6).

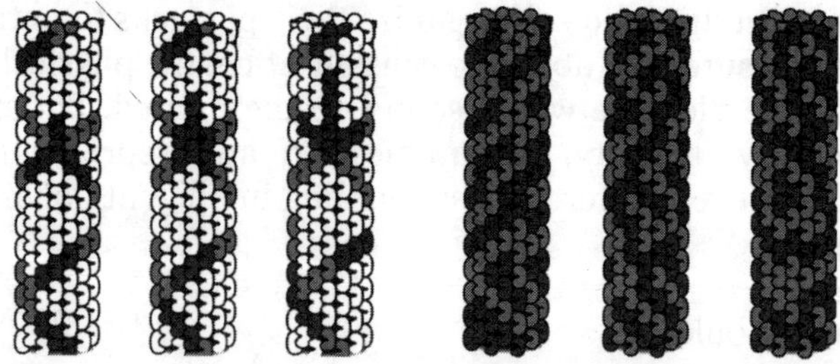

FIGURE 6

Three time-steps (e.g. at 10 megahertz) of a microtubule automaton which is classical. Tubulin subunit dipole states (black, white, gray) represent information. (a) Left: Spin currents interact and compute along spiral lattice pathways. For example (upper, middle in each microtubule) two upward traveling blue spin waves intersect, generating a new vertical spin wave (a 'glidergun' in cellular automata). (b) Right: A general microtubule automata process. With permission from Hameroff and Penrose, 2014.

But, what about consciousness? In the mid 1990s, Sir Roger Penrose and I teamed up to suggest microtubules in brain neurons 'orchestrated' OR events to produce conscious experience, and regulate conscious choice and action through neuronal firings and synaptic activities. The internal structure of microtubule protein subunits ('tubulin') appears analogous to the 'quantum underground' of pi resonance chromophores in plant photosynthesis. Computer models of tubulin structure show pi electron resonance clouds in aromatic amino acid rings of tryptophan, phenylalanine and tyrosine in clusters and channels (Craddock et al, 2012a, 2012b). Thus pi resonance regions in both photosynthesis proteins and tubulin in microtubules are buried and arrayed in a ('dry') non-polar solubility region shielded from ('wet') polar interactions - a 'quantum underground'. This particular solubility region is precisely where anesthetic gas molecules bind and selectively erase consciousness (the 'Meyer-Overton correlation' – see Section 3), and seems to be the origin of consciousness. Recent studies suggest anesthetics act by dampening terahertz (10^{12} Hz) quantum dipole oscillations in microtubule interiors (Craddock et al, 2015), these rapid oscillations being the 'inner apex' of a spatiotemporal hierarchy leading to electroencephalography ('EEG', see Figure 8).

According to Orch OR, quantum states and dipole oscillations in pi resonance clouds in a 'Meyer-Overton quantum underground' within neuronal microtubules are 'orchestrated' by synaptic inputs, memory and vibrational resonance. This enables superpositions to avoid random, non-cognitive interactions, and solely process purposeful and meaningful information. Thus when $E_G=h/t$ threshold is met in orchestrated conditions, fully conscious Orch OR moments are said to occur, resonating with deeper level 'Platonic values' in spacetime geometry. In pursuit of good feelings, Orch OR connects consciousness to the fine scale structure of the universe. Over appropriate time scales, Orch OR events optimize pleasurable qualia.

On the biological side, Orch OR is fully consistent with known neuroscience, action of anesthetic and psychoactive drugs, generates testable predictions (some validated, none refuted), has medical and philosophical implications, provides mental states with causal power and intentional awareness, and surpasses other theories of consciousness in terms of evidence and testability. Like panpsychism, Orch OR implies that qualia, i.e. feelings, preceded life.

It is suggested (Hameroff, 2016) that primitive 'proto-conscious' feelings occurred via Penrose OR in pi electron resonance clouds of micelle-like structures of dopamine-like molecules in non-polar regions of the prebiotic 'Primordial soup', the original 'quantum underground'. OR-mediated feelings provided feedback and motivation for self-organizing pi resonance clouds ('pi stacks') in the origin and evolution of life, and the brain. Intention and purpose optimized qualia. Life, microtubules and the brain evolved to 'feel good'.

Tubulin proteins comprising microtubules each have 8 tryptophan indole rings arrayed in a geometry strikingly similar to that in FMO photosynthesis proteins, and a total of 86 pi resonance clouds (including phenylalanine and tyrosine rings). Using molecular modeling, Craddock et al (2012a; 2012b) showed FRET-like excitons passing through tubulin among 8 tryptophan pi resonance clouds, driven by ambient energy, and blocked by anesthetics which bind naturally in non-polar regions.

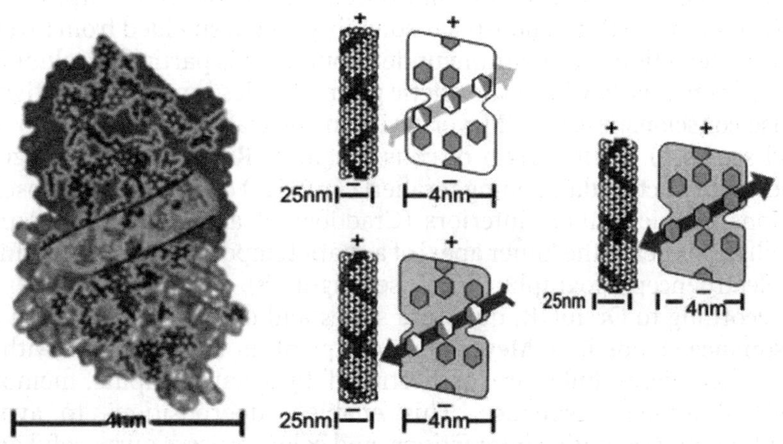

FIGURE 7
Left: the protein tubulin showing aromatic amino acid pi resonance clouds (tryptophan, phenylalanine, tyrosine) and sites of binding of anesthetic halothane (spheres). Band indicates non-polar cluster of aromatic rings ('quantum channel', or 'quantum underground') with anesthetic binding sites aligned along 5-start helix in microtubule lattice. Right: Dipole qubit in microtubule in Orch OR theory, with quantum dipole states oscillating, and forming quantum superposition of alternate states along '5-start' helical pathway in tubulin and microtubules. Dipoles may be electric or magnetic e.g. related to electronic (and/or nuclear) spin. Similar qubit pathways may occur along 8-start pathways, or other pathways.

Though electrically neutral and non-polar, pi electron resonance clouds are polarizable, and attract and couple by induced quantum dipoles (van der Waals London forces, quadrupoles, magnetic dipoles). Such coupling is enhanced by the 'hydrophobic effect' (oil and water don't mix), drives protein folding and results in 'pi stacking' in which resonance rings are arrayed at specific spacings and geometric orientations. At the van der Waals radius, electron clouds can couple and oscillate by van der Waals London forces, and 'excitons'.

The evolution of tubulin and microtubules is puzzling. Why would tubulin, a single protein, evolve as a cog in a machine, one brick in a skyscraper yet to be realized? According to conventional evolutionary theory, the feedback fitness function for tubulin would depend on higher order microtubule activities not yet present. Proponents of 'intelligent design' cite microtubules and their composites cilia and centrioles as structures which are difficult to explain through natural selection. They may have a valid objection, but lack a scientific alternative.

How *did* tubulin and microtubules (or their prokaryotic and archaebacteria counterpart proteins) evolve? Consider a possible scenario in the primordial soup. Pumped by ambient terahertz radiation, pi resonance rings on amphipathic molecules coalesced, coupled and oscillated in non-polar micelle interiors. Van der Waals forces provided separation between rings at quantum critical distances (Vattay et al, 2015). As micelles incorporated more pi resonance clouds (e.g. clusters of 3 or 4 rings), entangled quantum superpositions extended in an expanding quantum underground. The resultant increasing 'E_G' in each $E_G=\hbar/t$ OR event became, with feedback and developing over time, more purely coherent so that subjective 'proto-conscious' OR qualia became more cognitive and intense, good or bad. 'Good' feelings ensued from more energetically favorable pi stack geometry which resonated with Platonic values.

As the number of coupled coherent rings and E_G grew, intensity and quality of 'good feelings' also grew, providing feedback to pi stack geometry, e.g. flipping T and OP configurations within each micelle's quantum underground, optimizing qualia and experience. Rudimentary mental states exerted causal power, arranging pi resonance clouds within micelles which became proteins, membranes and nucleic acids. With repetitive feedback, clusters of pi resonance clouds optimized their geometry for pleasurable qualia as particular sequences of T and OP arrangements, coupling with other clusters by FRET and excitons, and absorbing and resonating with ambient terahertz, ultraviolet and cosmic microwave radiation. This all served to further optimize OR-mediated pleasure by pi cloud geometry.

But then what happened? Tubulins aligned by charge interactions and entropy, forming 'lattice patches' with pi resonance clouds extending from one tubulin to its neighbor, increasing OR-mediated pleasure. Cooperative information exchange developed a logic based on skewed hexagonal (Fibonacci) geometry of tubulin patches which rolled into cylinders, stabilized by ultra-violet absorption and megahertz mechanical resonances, reinforcing pi stack coherence, developing a hexagonal-based information code, ramping up OR pleasure even more. The microtubule was born, biological evolution accelerated, Orch OR, brains and full rich consciousness followed. Consciousness and feelings, from simple proto-conscious random events to full, rich 'orchestrated' conscious experience and perhaps collective coherence among populations, may be driving the evolution of life. Could consciousness also be driving evolution of the universe?

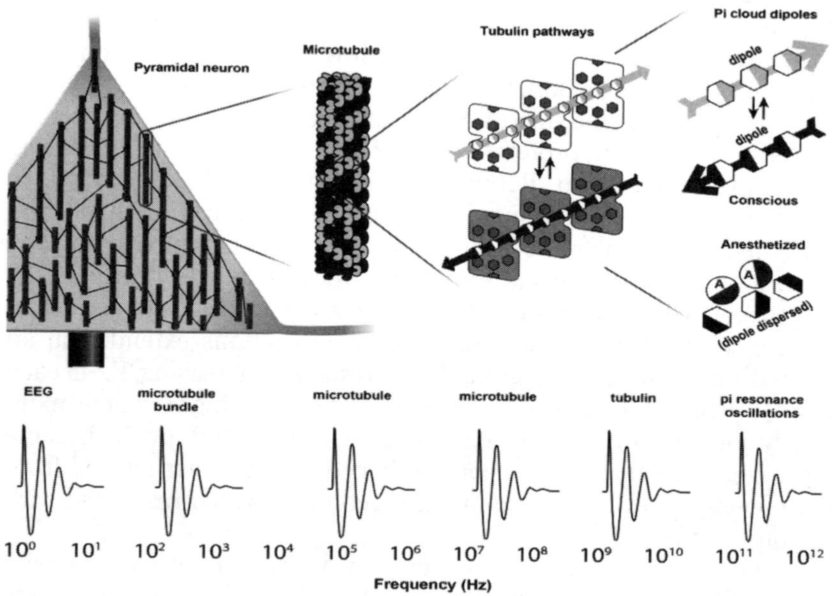

FIGURE 8
Resonance frequencies of microtubule-based quantum oscillations as discovered by Bandyopadhyay group (Sahu et al, 2013a; 2013b; 2014). Left-to-right: Pyramidal neuron cell body with internal microtubules; microtubule; row of tubulins with dipoles; dipoles with (below) anesthetic dampening. Resonances in spacetime geometry (not shown) would occur at higher frequencies, i.e. to the right, perhaps extending to Planck scale spacetime geometry.

Conclusion - The 'anthropic principle' and consciousness-driven evolution of the universe

'The anthropic principle' is the philosophical consideration that the universe is perfectly tuned to accommodate life and consciousness. The 20 or so fundamental constants which govern the universe (e.g. the mass of the proton, the gravitational constant, etc.) are all precisely, exactly what are needed for stars, life and consciousness – a coincidence of astronomically unlikely probability. We won the cosmic lottery. But how?

There are two types of explanations, the so-called 'weak' and 'strong' anthropic principles. The weak anthropic principle (e.g. as proposed by Brandon Carter, 1974) explains the apparent fine tuning as 'selection bias' in the context of the multiple worlds hypothesis. Only in this particular universe (out of an infinite number of possible universes) are conscious, living beings present and able to ponder this question. On the contrary, the 'strong anthropic principle', as advocated by John Barrow and Frank Tipler (1986), argues this one-and-only universe is somehow compelled to harbor conscious beings. But why would the universe be so compelled?

A logical answer is that consciousness is intrinsic to reality, as suggested in Orch OR, its quality woven into the 20 or so fundamental constants which regulate the universe. Could the values of such constants change over time, perhaps evolving to optimize consciousness? The nature of such constants is unknown, e.g. they could be akin to Platonic values and resonances intrinsic to the fine scale (and as yet unknown) structure of spacetime geometry? Their 'constancy' among different regions of spacetime is unknown, so the notion that they are mutable is not unrealistic. The OR process itself may induce slight alterations, with greater intensity and more pleasurable OR events having more profound effects. Or, consciousness-driven mutation and evolution of the universe may occur through more singular, cataclysmic happenings. For example, in 'Life of the Cosmos', Lee Smolin (1999) suggested that black holes give birth to 'baby universes', the physical constants changing and evolving with each such birth, leading to differing conditions in the offspring worlds.

Sir Roger Penrose has suggested 'Cyclic Conformal Cosmology' ('CCC') in which the universe is seen as a sequence of 'aeons', each aeon beginning with a (little) 'big bang', and ending with a heat death, re-scaling, another big bang, aeon, and so on. Smolin's black hole mechanism for mutating physical constants could apply to serial big bangs, optimizing consciousness. The serial universe evolves to optimize, tune and resonate consciousness....to feel good. Consciousness may be driving the universe.

References

Balestra, F. R., & von Tobel, L., Gonczy, P. (2015). Paternally contributed centrioles exhibit exceptional persistence in C. elegans embryos. *Cell Research, 25*, 642-644.

Barrow, J.D., & Tipler, F.J. (1986). The anthropic cosmological principal. Oxford: Oxford University Press.

Benioff, P. (1982). Quantum mechanical Hamiltonian models of Turing Machines. *Journal of Statistical Physics, 29*, 515-546.

Carter, B. (1974). Large number of coincidences and the anthropic principle in cosmology. IAU Symposium 63: Confrontation of Cosmological Theories with Observational Data. (pp. 291-298). Dordrecht: Reidel. Republished in *General Relativity and Gravitation* (2011) *43*(11), 3225-3233.

Chalmers, D.J. (1996). *The conscious mind – In search of a fundamental theory*. New York: Oxford University Press.

Craddock, T., St. George, M., Freedman, H., Barakat, K., Damaraju, S., Hameroff, S., & Tuszynski, J. A. (2012a). Computational predictions of volatile anesthetic interactions with the microtubule cytoskeleton: implications for side effects of general anesthesia. *PLoS ONE, 7*(6) e37521. Doi 10.1371/journal.pone. 0037251

Craddock, T., Tuszynski, J. Hameroff, S. (2012b). Cytoskeletal signaling: Is memory encoded in microtubule lattices by CaMKII phosphorylation? *PLoS Computational Biology, 8*(3) e1002421. doi:10.1371/journal.pcbi.1002421

Craddock, T. J. A., Hameroff, S. R., Tuszynski, J. A. (2015). Anesthetics act in quantum channels in brain microtubules to prevent consciousness. *Current Topics in Medicinal Chemistry, 15*, 523-533.

Damasio, A. (1999). *The feeling of what happens*. San Diego: Harcourt.

Dawkins, R. (1986). *The blind watchmaker*. New York: W.W. Norton & Company.

Dawkins, R. (1989). *The selfish gene*. Oxford: Oxford University Press.

Deutsch, D. (1985). Quantum theory, the Church-Turing principal and the universal quantum computer. *Proceedings of the Royal Society of London, 400*, 97-117.

Dyson, F. W., Eddington, A. S. (1920). A determination of the deflection of light by the sun's gravitational field, from observations made at the total eclipse of May 29, 1919. *Philosopical Transactions of the Royal Society Series A, 220*, 291-330.

Everett, H. (1957). Relative state formulation of quantum mechanics. *Reviews of Modern Physics, 29*, 454.

Feynman, R.P. (1986). Quantum mechanical computer. *Foundations of Physics, 16*, 507-531.

Freud, S. (1961). Beyond the pleasure principle (The Standard Edition). (J. Strachey, Trans.). New York: Liveright Publishing Corporation.

Frohlich, J. (1968). Long range coherence and energy storage in biological systems. *International Journal of Quantum Chemistry, 2*, 641-649.

Frohlich, H. (1970). Long range coherence and actions of enzymes. *Nature, 228*, 1093.

Frohlich, H. (1975). The extraordinary dielectric properties of biological materials and the action of enzymes. *Proceedings of the National Academy of Sciences, 72*, 4211-4215.

Garham, C. P., Vemu, A., Wilson-Kubalek, E. M., Yu, I., Szyk, A., Lander, G. C., Milligan, R. A., Roll-Mecak, A. (2015). Multivalent microtubule recognition by tubulin tyrosine ligase-like family glutamylases. *Cell, 21*, 161(5), 1112-23.

Haldane, J. B. S. (1929). The origin of life. *Rationalist Annual, 148*, 3–10.

Hameroff, S., & Watt, R.C. (1982). Information processing in microtubules. *Journal of Theoretical Biology, 98*, 549-561.

Hameroff, S. (1987). *Ultimate computing – Biomolecular consciousness and nanotechnology*. Amsterdam: Elsevier.

Hameroff, S., & Penrose, R. (2014). Consciousness in the universe: A review of the 'Orch OR' theory. *Physics of Life Reviews, 11*(1), 39-79.

Hameroff, S. (2006). The entwined mysteries of anesthesia and consciousness. *Anesthesiology, 105*, 400-412.

Hameroff, S. (2016). The quantum origin of life – How the brain evolved to feel good. In M. Tibayrenc, & F. Ayala (Eds.) *On human nature: Biology, psychology, ethics, politics, and religion*. Academic Press.

Hodgkin A. L., & Huxley A. F. (1952). A quantitative description of membrane current and its application to conduction and excitation in nerve. *Journal of Physiology, 117*, 500-544.

Koch, C. (2012). *Consciousness: Confessions of a romantic reductionist*. Cambridge: MIT Press.

Langton, C. G. (Ed.) (1995). *Artificial life: An overview*. Cambridge: MIT Press.

Margulis, L. & Sagan, D. (1995). *What is life?* New York: Simon Schuster.

Meyer, H. (1901). Zur theorie der alkolnarkose. *Naunyn Schmied Arch Exp Path Pharmakol, 46*, 338-446.

Miller, S., & Urey, H. C. (1959). Organic compound synthesis on the primitive earth. *Science, 130*(3370), 245-251.

Oparin A. (1924). *Proiskhozhedenie zhizni.* Moscow: Mosckovskii Rabochii. (J. D. Bernal, Trans. (1967). *The origin of life*. London: Weidenfeld and Nicolson.)

Overton, E. (1901). Studein ueber die narkosen. Switzerland: Verlag von Gustav Fischer.

Panksepp, J. (1998). *Affective neuroscience: The foundations of human and animal emotions*. New York: Oxford University Press.

Peil, K. T. (2014). Emotion: The self-regulatory sense. *Global Advances in Health and Medicine, 2*, 80-108.

Penrose, R. (1989). *The emperor's new mind: concerning computers, minds, and the laws of physics*. Oxford: Oxford University Press.

Penrose, R. (2010). Cycles of time – An extraordinary new view of the universe. New York: Knopf.

Pullman, B., & Pullman, A. (1963). *Quantum biochemistry*. New York: Interscience.

Rasmussen, S., Karampurwala, H., Vaidyaath, R., Jensen, K., & Hameroff, S. (1990). Computational connectionism within neurons: a model of cytoskeletal automata subserving neural networks. *Physica D: Nonlinear Phenomena, 42*, 428-449.

Sahu, S., Ghosh, S., Fujita, D., & Bandyopdhyay, A. (2014). Live visualizations of single isolated tubulin protein self-assembly via tunneling current: effect of electromagnetic pumping during spontaneous growth of microtubule. *Scientific Reports, 4*, 7303.

Sahu S., Ghosh, S., Ghosh, B., Aswanid, K., Hirata, K., Fujita, D., &

Bandyopadhyay, A. (2013). Atomic water channel controlling remarkable properties of a single brain microtubule: correlating single protein to its supramolecular assembly. *Biosensors and Bioelectronics, 47*, 141-148.

Sahu, S., Ghosh, S., Hirata, K., Fujita, D. & Bandyopadhya, A. (2013). Multi-level memory-switching properties of a single brain microtubule. *Applied Physics Letters, 102*, 123701.

Schrodinger, E. (1935). Diegegenwartesituationinderquantenmechanik. *Naturwissenschaften, 23*, 807-812, 823-828, 844-849. Translation by Trimmer, .T. in *Proceedings of the American Philosophical Society, 124*, 323-338.

Sherrington, C. S. (1951). *Man on his nature*. Cambridge: Cambridge University Press.

Shimony, A. (1993). *Search for a naturalistic world view, vol. II. Natural science and metaphysics*, Cambridge: Cambridge University Press.

Smith, S., Watt, R. & Hameroff, S. (1984). Cellular automata in cytoskeletal lattice protients. *Physica D: Nonlinear Phenomena, 10*, 168-174.

Smolin L. (1999). *The life of the cosmos*. Oxford: Oxford University Press.

Stapp, H.P. (2007). *Mindful universe: quantum mechanics and the participating observe*r. New York: Springer.

Szent-Gyorgyi, A. (1960). *Introduction to a submolecular biology*. Cambridge: Academic Press.

Tononi, G. (2012). *Phi: A voyage from the brain to the soul*. New York: Pantheon Books.

Whitehead, A. N. (1929). *Process and Reality*. New York: Macmillan.

Whitehead, A. N. (1933). *Adventures of ideas*. London: Macmillan.

Vattay, G., Salahub, D., Casbai, I., Nassimi, A., Kaufmann, S. A. (2015). Quantum criticality at the origin of life. *Journal of Physics: Conference Series*, DOI: 10.1088/1742-6596/626/1/012023.

III

Consciousness - Eastern Perspectives

Chapter 14

Perspectives on Consciousness: Indian Philosophical Traditions

P.SRIRAMAMURTI
Dayalbagh Educational Institute (Deemed University), Dayalbagh, Agra, India

Indian Philosophical Traditions are well known for their antiquity and continuity. The Vedic, Sramanic and Agamic traditions have their distinctive features which later got integrated into the philosophical systems of later times. The Sufi traditions developed from the Semitic lore of Judaism, Christianity and Islam and interacted with indigenous esoteric systems. The Sant traditions of Kabir, Guru Nanak and Radhasoamis amalgamated all these traditions , integrating their thought and practical methods of spiritual regeneration. They clearly stated the empirical and transcendental levels of consciousness and discussed the various practical methods adopted by different traditions to reach the highest level fixed by them for reaching by their methodologies as their *Summom Bonum*.

Thus the foundations of Spiritual Science were laid by the Rishis and Sages of yore. When they realized that the physical senses can only give us partial knowledge, they sought the help of some other senses to get at the truth. They discovered inside them in their head latent inner senses which when developed began to function. They found that the world was entirely different from what they had constructed by the knowledge of the physical senses. Pursuing the inner path further and further, they discovered more and more hidden senses or centres. They , then called the knowledge obtained through the physical senses Apara Vidya and that obtained through higher senses – *Para Vidya* or transcendental knowledge.

Chaitanya, the Primordial Reservoir of Consciousness, has the inherent characteristics of Sat (Truth), Chit (Intelligence), Ananda (Bliss) which also manifest as Energy, Light and Love: Shakti, Prakasha and Prema. This primordial consciousness (Chaitanya) is the Prime Cause of all Creation that came into being. It is infinite and eternal. This perception, is behind all the philosophical theories expounded differently by different visionaries of spiritual traditions in varied terminologies.

The Vedic tradition goes back to hoary past. In the earliest hymns we find expressions of these visions. In the Brihadaranyaka Upanishad, sage Yajnavalkya said to Gargi, "Verily, that Imperishable, is unseen but is the Seer , is unheard but is the hearer, is unthought but is the thinker, is unknown but is the knower." "There is no seer but Brahman, there is no other hearer; but Brahman , there is no other thinker but Brahman, there is no other knower but Brahman." "By this imperishable, O, Gargi! is this entire Space woven like warp and woof."

In the Chandogya Upanishad, it was said to Svetaketu by his father, "My dear! In the beginning 'Sat' alone existed without a second. It willed – "I shall become many" and created fire (Tejas), Tejas created water (apas), water created food (annam-earth). All the living beings are of three classes – born of egg (andaja) or another living being (jivaja) or sprout (udbhija). The 'Sat', the Para Devata willed again and entered the three – Tejas, Apas and Annam as their inner soul and developed different names and forms. In the course of the discourse, it was conveyed that "this world has the 'Self' as its subtle essence. That is 'Sat'. Every one including Svetaketu has that self as his origin. "That art thou, O, Svetaketu!" Several illustrations are furnished in support of this, such as Banyan Fig tree (Nyagrodha) and Salt & Water.

The course of Jiva after death is thus explained, "A hundred and one are the arteries of the heart. One of them leads up to the crown of the head; Going upward through that, one becomes immortal. The others serve for going in various other directions." Taittreya Upanishad describes – The state that is different from waking, dreaming, sleeping and fainting is – 'death'. It is the giving up of the gross body. After drawing together the organs of action and the organs of perception, their respective functions and the vital airs, the soul attended with desire and karmas (in the form of impressions left by our actions) and wrapped up in elements of ignorance goes to another world for attaining another body.

In an investigation into 'Brahman', it is taught that: That from which these beings are born, when born, by which they live and when they depart, into which they enter, that you seek to know – That is 'Brahman'. This is the functional definition of Brahman *(Thatastha Lakshana)* with its distinguishing features. *Satchidanandasvaroopam Brahma* is its definition giving out its real nature (*Svarupa Lakshana*) like *Satyam, Jnanam, Anantam Brahma.* We may compare it with the definitions given by Param Sants : *Sachidananda Swaroopam Chaitanyam; Sat, Chit , Premananda Prakasham Chaitanyam.*

Who Is the Real Agent in the Individual? "By whom willed and directed does the mind focus light on its objects? By whom commanded, does life make its first move? At whose will do people utter speech? And what God is it that prompts the eye and ear to function?" The questions put in this verse by the pupil imply that the passing things of experience are not the reality and they depend on a permanent reality. The necessity of a ground reality for the existence of finite beings is described here. These questions assume that there is a relation between ultimate reality governing the phenomenal and the phenomena. There is the Eternal Reality behind the mind , life and the senses as the mind of the mind and life of life and sense of senses namely, Brahman being the real agent. He who knows it becomes immortal.

In the Katha Upanishad, Yama, the Lord of Death, in his discourse to Nachiketa, explains the functioning of Jivatma (embodied soul) in the world by an analogy of chariot. The Atma is compared to the master of the Chariot – the human body. Buddhi, intellect is the driver (Sarathi). The horses are the sense organs, Manas (mind) is the reins by which the intellect controls the senses. The objects of the senses are the pathways that they traverse.

The Prashnopanishad speaks of Prana (bio-energy) thus: Prana is born of Self. It comes into body through the activity of mind. This Prana activates other Pranas. Atman dwells in the heart. There are a hundred and one arteries. To each one belong a hundred smaller arteries. To each one of these smaller arteries belong seventy two thousand branching arteries. Within these the Vyana (a type of Prana) moves. Prana is born out of Atman and comes into the body through mind and pervades it.

The syllable OM is described as bow and one's self is the arrow. Brahman is its target, which is to be hit carefully with concentrated mind so that the arrow becomes one with the target, i.e., the self becomes one with Brahman, the Universal Self.

Mandukyopanishad gives a comprehensive description of the three empirical states of consciousness common to all and distinguishes the fourth state of Turiya from them.

1. Jagrat - The perceptual self is the wakeful state , is called Vaisvanara (Visva);
2. Svapna - The imaginative self in the dream state is called Taijasa and
3. The conceptual self in the state of deep sleep is Prajna.

In the third state of consciousness, the self enjoys peace without the perceptual distraction of either external or internal objects. The transitory nature of state of deep-sleep is evident from the instantaneous relapse to dream or wakeful states. Only indiscriminate knowledge and veiled bliss are experienced in deep sleep. It is yet viewed as the cause of this worldly life. The three states of Jagrat, Svapna and Sushupti correspond to Virat, Hiranyagarbha and Avyakrita, in Macrocosm respectively while Turiya state corresponds to transcendental state of Brahman in Macrocosm. Hiranyagarbha is the Sutratma, the thread of subjectivity playing with the states of universal mind as Taijasa does in the dream world. The whole world rests in him in embryo form. When the world is projected in space and time it is "Virat". It is like the waking state, the sphere of Vaisvanara's activity. The waking and dream states correspond to exterior existence and interiorized state of the world (universal) spirit. When the universal spirit wills and exteriorizes its attention, the cosmos is created. When it turns inwards involution takes place, cosmos retreating to its latency. When universal spirit withdraws altogether it becomes Isvara. When it further retreats Isvara becomes Para Brahman. Shabda Brahma –Omkara represents both Isvara and Para Brahma.

According to Vedanta Pure consciousness is the prime source of the individual spirit entities as well as the objective world. Mula-prakriti, the primordial matter, came out of Pure Consciousness and created the world at the Will of It. Pure consciousness juxtaposed with Mula-prakriti became Witness-Consciousness. It reflected in Prakriti of Sattvic quality with Avarana Shakti of concealing and altering, thus it became Isvara Chaitanya. Reflecting in Rajas Prakriti with Vikshepa Shakti (distortion) it became Hiranyagarbha Chaitanya and when it reflected in Tamas Prakriti with Vikshepa Shakti it became Virat Chaitanya. The Virat with ego sense willed to create the world and gave rise to Akasha; Akasha to Vayu; Vayu to Agni; Agni to Apas; Apas to Prithivi. These are the subtle elements – Tanmatras. Virat willed to bring into existence further creation and embraced Tamas quality (inertia) and changed subtle elements into gross elements by a process called Panchikarana – quintuplication (1/2+1/8+1/8+1/8+1/8) and from those gross elements he created Brahmandas, macrocosms and also gross bodies appropriate to those worlds in respect of individual spirit entities. Bringing the Rajas quality (mobility) into action the five elements were divided into four parts. Out of three parts he created Prana, the life principle with five fold functions (Prana, Apana, Vyana, Udana and Samana). The fourth part originated five Karmendriyas – organs of action, the organ of speech, hands, feet, excretory organ and reproductory organ (Vak, Pani, Pada, Payu, Upastha).

Virat divided the Sattva (rhythmic property) of the five elements into four. With the sum of three parts the inner sense (Antahkarana) was created with its fivefold function, viz., Antahkarana, Manas, Buddhi, Chitta and Ahankara. With the fourth part he created organs of perception, five sense organs of eyes, ears, nose, tongue and skin. The totality of Sattva elements created the presiding deities of sense organs and they were cast into the macrocosm. Virat possessing self sense protected the gross elements. Hiranyagarbha rules over the subtle elements. The gross and the subtle elements and their products, the Pranas and organs of action and sense, could not function on their own. So he desired to make them conscious i.e. sentient. He pierced through the macrocosm and the caverns of the cranium of individual souls situated in their crests and entered them all.

Though non-conscious by nature, they now engaged in their

respective functions as if they were endowed with consciousness (*tat shrishtva tadevanupravishat*). Thus it is the Lord Himself, possessed of the particle of Maya, entered several bodies and attained the status of an individual soul. Entering the three bodies of Gross, Subtle and Causal, became the doer (*Karta*) and enjoyer (*Bhokta*) in all the states of waking, dreaming, sleeping, fainting and dying. Yajnavalkya explained about the five states namely, wakefulness, dream, dreamless sleep, swoon and death, and 'rebirth as per the results of past deeds', seeking liberation at the end of many lives and explained about bondage. About the secret of *Kaivalya* – 'aloneness' – being alone – Yajnavalkya explained - Brahman the Being, *Sat* alone existed at the beginning. He was ever free, indeterminate, truth, knowledge, (consciousness) bliss, ancient, without a second. In that Pure Being, undefinable (anirvachya), root principle of matter (*mula-prakriti*), existed. When it reflected in Brahman (Pure-Consciousness) it became *(Sakshi Chaitanya)* Witness Consciousness i.e., the eternal subject faced by objectivity, Subject-Object relationship developed later.

That Subject-Object relationship underwent change due to preponderance of Sattva Guna and became Avyakta the 'unmanifest' with the power of veiling the nature of Brahman. Brahman as reflected in it became Isvara Consciousness. With Maya under his control (mayantu prakritim vidyat, mayinam tu maheshvaram) He is all knowing, and the first cause of creation, sustenance and dissolution. On account of the karmas of the souls creation takes place. At the destruction of the karmas of the souls, it gets dissolved. From the powers of veiling (Avarana Shakti) of Isvara arises Mahat – the power of projection (Vikshepa Shakti) with the preponderance of Rajas. The consciousness reflected in Mahat is known as Hiranyagarbha – a manifest form distinct and indistinct. From the powers of projection, Vikshepa Shakti of Hiranyagarbha comes into being "Virat Chaitanya' – the power of making gross bodies – Ahankara 'Self Sense'. The Virat Consciousness conceiving the Self Sense as its own, becomes Vishnu the force sustaining gross creation. From Virat originates ether – Akasha, from Akasha Vayu, from Vayu – Agni, from Agni Jala, from Jala – Prithvi. These are the Tanmatras with three qualities. The creator embracing the quality of Tamas (inert property) created the gross elements from the Tanmatras by process of Panchikarana. From these quintuplicated elements many Brahmandas are created with their fourteen Brahmanda worlds and globular gross bodies.

Virat possessed with self-sense protected the gross elements. Hiranyagarbha ruled the subtle elements. He desired to make them all conscious (sentient beings). Piercing through macrocosm and caverns of cranium (*Brahmarandhras*) of the individual souls (microcosms), situated in their crusts, he entered them all. They who were non-conscious by nature, were engaged in their respective functions, as it endowed them with consciousness.

The Omniscient Lord possessed a particle of Maya on entering the several bodies and getting deluded by it attained the state of individual soul. By identification with the three bodies (gross, subtle and causal) he attained the state of doer (karta) ever performing the functions of waking, dreaming and sleeping, fainting and dying. Though all religious scripture contain some references regarding spiritual identity of man and the path to self realization, it is the Vedic and Sant traditions that give more specific and elaborate description of spiritual knowledge. Texts of Vedic and Sant traditions discuss creational process, levels of spiritual consciousness and methods of spiritual practices for their realization.

According to the paradigm of investigation given in the Taittiriya Upanishad, the Pure Spirit, the knower, is covered with five sheaths – Koshas: Annamya Kosha, the body, the material sheath on the surface, the Pranamaya Kosha, bio-energy sheath of vital airs, the Manomaya Kosha, the mind cover of sensory knowledge; the Vignaanmaya Kosa – the cover of higher mind of intelligence and discrimination of Buddhi, Anandamaya Kosha, the cover of reflected bliss of spirit in the deep sleep. The spirit characterized by Chit, pure consciousness is beyond these sheaths.

The Kathopanishad gives a somewhat different paradigm. It says that a man of subtle intellect sees the self within himself by following the said means of its attainment. He would withdraw and merge his attention focused on senses in mind. That mind he merges in intelligent self and then that intelligent self, in the universal consciousness, and that universal consciousness in the peaceful Self of Pure Consciousness. In this process the pseudo subject gradually shifts to real subject as has been succinctly explained in Drik-Drshya-Viveka by Sankaracharya-

"Form is seen by eye, the seer; that eye is seen by the mind – seer; the modifications of the mind are seen by the eternal seer, the Atman, the eternal Sakshi; The Atman is always the seer but never the seen."

KASHMIRI SHAIVISM:

Kashmiri Shaivism is exclusively a Science of Consciousness. Atman is defined as Chaitanya. "*Chaintyamatma*" (Shiva Sutra). The Self is Consciousness (Shiva Sutra 1.1). Pure Consciousness continually vibrates (Spanda). This vibration or pulsation at the macrocosmic level unfolds the Universe, holds it in place and withdraws it. On the microcosmic level it creates thoughts and beating of the heart. In meditation this vibratory movement can be contacted in stillness. This phenomenon is represented in a simple mandala diagram. Pure Consciousness continually pulsates from the centre creating the universe and densest matter on its periphery. It reverses the pulses in dissolution by Sadhana or Grace, back into Consciousness.

The first Sutra of Pratyabhijnahridaya says, Chiti Shakti, Universal Consciousness is supremely independent and it is the cause of the universe. In the next sutra it is said ' Of his own free will, chiti unfolds the universe on her own canvas.' Consciousness is immanent i.e., present everywhere in the universe and transcendent i.e., beyond the universe. Atman is consciousness. Consciousness is the primeval substance of universe. It is Paramashiva. He is eternally associated with Shakti. He is Chit Shakti. Kaishmiri Shaivism enunciates 36 Tattwas. Accepting the 25 Tattvas of Sankhya Darshana, they add 11 more at the top. The Chart below shows the Tattvas. In consequence of His limitation of Shakti (Shiva) the Reality which is all Consciousness becomes covered by malas i.e., imputities and becomes a *sansari* jiva of the creation i.e., a creature. The perfect powerful Shiva becomes

CHART

PARAMA SHIVA

(Shakti and Shaktiman)

1.Shiva (Chit Shakti)
2.Shakti (Ananda Shakti)

3.Sadashiva (Iccha shakti)	4.Ishvara (Jnana shakti)	5.Shuddha-vidya (kriya shakti)

6. Maya
(limits these shaktis with Kanchukas limitation /contraction)

7.Kala (Eternity)	8.Vidya (Omniscience)	9.Raga (Completeness)	10.Kata (Omnipotence)	11.Niyati (Omnipresence)

12. Purusha (Individual subject)	**13.Prakriti** (objective Experience)

14.Manas (mind)	**15.Buddhi** (Intelligence)	**16.Ahankara** (ego)
Jnanendriyas (organs of perception)	**Karmendriyas** (organs of action)	**Tanmatras** (subtle elements)
17.Shrotra (Ears)	22.Vak (Speech)	27.Shabda (Sound)
18.Tvak (Skin)	23.Pani (Hands)	28.Sparsha (Touch)
19.Chakshu (Eyes)	24.Pada (Legs)	29.Rupa (Form)
20.Jihva (Tongue)	25.Payu (Excretive)	30.Rasa (Taste)
21.Ghrana (Nose)	26.Upastha (Reproductive)	31.Gandha (Smell)

Mahabhutas

32.Akasha (Space) 33.Vayu (Air) 34.Agni (Fire) 35.Apas (Water) 36.Prithvi (Earth) imperfect jiva with limitations.

The **Buddhist meditation** popularly called mindfulness meditation is clear insight meditation, ***Vipassana.*** It focuses attention on every detail of our physical and mental experiences from moment-to-moment with an unbiased attitude. By this practice one develops seeing things as they are eliminating from the mind subjective association, which is the cause of physical and mental pain. It results in a state of stable happiness. Mindfulness is fourfold: (1) mindfulness with regard to the body, (2) mindfulness with regard to feeling, (3) mindfulness with regard to consciousness, and (4) mindfulness with regard to mental objects (dharmas). Stages of Meditation: Meditation or concentration in Buddhism is divided into four progressive stages. These are the stages of intense contemplation and absorption which finally lead the mind to an immovable tranquility. 1. The first trance is a stage of joy and happiness born of abstraction, reflection and investigation, the meditator is aloof from sensuality and sinful thoughts. 2. The second trance is a stage of joy and happiness born of profound inner tranquillity, without reflection and investigation; intuition predominates this stage. 3. The third stage of trance is characterized by the even-mindedness through happiness and cessation of passion; the monk is joyful and aware in his body of that delight which the saints call 'equanimity, mindfulness and bliss', (upeksa-smriti-samprajanya-sukha). 4. The fourth stage of trance is characterized by the destruction of both happiness and misery, by the rejection of joy and sorrow.

Each of these stages is divided into three orders–initial (paritta), middle (majjhima) and final (panita). The fourth stage of dhyana is free from inspiration, respiration, reflection, investigation, sorrow, pleasure, pain, and joy. The four stages of meditation keep the mind of the meditator monk within the limits of the material world. There are also four higher stages of dhyana which are called samapattis which the arhats obtain. The four arupas or formless and infinite objects of contemplation, mentioned earlier, lead an adept to the mastery of these four higher stages.

Vipassana is the quint essence of Buddhist spiritual practices. It is rightly attracting the attention of all nowadays. The scientific tests are also performed on its practioners. Vipassana is closely looking at things which will gradually lead to enlightenment. Anapanasati (Pranapanasati) concentration on the incoming and outgoing breath as well as concentration on Brahmaviharas forms part of this meditation. The four Brahmaviharas are Maitri (friendship), Karuna (compassion), Mudita (altruistic joy) in the well-being of others , Upeksa (sense of equality and justice towards all). These are found in Patanjali yoga also. In this way we find much in common in all yoga techniques calling for a scientific corroboration of all the techniques, in an integral way, after testing them independently in respect of different practitioners, to prove their scientific nature and efficacy for control of mind along with bodily well being and spiritual regeneration.

Vajrayana and Mantrayana of Buddhism use the formula "Om Manipadme Hum" accepting the efficacy of the Omkara. All these uses of Omkara in Vedanta Yoga, Jain and Buddhist traditions prove that the Shabda Sadhana is at the root of these practices. They show that the seekers and Sadhakas were after results only. The Christians speak of the Word and the Islamic Sufis speak of Lahut and Hut, which are of a high dimension of spirituality like Sat Nam of Sikhs and Radhasoami of Sants.

CONSCIOUSNESS IN JAINISM

Sramanas, munis of ancient times, were ancestors of Jains who devoted their lives for the attainment of spiritual wisdom and perfection through ascetic discipline and rigorous meditation. According to them life is full of misery and one should get rid of the cycle of births and deaths and attain spiritual emancipation. They did not accept Creator God who is also the dispensor of pleasures and pains. They believed that all potentialities are inherent in man. He has the capacity to uplift himself and raise to the highest level of spiritual attainment. They accepted a set of seven principles : 1. Jiva – Soul , the living matter who enjoys the fruits of his deeds and is capable of attaining infinite knowledge, faith and bliss. 2.Ajiva –Non living matter: When the Jiva and the Ajiva come together, the world comes into existence and the Jiva gets entangled in it. 3. Asrava : the inflow of karmic matter to Jiva which binds him. 4. Bandha bondage of jiva with karmic matter. It is also called kashaya. This is caused by false knowledge or ignorance. 5. Samvara: stoppage of inflow of karmaic matter . 6.Nirjara : Eradication of karmic matter , accumulated in the soul, thereby resulting in all bondage 7. Moksha : is the release from worldly bondage - Kaivalya.

Jainism teaches rigorous self discipline to enable man to develop his spiritual dimensions. Withdrawal and aloofness from the world – Nivritti Marga – is the life of Jainism. This helps awakening of spiritual consciousness leading to Kaivalya , complete dissociation of Atman from Karmic matter. The three spiritual practices of Jainism are Samyak Darsana, Samyak Jnana, Samyak Charitra – Right Perspective, Right Knowledge and Right Conduct. The five vows known as Panchamahavratas dictate the conduct to be followed by both monks and householders, which are Ahimsa, Satya, Asteya, Aparigraha and Brahmacharya. However, Rules are separately enjoined to householders (Shravakas) and mendicants (Sadhus) . They are almost like the eight limbs of Patanjali Yoga.

The Jain tradition too adopts the Shabda-sadhana for spiritual progress. In the Namaskara (Namukkaro) Mantra the contemplation on "Om" is prescribed. The contemplation of Pranava or Omkara is performed independently also. This forms part of Shukla Dhyana an advanced stage in spiritual progress. The Mantras used are : *Om Namo Arihantanam, Om Namo Siddhanam, Om Namo Ayariyanam, Om Namo Uvajjhayanam, Om Namo Savvasahunam.* Also the 16 letters: "*Arhatsiddhacaryopadhyayasarvasadhubhyo namah* II"

It is believed that this five fold Namaskara wards off all sins, secures all auspiciousness and results in Moksha. This is combined with Pranayama too. It is also said that the place of concentration is Nasagra (top of the Nose – the seat of spirit). Dharma Dhyana, Shukla Dhyana are said to be leading to salvation, a spiritual regeneration. Several stages of spiritual development are described in detail which are called *Gunasthanas.*

YOGAVÂSISTA

Yogavâsista is a later version of Ramayana of about 8th to 10th centuries ascribed to Valmiki, like the Adhdyatma Ramayana. The main characters of the text are Vasistha, the teacher and Rama, the taught. Vasistha played a vital role in the education of the sons of King Dasaratha in their early age. They were initiated by Vasistha and were taught the Vedas and Sastras. The origination of Universe forms the main thesis of the work which says that this perceptual universe does not exist at all. It is only an appearance, like a mirage or dream. This appearance of the Universe is destroyed in dissolution like dreams in deep sleep. It reappears in next creation. So appearance does not really exist. What appears is only mind's creation. The ultimate reality is the pure extinction and what remains is *pure consciousness* (*Nirvāna and paro bodhah*). The ultimate reality is the *Sankalpa-purusha* that is Citta-deha of the form of *Manas* a Shakti of Brahman. Brahman is Cit – pure consciousness. Citta evolves from Brahman. It is through Citta, mind with powers of action, *spanda,* root desires (*Vasanas*) and mental modifications arise.

The self born first vibration, assumes the form of Citta. From this first vibration Citta is not different. This creation arising from Citta is not different from it. It is like the vibrations or movements that arise in the air. 'Cit' is pure consciousness and its manifestations are infinite – It is '*cidvilāsa*' or a play of consciousness. "This entire space is sheer consciousness in all its infinitude, perpetuity and eternity; it has neither beginning nor an end." It is transcendent to time and space continuum.

Vasistha says that Bhut*ākāśa* is simply a creation of Citt*ākāsa.* Whatever we see outside is just a projection of what lies within. But the world outside the individual remains the same even after his demise along with his Citt*ākāsa*. Vasistha found a way out of this difficulty by discovering the presence of *Cidākāsa*, the space of pure consciousness, as the cause. Both are products of the space of pure consciousness in the same sense in which activities of a day time are products of that day. The fact is confused only due to our ignorance.

Our inner being is thus Citta which is the same as *Manas, Buddhi, Ahankara* and the four taken together form the *Antahkarana* the inner organ. Cit acts as Citta owing to its direct inherence in Citta which is the first focal point of pure consciousness(Cit) forming the personality of the individual.

Cit – pure consciousness is the ultimate reality, it is all pervasive. Its all pervasiveness manifests as Bhutak*âs'a* as such. The consciousness manifests in course of time apparently through inconscient nature (*Prakṛti*) as *Cittâkâsa*, as Cit- aspect only and later as the aspect of expansion i.e. expansive '*âkâs'a*'. Thus *Cittâkâsa* is formed. *Chidâksa* is everything in this world, remaining itself as such in the midst of all variations and forms, only Cit being the Ultimate reality. Cittâ*kâsa* works as a framework of the limitations of time and space. Its sense of continuation gives rise to the idea of time while that of expansion results in the sense of space. Citta covers Cittâ*kâsa* out of *Cidâkâsa* and the 'I'-sense makes it all inclusive to itself. On the other hand *Manas* operates the same *Cittâkâsa* projecting its own fantasies and images on it. The boundless and infinite power of *Atman* with his will power operates as an artisan on the drawing board of *Cittâkâsa*. Atman with his tools makes, unmakes and remakes the impressions of the world on the clean board of consciousness as per his predilections, *Karmas* his field of operations being real and unreal worlds. Weaving out the web of its own it keeps the individual bound to the falsity of the world.

Thus *Manas, Buddhi, Ahankara, Citta, Akarma, Kalpanā, Vāsanā, Vidyā, Smṛti, Indriya, Prakṛti, Māyā, Kriyā* are all expressions of Parabrahman, the pure consciousness conceived differently due to ignorance of the all-comprehensiveness of reality. Pure consciousness itself appears in diverse forms through the medium of Citta. It is a delusion created due to ignorance of the real nature of pure consciousness. चिदकाशो हि पुरुषः चिदकाशो भवानयम्। चिदकाशो–हमजरः चिदकाशो जगत्त्रयम्।।

The world therefore has got to be looked upon in its proper perspective as being the same as real Brahman and therein lays liberation. To attain this highest state Vasistha gives four essentials –*S'ama*: Tranquility of mind; *Vichara*: Right thinking- knowing the purpose of life in the light of scriptural knowledge. *Santosha*: Contentment with whatever one has attained by practice of *yoga* and perseverance on the path as a lifelong work of transformation. *Sādhu-sanga*: Living in the association of people that is congenial to his practice of *Yoga*.

Yogavâsistha has an important discourse on *'daiva'* and *'paurusha'* destiny and self-effort. It lays special emphasis on free will 'Paurusha' and its immense possibilities. One should exert physically and mentally with the proper advice of wise people to counteract destiny *'daiva'*. What we did wrongly in the past can also be overcome by present actions. All efforts have to be made with directions of *S'astras* and *Gurus*. The objective of our endeavors in this life should be to counter the effects of destiny 'daiva' and to exert to attain the Supreme end of life. Yogavâsistha calls 'daiva' a fiction and calls for the efforts to counteract it as *'Spanda'* activity at different levels. Thought movement *samvit-spanda* gives rise to movement of psychosis. *Chetas spanda* is *manasspanda,* which gives rise to movement of 'organs of sense and actions' (*aindriya spanda*) i.e *spanda* of *jnânendriyas* and *Karmendriyas.* There is no mention of *daiva*, destiny anywhere. There is nothing called *'daiva'* (destiny). Root inclinations of instinct become 'Vasanas' and get transformed into Karmas, they are potential and active states of the same thing. *Daiva* is Karma performed with strong desire which is *manas* itself. *Manas is the real agent – Karmapurusha.* The movement in the world is *Kriyaspanda* caused by *manaspanda* (*Karma bijam manasspandah*). *Manas, Buddhi, Ahankara, Citta, Karma, Kalpana, Samsmriti, Vasana, Vidya, Prayatna, Smriti, Indriya, Prakriti, Maya, Kriya* are different only in name. They signify active functioning of *manas* or *Citta* which is the first movement, *spanda* of Self-consciousness. First movement is *manas*. As static it is *Buddhi*. Associating with mind and body it is 'I-sense' – *Ahankara*. With reflective thought with memory and anticipations of future it is *Citta*. While in activity it is *Karma*. Thus the seed of Karma is *manas*. *Karmabijam manas spanda*.. The actions that follow is *Kriya* conative functions.

To sum up:

- First self-conscious activity is *manas* (मनस).
- Then *Buddhi* (बुद्धि) and *Ahankara* (अहंकार) – awareness and 'I-sense'.
- Reflective thought is *Citta* (चित्त).
- Activity undertaken consequently is *Karma* (कर्म).
- Reverting to previous impressions is – memory – *'Sm.ti'* (स्मृति).
- When certain impressions dominate, it is *'Vâsanâ'* (वासना).
- Self knowledge giving rise to world appearance is *'Vidyâ'* (विद्या).
- World-appearance leads to impure states – *'malâ'* (मल).
- The functions of five senses are – *'Indriyâs'* (इंद्रिय).
- As the origin of this appearance, it is called *'Prakriti'* (प्रकृति).
- As the true state cannot be called existent or non-existent, it is *'Maya'*.

In fact *Brahman* is no different at any time. *'brahma tattvam anyath¯nasti'* (ब्रह्मम अन्यथा नास्थि). Emancipation can be attained in this lifetime (*Jivanmukti*) or after death (*Videha mukti*).

Mind *'Citta'* transforms into different states – *'Vṛttis'* due to *Prânaspanda* i.e. vibration of *Prana* on the one hand and on the other hand due to strong desires – *'dṛdha bhāvanās'*. When *Prâna* vibrates it flows through the nerves, the mind is known to be full of thought process (*samavedanamaya* समवेदनामय) and when it lies dormant in the hollows of veins (*'sirâ-sarani-kotare*) there is manifestation of mind. It is this *Prâna vibration* (*Prâṇaspanda*) that manifests as world appearance from nothing, as it were. It means that cessation of *Pranaspanda* is cessation of cognitive functions. With the vibration of *Prâna* cognitive functions setting in, knowledge manifests. To stop knowledge of the appearances one has to stop the vibration of *Prâṇa,* and *Citta.* We have to see that *Citta* awakes to the inner sense while shuts to the extraneous cognitive activities to attain the highest state. For attaining cessation of *Cittta* vibrations *'yogins'* control *Prâna* through *Pranayama* (breath regulation) and *Dhyâna* (meditation) under the guidance of an expert adept Guru. *Vâsanâs* and *Pranaspanda* are related to each other as seed and sprout (*bājānkuravat*). From *Vâsana*, there is *Prâṛaspanda* and from *Prâṇaspanda* there is *Vâasana.* With the cessation of knowledge, the objects of knowledge too cease immediately *samūlam nas'yata.* *kṛipram mūlacchedā*diva druma. (YV V 91-66). *Prâna* is *spanda-s'akti* operating in the upper body and *apâna* operates in the lower part. In wakeful and dream states natural *prâṇâyâma* goes on. Mental outgoing tendency of *Prâṇas* from heart is *Recaka* and drawing of the *Prânas* by the *apâna* activity is *Pūraka.* The internal is *Kumbhaka* *Bhusunda*, the long living crow taught this to Vasistha (VI-24). Body is house with ego, *Ahankâra* as the householder. It is supported by three pillars – *Vââta* (air), *Pitta* (bile) and *Kapha* (phlegm) or bony structure consisting of skull, trunk and legs. It has nine doors – seven in the head two below. It is tightly fitted with tendons, *Snâyus* as fastening materials and cemented with blood, flesh and fat. On the two sides are *ida* and *Pingalā* - the *Nâdis* in passive and unmanifest condition. There is also a machine (*Yantra*) of bone and flesh (*asthimamsamaya*) in the shape of three double lotuses (*padmayugma traya*) with pipes attached to them running up and down closing upon one another.

When petals move, air increases and passes to different places and it is differently named as – *Prana, Apana, Samana, Vyana* and *Udana.* It is the threefold machinery located in the heart that runs the *Prana* forces operating in all directions. *Prâna* current helps exhalation (*Recaka*), inhalation (*Pūraka*), respite is *Kumbhaka*; *Prâna* functions are due to movement of *Cittâ*- ultimately the movement of thought currents. Thus *spanda-nirodha* and *prâna-nirodha* are reciprocal. From *Prana* movement *Citta* functions and produces knowledge. Yogavasista suggests second alternative for control of mind, *Citta* e.g. concentration on an object- fixed breath control with meditation. Concentration of attention between the eye-brows whereby right knowledge dawns and *prâna* activity ceases. It is interesting to note that nowhere in the *Ayurveda* texts there is such clear description of respiratory process.

Seven stages (*Bhumikas*) of progress towards attainment of salvation are described:

1. In the first stage, the seeker has to cultivate wisdom by study of scriptures and association of Adepts
2. In the second stage called *Vicārana*, he should critically analyze their teachings.
3. In the third stage – *asanga-bhāvanâ*, he should mentally practice dissociation from passions.
4. Fourth stage is *Vilâpini* in which he should see the truth that the world appearance is false through his right understanding.
5. The fifth stage is that of *Jivanmukta* in which he is in a state of pure knowledge and bliss (*suddha-samvidmaya-ânandarūpa*); he remains half asleep and half awake (*ardha-supta - prabuddha*).
6. In the sixth stage he is in a state like that of deep dreamless sleep of pure bliss (*susupta sadṛsa- sthiti*), *Turiya*.
7. The seventh and the last stage is transcendental state termed as *turīyātīta*, which is attained by a saint departing from this body according to Yogavâsistha.

Among the above stages, the first three are *Jāgrat*, (waking state), while *Svapna* (dream state) and *Sushupti* (dreamless sleep state) are the 4th and 5th stages. The sixth is *Turiya* and the seventh is *Turiyātīta*. The *Vâsanâs* can be eradicated by constant application with patience (*dhairya*) and perseverance. The last stage is without any *spanda* (*aspanda*) and outward consciousness (*āvedana*). *Citta* is destroyed completely. It is *bodhâtmaka* ultimate entity of consciousness. It is *avyapadeśya* – indescribable and is variously called Brahman, Siva or the realisation of *Prakṛti* and *Purusha*. According the Yogavâsistha it is absolutely transcendental and indescribable. With universal negation (*sarvā*pahnava). It is '*pāsānavat samam*' – like a feelingless stone.

Following the above descriptions the *Jivas*, living beings are classified into seven categories:

*Svapna jā*grata: dream-awake, dream persons.

*Sankalpa jā*grata: without sleeping they imagine all sorts of things.

Kevala jāgrata sthita: who are born in this life for the first time.

Cira jāgrata sthita: he, who passed through more than one life already.

Ghana jāgrata sthita: those who are born as trees etc., due to their sins.

Jāgrata svapna: those in course of their transmigration study and get good association and attain right knowledge.

Kshina jāgrata:those who reached the Turiya state of deliverance.

When all objects and knowledge cease, his bondage (*bandha*) is gone and deliverance results. The seeker can achieve this end through control of attachment and right knowledge.

Aesthetic experience : Camatkara or aesthetic delight is declared to be the effect of all the recognised seven factors contributing to poetic (artistic) beauty. In common parlance, the term 'Camatkara' means wonder. The term acquired a special signification in Sanskrit poetics, where it denotes poetic (aesthetic) delight. The traditional etymology of the word is that, 'camat' is the present participle of the verbal root 'cam' meaning taste, eat and hence enjoy. Thus, 'camattvam' means getting immersed in tasting or enjoyment of something, particularly of an aesthetic or mystical kind. The word may also be explained as a case of onomatopoeia—the imitation thus akin to 'Rasa' . Gnoli observes: "It is is compounded of 'camat' and 'kara'; 'camat', which occurs only in this expression, is probably no more than an interjection, expressing surprise or wonder while 'kara' (from 'kr') means the act of emitting such an interjection, of finding oneself in this state of consciousness." He says further that "it may be said equally that 'camat' is a nondiscursive phonic expression consisting of a vocality animated by a form of consciousness which arises from the very rhythm of our interior movement."

The first appearance of the word in the aesthetic literature is in the Abhinavabharati of Abhinavagupta, in course of the commentary on the famous Rasasutra. It is given there as a synonym of Rasa. Camatkara is described as an awareness devoid of obstacles. It is an uninterrupted state of immersion in an enjoyment, characterized by the presence of a sensation of inner fullness. It is also characterized by a kind of movement 'spanda', the inner rhythm of the aesthetic experience which is an inner perception, like pleasure, pain, etc., and in this sense is not of a discursive order. Ksmendra observes that Aucitya is the life of Rasa and the contemplation thereof brings about Camatkara or poetic delight. The word is taken from 'Prakasastra' as is the case with words like Rasa. It appears that originally the word Camatkara was an onamotopaeic word referring to the clicky sound we make with our tongue, when we taste something snappy and in the course of its semantic enlargements, Camatkara came to mean a sudden fillip relating to any feeling of a pleasurable type. Camatkara is what produces a continual experience of extraordinary pleasure in the mind of the learned. Poetry is defined as a linguistic expression possessing such a quality. All other poetic elements including Rasa, are considered as contributory factors.

The definition may be compared favourably with that of Jagannatha.

According to Jagannatha, Camatkara is aesthetic delight, produced by all art, and when it is produced through the communicative power of language such linguistic expression is known as Kavya. In this manner, the meaning of the word Camatakara is expanded and it has evolved into one that denotes aesthetic experience in the most comprehensive sense of the term. This includes the pleasurable effect of Rasa realization, the poetic appeal of Alamkaras, Aucitya, Riti etc. Bharatrihari, the great linguistic philosopher of India, speaks of Shabda Brahma as Ultimate Reality without beginning or end from which all objective world has manifested. It is one becoming many without losing its oneness. The manifestation is mulitiplicity in Being, itself becoming as experiencer, experienced and experience. A baby is born with seeds of knowledge and of know-how, when due to the working of its past karmas called adrista, which is the force generated by its deeds in previous lives, its Shabdabhavana, the capacity to express through language which is aroused in this life. The baby is enabled to understand and act. The creative capacity is called Pratibha which is explained as creative consciousness. This is later accepted as the source of artistic creations and experience all the more. It is at the source of art creation and art appreciation. It is *Prajna navanavonmeshasalini Pratibha mata* –Abhinavagupta. (Intuitive consciousness giving rise to ever new creations is called Pratibha).

Ayurveda – Science of Life and Living Beings

The purpose of life is to know or realize the Creator - Cosmic Consciousness and to express this divinity in day-to-day life. Ayurveda is the Science and Art of daily living in harmony for God Realization. Health and hygiene as well as curing diseases (disorders) are the aims of Ayurveda. Interdisciplinary and holistic approach is expected of the doctors. The source of our existence is Universal Spiritual Consciousness manifesting as *Purusha* and *Prakriti*. Ayurveda follows more or less the *Samkhya System* of philosophy with emphasis on the twenty-four *Prakritis* and *Purusha,* and three *Gu.as* of *Sattva, Rajas* and *Tamas*. Body, mind and soul exist together as one unit as tripod of life. All the things in the universe coexist in harmony. The combination of body, sense organs, mind and soul is called living being (आयु) life. Body and senses are perishable and insentient. Soul is imperishable and sentient. Body and sense organs establish contact with soul through mind. Synonyms of Ayu are Nityaga, Anubandha, Dhari and Jivita.

The constituent elements of the universe and the human body are the same. Whatever is there in the universe is present in the human body and whatever is there in the human body is present in the universe. Earth, water, fire, air and space along with unmanifest soul comprise individual Purusha. The same are there in the macrocosm. The

Upanishads explain – "आयु: प्राण: । य प्राण: सा वायु: ।" Ayu and Prana are one and the same principle and Prana and Vayu are identical. Everything in this world are waves of this ether endowed with motions (सर्वमित्याकाशं).

Vayu is the universal store of energy (संवर्ग:). In the physical (inanimate) world it is called Vayu and in the living (animate) world it is called *Prana*. The agent that adjusts the internal relations with external relations is Ayus and Ayus is life. That Ayus is a motion of the ethereal fluid which is "खं" in Sanskrit (akasha). It is sum total of various biological and a-biological energies which, under the names of heat, light, electricity, consciousness etc. manifest in the physical and metaphysical world. Prana is another name for that 'force'(Chaitanya Prana). In acting on an aggregated living body it divides itself into five distinct forces viz. *Prana, Apana, Samana, Udana* and *Vyana*. It also sub-serves the functions of correlation (*Vayu* or *Vata*), sustenance (*Pitta*) and controls oxidation (*Sleshma* or *Kapha*). In this way *Prana* continuously works and adjusts internal and external relations like the main-spring of a watch. Sankaracharya explains this clearly: The primary fluid that is endowed with motion in its evolution of life gets knotted into five divisions – Prana, Apana, Samana, Udana, Vyana and this acting on aggregated living mater is called Prana. This is the Biology of Hindus, Ayurveda on the basis of which Indian Medical Science is developed. Magnetism, Hydropathy, Genesiology and Anesthetics, Dissection, Avagharshana are parts of Ayurveda. The above facts viewed scientifically convince us about the truth that they contain gems of quite a few of present day achievements and help in improving upon the quality of our researches now for the benefit of humanity.

'Sankhya' system of philosophy is the basis for Ayurveda:

The Sankhya Philosophy is almost accepted in the Vedanta. It is also nearer to modern Science. The Sankhya theory of creation is adapted in many later systems like the Kashmiri Saivism, Yogavasishta and Ayurveda. The Sankhya System speaks of twenty five categories (Tattvas). In fact it recognizes two fundamental Tattvas – Purusha and Prakriti. Purusha is the intelligent principle that inspires Prakriti to create . He is neither the cause nor the effect while Prakriti in its unmanifest state forms (the Mulaprakriti), fundamental cause of Creation It inherently possesses three characteristics – Satva , Rajas and Tamas – intelligence, activity and inertia which in its unmanifeste state remain in equlibirium. From Prakriti came Mahat (Buddhi) which gives raise to Ahankara, Self-sense-individuation. The gunas inherent in it take different courses of development from Ahankara. From Sattva aspect of Ahankara also called Vaikarika are produced the Manas, the five organs of perception and the five organs of action. From the tamasa aspect of Ahankara (called also bhutadi) the fine five elements of tanmatras are created. The Taijas aspect namely Rajasa plays its role in the two processes. From the five Tanmatras are produced the five gross elements by preponderance of Tamas. In all these while one guna is prominent the others too help the process of evolution.

Pususha is pure consciousness, pure awareness. It is an abstraction of Universal knowledge. The Prakriti with all its evolutes forms the object of Buddhi while Purusha is aloof. He is mistaken to be the subject and hence the suffering. When he realises his Kaivalya aloofness, he is released. Experiences occur on account of false identity of the Purusha as doing something with Prakriti and its products. Once he realizes his folly he is freed and he shines in pristine consciousness.

Remaining static in his own state, the Purusha witnesses Prakriti as an observer. Purusha is the male principle and Prakriti is the female principle. Purusha wills and Prakriti creates the universe from its womb. Three universal qualities of Sattva, Rajas and Tamas (Pure existence, Movement and Inertia) belong to Prakriti and they remained in equilibrium in it before creation. When the equilibrium is disturbed by will of Purusha, interaction between the Gunas takes place affecting the evolution of creation. 'Rajas' is the active vital force while 'Sattva' and 'Tamas' are inactive potential energies. Sattva is the creative potential force of Brahma; Rajas is protective kinetic force of Vishnu and Tamas is resistance to change and is a destructive force of Mahesha. These are the three manifestations of Anahata Shabda 'AUM' – ॐ. Prakriti first manifests as Buddhi- (Mahat) Intelligence. It gives rise to 'I' sense – Ahankaara which comes under the influence of Gunas. Sattva and Rajas influence Ahankara to produce five organs of sense, five organs of action and the Mind. Under the influence of Rajas and Tamas, Ahankara produces the basic subtle forms of five elements – Tanmatras of Akasha, Vayu, Agni, Apas and Prithivi to create inorganic universe. Substances with sensory organization are sentient beings and others insentient.

Out of this absolute and Original Nature evolves the Universe. It is the material out of which the bodies of self-consciousness (*Karma Purusha*) working agent (who comes into being through the dynamical energy of the acts or *Karmas*) evolve. Out of that unmanifest original latent Avyakta Prakriti impregnated by atoms or elemental units of Consciousness or Purusha, Mahat is evolved – (Intellection) and out of Mahat, egoism.

Universal consciousness manifests as	
Purusha	*Prakriti*
(Passive energy) Witness to creation	With three *Gunas* is the field of action. When their equilibrium is disturbed creation takes place ⬇
	Mahat (Intellect) Buddhi ⬇
	Ahankara ('I' Consciousness) ⬇
	Tanmatras
	Five sense organs, five motor organs, five *pranas* and Mind (5+5+5+1)

Prakriti = Latent (unmanifest) supreme nature, self-begotten with three primary virtues of Sattva, Rajas and Tamas is the progenitor of all created things, imagined as embodied in the eightfold categories: Avyakta - Unmanifest; Mahan - intellection; Ahankara - Egoism.

Five Tanmatras are elemental properties of the senses. Mahat partakes of the three qualities Sattva etc., Egoism in its turn gets the three qualities –

Ahankara as Vaikarika (Sattvika), Taijasa (Rajasika) operative, Bhutadi (Tamasika) illusive.

Vaikarika and Taijasa Ahankara, cooperating with each other produced the eleven organs- five of cognition, five of communication and mind, partaking the character of intellectual and operative organs alike.

Sattva	Rajas	Tamas	
Adhesion	Cohesion	Disintegration	Physical plane
Affection	Love	Hate	Moral plane
Emancipation	Spiritual affinity	Sin	Psychic plane

Tutelary Gods are Buddhi–Brahma, Ahankara-Isvara, Manas-Chandra.

All 24 *Tattvas* as its prime cause, Mula Prakriti are bereft of consciousness. Purusha, the self-conscious subjectivity enters Mula Prakriti and its evolutes and makes them endowed with Self-Consciousness.

These twenty four primary principles, though unconscious in themselves, contribute towards making the self-conscious Self or the Universal individual (the aggregate of limited or conditional selves) for the purpose of working out his final liberation or emancipation i.e.

attainment of the stage of pure consciousness or perfect knowledge.

Purusha (individual soul) is nothing but a combination of a self-conscious self and the five kinds of (Mahabhutas) matter formed into an organic body. He is called *Karma purusha,* individual of action. The Purushas desire pleasure and avoid pain. They get associated with Prana, Buddhi and Manas. They have different temperaments – Sattvika, Rajasa and Tamasika. They undergo disease and death sooner. Thus the characteristics of three *Gunas* enter into successive elements.

Mind consists of five *Tanmatric* substances. External objects made up of gross elements come into contact with the senses which in their turn stimulate the inner senses- *tanmatras* constituting the mind. These five Tanmatras are our doorways of perception, the innermost instruments of experience. The outer objects stimulate the inner senses through which the mind comes into contact with the outer object by way of the inner *tanmatras* which results in our experience of perception. The Tanmatras are thus the doors of perception and instruments of experience. Manas is unconscious, yet active. Spirit activates it. Associated with the spirit, Mind is attributed with actions belonging to Spirit. Atman is endowed with consciousness and is hence called the *Actor*. Manas is unconscious, so it is not called *Actor* even though it acts. Mind is unitary and atomic in nature. Unity and atomicity are its characteristics. Mind has knowledge but knowledge is attributed to it when associated with Atman and Indriyas, it is then appears sentient. All that forms the object is called Artha. It includes whatever is thought of, reasoned, imagined, contemplated and intended.

Ten Dravyas(substances):

दस द्रव्य :- 0) तमस, 1) आकाश, 2) वायु, 3) अग्नि, 4) जल, 5) पृथ्वी, 6) काल, 7) दिशा (दिक), 8) मन और 9) आत्मा

0.	Tamas	6	Kala:	Nervous system
1.	Akash	7	Disha:	Mid Brain
2.	Vayu	8	Manas:	Limbic system
3.	Agni	9	Atma:	Nucleus
4.	Jal			
5.	Prithvi			

Tridoshas (Biological Humors):

Sattva	Rajas	Tamas
Vata	Pitta	Kapha
Air	Fire	Water

Three *Doshas* are Biological Humors: The five elements manifest in body as three basic principl es call ed 'Tridoshas'. Akasha and Vayu give rise to Vata, Agni and Apas give rise to Pitta and Apas and Prithvi give rise to Kapha. These three Doshas govern the functions of the body and determine its constitution. When they are in balance a person is normal and when they are out of balance disease is caused.

Dhatus - the biological tissues

Dhatus	**Upadhatus**	**Their Physical functions**
Rasa (chyle, lymph, blood plasma)	Stanya (mammary glands). Artava (menstrual blood and lactation)	Nourishment
Rakta (red bloodcells)	Shira (blood vessels) Kandara (muscles, tendons)	Invigoration
Mamsa (skeletal muscle)	Snayu (flat muscles) Tvacha (skin)	Covering the skeleton
Meda (fat in limbs and torso)	Sneha (subcutaneous fat)	Lubrication
Asthi	Danta (teeth)	Support
Majja (bone marrow)	Head hair	Filling space
Shukra and Artava(male and female reproductive fluids)	Ojas (produces aura & controls immunity)	Reproduction

Dhatus:

Food nourishes the body getting transformed into seven 'Dhatus' – (Tissues) one from the other successively according to Charaka, Rasa : blood plasma; Rakta : blood (red blood cells); Mamsa : skeletal muscle; Meda : fat in limbs and torso; Asthi : bones; Majja : bone marrow; Shukra & Artava : male and female reproductive fluids.

***Upadhatus*:**

Correspondingly there are seven Upadhatus arising from each one of them:

Rasa : Stanya (mammary glands - lactation), Artava (menstural blood)
Rakta : Shira (blood vessels), Kandara (muscle tendons)
Mamsa : Snayu (flat muscles), Tvacha (skin)
Meda : Snayu (subcutaneous fat)
Asthi : Danta (teeth)
Majja : Head's Hair
Shukra & Artava : Ojas (produces aura and controls immunity)

Ojas:

The white yellowish red fluid that is in the heart is called '*Ojas*' (the refined essence of all tissues in the body). It is life sustaining fluid. Owing to its loss a person dies. It is produced during the process of nutrition. It is – albumin, protein and globulin – contributing to immunity. Inferior Ojas moves all over the body; superior Ojas is in the heart. Ojas moves through plasma.

Tejas:

Tejas is like hormones and amino-acids. Tejas (Agni) is necessary for cellular and nuclear metabolism. It is responsible for intelligence, understanding and comprehension at the cellular level. Every cell is a centre of awareness and consciousness, and it is the unit of life.

Prana:

Prana is a continuous flow of consciousness between any two cells of the body. That 'flow' of consciousness i.e. flow of intelligence is called *Prana*. Prana is the bridge between mental and physical bodies. Spirit is consciousness which activates *Prana* and body through mind. Ayurveda assays physical, mental, emotional and spiritual components of life. Subjective experiences are reflected in mind while objective barometers are connected to the body. Objectivity is limited while subjectivity is unlimited.

Mind communicates with subtle forces of *Tanmatras*. Sum total of cellular consciousness.

Vibrations of thoughts, feelings and emotions from *manas* and body disturb the movement of *Pranas*.

The five sheaths of the soul are five energy fields. They resolve into three bodies. Physical body (*Annama ya Kosha*), Astral Body comprises *Pranamaya Kosha*, *Manomaya Kosha* and *Vijnanamaya Kosha* – Etheric Body, Mental Body and Emotional Body. They are Sheaths of Prana, Mind and Intelligence. Bliss Body is sheath of Bliss – *Anandamaya Kosha*. Sushumna passes through all these bodies centrally.

Chakras:

Chakras are energy centers or points of concentration of physical, mental and spiritual energies. If the flow of energy in any of these centers is blocked, stress is reflected in the physiology of man which can be detected by reading the pulse at appropriate level. In the Cranial Cavity of the head there is the brain – the meninges, duramater, archnoid, grey matter and white matter. Inside the core of white matter there is space. There are small spaces between neurons called Synaptic spaces. The synaptic space in between the neurons is functionally connected to the space within the brain called Chidakasha. It is within that space the pulsation of Prana and flow of Ojas and Tejas are felt. Chakras in Pind Desh, Material Region may be perceived in some yogic practices. They are reflections of six kamals in Brahmanda region of Universal mind which are themselves reflections of six Padams in the Pure Spiritual Region, Nirmal Chetan Desh. These are microcosmic centres corresponding to macrocosmic regions. It is only the human body that has all the eighteen centres. Saints advise their devotees to begin their practice of spiritual awakening from the seat of the spirit in the physical body namely Ajna Chakra/Tisra Til and further from Sahasdal Kamal in Brahmanda. The five chakras get dissolved at the time of death which is called Pinda Pralaya.

CHAKRA	POSITION	TATTVA
Ajna	Between Eyes	Atman/Surat
Vishuddha	Throat	Ether, Space/Akasha
Anahata	Heart	Air, Vayu
Manipura	Navel	Fire, Agni
Swadhisthana	Genital	Water, Jala
Muladhara	Rectal	Earth, Prithvi

Soul in Ajna Chakra controls all bodily functions through mind from here – physiological, biological, electrochemical;

Ajna : Do-dal kamal.
Pituitary gland and hypothalamus.

Vishuddha : Endocrinal glands thyroid and parathyroid

Anahata : Controls anabolism and catabolism (metabolism);
Protection and destruction of physical body through organization of Pranas, subtle

	life energy.
Manipura :	Controls pancreas, digestive system
Svadisthana :	Gonadal endocrine glands
Muladhara :	Solid aspects of body elimination; adrenal glands

The Yoga system of philosophy supplies the modus operandi of practical exercises for the Purusha to get released. Ego sense creates minds. Of the minds created, the one with originality controls all of them. That mind which is purified by Dhyana gets freed from Karmas, latent impressions and cravings. While the Karma of the yogi is neither white not black, the karmas of others are white (good) or black (bad) or mixed. Several tendencies(vasanas) are produced by the karmas and only those become manifest which have favourable conditions. The cause and effect chain of vasanas with impressions producing actions and thought continues through lives. It is operating beginning-less. Even the subconscious tendencies that exert in the mind are stimulated by the sense objects. Though the objects change, their impressions persist in the mind. The mind of the liberated soul without any impressions along with gunas is resolved back into Prakriti- undifferentiated matter. Ignorance, the cause of suffering ceases. Atman shines in its pristine nature of pure Consciousness.

Bhagavad Gita

According to Sir Sahabji Maharaj, the central teaching of the Gita lies in the concluding section of the XVth Chapter. There are two forces at work in this creation, kshara the perishable and akshara the imperishable. All the objects of the world are perishable and the unchangeable Atman is imperishable. There is another purusha superior to both these forces who is all pervasive and the basis of all the three worlds. He is called the Purushottama and according to the author of the Gita, Lord Krishna is the incarnation of this Purushottama and the highest spiritual benefit consists in attaining Him. Sant Mat states that the Nirmal Chetan Desh is above these regions of Kshara, Akshara and Niha –Akshara of Mahasunna. Sir Sahabji Maharaj says 'In my opinion, the basic teaching of the Gita is that man should seek the Lord in human form and when he comes into contact with Him, he should act according to His orders. However, if one is not able to meet the Lord in human form, he should remember Him as best as he can and perform his duty.'

Sant Mat

According to Param Guru Sahabji Maharaj – "The greatest discovery that has been made or that shall ever be and the highest truth that has been communicated to humanity or that shall ever be, is that there is nothing higher or nobler than Atman. There is no truth higher than God and no enjoyment higher than God realization."

The Supreme Being the Infinite Source of spirituality, *Sat, Chit, Anand, Prem, Prakash* in His unbounded Mercy and Grace incarnated in human form as *Param Purush Puran Dhani Soamiji Maharaj* and founded the Radhasoami Satsang on the auspicious day of *Basant Panchami* in 1861. It is only with the advent of Param Purush Puran Dhani Soamiji Maharaj that the Ultimate Consciousness or the Super Consciousness of the highest order has been revealed in the Religion of Saints.

The most significant Religious Phenomenon of Progressive Revelation is clearly enunciated by Soamiji Maharaj in Sarbachan (18-2) which starts with the Stanza:

गुरु की कर हरदम पूजा। गुरु समान कोइ देव न दूजा।। 1।।

....

गुरु ब्रह्मरुप धर आये। गुरु पार ब्रह्म गति गाये ।। 5।।
गुरु सत्त नाम पद खोला। गुरु अलख अगम को तोला ।। 6।।
गुरु रूप धरा राधास्वामी। गुरु से बड़ नहीं अनामी ।। 7।।

Worship the Guru every moment. There is no other God on par with Guru.....the Guru manifested himself in the form of Brahma and the Guru Himself talked about the Glory of 'Para Brahma'. Guru unraveled the abode of Sattnam and of Alakh and Agam Regions. 'Radhasoami' assumed the form of Guru, even Anami is not superior to the Guru.

Consciousness levels explained

Intensity of refulgence and subtlety of sounds has been the criterion by which, different levels of consciousness are distinguished. Analogies are given such as the brightness of candle flame, rising sun, moon and sun and further myriads of suns and moons. The music of gong, percussion instruments, string instruments, wind instruments, and so on is given as analogy of sounds. As the sounds are heard in trance, their expression in articulate speech nearing the spoken language of the revealing saints varies. However, the great teachers have also given their correspondence in clear terms thus emphasizing the truth that the internal path being the same, the pursuit of the reverberating primeval internal sound from the lower centers to that of its origin in the Pure Spiritual Region. Sarbachan Bachan 25 – Shabda2 substantiates this – explaining the states of consciousness in detail.

जग जाग्रत भौः दुःख मूल। सुपना भी दुःख सुख सूल ।।
सुशपति कुछ घर आराम। वह भी नहिं ठहरन धाम ।।
तीनों में भरमत आठों जाम। पूरा नहीं कहीं बिसराम ।।

....

कर दया भेद बतलाया। तुरिया पद मारग गाया।।
तुरिया के आगे बरना। फिर उस से आगे चलना।।
तिस के भी परे लखाया। उस के भी पार सुनाया।।
तिस परे और समझाया। कुछ आगे और बुझाया।।
वहाँ से पुनि आगे भाशा। निज धाम मुख्य यह राहा।।

....

सतगुरु फिर भेद बतावें। अब खुलकर तोहि सुनावें।।
तुरिया पद सहस कंवल में। तिस आगे चढ़ त्रिकुटि में।।
दस द्वारा सुन में खोलो। फिर महासुन्न चढ़ तोलो।।
चढ़ भंवरगुफा तब आई। फिर सत्तनाम पद पाई।।
वहाँ से भी चली अगाडी। हुई अलख पुरुष दरबारी।।
जाय अगम लोक को लीन्हीं। लीला सब वहाँ की चीन्हा।।
राधास्वामी धाम लखाया। अब यही ठीक घर पाया।।

-- *Sarbachan* B25,S2

Translation:

The wakeful state is a source of fear and pain and the dream state too is full of pains and pleasures. The deep sleep gives some relief but does not last long. One passes through these three states daily with no rest. The Satguru took pity on the Jiva and disclosed the secret of the fourth state and the way to attain it. He described the state beyond and also the one beyond that. He showed the state still beyond and also one further. He explained the state beyond and made known the one beyond that. Telling about the further state, He spoke of His Original Abode (The Regions of Param Sants) – The Satguru disclosed the secret in clear terms. The fourth state is in Sahasdal Kamal. The next state is up in Trikuti. In Sunn, the Tenth Gate of Saints opens. One goes up to the Mahasunn from there. Above that come Bhanwargupha and then the abode of Sat Nam. Going further up from there, the Spirit goes in front of Alakh Purush. Goes further to Agam Lok and sees the splendor thereof. Finally, the Sant Satguru showed the Region of Radhasoami, which is rightly, the Original Abode.

We may compare this with the Shabdas of Kabir Sahab to establish their correspondence:

कर नैनों दीदार महल में प्यारा है।।
कर नैनों दीदार पिंड से न्यारा है।।
है तिल के तिल के तिल भीतर बिरले साधू पाया है।।

Kabir Sahab quoted in Yatharth Prakash II P.302

The modern holistic studies in Human Possibilities, Spectrum of Consciousness and Emergence of Transcendental Systems, can be made inclusive of higher states of Consciousness that have been revealed by Rishis, Munis, Buddhas, Prophets, Sufis, Sants and Param Sants. The researchers so far have considered and included the states of Consciousness of practitioners of Yoga techniques known in the extant major religions but not those of Sufis, Sants and Param Sants.

In Sar Bachan (B24-1) (Maya Samvad) Soamiji Maharaj clearly states that the true Supreme Being is in the Fourth Loka which is beyond the three lokas i.e. 'the Region of Sants' by adopting the Surat Sabd Marg. The extant religions did not teach about that region. Guru Nanak, Kabir Sahab, have unequivocally spoken of *Sachch Khand* and *Satt Lok*:

नानक और कबीर बखाना। तुलसी साहब निज कर जाना ।। 122 ।।
उनकी बानी वह पद गावे। सच्चखंड सतलोक लखावे ।। 123 ।।

'Hidayatnama' contains the essential teachings of the Radhasoami Faith. It is, intended to *Adhikaris*, who earnestly seek instructions regarding the nature of Supreme Being and the method to reach Him. Proceeding in his investigations of True Religion, he (*Adhikari*) resorts to the company of a *'Guru'* who is an adept in the practice of listening to the internal sounds, that is a *Sant* practicing *'Surat Shabda Yoga'* or a *Fakir* practicing '*Sultan-ul-Azkar*'. Such a *Guru* explains to him the secrets of the true religion, when He is pleased. The glory of spiritual regions is explained in detail with enormous dimensions of time and space and the joy and bliss of experiences at the higher levels in terms of a picturesque imagery of sweet sounds and beautiful sights as also the fragrance of smell of the surroundings and delicious taste of ambrosial fluids of those regions.

At the conclusion, Soamiji Maharaj states that none except Sants and Fakirs know the secrets. The earlier seers and prophets taught about the intermediary stages. Our teachings do only appeal to persons who have abiding faith and trust in the Sants and Fakirs and their majesty and their exalted status. That is why those who have such full faith should alone be given these teachings.

Similarly, at the conclusion of *Barah Masa*, after singing the glory of *Jeth* Month, Soamiji Maharaj observes:- "I have not left out anything; I have spoken the truth repeating it several times in different ways. I have nothing to do with either victory or defeat being far above them. I conclude saying ' I have spoken the truth and nothing but the truth, the whole truth' - "Repeat the Name Radhasoami, chasten your mind for devotion and reverence to Him".

Soamiji Maharaj explained the teachings of earlier Seers, Prophets, Sufis and Sants giving them their right place. He has not only described the present state of their followers' indulgence in external worship but also brought out the profundity and depth of their esoteric philosophy and practices which the followers of those traditions themselves do not know now-a-days.

Huzur Maharaj explained the descent of the spirit in detail naming the various stations through which it traversed. The Original Abode of the spirit is Anami Pad (nameless abode Radhasoami). A sound wave came down through two stages of Agam and Alakh and settled in Satt Loka of pure spiritual luminosity. This is called as 'Hoot' by Mohammedans. Below Satt Loka is Bhavangupha which is called *Hootal Hoot* by Fakirs. Below that region is Sunn or Dasam-Dwar which is called Hahoot and below that is Trikuti, also called 'Lahoot'.

All these places high or low are inside the body. The material (coarse) stages end below the eyes, therefore, the limit of *Pind* is up to the eyes and on this account it is known as the area of the nine apertures. Above the eyes the region of *Brahmanda* starts from the plain of *Sahasdal Kamal* and it is what is known as *Parabrahma*. Beyond the plain of *Mahasunn* is *Dayal Desh*. Huzur Maharaj revealed the various stations the spirit traverses to attain the final abode with similar levels enunciated in Sufism also with details of the names and positions according to Sant Mat.

The following are the details of their names and positions according to the 'Religion of Saints' (*Sant Mat*):-

1. The ganglion at the rectum (*Guda Chakra*) – the *kamal* of four *dals* (four petalled Lotus) – the abode of Ganesh. As the *'Yoga Abhyas'* (spiritual practice) in earlier times was being commenced from this place, therefore the householders on observing the *yogis* do the *puja* of Ganeshji at the start of every work.
2. The ganglion at the organ of reproduction— (*Indri Kamal*) – of six *dals* (six petalled Lotus) – the abode of *Brahma* or the creative power.
3. The nervous centre at the navel (*nabhi kamal*) of eight *dals* (eight petalled Lotus) – the abode of Vishnu or power of preservation. These three places i.e. *guda, indri* and *nabhi kamal* are called ***Nasoot* by Mohammedans.**
4. Ganglion situated at the lower end of the sternum (*Hriday Kamal*) of twelve *dals* (twelve petalled Lotus) – the abode of *Shiv Shakti*.
5. The ganglion situated at throat (*Kanth Chakra*) of sixteen *dals* – (sixteen petalled Lotus) – the abode of *Durga* or the power of regulating desire and spirit.
6. Third *Til* or *Netra* which is also known as *Shiv Netra, Shyam Swet* etc. of two *dals* (two petalled Lotus) – the abode of the spirit i.e. *Param Atma*. The spirit should be concentrated here in the beginning. It is connected with the string of *Antahkaran* and the ten *indriyas* etc. are connected with the *Antahkaran*. The

Mohammedans call these three stations i.e. *Hriday Kamal, Kanth Chakra* and *Tisra Til* as ***'Malkoot'***. This is the limit of coarse or worldly stations.

7. *Sahasdal Kamal – Swet Shyam* of eight *dals* (eight petalled Lotus)— the abode of *Jyoti Niranjan*. Two heavenly sounds emanate from here i.e. two *Shabdas* manifest here. It is by following them the spirit ascends.
8. *Trikuti – kamal of* four *dals* – abode of *'Om'* – this is the *Trikuti* of Saints and not of *Jogeswars* and is known as *'Hamsamukhi'*. Mohammedans call these two *kamals* i.e. *Sahasdal Kamal* and *Trikuti* as ***Jabroot* and *Lahoot***.
9. *Sunn* or *Dasvan Dvar – kamal* of one *dal* – abode of *Parabrahma* – Muslim Fakirs call it *Hahoot*. The subtle or celestial regions end here.
10. *Mahasunn*—here four *Shabdas* (sounds) and five stations are hidden (occult).
11. *Bhanwargupha* – Mohammdens call it ***Hutalhoot***, abode of *Sohang Purush*. This is not the *Sohang* of the breath. These two places i.e. *Mahasunn* and *Bhanwargupha* are within the limits of *Dayal Desh.*
12. *Sat Loka* – Mohammedans call it ***Hoot*** – abode of *Sat Purush*. There are three more *pads* (stations) above it. Earlier Saints have not disclosed and mentioned them. By *Mouj*, Huzur Radhasoami Dayal has now clearly revealed and described them.

Thus, Radhasoami Faith propounds that the Cosmos consists of three Grand divisions, the purely material region called Pind, the material-spiritual region called Brahmand and the purely spiritual region called Dayal Desh or the Nirmal Chetan Desh as per the sub-divisions indicated in the chart below:

THE COSMOS			
Microcosm		Macrocosm	
PIND : PHYSICAL		**BRAHMAND : MENTAL**	**NIRMAL CHETAN DESH : SPIRITUAL**
Ajna -	Chandra	Sunn	Radhasoami
Visuddha-	Surya	Trikuti	Agam
Anahata -	Prithvi	Sahasdal Kamal	Alakh
Manipura -	Brihaspati	Vishnu Lok	Anami
Svadhisthana -	Sani	Brahm Lok	Sat Lok
Muladhara -	Varun	Shiv Lok	Bhanwargupha

The study of the human cosmos, the microcosm is the most practical and convenient method for a comprehension of universal cosmos, the macrocosm.

Correspondence and communion with macrocosm for the microcosm is made possible by means of apertures or gateways provided in the microcosm. At the lower level, we experience heat or cold outside through the sense of touch i.e., by means of sensory currents present in the pores of the skin. In the case of sense of sight it is the optic nerve through which communion with the outward light takes place. Light from the object penetrates the crystalline lens in the eye and produces an image on the retina. Perception takes place thereafter by means of the optic nerve and the sensory currents present therein. The optic nerve is phosphorescent containing light and by means of it communion with outward light takes place. The sensory currents complete the process of perception. Similar is the case with other senses as well. It may, therefore be propounded in the form of a law that for the perception of the macrocosm, the Spirit Current must get associated at the proper apertures in the microcosm with substances and powers similar to those that exist in the macrocosm. Communion between the various spheres of creation and the nerve centers, which correspond to them, is established in accordance with the law specified above. A special training is necessary by means of which alone the innermost functions of the nerve centers lying ordinarily dormant are developed and brought up to the condition in which communion is made possible.

The brain is the most important of the organs of the body. Though different parts of the brain have been mapped out with reference to their functions in regulating the lower nature of man, we do not yet have the knowledge of the functions of the brain with reference to its higher nature i.e., the dimensions of the higher mind and the spirit. Apparently, the nerves , nerve centers and brain are responsible for the growth and sustenance of the human frame. On close examination, we come to know that these functions take place automatically because even in the vegetable kingdom, where the nerves and ganglia are absent, growth and sustenance take place. This clearly shows that the nerves, nerve centers and brain, which is the reservoir of nerve-power, have other important functions to perform other than growth and sustenance of the physical frame. They are subjective functions of perception, volition etc. However, these functions too are not entirely dependent upon nerves etc. for their functioning. These functions are operative even in conditions like trance when they suddenly manifest. It is clear that the human body is possessing potentialities, which may manifest by proper training. Underlying the planes of ordinary functions there are subtler planes within the nervous system and the innermost part of each nerve center is associated with the subtle plane specific to that center. When these planes of nerve centers are acted upon, communion with the corresponding macrocosmic spheres is established and the powers of the presiding deities (reservoirs of power) of those macrocosmic spheres are imbibed.

There are twelve apertures situated in the fissure between the two lobes of the brain through which communion with the six subdivisions of Brahmand and six subdivisions of Pure Spiritual Region can be established. They are situated respectively in the grey matter and white matter of the brain. The innermost quarters of these apertures are the gateways as it were to the higher Spiritual Regions. The channels through which the spirit entity descends and ascends the various regions are also clearly explained in the Religion of Saints: Sushumna and Banknal upto Trikuti, Gandharpa Nal upto Sunn and Rukmani Nal upto Bhanwargupha.

Certain Yoga practices are prescribed by the Seers and the Saints for holding communion with higher spiritual planes and the higher spirituality of those spheres and their levels of consciousness. The Radhasoami Faith prescribes **Surat Shabda yoga** – the method of uniting the spirit with the Sound Current that would automatically take one to the Supreme Reservoir of Spirituality. It is the natural way – the natural Religion. Param Guru Sahabji Maharaj defined Religion as "Religion is one and the same and it is the way by which the Supreme Divine Current descends here and by getting hold of which we can ascend back to the Supreme Spiritual Source. This is truly Religion and it is the gift of God." He has pointed out that the spirit on entering the highest sphere, merges in the Highest Being i.e. the true Supreme Being and becomes one with Him. It then functions in its own attributes, which are self-existence, all-intelligence, all-bliss and light. This had been revealed in the form of a Sutra by Param Guru Maharaj Sahab thus:

Athah premasutram vyakhyasyamah
Sachchidanandaswaroopam Chaitanyam II

(Param Guru Maharaj Sahab)

It has since been further elaborated by Revered Prof. Prem Saran Satsangi Sahab:

Parama Sat Chit Premananda Prakasham
Shabda anahada nada swaroopam I
Radhasoami Dhvantyatmaka Shabda dhun
Aadi Anadi Chaitanyam II
Radhasoami Sarvakaranam ativikhyatam
moola parama tattvam bhaje II

(Rev. Prof. P.S.Satsangi)

We shall now explicate the Aphorisms of Love
Consciousness is of the nature of Truth, Intelligence and Bliss
(Param Guru Maharaj Sahab)

Radhasoami is of the form of Supreme Truth, Intelligence, Love, Bliss, Refulgence, the Original Mystic Name, the Resonating Unstruck Sound, the Beginning of All but Beginningless, Primeval Conscousness:
I adore 'Radhasoami' , the Original Cause of everything and the Extremely (Most) Well known Primal Supreme (Truth) Essence.
(Rev. Prof. P.S.Satsangi)

States of Consciousness according to Radhasoami Faith

1.	Jagrat
2.	Swapna
3.	Sushupti
4.	Turiya - Sahasdal Kamal
5.	Turiyatita - Trikuti
6.	Sunn
7.	Bhanwargupha
8.	Satlok
9.	Alakh
10.	Agam
11.	Radhasoami

According the teachings of *Saints,* there appears to be no chance of the any of the prevailing religious practices leading to true salvation of the *Jivas* because - there is neither a trace of love for the Lord in any of those activities, nor any desire for His Vision.

In the Religion of Saints, however, the spiritual practices pertain to internal activity, only within oneself, on higher planes. They start their spiritual practices from Sahasdal Kamal upwards. The external activities are a few viz. *Satsang, Seva* and *Arati.* Besides these, we may include four more external activities also: i) Rendering obeisance at the feet of Sant Satguru, ii) Offering garlands and flowers, iii) Using *Prasad,* iv) Taking *Charanamrit.*

The internal practices comprise of: 1) *Sumiran* -repetition of the True Name- Radhasoami internally with the tongue of the spirit, 2)*Dhyan* – Contemplation of the Holy Form of contemporary *Sant Satguru* and 3) *Bhajan* - listening to internal 'spiritual sounds' at different stages up to 'Radhasoami' in Radhasoami Dham.

The researchers so far have considered and included the states of Consciousness of practitioners of Yoga techniques known in the extant major religions but not those of Sufis, Sants and Param Sants. However, investigations into the nature of these levels of consciousness are being pursued earnestly as also their measurements with the state of art technology like the SQUID, at the Dayalbagh Educational Insititute, Agra, India.

In the words of Param Guru Sahabji Maharaj, the illustrious founder of Dayalbagh, the Head Quarters of Radhasoami Satsang at Agra, India, "nature is set to evolve slowly and steadily, a race of higher men in whom life and its attributes of spirit shall have the fullest expression, men through whom the gracious object of creation would be truly fulfilled. Humanity is steadily advancing towards a form of life that will be rich in knowledge, that will comprehend , control and appreciate its surroundings better and that will not rest till it has realized Ultimate Reality".

Efforts are being made at Dayalbagh to forge a meaningful dialogue between Yoga of the East and Science of the West. Religion and Science in recent years are progressing towards actualization of the highest human possibility of emergence of higher spiritual faculties of man. "Providence has located within the human body a special spiritual faculty and it is the exclusive function of religion to teach man all about that faculty. When that faculty is developed in us like our other physical and mental faculties, we shall be able to perceive Truth and Ultimate Reality in the same manner as we perceive Sun with our physical eyes. And when that takes place, you will be both astonished and amused to find that Truth – the goal of Science, Ultimate Reality – the goal of Philosophy and God – the goal of Religion, are but three names of the same Supreme Essence." (8th Agra University Convocation Address by Sir Sahabji Maharaj, Founder of Dayalbagh, 1935).

Summing up the current state of Consciousness Studies at Dayalbagh Educational Institute, Prof. Prem Saran Satsangi, Chairman, Advisory Committee on Education, Dayalbagh observed that : "At Dayalbagh, we have the rare blend of science and spirituality, with the DEI University providing the science and Dayalbagh community the spirituality.... We are pursuing at Dayalbagh 'Mission : Science of Consciousness' promoting and practicing Surat Shabda Yoga - uniting the Spirit with the Sound Current which is the true yoga for the well being of not only body but mind as well as spirit."

It is earnestly hoped that ere long beautiful flowers of spiritual well-being come to full bloom in this Garden of the Mericiful Lord and and spread their fragrance all over the world.

"-------- The Radhasoami Faith may be a harbinger of the religion of the future not only in India, but elsewhere in the world ---."

Mark Jurgensnmeyer

Select Bibliography

Dighe, A. B. (1981). *Jain Yog ka Alochanatmak Adhyayan*. Amritsar: Sohanlal Jaindharm Pracharak Samiti.

Frawley, D. (2011). *Ayurveda and the Mind: The Healing of Consciousness*. Wisconsin: Lotus Press.

Jurgensmeyer, M. (1991). *Radhasoami Reality – The Logic of a Modern Faith*. Princeton, NJ: Princeton University Press.

Param Purush Puran Dhani Soamiji Maharaj (1982). *Sar Bachan: Poetry*. Dayalbagh, Agra: Radhasoami Satsang Sabha 1982

Param Guru Huzur Maharaj (1985). *Catechism*. Dayalbagh, Agra: Radhasoami Satsang Sabha.

Param Guru Maharaj Sahab (2004). *Discourses on Radhasoami Faith*. Dayalbagh, Agra: Radhasoami Satsang Sabha.

Param Guru Sahabji Maharaj (2010). *Discourses Delivered in Satsang*. Dayalbagh, Agra: Radhasoami Satsang Sabha.

Rev. Prof. Prem Saran Satsangi Sahab (2010). *Expositions on Truth, Ultimate Reality and Supreme Being*. Dayalbagh, Agra: Radhasoami Satsang Sabha.

Swami Shankarananda (2013). *The Yoga of Kashmir Shaivism*. Delhi: Motilal Banarasidas.

Singh, S. P. (2010). *History of Yoga*, Vol. XVI, Part 2.

Sir Sahabji Maharaj (1932). *Bhagavat Gita ke Upadesh*. Dayalbagh, Agra: Radhasoami Satsang Sabha

Radhakrishnan, S. (2009). *Indian Philosophy* Vol. 1. New Delhi: Oxford India Paperbacks.

Chapter 15

Mystical (Religious) Experience and the Brain

VIJAI KUMAR and DAYAL PYARI KUMAR
Dayalbagh Educational Institute (Deemed University),
Dayalbagh, Agra, India

An intensive search for a "God Spot" in the brain has captured the imagination of the neuro-scientists in the present time.One of the areas of exploration in this field is to find out the neural correlates of the mystical manifestation of God.

A number of authors in the field have described the characteristics of such experience. A distillate of these as proposed by Cardena et al (2000),andJames (1902) and others is recalled below:

Ineffability.
Loss of all awareness of discrete, limited-being.
An obliteration of the self-other dichotomy.
Visual and auditory experiences.
Feeling of transcendence of space and time.
Feeling of cosmic union and consciousness.
Deep authoritative (noetic) knowledge.
Sense of presence of a higher being or reality.
Sense of sacredness.
Transience.
Passivity
Feelings of peace, bliss, joy and blessedness

Mystical experience according to Wulff (2000), diverges in fundamental ways from ordinary conscious awareness and leaves a strong impression on the experient of having encountered a reality different from and, in some crucial sense, higher than the reality of every day experience.

The region of the brain that has been implicated in the generation of fear, love,and intense emotions, as well as religious and spiritual belief, is the limbic system which comprises mainly of the hypothalamus, the amygdale, the hippocampus, the cingulated gyrus, the septal nuclei and the inferior temporal lobe (d'Aquili and Newberg (1993), (figure-1).

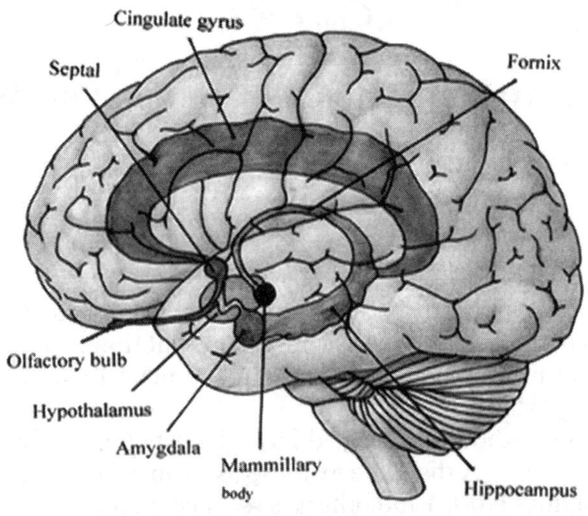

FIGURE 1
The Limbic System
After R. Joseph. TheLimbic System, 2012.
Published by Cosmology Science Publishes (Cambridge)

d'Aquili and Newberg believe that "............mystical states may be voluntarily or involuntarily induced and are dependent on the differential stimulation or degeneration of the limbic system nuclei including the hypothalamus, hippocampus, amygdale and the right frontal and temporal lobes. There is, however, a view that religious experiences are correlates of temporal lobe activity but this requires confirmation with more hard data. Nevertheless hyper-religiousness, or hyper spirituality, coupled with a need to preach or write about these experiences and feeling is not uncommon with temporal lobe epilepsy.

The medial areas of the temporal lobe have close anatomical connection with the limbic system which is the primary neural correlate of religious experience.Interestingly when the temporal lobes and/or the limbic nuclei buried within the depths of the brain are artificially or abnormally activated, it sometimes occurs that a variety of emotional reactions are evoked involuntarily which may take the form of complex hallucinations, dream like states, or confusional episodes. Such experiences seem to be associated with specific types of neuronal activity in the temporal lobes.

Likewise, when any person has "religious experience there is at least a partial common ground in biology, and specifically in brain"- a biological locus attuned to religious experience. Temporal lobe, specially its association cortex, is clearly important in spiritual and religious experience. Indeed, the temporal lobe, amygdale, and hippocampus enable humans to have religious, spiritual, and mystical experiences (d'Aquili and Newberg, 1993). It is further believed that those who appear to undergo seemingly supernatural happenings might have a more dominant right hemisphere.

Presumably, because all humans possess a limbic system and a brain that is organized in a similar manner, they have similar religious and mystical experiences, what Jung (1976) referred to as 'archetypes'- inborn tendencies to produce, create, dream of, and respond in a similar manner to specific images, symbols, and experiences.This commonality in "religious" or "archetypal" experience includes the capacity to experience "God" or "the personal soul". Of course interpretation of much of these phenomena relates to how spiritual experiences are defined.

An interesting hypothesis, proposed by William James (2002), based on Myers views (1892), states that a limen or threshold marks the boundary of the ordinary self, which is that section of conscious sensations and thoughts that best serve us in everyday life and, has proposed that mystical experiences originate in a region lying outside of normal awareness, a region he called the "subliminal" or "subconscious self".

There is a "gateway or barrier" between the subliminal and conscious regions which may be more readily responsive or "leaky" in some individuals in whom there is a free flow of ideational and affective inputs from the subliminal (Thalbourne and Delin, 1994).

Such experiences must involve mind-brain interaction which, according to Eccles, J.C. (1975) can be explained by the hypothesis that the self conscious mind can scan the activity of each module of the liaison brain or at least those modules, e.g. in the temporal lobe which may be attuned to its present interests e.g. a religious experience.

According to Biello (2007) more than single "God nodule" is at work—that a number of structures in the brain come together to "help us experience spirituality and religion". These states are well distributed throughout the brain but the temporal lobe is clearly important in this regard. These form the substrate on which the religious experiences arise.

We believe that these structures may be the components of the liaison brain of Eccles (1975) (Fig2). Such mind (Brahmandic)–brain (Pindic) interactions are not only a regular feature of every day existence but are also involved in higher order religious (spiritual) experience (Kumar and Sinha, 2010).

The liaison brain comprises a large part of the dominant hemisphere, particularly the linguistic areas, the poly-modal sensory areas the ideational areas and a large area of pre-frontal lobe.

While the proposed liaison brain establishes a means of interaction between the self-conscious mind and the brain, according to the Radhasoami Faith, communion can be established by a human entity with the six higher regions of the Spiritual Material Regions (Brahmanda) through apertures in the subtle planes of grey matter of the brain and with those of the purely spiritual Regions (Nirmal Chetan Desh) through six apertures in the subtle planes of the white matter (figure 2). The communion can be established through Surat-Shabd Abhyas, the spiritual practice of the Radhasoami Faith, performed under the guidance of a Perfect Master.

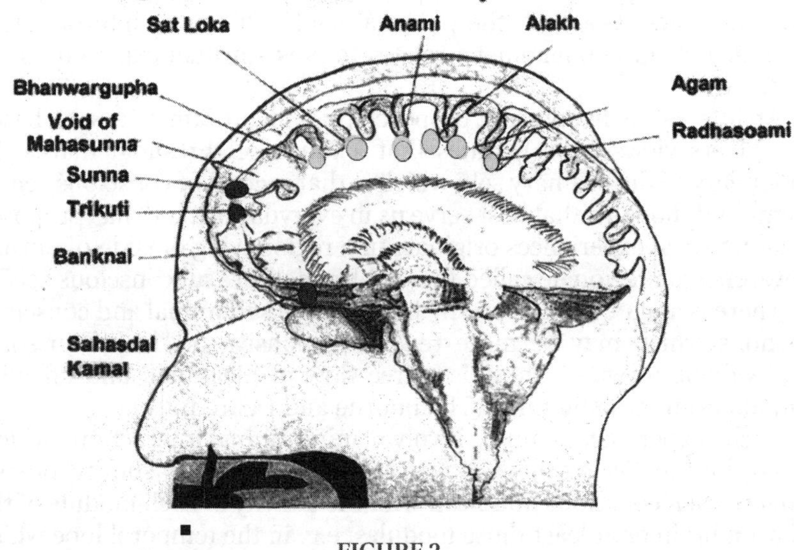

FIGURE 2
Apertures pertaining to Brahmanda
Apertures pertaining to Nirmal Chetan Desh

Many studies of Penfield and others (Penfield and Jasper, 1954) have shown that electrical stimulations of Heschl' sgyrus (Fig. 3) in the temporal lobe produce elementary hallucinations which include:

Buzzing,
Clicking,
Ticking,
Humming,
Whispering and
Ringing localized to the opposite side.

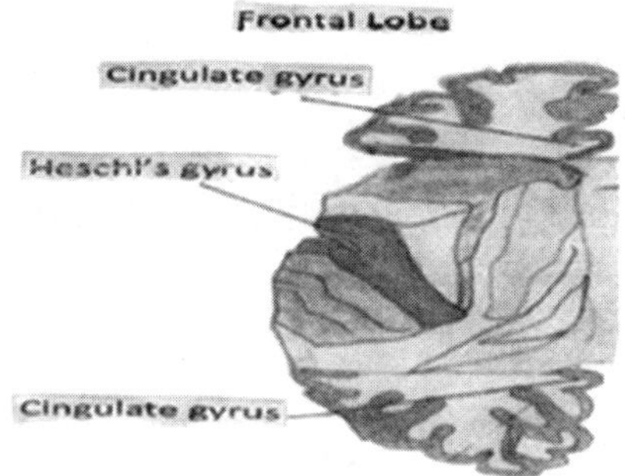

FIGURE 3
Coronal section of left Cerebral Hemisphere showing Heschi's gyrus.

The musical hallucinations are readily produced with electrical stimulation of the superior temporal gyrus of the right temporal lobe. In diseases of temporal lobe meaningful sounds such as clapping of hands or music may be produced as part of these.

Persinger (1983; 1987) calls momentary foci of electrical activity or micro-seizures, which yield the so called mystical and related experiences— the "temporal lobe transients" (TLTs). Over a period of time these TLTs produce alterations in the synaptic organization of limbic regions. He found that activity in temporal but not occipital lobes induced by exotic rhythmic sounds and pulsating lights correlated with measures of religious belief, paranormal or mystical experience, and a sense of presence. We believe that these are pseudo-spiritual experiences mimicking but not real spiritual experiences as discussed later.

It may be appropriate to recall here the Mystics concept of the religious experience, namely that it is generated at the spiritual plane of man at the primary level and the brain (limbic system) acts as a conduit (sheathing) through which it traverses and stimulates the limbic system to reach the physical level of consciousness of everyday experience as a secondary or tertiary phenomenon as mind may be regarded as providing a middle layer of the sheathing for the passage of the primary level spiritual signal (Satsangi 2012), (fig 4).

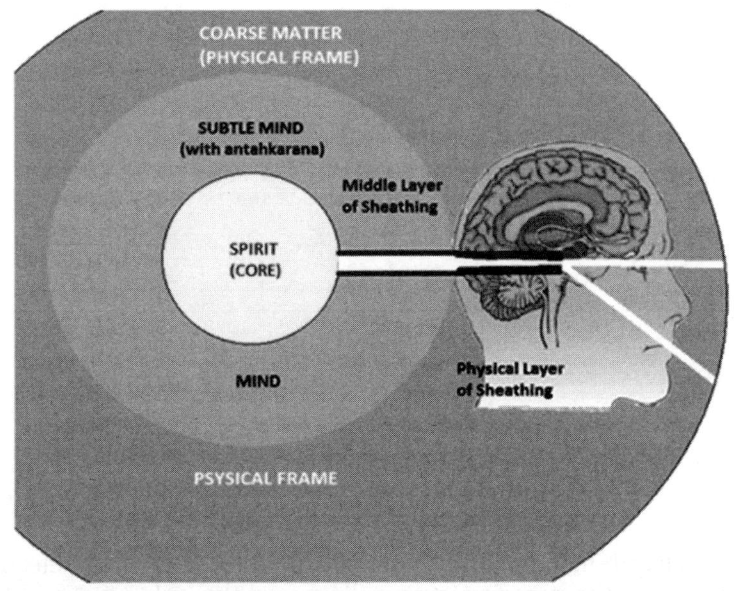

FIGURE 4

There seems to be an uncanny resemblance between listening to the music of the spheres in meditation, which may activate parts of the brain described above and trigger mystical or spiritual experience and the pseudo-spiritual experiences generated through stimulation of parts of medial lobe. The limbic system and medial temporal lobe, we propose are the final common pathway for the induction of spiritual experience and epileptic hallucination of the pseudo-spiritual experience. But the plane of origin of spiritual phenomenon is higher.

According to the Most Revered Dr. P. S. Satsangi Sahab, (2006) the Eighth Revered Sant Satguru of the Radhasoami Faith "....... One defining feature of any true religious experience is the listening of the internal sound. The only way that the One Lord God of Creation is going to manifest Himself is through mighty, luminous musical wave resounding with the original mystic name Radhasoami and no other.... A real religious experience is not without listening to internal sound."

The similarities of mystical (spiritual) experience and pseudo-mystical experience induced by hallucinenogenic drugs, temporal lobe epilepsy, and hallucinations involving temporal lobe have often been described. However, the experiences differ in fundamental ways as summarized below.

Differences Between True and Pseudo-mystical Experience

True Mystical Experiences	Hallucinogenic Drug induced Experiences (Pseudo mystical experiences)
Induce internal peace, tranquility.	Induce mental perturbations excitement.
Contentment	Disaffection.
Heighten the cognitive faculties	Inhibit cognitive faculties.
Induce feelings of love towards fellow beings.	Induce feeling of hostility and aggresiveness towards follow beings.
The experient moves from lower to higher plane of consciousness.	Lead to inhibition of consciousness.

It is our belief that the true and pseudo-mystical (spiritual) experiences use the same common pathway of temporal lobe and limbic system to reach conscious awareness in embodied spirits. Hence the superficial similarities in these.True mystical (spiritual) experience however originates at higher levels of consciousness.They are a pointer to the observation of the saints and "sadhs" over the ages that "the kingdom of God is within you" (Joseph 1996)

The true mosque that is built in the heart of saints is the
place of worship for all for God dwells there (Maulana Rumi).

References

Biello, D. (2007). Searching for God. *Scientific American*, 18(5).

Cardena, E., Lynn, S.J., & Krippner, S. (2000). Varieties of anomalous experience: Examining the scientific evidence. Vol. 299. Washington D.C.: The American Psychological Association.

D'Aquili, E.G., & Newberg, A.B. (1993). Religious and mystical states. *Zygon*, *28*, 177-200.

James, W. (1901). The varieties of religious experience: A study in human nature. Retrieved from http://www.hudevbooks.com/library/william_james_var.pdf

Jung, C.G. (1976). The Tavistock Lectures on the theory and practice of analytical psychology. In H. Read, M. Fordham, & G. Adler (Eds.), (R. F. C. Hull, Trans.). *The collected works of C. G. Jung* Vol. 18. Princeton, N.J: Princeton University Press.

Kumar, V., & Sinha, M. (2010). How brain gains access to self-conscious mind – and beyond. Convergence of Concepts of Neuroscience and Radhasoami Faith.

Myers, F. W. H. (1892). General characteristics of subliminal messages. In *The subliminal consciousness. Proceedings of the Society for Psychical Research*, *7*, 298. Retrieved from http://www.bbk.ac.uk/deviance/unconscious1/TheUnconsciousPsychicalResearch/Myers1/index.htm

Penfield, W., & Jasper, H. (1954). *Epilepsy and the functional anatomy of the human brain.* Oxford: Little, Brown & Co.

Popper, K. & Eccles, J. C. (1977). *The self and its brain: an argument for interactionism.*

Berlin Heidelberg: Springer-Verlag.

Persinger, M. A. (1983). Religious and mystical experiences as artifacts of temporal lobe function: A general hypothesis. *Perceptual and Motor Skills*, *57*(3), 1255-62.

Persinger, M. A. (1987). *Neuropsychological bases of god beliefs*. New York: Praeger Publishers Inc.

Joseph, R. (1996). *Neuropsychiatry, neurophysiology and clinical neuroscience* (2nd ed.). Baltimore, USA: Williams and Wilkins.

Satsangi, P. S. (2006). (Most Revered Prof. P. S. Satsangi Sahab. Discourse delivered in evening Satsang on 16th August, 2006.

Satsangi, P. S. (2012). Most Revered Professor P. S. Satsangi Sahab. Discourse delivered in the evening Satsang at Dayalbagh on September 22, 2012.

Thalbourne, M. A. & Delin, P. S. (1994). A common thread underlying belief in the paranormal, creative personality, mystical experience and psychopathology. *Journal of Parapsychology*, *58*, 3-38.

Wulff, D. M. (2000). Mystical experience. In E. Cardena, S. J. Lynn, & S. Krippner, S. (Eds.). *Varieties of anomalous experience: Examining the scientific evidence*. Vol. 299. Washington D.C.: The American Psychological Association.

IV

Consciousness - Integrating Eastern and Western Perspectives

Chapter 16

From Quantum Mechanics to Qualia Mechanics

DEEPAK CHOPRA
University of California San Diego
and
MENAS C. KAFATOS
Chapman University

ABSTRACT

Ever since quantum mechanics emerged in early 20th century, a new world view emerged, decidedly different from the world of classical physics. Quantum physics opened the door to consciousness in physical theories by introducing the participatory view of the cosmos: in the new quantum world, the observer, the measuring device, and the quantum system under study form an undivided process. The randomness of quantum phenomena, coupled to the ability to make choices, allows for free will to be an aspect of physical theories. The reliable world of the Newtonian paradigm, based on the five senses, was undercut by the quantum world. The repercussions of this new paradigm which challenges not only old classical concepts but also our common-sense perception of the world, are far-reaching. In this work we present the view that there is a complementary view to the way classical physics and more generally science are being practiced, namely that consciousness itself is primary and qualia form the foundation of experience. We outline the reasons why a new science of qualia, what we term qualia mechanics, is necessary for the next steps in evolution and understanding of the cosmos and humanity's role in it. As quanta are the constituents of quantum mechanics, the units of subjective experience, qualia are the constituents of qualia mechanics.

Keywords: consciousness, quanta, qualia, quantum mechanics, qualia mechanics, complementarity, recursion, process

1. INTRODUCTION

The quantum revolution unleashed in December 1900 with the publication of Max Planck's explanation of the black body radiation is reverberating until today. Quantum mechanics (QM) in contrast to Einstein's theories of relativity, was a collective product of many physicists spanning the first three decades of the 20th century (cf. Bohr, 1934, 1958; Heisenberg, 2007; Schrödinger, 1983; von Neumann, 1932/1955, etc.), and extended to the mid 20th century with quantum field theory (QFT) (Feynman 2006), up to today's superstring theory.

Central to the new QM were the concepts of measurement, implying a non-trivial role for the observer; quantum uncertainty; and probability theory for quantum events. However, the quantum revolution was only the first stage in directly addressing the role of consciousness, implied in measurement theory (Kafatos and Nadeau, 1990/2000; Stapp, 2004, 2007): It provided no answer to the actual experience of phenomena, an integral part of consciousness. The fact of life is, however, that we experience the world as qualia, the teeming subjective qualities of sensation, images, feelings, and thoughts, and as such, qualia are inescapable. If there is a reality that exists outside what we perceive, it is inconceivable. Once you subtract everything you can sense, imagine, feel, or think about, there's nothing left. Because qualia are subjective, they sharply challenge the dominant world view of modern science, which is reductionist, objective, and mathematical.

When qualia become fully integrated into a new science of consciousness, qualia mechanics will be seen as the reality that is most fundamental and direct to not just science but everyday life itself. A new way of triune reality will be accepted, comprising matter, mediators of interactions between matter and observers, and experiencing components of observers, or what we have called before the three-in-one, Q^3 reality: quarks (the primary particles of matter)-quanta (the mediators of quantum interactions)-qualia (the units of experience). Three-in-one reality reflects the history of philosophy and modern science. Discoveries unfolded in a line from the more inert and physical to the more subtle subjective. We believe that with qualia mechanics the process should be reversed and become the new Q^3, or experience-mediators of experience-matter (qualia-quanta-quarks), which recognizes the undeniable fusion of observer-observed-process of observation. This reversal maps the natural way in which the universe becomes manifest in our awareness and how it becomes aware of itself).

In the present work we examine the foundations of our proposed qualia mechanics, the emerging science of experience, whose principles must meet the demands of rigor, verifiability, experimentation, and falsifiability. The process of universal consciousness becoming the universe, within which all conscious experiences occur leads to the experience of matter and "the world out there." A blueprint for the evolution of the current object-based science into the future observer-based (qualia mechanics) science is outlined here. We also believe that unless and until this evolution unfolds, the dream of a Theory of Everything will remain just that.

In what follows, we use material from several blogs (see Chopra, Kafatos and Tanzi, 2012a,b,c,d) as well as our previous publication

(Chopra and Kafatos, 2014). However, we have updated these previous writings in important ways, taking into account recent works.

2. THE QUANTUM UNIVERSE, REALITY AND EXPERIENCE

The so-called "hard problem" (cf. Chalmers, 1996) is a statement of the inability of science and specifically neuroscience to account for experiencing the world, such as the colors we see, the thoughts we have, etc. Dennett (1988) states:

> "an unfamiliar term for something that could not be more familiar to each of us: the ways things seem to us."

As such, Qualia are the elements of experience. They exist at the crux where mind, operating "in here," and produce the sight, sound, texture, taste, and smell of the world "out there." We take the world as existing "out there" but in fact what is "out there" is an experience as well. To date, the perceived duality between "in here" and "out there" has forced science to choose data over experience, theories over experience, mathematics over experience. In fact, all these are modes of experience.

We hold the view that *Reality is Experience*. To qualify this statement, who is experiencing? We as conscious beings, experience reality and we call it "out there." But the experience of the underlying consciousness is the reality, it is the proverbial elephant in the room, a participant in every human activity – including mathematics the language of science. If this is accepted, then qualia science or qualia mechanics resolves the core problem in duality, the vexed relationship between mind and body, world and observers, mind and brain, etc. As we have argued before, instead of pursuing the fruitless goal of discovering how atoms and molecules, the constituents of matter, somehow evolved into life, cells, living beings and eventually humans with thinking faculties – in some ways implying that atoms have the ability to think – qualia science takes consciousness as primary in the universe, not a secondary product of life and brain processes. The "hard problem" becomes easy once this step is taken, because then the concept of external matter is another experience and one only has to account for the qualities of matter (solidity, weight, mass, momentum), which are adduced entirely from experience of these qualities.

To describe the nature of reality (see Chopra, Kafatos and Tanzi, 2012a,b,c,d), our contention is that qualia, not quarks or even quanta (matter and mediators of interactions), are the building blocks of Nature. QM finds itself trapped in a paradox without qualia, since it radically undercut the notion of solid physical objects while retaining the physical universe as a given. It opened the door to consciousness

(Kafatos and Nadeau, 1990/2000: Nadeau and Kafatos, 1999) but it cannot account for consciousness. Quantum physics needs to follow through with the fundamental implications of measurement theory, what John A. Wheeler (1983) calls the "Participatory Universe." Qualia science, as we envision it, resolves the paradox by showing how the universe operates as the *domain of consciousness*. The physical universe as a separate existence, existing in absolute terms without consciousness, is untenable in the post-quantum era. It requires radical extension of quantum mechanics (while keeping all its successes) to accept the active participatory universe experienced through qualia.

The obvious fact that science involves subjective experience doesn't negate the existence of facts, calculations, measurements, and data. These are to be understood as phenomena based on the underlying experiencing ability of consciousness, which has its own natural laws and reliable properties, including self-organization, similarity across different levels, complementarity, non-locality, least action, and fundamental aspects of process across all realms, as established in classical and quantum theory. The mistake of duality taken as an absolute was to turn reality into an either/or choice between subjectivity and objectivity, when in reality consciousness is the common element that unites "in here" and "out there", into an undivided wholeness (Kafatos, 2011).

Werner Heisenberg himself stated, "The atoms or elementary particles themselves are not real; they form a world of potentialities or possibilities rather than one of things or facts" (Heisenberg 1958). The process of undercutting the five senses is valid (Chopra and Kafatos, 2014), but the foundation of the senses, which makes any experience viable—consciousness itself—cannot be undercut. This distinction rescues objectivity and subjectivity at the same time and is the true meaning of complementarity, the first principle of how fundamental Consciousness (with a capital C) operates in experiencing itself and objects "out there."

The objection that qualia are only how the world seems to a particular observer is not valid, because even though people may have different experiences of color (such as green and red) they won't disagree on what "color" means. In neuroscience and psychology, the various personal experiences that we all have, such as pain, pleasure, dreaming, recollection of deep sleep, memory, etc., are the very things that lead researchers to investigate the brain in the first place (neuroscience) and how we perceive ourselves (psychology and psychiatry). Without qualia, brain activity as measured by EEGs and fMRIs, theories of the psyche, etc. are meaningless. In other words, the experience obviously comes first, and if a person says, "I'm not in pain," "I'm not depressed," or "I'm not in love with you," such reports are the last word—no brain scan or theory of neurons firing can prove them wrong.

Even denying the reality of experience, and as some philosophers and psychologists claim even the mind being illusion, one must nevertheless have an experience to begin with. This might be uncomfortable when a particle physicist tries to study the properties of particles of matter such as quarks, and quanta of energy such as photons, but the question that Heisenberg, Wheeler, Planck, Pauli (1954) and others answered is, how would we even know what properties would they have? Anything that might be proposed would be untestable and by definition inconceivable (concepts used in particle physics, such as "charm" and "spin," and even the Higgs boson itself, are qualia, too, including the mathematical theories such as QM, QED and superstring theories). Abstract thought doesn't have a privileged position as a non-experience. How could it? Our present understanding of space, time, matter, energy, and gravity as being fundamental, while at the same time failing to come up with a unified theory—not to mention the all but unknowable domains of "dark" matter and energy—may prove untenable. They exist in Consciousness but not outside Consciousness. There is no "outside" to Consciousness.

Understandably, there is considerable resistance placing Consciousness first, after so many decades of considering it a barely respectable subject for neuroscience. Reality shifts in ways that are unpredictable and strange, however. Time and space took very strange turns a century ago, for example, while cause-and-effect turned into a game of probabilities, and the solid physical universe dissolved into invisible energy clouds. Quantum theory has arrived, keeping pace with where reality led it. What Einstein calls the "spookiness" of activity at the quantum level has only become spookier ever since.

Here we refer to Chopra and Kafatos (2014):

> "Now it appears that reality is about to lead us into new, unexpected paths once more. A hint of the future was provided decades ago by one of the most brilliant quantum pioneers, Wolfgang Pauli, when he used a word that science shunned—psychic: "It is my personal opinion that in the science of the future, reality will neither be 'psychic' nor 'physical' but somehow both and somehow neither" (Pauli 1954). Pauli was pointing to a kind of ultimate mystery. What if the vast physical mechanism we call the universe behaves more like a mind than a machine? To thousands of working physicists, the riddle of mind and matter doesn't apply to their research. But the founder of quantum physics, Max Planck, has no doubt that mind will eventually become inescapable—an issue too massive and obvious to ignore: "I regard consciousness as fundamental.

> I regard matter as derivative from consciousness. We cannot get behind consciousness. Everything that we talk about, and we regard as existing, postulates consciousness" (Planck 1931).
> . . . Planck and Pauli were not alone in suspecting that consciousness was more than a given. Mind holds some kind of key to the nature of reality. But neither Planck nor Pauli followed up on the mystery they had uncovered. There was no need, not for a long time. Quantum physics blossomed into the most accurate and mathematically sophisticated model in the history of science. It achieved such precise results that its predictive powers were nothing less than stunning. As the eminent British physicist Sir Roger Penrose (2007) affirmed, Newton's gravitational theory as applied to the movement of the solar system was precise to one part in 10 million. Einstein's theory of relativity was improved upon Newton by another factor of 10 million.
> Reality, which cannot be denied, has led science along a very productive path. Leaving consciousness out of the equation is like leaving metaphysics out of cookbooks.... That time inevitably arises, however, for one simple reason: Reality is always more complicated than the models we use to explain it. Reality, as we investigate it more deeply, conforms to Planck and Pauli's intuition that consciousness will turn out to be the thing you cannot get behind. We think their intuition is right. We don't say this because we happen to be fans of the mind or have a personal stake in boosting it. Science has come to a turning point by following its own findings."

3. FROM QUANTA TO QUALIA—THE NEXT HORIZON

The deeper one looks, the more it appears that all three issues—a living universe, a human universe, and a universe that holds a place for Consciousness—start to merge. If they actually do merge, nothing will ever be the same again. Not just science but everyday existence will be completely overturned.

The new paradigm of QM began with the word quantum. Quanta as defined in an encyclopedia are "packets" of energy. The old quantum theory was non-relativistic and as such limited. It did however introduce the issue of measurement and the role of the observer. In the Copenhagen Interpretation, the role of observation was taken as primary. It was developed in a large body of published works, primarily by Bohr, Heisenberg, Pauli, Born, etc., such as Bohr (1934, 1958), Heisenberg (1958), etc. The so-called orthodox quantum theory, which followed and extended the Copenhagen Interpretation, was developed by the mathematician John von Neumann in his book (1955/1932), Mathematical Foundations of Quantum Mechanics. The philosophical implications of orthodox quantum mechanics have been explored as described above.

Central to the Copenhagen Interpretation is the double slit experiment, revealing a wave aspect or a particle aspect, which are tied to experimental choices. This dual situation is the core of complementarity, which forms the central pillar of the Copenhagen Interpretation: The quantum can be either a particle or a wave but never both in a given situation. What it is (or better what it is measured to be) depends on the observational choice that an observer made. The nature of the quantum is inexorably tied to choices of observers! This forms the core idea of the participatory universe. The strange but real world of the quantum, including non-locality, the Copenhagen Interpretation and the great successes of quantum mechanics are described several books and articles by Kafatos and co-workers. The connection of the quantum to cosmology is discussed in Kafatos (2009). While the role of universal Consciousness, hinted at in the *Conscious Universe*, was developed by Kafatos, Tanzi, and Chopra (2011).

Stuart Hameroff and Roger Penrose in a series of works developed the Orchestrated Objective Reduction model of how consciousness arises in the brain, utilizing space-time geometry at the fundamental Planck level (e.g. Penrose and Hameroff, 2011). Orch OR makes specific and interesting predictions on quantum coherence at microtubular levels, explored by experimentalists.

Whereas in classical physics objects, and presumably particles, were considered as hard and unchanging, QM reduced particles into possibilities of events, described by quantum probabilities. In modern QFT, particles are considered as vibrations of quantum fields. In the same vein, perhaps we can consider qualia as *vibrations of the field of Consciousness*. In this way we can begin to transition from quantum mechanics to qualia mechanics.

Qualia are the everyday qualities of experience—light, sound, color, shape, or texture. Since the only way we know reality is through experience, we have argued that qualia, not quanta, are the building blocks of nature. Qualia hold reality together. Looking at everyday experience through the perspective of the brain, psychiatrist and neural theorist Daniel Siegel (2012) describes reality "in here" to SIFT: sensation, image, feeling, and thought. No matter what's happening to us at any time, our brains are registering either a sensation, an image, a feeling.

Qualia make up our everyday experience, interfacing with the physical but they are not physical. The active participatory role of Consciousness manifests everyday reality through qualia. It is ironic that those we cannot do without are also beyond science as practiced today. This surely needs to change. As the great British physicist David

Bohm (1986) emphasized, "In some sense, man is a microcosm of the universe; therefore what man is, is a clue to the universe." This resonates with the ancient wisdoms, the Hermetic principle "as above, so below."

The horizon beyond current science as is being practiced today (but not as QM *implies)* that we need to perceive, is that going beyond the physical entails extending QM to include consciousness in a fundamental way. Since reality perceived, sensed and understood is an experience in Consciousness, pure reason leads us to the universality of Consciousness, Consciousness being the underlying reality, creating vast levels of experience. The quantum pioneers were very clear about this. "To divide or multiply consciousness is something meaningless" (Schrödinger 1983). We perceive the world through our individual minds, seeing differences which are nothing more than different experiences. However, all these experiences are in one universal field of Consciousness, as thoughts are different vibrations of the individual mind. There are not two realities—one for the outer world and one for the inner world, there is only one reality; and we are part of it. We don't have to throw out everyday reality, everyday experience, we don't have to throw out science. Guided from QM, we perceive, not with our senses but with our reason, that science, everyday experience and everyday reality, need to be extended, to show us that the current horizon can be extended to a greater wholeness. Qualia science brings in the observer, each one of us, to a participatory role—we all are the conscious agents who shape reality as we experience it, all aspects of the one reality.

4. QUALIA MECHANICS

To emphasize what we are saying: Any explanation that leaves consciousness out is incomplete and moreover creates a host of problems as objectivity cannot be complete without subjectivity. Experience is experience, there is no difference, as far as the visual cortex is concerned, between seeing a red rose and imagining it. The qualia of red is present in both. A specific wavelength of light isn't actually red—it takes a mind for redness to *exist in perception*. Indeed, it takes a mind for light to be bright in the first place. Photons are invisible without an eye to see. In the words of Sir John Eccles, the famous British neurologist, "I want you to realize that there exists no color in the natural world, and no sound—nothing of this kind, no textures, no patterns, no beauty, no scent" (Eccles 1995). When we dream of a rose, surely it is not "out there." Yet, in dream, it looks quite real. Where is the rose located? Perception creates reality, whether in "awake" state or "dream" state.

Realizing that perception the whole key to reality opens up a totally new way to view the world, including us. Roses are not red; rocks are not hard; water is not wet; light is not bright. These are all qualia created in the conscious mind, using the brain as a processing facility of the one Consciousness, "downloading" and "uploading" information, experiences from the mind to the universal Mind, as drops in an ocean are part of the ocean yet appear distinct. This does not mean that we are denying reality. Far from it, we now see that reality is not some mysterious "out there" stuff that makes no sense.

We affirm that qualia mechanics will have to be built on a set of operational or experiential statements. These statements about qualia are summarized and in fact lead, as we will see below, to three fundamental laws of how Consciousness operates. They are not mathematical in the usual sense of dynamical equations as we find in physics but are still subject to fundamental mathematical formalism, understanding that ultimately whatever formal logical system we use, it will have to lead to experiential principles. As a start, we provide here a set of statements of qualia experience that bridge the old and new paradigms, carrying us from quanta to qualia (for completeness and continuity, we present here ten statements, essentially what were presented in Chopra and Kafatos, 2014):

(1) The quantum universe exists as the one system that our nervous system allows us to perceive in the form of qualia—defined as all sensations, images, feeling, and thoughts experienced in a conscious mind.

(2) Quantum phenomena are not reified until registered by an act of observation. Observers participate in the phenomena they observe. The quantum world is a participatory world of events, not "hard" physical entities.

(3) Different phenomena that are applied in the quantum world are just as applicable to how consciousness operates. In brief, it includes the most basic discoveries of the quantum era: quantization; coherence, superposition and entanglement; complementarity; contextuality; primacy of process; non-locality; sentience. All can be expanded to describe the fundamental workings of Consciousness. The phenomena that are applied to the quantum world all are aspects of three fundamental laws that apply everywhere, in the inner and outer worlds: *Complementarity, Recursion,* and *Process* or *Interactivity* (see Kafatos and Nadeau 1990/2000; Nadeau and Kafatos 1999; Roy and Kafatos 1999, 2004; Theise and Kafatos, 2013a, 2013b, 2016). They provide the necessary links between quantum mechanics and qualia mechanics.

(4) All experience, whether of the body or the outside world, consists of qualia. Our world only exists because we perceive it and act as conscious agents, all interactions with the universe are experiential and subjective. What we call "objective" in science is that which we can measure within patterns of qualia dictated by mathematical laws. Quantum Mechanics is the best mathematical model we presently have for experiences in Qualia Mechanics.

(5) Consciousness is fundamental and indivisible. As such, Consciousness can only interact with itself. In life as in science, all experiences and measurements involve Consciousness interacting with itself. All reality originates from the potential field of Consciousness, which is a field of all possibilities, those manifesting in spacetime described by physics, and those that do not. Each possibility emerges as qualia. However, the field of pure Consciousness exists prior to qualia. Even our nervous system is a product of a possibility in universal Consciousness, or Awareness, which has evolved as a particular mode for interpreting consciousness from a human perspective. It does this by creating qualia (including sight, sound, touch, taste, and smell) as Consciousness interacts with itself.

(6) Qualia exist on the boundary between the perceived and the actual (pure Consciousness). Qualia mechanics will be developed to cross that boundary. The perceptual world is what our nervous system and those of other species experience. The actual world is pure Consciousness, which has no qualities, being the pre-created state.

(7) Pure Consciousness differentiates itself as the process of creation. Within the perceived universe, species-specific reality (e.g., that of humans) is a continuous and dynamic flow of Consciousness from the unmanifest field of all possibilities into matter, energy, worlds, and beings. Qualia mechanics captures the dynamic unfolding. True reality is acausal and non-local. Causality arises as the result of limited focus within specific nervous systems.

(8) As Consciousness interacts with itself, the resulting qualia self-organize or evolve. Self-organization is based on continuous feedback loops. Every qualia that manifests from existing qualia, in turn serves to regulate the qualia from which it manifested. Qualia emerge in layers of manifestation that make up a self-regulating program based on multifold feedback loops. This program can be a feeling, a human, the planet Earth, or the universe itself. Birth is the beginning of a particular qualia program, a particular human being, a planet, etc. An individual qualia entity emerges into the world with a potential in qualia that unfold as life. From birth, our reality is created via the resonance of shared qualia with others in our species and related species. As such, the perceived universe is, in essence, a collective agreement about qualia as experienced in human minds, with additional private or personal qualia. Death is the termination of a particular qualia program, i.e. qualia return to a state of *potentiality within Consciousness*, where they reshuffle and recycle as new living entities.

(9) The process of Consciousness interacting with itself is most obvious in humans as self-awareness imparting the sense of choice, purpose, and meaning. Self-awareness is the starting point for the next leap in our creative evolution as a species. Without self-awareness, the

universe would be devoid of meaning and therefore incomprehensible. Self-awareness is part and parcel of Awareness as water drops are the same "stuff" as the ocean.

(10) The future of qualia science will lead to the understanding of how qualia operate (qualia mechanics). They will lead to the emergence of new, dynamic, and self-organizing networks of qualia that will reshape the universe as we know it. In the process, quantum mechanics and classical science will remain necessary in their role of producing new technologies, measuring objects of observation, and interpreting mathematical laws. However, this activity will be subsumed under the reality of Consciousness unfolding as qualia, described by qualia mechanics. Exploring the actual (the "real" reality of Consciousness) qualia science in its workings as qualia mechanics will break down the barrier between a non-local field of all possibilities and the perceptions produced by our nervous system. The result will be a more connected and enlightened "human universe."

Specifying more (3) above, through the three fundamental laws, which apply at all levels, in all fields of human activity, all life, and everything that exists in the universe, Consciousness creates, sustains, and re-absorbs onto itself all in the universe. The fundamental laws consist of fundamental complementarity between object and subject, a projection from Consciousness into Consciousness. The second law states that Consciousness recursively applies in similar patterns, for objects to form similar relationships, appearances, and properties across vastly different scales. The third law states that everything interacts with everything else, process being the primary building block of what makes the universe (which for sentient beings is termed *sentience*), providing awareness and meaning to everything, sensing of the environment.

Through these laws, Consciousness unifies everything in undivided wholeness. All quantum phenomena spring out of the fundamental laws. At the same time, these laws limit (or focus) universal Consciousness, which otherwise would be unmanifest and unknowable. The universe is participatory as Consciousness is in partnership, or participation with everything in it. This participation manifests as sentience at all levels in all objects.

One important aspect of qualia mechanics is the veiling of underlying Consciousness. Without this veiling, there would be no experience of the "other", no sensory input, no human experience, no experience of the "external world." In QM and general relativity, the idea of veiling has been proposed by Kafatos and Kak (2015). We see that veiling is common to both quantum mechanics and qualia mechanics.

What must be common in both quantum mechanics and qualia mechanics is a language that would be similar. Recently, Kafatos (2015) has developed a mathematical formalism that ties together the observer with the observed in the most primary of relationships, the "I Am" and all derivatives such as "I Am That" statements (see Theise and Kafatos, 2016). The mathematical formalism accepts the view that universal Consciousness (or Awareness) is primary, operating through the three laws discussed above, applying at all scales. Five logical statements are developed wherein the object and the subject are one, yet in consecutive steps, the beginning of differentiation is set up. The mathematics allows for a rudimentary formalism of the qualia of experience that is a simplified version of Hilbert space convention encountered in quantum mechanics, using quantum concepts of vectors, corresponding to the subject and the object. The approach has the advantage of using the same familiar mathematics of QM, Hilbert space. It is a concrete step going from quantum mechanics to qualia mechanics. The mathematical formalism does, however, go beyond specific interpretations of quantum mechanics and has strong philosophical foundations in Western philosophy as well as monistic systems of the East. Kafatos (2015) explores the full development of this Hilbert-like axiomatic mathematical approach to the point where the identity of object and subject breaks down.

5. THE FUTURE

Qualia mechanics is needed to answer questions that conventional and externally-based science cannot answer and in fact it appears that it cannot even put in a coherent framework. We can place these questions into a few broad categories:

1. Questions about the mind: How does mind arise? What is its relation of mind to the physical world? How are mind and body connected (the body-mind problem)?
2. Questions about origins: Where does the universe come from? What existed "before" time and space?
3. Questions about life: How does life arise from lifeless matter? How is biology related to physics?
4. Questions about the laws of the physical universe: Are they permanent or changeable? Why is the universe so finely-tuned?
5. Questions about evolution: Is evolution universal or does it apply only to life forms? How is biological structure arise? Is self-organization fundamental at all levels of creation? Where is evolution going next?

If anyone wants to comprehend why a new paradigm is needed, these unanswered questions should suffice. They all depend upon the expansion of conventional science, and if it's too troubling to contemplate a reversal of object-based thinking, we are comfortable proposing an expansion instead. Reality, as currently conceived, involves a three-part structure: observer, observed, and process of observation. By focusing on the observer, the new paradigm is expanding beyond a narrow focusing on the observed. But that does not mean that the observed—i.e., everything that provides data, measurements, and information—is rendered invalid. Rather, its validity is placed in a wider context—human experience as a whole.

If the constituents of life and Awareness are inherent in the cosmos, human existence is no longer privileged, much less unique, yet it is of the outmost importance for us. We are a specific qualia program, within the cosmic qualia program. In everyday life, we engage with reality, which is triune, consisting of the observer, the observed, and the process of observation. The next horizon is to grasp that all three parts are within Consciousness. Setting aside any other argument, the most basic reason for qualia science is that it liberates us from arbitrary boundaries. The most arbitrary is the dividing line between inner and outer reality.

The road to reality as Penrose (2007) would call it, must involve going beyond the quantum. Qualia mechanics as the mathematics indicates (Kafatos, 2015) would include the observer, the observed and the process of observation. Science is not superior to common experience in that regard. It does not describe reality; it describes phenomena that fit various theories. As Peter Wilberg, a most gifted qualia theorist, has explained, we don't see because we have eyes. Eyes are physical organs evolved to serve the mind's desire to see. Mind comes first.

When qualia mechanics becomes fully developed and integrated into a new science of Consciousness, reality will be understood, through verifiable procedures, to be triune. What we have developed here is the beginning, the foundational framework of qualia mechanics. Qualia mechanics, similarly as quantum mechanics, follows non-locality and recursion, information being non-local and information being controlled by the brain, the brain being the processing center for all thoughts, feelings, sensations, and images—therefore the unbroken chain of qualia exists at every level in the body.

In a recent work, Theise and Kafatos (2016) state:

> "The ontologic framework of Fundamental Awareness proposed here assumes that non-dual Awareness is foundational to the universe, not arising from the interactions or structures of higher level phenomena. The framework allows comparison and integration of views from the three investigative domains concerned with the understanding nature of Consciousness: science, philosophy, and metaphysics. In this framework, Awareness is the underlying reality, not reducible to anything else. Awareness

and existence are the same. As such, the universe is non-material, self-organizing throughout, a holarchy of complementary, process driven, recursive interactions. The universe is both its own first observer and subject. Considering the world to be non-material and comprised, a priori, of Awareness is to privilege information over materiality, action over agency and to understand that qualia are not a "hard problem", but the foundational elements of all existence. These views fully reflect mainstream Western philosophical traditions, insights from culturally diverse contemplative and mystical traditions, and are in keeping with current scientific thinking, expressible mathematically."

Since qualia are the "units" of experience, qualia science will provide the working tools for a new way of dealing with reality. Qualia mechanics is reaching across the divide between contemplative traditions and rational science; between science and philosophy; and not, but not least, between the objective and the subjective. Object-based science has provided great discoveries. It's time now to realize that observer-based science, operating as qualia mechanics, can do the same by uncovering the underlying structure of reality, not simply a provisional model. It is perhaps then that we can truly understand how human awareness can unlock the secrets hidden in the infinite field of Consciousness, which now seem inaccessible.

References

Bohm, D. (1986). *Dialogues with scientists and sages: The search for unity*. London: Routledge & Kegan Paul.

Bohr, N. (1934). *Atomic theory and the description of nature*. Cambridge: Cambridge University Press.

Bohr, N. (1958). *Atomic physics and human knowledge*. New York: Wiley.

Chopra, D., Kafatos, M.C., & Tanzi, R. E. (October 8, 2012a). *From quanta to qualia: The mystery of reality, Part 1. [Blog post]*. Retrieved from http://www.huffingtonpost.com/deepak-chopra/from-quanta-to-qualia_b_1948416.html

Chopra, D., Kafatos, M.C., & Tanzi, R. E. (October 15, 2012b). *From quanta to qualia: The mystery of reality, Part 2. [Blog post]*. Retrieved from http://www.huffingtonpost.com/deepak-chopra/from-quanta-to-qualia-wha_b_1966954.html

Chopra, D., Kafatos, M.C., & Tanzi, R. E. (October 29, 2012c). *From quanta to qualia: The mystery of reality, Part 3. [Blog post]*. Retrieved from http://www.huffingtonpost.com/deepak-chopra/from-quanta-to-qualia-the_b_2038207.html

Chopra, D., Kafatos, M.C., & Tanzi, R. E. (November 12, 2012d). *From quanta to qualia: The mystery of reality, Part 4. [Blog post]*. Retrieved from http://www.huffingtonpost.com/deepak-chopra/from-quanta-to-qualia-the-mystery-of-reality_b_2118820.html

Chopra, D., & Kafatos, M.C. (2014). From quanta to qualia. *Philosophy Study, 4*, 287-301.

Chalmers, D. J. (1966). *The conscious mind: In search of a fundamental theory*. Oxford: Oxford University Press.

Dennett, D. (1988). Quining qualia. In A. Marcel and E. Bisiach (Eds.), *Consciousness in Modern Science*. Oxford: Oxford University Press.

Feynman, R. (2006). *QED: The strange theory of light and matter*. Princeton, NJ: Princeton University Press.

Heisenberg, W. (2007). *Physics and philosophy*. New York: Harper Collins (Original work published 1958 New York: Harper)

Kafatos, M.C. (2009). Cosmos and quantum: Frontiers for the future. *Journal of Cosmology, 3*, 511-28.

Kafatos, M.C. (2015). Fundamental mathematics of consciousness. *Cosmos and History: The Journal of Natural and Social Philosophy, 11*, 175-188.

Kafatos, M. (2011). The science of wholeness. In T. Tymieniecka & A. Grandpierre (Eds.), *Analecta Husserliana*, CVII, (pp. 69-80). Springer Science+Business Media, B.V.

Kafatos, M., & Nadeau, R. (2000). *The conscious universe: Parts and wholes in physical reality*. New York: Springer-Verlag. (Original work printed in 1990).

Kafatos, M., Tanzi, R., & Chopra, D. (2011). How consciousness becomes the physical universe. *The Journal of Cosmology, 14*, 3-14.

Kafatos, M. C., & Kak, S. (2015). Veiled nonlocality, cosmic censorship and local observations. *Physics Essays, 28*, pp.182-187. Retrieved from http://physicsessays.org/browse-journal-2/product/1242-9-menas-c-kafatos-and-subhash-kak-veiled-nonlocality-cosmic-censorship-and-local-observations.html and http://arxiv.org/abs/1401.2180

Nadeau R., & Kafatos, M. (1999). *The non-local universe: The new physics and matters of the mind*. Oxford: Oxford University Press.

Pauli, W. (1954). *On the nature of the psyche*. Collected Works Vol. 8, revised. para. 439n.

Penrose, R. (2007). *The road to reality: A complete guide to the laws of the universe*. New York: Vintage Books.

Penrose, R., & Hameroff, S. (2011). Consciousness in the universe: Neuroscience, quantum space-time geometry and Orch OR theory. *Journal of Cosmology, 14*. Retrieved from http://journalofcosmology.com/Consciousness160.html.

Pratt, D. (1995). John Eccles on mind and brain. Retrieved from http://www.theosophy-nw.org/theosnw/science/prat-bra.htm

Roy S., & Kafatos, M. (1999). Complementarity principle and cognition process. *Physics Essays, 12*, 662-8.

Roy, S., & Kafatos, M. (2004). Quantum processes and functional geometry: New perspectives in brain dynamics. *Forma, 19*, 69-84.

Schrödinger, E. (1983). *My view of the world* (pp. 31-34). Woodbridge. CT: Ox Bow Press.

Siegel, D. J. (2012). *The developing mind: How relationships and the brain interact to shape who we are* (2nd ed.). New York: Guilford Press.

Stapp, H. P. (2004). *Mind, matter and quantum mechanics* (2nd ed.). Heidelberg: Springer-Verlag.

Stapp, H. P. (2007). *The mindful universe: Quantum mechanics and the participating observer*. Heidelberg: Springer-Verlag.

Theise N. D., & Kafatos, M. (2013a). Complementarity in biological systems: A complexity view. *Complexity, 18*, 11-20.

Theise, N. D., & Kafatos, M. C. (2013b). Sentience everywhere: Complexity theory, panpsychism & the role of sentience in self-organization of the universe. *Journal of Consciousness Exploration & Research, 4*, 378-90.

Theise, N. D., & Kafatos, M. C. (2016). Fundamental awareness: A framework for integrating science, philosophy and metaphysics. *Communicative and Integrative Biology*, 9, e1155010. http://doi.org/10.1080/19420889.2016.1155010

Von Neumann, J. (1955). *Mathematical foundations of quantum mechanics*. Princeton:

Princeton University Press. (Original work published 1932).

Wheeler, J. A. (1983). In J. A. Wheeler & W. H. Zurek (Eds.), *Quantum theory and measurement*. Princeton: Princeton University Press.

Chapter 17

Wisdom of Both East and West has a Common Source, Consciousness

A. K. MUKHOPADHYAY
All India Institute of Medical Sciences, New Delhi, India

ABSTRACT

The division of civilization and culture into East and West is man-made and is a recent one, a few thousand years old, advanced during the era of imperialism, colonialism with a tangential desire of some nationalists for establishing racial supremacy. Present-day science is also only a few hundred years old as compared to the whole process of evolution starting from the origin of our universe to the culmination in state-of-art human being. The development of human brain, which is yet to complete its evolution, represents the pinnacle of the process. Irrespective of location in the East or in the West of this earth, the human brain with its cultural bias remains the common equipment for data acquisition with the help of its local resident like neurons and nonlocal 'influential' like self, mind, life-principle and consciousness. Acquired data (a space-time construct of information) is converted by mind *into meaningful information called informative knowledge. It is then filtered to the level of* self *as formative knowledge and* self *can use this knowledge without further deliberation on it. When knowledge is lived and experienced by several members through successive generation, formative knowledge transcends the barrier of time and space (culture) and consolidates into transformative knowledge and staggered as information-manifold within* life. *Finally with approval and concurrence of* consciousness, *transformative knowledge crystallizes into wisdom. Bottom-up, wisdom is accumulated experience over time, which has stood the test of life. Top-down, wisdom crystallizes only with the approval of consciousness.*

Holding human consciousness as invariant, it is easy to find out two groups of opinion-makers in the world, accomplished scientists and accomplished mystics corresponding to two ways of acquisition of knowledge, empirical and intuitive. However, because of disproportionate distribution of such opinion makers across the East and West of this planet earth, a distinction in the perspectives of population's collective consciousness is palpable at present. This paper is to discuss the difference and commonness in the two perspectives, and to suggest that the present day difference is to disappear in next two hundred years when the science of, and the science for consciousness is expected to percolate the mass culture.

THE PLAN OF THIS PAPER

In this essay we would begin with discussion on the differences in approach to consciousness in the east and the west. This would be followed by a brief review of western philosophies, which could be of help in developing a science for consciousness. Next, we would highlight the Indian philosophies, which could contribute to such development. The final section is on issue of reconciliation of the two.

EAST-WEST DIFFERENCE IN APPROACH TO CONSCIOUSNESS

East and west have approached consciousness differently with their respective cultural bias. As Huston Smith (Smith, 2000) puts it succinctly in the 'Cleansing the doors of perception', "Indian philosophy differs from Western in that Western philosophers philosophize from a single state of consciousness, the waking state, whereas Indian philosophizes from them all." All other differences crop up from this basic difference in approach. In the eastern culture, mystical views on consciousness predominate while in the western culture the scientific views are dominant. In *Prasna* Upanishad there are three unanswered questions, which the humanity has asked again and again, have been highlighted. What is God (read consciousness)? Who am I (read self)? What is this world? East has focused on 'self' to get into consciousness while west wades through the 'world' to get into it the same. Eastern and western cultures, however, are not monolithic. Inside the east there is west. Inside the west there is east. There are scientists with mystical mind. There are mystics who follow strident scientific methodology in recording their experience. Nevertheless, it is better to group the two approaches separately for convenience and understanding their complementarities.

East has accepted consciousness as a fact of underlying reality. It does not emerge from anywhere or any interaction. It is there! It is given! Any framework cannot define it. Although consciousness cannot be defined, consciousness could be qualified. Its first four qualities or attributes, all are transcendental in nature, are Immortality, Eternity, Infinity and *Ananda*. In contrast, the west has always sought a definition, at least a working definition, for consciousness. A consensus dictionary meaning of consciousness for them is awareness of self, awareness of surroundings (outside) and awareness of the feelings and thoughts inside. Expression and language could be included in this definition as the manifestation of consciousness for communicating in second and third person's perspectives. For the west, consciousness is an emerging property from the complexity of matter.

For the east, consciousness could not be localized. It is nonlocal. It is not bound by any space or time and it is also free any from causal matrix. The west has searched for consciousness within the locality of the brain. They have epitomized the concept of neurocentric consciousness. Consciousness for them at best is an emergent property of neural networking, a specific space-time geometry created by neuronal manifolds within the brain. To the eastern seekers, consciousness is independent of the brain, that is true for any brain anywhere any time. It is consciousness, which uses the infrastructure of the brain for its manifestation. For the western researchers consciousness confined to the brain vanishes with death. Consciousness is therefore mortal, time-bound (as long as the brain is there), and finite. Consciousness, for the west, is necessary for experiencing pleasure, sensing time and space and understanding causality. Cause, time, space and pleasure are four non-transcendental attributes of consciousness corresponding to its four transcendental properties as mentioned earlier as immortality, eternity, infinity and Ananda respectively.

In fact, all this could be seen as a matter of emphasis on 'noun' or 'verb' aspect of consciousness. The emphasis again differs in non-transcendental and transcendental realm. Broadly speaking, in the non-transcendental realm, in the mundane domain eastern culture lays emphasis on 'verb' (e.g., the work has been done, not being bothered by who has done it), while western culture highlights the 'noun' (e.g., Mr. John has done the work). In the transcendental realm, it is just the reverse. East focuses on ontological status of consciousness while the west concentrates on its epistemological implications. The eastern seekers want to know what consciousness is! The western researchers opine, should consciousness exist what does it do? Consciousness will be known to the world by the mechanics it plays.

The east distinguishes the hierarchy of matter mind and consciousness. Many of the western scholars have used the term mind and consciousness synonymously and interchangeably. For them our brain is a part of matter. In the eastern cultures, especially in Indian culture, mind has dual properties; dealing with matter in one hand and consciousness on the other hand. In the east, the brain is not just matter! It is a live organ. In the west there is little effort to find out the relation between 'life' and consciousness. They consider neuron-consciousness relationship as matter-mind relationship. For them, information handling by mind is all about and what is important and relevant in science for consciousness.

In the west, consciousness and knowledge have been often regarded as the same, if not identical. To know is to become conscious. To become conscious means to know. In the east, consciousness and knowledge are different. All knowledge is within consciousness. With gain of knowledge, which tends to concur with the holism of consciousness there is a concomitant process of becoming. Eventually, *Brahamabid brahamaiva Bhavati*. He who knows *Brahma* (unconditional consciousness) becomes *Brahman*.

While the east focuses on the possibilities of personification (individuation) of different levels of consciousness in human development, the west focuses on the mechanism of consciousness in nature, if any, which would be useful for innovative technology. The east offers the ontology of 'being', the west at least is eager to discover the process of 'becoming' in nature, to explore different invariants, laws and principles in deeper recess of nature, also their relationship, if any.

The eastern seekers seek consciousness within. They use self-consciousness as a tool to reconcile brain-independent consciousness with brain-trapped consciousness. Experience is recorded from first person's perspectives. Western researchers look for consciousness at other's brain. The subject they select may be a practitioner of meditation or a yogi. Technologies used are electron encephalography (EEG), nuclear magnetic resonance (NMR), positron emission tomography (PET), single photon emission computerized tomography (SPECT), magneto encephalography (MEG) etc. to find out the neural correlates/correspondence of consciousness. Their approach is from third person's perspective. Even if they ever adopt an internal method it still remains observational (intro *spection*) and cannot be said a method, which is realizational or experiential.

Eastern scholars close their eyes, minimize their sensory inputs and then turn towards unconditional consciousness. Western scholars with open eyes concentrate on the effect of stimulation of visual cortex to understand consciousness. They try to find out clues on consciousness, if any, following sensory stimulation of the visual cortex. Sensory curbing has been accepted as a must for consciousness-explorers of the east. Sensory enhancement has been the rule of observation for consciousness-explorers from the west. Non-sensory and extrasensory visual images during meditation are regarded as 'godly'/ divine for an eastern seeker. For a western seeker those are considered hallucination or illusion.

First person's direct experience in the eastern culture is self-evident.

It is considered as revealed truth. It has reflexive validity. In any problematic situation when there is any kind of suspicion in the process of experience, it is crosschecked from the pioneer, the precept they love to call as Guru, who has experienced it earlier and is able to guide the first person's experience. This may be accepted as evidence from second person's perspective. In western culture, the validity of any experience is based on evidence, which is public (third person's perspectives).

Even within the brain, the east and the west differ in approach to consciousness. East's focus is on imagination, non-sensory perception and on intuitive knowledge acquired by the brain. For them, the brain is an `open' system. It is open at its top level (*sahasrar chakra* on the top of the brain) and communicates with cosmic and supra cosmic plane. Its evolution as an organ is incomplete and has been still going on! For the west the functionality of the brain is limited 'within the system'. Its multi modal sensory-motor integration and acquisition of empirical knowledge are all about the brain. For the west, the brain is a closed system. Its crown, i.e. cerebral cortex, is informationally closed. Evolution of the brain for an orthodox western scientist is a closed chapter.

In the eastern philosophy, consciousness is simultaneously transcendental and immanent. In the west, such description could be found in Perennial Philosophy. However, the focus of the east is on the transcendental realm, especially on *consciousness as such*, which implies an informationally 'open' cerebral cortex of the brain. In contrast, the western emphasis remains on conscious experience that is sensible within the 'closed' box of the brain.

PHILOSOPHIES OF WESTERN ORIGIN THAT ARE OF HELP IN DEVELOPING THE SCIENCE FOR CONSCIOUSNESS

Modern western philosophy, in general, has been broadly built up on unity of science principle (USP). This trend has been followed after publication of a seminal treatise of Auguste Comte, *cours de Philosophie Positive* in 1842. According to the scheme of Comte, there are three sequential stages: (i) theological, where all observed events are explained by citation of will and intention (ii) metaphysical, where will and intention are replaced by abstract concept of power and force and (iii) positivistic, that works with the laws of co-existence, association and conjunction. There are, however, western philosophies, which are admixtures of both scientific and intuitive truths e.g. the works of Descartes, Leibniz and Whitehead. There are also exceptional modern western philosophers like William James who based their philosophy more on intuitive truth inviting scientific truth to adjust with the revealed truth.

Most of the western philosophies go by the name of the person who propounded it. Western philosophy, although could be stated to start from Thales (around 600 BC) about 150 years before Socrates, it is Socrates-Plato-Aristotle lineage, which makes the base of Western philosophy. Followings are a brief account, which seem relevant in developing a science for consciousness.

Socrates (469-399 BC), Plato (428-347 BC) and Aristotle (384-322 BC)

Greek philosophers Socrates, Plato (2007) and Aristotle (1976) have influenced developmental lines of science. No document written by Socrates is available. Socrates wrote nothing since he believed that he did not know anything. However, it is Socrates who is the first on historical record to pursue the art of disinterested enquiry. The gift of Socrates to science is the art of asking question to get a response without inconsistency (dialectics) and thus the art of reasoning which remains the principal tool for science. The gift of Socrates to consciousness and spirituality is his famous statement, "Know thyself". We quote the incident quite often when Socrates moves in the street with a lamp in his hand in broad day light in search of a pure man. This immediately reminds us of axiology of consciousness. Socrates taught that personal integrity was more important than gods, laws and Power. From the ethics of Socrates, arose many ethical schools, which served the human kind for worthy years. Modern scientific concept of consciousness that it emerges from the activity of neurons is supposed to scroll down from Socrates.

It is said that Socrates was the flame, which illumined Plato as candle while Aristotle represented the spark. While Socrates' gift was dialectics, Plato's gift to the west was logic. Plato's 'world' of 'Forms' is supposed to constitute the deeper reality. While Socrates had a leaning towards theology, will and intention, and Plato had a leaning towards metaphysics Aristotle was more worldly and positivistic. Most of the modern western philosophies could be traced back to Plato while most of the development in western science owes it to Aristotle. In the context of consciousness, Aristotle's '*unmoved mover*' seems to be a very important description for consciousness as an absolutely stable ground. The concept of teleology is of Aristotle's. Plato's '*entelechy*' is a similar description for the soul. Even today, Roser Penrose's (2004) *The Road to Reality* is based on three worlds, physical world, mental world and Platonic world. In Plato's theory on soul, one could see three parts, which correspond to three different kinds of interests, three kinds of virtues, three kinds of personalities. It depends on which part of the soul is dominant in a given individual. He also used to say, "God, forever, geometrizes". Plato's allegorical cave still inspires the modern truth seekers. We are inside the cave looking at the shadows, not yet in touch with the Reality.

According to Sir James Jeans (1931), "The outstanding achievement of twentieth century physics is not the theory of relativity with its welding together of space and time, or the theory of quanta with its present apparent negation of the laws of causation, or the dissection of the atom with the resultant discovery that things are not what they seem; it is the general recognition that we are not yet in contact with ultimate reality. We are still imprisoned in the cave, with our backs to the light, and can only watch the shadows on the wall."

Both Plato and Aristotle have contributed to development of human ethics. Jonathan Shear (2006) has mentioned that there are two major character-development approaches, external and internal. The former had been the approach of Aristotle and the latter of Plato. "The external approach emphasizes internalization of accepted norms and emulation of ethical exemplar. The internal approach relies on what are taken to be culture-invariant aspects of human consciousness, and emphasizes development of the individual from within." Aristotle was tutor of Alexander, the Great, who wanted to unite Indian and Greek cultures but Aristotle never approved the idea.

Other Greek Philosophers of peri-Socrates era

Thales himself was a Greek who lived in what is now Turkey. He propounded that all things are made up of one substance, which is water. His disciple, Anaximander, however, stated that this substance is beyond space and time. It is he who brought the concept of mind in western philosophy. Pythagoras was a mathematician as well as a mystic. The words, 'cosmos', 'theory', 'philosophy' are attributed to Pythagoras. He believed in existence of soul and its transmigration. According to Bernard Russell, 'Platonism' in essence is 'Pythagoreanism'. While most of the Greek philosophers laid emphasis on static form and geometrical symmetries, it is Parmenides (? 460 BC) who made an advancement by stressing more on the process. The idea that the essence/substance of everything continues to exist came in western philosophy from Parmenides. In the context of individuation and science for consciousness, Parmenides will be remembered for stressing on the skill of 'surrender' for attaining higher spiritual goal. There was Anaxagoras (?500 BC), who found mind beyond all physical changes and distinguished entity with mind, and without mind. Leucippus (?440 BC) and Democritus (?420 BC) were atomists, who brought the concept of atom, which are indivisible, always in motion and remain separated by space.

Plato's Academy was established in 386 BC. It served for about 900 years and was closed down by Christian King Justinian in 529 AD, which ushered the dawn of 'Dark Ages' which continued about 1000 years. The Dark Age, 'the mediaeval period' was full of skeptics as well as cynics and stoics (spiritually inclined with intellectual mind). Two saints, Augustine and Aquinas, were instrumental to amalgamate Christianity with philosophy of Plato and Aristotle respectively. Augustine realized and propounded that without the Grace of Lord (read unconditional consciousness personified) it is not possible to know him. Aquinas introduced the terms and concepts of 'existence' and 'essence'. Ockham put forward his view that any explanation on a new advancement should be done in the simplest way possible with minimum number of invariables (popularly known as Ockham's razor).

Following this dark period came a new breed of thinkers in the west in late sixteenth century onwards.

Rene Descartes (1596-1650)

Rene Descartes, the French mathematician, philosopher and scientist is the first person to recognize consciousness in his publications. "*Cogito ergo sum*". "I think therefore I am", said Descartes. To keep Church away from interfering with science he postulated *substance dualism,* which is popularly known as the Cartesian cut, the deep chasm between matter and mind. Arrival of Descartes ushered the end of Dark Ages. In 1633, he wrote the book, 'The World', but because of the fear of Church it was not published; His 'Discourse on Method' was published in 1637 and 'Meditation' in 1641. However, following his death the church put his all books in 'The Index of Banned books'.

Spinoza (1632-1677)

Born Jewish, short lived (only 45 years), led a life of saint. He was a firm believer of Pantheism. Spinoza drew inspiration from Descartes but went beyond him. For him, at the fundamental level, mind and body are same which surface as two aspect of one reality. Both the aspects are independently infinite (compare *Purusha* and *Prakriti* of Samkhya philosophy, where they are standing back to back. Each one is independently infinite).

John Locke (1632-1704)

'No man's knowledge can go beyond his experience', - was his famous statement. However, for him, only sense organs are conduits of experience. He is, therefore, considered as the father of 'Empiricism'.

Wilhelm Leibniz (1646-1710)

The great mathematician, inventor of calculus, Leibniz's philosophical contribution of 'monad' may seem important for us. According to him, the universe is composed of monads. Monads have a hierarchy and each grade in this hierarchy reflects a corresponding degree of the universe (cf., holography). Leibniz's worldview was not confined to one universe only. It extended over several universe(s), which in the terminology of modern cosmologists has been called multiverse. He described the concept of 'analytic' and 'synthetic'. He also offered the 'Principle of sufficient reason'.

George Berkeley (1685-1753)

"To be is to be perceived', said Berkeley. This is reflected in John Wheeler statement, "a phenomenon is a real phenomenon only if it has been observed by a conscious entity'. Being a Bishop in Ireland, Berkeley was a believer in God and in existence of self.

Immanuel Kant (1724-1804)

Newtonian Science and Euclidian geometry influenced Kant. Kantian philosophy (Kant, 1781) is well known for his 'categorical imperatives' and ethics (Kant's moral philosophy), which are important for attitudinal disposition of a consciousness-scientist. As Leibniz introduced the term 'Synthetic' and 'Analytic', Kant introduced the concept of 'a priori' and 'a posteriori'. The 'thing-in-itself', according to Kant, is the noumenon which becomes phenomenon after being perceived by mind of conscious entity (cf. Berkeley and Wheeler). For Kant, all rational wills are autonomous. That mind makes nature has been accepted now as Kant's Copernican revolution. That mind of the knower actively contributes to acquisition of experience of object around us is the key to understand Kant's transcendental idealism. According to Kant, transcendental consciousness is the ultimate source of conceptual synthesis. Since consciousness can never be an object of senses categories cannot be applied to it. He also believed that law could not bind creativity. Freedom is the most important necessity for creativity and, to say, for any human endeavor. Kant did not avoid existential issues. He discussed the existential issues and differentiated sensual from the transcendental and also the sublime from the beautiful.

Kant was, however, of the opinion that humanity is the end in itself. In emphasizing categories, he neglected the process. Kant never tried to define what he meant by transcendence. Kant is said to be a failure in reconciling the masculine with the feminine components of the Reality.

George Wilhelm Friedrich Hegel (1770-1831)

Hegel belonged to the period of German Idealism. In the post Kantian period, he presented us with a comprehensive and systematic ontology as said by R.P. Singh (2008). From a logical starting point, Hegel's notion of the Spirit (*Geist*) has been compared with Sankaracharya's notion of Absolute consciousness. The difference is that Hegel would never accept pure immediacy in the Absolute whereas immediate experience is the very heart of Sankar's absolutism. For Hegel, "Philosophy is itself, in fact, worship; it is religion, for in the same way it renounces subjective notions and opinions in order to occupy itself with God...". ..... "The central claim of Hegel's philosophy as against Kant is that we cannot speak of the Absolute without at the same time speaking of self-consciousness of human mind, nor fruitfully pursue that interrogation itself unless we conceive our activity in doing so as one sustained and made possible by the Absolute." Singh also points out that Hegel's teleological account of history, estrangement and dialectical unification was later taken over by Karl Marx who "inverted" this into a materialistic theory which culminated into communism.

Alfred North Whitehead (1861-1947)

Whitehead (1920; 1926) was influenced by Einstein's theory of Relativity. For him the reality is a process. His philosophy is called process philosophy. "The creative process is thus to be discerned in that transition by which one occasion, already actual, enters into the birth of another instance of experienced value. There is not one simple line of transition from occasion to occasion, though there may be a dominant line. The whole world conspires to produce a new creation. It presents to the creative process its opportunities and its limitations."

It is argued (de Quincey, 2008) that Whitehead's process philosophy takes us beyond both ontological Cartesian Schism (substance dualism of mind and matter) and epistemological Kantian impasse (we can never know anything about the physical world other than as ideas or forms in the mind) by simply accepting the view that matter and mind are related as phases in process; 'Now subject, then object'.

There are three more important philosophies of Western origin that could contribute considerably in development of a science for consciousness.

Aldous Huxley (1894-1963): Perennial Philosophy

Transcendental essence is hierarchically immanent is the dictum of Perennial philosophy. Although the 'transcendental' element poses the problem of subjectivity in science, the emphasis on hierarchy of nature and hierarchical transcendentalism is relevant in developing a science for consciousness. Perennial philosophy misses the process in nature.

Jan Christian Smuts (1870-1950): Systems Holism

Systems theory is based on holography – the whole is represented in every fragment, every part and every point of the system. Therefore, the more you know the part in detail the more you could have glimpse of the whole. The theory has its reflection in self-organizing system. The theory talks of the process but all processes must be within the system. Following this, the brain has also been compared with a hologram, interpreting a holographic universe (Karl Pribram). It is not static. It is all flux (David Bohm).

Systems holism is limited by its boundary-problem. All processes are within the system. The boundary is impervious. No extraneous influence is acceptable in explaining the function of the system. Therefore, the theory suffers from the problem of vertical depth.

Johann Wolfgang Von Goethe (1749-1832)

German Scientist and poet Goethe preferred to derive multiplicity from a preexisting reality rather than reducing pluralism to a commonality. The process of blooming of a whole tree from its seed is an important example. Goethean Philosophy and Goethean phenomenology advocates an inside-out and outside-in phenomenon in the process of describing total reality. Inside-out and outside-in phenomena of Goethean science pose existential issue which science in its present form is not ready to address.

We will fall short of our referral till we do not mention five modern American philosophers of science who have been influencing the development of science for consciousness.

Patricia Churchland

According to Churchland (Churchland, 1995; Churchland & Churchland, 1998), consciousness is too vague for empirical research. If we know all about the brain, consciousness could be explained. Till such time, it would be fare not to confuse and mislead science with consciousness. She therefore propounded the view, which is known as Eliminative Materialism. "Electrical current in a wire is not caused by moving electrons; it is moving electrons. Genes are not caused by chunks of base pairs in DNA; they are chunk of base pairs."

Daniel Dennett

His approach is strictly that of a physicalist, functionalist and heterophenomenologist. Dennett (Dennett, 1991; 2006) upholds the philosophy followed by cognitive scientists; mind is consciousness. To him consciousness is all about neural networking and information flow. Mind works like a computer. Consciousness is not required for mind to function as mind. "What RoboDennett still does not know" has been written by Michael Beaton (2005).

Colin McGinn

"Consciousness is terminally mysterious", says McGinn (1991) (new mysterianism). The problem of consciousness is insoluble. Even if consciousness is not super-material or supernatural, "Human mind lacks the cognitive ability to understand the nature of Consciousness, just as monkeys cannot understand particle physics". To the critics, this is known as cognitive closure hypothesis. Evolution of the brain and therefore of cognitive ability has been ignored in McGinn's viewpoint.

John Searle and Thomas Nagel

It is John Searle who is optimistic to opine, "Consciousness is one of the rare philosophical problems that will have a scientific solution". Both Searle and Nagel (Nagel, 1974; 1986) distinguish consciousness from conscious experience. Three characterizing features ascribed to awareness, are (i) Privacy (ii) Unity and (iii) Intentionality. However, Negal pointed out an intrinsic asymmetry between subjective and objective aspects of consciousness that keeps it removed from naturalistic understanding. Nagel also emphasized a lacuna in consciousness-research by saying, "What we lack in a science of consciousness are rules for extrapolating subjective properties (consciousness) from the properties of objects (interconnected nerve cells)"..., Nagel continues, "......To arrive at that theory, we will first have to discover the elementary components of subjective consciousness." "This discovery", Nagel argues, "will be of enormous magnitude and implication and one that may require a revolution in biology and most likely a complete transformation of scientific thought", quoted by Kandel (2000).

John Searle distinguished two types of emergence (Searle, 1992). Searle pointed out that consciousness could be best understood as a *causally emergent* feature of the brain. "The existence of consciousness can be explained by the causal interactions between elements of the brain at the micro-level, but consciousness cannot itself be deduced or calculated from the sheer physical structure of the neurons without some additional account of the causal relations between them" (Searle, 1992, p. 112). This is what he calls Type I emergence. "A much more adventurous conception" in emergence, what he describes as Type II emergence, would be when the emergent has independent life and causal power to influence the parts from which it emerges. He calls this idea 'naïve'. "If consciousness were emergent 2, then consciousness could cause things that could not be explained by the causal behavior of the neurons. The naïve idea here is that consciousness gets squirted out by the behavior of the neurons in the brain, but once it has been squirted out, then it has a life of its own (Searle, 1992). This roughly conforms to Robert Van Gulick's radical kind of emergence (Gulick, 2001) and also to the proposition of Michael Silberstein (2001).

Finally, we like to mention the works of two accomplished mystical philosophers from west; both are from America, whose philosophical works are not biased by scientific formulations of the past or present but are endowed with the ability to help in developing a science for consciousness.

William James (1840-1910)

Considered as Father of American psychology, James' book, *The Varieties of Religious Experience* (2004) remained in print continuously since its first publication in 1902. He describes experiences ranging from mundane to higher consciousness, superficial psychology to depth psychology, ordinary experience to ineffable experience. Journal of Consciousness Studies published centenary essays on James in their September-October issue of 2002. The same Journal in July 2005 reproduced James communication on *The Notion of Consciousness*, at the fifth International Congress of Psychology held at Rome in 1905 (a strange coincidence of the year of publication of Relativity by Einstein). His characterization of transcendence offers valuable clues for development of its science. It is interesting to note that William James described Swami Vivekananda from India as the 'Ambassador of the East'.

Ken Wilber

Ken Wilber (1982; www.theworldofkenwilber.com), the modern philosopher from USA who is well versed with Sri Aurobindo's work (Wilber, 2001), popularized the concept of what is meant by `integral'. He used this concept extensively in his personal development and therefore also in his writings, which he labels as fourth phase of writing. Following Sri Aurobindo, he also advocates an integral approach by which he means that "transcends and includes". Like Sri Aurobindo, he also talks of levels, planes and hierarchy. "The 'higher' comes through the 'lower', rests on the lower but does not come from the lower. All of the lower is in the 'higher' but not vice versa. It is this not vice versa which makes hierarchy".

Wilber has established an Integral Institute in USA. His propositions for an Integral University and for Integral Medicine are getting acceptance in USA. He builds up this on his four-quadrant model; Individual and Collective, each having an Interior and an Exterior. Individual-Interior determines 'Intention'. Individual-Exterior determines 'Behavior'. Collective-Interior is reflected as 'Culture'. Collective-Exterior is what is known as 'Social'. He distinguishes states of consciousness, levels of consciousness, lines of consciousness and planes of consciousness. One has to consider all four Quadrants, at all Levels, in all developmental Streams and at all States. Therefore, it is called AQAL (short form of All Quadrants, All Levels, All Streams, All States) model.

The model has not worked as expected. Why? The causal force for effecting an integral process is conspicuous by its absence in this scheme. Development of anything integral is not merely an intellectual endeavor. Essential for its development is the causal factor/agent/force. Till we get into what could be this causal agent, we are far away from any practical solution.

Indian Philosophies that help in developing a Science for Consciousness

> "The spiritual heritage of India is one of the world's standing miracles. It would rank among its greatest human achievements were it not that "achievement" isn't really the right word. It is more like a reception - the opening of a people to receive, through inspiration, the Breath of the Eternal." - Huston Smith (2000).

Leaving aside some materialistic philosophy like that of Carbaka, Indian philosophy is mostly based on intuitive knowledge and although interconnected and co-evolving with individuation, every teaching here has to stand on its own merits irrespective of who is the teacher. The message is more important than the messenger. In this sense, it leans towards characteristics of science. Indian philosophy is not monolitithic. "For every psychological term in English, there are four in Greek and forty in Sanskrit" (A. K. Coomaraswamy). Broadly, there are Hindu philosophy, Buddhist philosophy and Jain philosophy. Buddhists and Jains, although, do not accept Vedanta of Hindu philosophy as authoritative, (may be for historical reasons) they accept the authority of transcendental and revealed truth and therefore in essence there is little difference between the three in the context of human knowledge. The

Buddhist philosophy has already been cultivated in the west and has been helping in developing a science for mind, if not for consciousness. While Buddhist philosophy remained mostly confined to brain-bound consciousness and ignored cosmology, Hindu philosophy stretches out to cosmology, primordial creation and brain-independent consciousness. Such Hindu philosophy is thus inclusive of inner and outer cosmos.

There are six systems of Hindu thoughts (called six *darshans*)
1. *Nyaya* of Gotama, deals with reasoning and logic
2. *Vaisesika* of Kanada, deals with notion of space, time, matter, causation
3. *Samkhya* of Kapila, deals with creation based on twenty five different elements
4. *Yoga* of Patanjali, deals with eightfold path of union of body, mind and soul
5. *Mimamsa* (also called Purva Mimamsa) of Jaimini, deals with righteousness in action, ethics and aesthetics in rituals
6. *Vedanta* (also called Uttara Mimamsa) of Vyasa, deals with pathway to Supreme knowledge

Very grossly speaking *Nyaya* describes the cognitive aspect of the brain function, *Vaisesika* the material world, *Samkhya* the cosmology, *yoga* the psychology, *Mimansa*, the hermeneutics and *Vedanta* deals with the notion of the Absolute.

Six systems make three pairs; Nyaya-Vaisesika, Samkhya-Yoga and Purva Mimamsa-Vedanta. In the gradation of ascending order of experiential truth, Vedanta is held as the final word. Common to all of these systems is existence of a hierarchy of matter, mind, self/consciousness. All agree upon the supremacy of self/consciousness.

Distinction between self and consciousness is more clear in Sankhya and most clear in Vedanta. "Unlike in Advaita and Samkhya, consciousness in Nyaya-Vaisesika is not substance but an attribute of the self". "Consciousness in Nyaya is more like empirical consciousness (mind) in Advaita which manifests as intentional awareness" [29]. However, all six systems are in agreement that mind has a physical aspect and a consciousness aspect. Let us describe those in brief.

Monistic Materialism of Carbaka

Although nothing is definitely known about Carbaka from historical perspectives, India never ignored Carbaka's philosophy of materialism, sensuality, space-time matrix of the experiential reality. Carbaka's philosophy is the philosophy of a sensualist in combination with skepticism for any other realm of existence. According to Carvakas, when four elements namely, earth, water, fire and air (Carbaka did not accept the existence of fifth element, *akash*) combine together, consciousness is generated, - a view similar to many neuroscientists that consciousness is nothing but combined activity of a pack of neurons. In totality of India's philosophical spectrum, Carbaka's materialism has a limited, nevertheless a specific room.

Dualism

Unlike substance dualism in the West, where mind and matter are separate substances, the dualism in India indicates 1) a relationship between the same 'substance' separated by space, time and purpose, 2) between two facets of the same Reality or 3) a combination of one and two.

1. *Dualism between the same 'substances' separated by space time and purpose*

Dualism of Madhavacharya (1238-1317) deals with relationship between small 'i' and capital 'I' through a refined emotional playing (*Bhakti*). Madhvacharya was the most profound advocate of dualistic philosophy in *Bhakti-Vedanta*. It is the refined and directed emotion, called devotion, which is considered as the vehicle of communication between the two, the soul and the God, the self and unconditional consciousness *Jivatman* and *Paramatman*, brain-bound consciousness and brain-independent consciousness.

2. *Dualism between two facets of the same Reality (Samkhya Dualism)*

Consciousness and Nature could be expounded as the masculine and feminine components of the Reality. While the mystics explore the masculine (Consciousness) component, the scientists are engaged with the feminine (Nature). The mystics explore consciousness (*Purusha*) and offer us intuitive wisdom. Scientists explore nature (*Prakriti*) and offer us empirical truth.

The dualism of *Samkhya* is between the masculine and feminine components of the Reality. Consciousness (masculine, *Purusha*) and nature (feminine, *Prakriti*) form an inseparable duo but facing the opposite direction. The strategic flaw here is, as if nature and consciousness are two different entities standing back to back, facing the opposite direction and is independently infinite. Therefore, the idea, opinion, doctrine originated from this type of notion is uni-faceted. There is no scope for any process like evolution. It is good for analysis and that too to a specific extent and is not probably useful for any synthesis of the Whole.

Therefore Purusha of Samkhya is a non-evolving purusha. Samkhya accounts for two Purusha(s) (*Khasara* and *Akhsara*). Khasara is the perishable world-consciousness. Akhsara is the imperishable self-consciousness. In contrast Vedanta accounts for three Purusha; *Khasara, Akhsara* and *'Uttama'* (compare *Purshosttama* concept of Gita). Purushottama there is a personified unconditional consciousness, supracortical autonomy, Sadguru, who acts as the magnet for human evolution en-masse.

3. *A combination or 1 & 2: Dualistic Non-dualism*

This deals with relationship between small 'i' and capital 'I' in the context of both consciousness and nature. This is one of the five kinds of non-dualisms, which takes dualism within its fold (see below).

Nondualism

In consciousness study, the absolute nondual consciousness has been regarded as the Ultimate. In India, even non-dualism has six sub-schools. All of them seem to have relevance in developing a science for consciousness.

1. **Sankara**

Non-dualism of Sankara (788-820 AD), called *Kevaladvaita,* accepts nondual consciousness as the only ultimate. (As Niels Bohr derived his complementary principle in QM from Chinese Yang-Yin version of reality, many other doyens of QM like Schrödinger and Heisenberg drew their philosophical nourishment from nondualism of Sankara). The school completely disregards nature, the feminine component of the Reality and therefore, any creative feat according to this philosophy is a self-deception or illusion (*Maya*). Brahman is the only truth and the world is false. Self is as inactive as Brahman. It is non-anthropomorphic and excludes possibility of any personal God. When we take the view that consciousness is absolutely impenetrable, it is attributeless, indeterminate, a-cosmic or, non-definable consciousness, we have been speaking from *Kevaladvaita* position.

2. Ramanuja

Consciousness cannot be defined. However, it can be qualified. It is immortal, eternal, infinite and is perceived biologically as *Ananda*. This kind of statement emanates from *Visistadvaita* (first propounded by Ramanuja, 1017-1137 AD) position. There is non-duality of the qualified Whole. When we say consciousness is biologically perceived as *Ananda*, we are acknowledging anthropomorphic tilt in non-dualistic view. Isvara (the Supreme), chit (self) and achit (world) are three essential One in this philosophy.

3. Vallabhacharya

Instead of brushing aside the nature/prakriti, the school of *Shuddadvaita* accepts it as a Reality. Since consciousness is not illusory and the nature is in its possession, nature cannot be said illusory too. Nature of consciousness is as pure or as untainted as consciousness itself. Nature is thus distinguishable but not different from consciousness. Nature works as the kinetic facet, mobile pole, and executive front of consciousness. This nature could also be personified. This is the position of *Shuddadvaita*. Vallabhacharya first advocated this in the first half of sixteenth century (or fifteenth century). Supreme Brahman/Immutable Brahman (Parabrahaman), the Self (Akshara Brahman), and the Brahman as the World (Shakti) are three essential One in his philosophy.

4. Nimbarka

May I be many! There are occasions when consciousness duplicates itself (self replication). It creates a self-image in nature to experience tension in the act of union (enjoyment) and tension in separation (suffering) in the state of duality. Consciousness could reflect, crystallize and even `personify' in nature. This is a duality in unity, described as Dualistic non-dualism. *Sadguru* (Supracortical Autonomy) and Consciousness Absolute, are therefore identical (Guru, the Master, is *Brahman. Brahman* is Guru, the Master). The view could be an example of *Dvaita-Advaita* (first propounded by Sri Nimbarka (?) – 1162 AD).

5. Sri Chaitanya

Distinction between nature and consciousness is not that important. It is rather irrelevant! Consciousness is nature and nature is consciousness. Nature is naturally intoxicated with consciousness and consciousness is purposeless without nature. This is inconceivable oneness and difference, the *Achintabhedabhed* (Sri Krishna Chaitanya, 1486-1533) school of Non-dualism. Let our nature get completely intoxicated with consciousness and we will be in a position to experience both consciousness and nature. When one's nature becomes pure nature one is consciousness. There is thus a process that is evolutionary that acknowledges *becoming* of nature. *Achintabhedabhed* seems more relevant for those scientists engaged in consciousness-based study of nature. While (matter)/nature-based studies of consciousness are mostly disappointing and even frustrating in science, consciousness-based study of nature (matter) appear rewarding in the sense that it promises to reveal a few radical laws/principles of nature that could not be known by matter-based study of nature or consciousness.

6. **Advaita Saivaism**,

This originated in Kashmir (8th-16th century), propounded nature and consciousness as indivisible 'Biune Reality'. The ultimate Reality, the *Parama Shiva* (in the present context, Consciousness) is indivisible from *Shakti* (in the present context, Nature) at every point of space and/or time or even at no space no time domain. As the burning ability of fire cannot be studied separately or independently from the fire itself, similarly the mechanics of *Shakti* cannot be completely explored totally detached from consciousness. Consciousness and nature, therefore, are interdependent both ontologically and epistemologically. This leap from nature to 'shakti' is a huge one. In Advaita Saivism one sees the primordial 'vibration', the dynamism in the inseparable operation of the masculine and the feminine component of the Absolute Reality, This philosophy offers a new linguistic approach to consciousness. Three primary qualifications of Nondual Consciousness namely, Existence (*Sat*), Knowledge (*Chit*) and Bliss (*Ananda*) are embedded in Advaita Saivism as two aspects of *Shakti* namely, *icchashakti* (Power of Will) and *kriyashakti* (Power of Action) (Singh, 1985; SenSharma 2009).

In the recent past, there are three phenomenal spiritual upheavals in India in ninetieth-twentieth century.

1. Ramakrishna-Vivekananda lineage with revival of Vedanta in the West.
2. Sri Aurobindo and the legacy of his profound work.
3. Akhandamadleswar Sri Sri Swami Swarupananda Paramahansa Dev

The philosophies of Sri Ramakrishna and Sri Aurobindo have made finer improvements on this Biune Reality. Sri Ramakrishna replaced the phrase *Shakti* of Advaita Saivaism with *Mother*. This is an unprecedented leap, which had been demonstrated in his personal life wherein he worships his married wife as Mother. The whole philosophy of Sri Aurobindo stands on this Mother's strength (Sri Aurobindo, 2011). For Swami Swarupananda Paramahansa, all and any feminine component as a person or an entity in nature, from the bottom to the top is Mother or Mother Nature. All these developments led to the culmination of a synthesis, called the Akhanda philosophy.

Ramakrishna-Vivekananda

Sri Ramakrishna at his full fruition was a personification of an ideal that reflects Advaita-Saivism, the biune reality of Consciousness-Mother Nature. His direct disciple, Swami Vivekananda said, "I have a message for the West, as Buddha had a message for the East". Vivekananda redefined religion, the goal of humanity and its methodology. "Each soul is potentially divine", thundered Vivekananda in America,.....".

"The goal is to manifest this Divinity within by controlling nature, external and internal. ....Do this either by work, or worship, or psychic control, or philosophy by one, or more, or all of these and be free"... "This is the whole of religion. Doctrines, or dogmas, or rituals, or books, or temples, or forms, are but secondary details".

Sri Aurobindo (1872-1950)

Sri Aurobindo ushered the descent of the 'Divine' on this very earth. He himself experienced and eloquently expressed this descent from 'supramental' to mind and from the mind to the material. The process is divine materialism. He demonstrated in life the physical conquest of death in his seminal work *Savitri* (Sri Aurobindo, 1940) and opened up the door for a greater psychology with layers of mind like ordinary mind, higher mind, over mind, intuitive mind, illumined mind and super mind. It has led to a great synthesis involving the inner and outer cosmos both as a system and a process. He reconciled evolution and creation by introducing the concept of involution in between. His views and concept of 'Mother' as the prime Force of Consciousness is extremely useful in connecting the `material' with `spiritual'. The nature of consciousness could be called Mother Nature of which the rest of the nature is an extension. In contrast to a mystic who engages directly with consciousness, the scientist deals with nature and as consciousness also possess a nature, there emerges a possibility of a science for consciousness.

Akhandamandaleswar Sri Sri Swami Swarupananda Paramahansa Dev (1890-1984)

Swami Swarupananda had been more practical in terms of knowledge, skill and attitude, in his philosophy, work and devotion (Akhandamandaleswar, n.d.). As a great human resource developer he operated with humanity's 'stem cell pool' from the countryside of Bengal, Tripura, Assam, Bihar, Jharkanda and Orissa and erstwhile East Bengal (now Bangladesh) initiated the beings to proliferate and to differentiate on their respective natural direction. For him, the Source pool for this material world is the *Essence* of the system of multiple universe(s), the Multiversity. The *Essence of the Multiversity* in form of a cosmological realism offers nourishment to the roots of the inverted neuraxis (tree) of human tabernacle.

THE AKHANDA PHILOSOPHY

The Akhanda Philosophy deals with Indivisible with Divisions, plurality without compromise of the autonomy of the individual within the whole, which encompasses multiple universe(s) (Akhandamandaleswar, n.d.). There is no reduction anywhere. It accepts *nature as an indivisible extension of consciousness*. Feminine component here is not *Shakti* (of Advaita Saivism) but *Mother* (like Sri Ramakrishna and Sri Aurobindo). Unlike Advaita Saivism, which focuses on the Ultimate reality, the Akhanda philosophy zooms on the Total reality. The view upholds the parental Biune concept of *Advaita Saivism* down up to the basic and rock bottom of the matter where any, every and all feminine elements is considered as 'Mother'. The ideology is not of *maya* or renunciation but is rooted in Love. In the Akhanda philosophy, with Mother's love, the matter and the senses are also real. The 'matter' here does not produce self-deception and could not be ignored also as 'illusion'. Consciousness, matter and all in between, are real. The process in the Akhanda Philosophy, like Sri Aurobindo's, is integral, in contrast to Adavita Saivism where the process is Real-Ideal/Ideal-Real.

In contrast to Advaita Saivism where the operation is always a joint mechanics of consciousness-nature (Akhandamandaleswar, n.d.), activities are five in number; Self-concealment, Creation, Sustenance, Destruction and Grace, the Akhanda Worldview upholds operation of consciousness of his own, a joint operation of consciousness-Mother Nature and the operation of Mother Nature of her own (see the Table below) and there is scope for Grace in all three.

Operation of Consciousness	**Joint operation of Consciousness-Mother Nature**	**Operation of Mother Nature**
Absolute Ease Self-concealment Maintenance of its own supreme sovereignty and independence Power of Will Grace of Consciousness	Creation Destruction Grace of Consciousness-Mother Nature	Sustenance Determination of Purpose Scrutiny on unconditionality during bidirectional transformation Execution of upside-down, inside-out and outside-in phenomenon, Grace of Mother Nature

According to the Akhanda Worldview, consciousness remains the only invariant in all equations or relationships what the science intends to explore. All other invariants and constants, natural or man-made (e.g., Einstein's constant, Planck's constant etc.), are considered flux in nature. The roots of the Akhanda are in the systems Multiversity, the largest intellectually comprehensible pluralistic system of multiple universe(s). Therefore, the vertical depth of the *Akhanda* metaphysics extends far beyond the Z.P.F. (zero point field), and dark matter and dark energy in sub-Planckian scale. It penetrates into the essence of the Multiversity (the system of multiple universe), the Ultimate Source Field.

The Akhanda Philosophy incorporates Perennial philosophy, Systems holism and Goethean philosophy into an overarching One. Multiple universe(s) form the highest comprehensible systems (cf. systems holism). At the boundary of the universe, there is an inside-out phenomenon (cf., Goethean philosophy). The human neuraxis behaves like an inverted tree with roots open to the eternity and the branches down as peripheral nerves. The transcendental reality (Consciousness-Mother Nature), although, is beyond this farthest inversion point (cf. Transcendental Essence of Perennial philosophy) there are cascades of such inversions in different nests of nature. Nature shows a hierarchically nested organization. The determinism seen in the most superficial nest of nature, i.e., in the classical world resembles the certitude observed in the transcendental world of consciousness.

The Akhanda Worldview represents the culmination of Indian philosophical thoughts through materialism (of *Carbaka*), unbreakablity of self (*atman*) and dualism of *Samkhya,* the discipline of *Bhakti*, unconditional non-anthropomorphic non-dualism of Sankara, other non-dualistic schools of philosophy, the biune reality of *Advaita Saivites*, 'Mother' of Sri Ramakrishna and Sri Aurobindo, also taking into consideration of the ongoing evolution of the present human species towards the divine being (Sri Aurobindo) / divine-human (Swami Swarupananda) / *Homo spiritualis* (in science). Development of science for consciousness cannot be dissociated from individuation, the personal growth of the scientist. The Akhanda philosophy predicts arrival of divine-human (*Homo spiritualis*) within a time frame of 300 years. This period covers nine generation of conscious effort by present humanity for production of necessary genetic infrastructure to sustain consciousness of higher domain. Finally, we concede that the Akhanda philosophy itself is an open-ended and evolving philosophy and the followers are welcome to contribute to its further development and ramifications.

Unique position of the Brain in the practitioners of the Akhanda Philosophy

The Akhanda philosophy transcends and includes all. The brain stationed at, and functioning in the Akhanda state could be said to have tasted the experience of every individual station of the base camps, which are in parallel and in series at different altitude and that of the summit, and in the process has acquired the ability of having freedom from any territorial enslavement without losing the capacity to enjoy the richness of every territory in fitness of the proper context. This positioning of the brain is unique in the Akhanda Worldview.

There is an assumption in Nondual philosophy that the pathway from dualistic base to the terminals of non-dualism, from anthropomorphic non-dualist post to the summit of non-anthropomorphic non-dualistic apex is a one-way. Once at the top, it is impossible, or is extremely difficult for 'self' to come down. The Akhanda philosophy as lived by its founder, does not support such stand. Accordingly, there are ways to climb up and also to come down. In this sense, the Akhanda State of the Being indicates a much more mature and flexible state of the brain upholding its (brain's) openness, plasticity and integrating capacity. The *primal essence* (read consciousness), which drives 10^{11} neurons and almost similar number of glial cells within the brain, is also the driving force of 10^{11} stars in a galaxy and 10^{11} galaxies of the universe!

The Akhanda

The *Akhanda* is the one in whom the Akhanda worldview has been personified. For those who all are familiar with the Indian vocabulary of spiritualism, the *Akhanda* as a person is an embodiment of *sat*, *chit* and *ananda*, respectively of the world, self and *Brahaman*, three purushas; *kshara*, *akshara* and *uttamo*, three prakritis; *apara*, *para* and *parama*. The Akhanda is a personification of the three 'Alternate Absolutes' of World, Self and *Brahman* as introduced by (K.C. Bhattacharya). This is a new way of expressing the Upanishadic *Om* (Brahaman) *Tat* (Self), *Sat* (World) or *Sat Chit Ananda* (World-Self-Ananda)!

Following is a tentative comparative table of similar ideas in the east and the west on World Self and Brahman.

	World	Self	Brahman
1. Philosophy of	Object	Subject	Absolute
2. Approach	Cosmo centric	Anthropocentric	Theocentric
3. Movement of spirit to free itself from nature delivers,	Anthropology	Psychology	Phenomenology
4. In the language of Spinoza	Matter	Mind	God
5. In the language of Kant	Rational Cosmology	Rational Psychology	Rational Theology
6. In the language of Hegel	The science of idea in its otherness	The science of Idea in and for itself	The science of Idea coming back to itself out of that otherness
7. In the language of Bhagavad Gita			
(i) Three Purusha (ch. 15)	*Khsara Purusha*	*Akhsara Purusha*	*Purshottama*
(ii) Three Prakriti (ch. 7)	*Apara Prakriti*	*Para Prakriti*	*Parama Prakriti*
(iii) Movement of the Aspirant	*Karma Yoga*	*Jnana Yoga*	*Bhakti Yoga*
8. In the language of Vedanta			
(i)	*Sat*	*Chit*	*Ananda*
(ii)	*Sat*	*Tat*	*'Om'*

RECONCILIATION: WEST AND EAST

Reconciliation of East and West! Where was the East and where was the West, asks Thomas McEvilley (2002) before colonialism, imperialism and before the ruthless advancement of the desire to establish racial supremacy? In the ancient world, Indus valley civilization was said to be the matrix of three civilizations namely Greek, Mesopotamian and (?) Egyptian. Neither there was good transport nor communication technology as it is in the present. There was no fixed boundary of nations even. Moreover there were not nationalists in the narrow sense of its following. There were, however, free flow of thoughts and culture across all four civilizations, which had their own rational, non-rational and trans-rational documents of experiences. Sanskrit, like German, Latin and Greek was a rich Indo-European language prior to the Pre-Socratic Greek, the Thales of Miletus. The barrier between East and West is simply a recent discovery, a construct of mind infected with imperialism, colonialism, racism and most recently the scientism.

> "But there is neither East nor West, Border, nor Breed, nor Birth,
> When two strong men stand face to face,
> though they come from the ends of the earth!"
> \- *Rudyard Kipling*

Is reconciliation necessary?

Certainly! Wisdom of both East and West has a common source, Consciousness. This reconciliation is necessary both for harmonization of knowledge from different sources and for ordered individuation in the globalised world. It is required for the totality of the process of acquisition of knowledge and skill, and also for complete fulfillment of the individual with appropriate attitudinal disposition. Reconciliation is necessary for reconciliation of top-down and bottom-up skills. This is also necessary for accomplishment of the *purpose* of evolution of the brain as an organ of consciousness.

Is reconciliation possible in practice?

In all likelihood the answer will be in affirmative. Reconciliation of two complementary approaches of mystics and scientists, east and west is possible when the rigid distinction between nature and consciousness is dissolved! The work might begin with an *assumption* that nature and consciousness are indissolubly wedded. There is no boundary but only a spectrum across transcendentalized nature and naturalized transcendental. There are autonomous operations interconnected, hierarchically nested but all within the ambits of systems science of "The Multiversity".

In practice, this could be made possible when the mystic becomes a scientist and the scientist becomes a mystic. This presupposes conscious transcendence of death by the being while alive, a very difficult process indeed but not impossible to accomplish! This realization is likely to facilitate consolidation of the *Akhanda worldview,* which in turn admits co-evolution of Humanities, Science and the Spirit. Final reconciliation thus waits for emergence of those individuals who are both scientist and mystic by all parameters of brain functions. In developing the science for consciousness, we need in one person a spiritualist, a philosopher and a scientist. And, we need plenty of them.

Reconciliation has already started in the West, which might be complemented from the east.

Natural evolution of the brain is beyond the boundary of east and west. One can see the trend of movement in the west itself. We may start with the Philosophy of Mind as originated in the west with Copernicus, Galileo and Descartes. They took leave from the earlier prevalent philosophy by advocating a *'substance dualism'* meaning mind (consciousness) and matter (body) are two different substance altogether. The observation is practically relevant in the sense that the matter is amenable to senses and falls within the objective realm. On the other hand, mind/consciousness appears beyond the realm of senses and better comes under subjective realm. However, should we remain 'open' to only our 'senses' we land up becoming an advocate of *material monism* and in the extreme stage become an *eliminative materialist* (like Patricia Churchland). On the other hand should we ignore the senses and its domain the space time bound classical world, with a total tilt and emphasis on 'mind' only, we are labeled as *panpsychist.* As a group, both sides collapse the hierarchy on their respective side. Those who eliminate 'consciousness', in fact do it so by their brain consciousness (an example of *reductio at absurdatum*)! And a panpsychist excludes matter only by the activity of the 'matter' (I mean neurotransmitters) in his brain!

It is Leibniz who emphatically propounded the view that there is a *pre-established harmony* between the two substances, mind and matter. However, the 'harmony' between the two substances could not be effected unless there exists a connection and interaction between the two. Mind (consciousness) and matter (body) are, therefore, connected to each other (cf., *Connectionism* of John Searle). And, they do interact (cf., *Interactionism*, e.g. Descartes). Their connection, according to Leibniz, is already established (pre-established).

Common mortals like us are not aware of this connection and interaction. As monkey's brain is not in a position to understand quantum physics, so the human brain is not equipped enough to understand consciousness. This is the view/propounded in *Cognitive closure hypothesis* of Colin McGinn. McGinn could be correct! But only partially! Since *evolution* of human brain is not yet complete. Ongoing process of evolution of the brain, however, rescues us from this blinding pessimism. The stem cells in the 'brain-marrow' could be a rich resource for renewal of the brain.

Mind and body do interact, may be occasionally (cf., Malebranche's *Occasionalism*), the interaction might be in the realm of *phenomenology* (cf., Husserl's *psychologism*). Whether they do or, they do not, it would be better not to abandon *positivism* (cf., Comte) and *behaviorism* (cf., B.F. Skinner) in any and all situations where one is able to quantify the stimulus/response relationship by measurable yardstick. In fact, this was the rationale adopted following the 'behaviorist's coup' in 1913. The approach seems most practical as long as the complex picture beyond the mindscape is not very clear. Beyond the realm of mind, the science is of quality and relationship, rather than of measurement and equation.

Following advocacy of the *Process philosophy* of Whitehead in the west and scientific openness to new ideas and thoughts to connect through the prevailing gaps, the scenario has changed considerably, particularly following 1980s. The humanities in general, and the scientists in particular, have been coming across attitudinal transformation with ongoing evolution in their brain.

The gap between two different 'substances' of Descartes is bridged now with interacting *field, energy, 'form'* and different kinds of *information*. In the course of processing of this variety of information, mind does resemble a 'computer', but only to a limited extent (cf., *computational models of mind*). That is to say that the mind, whether it arises out of function of the neurons (cf., *Functionalism*, Putnam, Neisser) or is a combined product of consciousness and functioning neurons, it does possess computable properties. Some of the computational functions of the mind, it seems, could be externalized with far more precision and time-economy as has been done in *Artificial Intelligence* or *Expert system*. Mind/Consciousness, however, has been found to have more skills and functions other than what have been mimicked or simulated in a computer or in an expert system so far. The expert system has access-consciousness (rather to say access to information), monitoring consciousness (rather to say monitoring information) and decision-making consciousness within the bounds of a large number of probabilities. However, expert system developed so far has no hints of having self-consciousness, meta-self-consciousness and phenomenal consciousness. The probability remains high that in future more of such new skill/functions of mind/consciousness would be externalized in expert system taking help from the disciplines of neuroinformatics, informational geometry in the context of neuronal manifolds, different types of nonlocal communications and advancement in our understanding of 'life', which has supposed access to the sub-Planckian nature of dark energy and dark matter.

We trust on developmental possibilities in the human brain as well. The gap is likely to be filled up not merely through deep introspection (cf., *Introspectionsim*) but through direct experience of the Reality and more in-depth research in phenomenology. This is likely to unravel the most private aspects/facets of 'self' (Thomas Nagel's *elements of subjectivity*) and the speculated connections between psychic mechanics and information mechanics.

This may warrant us to consider critically the state of informational openness of the brain across the cerebral cortex. When the transcortical information exchange between 'inside' and `outside' of the brain achieves *harmony* (Leibniz's ideal), the evolutionary accomplishment of the brain as an organ is completed for manifestation of consciousness. At that time, mind and matter may work in an identical way (cf., *Identity theory*). The outcome is a kind of divine materialism, where there is an explicit layout of integration of consciousness mind and matter.

If not exactly 'identical', mind and matter might be considered at best as two facets of one coin. We are reminded of Spinoza's *Double aspect theory,* which states that mind and matter are two facets of the one and the same. Consciousness and nature represent the two facets of the one, not as in Samkhya philosophy but as a Biune Reality of Advaita Saivism.

In the Akhanda worldview there is a terrain, in between matter and mind, of elementary phenomena with operations of mind, information, informational memory and intelligence. Between mind and consciousness sandwiched is another terrain, the nest of Mother Nature with operators like 'self' and 'life' ('life' has access to the domain of dark energy). and their operations like access to the domain of dark energy etc. At the micro level, cellular cognition could be a testable model, while at macro level the testable model is the brain itself. The brain is the 'play ground' and the meeting point of consciousness, mind and matter, self, life principle and information.

Final reconciliation, however, would wait till we could (i) develop a science for transcendence (of death) and (ii) connect different nests of nature through their respective but interconnected mechanics (iii) emergence of those individuals who are equally a scientist and a mystic.

How is reconciliation going to happen?

It requires a continued *education* program on the science of transcendence. Education is formally defined as the process of bringing desirable changes in the behavior of the learner in terms of knowledge, skill and attitude contributed respectively by the cognitive, psychomotor and affective aspects of the brain. The goal of education is to know the Truth, achieve the skill of Freedom and experience the joy of accomplishment/fulfillment, which in mystical version has been described as *Ananda*. Education on transcendence and the skill of projecting First Person's experience in Third Person's perspectives would facilitate reconciliation.

Is there any working Model?

Consciousness is the reality independent of any experiential or experimental realities. This is consciousness's ontological status. Consciousness could be known by what consciousness does. Consciousness has an operational mechanics. This is its epistemological perspective. The mechanics of consciousness is connected to nature's mechanics on the surface level, quantum mechanics and classical mechanics. The connection becomes effective only in accordance with the mutually agreed value-systems working in between its constituents. This axiology of invariants does not violate the status of ontological consciousness. Phenomenology of consciousness, i.e., not-happening, happenings and the set of happenings, like generation of self, life-principle, mind and information, and also of space, time and energy are subject to acceptance of this ontological status of consciousness and its axiological ramification. Creative phenomenology demands an absolute freedom, which is achieved by total submission, a complete 'surrender' to the axiology of consciousness. The phenomenology of consciousness requires approval, a sanction from the axiology emanating from consciousness's ontological status. There are, it is admitted, epistemic constrains to realize this agenda of consciousness within the brain. And, this fundamental epistemic constrain introduces perception *of uncertainty*. This is the reason the reality looks probabilistic in quantum approach to consciousness.

The model that we expect for a science of consciousness is non-reductive, holistic and without any boundary problem. To have models accommodating autonomy within holism, pluralism without contradicting individual aspiration and that too all within the ambits of systems science is our aim. The present author has been working on this line since 1985 and the following few are his important contributions.

1. Supracortical Consciousness (an example of interface between systems-independent consciousness and systems (brain)-confined consciousness) Mukhopadhyay, 1985; 1987; 2006).
2. Five-nest (Pentaune) model of nature-consciousness as depicted in The Millennium Bridge (Mukhopadhyay, 2000). Classical mechanics, quantum mechanics, information mechanics, mechanics of 'life' and 'self' cascade to mechanics of consciousness.
3. A radical view of Information. Its nature and science (Mukhopadhyay, 2008; 2013; 2012). Information serves as the bridging operator between local and non-local domain.
4. Model connecting Systems neuroscience, systems psychology and consciousness (Mukhopadhyay, 2015a), and model connecting systems psychology with cell biology at molecular level (Mukhopadhaya, 2015b).
5. Simplifying the complexity by identifying non-observable operators, their operations and hierarchically nested interaction within it (Mukhopadhyay, 2016). Here we understand the pathway from signal to information, knowledge and wisdom and vice versa. Knowledge organization is a function of 'life' and it is possible because of 'life's supposed access to the domain of dark energy.
6. Communication between Systems-bound consciousness and systems-independent consciousness requires an extraordinary inter-phase constituted by five irreducible operators like consciousness, self, life, mind and information. How this narrative can be an important part of future science has been elaborated (Mukhopadhyay, 2010).

Where this reconciliation is likely to lead us?

(i) This reconciliation is to set the development of a much-desired science for consciousness as an open-ended process and (ii) would help and facilitate emergence of the individuals who could be designated as *First-Person-Universal* swimming comfortably in the *Inter-universal Essence*, an individual indivisible from the Whole (*Akhanda*), an individual who has the complete knowledge as well as skill and is having the required attitudinal disposition towards the service for the mankind. In the terminology of evolutionary process, this may mean emergence of a new species on this earth. We may call them *Homo spiritualis* emerging from present *Homo sapiens* (Mukhopadhyay, 2010).

Having known all that is possible, having acquired the leadership skill and attitudinal disposition towards philanthropic service, what one is prepared for? It is to serve and serve only. This is probably what Robert Greenleaf, in 1971, called *servant leadership* in the context of management. The concept of servant leadership itself is very old in India and goes back to Bheeshma's dialogue with Yudhisthir in the Shanti Parva of the *Mahabharat.* It could also be found in the description of Governance in Kautilya's Arthashastra. In the second half of the 1990s the academicians picked up the idea as a possible synthesis in East-West leadership style for a globalized world. In the West, political leader such as Martin Luther King Jr. and Abraham Lincoln best symbolized this style in the past. In India, political leader like Mohondas Karamchand Gandhi has exemplified it. Huzur Dr. Prem Saran Satsangi Sahab is a living example of such servant leader in Dayalbagh Educational Institute. The individuals working locally and having the ability to communicate globally with knowledge universal is a servant leader. We need plenty of such servant leaders as Scientist, Humanist and Spiritualist.

References

Akhandamandaleswar Sri Sri Swami Swarupananda Paramahansa Dev (n.d.). *Akhanda Samhita* (1-24 parts) (in Bengali). Varanasi: Ayachak Ashrama.

Barnes, J. (1976). *Introduction to the Ethics of Aristotle: The Nicomachean Ethics.* (J. A. K. Thomson, Trans.). Harmondsworth: Penguin.

Beaton, M. (2005). What RoboDennett still doesn't know. *Journal of Consciousness Studies, 12*(12), 3-25.

Churchland, P. M. & Churchland, P. S. (1998). *On the contrary.* Cambridge, MA: MIT Press.

Churchland, P. M. (1995). *The engine of reason, the seat of the soul: A philosophical journey into the brain.* Cambridge, MA: MIT Press.

de Quincey, C., (2008). Reality bubbles: Can we know anything about physical world? *Journal of Consciousness Studies, 15*(8), 94-101.

Dennett, D. C. (1991). *Consciousness explained.* New York: Little Brown.

Dennett, D. C., (2006). What RoboMary knows. In T. Alter & S. Walter (Eds.) *Phenomenal concepts and phenomenal knowledge: New essays on consciousness and physicalism.* New York: Oxford University Press.

Gulick, R. V. (2001). Reduction, emergence and other recent options on the mind/body problem. A philosophic overview. *Journal of Consciousness Studies, 8*(9-10) 1-34.

James, W. (2004). *The varieties of religious experience.* New York: Barnes & Noble Classics. (Original work published 1902).

Jeans, J. (1931). *The mysterious universe.* (p. 111). Cambridge: Cambridge University Press.

Kandel, E. R. (2000). From nerve cells to cognition. In E. R. Kandel, J. H. Schwartz, & T. M., Jessel (Eds.) *Principles of neural science.* (International 4th ed.) (pp. 381-403) McGraw Hill, New York, London, Singapore, New Delhi: McGraw Hill.

Kant, E. (1781/1929). *Critique of pure reason.* (N. K. Smith, Trans.). London: Macmillan.

McEvilley, T. (2002). *The shape of ancient thought: comparative studies in Greek and Indian philosophies*. New York: Allworth Press.

McGinn, C. (1991). *The problem of consciousness*. Oxford: Blackwell.

Mukhopadhyay, A. K. (2010). On the landscape of human possibilities: tendencies of *Homo sapiens* to become *Homo spiritualis*. In S. C. Mishra, A. B. Samaddar, & S. Ghosh, *Bridging science and spirituality*, (pp. 69-87). Published jointly by Bhakti Vedanta Institute, Kolkata and Motilal Nehru Institute of Technology, Allahabad. Retrieved from http://akmukhopadhyayconsciousness.com/pdf/LINK9.pdf

Mukhopadhyay, A. K. (1985). States of consciousness: a holistic hypothesis. Supracortical consciousness: an existing reality. In *Frontiers of research for human biologists. Next hundred years* (pp. 1-6). New Delhi: Conscious Publications.

Mukhopadhyay, A. K. (1987). *The dynamic web of supracortical consciousness*. New Delhi: Conscious Publications.

Mukhopadhyay, A. K. (2000). *The millennium bridge*. New Delhi: Conscious Publications.

Mukhopadhyay, A. K. (2008). A radical view of information. On its nature and science. *Frontier Perspectives, 16*, 19-28.

Mukhopadhyay, A. K. (2013). Setting the agenda for science of information. [PowerPoint presentation] at Towards a Science of Consciousness, Dayalbagh, Educational Institute, Dayalbagh, Agra, India. Retrieved from http://akmukhopadhyayconsciousness.com/pdf/LINK14.pdf

Mukhopadhyay, A. K. (2015a). Neural fabrics of the mind: systems neuroscience, systems psychology and consciousness. *Annals of Psychiatry and Mental Health, 3*, 1049. Retrieved from from http://www.jscimedcentral.com/Psychiatry/psychiatry-3-1049.pdf.

Mukhopadhyay, A. K. (2015b). Systems cell: a testable model for systems holism, *International Archives of Medicine, 8*, 1-10. http://dx.doi.org/10.3823/1703

Mukhopadhyay, A. K. (2016). Emerging patterns in the complexity: Their organization in systems science. *International Journal of Applied Science and Engineering Research, 5*, 3, 208-234. doi:10. 6080.ipajaser. 05023

Mukhopadhyay, A. K., (2006). Supracortical consciousness. An opening to multiple new doors of science. In R. Balasubramanian (Ed.), *The enworlded subjectivity. Its three worlds and beyond* (pp. 380-446). Project History of Indian Science, Philosophy and Culture (PHISPC). Vol. XI, Part 4. New Delhi: Center for Studies in Civilization. Retrieved from http://akmukhopadhyayconsciousness.com/pdf/LINK2.pdf.

Mukhopadhyay, A. K., (2012). Information holograph. The structure, the source and its operation, *International Journal of BioEngineering, NeuroSciences and Technology*, 2, 12-32. Retrieved from http://akmukhopadhyayconsciousness.com/pdf/LINK13.pdf.

Nagel, T. (1974). What is it like to be a bat? *Philosophical Review, 83*, 433-50.

Nagel, T. (1986). *The view from nowhere*. New York: Oxford University Press.

Penrose, R. (2004). *The Road to Reality*. London: Jonathan Cape

Plato (2007). *The republic*. Penguin.

Rao, K. R. (2005). Perception, cognition and consciousness in classical Hindu psychology. *Journal of Consciousness Studies, 12* (3), 3-30.

Retrieved from http://akmukhopadhyayconsciousness.com/pdf/LINK6.pdf.

Searle, J. R. (1992). *The rediscovery of the mind*. Cambridge, MA: MIT Press.

SenSharma, D. (2009). *An introduction to the advaita saiva philosophy of Kashmir*. Varanasi, India: Indica Books.

Shear, J. (2006). Ethics, meditation and development of consciousness. In *Understanding consciousness: Recent advances*.(pp. 131-147). Kolkata, India: Ramakrishna Mission Institute of Culture.

Silberstein, M. (2001). Converging on emergence, consciousness, causation and explanation. *Journal of Consciousness Studies, 8*(9-10), 61-98.

Singh, J. (1985). *Vedanta and advaita saivagama of Kashmir*. GOl Park, Kolkata: The Ramakrishna Mission Institute of Culture.

Singh, R. P. (2008). Hegel's notion of the spirit (Geist), estrangement and dialectical unification. In *Consciousness: Indian and western perspectives*. (pp. 206-317). New Delhi: Atlantic Publishers & Distributors Pvt. Ltd.

Smith, H. (2000). [Foreword], In *The spiritual heritage of India* by Swami Prabhananda. Mylapore, Chennai: Sri Ramkrishna Math.

Smith, H. (2000). *Cleansing the doors of perception: the religious significance of entheogenic plants and chemicals*. New York: J. P. Tarcher/Putnam.

Sri Aurobindo (1940). *Savitri* (Vol. 28 & 19). Pondicherry, India: Sri Aurobindo Ashram.

Sri Aurobindo (2011). *The Mother* (Vol. 25). (Original work published 1928) Retrieved from http://www.aurobindo.ru/workings/sa/25/25_eng.pdf

Whitehead, A. N. (1920). *The concept of nature*. Cambridge: Cambridge University Press.

Whitehead, A. N. (1926). *Religion in the making*. New York: Macmillan.

Wilber, K. (2001). [Foreword]. In A. S. Dalal (Ed.), *A greater psychology* (p. viii). New York: Putnam.

Wilber, K. (Ed.) (1982). *The holographic paradigm and other paradoxes*. Boston & London: New Science Library, Shambhala.

www.worldofKenWilber.com accessed on May 12, 2016, 5PM, IST

Chapter 18

Chaitya Purusha or The Principle of Sentiency as Anthropic Evolutionary Consciousness- Integration of Eastern and Western paradigms

TANIMA BHATTACHARYA
Ranbir and Chitra Gupta School of Infrastructure Design & Management
Indian Institute of Technology, Kharagpur, India

and

JOY SEN
Department of Architecture and Regional Planning and
Ranbir and Chitra Gupta School of Infrastructure Design & Management
Indian Institute of Technology, Kharagpur, India

It is not the psychic being itself that develops, but it guides the evolution of the individual being by increasing the psychic element in the nature of the individual. It is these personalities in nature that are bound.....

.....I wanted to know if the word has a fixed connotation. If it has not, then one can use the word "Chaitya Purusha" for the "Psychic being". It has the advantage of carrying both the functions of the Psychic being : it is the direct portion of the Divine in the human and it is also the being that is behind the Chitta.

Sri Aurobindo on 'The *Chaitya Purusha*'

INTRODUCTION

Deep within an inner cave (*guhahitam*) present in the very heart of hearts of our existence, is our potential Divinity. It is the place where our reflected sentient being (*which can be compared to the symbolic Second bird of the Upanishad sitting on the lower branches and tasting the fruits and vagaries of mortal existence*) is trying to probe deeper and recover the hidden sun (*which is the glow of the First or upper Bird sitting but detached on the crown of the Tree*). The idea of the two movements, the two birds are evident in **the parable of the Cave** preached by the Upanishads and much later by Gnostic Greek philosopher Plato in his famous work 'The Republic'. The First Bird, the potential seat of a guiding consciousness is within us and its presence makes our evolution surge. Finally, the human mind merges with the resplendent celestial blue as the full radiance of a solar like expanse transcends the limitations of all ignorance and division: *Aditya varnang tamaso parastat*!

Till the end of the journey is attained, there exist two Birds. One, the psychic being which is our reflected consciousness and two, the direct portion of the Divine, who is constantly trying to guide and work within us, to make the two ONE – the *Param Purusha*. In the words of Sri Aurobindo, it is *Chaitya Purusha*, the first bird or the direct portion of the divine. As explained by an ancient primordial Sage Kapila evident in the ancient *Swetaswatara Upanishad* and also in the remnants of a later Bhagabat Purana, the evidence continues in the subsequent chronicles of ancient Buddhism closest to the times of Gautama the Buddha, who himself had derived the principle of empathy and compassion based on the inner working on a guiding light of consciousness immanent within the human soul. As the Buddha said:

Atmo Dipa Bhava
(You be that Light)
By extinguishing desire (Nirvana)
and reaching that ever-effulgent light (*Anirvana*)

The principle of sentiency is Çhaitya Purusha, the direct portion of the Divine in the human. It is also the being that is behind the Chitta, as Sri Aurobindo says. The inspired Architects in the most ancient of all Buddhist ages had carved the idea as rock-cut expressions called the *Chaitya* hall. As the Mahayana Sutra of the *Foremost Shurangama* at the Crown of the Great Buddha says:

...the way of practicing the Samadhi is not singular and its actual method of cultivation depends upon the functioning of mind and mental concomitants (Citta-Chaitya pravritti) of each being and their interconnectedness (Mahat)

The present chapter is a systematic contribution of the presence of consciousness individually within each of us (*Aham*) and in the universal or collective consciousness (the Mahat) for a purpose of existence that transcends limited notions of one life and one death. The aim of this chapter is presented in three parts:

Part 1. To decipher the hidden elements and their interconnection that reinvigorates the edifice of *Sanatana* (universal and timeless) Vedic cultural, architectural and mythical orientation. The iconography of '*Chaitya*' as a cosmological archetype has been explored to which the earliest forms of Buddhist iconography are perhaps original continuities. To best capture the spirit of continuity, the iconography of '*Chaitya*' has been earmarked to bridge the gap between Vedic times and archaic Buddhism and provide means to understand the deep implications of individual salvation and its relationship with collective and cosmic resurgence. The present chapter has expanded the iconographic enquiry along with Indic convergences between ideologies, philosophy, language behind the iconography of '*Chaitya*'. At the outset, the chapter has mainly reviewed the term '*Chaitya*', both in the physical and cognitive levels of human interaction with the divine. The literature review forwards an initial understanding and textual interpretation enacted as the supportive material to explain the philosophical correlation between the two periods. The objective is to probe into an understanding of the continuity of the periods, which is still a grey area of Indian history, through the iconography of '*Chaitya*'.

Part 2. To investigate the iconographical elements and their propinquity that resuscitates the architectural expression of Early Buddhism and established its *Sanatana* (universal and timeless) Vedic cultural, architectural and mythical orientation. The iconography of '*Chaitya*' as a physical manifestation of philosophical prototype has been explored, which can be regarded as the earliest forms of Buddhist iconography. To tap on the spirit of continual architectural and formal development, the iconography of '*Chaitya*' has been append to dissect its form and expression of archaic Buddhism and provide means to understand the deep implications of deep ecological conscience to the physical built form. The present chapter has forwarded the iconographic enquiry of the origin, purpose, iconographical connotations that connects *Chaitya* as a specimen of built environ of early Buddhism of India to the rest of the world. Furthermore, the chapter has mainly reviewed the term '*Chaitya*', in the physical levels of human interaction with the divine. The methodological construct would apprehend the architectural and symbolical assay of the built form of '*Chaitya*', which can be best captured from the comparative analysis of the earliest specimen of Buddhist architecture and its later formal rejuvenation in temple architecture and in formation of Christian basilica plan churches. Thus, the objective is to probe into an architectural iconographical assay of the term *Chaitya* to arrest the contribution of Buddhist elements in forming the architectural shape grammar of the Western world.

3. To evaluate a Post-Cartesian Departure in our own times that traces the guiding light:

- The first break-way from the narrow viewpoint of reductionism had come through from the very world of fundamental Physics

– with the works of Werner Heisenberg (the dual wave-particle theory), Albert Einstein (the principles of relativity), Neils Bohr (the quantum theory) and the scientists of the EPR (Einstein-Podolsky-Rosen) experiment under the leadership of Einstein himself (Bohm, 1951[1]; 1980[2]). The resultant was the birth of the Quantum reality of nature recognizing non-local connections of energy systems and it's interconnectedness amongst different parts in nature signifying a universal holism.

- **Post-Darwinian shift:** In the recent times, advances in genetic microbiology and evolutionary sciences have further shown that mutations are only one among the three avenues of evolutionary changes, the other two being the trading of genetic codes in the network of various organisms in the web of life and the process of sym-biogenesis that suggests an **element of creativity** – a creation of new living systems and approaches by merging of different species. These advances have led to a conceptual shift – from neo-Darwinian emphasis on 'chance and necessity' to a system's viewpoint that sees evolutionary change as a manifestation of the principle of life as a whole and its self-organization in the planetary and universal scale (Margulis, 1998[3]; 1997[4]). The point has been expanded later in the chapter.

4. On the system's viewpoint to Human evolution and progress, its purpose and perfection, and returns to scale as a future teacher (what we call involution) Swami Vivekananda provides the clue to the Turning point, in his seminal work, 'Raj Yoga'. It shows how Darwinian evolutionary scales based on competition and the limited gratification forwarded by Freud:

"Today the evolution theory of the ancient Yogis will be better understood in the light of modern research. And yet the theory of the Yogis is a better explanation. The two causes of evolution advanced by the moderns, viz. sexual selection and survival of the fittest, are inadequate. Suppose human knowledge to have advanced so much as to eliminate competition, both from the function of acquiring physical sustenance and of acquiring a mate. Then, according to the moderns, human progress will stop and the race will die. The result of this theory is to furnish every oppressor with an argument to calm the qualms of conscience. Men are not lacking, who, posing as philosophers, want to kill out all wicked and incompetent persons (they are, of course, the only judges of competency) and thus preserve the human race! But the

[1] 'Quantum Theory' (1951), New York: Prentice-Hall
[2] 'Wholeness and the Implicate Order' (1980), London: Routledge and Kegan Paul
[3] 'Symbiotic Planet' (1998), Basic Books, New York
[4] 'Microcosmos' (199), California Press, Berkley

great ancient evolutionist, Patanjali, declares that the true secret of evolution is the manifestation of the perfection which is already in every being; that this perfection has been barred and the infinite tide behind is struggling to express itself. These struggles and competitions are but the results of our ignorance, because we do not know the proper way to unlock the gate and let the water in. This infinite tide behind must express itself; it is the cause of all manifestation.

Competitions for life or sex-gratification are only momentary, unnecessary, extraneous effects, caused by ignorance. Even when all competition has ceased, this perfect nature behind will make us go forward until everyone has become perfect. Therefore there is no reason to believe that competition is necessary to progress. In the animal the man was suppressed, but as soon as the door was opened, out rushed man. So in man there is the potential god, kept in by the locks and bars of ignorance. When knowledge breaks these bars, the god becomes manifest."

It is important to understand the larger tide, the infinite tide that is behind our evolution and how it must express itself and how it is expressing itself; it is the cause of all manifestation. The present chapter accordingly unfolds a story in three parts starting with the recovery of a story of evolution and realization of a timeless principle of Sentiency or Immanent Consciousness. The principle hailed by the Upanishads and the philosophy of Kapila is still evident in the works of Sri Aurobindo. The living principle is called the Chaitya Purusha, the spark of consciousness immanent in all living beings; more evolved in human beings; and fully recovered in a raised human being whom we call a Rishi or a Yogi.

PART 1

1.0 Introduction

A discussion may be initiated on the bases of a study of the emergence and evolution of *Chaitya* in physical, philosophical and spiritual terms. The analysis is prorated more or less into three clefts. The first one deals with the much deeper ecological aspect of etymology and vocabulary (coinage of the term '*Chaitya*'). Secondly, a review has been laid based on the findings of the earlier and contemporary pedagogues; and thirdly, a concluding discussion on the physical, iconographical and architectural specifics of *Chaitya* has been forwarded.

Architecture is a study of forms about plans, designs, motifs and how they have evolved over time. Thus, built spaces are a medium to study the prevailing practice, beliefs, structure of the societies as well. Architectural spaces, both sacred and secular have a functional aspect in relation to mundane or ritualistic life, in the sense that they fulfil the need for what they were created. Architecture is also a medium to study the formation of the society because built spaces delineate communities, give them a sense of belonging and cultural identity. In the case of Indian art and architecture, it is basically developed out of the socio-physical needs of religion, embodying an idea representing an inner world of beauty that may have an intrinsic meaning seeking physical manifestation. It may be said that Indian architecture, conforming to classical norms of Neo-Platonist doctrines, holds the potentials of organic creativity which is allowed to embrace all arenas of tangible Indian art as carriers of intangible spiritual truths.

The spirituality of Indian art was underlined when A. K. Coomaraswamy (The Origin of the Buddha Image) informed that nature was transcendental and existed on a metaphysical plane in the artist's mind, which was then externalized and represented in material art form in his work. Coomaraswamy was right in assessing the role of religion in Indian art. However, when it comes to explain the precise relation between art and religion or the nature of Indian art, he took recourse to collective metaphysical generalizations. Two aspects, one a need and the other, an issue, are important in his works that emphasizes how a research may be best activated:

i. There is a need for an assessment of the traces of relation between religion and art that was found dating back to the period of Buddhist circumference during the Mauryan era.

ii. There is a complementary issue of exploring an honest relationship between the architectural form and the meaning, which can be derived, or read by virtue of its intrinsic properties.

Much of commentary and researches today explain the exact nature of this relationship in more concrete and individual ways, rather than in generalized collective notions. In this connection, architecture has to be studied in specific religious, cultural, political and social contexts. Accordingly, different endeavours and forms have to be clearly assessed from their own specific contemporary positions and perspectives, and as well as historic continuity.

1.1 In Search of Continuity

The connection between the words *Sanatana* (universal and timeless) as a Vedic precursor and a multitude of Buddhist phraseology has conspicuously retained some analogy in phases, say between Indus valley civilization and the emanation of Buddha. Intermittence of same words, both in phonemics and syllabification, purposefully bolstered the affinity between the two distinct phases of religious history but built upon the common edifice. So what could have been that edifice? Will '*Chaitya*' venture to arrest, at least a set of indicators, to construct that lost edifice?

Contemporary versions and appreciation of Indian Art often propagates a discontinuity from a biased perspective as approached by diverse and shallow local and foreign influences, as there is no holistic attempt to collate a pool of art and architectural evidences found in the interim period between Vedic and Buddhist eras. Here the word *Chaitya can* come forward to construct both form and concept driven philosophical notion linking Vedic period and Buddhist architectures and all that can be explored through a correlation of 2D footprints in 3D format corroborating the actual shape grammar in reality. In view of this correlation, two objective statements can be simulated:

- To establish the practice and socio-cultural linkage underlying the popular Buddhist terminology of Chaitya and trying to identify the traces of it traversing both periods
- To bring to light the 'architectural design elements' unveiling Chaitya as an intrinsic-ecological form and its meaning representing the aspiration of the seeker and its conscious or sentient relationship with the cosmos.

2. Literature review: *Chaitya*

Scholars of the twentieth century and even the intellectuals of the contemporary period followed and continuously re-evaluated fresh aspects of architectural evaluation articulated by Fergusson during 19th century. He opined on the religious dominance over Indian art, and the idea got established to some extent due to Nineteenth century European methodology and Indic scholarships, an approach that was piecemeal and fragmentary. According to Niharranjan Ray, prominent art historian of twentieth century, *"This scholarship created a number of stereotyped images of India, only loosely connected with one another, the establishment of which brought about a distorted perspective in the perception of Indian culture."* As evident in table 1, he takes issue of Ananda K. Coomaraswamy for his contribution to the distorted perspective emanating from his underlying assumption that Indian art is based on religion and it is articulation of the intellectual and the transcendental. As Coomaraswamy's interpretation of Indian art had been religiously conditioned, his emphasis was too frequently on the *"... literary, religious, symbolical and metaphysical content of Indian art at the expense of considerations of important, imaginative and aesthetic questions, problems of artistic forms and its evolution and the human and social context of art."*

TABLE 1
Literary representation on *Chaitya*

TIME LINE / ELEMENTS & ORIGIN	Evidences in literary Formats
Vedic Era	Concept of *Chaitya* is present in the Vedas, especially through the story of the two birds metaphorically mentioned as Jivan and Atman in Rig Veda.
Ramayana/ Upanishadas and Puranas	*Others see in the meditation upon Him within their own body the Personality of Godhead residing in the region of the heart measuring eight inches, having four arms, carrying the lotus, the wheel of the chariot, the conchshell and the club.* (Bhagabat Purana 2.2.8)
Gita/ Mahabharata/ Buddhist Texts	The ***Anguttara Nikâya*** mentions several discourses preached to the Cetis, while the Buddha dwelt in their town of Sahajâti. The ***Pâcînavam sadâya*** confirms Buddha dwells in the Ceti country.
17th to 19th century findings	**James Fergusson** Rediscovery of the Indian art and archaeological section Fergusson played the pivotal role to shape up the base of Indian archaeology. **Percy Brown** kept aside the concept of religious codification by stressing on the broader range of *caityagriha* morphologies than conveyed by earlier definition.
Contemporary re-readings	*"The hall is really a Buddhist church, and like a Christian church"* **Ananda K. Coomaraswamy.** **Niharanjan Ray** Ray associated architectural evolution of Buddhist *Catiya griha* as being response for the socio economic needs as the community dedicated to serve the greater society. **John Irwin** According to J. Irwin the *stupa* in the beginning, even before the advent of Buddhism was a cosmogram or a permanent cosmogony stating that the *stupa* is a cosmogram embodying Mount Meru. **Louise Renou** In his article called *"La maison védique"* (The Vedic house) that appeared in Journal *Asiatique* in 1939 opined that *Chaitya* s had a broader implications devoid of the religious functionality. **Walter Spink** He has termed and analyzed catiya in a restricted manner with a parallel Comparative study with Western architecture i.e. earlier basilica plan church. **Vidya Dehejia** She has approached *Chaitya*'s symbolism via a universally valid system of 'Fundamental Symbols of Sacred Science'.

While exploring the art panorama of Indian subcontinent A.K. Coomaraswamy utilized the term *catiya* hall in his survey of Indian an Indonesian Art. Discussing the existence of the *catiya* hall of Karle,

Bahaja, Ajanta, he opined that "*The hall is really a Buddhist church, and like a Christian church, consists of a nave, apse and aisles, the latter separated from nave by pillars, the apse containing the space for altar, a solid stupa, the whole excavated in the living rock or built of wood and brick. The aisle is continued round the apse, thus providing of circumambulation and corresponding to the outer hall or veranda of structural temples*"- in this quotation he is continued to associate *catiya* halls with that of the plan of the Christian churches and an enumeration of shared components. Coomaraswamy initially augmented the idea simulated by Fergusson but very surely avoids the claim of commonalities between the two (Buddhist and Christian architecture), rather established his concept of religious dependency by stressing on the importance of circumambulation within it. Though he mentioned about varied interior morphologies still abide the concept of Indian architecture in a much narrower corpus by asserting that "*... it is nevertheless becoming more apparent every day that the content of Buddhism and Buddhist art is far more orthodox than was at first imagined, and orthodox not only in a Vedic sense, but even universally.*"

Alike Coomaraswamy, Percy Brown also exhibits a disjunction between the definition of *Chaitya* halls and its wider application. He has concentrated on the architectural morphology, shape and built forms of *Caitya griha* and later on kept aside the concept of religious codification by stressing on the broader range of *Caityagriha* morphologies than conveyed by earlier definition. Louis Renou in his article called "La maison védique" (*The Vedic house*) that appeared in *Journal Asiatique* in 1939 shared the same tune with the other scholars. Similar to Brown Walter Spink termed and analyzed *catiya* in a restricted manner with a parallel comparative study with Western architecture i.e. earlier basilica plan church.

TABLE 2
Philosophy of *Chaitya* over the ages

TIME LINE ▾ | ELEMENTS & ORIGIN ▸	**Philosophy of *Chaitya***
Vedic Era	In Rig Veda, *Man* is said to have a transient frontal personality coupled with an inner eternal soul or Divine Self or *Chaitya Purusha*, referred to as the metaphor of "two birds on the tree" (*Rig Veda 1.164.20)*
Ramayana/ Upanishadas and Puranas	The inner Self, no larger than the size of a man's thumb... *(Katha Upanishad 2.3.17, Svetasvatara Upanishad 3.13)*

Ancient Buddhist Texts	Cetiya is meant for "reminders" or "memorials", are objects and places used by Theravada Buddhists to remember Gautama Buddha. These are traditionally divided into three categories: **Sarîraka**, pieces of the body, **paribhogaka**, things he used, and **udeśaka,** reminders.
Late Buddhist	Amaravati school initiated in 3rd century BCE exhibited an array of sculptures that reflect both, aniconic and iconic depiction of philosophies of that time.
Contemporary re-readings	*The psychic being is formed by the soul in its evolution. It supports the mind, vital, body, grows by their experiences, and carries the nature from life to life. It is the psychic or Chaitya purusha. At first it is veiled by mind, vital and body, but as it grows, it becomes capable of coming forward and dominating the mind, life and body; in the ordinary man it depends on them for expression and is not able to take them up and freely use them...* ***Shri Aurobindo*** *(pp.282-284* *Jivatman, Spark-soul and Psychic Being)*

Countered with the hypothesis of Coomaraswamy, as evident from the table no 2, Niharranjan Ray contended that the religious extrapolation of Indian architecture cannot be ignored but the proper perspective contains a broader periphery i.e. essential sociality and the integral part of temple in Indian social life as market centre, public forum, communal bank, treasury and he argues that it was naturally a communal centre of Indian culture focussing on the visual and performing arts. Ray associated architectural evolution of Buddhist *Caityagriha* as being response for the socio economic needs as the community dedicated to serve the greater society. Ray broadened the notion by aberration of the two ideas, one is religiosity and another is spirituality or deep ecology that is profusely intertwined in orientalised objectives.

Much contemporaries like Vidya Dehejia avoided the compound entirely while depicting cave morphology along with a *stupa* and circumambulatory passages as is evident in table 2. Much recent scholarly disputation on the subject has once more centred on the question of whether we should approach *Chaitya*'s symbolism via a universally valid system of "Fundamental Symbols of Sacred Science", of unspecified ancient Indic and largely pre-Buddhist provenance – or depending solely on what Buddhist scriptural and epigraphic tradition has to say on the subject. The ideas of one protagonist in the debate, John Irwin (1980), barely represent much more than the overviews held by Ananda K. Coomaraswamy i.e. an innate universal symbolism that only awaits detection by the modern visionary. According to J. Irwin the *stupa* in the beginning, even before the advent of Buddhism was a cosmogram or a permanent cosmogony stating that the *stupa* is a cosmogram embodying Mount Meru. He relied on the notion of the Primordial Hillock floating on the Primordial Ocean is all-pervasive. According to him the *yaús´* or the centre line of the *Caitya* must be seen as

"none other than the Axis Mundi itself, metaphysically identified with the World Tree and the World Pillar as interchangeable images of the instrument used to both separate and unite heaven and earth at the Creation. Both are in turn identified with the sun, which was released from the Cosmic Ocean at the moment of separation to create Time and the Seasons. By its orientation to the four cardinal points, the Axis expresses the unity of Space-Time and enables the worshipper, by performance of the rite of sun wise circumambulation, to identify with the rhythm of the cosmic cycle".

3.0 Methodology

As can be seen from figure no 1, distinct words can decipher the Vedic connection of the Buddhist terminologies that has further determined the thread of emergence of Buddhism. This underlying relation can be elucidated through the terms as '*Rishi Asit Devala*', 'The clan of *Goutama*', '*Nikaya* as a process', '*Shakya* clan', '*Astangik Marg*', '*Odana*', '*Buddhi Yoga*', '*Stupa* as an objective', '*Chaitya* ' etc.

As for example, *Nikâya* is a Pali word meaning 'volume'. It is used like the Sanskrit word *âgama* 'basket' to mean 'collection', 'assemblage', 'class' or 'group' in both Pâḷi and Sanskrit. It is most commonly used in reference to the Buddhist texts of the *Sutta Piṭaka* but can also refer to the monastic divisions of Theravâda Buddhism. Again Buddhist *Stupa*, both in its physical and philosophical orientation followed the prevailing notions of *Sanatana* Vedic philosophy. The Physical structure of stupa simulated the idea of a pit or a mound even present in the Indus valley civilization and in terms of its philosophical articulation it divulged the axioms of *Panchatatwa* i.e. *Khsiti* (earth), *Op* (Water), *Tej* (Fire), *Marut* (Wind) and *Bom* (Sky).

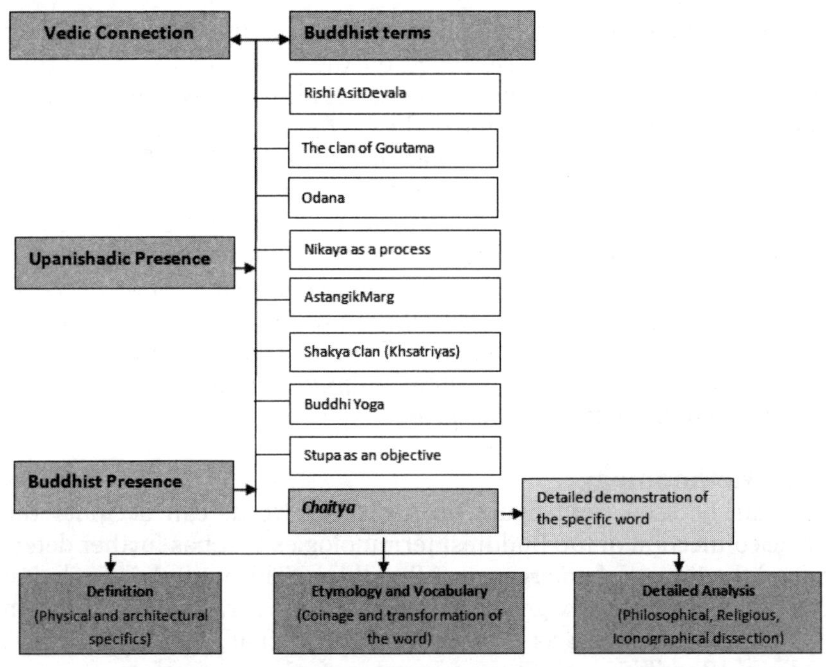

FIGURE 1
The position of Chaitya in a combined hierarchical format

Therefore the words like *Nikaya*, *Stupa* can be traced back to the time of Vedic period and shows its origin from Sanskrit. Formulation of the convergence between the two religions will unfurl the new pages in the history of Indian civilization. Likewise, this chapter is concentrating on the term '*Chaitya*', seeking to unveil the philosophical and iconographic overlays of ideas. Initially the term '*Chaitya*' is demonstrated as the specific word, developing through different ages that can be elaborated from different perspectives. Diversification even in the origin of the word can give us a glare of its multifarious dimension.

3.1 Emergence and Condensation of the term *Chaitya*

Buddhism was the earliest Indian religion to require large communal spaces for worship which led to three types of architectural forms: the *stupa*, the *Vihara* and the *Chaitya* . Many religious Buddhist shrines came up between the 2nd century BCE - 1st century CE. Amongst them *Chaitya* is the place of community congregation. A *Chaitya* is a Buddhist shrine or prayer hall with a *stupa* at one end[1]. In modern texts on Indian architecture, the term *Chaitya-griha* is often used to denote an assembly or prayer hall that houses a *stupa*. *Stupa*, originally focuses the popular cult of the dead, is a large burial mound containing a relic of the Buddha.It celebrates the Buddha's *parinirvana*, symbolizes his eternal body, and is an object of worship.

3.2 Etymology of *Chaitya*

The emergence of the word '*Chaitya*' can be a debatable ground as it spanned as a philosophical perception during Vedic period. It left evidences in the field of anthropology, religion, geographical terrain and at last consolidated as the term to denote architectural overbearing.

- The word *Chaitya* is actually derived from the Sanskrit word *Caitya*, which is again a derivative of *citâ* (funeral pyre), akin to *cinoti* (piles up).
- The coinage of the term *Chaitya* and its meaning is directly related to the first public speculation of thoughts of Lord Buddha at Senani Village, near present Hazipur (Bihar), where he delivered his first public speech even prior to his 'First Sermon' at Mrigadava, Sarnath. He uttered that, "***One should not chase behind Anatma***". His direct reference of *Anatma*, established the notion of *Atma*.
- *Catiya* is a tumulus, a mausoleum, a place where the relics of Buddha were collected; hence, a place where the sutras or images are placed[2].
- The Sanskrit word '*Caitika*' was an early Buddhist school, and was a sub-sect of the *Mahâsâṃghika* School. They were also known as the Caityaka sect. The Caitikas proliferated throughout the mountains of southern India, from which they derived their name. In Pali writings, members of this sect and its offshoots were generally referred to as the Andhakas, meaning those of the Ândhra region.

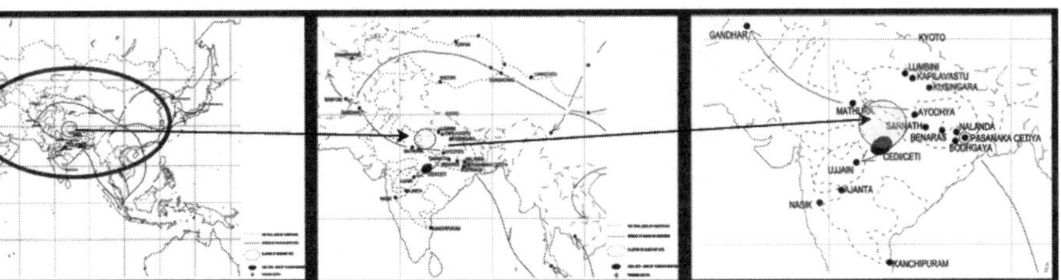

FIGURE 2

Maps showing the presence of the term Ceti/ Cedi/ Caitika even prior to the advent of Buddhism

- Epigraphic evidence of the *Mahâsâṃghikas* in the Mathura region dates to the first century BCE, and the *Sâriputraparipṛcchâ Sűtra* dates the formation of the *Caitikas* to 300 years after the Buddha. However, the ancient Buddhist sites in the lower Krishna Valley, including Amaravati, Nagarjunakonda and Jaggayyapeṭa "can be

traced to at least the third century BCE, if not earlier.[3]
Ceti or Cetiya was regarded to be one of the sixteen Mahâjanapadas[4], probably identical with Cedi of the older documents[5]. The people of Ceti seem to have had two distinct settlements: one, perhaps the older, was in the mountains, probably the present Nepal[6]. It is evidently this older settlement which is mentioned in the Vessantara Jâtaka.

- An eminent art historian of Modern India Sukumar Dutta opines Cetiya vada or Caitika flourished in Amaravatischool.[7]

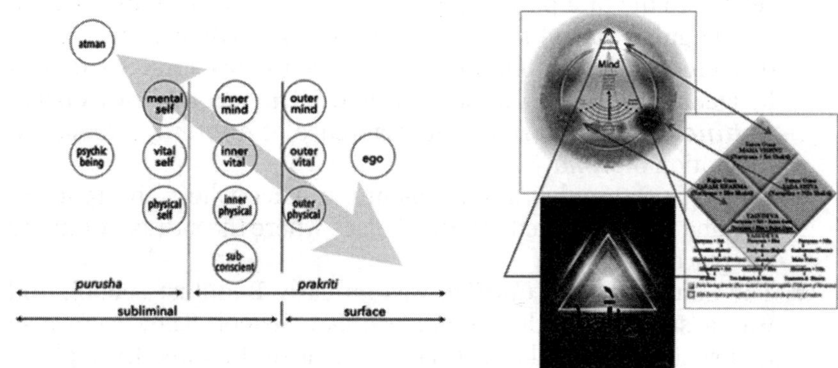

FIGURE 3
Relation of Purusha and Prakriti that established the presence of Chaitya

3.3 Concept of *Chaitya* and *Chaitya Purusha*

Concept of *Chaitya purusha* is an antiquated concept that was prevailing since the time of Vedas which is later corroborated through the principles of Shri Aurobindo in his *Spark Soul and Psychic Being*. According to his idea of *Chaitya purusha* in the contemporary context is actually-

"The psychic being is formed by the soul in its evolution. It supports the mind, vital, body, grows by their experiences, carries the nature from life to life. It is the psychic or Chaitya purusha. At first it is veiled by mind, vital and body, but as it grows, it becomes capable of coming forward and dominating the mind, life and body; in the ordinary man it depends on them for expression and is not able to take them up and freely use them..."

Shri Aurobindo[8]

3.4 Presence of *Chaitya* in Vedas

The term *Chaitya* was not persisting during the phases of the Vedas but the concept was there in *Katha Upanishada* it is said that *Chaitya* or *Chitta* is '*The inner Self, no larger than the size of a man's thumb...*'[9]. According to Vedas *Chaitya* is divided into two segments *Purusha* and *Prakriti*. While *Purusha* deals with the Psychic being or atman on the cognitive level on the other *prakriti* denotes our outer mind occupying our mundane life which can be termed as Ego.

"In the space lying inside the heart, the Purusha assumes the form of manas which is immortal and golden in look."[10]

3.5 The Principle of *Chit*

As can be seen from the figure no 4 that the principle of sentience or '*chit*' (Ability to feel, experience, perceive subjectively) was first articulated by sage Kapila in his philosophy of *Samkhya Darshana*[11] (7th century BCE), which was continued even in the period of *Svetaswatara Upanishada* (4th to 3rd cent BCE.). According to Kapila's spiritual philosophy *Chaitya purusha* is equalled with the Sentient Being.

- Prior to the calculative appreciation of *Samkhyatatwa*, Rig Veda stimulated the concept through the story of two birds on a tree i.e. '*Jiva*' (the individual) and '*Atman*' (Chaitya Purusha).

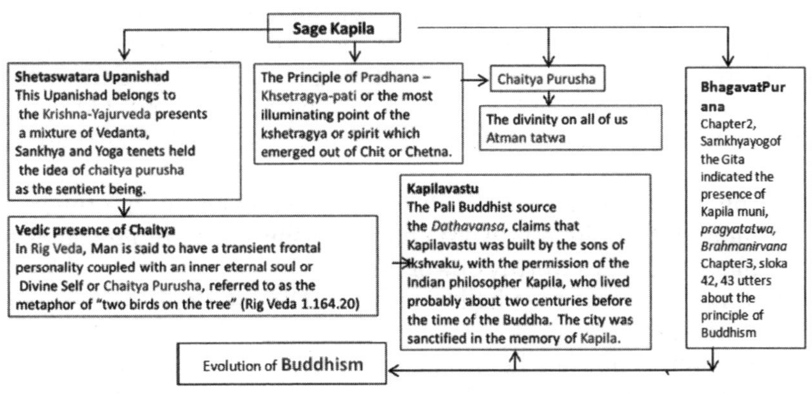

FIGURE 4
A continuity tracing Buddhism from sage Kapila

- Therefore the presence of *Chaitya Purusha* indicates the divinity within the physic being, from which the principle of '*Pradhana-Khetragyapati*' has sprung up.
- According to the Buddhist text *Dathavansa*, the city of Kapilavastu was sanctified after the sage Kapila who articulated *SamkhyaDarshana* and almost after two centuries the ideas of

Kapila was corroborated through Buddhism.

- The Gita asserts the presence of the ideals of 'Pragyatatwa', 'Brahma Nirvana', 'Buddhi Yoga' which had laid the basis of Buddhism. The chapter III, Karmayoga (Sloka 42) has attested the idea of -

"Indriyaniparaniahuhindriyebhyahparammanah I
Manasahtuparabuddhih yah buddhehparatahtusah II"

The psychic being is the evolving soul within us, which sits behind our heart, which develops life after life through life experiences. It is the portion of the Divine which holds together our mental, vital and physical sheaths.

Shri Aurobindo

4. *Chaitya*: An Architectural Icon

Shrines and images in Buddhism are generally complex as emerged out of conglomeration and consolidation of a long period between Vedic era and appearance of Buddhism. The philosophical and ideological orientation of Lord Buddha first manifested in the built form that can be read in many ways depending on the context; the country, the sect of Buddhism, and sometimes the artists' own aesthetic tastes which often shape how to interpret these symbols – especially when it is the element directly related to their religiosity and mundane life.

This chapter is concentrating on the metamorphosis of the cognitive speculation to a more concrete iconographic format of built architecture. When the concept of *Chaitya* corroborated within Buddhism it has first taken the shape of architectural interventions during Mauryan period.

- The word *Chaitya* is often taken to have its origin in a funerary mound, from its root word *chita* i.e. ashes; so *Chaitya* comes to mean the ashes worthy of worship.
- *Chaitya*s are the halls enclosing the *stupas* for showing veneration.
- In order to house a hemispherical *Stupa* and to provide path for circumambulation, building had conceptualised in circular plan and had a domed roof. The dome shaped roof reveals an iconographic semantics as it sometimes compared with the back of an elephant. In Buddhist context elephant is a symbol interspersed in different spheres. Metaphorically it denotes the dream of queen Mayadevi of a white elephant entering into her womb and also has an implication in Buddha's birth in a royal family.
- It is a large vaulted hall with apsidal end and divided longitudinally by two colonnades into a broad nave and two aisles.
- A *Chaitya griha* or Buddhist cave (*stupa* hall) is a meeting or

assembly chamber often used for purposes showing veneration similar to a *stupa*. Aisles and apsidal end used for circumambulation and nave for congregational service.

- Architecturally they show similarities to Roman design concepts of column and arch.

4.1. Distinction according to Philosophical orientation

Generally *Chaitya* is the prayer hall of the Buddhist enclosing the *stupa* of all three different types, i.e. ***Saririka***, ***Poribhagika*** and ***Uddyeshika*** for showing veneration to the Lord Buddha.

- The *Sariraka* or *dhâtu Cetiya*, contains the relics of Buddha which were responsible for major forms of Buddhist art and symbolism.
- The *paribhoga Cetiya*,contains the things used by the Buddha for '*Bhoga*' (used in mundane life). It can be compared to the contentious Shroud of Turin temples such as Tongdosa in South Korea claim to keep his robe and begging bowl.
- The final category, *udeśaka* or *uddesika Cetiya*, literally translates as "indicative reminders" or "votive objects", for example images of the Buddha.
- A fourth category, *dhammaka*, was introduced later to remind monks that the true memory of Gautama Buddha can be found in his teachings. The *Dhammaka* category is actually a votive object to remind of the *Dhammachakkapavartana* of Lord Buddha. It emphasizes on the historicity of the religion rather than a metaphorical concept.

4.2 From Deep Ecology to Built Architecture

Tracing the development of an architectural built environ forming out of the deep ecological consciousness reckoning on a range of interests from archaeology, anthropology, sociology, technology and aesthetics, to the evolution of consciousness and theology. Thus here presents the regulatory aspects that enable the gradual transformation. In the following section five concomitants of architectural development are presented as the determining factors:

(1) social and cultural considerations,
(2) exigencies of liturgical ritual and function,
(3) symbol and meaning in architectural conception,
(4) technique and structural possibilities
(5) Concepts of form.

Social and cultural considerations: This interdependency between architecture and society has led to regard architecture as a mirror of a society's cultural progress. For V. Hugo, for example, "Architecture is the book of human history... the handwriting of humanity." Architecture is the most useful in tracing the origins, growth, and decline of various cultures in history. Socio-cultural determination and architectural formation is one of mutual specification that can best be revealed in the aphorism that "as we shape our buildings, likewise do our buildings shape us."

Exigencies of liturgical ritual and function: Ritualistic elaborations inhibited the architectural forms. The architectural significance of ecclesiastical structures is at the inception necessarily dependent upon the degree of ritual determination that has formed the apsidal nave of the Buddhist *Chaitya* s and the materialization of the basilica plan church at the West.

Symbol and meaning in architectural conception: The use of symbol or other modes of conceptualization may support the ritual utility and make it visible form that is expressive of the supernatural. Symbolism, myth, analogies of proportion, light, number, or other factors might be employed in architectural conception. These influence the propensity of structure and are of particular importance in elevating the sacred architecture.

As for example, Christian architecture was the direct heir to Roman architectural practices, which evinced tedium with the plan of Buddhist *Chaitya* halls. Christianity favoured a merging of the longitudinal and centripetal plans, which served the public nature of the Mass and complemented the concept of Christ as Pantokrator. While the West kept a predilection for the pure basilica plan, the East favoured the domical-basilica plan.

Techniqueandstructuralpossibilities: Thestructuralmotivation for the prevalent conception comes up with techniques and structural potentialities that have augmented over time with the incorporation of scientific tools. For example, the eastward ontogenesis certainly marked by the desire to incorporate domical centripetal arrangements, which were regarded as symbolic of cosmic authority, with the traditional longitudinal temple plan (derivation from the *Chaitya*) and to combine the two disparate systems required ingenuity.

Concepts of form: The architecture does not stand for sacredness but is identified with sacredness. C. Yavis's study of Greek altars documents the origins of certain cult localities as an evolution from immediate manifestation (momentary deification), to site deification, altar deification, and anthropomorphic image deification, until final enclosure by the temenos wall and construction of the temple. The longitudinal form promoted the congregation forms a linear procession toward a terminally located sacred object. The type has conceptual value and has determined architectural form for centuries.

Initial Observations

Literature review (through the ages) and social-anthropological footprints revealed a significant chronological development of thought and physical built archetype of the term '*Chaitya* '. The huge spectrum commenced with Vedic literature, *Upanishads*, *Puranas* to the findings and re-readings of contemporary analysts, art historians, philosophers, postulating the persisting concept of *Chaitya*, actually advocated the unceasing flow of development of Indian art panorama. The commonality through the different phases of history underscores adequate connection between the proto historic phase of Harappa-Mohenjodaro and the Mauryan era. This will further validate the integral relationship between the Vedic tradition and Buddhist culture. The close association of both of the phases will help to unveil the darkness of the interim periods of the two i.e. between 3500 BCE (Indus valley civilization) and 550 BCE (time of Buddha's incarnation). This connection also proves the maturation of the cosmic archetype to a physical built space with iconographic connotations.

Authentication of the fact will throw light on the so called dark phase (colonial version of Indian Ancient History) and will create a new paradigm of Indian historical, cultural and traditional parts that yields a threshold of a new legacy. Finally, the studies of the linkages between, scriptures, written documents from the past, myths and mythologies has substantiated the hypothesis and also tap on the question that how the gradual evolution of Indian architectural components seeped into the dominion of larger global arena to inculcate a new language of expression and demonstration.

PART 2

5.0 Introduction

A discourse may be proposed based on the study of the emergence and evolution of *Chaitya* as a physical, iconographical built environ. The analysis has been forwarded in three parts. In Part I, a review has been laid based on the findings of the earlier and contemporary pedagogues and therefore a methodological diagram has been proposed accordingly. Part II deal with a thorough discussion on the physical, iconographical and architectural specifics of *Chaitya* and in Part III, a connection has built to the rest of the world in terms of architectural iconography and expression, focusing on its later development.

The study of iconographic reinterpretation of the built environmental patterns of Vedic and Buddhist period has focussed to establish the integral relationship between the Vedic tradition and Buddhist culture. Buddhist symbolism, in art and religion, is nothing but a part of the main current of the Indian religion, art and architecture and has to be studied in that context. Early Indian philosophy, art and architecture are thus, essentially, the continuation of an aniconic 'Vedic' style and the compositions are comprehensible with reference to the Vedic notions. According to the genealogy of this persisting tradition the affinity and the disparity lies within can be elucidated through studies the fundamental elements of Buddhist symbolism which predominated the early aniconic art and never dispensed with in the later imagery, though they are subordinated to the "human" icon. The study of these cognate symbols reveals that they represent a universal Indian symbolism along with the set of theological concepts as can be seen in the presence of *stupika* within the built form of *Chaitya* as an aniconic form of Buddha to offer veneration.

According to the initial thoughts of abridging the gap between Vedic and Buddhist eras through dissection of the word *chaitya*, will also engulfs the rifts and interstices between the two periods, as the nomenclature of the popular phrases, consolidation and codification of the architectural specifics and norms. Evolution of the dialectics of Buddhism, iconographic and iconological transformation has altered the behavioral patterns and therefore affected the overall psychological and physical built environ. Therefore, it can be said that, Indian architectural traditions are synonymous with Indian cosmic traditions having footprints in the ancient ground plan and cosmological models as an imprint. The relations are **complementarities between Indian building physics and the metaphysics of shape grammars leading to a footprint** derived from the macrocosmic model imprinted on the user (both the deity and the devotee as one).

The close association of both of the phases will help to unveil the interim periods of the two i.e. the period between 3500 B.C. (Indus valley civilization) and 550 B.C. (time of Buddha's incarnation). Establishment of the fact as derived from various orders of correlation will throw a light on the so called dark phase (Often interpreted by Classical version of Indian Ancient History) and will create a new paradigm of Indian historical, cultural and traditional parts.

5.1 Tracing the trail of linkage between Vedic and Buddhist period since antiquity

Propensity of both the ideological paradigm (Vedic and Buddhist) towards a central point would imply to the formulation of theory of sharing the same edifice. In the case of tracing the trail of linkage between the two, discerning of the emergence of Buddhism as a parallel archetype of religion takes on the prime position. The postulated theory of Buddhism as a counterpart of *Brahmanical* Hinduism relies on the search and comments of the historians and theoreticians.

Sir Mortimer Wheeler opined,

"it cannot be denied that during the seven centuries between 250 BCE and CE 450 most of the surviving sculpture of the highest quality in India was associated with Buddhism, and it was, above all, Buddhism that during the same period (and particularly the latter part of it) spread Indian art and idiom through the highways and byways of Asia."

The pedagogue of the recent past, the poet-philosopher Rabindranath Tagore[13] expounded the view that Buddhism and Jainism represented the ideals of the *kshatriyas* which conflicted with those of the *brahmanas*, that the history of ancient India is a record of ,

"the pull of the two opposite principles, that of self-preservation represented by the brahmana, and that of self-expansion represented by the kshatriya."

---The Poet-Philosopher Rabindranath Tagore

The discussion is forwarded in three sections: First, the Philosophical or realization construct; second, the architectural or built manifestations; and third, tracing a later development.

SECTION 1

5.2 A Construct

Upanishads also were inspired by a desire to struggle for the supremacy of their supposed ideal of "self-expansion" against that of the priestly "self-preservation."[14] The Buddha though was from a Kshatriya background, emphasized the ideal of self-abnegation and taught the tenet of "not-self", therefore propounded the notion of *Chaitya Purusha* integrated within the physical built form of *Chaitya*.

From the matrix (Table 3) of scientific and heritage dimensions of *Chaitya,* tangible iconographical delineation coupled with deep ecological approach can be deciphered through the ages (Sanatana to Buddhist period). Different dimensions can be tapped in regard to anthropometric, mathematical and geo-spatial arrangements that supported the theory of deep ecological, cultural, social and architectural continuation between the periods.

SCIENTIFIC DIMENSION ▸ / HERITAGE DIMENSION ▾	Social Science and Cultural Aspects	Mathematical Approach	Deep ecological Science	Archaeology	Anthropometric measurements	Geo-spatial setting
Tangible Iconographic delineation	Ritualistic Traditions existing since antiquity as Mandala, Fire Altars	Connections between holy diagrams and Maslow's hierarchy of needs (while inverted denotes *Urddhamulam Adhaswakam*), Cartesian's theory etc.	Consistency of the legendary figures from Vedic to Buddhist era.	Found objects, potteries, terracotta, Epigraphic evidences and scriptures	Presence of anthropometric influence in the iconographic presentation as seals, potteries, Plucks etc.	Geo-spatial settings went to influence cultural specifics and therefore icons.
Built Architecture	Socio-cultural footprints and transformations according to necessity	Mathematical measurements in plan (2D) and elevation (3D) of architectural parts.	Chaitya, Stupa, *vedica* etc. Vastupurusha	Initial stage of rock cut architecture to its maturation in Buddhist era	Elevation of Built architecture after the shape of animal. Ex, chaitya was formed after the shape of an elephant's back	Geo-spatial setting affects atmosphere thus altars architectural idioms Ex. Variation in the forms of stupa
Deep Ecological/ Cognitive Domain	Social aspects of Idolatry, Vedic *Upanishads*, *Puranas* and Myths.	*Samkhya Tatwa* of Kapilamuni to *Dathavansa* of the clan of Goutama	Spark and soul theory (Jivan and atmaan)			

TABLE 3
Matrix of Scientific and Heritage dimensions of Chaitya

5.3 Methodology

As can be seen from figure no 5, the term *Chaitya* is identified to decipher the connection of the architectural expression on the edifice of Sanatana culture. This underlying relation can be elucidated through the steps as, a brief literature review that has laid the basis for the further search based on the ideas of contemporary pedagogues. Therefore presented an analysis of the collaborating ideas that enforce to transform the deep seated ecological postulation to shape a 3D built architectural form as can be seen from figure no 5. Here the built architectural form and the deep ecological stratum correspondence to each other.

Therefore the word *Chaitya* can be traced back to the time of early Buddhist era. Formulation of the convergence between the archi-

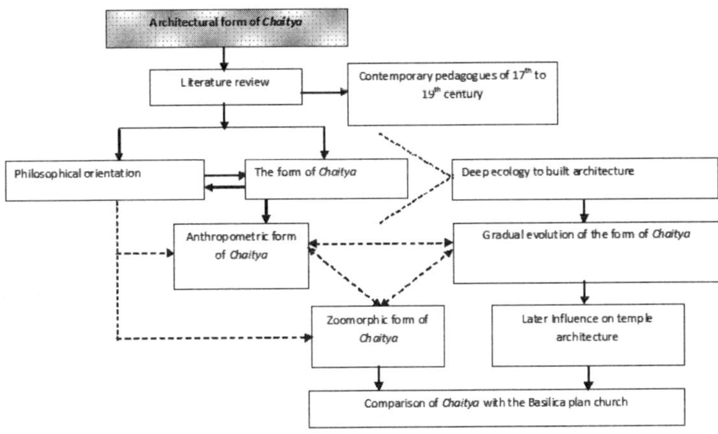

FIGURE 5
Methodological diagram to decipher the architectural specifics of *Chaitya*

tectural and philosophical notion will unfurl the new pages in the history of Indian civilization. Likewise, this chapter is concentrating on the term '*Chaitya*', seeking to unveil the iconographic overlays of ideas. Initially the term '*Chaitya*' is demonstrated as an architectural form, developing through different ages that can be elaborated from different perspectives. Diversification even in the origin and the ontogenesis of the form can give us a glare of its multifarious dimension.

SECTION 2

5.4 Anthropometry of Chaitya

Anthropometry deals with the measurements and proportions of the human body, and anthropometrics is the comparative study of these measurements. Inclusion of anthropometric measurement in architecture is a traditional practice since the emergence of Buddhist rock cut architecture.

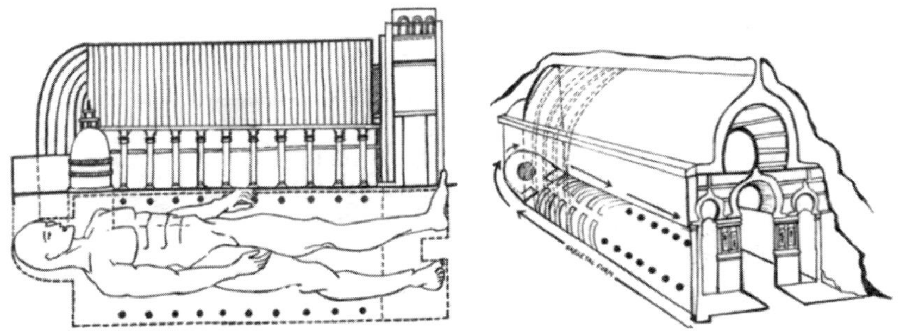

FIGURE 8
Plan and elevation of Chaitya follows the anthropometry of human form

The ground plan of *Chaitya* followed the plan of a humanbody where the heart and *stupa* lies in the same axis. The stupa and the '*Gabakkha*' or *Chaitya* window creates a diagonal axis from where the sunlight pours in. Here the light doesn't only exemplify the physical entity rather the inner consciousness i.e. *Chaitya.*

5.5 Zoomorphic form of Chaitya

Symbolism played a predominant role in the religious and funerary architecture since antiquity, and still does today. However, symbolic elements of architecture belong to an advanced stage in the development of representation. A much more primary stage is the one where the actual deity is represented architecturally as a structure formed according to his shape. This shape could be conceptual to suggest cosmic elements; for instance, the world itself as in the stupa of India. Drawings from the Archaic Period in Egypt (2800 BCE) represent an edicule, probably religious or funerary, characterized by an irregular upper outline.

As evident from the figure no 9, the ideological concept of the embodiment of a god into zoomorphic shrine is actually the first step of derivation of these structures in built form. In the case of *Chaitya* the roof has taken the shape of an elephant's back. Elephant implied as the symbolic icon in Buddhism as it denotes the dream of Mayadevi,

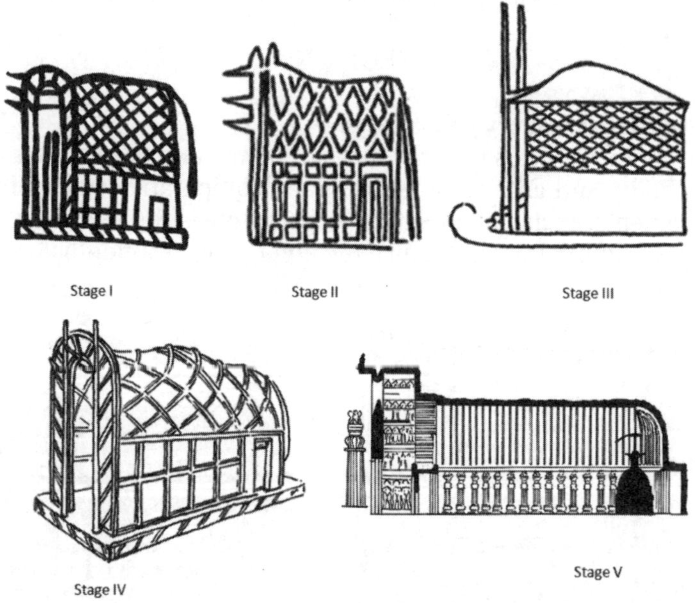

FIGURE 9
Stages of Development of the zoomorphic form of *Chaitya*

Buddha's born in a royal family and architecturally infringes at the iconographic level.

5.6 Examples of Gradual evolution of the form of *Chaitya* :

The preliminary time of consolidation of the philosophical ideas the form gradually developed and took the shape of 3D built architectural form to express the essence of contemporary art and culture. *Chaitya* as a Buddhist architectural, term emerged in India during the early phases of expansion of Buddhism and gradually condensed with maturated form, plan and elevation. Thus, the process of evolution is going to be analyzed here chronologically, to tap onto the addition and elimination process of form and function coupled with aesthetic parameters.

BARBAR HILL

Barabar Hill contains four caves, namely, Karan Chaupar, Lomas Rishi, Sudama and Visva Zopri. Sudama and Lomas *Rishi* Caves are the earliest examples of rock-cut architecture in India, with architectural detailing, made in the Mauryan period, and became a trend the subsequent centuries, like the larger Buddhist *Chaitya*, that were found in Maharashtra, such as in Ajanta and Karla Caves, and greatly influenced the tradition of South Asian rock-cut architecture. Barabar caves have magnanimous arches which are rare in ancient history.

- Lomas Rishi cave: The arch-like shape facade of Lomas Rishi Caves, imitate the contemporary timber architecture. On the doorway, a row of elephants proceed towards stupa emblems, along the curved architrave.
- Sudama cave: This cave was dedicated by Mauryan Emperor, Ashoka in 261 BCE. The arches of Sudama cave are of bow shape. The caves consist of a circular vaulted chamber with a rectangular mandapa.

CHAITYA CAVES AT BHAJA – C.250BC

Chaitya at Bhaja can be regarded as one of the ancient example the consists of a simple *Chaitya* hall with no decoration comprising to other *Chaitya* hall representing the initial stage of construction pertaining to Hinayana style.

- Entrance is an open archway leading to the interior hall 16.7m x 8m wide , side aisles of 1 m width
- Pillars are 3.4m high, the vaulted ceiling is at a height of 8.8 m from the floor level
- The *stupa* is plain with a cylindrical base supporting a huge dome with railing like finial
- Use of timber work in the *Chaitya* window trellis

CHAITYA CAVE AT KARLE – C 78 BC

Chaitya hall at Karle consisted of a Gigantic hall (14m x 46m) with 13.7m high vaulted roof, is very unique and extra ordinary than other *Chaitya* hall as it offers visual drama. A large platform built at the sloping hill side leading to the magnificent cave. Entrance is guided by 2 enormous 15.2 m high free standing stone column crowned with lion. The next important part is a transitional vestibule with double height. The walls are magnificently carved with recessed sun window set in horse shoe archway. The hall contains 2 rows of column forming nave at the centre and aisles all around which was used for circumambulation.

- Each column is 7.32 m high with 1.22m diameter
- The shaft is octagonal with vase shaped base
- Capital is bell shaped and sculpted
- The stupa at the end is carved with railing and has inverted pyramid type finial
- The marvelous things of the cave are magical quality space, light and sculpture along with their relationship
- This magical experience is created by light that is filtered in through the columns, screen and the Chaitya window offering soft and peaceful light
- It is the unending source for architectural inspiration
- The roof is supplemented by a series of wooden ribs

FIGURE 6
Ajanta Cave 19

FIGURE 7
Chaitya Griha – this sitting pose of Buddha (instead of lotus pose) enables devotees to touch his feet

AJANTA CAVES (2nd century BC)

Caves of Ajanta are situated in a horse shoe shaped valley spread over a length of 500 m East-West and the cliff is 79 m high. Out of 30 caves 9, 10, 19, 26 and 29 are *Chaitya* halls and other remaining are *viharas* excavated on the face of almost vertical cliff. Walls are carved with figures of myths and deities related to Buddha. Among all *Chaitya* hall no 26 is the most wonderful and popular.

- It has a small rectangular door way with horse shoe shaped window opening above it with tracery work, through which light is admitted into the vaulted hall
- Vaulted hall has an apsidal end and is divided longitudinally by 2 rows of columns forming broad nave and 2 aisles
- At the end , a stupa carved out of living rock with statue of Buddha seated in front of with his feet down and surrounded by his attendant and heavenly flying figures
- The vaulted roof is supplemented by closely space ribs carved out from rock representing prototype timber member
- At the entrance of hall, there is a standing statue of Bodhisattva

- Ajanta caves are popular for their fresco painting, depicting Buddha's life. These are ranked as world's finest fresco painting
- Use of plaster of 1 cm thick, made from clay, cow dung, straw, rice husk and gypsum. On it outlines are drawn and finally coated with colours made of natural dyes
- Work of arts in dark cave were made bright by reflecting rays of sun from large metal reflectors installed outside

CAVES AT ELLORA

Ellora demonstrates quite mature form and aesthetic development of *Chaitya* . The name Ellora was derived from Ellapur, a village named after the king Ela who ruled over there. Nagarjuna – Founder of the Mahayana school is said to have had them excavated in 1st century AD. Out of 12 caves, only one is *Chaitya* hall i.e. vishwakarma that exemplifies the pattern of construction is similar to Ajanta caves and the interior manifests the sameness with Ajanta.

- Columns are rectangular with shallow flutes and wide capitals of elaborately carved sculptures
- Vaults of roof are supplemented by natural rock ribs
- There are 17 Hindu caves(8th and 9th c AD) and 5 Jain caves(9th and 11th c AD)

MONASTERY OF TAKHT-E-BAHI

Takht-i-Bhai is a Parthian archaeological site in Mardan, Khyber-Pakhtunkhwa, Pakistan was first a Zoroastrian complex which, after the later arrival of Buddhism, was then converted into a Buddhist monastic

Barbar Hills, Lomasha Rishi Cave, 3rd century BCE. The first example of Rock cut Chitya with a horse shoe shaped window and plain interior.

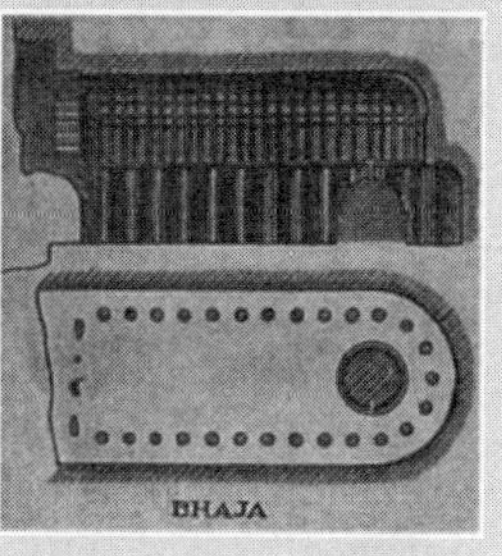

Located in Maharashtra, Bhaja is a group of caves at the valley of Indrayani river. These caves were created approximately 2200 years ago and they are very important early Buddhist rock-cut architecture in Deccan region.

Kondana Caves are located in small village, Kondana, 33 km north of Lonavala and 16 km nrth west of Karla Caves. This cave group has 16 Buddhist caves. The caves were excavated in first century BCE

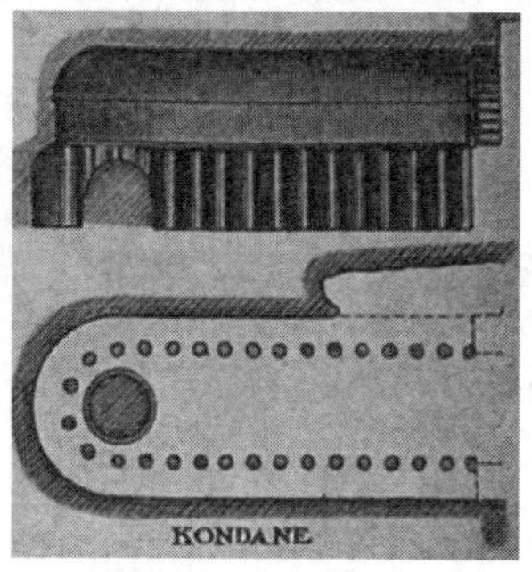

complex. It is dated to the 1st century BCE. The complex is regarded by archaeologists as being particularly representative of the architecture of Buddhist monastic centres from its era.

- Mahayana monastery
- One of the most impressive and schematically planned
- Built in stone
- Use of lime
- 15.2m high stupa rested on 6 m wide square platform set with in 23.7m x16.7m area
- Stupa was surrounded by cells and in turn they had alternate

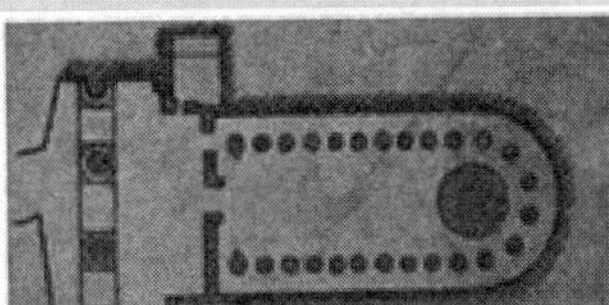

Exterior façade, ground plan and elevation of Kondana Caves, located in small village, Kondana, 33 km north of Lonavala and 16 km north west of Karle Caves. This cave group has 16 Buddhist caves. The caves were excavated in first century BCE

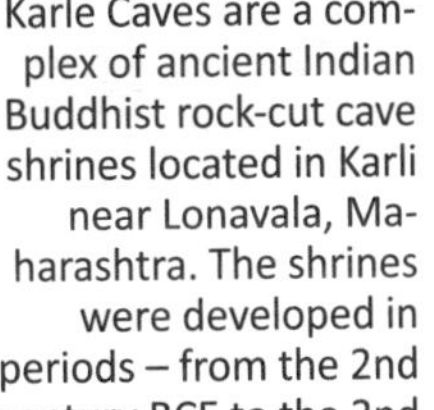

Karle Caves are a complex of ancient Indian Buddhist rock-cut cave shrines located in Karli near Lonavala, Maharashtra. The shrines were developed in periods – from the 2nd century BCE to the 2nd century CE.

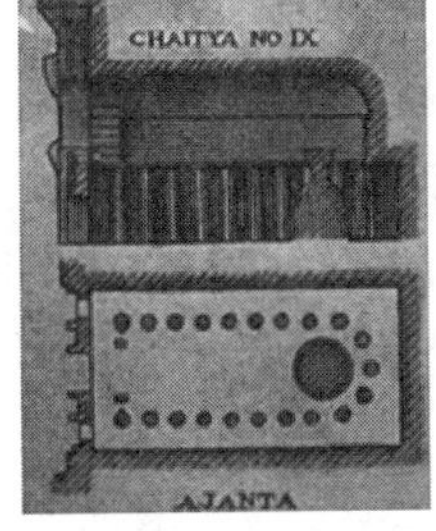

Exterior, elevation and ground plan of Ajanta cave no 9, more matured phase of *chaitya* created in 2nd cent BCE.

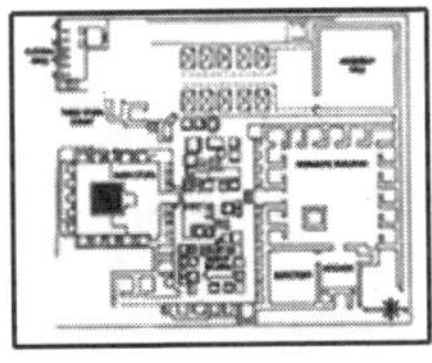

Takht-i-Bhai is a Parthian archaeological site in Mardan, Pakistan. It was first a Zorostrian complex which, after the later arrival of Buddhism, was then converted into a Buddhist monastic complex. It is dated to the 1st century BCE.

roofs of domical and barrel vault shapes derived from Chaitya

- Cells were for housing image of Bodhisattavas

5.7 Comparison of Chaitya with Basilica plan Church

"*The hall is really a Buddhist church, and like a Christian church, consists of a nave, apse and aisles, the latter separated from nave by pillars, the apse containing the space for altar, a solid stupa, the whole excavated in the living rock or built of wood and brick. The aisle is continued round the apse, thus providing of circumambulation and corresponding to the outer hall or veranda of structural temples*"-A.K.Coomaraswamy.

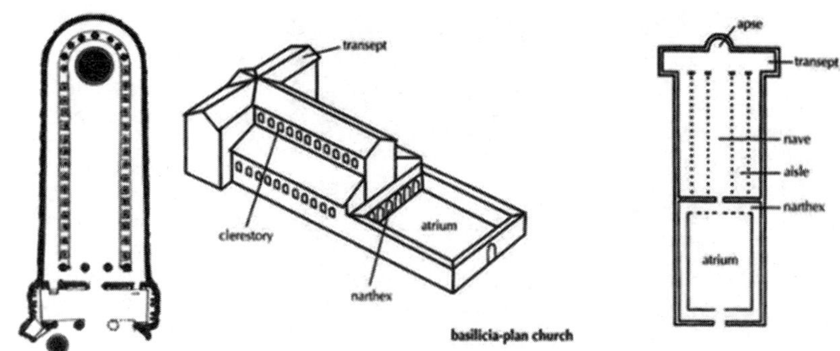

FIGURE 10
Similarity between the arrangement of the pillars, nave, aisles, apsidal form & the position of the stupa at the Buddhist *Chaitya* and Christian Basilica church

The plan of the Buddhist rock cut *Chaityas* manifests a unique semblance to the plan of the Christian church and cathedrals. The rounded apse, nave, pillared aisles except the addition of the transepts, echoes the sameness of the two. The rounded apse in a church and in Buddhist *Chaitya* halls are basically used as the circumambulatory pathway for the devotees and worshipers.

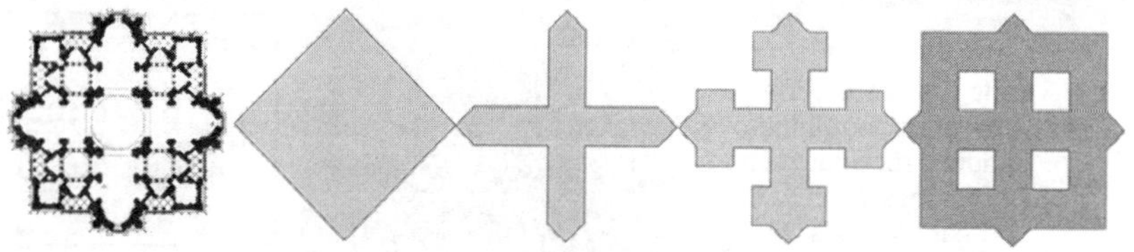

FIGURE 11
The cruciform Vajra shaped plan or the Asian Mandala and Half Mandala based on the square formation khsiti tatwa

While tracing the convergences of the ancient Buddhist and early Christian architecture there are few other grounds to be reconsidered, as,

a. The commonality of the rituals of Agni and Soma with the presence of the Holy Spirit and divine intoxication.
b. An uncanny resemblance between the monastic tradition and rituals.
c. The feasibility of light and shade is the substructure of the Indian spirituality which on the other hand best be exemplified in the Christian churches.
d. In the ground plan both are following the cross plan of the symmetrical Greek cruciform, which is the symbol of Vajra in India. Both the symbols are 'symmetrical and following the pure

circle of Mandala'[12].

e. Both the religions, ancient Buddhism and early Christianity are the revolution from the orthodox religious traditions. The former one is the condensation of the Brahmanical phase and the later one eradicated the petrified priestly tradition of Judaism.

SECTION 3

5.8 Later Development plan of *Chaitya*

The shape of the temple, in Indian traditional architecture, is known as *Gajaprasta* which means the resemblance to the back of an elephant. The plan of *Durga* temple of Aihole has unusual apsidal form which is thought to imitate the earlier Buddhist *Chaitya* Halls

A pillared corridor runs around the temple, enveloping the shrine, *mukhamantapa*and the *sabhamantapa*. In reference to figure no 12, shows there is a high entrance with steps leading up to a tall base; the roof is almost double in height and in this particular case the turret is

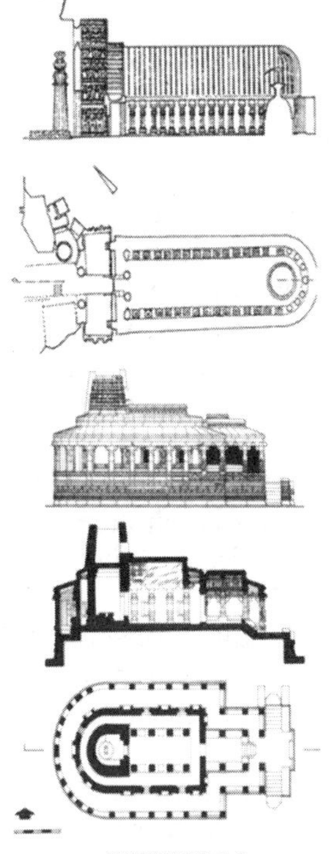

FIGURE 12
Durga temple, Aihole, 8th century; a semi-circular ended plan is rare in structural Hindu architecture, deriving from rock-cut Buddhist sanctuaries

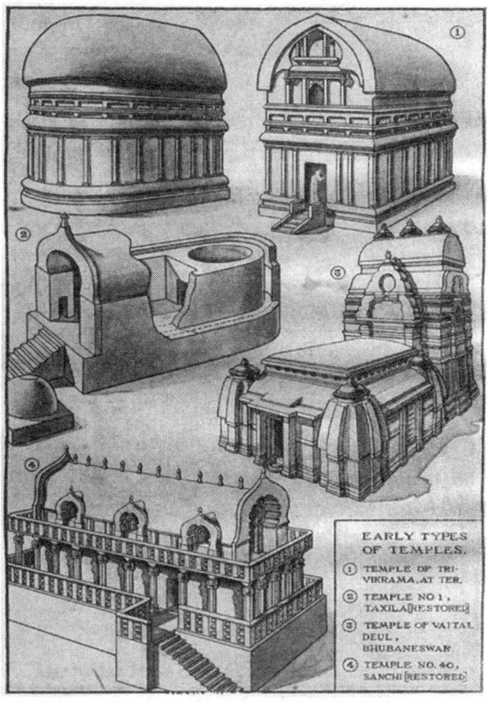

FIGURE 13
Early types of Temples developing from the form of *Chaitya*

beginning to take the shape of a little spire, which, during the course of the next centuries; evolved into a towering *Shikhara*.

The reference to temples in literature go back early with Panini (520 BC - 460 BC) and Patanjali mentioning temples which were called prasadas. The principles of temple architecture were codified in treatises and canons such as Manasara, Mayamatam, and Vaastu Shastra. These offered an ordering framework yet allowed certain latitude for contextual articulation. Early beginnings of Hindu temple architecture have been traced to the remains at Aihole and Pattadakal in present day Karnataka, and have Vedic altars and late Vedic temples as described by Panini as models. Buddhist elements, motifs and especially technicality regarding rock cut architectural complexes have influenced temple architecture to a considerable extent.

PART 3

6.0 Integrating with Western perspectives

It is important to understand the larger tide, the infinite tide that is behind our evolution and how it must express itself and how it is expressing itself; it is the cause of all manifestation. From the limited subconscious of the animal, where the man was once suppressed, with evolution, as soon as the door was opened, out rushed the human conscious mind, more guided by reason and lesser and lesser by instinct. In the next rung of evolution, as in the human there is the potential godhead kept in by the inner locks and bars of higher ignorance, a larger and a greater policy of humanity is required as and when knowledge already potent will break these bars, the divinity will become manifest. The Changes which are happening now are in effect is a part of the making of that greater policy to unleash a systems evolution in this chapter. At this point, it will be extremely important to understand at least four of these force-changes that is happening and bringing about the change itself. They are the recognition of the ancient wisdom (heritage) through a scientific view – that of:

- Akashi records: the science of the Collective Consciousness (Mahat) and passage of Individual (Aham) impressions through metempsychosis and transmigration (Purva-pragna and Chaitya purusha);
- it leads to **the Architecture of interpenetration or Chaitya conjugate:** parable of the double intender – the mirror of wave mechanics (Vajra) (Viparita-ratatura and samarasyam)

In each, as a systems dimension, the principle of sentiency in the individual; in the universal and in the state that is beyond the cave of the universal experience (bhamaraguha) have been explained.

6.1 Cosmic Architecture: Recognition of Akashi records: the Universe as Mahat (Collective Mind)

- The science of the Collective Consciousness (*Mahat*) and Individual (*Aham*) metempsychosis and transmigration (*Purva-pragna* and *Chaitya Purusha*)

FIGURE 14
The contemporary history of Akashi records

Swami Vivekananda (see left) meets Nikola Tesla (see top order left) in 1893 after the City Beautiful Movement in Chicago; the knowledge on Akashi records travels to next generation: it reaches Ervin Lazlo and Erich Jantsch (see top order middle and right); philosophically it influences William James and Alfred North Whitehead (middle vertical order); partly influences Helena Blavatsky and Edgar Cayce (see lower right order) at some deeper normative level (through ideas of *Vasana* or *Samskara* (desire),*Chaitya* (the guiding flux) and *Pragna* (wisdom) in Buddhism.

Akasha is the enduring memory of the cosmos The *Akashic* Records refer to a database of every word, thought or action that is stored energetically and encoded in a non-physical plane of existence. They are said to contain the information of every Soul or Being in the cosmos. The Records are continually updated, with each new thought, word or action that every Soul or entity makes. The *Akashic* Records therefore contain the energetic prints about the origination and journey of every Soul through its lifetimes. They connect each of us to one another. Having in ancient origin in the Vedas and particularly, the Upanishads, *Akashi* forms the complementary basis of the universal (*Mahat* or collective or cosmic ego driven) consciousness and the discrete (*Aham* or individual ego driven) causations of the individual human mind and the interconnection between the two. In the book, 'The *Akashic* Experience: Science and the Cosmic Memory Field', Ervin Laszlo says:

> *...it is the* "Akashic Record." *In his classic Raja Yoga, Swami* Vivekananda *described the ancient concept of ... About a hundred years ago the maverick genius Nikola* Tesla *revived this idea.*

Nikola Tesla used ancient Sanskrit terminology in his descriptions of natural phenomena. As early as 1891 Tesla had described the universe as a kinetic system filled with energy which could be harnessed at any location. His concepts were then greatly influenced by the teachings of Swami Vivekananda. Swami Vivekananda was the first of a succession of eastern yogi's who brought Vedic philosophy and religion to the west. After meeting the Swami, Tesla began using the Sanskrit words *Akasha,* and *Prana,* and the concept of luminous ether to describe the source, existence and construction of matter. It was at a party given by Sarah Bernhardt in Chicago that Nikola Tesla had probably first met Swami Vivekananda. Sarah Bernhardt was playing the part of 'Iziel' in a play of the same name. It was a French version about the life of Bhudda. The actress upon seeing Swami Vivekananda in the audience arranged a meeting which was also attended by Nikola Tesla (see Figure 15). In a letter to a friend, dated February 13th, 1896, Swami Vivekananda noted the following:

> *..Mr. Tesla was charmed to hear about the Vedantic Prana and Akasha and the Kalpas, which according to him are the only theories modern science can entertain.....Mr Tesla thinks he can demonstrate that mathematically that force and matter are reducible to potential energy. I am to go see him next week to get this mathematical demonstration."*

In deep theosophy and anthroposophy, where one explores the deeper connections between human thought currents and patterns of the universe and its variety, the Akashic records are believed by Theosophists to be encoded in a non-physical plane of existence known as the astral plane. Akasha as a Sanskrit word entered the language of theosophy through H. P. Blavatsky, who characterized it as a sort of life force; and she also referred to some "indestructible tablets of the astral light" at the cosmic or universal plane. According to Marshal McKusick, former professor of Anthropology at the University of Iowa, the term Akashicrecord was augmented by Rudolf Steiner, who had probably inherited the doctrine from a preceding history in the Mid-West and particularly, the Illinois-Iowa region. Similarly, Edgar Cayce was no exception emphasizing a New Age Movement coming to late 21st century world based on the acceptance of reincarnation and Akashi records.

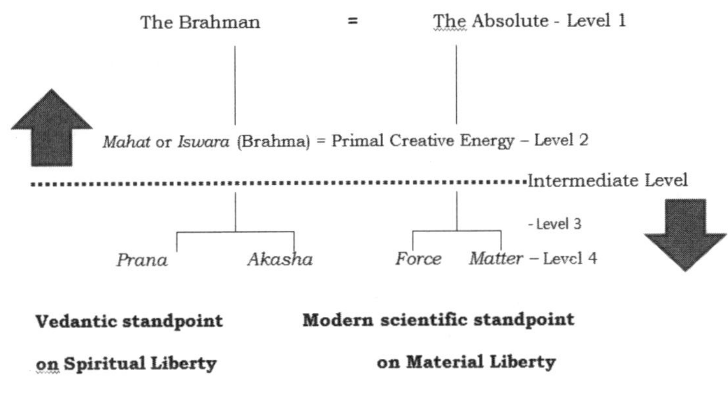

FIGURE 15
A normative and positive schema of Akashi records

Note:

There is a complementarity of *Prana* (elen vital) and *Akasha* (mind space) in the subtle human world to Force and matter conjugate in the material or the gross phenomenal world

(Based on the letter dated February 13th, 1896 by Swami Vivekananda)

László's 2004 book entitled 'Science and the Akashic Field: An Integral Theory of Everything' posits a field of information as the substance of the cosmos. Using the Sanskrit and Vedic term for space, Akashi, he calls this information field at the level of the Universe, which is analogous to Kapila's *Mahat* from the ancient *Swetaswatara* Upanishad. Lazlo posits that the 'quantum vacuum' is the fundamental energy and information-carrying field that informs not just the current universe, but all universes past and present. This he calls 'Metaverse', which transcends a single Universal theory. László believes that such an informational field can explain why our universe appears to be fine-tuned so as to form galaxies and conscious life forms within it; and why evolution is an informed, not random, process, that is based on long time based or Aeon based ranges of causation, its patterns and cycles. He believes that the hypothesis solves several problems that emerge from quantum physics, especially non-locality and quantum entanglement.

Recently, trans-personal psychologist Stanislav Grof has compared László's work to that of Ken Wilber, saying 'Where Wilber outlined what an integral theory of everything should look like, Laszlo actually created one.' Jennifer Gidley, President of the World Futures Studies Federation has recently stated:

A major distinction appears to be that László (2007) builds his general evolution theory in a more formal, systematic manner. He claims that he built significantly on the theoretical traditions of Alfred John Whitehead's process theory, Bertalanffy's general system theory and Prigogine's non-linearly bifurcating dissipative structures.

Ken Wilber's process appears to have been much broader and more diverse—but perhaps less systematic—gathering together as many theorists in as many fields of knowledge as he could imagine, then arranging them according to the system that he developed—which he calls an integral operating system. Both Wilber's and particularly, Abraham Maslow's approach to an advanced transpersonal approach to human evolution had been influenced by Professor William James of the Harvard University, who had come in contact with Swami Vivekananda like Electrical Engineer and scientist Nikola Tesla. Akashi Records in the west is still at its nascent stage. With the works of Ervin Lazlo, Erich Jantcsh and others, one day, it will arrive at the science of the Collective Consciousness (*Mahat*), which is the repository of the Individual (*Aham*) consciousness and holds the clue to all possibilities of causation. Hence, metempsychosis and transmigration of souls and their evolution based on the impact of the past patterns (*Purva-pragna*) of the lower immanent soul and the upper immanent or guiding soul from the cosmos (*Chaitya Purusha*) may one day enter the contemporary realms of human sciences and realization.

6.2 Architecture of Chaitya: Fractals and Holism: the double intender: the mirror (Vajra)

The Spring and Autumn Annals is an ancient Chinese chronicle that by the time of Confucius, in the 6th century BCE, had come to mean "year" and was probably becoming a generic term for 'annals' or 'scribal records'. Closest to these annals are the Book of I Ching, which is also known as the Classic of Changes or Book of Changes. It is an ancient divination text and the oldest of the Chinese classics.

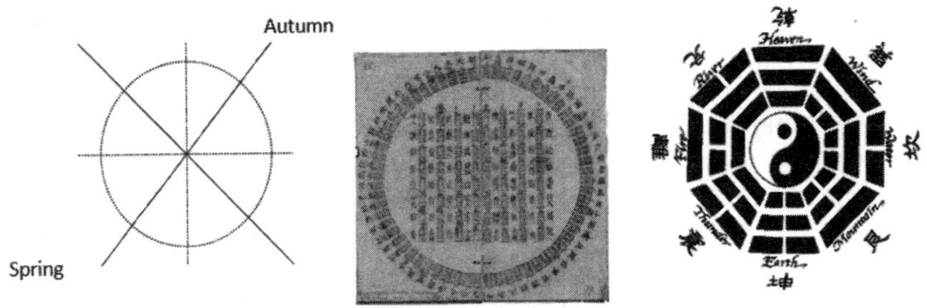

FIGURE 16
Cyclic Changes: Spring and Autumn and I-Ching Hexagram

Note:
On the middle is the diagram of I Ching hexagrams, which was sent to Gottfried Wilhelm Leibniz from Joachim Bouvet. The Arabic numerals were added by Leibniz. Joachim Bouvet was a French Jesuit who had worked in China. Psychologist Carl Jung took interest in the possible universal nature of the imagery of the I Ching, and he introduced an influential German translation by Richard Wilhelm by discussing his theories of archetypes and synchronicity.

Chinese writers often had offered parallels between the I Ching and subjects such as linear algebra and logic in computer science. Much of their efforts aimed at demonstrating that ancient Chinese cosmology had influenced the Western discoveries. There is a possible connection which could have been disseminated to Europe prior to and during the Dark Ages through the upper Silk Route (Tartary) from East Asia to Anatolia (Turkmenistan). Biochemist Joseph Needham also referred to the Book of Changes.

6.3 Interpenetration: All in ONE and One in the All

The I Ching uses a type of divination, which produces apparently random numbers, and is turned into a hexagram. It is arranged in an order known as the King Wen sequence. The hexagrams themselves have often acquired cosmological significance and paralleled with many other traditional names for the processes of change such as yin and yang. The Book often provides guidance for moral decision making as informed by Taoism and Confucianism. It is to be noted that:

1. The I Ching is essentially the fundamentals of Returning to the Unity and Balance of the Tao. It is not a system to be understood solely with the mind, but lived fully through the human experience. The Book of Changes describes the eternal dance of cycles occurring

in our life an evolution itself. For thousands of years sages and mystics have used the binary code of this system to unlock deeper layers of profound wisdom.

2. The I Ching is also an intricate expression of the fundamental patterns of the universe, based on the principles of yin (feminine) and yang (masculine) energy. This binary pattern forms 8 Elemental Trigrams, the Ba Gua (akin to Vak or soul itself). An Elemental Trigram expresses a specific primary energy. A Hexagram is formed by combining two elemental trigrams, thus revealing the 64 possible combinations of yin and yang. Each Hexagram is a pictographic binary expression of two elements interacting with one another, the basis of all the phenomena of life. Finally, the turning and the return (tropics) is the Motion of the Tao, which explains the flux both as stability and change akin to the Dynamic Equilibrium of modern science. Thus Atman is Brahman, as the Vedas say, and the equivalence is both the dynamism (flux and changes) and also the equilibrium (order and fixity). Thus Soul is not a fixed identity but essentially a Circuit of Changes as the Universe itself. That is Mahat. In the center is the immutable which supports all changes and is beyond it. Seen in this light, all are contained in the Whole as parts, as the Whole or Equilibrium itself is embedded in the chain of changes i.e., all it parts. Here, the ancient conception of Soul and No-soul, both are transcended and truth emerges as an undifferentiated unbroken whole (Akhanda), which is the reality within everything and also the reality all pervading.

That is what Swami Vivekananda meant by saying in his seminal talk – 'The Mother Worship', while referring to Confucius, who touched the universal *Mahat* and the level of *Matariswan*:

The two conjoint facts of perception we can never get rid of are happiness and unhappiness—things which bring us pain also bring pleasure. Our world is made up of these two. We cannot get rid of them; with every pulsation of life they are present. The world is busy trying to reconcile these opposites, sages trying to find solution of this commingling of the opposites. The burning heat of pain is intermitted by flashes of rest, the gleam of light breaking the darkness in intermittent flashes only to make the gloom deeper.

... Confucius alone has expressed the one eternal idea of ethics. "Manu Deva" was transformed into Ahriman. In India, the mythological expression was suppressed; but the idea remained. In an old Veda is found the Mantra, "I am the empress of all that lives, the power in everything."

(Fragmentary notes taken on a Sunday afternoon in New York in June, 1900)

So it is said:
Returning is the motion of the Tao; going far is returning.

Lao Tzu
'Tao Te Ching'

'The seer-wisdom realizes that supreme solar world in the form of a Asswattha (pippal) tree, where the branching of rays carrying the immortalizing waters (the madhu) reverts back to its roots at night and resurges again to flood the universe with the day light – they know the truth who are one with their 'Father in the heaven'.

Seer Dirgha-tama
Rig Veda: *mandala* one, 164:20

Note: As a whole, the Book of I Ching forwards a perfect depiction of a unified field theory which includes the description of absolute as the integration of Changes and equilibrium.

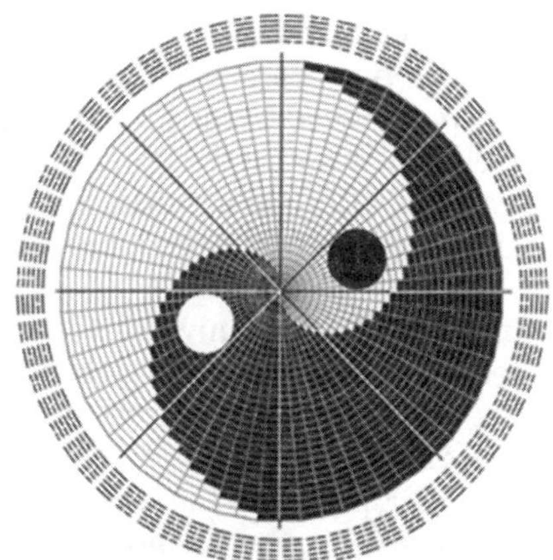

FIGURE 19
Cyclic Changes: Spring and autumn and I-Ching Hexagram The flux which called a Chaitya flow (Basis of transit consciousness in Buddhism)

6.4 The two-way ladder

The description in the turning of the Cosmic Wheel and its symbolic representation by the twelve months, of which the zenith is the tenth month, is forwarded in the following words:

These are the four eternal worlds hidden in the guha (the inner cave), the secret, unmanifest or superconscient parts of being which although in themselves eternally present states of existence (sanabhuvan ¯a ¯) are for us non-existent and in the future; for us they have to be brought into being, they are yet to be created. Therefore the Veda sometimes speaks of Swar being made visible, as here (vyacaks.ayatsvah.), or discovered and taken possession of, vidat, sanat, sometimes of its being created or made.

These secret eternal worlds have been closed to us, says the Rishi, by the movement of Time, by the months and years; therefore naturally they have to be discovered, revealed, conquered, and created in us by the movement of Time, yet in a sense against it.

This development in an inner or psychological Time is, it seems to me, that which is symbolised by the sacrificial year (samvatsara / sana) and by the ten months (dasagwas) that have to be spent before the revealing hymn of the soul (brahma) is able to discover the seven-headed, heavenconquering thought which finally carries us beyond the harms of Vritra and the Panis (darkness).

Sri Aurobindo
The Secret of the Vedas

The Book of Changes: I Ching explicitly denote the same turning of the wheel. The explanatory discussion is quoted from the two lectures on 'microcosm' and 'macrocosm' delivered in New York, USA on 19th and 26th of February in 1896 by Swami Vivekananda:

■ **Parable of the seed and the cyclic process:** What does man see around him? Take a little plant. He puts a seed in the ground, and later, he finds a plant peep out, lift itself slowly above the ground, and grows and grows, till it becomes a gigantic TREE. Then it dies, leaving only the seed. It completes a circle – it comes out of the seed, becomes the tree, and ends in the seed again.

■ **Cycles or waves of cause and effect:** The universe with its stars and planets has come out of a nebulous state and must go back to it. What do we learn from this? That the manifested or the grosser state is the effect, and the finer state, the cause.

■ **The rise and fall of waves:** The TREE produces the seed, which again comes up as another TREE, and son and on; there is no end to it. Water drops roll down the mountains into the ocean, and rise gain as vapor, go back to the mountains and gain come down to the ocean. So, rising and falling, the cycle goes on. So with all lives, so with all existence that we can see, feel, hear or imagine. Everything that is within the bounds of our knowledge is proceeding in the same way, like breathing in and breathing out in the human body. Everything in creation goes on in this form, one wave rising, another falling, rising again and falling gain. Each wave has its hollow; each hollow has its wave. The same law must apply to the universe taken as a whole, because of its uniformity.

■ **The periodic nodes of turning or tropics:** There is one more fact about this rising and falling. The seed comes out of the TREE, but has a period of inactivity or rather a period of very fine unmanifest action. The seed has to work for some time beneath the soil. It breaks into pieces, degenerates (dies) as it were, and regeneration (resurrects) comes out of that degeneration.

■ **Out of what has the TREE been produced?**Out of the seed; the whole of the TREE was there in the seed. It comes out and becomes manifest. So, the whole of this universe has been created out of this very universe existing in a minute form. It has been made manifest now. It will go back to that minute form, and again will be made manifest. This coming out of the fine and becoming gross, simply changing the arrangements of its parts, as it were, is what in modern times called evolution.

■ **Involution precedes evolution:**We have to go one step further, and what is that? That every evolution is preceded by an involution. The seed is the mother of the TREE, but another TREE was itself the mother of the seed. The seed is the fine form out of which the big TREE comes, and another big TREE was the form, which is involved in that seed. The whole of this universe was present in the cosmic fine universe.

■ **A priori - Recognition of the involutionary principle in an evolutionary process:**This involution and evolution is going on throughout the whole of nature. The whole series of evolution beginning with the lowest manifestation of life and reaching up to the highest, the most perfect man (Anthropic Principle), must have been the involution of something else. The question is: The involution of what? What was involved?

■ **Unfolding of involved a priori universal intelligence as evolving individual and social intelligence:** The TREE comes out of the seed, goes back to the seed; the beginning and the end are the same....applying the same reason to the whole of the universe, we see that intelligence must be the lord of creation, the cause. At the beginning that intelligence becomes involved, and in the end that intelligence gets evolved. The sum total of the intelligence displayed in the universe must, therefore, be the involved universal intelligence unfolding itself.

■ **Complete or perfect anthropic principle:**This cosmic intelligence gets involved, and it manifests, evolves itself, until it becomes the perfect man.

■ **Macrocosm and microcosm are built on the same plan:** Applying the law we dwelt upon under macrocosm, that each involution presupposes an evolution, and each evolution an involution, we see that instinct – of the personal ego-animal level is involved or down turned reason. In this manner, each lower level is an evolution of a preceding involvement of a higher level. The latest scientific man admits that each man and each animal is born with a fund of experience, and all these actions in the mind are the result of past experience.

6.5 Integrating Western perspective

To create an atmosphere of comparative analogy, here is a brief of the other side. These are the current changes in modern physics since the days of Sir Albert Einstein, which have led to the theory of our present discussion, the theory of non-locality. The brief outlines a sequence of events:

1. In May 1935, Sir Albert Einstein and two of his colleagues, Boris Podolsky and Nathan Rosen published the first description of a reality that is non-local (meaning traveling faster than the speed of light) as something unbelievable. Einstein called this 'spooky action' and this publication was eventually called the EPR paradox. It includes two major enigmas:
   - The collapse of the wave function as interpreted through the wave equation of Erwin Schrödinger
   - A probabilistic notion that every part of a quantum system responds instantaneously to a stimulus affecting any other part of a system. They suggest instantaneous connection with the universe as a whole.
2. The EPR experiment inspired other areas of research like polarization of light[15] seen from a quantum viewpoint. These emissions suggested information transfer in opposite directions to points far apart. Whether such transfer actually takes place at a speed exceeding that of light is another question.
3. Two later works emerged. One was of David Bohm (London, U.K.) in the 1950s and the other was by John Bell at CERN (European Center for Particle and Nuclear Physics, Switzerland) in the 1960s. Bohm proposed the 'Scattered-Matrix' theory and John Bell his 'Bell's Theorem' to take the notion of 'non-locality' further. But all these were theories.
4. In 1980s, Alain Aspect and his colleagues (in Paris) for the first time experimentally confirmed the EPR enigma and posed new avenues to review the Copenhagen interpretation of Schrödinger.
5. In the early 1990s John Cramer at the University of Washington, Seattle pointed out a unique thing implied in Schrödinger's wave equation. Cramer reviewed the equation and explained a bi-polarity meaning a conjugate of opposites. His wave equation is based on the simple idea of complex numbers which is: $Y = A + Bi$

And this stands for a complex number:

If $Y = A + B$ then $Y.Y = (A + B) . (A + B)$
In case of complex numbers, we know that $Y.Y = (A + Bi).(A - Bi)$

In other words, this complex conjugate form implies backward and forward linkages of the B factor, which stands for Time in the wave equation.
So, implicitly or explicitly, the use and application of the wave equation involves backward and forward linkages in time (Gribbin, 1995)[16] in any quantum calculation or experiments.

Cramer's deliberations imply that a wave function has a bi-polarity of backward and forward linkages of time. Backward linkage of time takes creation backward to its roots, its origin. In other words, the linkage is one of anti-creation (deconstruction taking everything to its seed form). Forward linkages of time, on the contrary, take us to future. It takes us to the full bloom and the highest creative possibility. The two concepts are however juxtaposed in the above equation. The findings in ancient wisdom of the Vedas are akin to what is happening in Science. **The Religion of the rise and fall of waves holds the key.**

7.0 CONCLUSIONS

The macrocosm and the microcosm are built on the same plan.

The Eastern perspective of consciousness has mostly focused in the smaller reality, the microcosm and its evolution to re-interpret our idea of the external world, the macrocosm. The eastern viewpoint has looked for ages deep within an inner cave (*guhahitam*), which is present in the heart of hearts of our existence. The deep eastern conception which is just not a philosophy but diret realization is based on the re-envision of the external world based or guided by our very potential Divinity. It is this principle of sentiency that is *Çhaitya Purusha*, the very direct portion of the Divine in the human, which has been forwarded by the present Chapter. It is also the being that is behind the *Chitta*, the mind-stuff and the mind-flux as Sri Aurobindo says.

The Western perspective has focused and started from the external world, through logic and experimentation of the macrocosm. The journey of Western sciences since the days of Aristotle and up to Descartes, Newton and Francis Bacon has been restricted by a machine driven idea of reality. However, since the days of the EPR experiment opening up chances of an inclusion of a quantum reality; the role of the participant in that reality and the possibility of the reality driven by quantum interpenetration and teleportation, the Western perspective has come closer and even more closer to the Eastern deep psychological perspective, which is based on direct perception of reality intuitively. In the Eastern perspective, first it is achieved through deep and sustained concentration, as the mind is purified (*nir-vasana*), which is *Dhyana* or Meditation and then it is augmented through a penetration into the direct perception of the reality within, which is *Yoga*.

1. The first stage is extermination of desire or destruction of individual personality, which is *Nirvana*
2. The second and the highest stage is the opening up of the reality within to a world view that is guided the principle of sentiency. This is *Anirvana.*

The key to bridge the two perspectives, Eastern and Western is perhaps the ancient realization of Sage Kapila and the evolution of deep Buddhist Iconography born from a great soul born in Kapila Vastu and particularly from Mahayana Buddhism, it's most powerful derivate, which the authors think is more original and much closer to the original teachings of that soul. To revert back to the critical point of historical evaluation with which the chapter had started:

- The inspired Architects in the most ancient of all Buddhist ages had carved the idea as rock-cut expressions called the *Chaitya* hall. As said before, the *Mahayana Sutra of the Foremost Shurangama* at the Crown of the Great Buddha says:
  ...the way of practicing the Samadhi is not singular and its actual method of cultivation depends upon the functioning of mind and mental concomitants (Citta-Chaitya pravritti) of each being and their interconnectedness (Mahat).

References

1. "Shikarakuta (small temple) *Chaitya* ". Asianart.com. Retrieved 2012-04-24

2. Source: Buddhism Study and Practice Group: Buddhism Glossary.

3. Padma Sree, A. W. Barber (Eds.). (2008). Buddhism in the Krishna river valley of Andhra. (p. 2). Albany, NY: SUNY Press.

4. A.i.213, etc.

5. E.g., Rig Veda.viii.5, 37-9

6. Bud. India, p.26

7. Dutt, S. (1988). *Buddhist monks and monasteries of India: their history and their contribution to Indian culture* (p. 221). New Delhi: Motilal Banarsidass.

8. Pp.282-284Jivatman, Spark-soul and Psychic Being

9. *Katha Upanishad* 2.3.17, *Svetasvatara Upanishad* 3.13

10. *Taittiriya Upanishad* I.6

11. *Samkhyadarshana* (*Sâṃkhya* is said to be one of the oldest metaphysical worldviews and philosophies of salvation. The word *Sankhya* means count, and *Sâṃkhya* is called so because it describes the world in an enumerative way. Twenty five principles are enlisted in *Sâṃkhya.* In an alternate and more elaborate version, these principles along with their attributes are enlisted as sixty principles. For this reason *Sâṃkhya* is also called *Ṣaṣṭhi Tantra* (meaning the philosophy of sixty principles)

12. Sen, J. (2006). *Concept of complete religion.* Kolkata: Cygnus Publication.

13. Sen J. (2008). *Principles of Indian architecture - a timeline study of her contribution to the global patterns of civilization* (p. 157). Kolkata: Cygnus Publication.

14. Sen, J. (2016). *A systems evaluation of global history of Indian architecture.* New Delhi: Copal Publishing House.

15. Tagore, R. (1951). *A vision of India's history*. Kolkata: Visvabharati Publication.

16. Joshi, L. M. (1970). Brahmanism, Buddhism, and Hinduism: An essay on their origins and interactions. Kandy, Sri Lanka: Buddhist Publication Society.

Bibliography

1. Tomory, E. (1989). A history of fine arts in India and the west. Orient BlackSwan

2. Huntington, S. History of Indian Art

3. Alexander Badawy; Shrines in Egypt and India; University of Kansas

4. The Buddhist and Hindu Architecture of India. Journal of the Royal Society of Arts. Retrieved from JStor 203.110.246.22

5. Badawy, A.; Buddha in Art: Form, Symbol to Image

6. Kak, S. (2005). Early Indian architecture and art. *Migration & Diffusion*, 6(23), 6-27.

7. Coomaraswamy, A. K. (1927). The Origin of the Buddha image.

9. Mortimer Wheeler, R. E. (1949). Romano-Buddhist art, and old problems restated. *Antiquity*, *XXIII*(89), 5.

However, the Buddhist sculpture of the Gandhara School can scarcely be called 'Romano-Buddhist'

Bose, A. (1945). Social and rural economy of Northern India, Vol. II. (pp. 481f) Calcutta.

Kosambi, D. D. (1951). Ancient Kosala and Magadha. *Journal of the Bombay Branch of the Royal Asiatic Society*, (pp. 186f).

Pande, G. C. (1957). *Studies in the origins of Buddhism* (p. 317). Allahabad: University of Allahabad.

Ancient Indian architecture. Retrieved from http://www.crystalinks.com/indiarchitecture.html

Buddhist architecture in India. Retrieved from http://himalaya.socanth.cam.ac.uk/collections/journals/bot/pdf/bot_11_03_02.pdf

Chapter 19

A Science of Human Experience to Help Solve Mysteries of Consciousness and its Place in Nature

DONALD D. PRICE
Division of Neuroscience, OMS, University of Florida, U.S.A.
and
JAMES J. BARRELL
University of West Georgia, U.S.A

This chapter provides an overview of an experiential science that we have developed for over 30 years and then focuses on how it can be applied to some deep questions about consciousness and its place in nature. We initially explain an experiential method in which co-investigators and participants are trained to observe (i.e., notice, be aware of) their direct experiences. This method focuses on a form of phenomenological analysis in which co-investigators and participants explore, confirm, and understand various topics of conscious human experience. We initially summarize this program of research that has been extensively described and explained in our recent book "Inner Experience and Neuroscience" (Price D.D. and Barrell J.J., 2012). We go on to emphasize that the first steps of this paradigm cannot be ignored or bypassed in experiential science. For reasons to be explained, we think that a science of conscious experience is not feasible unless investigators begin with their own direct experiences (Barrell J.J. and Barrell J.E., 1975; Price and Barrell, 1980; 2012). Based on repeated observations of direct experience, testable hypotheses are derived and when tested they ultimately help us to understand the structures of types of human experiences. Results of using this method can interface with traditional psychological and neuroscience observations as well as with philosophical reflections. This strategy can be used to help answer deep questions about consciousness and its relationship to other phenomena. Thus, the approach can be used to understand states of consciousness, including "ordinary" and "higher" states. States of consciousness are also intimately related to the issue of volition, a phenomenon that is relevant to both eastern and western perspectives. Finally, experiential science might help explain the role of observation in understanding quantum mechanics and consciousness. The solutions to both of these mysterious phenomena may be facilitated by a science of human experience, one that includes the paradigm described in this chapter.

Overview of the Experiential Method

Investigators that would be interested in the experiential methods would focus on specific phenomena or questions about them, such as the nature of specific types of emotional feelings, pain, pleasure, or background states of consciousness. Perhaps an ideal method would be one that addresses specific questions about experience yet is both exploratory and confirmatory. It would have two stages of verification. The purpose of the first stage would be to generate hypotheses and would be mainly exploratory while the second stage would explicitly test hypotheses generated in the first stage. We developed an experiential method that contained both stages (Barrell and Barrell, 1975; Price and Barrell, 1980; 2012). The cornerstone of this method is awareness of experience as it has just taken place in the moment. An independent summary and evaluation of this method is provided by Max Velmans (2013). To study specific topics of interest, such as emotions and states of consciousness, certain outer and inner conditions have to be arranged. The following discussion is about the purpose of this paradigm, the nature of the procedures, the form of the results, and how the data are interpreted and understood.

1. The Outer and Inner Conditions of the Experiential Method

The experiential method begins with a study group posing a general question to their experiences such as absorption, active attention, emotions, or background states of consciousness such as associative thinking or meditative states (Price and Barrell, 1980; 2012). The question is general, clearly understandable, and specifically directed to *how* one experiences a given phenomenon rather than only the target of experience or the stimulus conditions in which the phenomenon manifests itself. Thus, if the question is about a specific type of background state of consciousness, such as a hypnotic state, we focus on the experience of being in this state rather than the hypnotic instructions or on specific sensory contents (i.e., the target). The assumption is that the process of experiencing rather than the specific targets of experience leads us to an understanding of the essential factors within the phenomenon. For example, the specific targets of attention and the specific physical contexts may vary considerably from one situation to another. However, noticing *how* we experience a given phenomenon such as a hypnotic state is more likely to reveal the content of experience that is common across situations and across individuals. Most important, the study group members are to pose the question to their own experiencing of the phenomenon. Our idea is that an understanding of the reality of an experiential phenomenon is most accurate if it includes one's *own* experiences and those of others.

Accounts of such experiences last several seconds and usually not much longer. These accounts are obtained by having co-investigators (also known as co-participants) notice and then write brief descriptions of these moments. The descriptions follow certain guidelines as follows:

1. Briefly describe the setting in which your experience takes place. Where were you? What were you doing?
2. Attempt to get back into and re-experience a short interval of time when you had the experience of X (e.g. hypnotic state, associative thinking).
3. Make the interval between the actual experience and your description as short as is feasible, preferably right after the experience. Do not write descriptions hours after the actual experience.
4. Make the descriptions brief, a few sentences or a short paragraph.
5. Just describe what was in your experience, without interpreting, judging, or adding anything to make the description poetical, amusing, or clever.
6. Write the descriptions in first-person, present tense since even an immediately past experience is to be re-experienced at that moment.

2. *The Act of Observing in the Experiential Method*

Similar to other experiential methods (described and compared in Price and Barrell, 2012), our experiential method describes and characterizes phenomenal experience as it is lived in the moment. Since people find it difficult to notice at exactly the same moment one is experiencing a phenomenon, this form of observation often consists of an immediate retrospective account of what has just occurred in experience. It is a form of self-observation that is very different from armchair reflections, filling out detailed psychological questionnaires, engaging in phenomenology or the usual manner of providing self-reports during psychological experiments. What we mean by self-observation is taking an immediate impression of what is taking place in a moment of consciousness, like taking a snapshot of what is happening (Givot, 1998). The content can include sensations, perceptions, feelings, beliefs, moods, movements, thoughts, and images. For example, self-observation for the experiential method requires *awareness* rather than absorbed reflection ... unless one is studying absorbed reflection. However, even if someone is observing absorbed reflection, he or she would have to wake up momentarily to notice it. Awareness includes simply noticing whatever is present in experience. This is not an active effort but rather an intention to notice.

The experiential method addresses questions that pertain to specific topics, such as the nature of human emotions and states of consciousness. However, consistent with the principles of phenomenology, the questions are open-ended and exploratory. For example, we have asked "What is like to feel anger toward someone?" or "What is like to feel anxious about an outcome?" The results of these explorations are descriptions of experience that contain common factors or meanings.

3. Describing Experiences

The first part of this descriptive task in re-experiencing is that of briefly (in one or two sentences) describing the situation wherein the experience takes place in order to set the context of the experience and to foster an optimum mindset for re-experiencing. For example, if someone was re-experiencing anxiety about an outcome, he or she would initially describe the physical and/or social situation in which the experience has just taken place. The rest of the description records simply what the individual is noticing in his or her experience—thoughts, images, feelings, and so on. This part of the description is also relatively brief, consisting of no more than a single paragraph. Let us take a simple example from a study that we conducted on hypnotic states, one that relied on participation of investigator–participants:

I was sitting in a large recliner in a faculty office. Someone was sitting to my right speaking softly.

> I feel more and more relaxed as time goes by. I feel heaviness in my eyes as I watch her [the hypnotist]. I see her very clearly and notice very little else. As she speaks about my arm lifting, I notice that my arm makes a smooth arc all by itself and my finger touches my forehead. I am amazed by my experience. The room seems to be glowing and I feel a deep relaxation and quietness while everything takes place. (From Price and Barrell, 1990)

Participants could not help but sometimes reflect on changes in their conscious state. This reflection often came at the end or beginning of the experience when suggestions were given to induce or terminate the period of hypnosis but could also occur during hypnosis as in the situation above. Notice that the description of the setting and context (recliner, faculty office) is separated out from the thoughts and images that are more integral to the experience. Relaxation and focused attention is clearly evident in this description ("....more relaxed as time goes by" "I see her very clearly and notice very little else"). The sense of agency is that this person's action happens automatically and does not originate from a deliberate intention to move ("I notice that my arm makes a smooth arc all by itself..."). There is a feeling that relates to some or all of this despite the lack of exact certainty of where this feeling occurs during the experience ("glowing" "deep relaxation" "quietness).

The experiential method allows the capacity to capture most or all of an entire episode of an emotion or type of background state of consciousness, so that most or all of the factors that constitute a type of experienced phenomenon (e.g., hypnotic state) can be identified and characterized in a single episode. It also provides a means of allowing the experiencing person to provide the report. Of course, the report itself has to be discussed and described in group meetings with other co-investigators.

To further clarify the nature of an experiential report, we can distinguish it from those reports which would not be considered experiential. These alternative report styles would include *interpretative, poetical,* and *historical* accounts. For example, an interpretative report of hypnotic state might be, "I feel that my mind is being taken over by this person" "I have physiological activity which continues to increase during hypnosis". "Hypnosis happens when someone has reduced my mental activity" What is specified in this type of reporting are concepts, ("physiological activity"), causes ("...reduced my mental activity"), and inferences (i.e., "...my mind is taken over...") that are not immediately given in experience. Thus, only after a reflection disconnected from immediate experience do we classify a type of conscious state or infer its causes (Barrell and Barrell, 1975; Price and Barrell, 1980; 2012).

Poetical or historical self-reporting also doesn't reflect what is directly given in experience. A poetical account of hypnotic state might consist of statements such as, "It is like a room filling up with a glowing wonderment". In this case, imagination and metaphor interferes with the precise structure of the experience itself and the experience is from an outside viewpoint without explicitly acknowledging this viewpoint. Similarly, an historical account of experience necessitates that one view oneself in the past instead of in the present. For example, "When I was hypnotized, I became very still and moved automatically." This statement may or may not be correct and it ambiguously conflates the *experience* of automaticity with a third-person account of automatic behavior. In contrast, the experiential report is an account of immediate experience and is written in the first person, present tense, since even previous data reflect re-experiencing of those situations. With continued descriptions of experiences, types of experiences (e.g. hypnotic state) are seen to contain felt meanings, such as "deep physical and/or mental relaxation" and "events/actions happening by themselves automatically". In the studies that we conducted, each group member contributed several descriptions of experience that were in the first person, present tense, and either written or transcribed from tape. As in the example above, each description was preceded by a sentence or two that described the situation in which the experience occurred in order to frame the context of the experience and to re-experience the episode of interest.

Another critical issue is to what extent descriptions are reconstructions of the original lived experience. It is unlikely that the descriptions lead to an exact replica of the original lived experience. In re-experiencing an episode, participants may engage in a kind of abstract remembering that doesn't necessarily involve putting oneself back in the original situation. Or they may imaginatively put themselves back in the previous situation and think/feel the experience anew. In using the experiential method, we have emphasized getting as close to the original experience as much as possible (i.e., reliving). Like other methodologies (e.g., psychophysics), it is largely a matter of training. There is no way to absolutely eliminate the possibility that some participants "recreate" or even fabricate their accounts. If such distortions were systematic, however, it would seem unlikely that all co-investigators would arrive at the same common factors that characterize a type of experience. The use of multiple descriptions from each co-investigator and guidelines for participation help establish group consensus. Descriptions that didn't follow the guidelines of this method were eliminated from the collected data. Such descriptions were noticed sometimes by the author of the description and sometimes by others. Importantly, each description was read and discussed by the group.

4. Discovering the Common Factors

Once group members produced several descriptions that pertained to the topic of interest (e.g., anger, anxiety), members would each begin to identify the common meanings or factors within all of their descriptions of a given kind of experience (e.g., hypnotic state, emotions), and they would do this prior to group meetings. They began this process by analyzing the descriptions in such a way as to determine what is present in all situations in which this phenomenon occurs. The aim of this approach is to reflect in such a way that no preconceptions are brought in for the purpose of interpretation. The common factors of a type of experience were evident from descriptions of the experiences themselves, yet each co-investigator found that all factors are explicit or strongly implicit in his or her own experience. For example, one experiential study (Price and Barrell, 1990; Price, 1996) was guided by 21 participants who continued to ask, "What is present in all situations wherein a hypnotic state occurs?" "What common factors are necessary or sufficient for this type of experience?" Preliminary lists of common meanings/factors were submitted for group discussion and analysis at regular meetings. Each of five factors was unanimously agreed upon as being part of the unique altered state that occurred during hypnotic inductions:

1. An absorbed and sustained focus of attention on one or few targets.
2. A feeling of mental/physical ease or relaxation.

3. An absence of judging, monitoring, censoring.
4. Suspension of usual orientation toward time, location of self, and/or sense of self.
5. Own responses experienced as automatic/without deliberation or effort.

Factors 1, 2, and 5 were clearly and usually explicitly evident in the descriptions of participants because the descriptions contained words that conveyed this same type of meaning. The representative description given earlier serves as an example. Factors 3 and 4 were found to be different in that they were sometimes discerned only after reflecting on the experience that had just occurred. Similar to immediate accounts of dreams, the absence of monitoring and the suspension of usual self-orientation was noticed retrospectively. These factors have been independently verified in other studies that used other methods to study the hypnotic state.

5. *Discovering Relationships*

Once the common factors were agreed upon, the factors were subjected to an analysis in which the study group reflected upon two kinds of relationships within the phenomenon. The first is the discovery of *definitional hypotheses*, statements about the necessary and sufficient experiential factors for the occurrence of a given phenomenon. A definitional hypothesis is facilitated by performing an analysis in which we determine whether each experiential factor is necessary or sufficient for a given phenomenon. To do this, we would attempt to place ourselves in or re-experience situations in which the phenomenon is present and the factor is absent and vice versa.

The second is the discovery of *functional hypotheses*, statements about the relationships between these experiential factors, including quantitative relationships between one factor and another. These relationships must apply to the several situations that one has experienced. Once the relevant causal paths are identified in an experiential study, they can be tested in other groups of participants unfamiliar with the hypothesized paths. In other words, they can be tested with conventional psychological methods. Thus, it is possible to develop and validate scales of these experiential dimensions so that these hypotheses can be tested with methods traditionally used in psychophysical studies. For example, our experiential-phenomenological study was followed up in a second study in which 62 participants rated each of the 5 factors listed above under conditions of "normal wakefulness" "mild hypnosis" and "deep hypnosis. A model was tested during experimental conditions designed to produce "normal waking," mild, and deep hypnotic states (Price, 1996). As can be discerned from Figure 1, structural equation modeling provided a reasonable confirmation of this model. For example, the links (beta weights) between the factors in this model were stronger in comparison to alternative models that were tested. The five factors and relationships between them were agreed upon by all members of

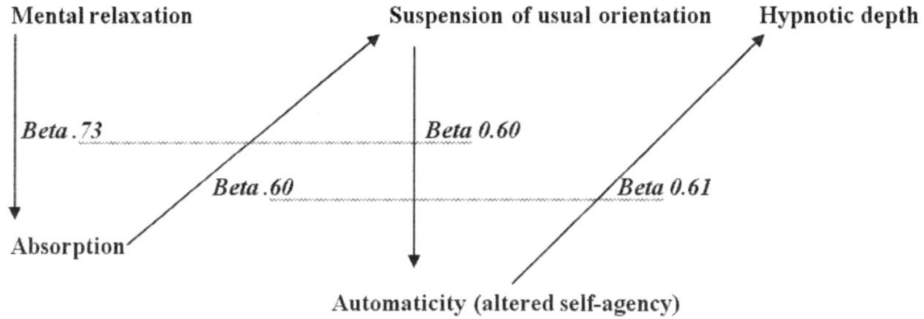

FIGURE 1

Simplified version of structural equation model based on ratings of 62 participants (from data based on Price and Barber, 1996). Beta weights are estimates of strength of connection between these variables.

the study group and supported by the large majority of descriptions obtained from group members.

The experience of a hypnotic state begins with a relaxed condition of mental (and often physical) ease in combination with an absorbed and sustained focus on an object or objects of attention. Thus, initial suggestions for induction of those changes are commonly directed toward these two dimensions (mental ease and absorption). With time one proceeds from an active form of concentration to a relaxed passive form. There is often (though perhaps not necessarily) an inhibition or reduction in the peripheral range of experience. This relaxation and/or reduction in range of active attention supports a lack of monitoring and censoring of that which is allowed into experience (altered self-regulation). Hence, inconsistencies are now more tolerable. Contradictory statements, which once arrested attention and caused confusion or disturbance, now no longer do so. The uncensored acceptance of what is being said by the hypnotist is not checked against one's associations. Consequently, one no longer chooses or validates the correctness of incoming statements. This allows thinking and meaning-in-itself that is disconnected from active reflection. From this way of experiencing, there emerges the sense of automaticity wherein thinking is no longer felt as preceding action but action is felt as preceding thought. Thus, if the hypnotist suggests a bodily action, a sensation, or a lack of sensation (e.g., pain), there is no experience of deliberation or effort. One simply and automatically identifies with the suggested action, sensation, or lack of sensation, as it is suggested. Changes in perception, mental activity, and behavior are simply felt as happening. Little consideration is given to the possibility of *not* carrying out the action or *not* experiencing the suggested changes in sensation. These changes experienced during hypnosis facilitate the incorporation of suggestions, such as analgesia. For example, the words of the hypnotist can be incorporated into the thoughts and the meanings of the subject.

6. Extending Experiential Validation in Conventional Psychological Studies

An aim of the experiential method is to generate qualitative descriptions of given kinds of experience, descriptions that express phenomena as they reveal themselves to the experiencing subject. They are to be agreed upon and well understood by all those capable of having the experiences in question. Each final description is to contain precise explicit statements about what is essential for the experience, omitting particulars. The experiential method (1) enlists co-investigators to form these descriptions, (2) specifies the mode of attending and questioning, (3) includes a strategy of determining the necessary and sufficient factors for the experience in question (definitional hypotheses) and (4) allows the investigators to discover the functional relationships of common factors of given kinds of experience. This strategy can generate both *definitional and functional* hypotheses as we have described. It is important to emphasize that unlike other sciences and psychology in particular, the experiential method doesn't *begin* with theories or hypotheses. Rather it begins with general questions posed to experience and *arrives* at definitional and functional hypotheses through self-directed experiences. Both types of hypotheses can then be tested in studies that use quantitative methods in conventional psychological studies. The "conventional" studies can use large numbers of participants who are unfamiliar with the definitional and functional hypotheses under study.

7. Testing Relationships in Neuroscience Research

These common factors of a hypnotic state and their interrelationships have since been integrated with neuroscience, thereby illustrating how the results of an experiential science interface those of the natural sciences, including cognitive neuroscience (Price and Barrell, 2012). For example, in one study 10 normal volunteers underwent brain scanning (positron emission tomography) before and after the induction of hypnosis (Rainville et al., 2002). They rated their experienced level of "mental relaxation" and "mental absorption" two of the key dimensions characterized in our earlier study of the experience of being in a hypnotic state. Correlations (i.e. regression analyses) between measures of neural activity (as measured by regional cerebral blood flow) and self-ratings confirmed the hypothesized increased activity of the of the brains arousal system in combination with decreased activity in brain regions involved in the sense of self-agency. As one might expect, ratings of *absorption* were positively correlated with midbrain, midline thalamus, and anterior cingulate brain regions involved in arousal and attention. In contrast, *decreases* in neural activity in regions of the brain involved in self agency, were positively correlated with ratings of "relaxation". Some relaxation-related areas were within the right parietal cortex. (Rainville et al., 2002). Although other studies further support these relationships, much more needs to be done to relate all five dimensions of hypnotic state to distributed patterns of brain activity. Similar to consciousness in general, the experience of a hypnotic state is highly modifiable on a moment-to-moment basis, depending on attentional, emotional, and other psychological factors. All of these facets of experience can be captured in observers trained to notice details of their experience, using experiential methods. If that is the case, then variation can be induced in the experience of the magnitudes of factors that comprise a hypnotic state. The experiential variation can then be linked to variation in levels of activity within multiple brain areas and in the functional connections between them. It may then be possible to more rigorously test the relationships between neural activity and hypnotic state, thereby providing a more refined way to explain and understand this type of conscious experience.

The strategy of using these seven steps has been applied to many types of conscious experiences and topics. For example, different types of pain have been characterized using an experiential approach and the neural correlates of "second" pain have been characterized to some extent (Chapter 8, Price and Barrell, 2012). In addition to neuroscience studies (step7), the experiential method has also been used to discover the common factors and their functional interrelationships in various emotions, such as depression, anxiety, relief, satisfaction, and excitement (Chapters 4-6, Price and Barrell, 2012). Finally, this approach and method is also ideal for studies related to consciousness. The same stages of research can be carried out to experientially define and differentiate states of consciousness such as dreams, higher states of consciousness and as well as different types of waking states.

The First Steps of the Experiential Method

The first steps of this experiential method are critical and cannot be bypassed. It is important to distinguish the paradigm that we have outlined above with that of traditional psychology and neuroscience. Traditional approaches almost always begin with theories that are influenced by presuppositions and even beliefs about the nature of the subject of study. The distinctive feature of our experiential method is that it adds an initial, structured exploration of experience to the usual scientific method, with the intent of avoiding theoretical biases and presuppositions before further investigation is conducted. Yet for this approach to work, investigators must carefully design and conduct the steps 1-4 discussed above. These steps have the unique requirement that co-investigators/participants have a trained or at least well-instructed preparation to observe *how* they experience conscious phenomena of interest. As we have already discussed, they must be willing and able to witness their experiences. Much of this witnessing is immediate retrospective and is only feasible during awareness. Other conscious conditions make it difficult or impossible to observe and self-report. For example, people may be in states of vague wakefulness (e.g. associative thinking), or simple attention that is only focused on things or targets outside oneself. In the state of *awareness*, both the targets of our attention and the reactions and meanings of the one who is attending are within experience. This allows critical noticing of both 'how' one is experiencing and 'what' is in experience. For example, in the report of being in a hypnotic state described earlier, the participant described his own motor act as happening all by itself. This was not an interpretation or conclusion but rather an account of what this experience was really like. Implicit in this report is the absence of the implicit or explicit presence of the intention to move. Had the participant been vaguely awake, or multitasking at the time of making this observation, the report would not likely have contained the common factors reported by most participants in this study.

Regardless of whether the list of common factors is decided by co-investigators or investigators who do not participate in their own experiments, the participant and the investigator must train their sensibility to each other so that interpretations of experiences ultimately and accurately follow the observations (i.e., the direct experiences). The participant must train his or her skills in noticing and reporting experiences, and the investigator must train his or her ability to provide an undistorted report of what the participant is experiencing. As Kordes (2009) notes, "This confirms the need (and ethical urge) for a dialogical approach..." Both participants and investigators are researchers in an important sense because observation of experience is not "from the outside" but one of participatory co-research. Kordes asks, "Is it possible to research the experience of another being unless that person has an honest and deeply existential interest in observing his/her experience?" We think this interest must occur in both investigators and participants. Thus, the investigator-participant model is the key feature of our experiential method. The steps of learning to observe and report experience cannot be bypassed in experiential science.

Definitional and functional hypotheses must come from direct lived experience rather than just theories or presuppositions. Groping in the dark for hypotheses is not an option for the method we have practiced and outlined above.

The resistance to looking at ourselves must be overcome to have a truly objective science of conscious experience. Through the practice and application of awareness, the objective observer emerges. This has been and continues to be a fundamental goal for traditional science. From this perspective, the meaningfulness of data and the deep understanding of consciousness and human experiences far exceed mere speculations and theoretical explanations.

Using the experiential method to characterize various background and higher states of consciousness

The experiential method with its stages of observing, describing and understanding can be used for studies related to both ordinary background and extra-ordinary states of consciousness. Using this methodology, we can arrive at common meanings defining such ordinary states as *vague wakefulness, absorption, and attention* as well as extra-ordinary states such as *awareness, self-remembering and pure awareness*. The common meanings or factors within these states can then be put into the form of definitional hypotheses and functional hypotheses as we have described above for the hypnotic state.

Vague wakefulness and other ordinary states

A common background state of consciousness occurs when subjects of brain imaging experiments are told to "rest" during control baseline conditions (Price and Barrell, 2012). When left without external or internal demands, the default mode of consciousness is often that of vague wakefulness, something between "waking" and "sleep". It has been characterized as a state wherein subjects make unconstrained loose associations that are unrelated to the immediate external environment. Images and/or thoughts are linked closely together and quickly (e.g., brain scanner—dark—end of daylight savings---got to set clock tommorro---can't be late for work). This default mode of consciousness is accompanied by activation within a network of brain structures: ventromedial prefrontal cortex, anterior and posterior cingulate cortex, and areas in the medial parietal and temporal cortices. These areas are involved in short and long term memory, attention, and other factors related to consciousness regulation. Activation is minimal in areas involved in early stages of sensory processing, consistent with the experience of vague wakefulness and associative thinking that are not linked to anything directly in the immediate environment. A more refined experiential characterization of this state could lead to identification of common factors that constitute it.

Through application of the experiential method we could discover common meanings or factors of other ordinary states. Examples may include multi-tasking, planning or simply thinking about the future or dwelling in the past. In deep absorption, one can be totally lost in the moment with no sense of self or body. As discussed earlier, this kind of experience is a component of the hypnotic state. Attention may include some sense of self but without a separation or distance between the object of attentions and self.

Awareness, self-remembering, and presence

For extra-ordinary states, we may also discover some common meanings or themes. In *absorption* one is lost in target of experience. In *attention* there can be both judgment and separation from the target. In contrast to both *absorption* and *attention,* in *awareness* there is sense of presence with the target. This allows us to be more objective to the target and supports a direct noticing without presuppositions, imagined results, and theorizing that foster a subjective orientation. Awareness, on the other hand, is closer to an objective orientation since it allows the contents and the "how" of experience simply to be there. Within the experiences of self-remembering or the experience of "*I am*", there is the experience of nothing outside the self (Ouspensky, 1971. All is *one*. There is only *presence*. It is possible to access this experience starting with feeling your whole body at once. Finally, a common meaning for *pure awareness* includes the complete absence of any sense of self or presence. You simply dissolve into and become the awareness. It is like everything being in the awareness of "something higher". Interestingly, in the Hindu Religion, Atman can correspond to the experience of self-remembering or "I AM" and Brahman can relate to pure awareness (Balsekar, 1998; Maharaj, 2001; Sriamamurti, Prashant, and Mohan, 2013). These are just a few examples of states of consciousness that could be studied using an experiential perspective and method. The emphasis on observation of direct experience is quite different from methods based on theory and conceptualizations. Immediate retrospective noticing of these states, as provided by our experiential method, could be used for their study and analysis.

Are there common factors within the experience of volition?

What if this approach was taken to study the experience of volition. Our studies of hypnotic and other background conscious states revealed distinctions between experiencing oneself as the agent of one's actions versus automaticity (Price and Barrell, 2012), a distinction that has received a lot of attention in cognitive neuroscience (e.g., Rainville et al., 2002). It also compared states that included self-orientation versus those which do not include this factor. Unlike hypnotic states, volitional states of consciousness may include "presence"/awareness. The difference between volitional and non-volitional choice may be related to differences in background states of consciousness that optimize or reduce awareness of one's values and information that would lead to expectations. Consider then the possibility that a mind-set that characterizes volitional choice might include some or all of the following common factors:

1. lack of identification and attachment (Ouspensky, 1971)
2. awareness of relevant information, meanings and feelings (desires, expectations, etc) associated with the different options*
3. based on 2, a conscious weighing of feelings associated with each option, leading to a deliberate choice**.
4. a feeling of being the agent of one's choice***

*Chapter 4-6, **Chapter 6, ***Chapter 10, Price and Barrell, 2012

This list is not meant to be a definitive characterization of conscious choice, but merely suggested possible factors that are included in the *experience of volitional choice*. Some of the factors, such as "lack of attachment", may be present in both hypnotic states and in 'mindful' choice. On the other hand, other factors such as feeling to be the agent of one's choice versus the automaticity that occurs during hypnosis appear to be at opposite ends of a continuum. The list is also based on a consideration of 'mindfulness', a subject that has gained considerable attention in psychology and neuroscience (Bohdi, B. 2005; Grant, Courtenmanche, and Rainville, 2011; Ives-Deliperi, Solms, Meintjes, 2011; Zeiden et al., 2011). Mindfulness also follows eastern psychological traditions, most particularly Bhuddism. However, it may not be necessary to practice Bhuddism or any other ancient teaching to arrive at an understanding of the structure of volitional action. Nevertheless, to the extent to which such teachings foster the practice of awareness, the practice of meditation would likely facilitate the process of understanding. The experiential approach and method could be used to arrive at the common factors and test interrelationships between them, just as it was used to characterize the hypnotic state and distinguish it from other background states of consciousness, such as vague wakefulness.

Regardless of the exact experiential method used to study it, volition seems to require awareness. Awareness means the experience of feeling present to the moment, being embedded in the experience yet remaining impartial. Awareness contrasts with absorption where one is lost in the moment and forms of attention where one lacks presence. Put another way, it contrasts with 'identification' which is losing one's sense of presence (Ouspensky, 1971; Givot,1998) and 'attachment' which is an inability to let go of what one is identified with (Bohdi, 2005; Ouspensky, 1971). An experiential approach to this problem may help distinguish what does and does not constitute volition, a phenomenon that has been debated and redefined for centuries. A dictionary definition of volition is *an act of making a choice or decision.* This definition refers only to a behavior and does not differentiate between the conscious experience of choosing and unconsciously making choices. The experience of choosing must include the feeling that *I am choosing* (self-agency) which is based in part on knowing that *I can choose.* Knowing that one can choose is constrained by external conditions but may not be fully determined by them. Clearly, there are physical, social, and political circumstances under which someone experiences their ability to choose as severely limited, or alternatively, greatly enhanced. Knowing that one can choose is required for the feeling that one is choosing and is a measure of relative freedom. It is relative since we have no absolute control over external circumstances or the outcomes of our choices. That our choices are influenced by our values and hence our genes and learning history does not negate the possibility that we can choose with perspective and awareness.

Our current experiential methodology is based on a learned ability to notice, be objective, and most importantly be aware of *how* and *what* we are experiencing (i.e. thoughts, feelings, sensations, imaginings, actions etc.). Awareness, which has traditionally been of great value for those in the East, is the centerpiece of the Experiential Method and is necessary for objectivity within both Eastern and Western perspectives. Awareness appears to be a primary integrating factor for Eastern and Western perspectives. Western science has carried out much research on hypnosis, sleep and dreams while Eastern research has focused on meditative practices and higher states of consciousness. Although ordinary waking states appear to be largely ignored, states related to pain and suffering, as part of the ordinary waking state, have been of great interest for both East and West.

Using experiential methods to address the quantum measurement problem (QMP) in quantum mechanics

Problems related to approaches and methods of observation exist not only for psychology but also physics. For example, there is a continuing controversy in quantum mechanics about the role of human observation in quantum phenomena (Schwartz and Begley, 2002). The standard formulation of quantum mechanics is that the state of physical systems is to be described by a wave function, according to which physical entities such as electrons, ions, or photons, are in a superposed state (i.e., in a superposition of different positions) when they are left unobserved. The wave function can then evolve in two ways: 1) linear evolution by the Shrodinger equation that tends to maintain superposed states or 2) nonlinear *collapses* which occur only upon measurement. Thus, the wave function of a subatomic particle collapses and its position can be known when a *measurement* occurs. Before measurement, the position of the particle is in an indeterminate state and is actually considered to have statistical probabilities of being in different places at the same time. Upon measurement, the position is fixed in place, i.e. it is collapsed. Although there may be no widely agreed upon definition of what a measurement is, measurement requires *observation by a conscious observer*. On some accounts of quantum mechanics, the experience of the observer is ontologically part of the quantum mechanical phenomena that are about the behavior of particles and waves. In the earliest and in some present interpretations of quantum mechanics, there is a clear separation between the process taking place in the observer (Process 1) and the process in the system being observed (Process 2) such as the interference pattern of light passing through double slits. Process 1 has always been very problematic because of the unresolved issue of what aspects of observation are critical for the results of an experiment. Thus, the observation might include the measuring instrument (e.g., a Gieger counter) as well the body, brain, and conscious experience of the observer. For example, it could be the case that quantum events are actualized at the time they are recorded by an instrument rather than when they are consciously experienced. The latter alternative would then have little consequence for the causal impact of conscious experience on the physical world.

The ambiguities in quantum physics are mainly about which aspects of observation influence the outcome (particle or interference pattern). The calculations and equations of quantum mechanics are mostly agreed upon by physicists, in contrast to views about observation. Physicists on the materialistic side of this divide have invoked the many-worlds theory in order to eliminate the role of human observation entirely and to preserve materialism (Schwartz and Begley, 2002). This interpretation of quantum mechanics holds that superposed waves exist for quantum phenomena, but collapse never happens. Instead, the wave function continues to evolve. At the point of measurement, the wave function splits into multiple possibilities, each of which can be potentially witnessed by corresponding minds. Thus, the many-worlds theory entails a many-minds theory. For example, if the wave function gives a fifty-fifty probability that a radioactive atom will decay after thirty minutes, then in one world it will have decayed in thirty minutes and in another world it will have not. At the point of measurement, the mind of the observer also splits into two corresponding realities, one perceiving a decayed atom and another perceiving an intact one. As might be expected, there are physicists who strongly oppose the many-worlds/many minds theory (see references and discussion in Schwartz and Begley, 2002). Instead, they claim that human observation is part and parcel of the very quantum phenomena that exist. Yet the latter group doesn't specify the exact nature of human observation---they leave out the phenomenology of the observing experience. In conducting an experiment in quantum mechanics, a physicist *chooses* which physical property of matter and energy to observe as well as when and how often to observe it. These choices are critical for what actually happens in the experiment. But what is the experience of choosing like? Do the results vary as a function of the attentiveness, absorption, or awareness of the observer? Or does any of this matter? Thus, almost regardless of the metaphysical positions taken with respect to the role of observation in quantum phenomena, the experience of the observer is either eliminated from the explanation or remains a "blind spot" in it. This is also the state of affairs for other sciences, including neuroscience and psychology. Through a return to an experiential perspective, it is given directly that the observed is *within* the observer's experience.

The results of interfacing psychological variables with experiments on quantum mechanisms have recently shown critical progress in several experiments conducted by Dean Radin and his colleagues (Radin et al., 2012). They tested the possible role of consciousness in the collapse of the quantum wave function, using a double slit optical system. They initially point out (quoting Feyman, 1965) that the double slit experiment has in it the heart of quantum mechanics and contains its deepest mystery. When light is passed through the two slits at separate times, the resulting spectral patterns are consistent with the interpretation of light as particles but when light is passed through both slits simultaneously, the resulting spectral patterns are consistent with a wave interpretation. The interference pattern's double-slit spectral power (i.e., "wave-likeness", termed D for double slit) and single-slit spectral power (i.e., "particle-likeness" termed S) were quantified precisely in Radin et al.s experiments. The dependent variable was the ratio (R) of wave-like to particle-like spectral power, expressed as R= D/S. Data contributed by 137 people in six experiments totaling 250 test sessions showed that this ratio decreased when the participants' *attention* was focused toward the double slit as compared to when they did *not* focus toward the double slit. To put it more succinctly, attention to the double slit resulted in spectral patterns more particle-like than wave-like, as they predicted. For groups of participants as a whole, the size of these effects were small (Ca. -.2) but certainly not negligible and they were statistically significant (e.g., P = .015 to .0097). Psychological factors seemed to be much more influential than immediate physical factors such as temperature, vibration, and signal drift. Except for zen meditators, participants who practiced meditation showed larger effect sizes (-.46) than non-meditators (+.19) and a number of psychological factors significantly correlated with changes in double slit interference pattern. Thus, effect sizes in these types of experiments are not necessarily small or negligible. In contrast, no effects were found in control sessions in which no participants were present and wherein only physical variables were tested. Thus, it appears that conscious phenomena, from observers inside and outside laboratories, influence the extent to which photons behave as waves or particles!

But what is the nature of these conscious phenomena and how can we study them in relationship to the kinds of experiments that Radin et al conduct? As noted by Radin et al, it should be noted that some meditation styles, such as mantra repetition, tend to use a more focused concentrated attention, while others, such as mindfulness meditation, tend to expand one's awareness capacities. No attempt was made in the present studies to assess differences among reported meditation styles, or to independently measure participants' capacity for sustained focused attention (Radin et al., 2012).

Motivation, belief, focused attention, and background states of consciousness appeared to influence the outcomes in Radins experiments, but it is not clear which factors were critical. If we knew these answers, we might be closer to understanding the nature of relationships between mental and physical aspects of reality. We need to move far beyond responses to questionnaires and personality constructs to understand how human experience interacts with nature. The experiential methods outlined earlier offer the opportunity to select experiential variables prospectively by determining 'What it is like' to influence the outcomes of these double slit experiments. Thus, possible independent variables of imaginative involvement, absorption, awareness, desire for an effect, and degree of expectation may exert their influence to varying extents in these types of experiments. The experiential data may consist of both qualitative (e.g., first-person present tense descriptions of phenomenal experience) and quantitative data (ratings of critical variables such as absorption) as outlined above in our account of the experiential method. Combining the methods of an experiential science with those of quantum physics might help solve two mysteries at the same time---that of consciousness and quantum mechanical phenomena. The possible entailment between the two phenomena has been suggested by others, including Chalmers (2003).

Conclusions

We have outlined an experiential research paradigm that consist of seven steps—1) arranging for co-investigator-participants to question and explore a given phenomenon of consciousness (e.g., hypnotic state, vague wakefulness); 2) noticing particular experiences of this phenomenon; 3) describing these experiences just as they occurred in an immediate retrospective manner; 4) determining the common factors or meanings for a given type of phenomenon; 5 arriving at *definitional* and *functional* hypotheses; 6) testing these hypotheses in large groups of participants unfamiliar with the hypotheses; and 7) conducting research on the neural causes and/or correlates of these hypotheses. The first 6 steps may be crucial for a science of conscious experience, one that could be integrated with the rest of science. There is often a tendency to avoid experiential phenomenology and instead test ideas and beliefs with impressive technologies and sophisticated experimental designs. The latter approach is not necessarily based on data from direct human experience or by the steps of that we have outlined in this chapter. **We need to decide on whether we want a science of consciousness to be *based* on theories and beliefs or the realities of our own direct phenomenal experiences.** For example, both ordinary and extraordinary states of consciousness can be characterized along several dimensions and/or meanings. These factors are *within experience* that can serve as independent variables that scientifically relate experiential reality to the brain, body, and even physical reality. These independent variables can be used in neuroscience, as exemplified in some neuroimaging studies of self-agency and hypnosis. And they can be independent variables of studies such as those conducted by Radin and his colleagues (Radin et al., 2012). This approach would be illuminating and profound for understanding consciousness-brain-body relationships and consciousness-matter relationships. Thus, replications of Radin et al.'s studies of psychological modulation of electromagnetic interference patterns (e.g. double slit studies) might achieve a level of analysis that could answer deep questions about relationships between phenomenal experience and the physical universe.

References

Balsekar, R. (1998). *Your head in the tiger's mouth*. Redondo Beach, CA: Advaita Press.

Barrell, J. J. & Barrell, J. E. (1975). A self-directed approach for a science of human experience. *Journal of Phenomenological Psychology, 6*, 63-73.

Bohdi, B. (2005). *In the Buddha's words: An anthology of discourses from the Pali canon*. Boston: Wisdom Publications.

Chalmers, D. J. (2003). Consciousness and its place in nature. In S. Stich and T. Warfield (Eds.), *Blackwell Guide to the Philosophy of Mind* (pp. 1-37). Malden, MA: Blackwell.

Feyman, R., Leighton, S., & Sands, M. (1965). *The Feyman lectures on physics*. New York: Addison-Wesley.

Givot, I. (1998). *Seven aspects of self-observation*. Aurora, OR: Two Rivers Press.

Grant, J.A., Courtenmanch, J., & Rainville, P. (2011). A non-elaborative stance and decoupling of executive and pain-related cortices predicts low pain sensitivity in Zen meditators. *Pain, 152*, 150-156.

Hurlburt, R. T. & Schwitzgebel, E. (2007). *Describing inner experience? Proponent meets skeptic*. Cambridge MA: MIT Press.

Ives-Deliperi, V. L., Solms, M., & Meintjes, E. M. (2011). The neural substrates of mindfulness: An fMRI investigation. *Social Neuroscience, 6*(3): 231-242.

Kordes, U. (2009). The phenomenology of decision making. *Interdisciplinary Description of Complex Systems, 7*(2), 65-77.

Maharaj, N. (2001). *The ultimate medicine*. San Diego, CA: Blue Dove Press.

Mellers, B.A., Schwartz, A., & Ritov, I. (1999). Emotion-based choice. *Journal of Experimental Psychology, General, 128*, 1-14.

Ouspensky, P. D. (1971). *The fourth way*. New York: Vintage Books.

Price, D. D. (1996). Hypnotic analgesia: psychological and neural mechanisms. In J. Barber (Ed.), *Hypnosis and suggestions in the treatment of pain* (pp. 67-84). New York: Norton.

Price, D. D., & Barber, J. (1987). An analysis of factors that contribute to the efficacy of hypnotic analgesia. *Journal of Abnormal Psychology, 96*, 46-51.

Price, D. D., & Barrell, J. J. (1990). The structure of the hypnotic state: a self-directed experiential study. In J. J. Barrell (Ed.), *The experiential method: Exploring the human experience* (pp. 85-97), Acton, MA: Copely Publishing Group.

Price, D.D., & Barrell, J. J. (1980). An experiential approach with quantitative methods: A research paradigm. *Journal of Humanistic Psvchology, 20*, 75-95.

Price, D. D. & Barrell, J. J. (2012). *Inner experience and neuroscience: Merging both perspectives*. Cambridge, MA: MIT Press.

Rainville, P., Hofbauer, R. K., Bushnell, M. C., Duncan, G. H., & Price, D. D. (2002). Hypnosis modulates activity in brain structures involved in the regulation of consciousness. *Journal of Cognitive Neuroscience, 14*, 887-901.

Radin, D., Michel, L., Galdamaez, K., Wendland, P., Rickenbach, R., & Delorme, A. (2012). Consciousness and the double-slit interference pattern: Six experiments. *Physics Essays, 25*, 157-171.

Schwartz, J. M. & Begley, S. (2002). *The mind and the brain*. New York: HarperCollins.

Sriramamurti, P., P. Prashant, P. & M. Anand, (Eds.) (2013). *Spiritual Consciousness*. New Delhi: New Age Books.

Velmans, M. (2009). *Understanding consciousness*. London: Routledge.

Velmans, M. (2013, January). [Review of the book *Inner experience and neuroscience: Merging both perspectives*, by D. D. Price & J. J. Barrell]. *Journal of Consciousness Studies, 20*, 208-215.

Zeiden, F., Martucci, K., Kraft, R., Gordon, N., McHaffie, J., & Coghill, R. (2011). Brain mechanisms supporting the modulation of pain by mindfulness meditation. *Journal of Neuroscience, 61*, 5540-5548.

Chapter 20

Modelling Microtubules in the Human Brain as a Generalization from two-(state) Qubit to n-Qudit Quantum Hopfield Network and Beyond

DAYAL PYARI SRIVASTAVA
Department of Physics and Computer Science and Quantum-Nano Systems Centre, Dayalbagh Educational Institute (Deemed University), Dayalbagh, Agra, India

VISHAL SAHNI
Quantum-Nano Systems Centre and Centre for Consciousness Studies, Dayalbagh Educational Institute (Deemed University), Dayalbagh, Agra, India

and
PREM SARAN SATSANGI
Chairman, Advisory Committee on Education, Dayalbagh Educational Institutions, Dayalbagh, Agra, India

Keywords : Quantum Hopfield Network, Qudits, Contextuality, Power Laws

ABSTRACT

The scientific approach to understand the nature of consciousness revolves around the study of human brain. Neurobiological studies that compare the nervous system of different species have accorded highest place to the humans on account of various factors that include a highly developed cortical area comprising of approximately 100 billion neurons, that are intrinsically connected to form a highly complex network. Quantum theories of consciousness are based on mathematical abstraction and Penrose-Hameroff Orch-OR Theory is one of the most promising ones. Inspired by Penrose-Hameroff Orch-OR Theory, Behrman et. al. (Behrman, 2006) have simulated a quantum Hopfield neural network with the structure of a microtubule. They have used an extremely simplified model of the tubulin dimers with each dimer represented simply as a qubit, a single quantum two-state system. A qubit, unlike a bit, can exist in a superposition of the two states. They have included Coulombic interactions between qubits, and thermal effects for the qubits themselves.

This chapter presents an extension of this model to n-dimensional quantum states, or n-qudits which holds considerable promise for even higher mathematical abstraction in modelling consciousness systems. We start with the simplest case of a qubit with $n = 4$ *discretization points in a system of* $N = 3$ *qubits (d=2) and then proceed to* *a qudit (d=3) with $n=8$ discretization points in a system of $N=3$ qudits, where each qudit is now represented by a sphere with 8 discretization points. It is extended to a qudit (d=5) with $n=32$ discretization points in a system of $N=5$ qudits. In this solar system model, each 3-dimensional sphere is rotating in a loop / circle to give five degrees of freedom. It is further extended to a qudit (d=7) with $n=128$ discretization points in a system of $N=3$ qudits. In this galaxy model (comprising planet, sun and galaxy), each 3-dimensional sphere (planet) is revolving in a circular orbit around an (imaginary) sun, and the solar system (with associated planets) is in turn, revolving in a circular orbit around the galaxy.*

We see significant jump in the level of discretization and level of fineness (fine-grained quantum geometry) while invoking higher and higher level of unified quantum field theory and correspondingly subtler and subtler particle size of fine grained geometry. We conclude that by using n-qudit based model ($n \to \infty$), we should be able to access at least in the abstract world of mathematics and physics, the primary ultimate source of consciousness in the whole universe.

1. MODELLING MIRCOTUBULES AS QUANTUM HOPFIELD NETWORKS

Hopfield neural networks are a class of neural network models where non-linear graded response neurons organized into networks with effectively symmetric synaptic connections are able to implement interesting algorithms, thereby introducing the concept of information storage in the stable states of dynamical systems. The dynamics of the state-space trajectory as well as time domain evolution of sensitivities of the states with respect to circuit parameters using system dynamics simulation has been extensively studied (Kumar and Satsangi, 1993).

Behrman et. al. (Behrman, 2006) have simulated a quantum Hopfield neural network with the structure of a microtubule. They have used an extremely simplified model of the tubulin dimers: each is represented simply as a qubit, a single quantum two-state system, the quantum analog of a classical bit. A qubit, unlike a bit, can exist in a superposition of the two states. They have included Coulombic interactions between qubits, and thermal effects for the qubits themselves. This is a kind of quantum Hopfield network. Each of the individual processing elements or neurons (here, the qubits) interacts with each of the others (a fully interconnected network); the elements (qubits) are initialized in some state, and allowed to evolve towards a local minimum. These networks store information and are also called "associative memory" or "content addressable memory" models. The final stable state is a pattern that is recalled by the network.

Inspired by Penrose-Hameroff Orch. OR theory, Behrman et. al.

(Behrman, 2006) use an extremely simplified model of tubulin dimers, each represented simply as a qubit, a single quantum two-state system. In order to obtain the Quantum Hopfield Net (QHN), they consider an array of N qubits. Hamiltonian or energy function operator for each qubit j is given by

$$H_j = K\sigma_x + A\sigma_z \qquad (1)$$

where $\sigma_x = \begin{bmatrix} 0 & 1 \\ 1 & 0 \end{bmatrix}$ and $\sigma_z = \begin{bmatrix} 1 & 0 \\ 0 & -1 \end{bmatrix}$ are respectively the Pauli X and Z matrices; and the full Hamiltonian Operator $H = \sum_{j=1}^{N} H_j$.

The first term in Eq. (1) represents the flipping of the qubit from one state to the other, called "tunneling", with amplitude K.

The second term in Eq. (1) represents the energy-difference 2A between the two states. This difference can be the result of external fields or interaction with other qubits. The Pauli Matrix σ_z measures the state of the system; e.g. $\sigma_z \begin{bmatrix} 0 \\ 1 \end{bmatrix} = (-1)\begin{bmatrix} 0 \\ 1 \end{bmatrix}$, telling us that the system is in the (-1) state. Thus each qubit j may be visualized as a loop having n discretization points, propagating in imaginary time from 0 to β. [A discretization point at any instant of imaginary time is the instantaneous state of the qubit at that corresponding value of the inverse temperature].

Let $|\Psi\rangle = \delta|0\rangle + \gamma|1\rangle$ represent a qubit in terms of Quantum Terminal Graph (QTG) (Srivastava et. al. 2011, 2014) in Figure 1 where $|0\rangle$ is the (+1) state $\begin{bmatrix} 1 \\ 0 \end{bmatrix}$ and $|1\rangle$ is the (-1) state $\begin{bmatrix} 0 \\ 1 \end{bmatrix}$. Notice that $\sigma_x \begin{bmatrix} \delta \\ \gamma \end{bmatrix} = \begin{bmatrix} \gamma \\ \delta \end{bmatrix}$ which flips the probability amplitudes. For example, the (+1) state $|0\rangle$ is flipped to the (-1) state $|1\rangle$, and vice-versa. The Quantum Terminal Graph (QTG) in Figure 1 (Srivastava et. al. 2011, 2014) is shown as the union of two separate parts such that $a_1a_1^{'}$ denotes the "ket 0"-part and $b_1b_1^{'}$ denotes the "ket 1"-part (which form an orthonormal basis for the Hilbert space). Here δ and γ are complex numbers such that $|\delta|^2$ is the probability of qubits of "information / computation data" flow-rate along unit directional (quantum across variable) vector $|0\rangle$; and $|\gamma|^2$ is the probability of "information / computation data" flow-rate along unit directional (quantum across variable) vector $|1\rangle$. Notice that the sum of probabilities of flows along $|0\rangle$ and $|1\rangle$ adds to 1, i.e. $|\delta|^2 + |\gamma|^2 = 1$. Accordingly, the probable qubit states can be said to be normalized to length 1.

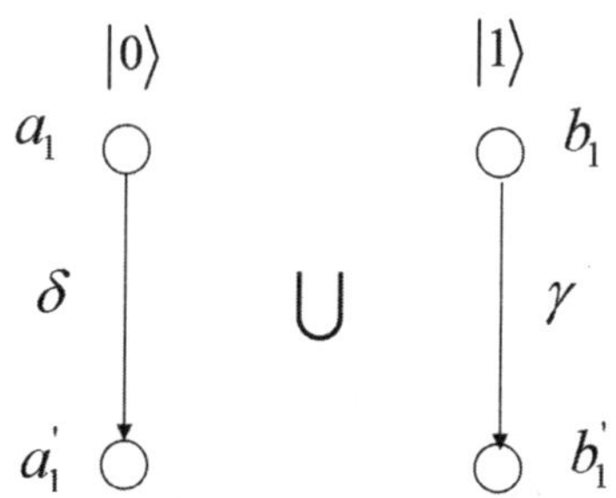

FIGURE 1
Quantum Terminal Graph

Srivastava et. al. (2014) have applied Graph Theoretic Quantum System Modelling (GTQSM) in continuum of protein heterodimer tubulin molecules of self-assembling polymers, viz., microtubules in the brain as a holistic system of interacting components representing hierarchical clustered quantum Hopfield network (hQHN) of networks. The quantum input-output ports of the constituent elemental interaction components (or processes) of tunneling interactions and Coulombic bidirectional interactions are in cascade and parallel interconnections with each other while the classical output ports of all elemental components are interconnected in parallel to accumulate micro-energy functions generated in the system as Hamiltonian (or Lyapunov) energy function. They have presented an insight, otherwise difficult to gain, for complex system of systems represented by clustered quantum Hopfield network (h-QHN), through application of graph theoretic quantum system modelling (GTQSM) construct presented in the next section.

While the detailed system graphs and equations are available in Srivastava et. al. (2014), Hierarchical Clustered Quantum Hopfield Network (h-QHN) System Schematic is reproduced for reference in Figure 2 as parallel and cascade interconnections of constituent transfer function operator blocks between quantum input-output ports together with parallel interconnections at the common classical output port, marked as $R - R'$. Hierarchical Clustered Quantum Hopfield Network (h-QHN) System Graph is represented by Figure 3 portrays interconnections between quantum input-output ports. With reference to System Schematic in Figure 2 and System Graph in Figure 3, consider the Quantum Subsystem Graph showing cascade interconnection between quantum output port $(i+1) \equiv n$ of σ_x-block, with quantum input port $(i) \equiv (n-1)$, of qubit j_l at level l with the quantum input port n

of σ_x-block of the same qubit j_l at level l, as redrawn in Figure 4 for the sake of clarity, such that output terminal graph is in dotted lines and input terminal graph is in continuous lines. Quantum subsystem graph vertex equation for Figure 4 is given by

$$y^{j_l^i}_{\underset{0n}{(\sigma X)}} = y^{j_l^\phi}_{\underset{0n}{(\sigma X)}},\ y^{j_l^i}_{\underset{1n}{(\sigma X)}} = y^{j_l^\phi}_{\underset{1n}{(\sigma X)}};$$

and quantum subsystem graph for circuit equation is given by

$$x^{j_l^i}_{\underset{0n}{(\sigma X)}} + x^{j_l^\phi}_{\underset{0n}{(\sigma X)}} = 0,\ x^{j_l^i}_{\underset{1n}{(\sigma X)}} + x^{j_l^\phi}_{\underset{1n}{(\sigma X)}} = 0.$$

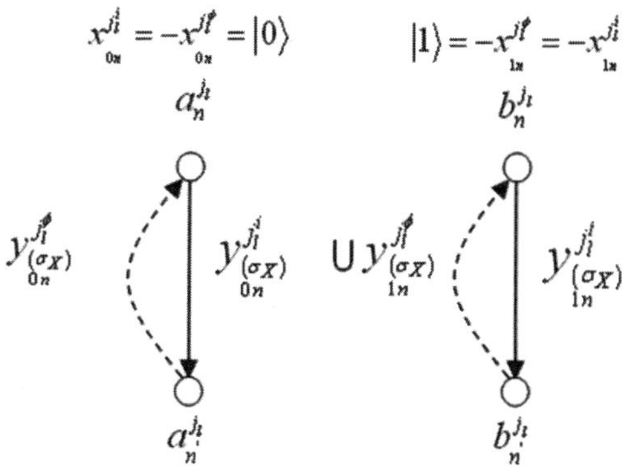

FIGURE 4
Quantum Subsystem Graph – Cascade Interconnection, as the union of constituent quantum terminal graphs (QTGs)

2. GENERALIZATION OF QUANTUM HOPFIELD NETWORK MODEL FOR *n*-QUDITS

Let $|\psi\rangle = \alpha|0\rangle + \beta|1\rangle + \gamma|2\rangle + \delta|3\rangle + ... + \nu|n-1\rangle$ represent a generalized quantum odd prime based qudit (with dimension $d=n$) in comparison to the commonly used even-prime based quantum bit (qubits with dimension 2) in terms of Quantum Terminal Graph (QTG) in Figure 5 where $|0\rangle$ is the state $\begin{bmatrix}1\\0\\0\\.\\.\\0\end{bmatrix}$ and $|1\rangle$ is the state $\begin{bmatrix}0\\1\\0\\.\\.\\0\end{bmatrix}$ and $|2\rangle$ is the state $\begin{bmatrix}0\\0\\1\\.\\.\\0\end{bmatrix}$, and $|n\rangle$ is the state $\begin{bmatrix}0\\0\\0\\.\\.\\1\end{bmatrix}$.

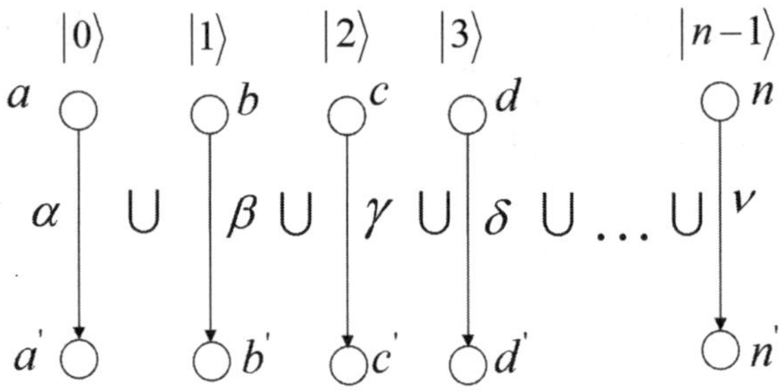

FIGURE 5
Generalized Qudit (dimension *d*=*n*) as union of *n* separate parts

The generalized quantum terminal graph (QTG) with dimension (d=n) is shown in Figure 5 as the union of n separate parts such that $a\,a'$ denote the first "ket-0" part, $b\,b'$ denotes the second "ket-1" part, $c\,c'$ denotes the third "ket-2" part, $d\,d'$ denotes the fourth "ket-3" part and so on, upto $n\,n'$ which denotes the "ket-(n-1)" part (which form an orthonormal basis vector-set for the Hilbert space). Here $\alpha,\beta,\gamma,\delta,\nu$ are complex numbers such that $|\alpha|^2$ is the probability of qubits of "information / computation data" flow-rate along unit directional (quantum across variable) vector $|0\rangle$; $|\beta|^2$ is the probability of qubits of "information / computation data" flow-rate along unit directional (quantum across variable) vector $|1\rangle$; $|\gamma|^2$ is the probability of qubits of "information / computation data" flow-rate along unit directional (quantum across variable) vector $|2\rangle$; $|\delta|^2$ is the probability of qubits of "information / computation data" flow-rate along unit directional (quantum across variable) vector $|3\rangle$; $|\varepsilon|^2$ is the probability of qubits of "information / computation data" flow-rate along unit directional (quantum across variable) vector $|4\rangle$ and so on, and $|\nu|^2$ is the probability of "information / computation data" flow-rate along unit directional (quantum across variable) vector $|n-1\rangle$. Notice that the sum of probabilities of flows along $|0\rangle$, $|1\rangle$, $|2\rangle$, . . . and $|n-1\rangle$ adds to 1, i.e.

$$|\alpha|^2+|\beta|^2+|\gamma|^2+|\delta|^2+...+|\nu|^2=1 \qquad (2)$$

Accordingly, the probable qudit states can be said to be normalized to length 1.

Eq. (2) is the equation of an n-dimensional sphere. Thus each qudit j may be visualized as a d-dimensional hyper sphere (instead of a loop for qubit which has only 2 states, i.e. $|\alpha|^2+|\beta|^2=1$, a qudit which has only 3 states, i.e. $|\alpha|^2+|\beta|^2+|\gamma|^2=1$, the equation of a sphere) having n discretization points, propagating in imaginary time from 0 to β (this is different from the index β for $|1\rangle$). [A discretization point at any instant of imaginary time is the instantaneous state of the qudits at that corresponding value of the inverse temperature].

Figure 6 shows a qubit with $n = 4$ discretization points in a system of $N = 3$ qubits (*d*=2) (Srivastava et. al., 2014).

Figure 7 shows a qudit (*d*=3) with $n = 8$ discretization points in a system of $N = 3$ qudits shown in different colours. Each qubit is now represented by a sphere with 8 discretization points.

Figure 8 shows a qudit (*d*=5) with $n = 32$ discretization points in a system of $N = 5$ qudits. In this solar system model, each 3-dimensional sphere is rotating in a loop / circle and sample connections are shown for discretization points i = 9 to 16. Similar connections exist for i = 1 to 32 as shown by black lines. If radius of the sphere (planet) is r_1 and radius of the orbit is r_2 (r_1 and r_2 are labelled in qudit j = 3 for illustration), then

$r_1^2 = |\alpha|^2 + |\beta|^2 + |\gamma|^2$ (equation of a sphere)
$p = 3$ degrees of freedom
$r_2^2 = |\delta|^2 + |\varepsilon|^2$ (equation of a loop / circle)
$q = 2$ degrees of freedom

Total degrees of freedom $n = p + q = 5$
Discretization Points used = $2^p.2^q = 2^3 \times 2^2 = 8 \times 4 = 32$

We will have $r_1^2 + r_2^2 = 1$ as the system equation for j which is the same as Eq. (2), i.e. $|\alpha|^2 + |\beta|^2 + |\gamma|^2 + |\delta|^2 + |\varepsilon|^2 = 1$ for a 5-dimensional qudit.

Figure 9 shows a qudit (*d*=7) with $n = 128$ discretization points in a system of $N = 3$ qudits. In this galaxy model (comprising planet, sun and galaxy), each 3-dimensional sphere (planet) is revolving in a circular orbit around an (imaginary) sun, and the solar system (with associated planets) is in turn, revolving in a circular orbit around the galaxy. Sample connections are shown for discretization points i = 1 to 32. Similar connections exist for i = 1 to 128 as shown by grey lines.

If radius of the sphere (planet) is r_1, radius of its orbit around sun is r_2, and radius of orbit of solar system around galaxy is r_3 (r_1, r_2 and r_3 are labelled in qudit j = 3 for illustration), then

$r_1^2 = |\alpha|^2 + |\beta|^2 + |\gamma|^2$ (equation of a sphere : Planet)
$p = 3$ degrees of freedom
$r_2^2 = |\delta|^2 + |\varepsilon|^2$ (equation of circle : Planet orbit around Sun)
$q = 2$ degrees of freedom
$r_3^2 = |\zeta|^2 + |\eta|^2$ (equation of circle : Sun orbit around Galaxy)
$r = 2$ degrees of freedom

Total degrees of freedom $n = p + q + r = 7$
Discretization Points used = $2^p.2^q.2^r = 2^3 \times 2^2 \times 2^2 = 8 \times 4 \times 4 = 128$

We will have $r_1^2 + r_2^2 + r_3^2 = 1$ as the system equation for j which is the same as Eq. (2), i.e. $|\alpha|^2 + |\beta|^2 + |\gamma|^2 + |\delta|^2 + |\varepsilon|^2 + |\zeta|^2 + |\eta|^2 = 1$ for a 7-dimensional qudit.

This idea can be similarly extended for even higher dimensions of d.

We see the significant jump in the level of discretization and level of fineness (fine-grained quantum geometry) while invoking higher and higher level of unified quantum field theory. We are thus getting subtler and subtler particle size of fine grained geometry. So, our thesis is that by using n-qudit based model ($n \to \infty$), we should be able to access at least in the abstract world of mathematics and physics, the primary ultimate source of consciousness in the whole universe. This opens up the immense possibility of going far beyond the presently obtaining highest dimension 10 of strings of the M-theory group of models. This is inspired by a study carried out by a group of researchers (Howard et. al., 2014) at University of Waterloo published in Nature. Their motivation had been to discover necessary and sufficient conditions for maintaining coherence in a quantum computing system, so that quantum computers could become a reality. So, in this context, they came up with a suggestion, (and thereby they did prove the necessary conditions), to the effect that if they generalize the concept of qubit to that of qudit, that is instead of considering two-state quantum bits, once could get three state quantum odd prime based bits. But why remain limited to three states only? So that is what we have been arguing. In our Physical System Theory Model and its counterpart as consciousness system model, it takes only a step forward to generalize it to higher dimensions. We could generalize to any odd prime based higher dimension even beyond 3, say 5, 7, 11, 13, 17, 19, 23, 29, 31, 37, 41, 43 and so on. So it could almost tend to infinity, and that is the hope which brings us to the threshold of being face to face mathematically in abstract terms with the ultimate source of consciousness, mind you, not physically, but in abstraction.

We generalize the quantum mechanical representations based on qubits to qudits and show that this gives us a handle at abstracting things to a level where these become realities mathematically at least, that is we endow these with almost infinite degrees of freedom mathematically, that qudits of high order tending towards infinity and they are accompanied by size or dimensions tending towards zero, infinitesimally small. So we are wedding both worlds, infinitesimally small and infinitely large and this is what scientists are also attempting. Qudit makes it possible to do so within the scientific framework, if we postulate qudits and generalize it as we have done, it is easy to perceive that they do exist mathematically.

These diagrams also lead to an interesting point which has been brought out in our work and it is that in terms of the large picture of cosmology, cosmology beyond physical world, going to the universe of mind and universe of consciousness, we can see that these would simulate trajectories which are noticed in cosmology. We have trajectory of a planet, or orbit of a planet, planet is a sphere, so it is approximated as $r_1^2 = |\alpha|^2 + |\beta|^2 + |\gamma|^2$, that would be the equation of a sphere and equation of a circle will be $r_2^2 = |\delta|^2 + |\varepsilon|^2$, so one can in fact, in this manner, build up and show that this would simulate the trajectory of a planet around sun, a spherical object making a circular orbit around sun and then, this larger planetary system around sun, making its own trajectory around its galaxy, so that is simulated by the next dimension d=7, such that we have the degrees of freedom as 7, then that is simulated and if we go higher, we have higher level suns and higher level galaxies, i.e., super clusters, which may be further simulated.

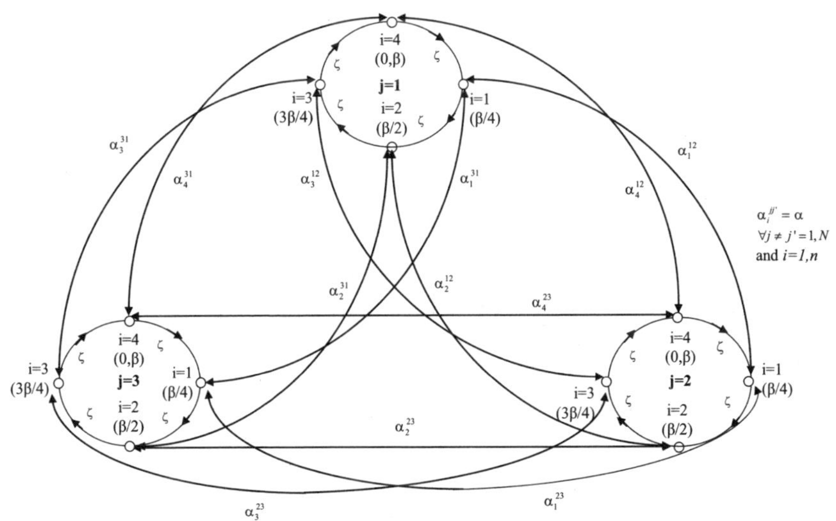

FIGURE 6
A qubit with $n = 4$ discretization points in a system of $N = 3$ qubits

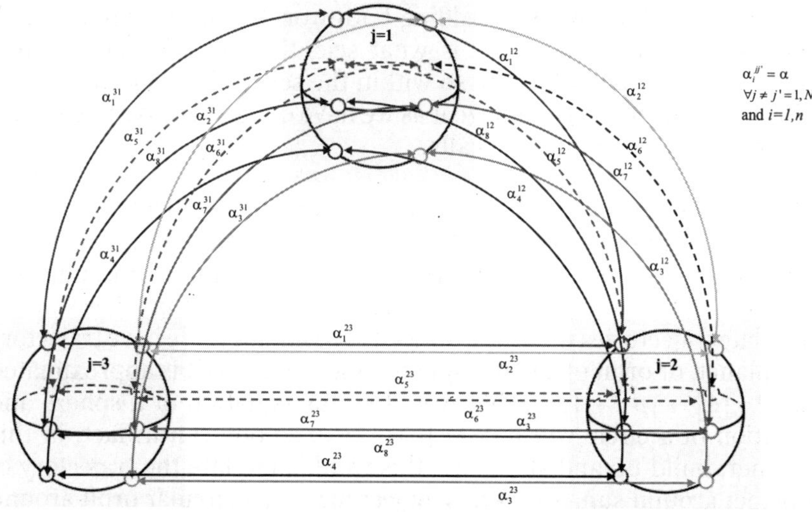

FIGURE 7

A qudit (d=3) with $n = 8$ discretization points in a system of $N = 3$ qudits

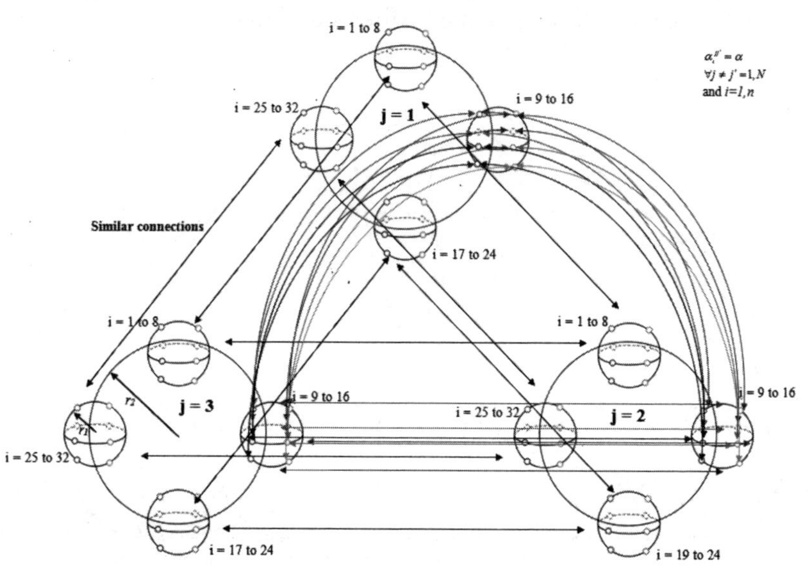

FIGURE 8

A qudit (d=5) with $n = 32$ discretization points in a system of $N = 3$ qudits
Sample connections are shown for discretization points *i*= 9 *to* 16. Similar connections will exist for all *i* as shown by black lines

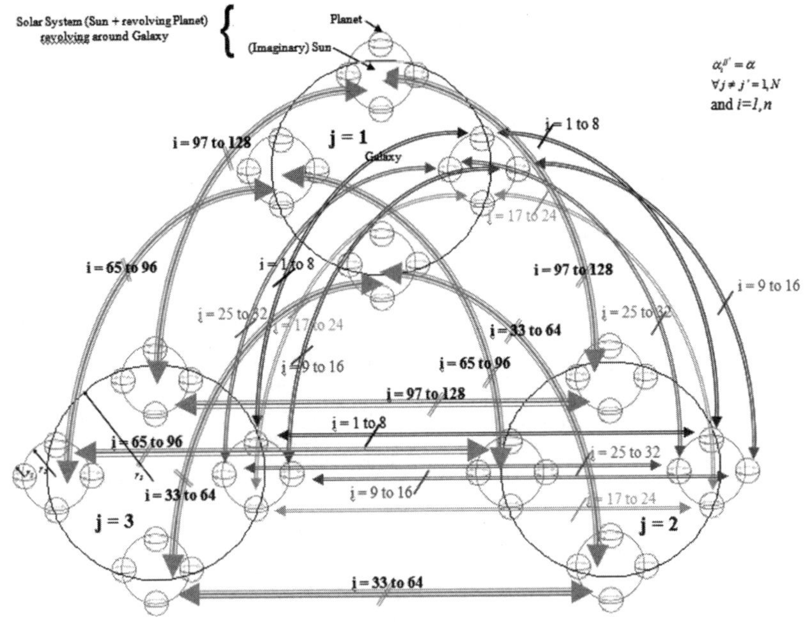

FIGURE 9

A qudit (d=7) with $n = 2^7 = 128$ discretization points in a system of $N = 3$ qudits Sample connections are shown for discretization points $i = 1$ *to* 32. Similar connections exist for all *i* as shown by grey lines

3. CLUSTERED HIERARCHICAL LEVEL MODEL OF THE BRAIN

Woolf N. (2006) has proposed five hierarchical levels of quantum entanglement-based neural interaction microtubules spread among 13-23 billion neurons in the human cortex of the estimated 100 billion neurons in brain. We can thus extend the graph-theoretic modelling framework to these, in general, *l* levels.

An estimate of N_l and degree of entanglement α_l for $l = 1$ to 5 by Woolf (2006) and adapted by Srivastava et. al. (2014) is summarized in Table 1. The cluster approach propounded by Srivastava et. al. (2014) views the quantum Hopfield network as *Nn* information processing subunits (each with states ± 1), corresponding to *N* qubits of tubulin molecule, which converge to $2^{(Nn)}$ corners of an (Nn)-dimensional box.

TABLE 1
Hierarchical levels of quantum entanglement

Hierarchical Level of Quantum Entanglement	Quantum entanglement among	Estimate of number of qubits N_l by Woolf (2006) as adapted by Srivastava et. al. (2014)	Estimate of α_l by Woolf
1	Tubulins of the same microtubule	$N_1 \rightarrow 10^4$ tubulins of the same microtubule in any one of $m_1 = 10^{15}$ possible clusters Srivastava et. al. (2014)	likely to be high
2	Pairs of microtubulins (qubits) in the same neuron	$N_2 \rightarrow 10^4$ different microtubules in the same neuron in any one of $m_2 = 10^{15}$ possible clusters Srivastava et. al. (2014)	$\alpha_2 << \alpha_1$
3	pairs of microtubulins (qubits) belonging to different neurons	$N_3 \rightarrow 10^3$ different microtubules belonging to different neurons in same modules in any one of $m_3 = 10^{16}$ possible clusters Srivastava et. al. (2014)	$\alpha_3 << \alpha_2$
4	highly interconnected cortical areas	$N_4 \rightarrow 10^7$ different neurons in any one of $m_4 = 10^{12}$ possible clusters Srivastava et. al. (2014)	$\alpha_4 << \alpha_3$
5	entanglement among cortical areas having few or no axonal connections	$N_5 \rightarrow 10^{10}$ different neurons in any one of $m_5 = 10^9$ possible clusters (Teleportation invoked by Srivastava et. al. (2014))	$\alpha_5 << \alpha_4$

4. CONTEXTUALITY

In a recent paper in Nature, Howard et. al. (2014) show that contextuality, an abstract generalization of nonlocality is a necessary condition for magic state distillation. They make an abstract graph called an exclusivity graph to obtain their results. Qudits of odd prime dimensionality are naturally differentiated from qubits in their analysis. In exclusivity graph in Figure 10(a), each of the 30 vertices corresponds to a two-qubit stabilizer state; connected vertices correspond to orthogonal states. A maximum independent set (representing mutually non-orthogonal states) of size 8 is highlighted in red. They have proved a remarkable equivalence between the onset of contextuality and the possibility of universal quantum computation via 'magic state' distillation, which is the leading model for experimentally realizing a fault-tolerant quantum computer. This is a conceptually satisfying link, because contextuality, which precludes a simple 'hidden variable' model of quantum mechanics, provides one of the fundamental characterizations of uniquely quantum phenomena. Furthermore, this connection suggests a unifying paradigm for the resources of quantum information: the non-locality of quantum theory is a particular kind of contextuality, and non-locality is already known to be a critical resource for achieving advantages with quantum communication.

In the case of qubits, it is a pressing open question whether a suitable operationally motivated refinement or quantification of contextuality can align more precisely with the potential to provide a quantum speed-up. For qudits, the set of states proven to be contextual by construction (Howard et. al., 2014) have been previously conjectured to be sufficient to promote stabilizer circuits to universality. Proving this conjecture would require proving that any state can be distilled to a magic state. While substantial progress in this direction has been made, it is still an open problem. In our Physical System Theory Model, we have taken a step forward to generalize qudits to higher and higher dimensions which could almost tend to infinity, which will bring us to the threshold of being face to face mathematically in abstract terms with the ultimate source of consciousness in abstraction (Satsangi, 2015). This opens up the immense possibility of going far beyond the presently obtaining highest dimension 10 of strings of the M-theory group of models (Zee, 2010).

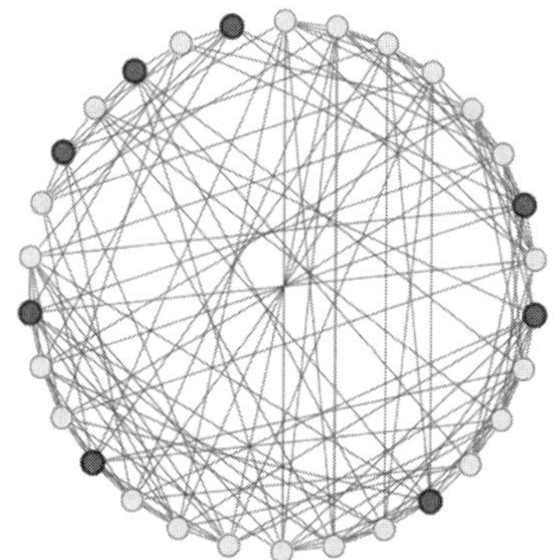

(a) Exclusivity graph proposed by Howard et. al. applied to two qubits

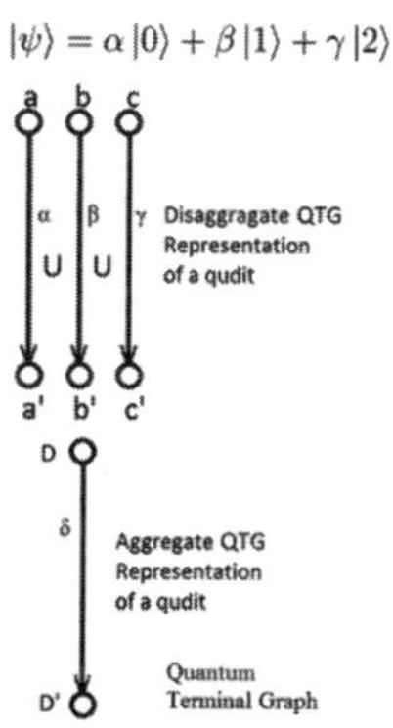

(b) QTG Representation

FIGURE 10

Based on insights given from Srivastava (2013) and Srivastava et. al. (2014), it is proposed to derive exclusivity graph in Figure 10(b) by representing Quantum Terminal Graphs (Srivastava 2013, Srivastava et. al. 2014) as composite Quantum Terminal Graphs each represented by a single composite quantum terminal graph which may be further reduced to a representation in terms of a single composite quantum vertex or node as in Figure 10(b) by rendering the composite datum node as a floating unspecified datum node.

We believe that our graph theoretic approach based on physical systems theory, will give a simpler derivation of their results potentially allowing us to demonstrate that contextuality is not only necessary but also sufficient for magic state distillation. We are attempting to address the important question of how does the brain overcome decoherence using topological, fault tolerant computing and magic state distillation.

We are working on simulating a functional model of the brain based on quantum Hopfield networks with neurons selected from the various regions of the brain, based on functional layer diagram. Such models should be able to handle association and contextuality both as they will have neurons from portions of the brain tasked with association (association cortex) as well as contextuality (pre-frontal cortex). Table 2 gives a summary of the macrocolumn functional units mentioning number of columns, which is believed to be the fundamental computational unit of the cortex, and an estimate of the neurons in various lobes of the brain.

TABLE 2
(a) Macrocolumn functional units of the cortex

Functional Unit	**Columns**	**Billion Neurons**
Visual Cortex	232 million columns	68.3
Auditory Cortex	83 million columns	24.0
Somatosensory cortex	21 million columns	6.0
Association cortex	5 million columns	1.4
Motor cortex	1 million columns	0.3
TOTAL	**342 million columns**	**100 billion**

(b) An estimate of the neurons in various lobes of the brain

Frontal Lobe	35 billion
Motor cortex (precentral gyms)	6 billion
Temporal Lobe	19 billion
Parietal Lobe	16 billion
Occipital Lobe	14 billion
TOTAL	**90 billion**

5. POWER LAWS

To gain a picture of emergent patterns of brain activity, investigators need new sensing devices that can record from assemblages of thousands of neurons. Nanotechnology, with novel materials that sometimes measure less than the dimensions of individual molecules, may assist in making large-scale recordings. Prototype arrays have been built that incorporate more than 100,000 electrodes on a silicon base; such devices could record the electrical activity of tens of thousands of neurons in the retina.

Electrodes are only one way to track the activity of neurons. Methods that move beyond electrical sensors are making their way into the lab. Biologists, borrowing from technologies developed by physicists, chemists and geneticists, are beginning to visualize living neurons in awake animals going about their daily paces using electro-encephalography (EEG), magento-encephalography (MEG) and functional Magentic Resonance Imaging (fMRI) and further analysis by Fourier transform methods.

An interesting conclusion we can draw from a course on noise is that the $1/\rho$ behaviour of EEG and MEG (i.e. "one over of" power-spectrum) is a special noise (also called 'pink' noise) is the golden means between the disorder with high information content (white noise with $1/\rho^0$ flat (constant power spectrum) and the predictability with low information content (brown noise with "one over ρ^2 power spectrum"). The cerebral cortex with its most complex architecture generates the most complex noise known to physics (Buzsaki, 2006).

The anatomical-functional organization of the cerebral cortex should have consequences and limitations on cognitive behaviours as well. A well-known psychological law that comes to mind in connection with the $1/f$ nature of the cortical EEG / MEG is that of Weber and

Fechner: the magnitude of a subjective sensation (a cognitive unit) increases proportionally to the logarithm of the stimulus intensity (a physical unit).

This collective behaviour of neurons, summed up crudely as the mean field (EEG / MEG) is a blend of rhythms. Neuronal network in the mammalian cortex generates several distinct oscillatory bands, covering frequencies from <0.05 hertz to >500 hertz.

Brain evolution opted for a complex wiring pattern in the mammalian cortex. The resulting $1/f^{\alpha}$ temporal statistic of the mean field are the hallmark of the most complex dynamics and imply an inherently labile, self-organized state.

Unlike so-called normal distribution (such as for human brain weight (e.g. 1.35 kg or 3 lbs.), in scale-free systems (governed by power law), things are different. There is no typical example in a scale-free system. A power law implies for the case of fracture, that if we plot the numbers of different size of pieces on a log-log scale, we will get an oblique line.

In fractal geometry, fractals are usually defined in statistical or qualitative terms, loosely indicating anything that "looks like itself". The scale invariance of fractals implies that knowledge of the properties of a model system at any scale can be used to predict the structure of the real system at larger or smaller scale.

6. CONCLUSIONS

Price and Barrell (2012) show how a science of human experience can be developed through a strategy by integrating experiential paradigms with methods from the natural sciences. A science of human experience would largely be about human meanings and also would constitute a science of consciousness. Psychophysics includes a rudimentary form of introspection that is critical for developing a science of human meanings and consciousness. The qualitative aspects of human experience serve as a foundation for developing hypotheses to be used in experiments that have quantitative methods. This model serves as a useful example for correlating first person and third person approaches for explaining a conscious experience.

Interesting conclusions can be drawn from a study of $1/f^{\alpha}$ behaviour of brain-scans of humans, particularly during Eastern Meditational Practice. The cerebral cortex with its most complicated architecture generates the most complex noise known to Physics. One over f $(\alpha \equiv 1)$

power spectrum (also called "pink noise") is a golden mean between the white noise ($\alpha \equiv 0$, i.e. constant power spectrum) representing disorder with high information content, and brown noise ($\alpha \equiv 2$) representing predictability with low information content. The anatomical functional organization of the cerebral cortex brings to mind a well-known psycho-physical law credited to Weber and Fechner (Price and Barrell, 2012). Accordingly, the magnitude of a subjective sensation such as meditational consciousness in cognitive and meta-cognitive domains increases proportionally to the logarithm of the stimulus intensity, "one over *f* (i.e. rhythmic frequency)", a physical unit. Notably, scale-free systems or fractals are governed by Power Laws (Satsangi and Sahni, 2015).

The formulation of power law of meditational consciousness requires invoking a family of models based on Omni quantum theory and physical system theory (including fuzzy analytical hierarchy process), and requisite integration of first person inner experiences of meditationists as co-investigators with the third person scientific methodology of observing, reporting, understanding and hypothesis-testing. There is hope for making abstractions and if we wed the inner experiences with the outer world experience, we will have the full closure with the system which is desirable in order to achieve the dream of Einstein as a theory of everything (Satsangi, 2015).

REFERENCES

Bandopadhyay A. (2011), Direct experimental evidence for quantum states in microtubules and topological invariance, Abstracts : Towards a Science of Consciousness, 2011, Stockholm, Sweden, http://www.consciousness.arizona.edu/TSC2011MicroTub.htm.

Behrman E.C. (2006), Gaddam K, Steck JE and Skinner SR, Microtubules as a Quantum Hopfield Network, The Emerging Physics of Consciousness, ed. J.A. Tuszynski, pp.351-370, Springer, New York, 2006.

Buzsaki G. (2006), *Rhythms of the Brain*, Oxford University Press, USA, 2006.

Hameroff S, Hagan S and Tuszynski JA (2002), Quantum computation in brain MTs: Decoherence and biological feasibility, Physical Review E 2002;65:061901 1-11.

Henry, Stapp, (2006), "Quantum Interactive Dualism: Libet and Einstein-Podolsky-Rosen Causal Anomalies." Invited contrib. to Erkenntnis, Feb. 2006.

Howard M., Wallman J., Veitch V., Emerson J., "Contextuality supplies the 'magic' for quantum computation", Nature, Vol. 510, pp. 351-355, June 19, 2014.

Kumar and Satsangi (1993), "System Dynamics Simulation of Non-degenerate and Degenerate Circuits and Systems", Paritantra (A Journal of Systems Science and Engineering, Systems Society of India, Wiley Eastern Limited, New Delhi) 1(1), 11-39.

Penrose and Hameroff (2011), Consciousness in the Universe: Neuroscience, Quantum Space-Time Geometry and Orch OR Theory, Journal of Cosmology, Vol. 14, April-May 2011.

Price D. and Barrell J. (2012), *Inner Experience and Neuroscience : Merging both Perspectives*, MIT Press, USA, 2012.

Sahni V., Lakshminarayanan V., Srivastava D.P. (2011), *Quantum Information Systems*, ISBN 9780070707078, Tata McGraw Hill, New Delhi, April 2011.

Satsangi P.S. (2006), "Generalizing Physical Systems Through Applied Systems Research from "Real" Physical Systems through "Conceptual" Socio-Economic-Environmental Systems to "Complete" (Physical-Mental-Spiritual) Creational Systems", International Journal of General Systems, Vol. 35, No. 2, 2006, pp. 127-167.

Satsangi P.S. (2010), Cosmology from the Twin Vantage Points of Radhasoami Faith and Systems Science, Vision Talk at International Seminar on Religion of Saints ('Sants') – Radhasoami Faith, Spiritual Consciousness Studies (SPIRCON 2010), Nov. 12-13, 2011.

Satsangi P.S. (2011), Cosmology of Consciousness : Towards Quantum-Theoretic Systems Modelling; Spirit-Mind-Brain Interactions, Vision Talk at Inaugural Workshop of DEI Centre for Consciousness Studies (CONCENT 2011), Oct. 1-2, 2011, Abstract Book, pp. 50-67.

Satsangi P.S. (2015), Rhythms of Macrocosmic Universe and Human-Microcosm: Consciousness Systemology Perspective, Vision Talk at the East-West Forum, Toward a Science of Consciousness (TSC 2015), Helsinki, Finland, June 8, 2015, Abstract Book, pp. 373.

Satsangi P.S. (2015), "Towards An Ultimate Consciousness Conjecture (for the Human Microcosm and the Grand Macrocosm)", Vision Talk at Special Forum on "Consciousness : Integrating Eastern and Western Perspectives" at International School on Quantum and Nano Computing Systems and Applications (QANSAS 2015), Dayalbagh Educational Institute, November 25, 2015.

Satsangi P.S., Sahni V. (2012), "Cosmic Consciousness Hierarchization : Analytic, Experimental and Experiential", Concurrent Session on Science and Spirituality, Toward a Science of Consciousness (TSC 2012), Tucson, Arizona, USA, April 2012, Abstract Book, pp. 193.

Satsangi P.S., Sahni V. (2015), "Power Law of Meditational Consciousness", Concurrent Session on Meditation, Toward a Science of Consciousness (TSC 2015), Helsinki, Finland, June 2015, Abstract Book, pp. 340.

Srivastava D.P., Sahni V. and Satsangi P.S. (2011), "Graph Theoretic Quantum System Modelling for Information / Computation Processing Circuits", *International Journal of General Systems*, Vol. 40, No. 8, ISSN 0308-1079, Taylor & Francis, UK, pp. 777-804.

Srivastava D.P. (2013), "Graph Theoretic Quantum Field / System modelling for Quantum Information / Computation Circuits and Algorithms" Ph.D. Thesis, Dayalbagh Educational Institute, Dayalbagh, Agra, September 2013.

Srivastava D.P., Sahni V., Satsangi P.S. (2014) "Graph Theoretic Quantum System Modelling for Neuronal Microtubles as Hierarchical Clustered Quantum Hopfield Networks", International Journal of General Systems, Taylor & Francis, UK, Vol. 43, No. 6, pp. 633-648.

Srivastava D.P., Sahni V., Satsangi P.S. (2015), "Modelling Microtubules in the Brain as n-qudit Quantum Hopfield Network and Beyond", International Journal of General Systems, Taylor and Francis, UK, January 2016, DOI: 10.1080/03081079.2015.1076405.

Srivastava D.P., Sahni V., Satsangi P.S. (2015), "Modelling Microtubules in the Brain as n-qudit Quantum Hopfield Network and Beyond", Neurons and Cognition (q-bio.NC); Quantum Physics (quant-ph), arXiv:1505.00774, May 2015.

Stapp (2007), *Quantum Approaches to Consciousness*, Chapter 31, Cambridge Handbook of Consciousness.

Woolf N. (2006), Microtubules in the Cerebral Cortex : Role in Memory and Consciousness, The Emerging Physics of Consciousness, ed. J.A. Tuszynski, pp. 49-94, Springer, New York, 2006.

Zee Anthony (2010), *Quantum Field Theory in a Nutshell*, Second Edition, Princeton University Press, USA, 2010.

Chapter 21

From n-Qubit Multi-Particle Quantum Teleportation Modelling to n-Qudit Contextuality based Quantum Teleportation and Beyond

DAYAL PYARI SRIVASTAVA
Department of Physics and Computer Science and Quantum-Nano Systems Centre, Dayalbagh Educational Institute (Deemed University), Dayalbagh, Agra, India

VISHAL SAHNI
Quantum-Nano Systems Centre and Centre for Consciousness Studies, Dayalbagh Educational Institute (Deemed University), Dayalbagh, Agra, India

and
PREM SARAN SATSANGI
Chairman, Advisory Committee on Education, Dayalbagh Educational Institutions, Dayalbagh, Agra, India

ABSTRACT

Quantum entanglement is a key resource for several applications in quantum information processing. Thus, it is important to quantify the degree of entanglement in multi-particle systems. Experimental realization of multi-particle systems and the detection of all orthogonal basis states forming a complete set of entangled states remain a challenge, nevertheless, efficient theoretical construction and characterization of different multi-particle entangled channels for analyzing information processing protocols is an important precursor to successful design of experiments.

This chapter further generalizes the modelling framework for contextuality based quantum teleportation to n-dimensional quantum states, or n-qudits (quantum odd-prime based units) which holds considerable promise for even higher mathematical abstraction. The proposed generalization for n-qudits extends the two states in the qubit model, to n states and this n could tend towards infinity. In terms of mathematical abstraction, there is no limit imposed. We can see that we are heading towards point-sized loops or fine-grained particles of nature, which have been rejected out of hand by string theorists, that it is not unique. It is not physical reality when measured from the sense of Planck's length of 10^{-35} metre, but finer-grained particles than Planck's length 10^{-35} metre may exist, although they are not matter anymore. Pursuing such abstraction further is the purpose of this chapter and *we argue that why stop at degree of freedom of three; instead, why not pursue quantum odd-prime based units with higher degree n such as 5, 7, 11, 13, 17 and so on till n^{th} degree of freedom even tending to infinity so that we have the highest abstraction. It involves only a mathematical description of the gates and their matrices as shown in this chapter. Recall that while claiming uniqueness for string theory, they admit its multiple landscapes with higher degrees of freedom which in a sense fouls up its uniqueness both for particles finer than 10^{-35} metre as well as distances greater than 10^{10} light years.*

Section 1 discusses n-qubit multi-particle quantum teleportation modelling, starting with example of three-particle quantum teleportation and extending it to n-particles, while referring to Srivastava (2013) which contains a detailed explanation including the terminal graph models. Section 2 extends the model to n-qudit contexutality based quantum teleportation, with definitions and discussion of the various stages of the circuit. Section 3 presents the contextuality based models. Discussion appears in Section 4 and the Conclusions are presented in Section 5.

Keywords : Qudits, Teleportation, Contextuality

1. *n*-QUBIT MULTI-PARTICLE QUANTUM TELEPORTATION MODELLING

Graph-theoretic system modelling framework (Seshu and Reed, 1961, Koenig et. al. 1967, Satsangi 2006a, 2006b, 2009) has been extended to model a problem of quantum teleportation of a two particle entangled system (Srivastava et. al. 2011). In the current chapter, graph theory has been used to model a three particle entangled teleportation system. Sender Alice, intermediary supervisor Charlie and receiver Bob are quantum entangled through a triplet called a GHZ state. The classical measurements communicated to Bob encode information for applying requisite Pauli spin matrices to correctly recover the qubit sent by Alice for Bob at receiver end, through quantum teleportation. Notice that measurement of Charlie is made according to basis vector pair $|0^*\rangle$ and $|1^*\rangle$ (where $|0^*\rangle = (|0\rangle + |1\rangle)/\sqrt{2}$ and $|1^*\rangle = (|0\rangle - |1\rangle)/\sqrt{2}$), unlike measurements by sender Alice which are according to normal basis vector pair $|0\rangle$ and $|1\rangle$. An alternative approach has been shown as feasible by adding a Hadamard gate at Charlie's port before measurement gate. In this case, we do not have to change the basis vector pair for Charlie. The results have been further generalized by considering n-particle entanglement between sender Alice, $(n-2)$

intermediary supervisors Charlie and receiver Bob for multiparticle quantum teleportation.

1.1 Three-Particle Quantum Teleportation

This sub-section presents a circuit for three particle quantum teleportation. Similar to Bell states used in two location quantum teleportation, three-particle quantum entangled states called as GHZ states (Greenberger-Horne-Zellinger, 1989) are used for three-particle teleportation. An example of GHZ state is $\left[\frac{|000\rangle+|111\rangle}{\sqrt{2}}\right]$ and this entangled state has been used shared between sender Alice, receiver Bob and supervisor Charlie.

The circuit for three particle quantum teleportation is shown in Figure 1. The sender Alice has a qubit $|\psi\rangle = \alpha|0\rangle + \beta|1\rangle$ which she wishes to send to the receiver, Bob. The supervisor Charlie, along with Alice and Bob share one particle each of the GHZ state. Measurement is made according to basis vectors $|0^*\rangle$ and $|1^*\rangle$ where $|0^*\rangle = \frac{|0\rangle+|1\rangle}{\sqrt{2}}$ and $|1^*\rangle = \frac{|0\rangle-|1\rangle}{\sqrt{2}}$.

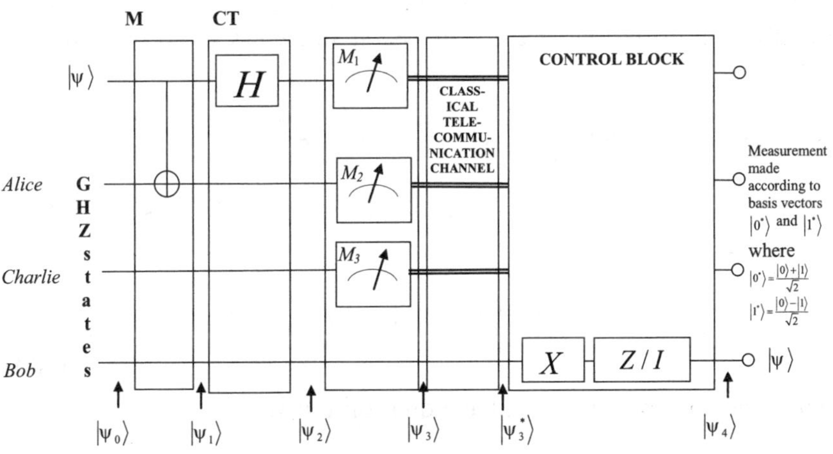

FIGURE 1
Three particle quantum teleportation circuit

Step-1 (Stage 0)

Quantum information vector state supplied at the sending end $\left|\psi^{0\phi}\right\rangle$ and quantum information vector state received at the receiving end $\left|\psi^{4i}\right\rangle$ are given by Equations 1.1(a) and 1.1(b) respectively,

$$\left|\psi^{0\phi}\right\rangle = \left|\psi^{0i}\right\rangle \triangleq |\psi_0\rangle = |\psi\rangle\left[\frac{|000\rangle + |111\rangle}{\sqrt{2}}\right] = (\alpha|0\rangle + \beta|1\rangle)\left[\frac{|000\rangle + |111\rangle}{\sqrt{2}}\right] \quad 1.1(a)$$

To save confusion, y^0 is defined to be probability parameter associated with $|0\rangle$ and y^1 is probability parameter associated with $|1\rangle$

$$\text{and } \left|\psi^{4i}\right\rangle = \left|\psi^{4\phi}\right\rangle \quad 1.1(b)$$

Step II (Stage 1)

Processing $|\psi_0\rangle$ from stage 0 through CNOT gate, there results $|\psi_1\rangle$ at stage 1 given by Equation (1.2)

$$|\psi_1\rangle = \alpha|0\rangle\left[\frac{|000\rangle + |111\rangle}{\sqrt{2}}\right] + \beta|1\rangle\left[\frac{|100\rangle + |011\rangle}{\sqrt{2}}\right]$$

$$= \frac{\alpha}{\sqrt{2}}|0000\rangle + \frac{\alpha}{\sqrt{2}}|0111\rangle + \frac{\beta}{\sqrt{2}}|1100\rangle + \frac{\beta}{\sqrt{2}}|1011\rangle \quad (1.2)$$

Step III (Stage 2)

On processing through Hadamard gate between stages 1 and 2, quantum information vector state $|\psi_2\rangle$ at stage 2 is given by Equation 1.3(a)

$$|\psi_2\rangle = \frac{1}{\sqrt{2}}\left[(|000\rangle + |111\rangle)\alpha\left(\frac{|0\rangle + |1\rangle}{\sqrt{2}}\right) + (|100\rangle + |011\rangle)\beta\left(\frac{|0\rangle - |1\rangle}{\sqrt{2}}\right)\right]$$

$$= \frac{\alpha}{2}|(000)0\rangle + \frac{\alpha}{2}|(111)0\rangle + \frac{\alpha}{2}|(000)1\rangle + \frac{\alpha}{2}|(111)1\rangle + \frac{\beta}{2}|(100)0\rangle + \frac{\beta}{2}|(011)0\rangle - \frac{\beta}{2}|(100)1\rangle - \frac{\beta}{2}|(011)1\rangle$$

$$= \left\{\frac{\alpha}{2}|(000)0\rangle + \frac{\beta}{2}|(011)0\rangle\right\} + \left\{\frac{\alpha}{2}|(111)0\rangle + \frac{\beta}{2}|(100)0\rangle\right\} + \left\{\frac{\alpha}{2}|(000)1\rangle - \frac{\beta}{2}|(011)1\rangle\right\} + \left\{\frac{\alpha}{2}|(111)1\rangle - \frac{\beta}{2}|(100)1\rangle\right\}$$

1.3(a)

which can also be rearranged as Equation 1.3(b)

$$|\psi_2\rangle = \frac{1}{2}|000\rangle(\alpha|0\rangle + \beta|1\rangle) + \frac{1}{2}|011\rangle(\beta|0\rangle + \alpha|1\rangle) + \frac{1}{2}|100\rangle(\alpha|0\rangle - \beta|1\rangle) + \frac{1}{2}|111\rangle(-\beta|0\rangle + \alpha|1\rangle)$$

1.3(b)

Step IV (Stage 3)

This involves Alice's measurement as ports 1 and 2 and Charlie' measurement at port 3 as below.

Alice's measurement at ports 1 and 2 according to basis vectors $\|0\rangle$ and $\|1\rangle$ and Charlie's measurements at port 3 according to basis vectors $\|0^*\rangle$ and $\|1^*\rangle$	$\|\psi_3\rangle$ state of qubit 4 at port 4
000^*	$y^0\|0\rangle + y^1\|1\rangle$ where $y^0 = \alpha$, $y^1 = \beta$
001^*	$y^0\|0\rangle + y^1\|1\rangle$ where $y^0 = \alpha$, $y^1 = \beta$
010^*	$y^0\|0\rangle + y^1\|1\rangle$ where $y^0 = \beta$, $y^1 = \alpha$
011^*	$y^0\|0\rangle + y^1\|1\rangle$ where $y^0 = -\beta$, $y^1 = -\alpha$
100^*	$y^0\|0\rangle + y^1\|1\rangle$ where $y^0 = \alpha$, $y^1 = -\beta$
101^*	$y^0\|0\rangle + y^1\|1\rangle$ where $y^0 = \alpha$, $y^1 = -\beta$
110^*	$y^0\|0\rangle + y^1\|1\rangle$ where $y^0 = -\beta$, $y^1 = \alpha$
111^*	$y^0\|0\rangle + y^1\|1\rangle$ where $y^0 = \beta$, $y^1 = -\alpha$

Step V (Stage 3*)

Input from stage 3 is applied by the sender "S" to the classical telecommunication channel CT in Figure 1 for telecommunicating the measurement information from ports 1, 2 & 3 at stage 3 as the output at stage 3* to Receiver R.

Step VI (Stage 4)

Quantum information vector state retrieved at the receiving end is given by

$$|\psi^{4i}\rangle = [Y^{4i}]^T [X^{4i}] = \{(0)(0)(0^*)(\alpha|0\rangle + \beta|1\rangle)\}$$

$$|\psi^{4i}\rangle = [Y^{4i}]^T [X^{4i}] = \{(0)(0)(1^*)(\alpha|0\rangle + \beta|1\rangle)\}$$

OR $$|\psi^{4i}\rangle = [Y^{4i}]^T [X^{4i}] = \{(0)(1)(0^*)(\alpha|0\rangle + \beta|1\rangle)\}$$

OR $$|\psi^{4i}\rangle = [Y^{4i}]^T [X^{4i}] = \{(0)(1)(1^*)(\alpha|0\rangle + \beta|1\rangle)\}$$

OR $$|\psi^{4i}\rangle = [Y^{4i}]^T [X^{4i}] = \{(1)(0)(0^*)(\alpha|0\rangle + \beta|1\rangle)\}$$

OR $$|\psi^{4i}\rangle = [Y^{4i}]^T [X^{4i}] = \{(1)(0)(1^*)(\alpha|0\rangle + \beta|1\rangle)\}$$

OR $$|\psi^{4i}\rangle = [Y^{4i}]^T [X^{4i}] = \{(1)(1)(0^*)(\alpha|0\rangle + \beta|1\rangle)\}$$

OR $$|\psi^{4i}\rangle = [Y^{4i}]^T [X^{4i}] = \{(1)(1)(1^*)(\alpha|0\rangle + \beta|1\rangle)\}$$

$$= \begin{bmatrix} (000^*)|\psi\rangle OR (001^*)|\psi\rangle OR (010^*)|\psi\rangle OR (011^*)|\psi\rangle \\ OR (100^*)|\psi\rangle OR (101^*)|\psi\rangle OR (110^*)|\psi\rangle OR (111^*)|\psi\rangle \end{bmatrix}$$

Charlie measures his qubit and conveys binary result (whether he measured $\left(\frac{|0\rangle+|1\rangle}{\sqrt{2}}\right)$ or $\left(\frac{|0\rangle-|1\rangle}{\sqrt{2}}\right)$ to Bob. The two measurements of Alice and one of Charlie are used in control block as shown in Table 1 and Table 2 to obtain the final result of Bob $|\psi_4\rangle = |\psi\rangle$.

Alice's result (Stage 3)	State of qubits 3 and 4 after Alice's measurements between stages 2 and 3	Charlie's measurements (between stages 2 and 3)	State of Bob's qubit after Charlie's measurement (between stages 2 and 3)	Gates to be used in control block of Bob to obtain $\|\psi_4\rangle = \|\psi\rangle$
00	$\left(\frac{\|0\rangle+\|1\rangle}{\sqrt{2}}\right)(\alpha\|0\rangle+\beta\|1\rangle)+\left(\frac{\|0\rangle-\|1\rangle}{\sqrt{2}}\right)(\alpha\|0\rangle-\beta\|1\rangle)$	$\left[\frac{\|0\rangle+\|1\rangle}{\sqrt{2}}\right]\triangleq 0^*$	$(\alpha\|0\rangle+\beta\|1\rangle)$	None
10	$\left(\frac{\|0\rangle+\|1\rangle}{\sqrt{2}}\right)(\alpha\|0\rangle-\beta\|1\rangle)+\left(\frac{\|0\rangle-\|1\rangle}{\sqrt{2}}\right)(\alpha\|0\rangle+\beta\|1\rangle)$	$\left[\frac{\|0\rangle+\|1\rangle}{\sqrt{2}}\right]\triangleq 0^*$	$(\alpha\|0\rangle-\beta\|1\rangle)$	Pauli Z Gate
01	$\left(\frac{\|0\rangle+\|1\rangle}{\sqrt{2}}\right)(\alpha\|1\rangle+\beta\|0\rangle)-\left(\frac{\|0\rangle-\|1\rangle}{\sqrt{2}}\right)(\alpha\|1\rangle-\beta\|0\rangle)$	$\left[\frac{\|0\rangle+\|1\rangle}{\sqrt{2}}\right]\triangleq 0^*$	$(\alpha\|1\rangle+\beta\|0\rangle)$	Pauli X Gate
11	$\left(\frac{\|0\rangle+\|1\rangle}{\sqrt{2}}\right)(\alpha\|1\rangle-\beta\|0\rangle)-\left(\frac{\|0\rangle-\|1\rangle}{\sqrt{2}}\right)(\alpha\|1\rangle+\beta\|0\rangle)$	$\left[\frac{\|0\rangle+\|1\rangle}{\sqrt{2}}\right]\triangleq 0^*$	$(\alpha\|1\rangle-\beta\|0\rangle)$	Pauli X Gate followed by Pauli Z Gate
00	$\left(\frac{\|0\rangle+\|1\rangle}{\sqrt{2}}\right)(\alpha\|0\rangle+\beta\|1\rangle)+\left(\frac{\|0\rangle-\|1\rangle}{\sqrt{2}}\right)(\alpha\|0\rangle-\beta\|1\rangle)$	$\left[\frac{\|0\rangle-\|1\rangle}{\sqrt{2}}\right]\triangleq 1^*$	$(\alpha\|0\rangle-\beta\|1\rangle)$	Pauli Z Gate
10	$\left(\frac{\|0\rangle+\|1\rangle}{\sqrt{2}}\right)(\alpha\|0\rangle-\beta\|1\rangle)+\left(\frac{\|0\rangle-\|1\rangle}{\sqrt{2}}\right)(\alpha\|0\rangle+\beta\|1\rangle)$	$\left[\frac{\|0\rangle-\|1\rangle}{\sqrt{2}}\right]\triangleq 1^*$	$(\alpha\|0\rangle+\beta\|1\rangle)$	None
01	$\left(\frac{\|0\rangle+\|1\rangle}{\sqrt{2}}\right)(\alpha\|1\rangle+\beta\|0\rangle)-\left(\frac{\|0\rangle-\|1\rangle}{\sqrt{2}}\right)(\alpha\|1\rangle-\beta\|0\rangle)$	$\left[\frac{\|0\rangle-\|1\rangle}{\sqrt{2}}\right]\triangleq 1^*$	$(\alpha\|1\rangle-\beta\|0\rangle)$	Pauli X Gate followed by Pauli Z Gate
11	$\left(\frac{\|0\rangle+\|1\rangle}{\sqrt{2}}\right)(\alpha\|1\rangle-\beta\|0\rangle)-\left(\frac{\|0\rangle-\|1\rangle}{\sqrt{2}}\right)(\alpha\|1\rangle+\beta\|0\rangle)$	$\left[\frac{\|0\rangle-\|1\rangle}{\sqrt{2}}\right]\triangleq 1^*$	$(\alpha\|1\rangle+\beta\|0\rangle)$	Pauli X Gate

TABLE 1
Measurements on Control Block

Port	Input	Rule
I	$\|\psi_3\rangle_I$	(i) If $CCC = (000^*)$ at Ports I, II and III, apply Pauli I gate (matrix) = $\begin{bmatrix} 1 & 0 \\ 0 & 1 \end{bmatrix}$ at port IV
		(ii) If $CCC = (100^*)$ at Ports I, II and III, apply Pauli Z gate (matrix) = $\begin{bmatrix} 1 & 0 \\ 0 & -1 \end{bmatrix}$ at port IV
		(iii) If $CCC = (010^*)$ at Ports I, II and III, apply Pauli X gate (matrix) = $\begin{bmatrix} 0 & 1 \\ 1 & 0 \end{bmatrix}$ at port IV
II	$\|\psi_3\rangle_{II}$	(iv) If $CCC = (110^*)$ at Ports I, II and III, apply Pauli X gate followed by Pauli Z gate, i.e. XZ (matrix) = $\begin{bmatrix} 0 & 1 \\ -1 & 0 \end{bmatrix}$ at port IV
		(v) If $CCC = (001^*)$ at Ports I, II and III, apply Pauli Z gate (matrix) = $\begin{bmatrix} 1 & 0 \\ 0 & -1 \end{bmatrix}$ at port IV
III	$\|\psi_3\rangle_{III}$	(vi) If $CCC = (101^*)$ at Ports I, II and III, apply Pauli I gate (matrix) = $\begin{bmatrix} 1 & 0 \\ 0 & 1 \end{bmatrix}$ at port IV
		(vii) If $CCC = (011^*)$ at Ports I, II and III, apply Pauli X gate followed by Pauli Z gate (matrix) = $\begin{bmatrix} 0 & 1 \\ -1 & 0 \end{bmatrix}$ at port IV
IV	$\|\psi_3\rangle_{IV}$	(viii) If $CCC = (111^*)$ at Ports I, II and III, apply Pauli X gate (matrix) = $\begin{bmatrix} 0 & 1 \\ 1 & 0 \end{bmatrix}$ at port IV

TABLE 2
Receiving end (R) : Triple Qubit Input-Output Pauli Gate (Triple Qubit Controlled Pauli (I / X / Z / (XZ)) Gate

1.2 Three-Particle Quantum Teleportation with Alternative Basis of Measurement

This sub-section presents Graph Theoretic Quantum System Modelling with measurement in the basis $|0\rangle$ and $|1\rangle$, as compared to sub-section 1.2, where measurement was made according to basis vectors $|0^*\rangle$ and $|1^*\rangle$ where $|0^*\rangle = \frac{|0\rangle + |1\rangle}{\sqrt{2}}$ and $|1^*\rangle = \frac{|0\rangle - |1\rangle}{\sqrt{2}}$.

The circuit for three particle quantum teleportation is shown in Figure 2. The sender Alice has a qubit $|\psi\rangle = \alpha|0\rangle + \beta|1\rangle$ which she wishes to send to the receiver, Bob. The supervisor Charlie, with Alice and Bob share one particle each of the GHZ state. Three particle quantum entangled states called GHZ states are used for three-particle teleportation.

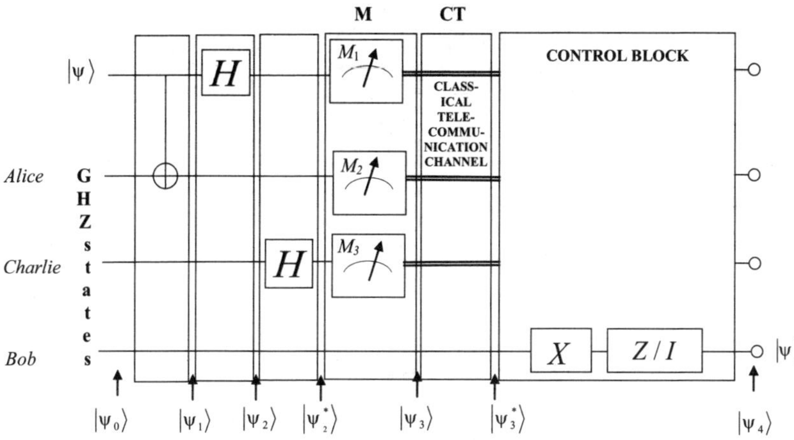

FIGURE 2
Three-particle Quantum Teleportation Circuit

A detailed analysis of the various stages along with the terminal graphs appears in Srivastava (2013).

1.3 n-Particle Quantum Teleportation

Three particle quantum entangled states called GHZ states are used for three-particle teleportation. An example of GHZ state is $\left[\frac{|000\rangle + |111\rangle}{\sqrt{2}}\right]$ and this entangled state has been used, shared between sender Alice, receiver Bob and supervisor Charlie. n-particle quantum entangled states called GHZ states are used for n-particle quantum teleportation. There will be n-fold entanglement. The entangled GHZ state $\frac{|0\rangle^{\otimes n} + |1\rangle^{\otimes n}}{\sqrt{2}}$ has been shared between sender Alice, receiver Bob and $(n-2)$ supervisors Charlie. There will be 2^n cases.

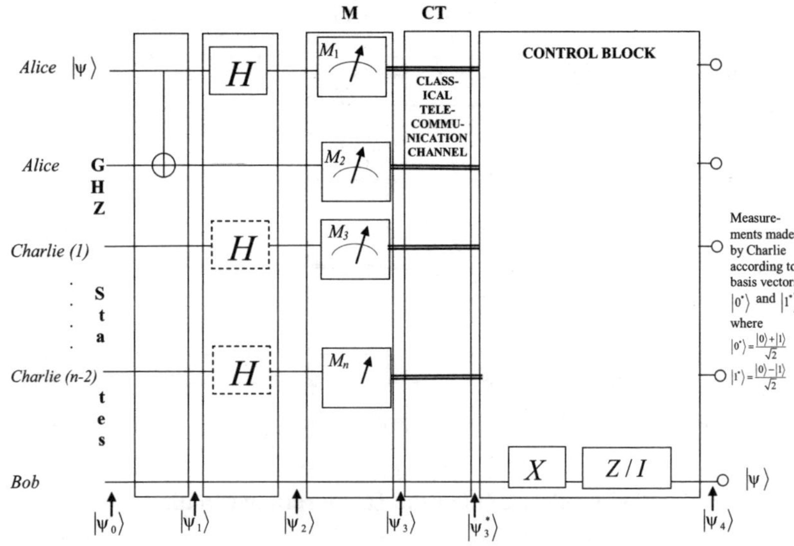

FIGURE 3
n-particle Quantum Teleportation Circuit

The circuit for n-particle quantum teleportation is shown in Figure 3. The sender Alice has a qubit $|\psi\rangle = \alpha|0\rangle + \beta|1\rangle$ which she wishes to send to the receiver, Bob. The supervisors, Charlie, with Alice and Bob share one particle each of the GHZ state. Measurements for Charlie are according to basis vector pair $|0^*\rangle$ and $|1^*\rangle$ unlike measurements made by sender Alice which are according to normal basis vector pair $|0\rangle$ and $|1\rangle$.

An alternative approach would be adding Hadamard gates in the circuit for each of the supervisors between stages 2 and 3 (i.e. stage 2^*) as shown by dotted lines. By doing so we need not change the basis vector pairs for the supervisors to $|0^*\rangle$ and $|1^*\rangle$. A detailed analysis of the various stages along with the terminal graphs appears in Srivastava (2013).

2. MODELLING *n*-QUDIT CONTEXTUALITY BASED QUANTUM TELEPORTATION AND BEYOND

Srivastava et. al. (2016) have applied Graph Theoretic Quantum System Modelling (GTQSM) to qudits of d-dimension, generalizing the graph models proposed by Srivastava et.al. (2011, 2014). The graph-theoretic model of a qudit is briefly presented below.

Let $|\psi\rangle = \alpha|0\rangle + \beta|1\rangle + \gamma|2\rangle + \delta|3\rangle + ... + \nu|n-1\rangle$ represent a generalized quantum odd prime based qudit (with dimension d=n)

in comparison to the commonly used even-prime based quantum bit (qudits with dimension 2) in terms of Quantum Terminal Graph (QTG) in Figure 4. where $|0\rangle$ is the state $\begin{bmatrix}1\\0\\0\\.\\.\\0\end{bmatrix}$ and $|1\rangle$ is the state $\begin{bmatrix}0\\1\\0\\.\\.\\0\end{bmatrix}$ and $|2\rangle$ is the state $\begin{bmatrix}0\\0\\1\\.\\.\\0\end{bmatrix}$, and $|n\rangle$ is the state $\begin{bmatrix}0\\0\\0\\.\\.\\1\end{bmatrix}$.

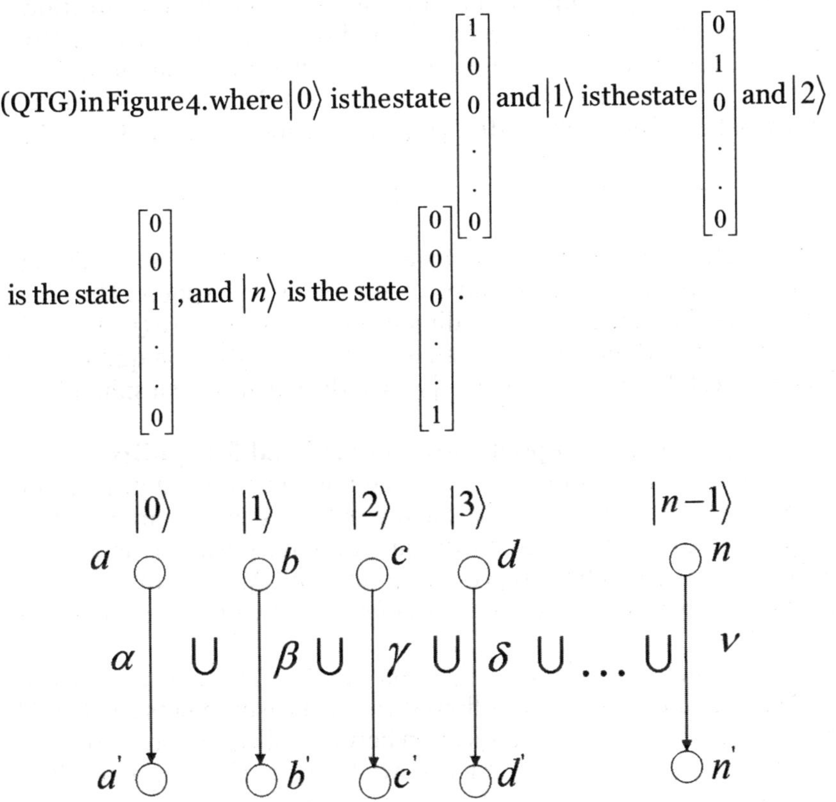

FIGURE 4
Generalized Qudit (dimension d=n) as union of n separate parts

The generalized quantum terminal graph (QTG) with dimension (d=n) is shown in Figure 4 as the union of n separate parts such that $a\ a'$ denote the first "ket-0" part, $b\ b'$ denotes the second "ket-1" part, $c\ c'$ denotes the third "ket-2" part, $d\ d'$ denotes the fourth "ket-3" part and so on, upto $n\ n'$ which denotes the "ket-(n-1)" part (which form an orthonormal basis vector-set for the Hilbert space). Here $\alpha,\beta,\gamma,\delta,\nu$ are complex numbers such that $|\alpha|^2$ is the probability of qubits of "information / computation data" flow-rate along unit directional (quantum across variable) vector $|0\rangle$; $|\beta|^2$ is the probability of qubits of "information / computation data" flow-rate along unit directional (quantum across variable) vector $|1\rangle$; $|\gamma|^2$ is the probability of qubits of "information / computation data" flow-rate along unit directional (quantum across variable) vector $|2\rangle$; $|\delta|^2$ is the probability of qubits of "information / computation data" flow-rate along unit directional (quantum across variable) vector $|3\rangle$; $|\varepsilon|^2$ is the probability of qubits of "information / computation data" flow-rate along unit directional (quantum across variable) vector $|4\rangle$ and so on, and $|\nu|^2$ is the probability of "information / computation data" flow-rate along unit directional (quantum across variable) vector $|n-1\rangle$. Notice that the sum of probabilities of flows along $|0\rangle$, $|1\rangle$, $|2\rangle$, . . . and $|n-1\rangle$ adds to 1, i.e.

$$|\alpha|^2+|\beta|^2+|\gamma|^2+|\delta|^2+...+|\nu|^2=1 \tag{2.1}$$

Accordingly, the probable qudit states can be said to be normalized to length 1. Eq. (2.1) is the equation of an n-dimensional sphere. Thus each qudit *j* may be visualized as a *d*-dimensional hyper sphere (instead of a loop for qubit which has only 2 states, i.e. $|\alpha|^2+|\beta|^2=1$, a qudit which has only 3 states, i.e. $|\alpha|^2+|\beta|^2+|\gamma|^2=1$, the equation of a sphere).

2.1 Quantum Teleportation generalized for qudits

Quantum teleportation involves sending quantum states around without a quantum channel, involving only classical communication. Figure 5 shows the well-known quantum teleportation circuit for qubits. The top two lines represent qubits with Alice and the last line is the qubit with Bob. Ultimately, the first qubit with Alice, having the quantum state $|\psi\rangle=\alpha|0\rangle+\beta|1\rangle$ is sent to Bob. This circuit involves a CNOT gate, Hadamard gate, followed by two measurements and Pauli X and Z gates. The only communication between Alice and Bob is through classical communication channel shown by double lines. The results of the two measurements (00, 01, 10 or 11) are conveyed by Alice over this classical channel to Bob, who applies the Pauli X gate, or Pauli Z gate, or both, or neither depending on the measurement outcome.

Extending this circuit to qudits would require hybrid definitions for the two-qubit gates used so far, namely the CNOT gate, Hadamard gate, measurement operators and the Pauli gates. We propose the simplest case of qudits of dimension d=3, or qutrits. The quantum teleportation circuit for qudits with dimension d=3 is shown in Figure 6. It involves hybrid CNOT and Hadamard gates and the result of measurement is conveyed over a classical channel depicted by a triple line, as the result could now be 0 or 1 or 2, since our state is now $|\psi\rangle=\alpha|0\rangle+\beta|1\rangle+\gamma|2\rangle$. Thus, there are nine possible measurement results (00, 01, 02, 10, 11, 12, 20, 21, 22) which can be conveyed by Alice to Bob, and Bob will have to apply 1 of 9 operators to get the original qudit of dimension d=3 sent by Alice.

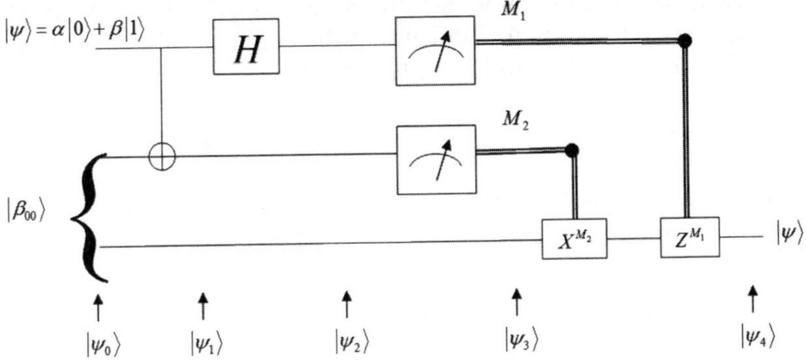

FIGURE 5
Quantum teleportation circuit for qubit (d = 2 dimensional qudit)

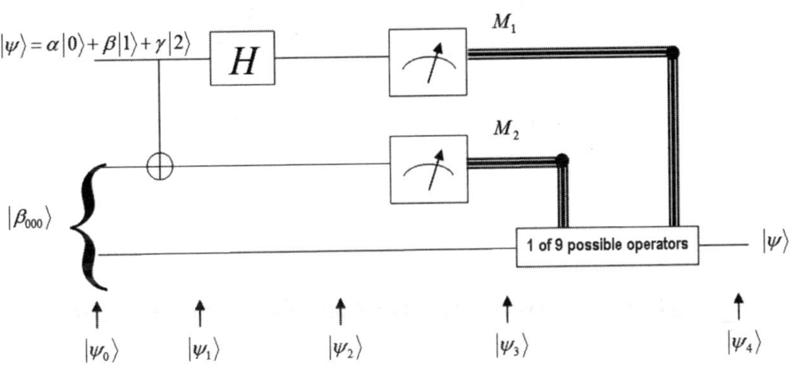

FIGURE 6
Quantum teleportation circuit for qutrit (d = 3 dimensional qudit)

2.2 Definitions of qudit states and gates

We list the definitions for the hyrbid gates, states and operators used for d=3 dimensional qudit teleportation.

2.2.1 Three-dimensional Qudit (d=3) or qutrit state

As already discussed in Section 2, we propose to teleport a qudit of dimension d=3, or qutrit state, which can be mathematically expressed as :

$$|\psi\rangle = \alpha|0\rangle + \beta|1\rangle + \gamma|2\rangle \qquad (2.2)$$

The measurement outcome has probability $|\alpha|^2$ for state 0, $|\beta|^2$ for state 1 and $|\gamma|^2$ for state 2. Notice that the sum of probability magnitudes of states $|0\rangle$, $|1\rangle$ and $|2\rangle$ adds to 1, i.e.

$$|\alpha|^2+|\beta|^2+|\gamma|^2=1 \tag{2.3}$$

which is the equation of a 3-dimensional hypersphere as shown in Figure 7 below.

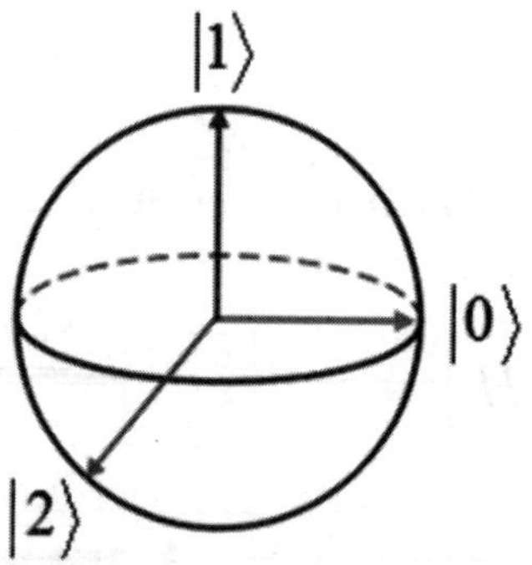

FIGURE 7

A 3-dimensional hypersphere with probability magnitudes $|\alpha|^2+|\beta|^2+|\gamma|^2=1$

2.2.2 (Hybrid) Controlled-NOT Gate for qudits of dimension d=3

Wilmott et. al. (2011) have proposed the 9 x 9 matrix for hybrid CNOT gate for 3-dimensional qutrits, extending the definition of 4 x 4 matrix normally used for qubits.

$$CNOT_{qutrit} = \begin{bmatrix} 1 & 0 & 0 & 0 & 0 & 0 & 0 & 0 & 0 \\ 0 & 1 & 0 & 0 & 0 & 0 & 0 & 0 & 0 \\ 0 & 0 & 1 & 0 & 0 & 0 & 0 & 0 & 0 \\ 0 & 0 & 0 & 0 & 0 & 1 & 0 & 0 & 0 \\ 0 & 0 & 0 & 1 & 0 & 0 & 0 & 0 & 0 \\ 0 & 0 & 0 & 0 & 1 & 0 & 0 & 0 & 0 \\ 0 & 0 & 0 & 0 & 0 & 0 & 0 & 1 & 0 \\ 0 & 0 & 0 & 0 & 0 & 0 & 0 & 0 & 1 \\ 0 & 0 & 0 & 0 & 0 & 0 & 1 & 0 & 0 \end{bmatrix} \tag{2.4}$$

The action of the control qubit which could be in either of the states 0, 1,2 or their superposition, on the target qubit is also summarized in Table 3. The three possible outcomes or their superposition of action of control qubit on target qubit is also shown as a quantum graph in Figure 8, using the hypersphere proposed in Figure 7. It is simply a rotation of the axes.

Control Qubit	Action on Target Qubit
0	No action
1	0 → 2, 1 → 0, 2 → 1
2	0 → 1, 1 → 2, 2 → 0

TABLE 3
Hyrbid CNOT Gate operation for qudit of dimension d=3

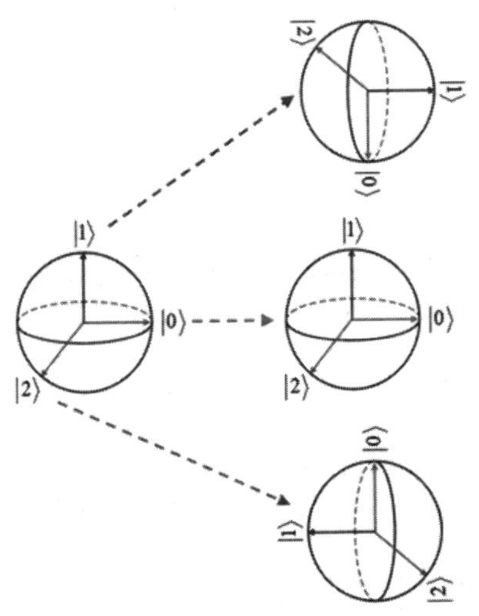

FIGURE 8
Quantum graph depicting effect of hybrid CNOT gate

2.2.3 (Hybrid) Hadamard Gate for qudits of dimension d=3

For d=2 (qubit), the Hadamard gate (or 2-dimensional Fourier gate) converts $|0\rangle \rightarrow \frac{|0\rangle + |1\rangle}{\sqrt{2}}$ and $|1\rangle \rightarrow \frac{|0\rangle - |1\rangle}{\sqrt{2}}$ and the matrix representation is $H = \frac{1}{\sqrt{2}}\begin{bmatrix} 1 & 1 \\ 1 & -1 \end{bmatrix}$. For d=3 (qutrit), the corresponding

Fourier gate is named as Chrestonson gate C and its matrix has been given by Dogra et. al. (2015) as

$$C = \frac{1}{\sqrt{3}} \begin{bmatrix} 1 & 1 & 1 \\ 1 & e^{\frac{2\pi i}{3}} & e^{\frac{4\pi i}{3}} \\ 1 & e^{\frac{4\pi i}{3}} & e^{\frac{2\pi i}{3}} \end{bmatrix}, \tag{2.5}$$

Considering that exponentiations $e^{\frac{2\pi i}{3}}$ and $e^{\frac{4\pi i}{3}}$ are simply rotations by $\angle 120^\circ$ and $\angle 240^\circ$ respectively, we use the phasor notation of electrical engineering to obtain,

$$C = \frac{1}{\sqrt{3}} \begin{bmatrix} 1 & 1 & 1 \\ 1 & \angle 120^\circ & \angle 240^\circ \\ 1 & \angle 240^\circ & \angle 120^\circ \end{bmatrix} \tag{2.6}$$

Upon measurement, only the magnitudes are considered and the phases collapse.

2.2.4 (Hybrid) Entangled State for qudits of dimension d=3

The entangled state used for illustrating teleportation for qubits, is usually the first Bell state β_{oo}, which is $\beta_{oo} = \frac{|00\rangle + |11\rangle}{\sqrt{2}}$.

Extending teleportation to qudits would involve higher-dimensional entangled states and for the 3-qudit model, we use the state, β_{ooo} which is

$$\beta_{ooo} = \frac{|00\rangle + |11\rangle + |22\rangle}{\sqrt{3}} \tag{2.7}$$

Each outcome has a probability 1/3 of measurement. Figure 9 uses the hypersphere notation used so far to depict this entangled state β_{ooo}.

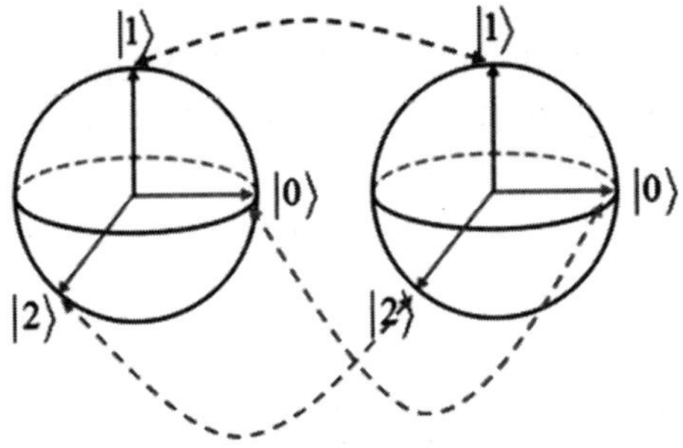

FIGURE 9

d=3 dimensional quantum entangled state $\beta_{ooo} = \frac{|00\rangle + |11\rangle + |22\rangle}{\sqrt{3}}$

2.3 Modelling Teleportation for Qudit of Dimension Three (d=3)

The various qubit states and their graph theoretic representation for teleportation circuit of Figure 6 are discussed below.

Step I

The state input to the circuit has the first qudit as $|\psi\rangle$ and the second and third qudits are the Bell states β_{ooo}. So the input state becomes The input state (Figure 10) is the tensor product of the qudit proposed in Figure 7 and the entangled state of Figure 9.

$$|\psi_0\rangle = |\psi\rangle \beta_{000}$$

$$= \frac{1}{\sqrt{3}}\left[(\alpha|0\rangle + \beta|1\rangle + \gamma|2\rangle)(|00\rangle + |11\rangle + |22\rangle)\right]$$

$$= \frac{1}{\sqrt{3}}\left[\alpha|0\rangle(|00\rangle + |11\rangle + |22\rangle) + \beta|1\rangle(|00\rangle + |11\rangle + |22\rangle) + \gamma|2\rangle(|00\rangle + |11\rangle + |22\rangle)\right]$$

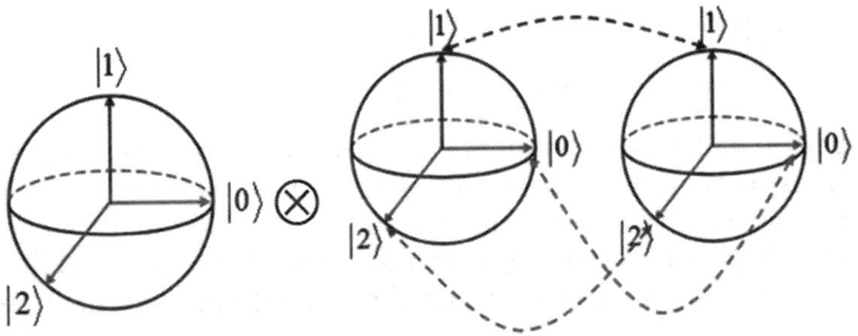

FIGURE 10

$|\psi_0\rangle = |\psi\rangle \otimes \beta_{000}$ as the tensor product of Figures 7 and 9

Step II

Alice sends her qubits through a hybrid CNOT gate whose working and graph theoretic representation has already been discussed, obtaining

$$|\psi_1\rangle = \frac{1}{\sqrt{3}}\left[\alpha|0\rangle(|00\rangle+|11\rangle+|22\rangle)+\beta|1\rangle(|20\rangle+|01\rangle+|12\rangle)+\gamma|2\rangle(|10\rangle+|21\rangle+|02\rangle)\right]$$

Step III

Alice then sends the first qubit through a Chrestonson (hybrid Hadamard or Fourier) gate, obtaining

$$|\psi_2\rangle = \frac{1}{3}\begin{bmatrix} \alpha(|0\rangle+|1\rangle+|2\rangle)(|00\rangle+|11\rangle+|22\rangle)+ \\ \beta(|0\rangle+|1\rangle\angle 120^\circ+|2\rangle\angle 240^\circ)(|20\rangle+|01\rangle+|12\rangle)+ \\ \gamma(|0\rangle+|1\rangle\angle 240^\circ+|2\rangle\angle 120^\circ)(|10\rangle+|21\rangle+|02\rangle) \end{bmatrix}$$

or

$$|\psi_2\rangle = \frac{1}{3}\begin{bmatrix} \alpha(|000\rangle+|011\rangle+|022\rangle+|100\rangle+|111\rangle+|122\rangle+|200\rangle+|211\rangle+|222\rangle)+ \\ \beta(|020\rangle+|001\rangle+|012\rangle+|120\rangle\angle 120^\circ+|101\rangle\angle 120^\circ+|112\rangle\angle 120^\circ)+|220\rangle\angle 240^\circ+|201\rangle\angle 240^\circ+|212\rangle\angle 240^\circ \\ \gamma(|010\rangle+|021\rangle+|002\rangle+|110\rangle\angle 240^\circ+|121\rangle\angle 240^\circ+|102\rangle\angle 240^\circ)+|210\rangle\angle 120^\circ)+|221\rangle\angle 120^\circ+|202\rangle\angle 120^\circ) \end{bmatrix}$$

which on re-arranging terms, can be looked upon as 9 individual terms for $|00\rangle$, $|01\rangle$, $|02\rangle$, $|10\rangle$, $|11\rangle$, $|12\rangle$, $|20\rangle$, $|21\rangle$ and $|22\rangle$. (We have 4 such terms in case of 2-qubit teleportation).

$$|\psi_2\rangle = \frac{1}{3}\begin{bmatrix} |00\rangle(\alpha|0\rangle+\beta|1\rangle+\gamma|2\rangle)+ \\ |01\rangle(\alpha|1\rangle+\beta|2\rangle+\gamma|0\rangle)+ \\ |02\rangle(\alpha|2\rangle+\beta|0\rangle+\gamma|1\rangle)+ \\ |10\rangle(\alpha|0\rangle+\beta|1\rangle\angle 120^\circ+\gamma|2\rangle\angle 240^\circ)+ \\ |11\rangle(\alpha|1\rangle+\beta|2\rangle\angle 120^\circ+\gamma|0\rangle\angle 240^\circ)+ \\ |12\rangle(\alpha|2\rangle+\beta|0\rangle\angle 120^\circ+\gamma|1\rangle\angle 240^\circ)+ \\ |20\rangle(\alpha|0\rangle+\beta|1\rangle\angle 240^\circ+\gamma|2\rangle\angle 120^\circ)+ \\ |21\rangle(\alpha|1\rangle+\beta|2\rangle\angle 240^\circ+\gamma|0\rangle\angle 120^\circ)+ \\ |22\rangle(\alpha|2\rangle+\beta|0\rangle\angle 240^\circ+\gamma|1\rangle\angle 120^\circ) \end{bmatrix}$$

Now Alice makes measurement of her 2 qubits and there are 9 possibilities (as compared to 4 possibilities (00, 01, 10, 11) in qubit teleportation). She conveys the measured result, with 9 possibilities each of which has a probability of 1/9 over the classical channel to Bob. Bob applies one of the 9 rotation operators, based on the measurement result conveyed by Alice, to get the teleported qubit $|\psi\rangle=\alpha|0\rangle+\beta|1\rangle+\gamma|2\rangle$. Table 4 summarizes the 9 possibilities.

Alice measures	State of Bob's qubit	Action required by Bob
$\|00\rangle$	$(\alpha\|0\rangle+\beta\|1\rangle+\gamma\|2\rangle)$	No further action required
$\|01\rangle$	$(\alpha\|1\rangle+\beta\|2\rangle+\gamma\|0\rangle)$	$\begin{bmatrix}0&1&0\\0&0&1\\1&0&0\end{bmatrix}\begin{bmatrix}\gamma\\\alpha\\\beta\end{bmatrix}=\begin{bmatrix}\alpha\\\beta\\\gamma\end{bmatrix}$
$\|02\rangle$	$(\alpha\|2\rangle+\beta\|0\rangle+\gamma\|1\rangle)$	$\begin{bmatrix}0&0&1\\1&0&0\\0&1&0\end{bmatrix}\begin{bmatrix}\beta\\\gamma\\\alpha\end{bmatrix}=\begin{bmatrix}\alpha\\\beta\\\gamma\end{bmatrix}$
$\|10\rangle$	$(\alpha\|0\rangle+\beta\|1\rangle\angle120^\circ+\gamma\|2\rangle\angle240^\circ)$	$\begin{bmatrix}1&0&0\\0&1\angle240^\circ&0\\0&0&1\angle120^\circ\end{bmatrix}\begin{bmatrix}\alpha\\\beta\angle120^\circ\\\gamma\angle240^\circ\end{bmatrix}=\begin{bmatrix}\alpha\\\beta\\\gamma\end{bmatrix}$
$\|11\rangle$	$(\alpha\|1\rangle+\beta\|2\rangle\angle120^\circ+\gamma\|0\rangle\angle240^\circ)$	$\begin{bmatrix}0&1&0\\0&0&1\angle240^\circ\\1\angle120^\circ&0&0\end{bmatrix}\begin{bmatrix}\gamma\angle240^\circ\\\alpha\\\beta\angle120^\circ\end{bmatrix}=\begin{bmatrix}\alpha\\\beta\\\gamma\end{bmatrix}$
$\|12\rangle$	$(\alpha\|2\rangle+\beta\|0\rangle\angle120^\circ+\gamma\|1\rangle\angle240^\circ)$	$\begin{bmatrix}0&0&1\\1\angle240^\circ&0&0\\0&1\angle120^\circ&0\end{bmatrix}\begin{bmatrix}\beta\angle120^\circ\\\gamma\angle240^\circ\\\alpha\end{bmatrix}=\begin{bmatrix}\alpha\\\beta\\\gamma\end{bmatrix}$
$\|20\rangle$	$(\alpha\|0\rangle+\beta\|1\rangle\angle240^\circ+\gamma\|2\rangle\angle120^\circ)$	$\begin{bmatrix}1&0&0\\0&1\angle120^\circ&0\\0&0&1\angle240^\circ\end{bmatrix}\begin{bmatrix}\alpha\\\beta\angle240^\circ\\\gamma\angle120^\circ\end{bmatrix}=\begin{bmatrix}\alpha\\\beta\\\gamma\end{bmatrix}$
$\|21\rangle$	$(\alpha\|1\rangle+\beta\|2\rangle\angle240^\circ+\gamma\|0\rangle\angle120^\circ)$	$\begin{bmatrix}0&1&0\\0&0&1\angle120^\circ\\1\angle240^\circ&0&0\end{bmatrix}\begin{bmatrix}\gamma\angle120^\circ\\\alpha\\\beta\angle240^\circ\end{bmatrix}=\begin{bmatrix}\alpha\\\beta\\\gamma\end{bmatrix}$
$\|22\rangle$	$(\alpha\|2\rangle+\beta\|0\rangle\angle240^\circ+\gamma\|1\rangle\angle120^\circ)$	$\begin{bmatrix}0&0&1\\1\angle120^\circ&0&0\\0&1\angle240^\circ&0\end{bmatrix}\begin{bmatrix}\beta\angle240^\circ\\\gamma\angle120^\circ\\\alpha\end{bmatrix}=\begin{bmatrix}\alpha\\\beta\\\gamma\end{bmatrix}$

TABLE 4
9 possible measurement outcomes of Alice and action required by Bob

3. CONTEXTUALITY BASED MODELS

Howard et. al. (2014) at University of Waterloo in their celebrated paper in Nature were motivated to discover necessary and sufficient conditions for maintaining coherence in a quantum computing system, so that quantum computers could become a reality. In this context, they came up with a suggestion, (and thereby they did prove the necessary conditions), to the effect that if they generalize the concept of qubit to that of qudit, that is instead of considering two-state quantum bits, one could get three state quantum odd prime based bits. While quantum computers promise dramatic advantages over their classical counterparts, but the source of the power in quantum computing has remained elusive. Howard et. al. have proved a remarkable equivalence between the onset of contextuality and the possibility of universal quantum computation via 'magic state' distillation, which is the leading model for experimentally realizing a fault-tolerant quantum computer.

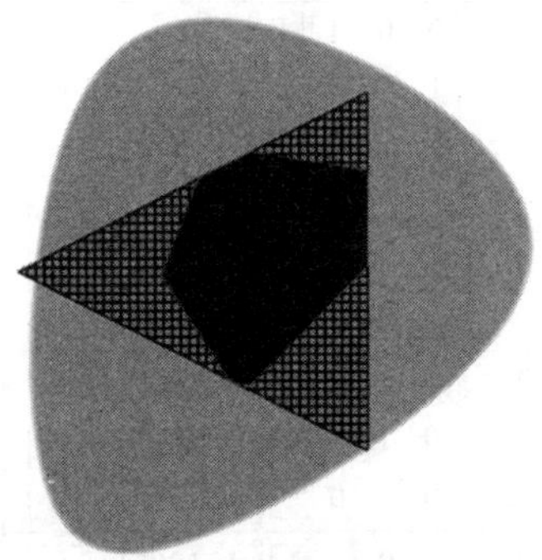

FIGURE 11
Two-dimensional slice through qutrit state space (Howard et. al., 2014)

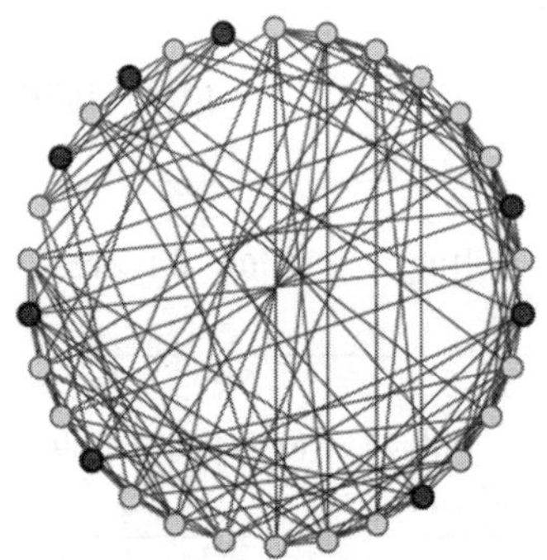

FIGURE 12
Construction applied to identify 'magic' state (Howard et al, 2014)

Figure 11 shows the idea proposed by Howard et. al. for a two-dimensional slice through qutrit state space with three distinct regions in the space of 3 x 3 matrix operators. Figure 12 shows the construction applied by them to two qubits to identify a maximum independent set, or 'magic' set.

Our model offers a better view and a close examination of Table 4 will reveal that there are three distinct states in the last column, with further rotations by $\angle 120^\circ$ and $\angle 240^\circ$, which eventually collapse since the measurement involves only magnitudes. This insight from electrical engineering has helped us to come up with a simpler model for Figure 11 and 12, in Figure 13, depicting the possible outcomes in contextuality based quantum teleportation. $|\alpha|^2, |\beta|^2$ and $|\gamma|^2$ are coordinates on all the three axes since there is interchange of the coefficients α, β and γ for $|0\rangle$, $|1\rangle$ and $|2\rangle$ axes in the last column of Table 4, with only phase rotations.

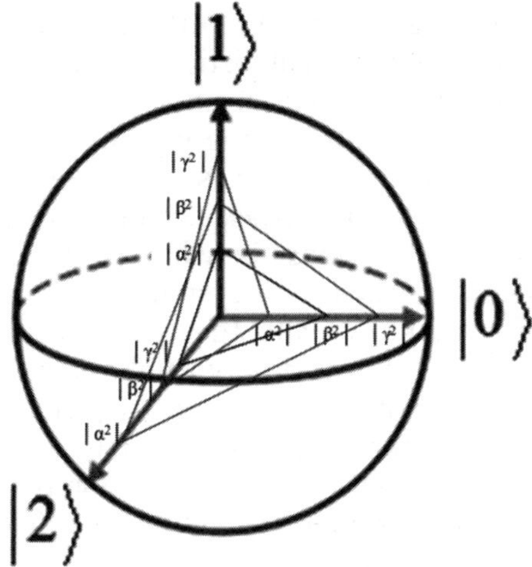

FIGURE 13
Simpler model for contextuality based quantum teleportation with insights from phasor representation of electrical engineering

Our argument is that we should not remain limited to three states only. In our Physical System Theory Model and its counterpart as consciousness system model, it takes only a step forward to generalize it to higher dimensions. We could generalize to any odd prime based higher dimension even beyond 3, say 5, 7, 11, 13, 17, 19, 23, 29, 31, 37, 41, 43 and so on, tending to infinity, and that is the hope which brings us to the threshold of being face to face mathematically in abstract terms with the ultimate source of consciousness.

4. DISCUSSION

This chapter presents application of Graph Theoretic Quantum System Modelling (GTQSM) to three-particle quantum teleportation circuit using GHZ (Greenberger, Horne and Zeilinger, 1989) states. The system models have been drawn using two different basis states in sub-sections 1.1 and 1.2. It also generalizes the teleportation circuit for n-particle quantum teleportation in sub-section 1.3. It may be observed that GTQSM presented in this chapter does not require any quantum field (or continuum) equations nor any spatial discretization process, unlike graph-theoretic approach to classical field problems (Savage et. al. 1977, 1980) since the components used are discrete at the nanometer scale of realization. Also, quantum teleportation has been enabled as a result of classical telecommunication and the phenomena of quantum entanglement. Accordingly, the graph theoretic modelling would seem to integrate seamlessly classical and quantum models in the context of processing between stages 3 and 3*. Furthermore, quantum theoretic model is essentially a linear probabilistic model in which measurement results in disappearance of superposition of probable states (i.e. in nonlinearity) with the collapse of the measured quantum state into one of the probable states i.e. a classical state. Accordingly, post-measurement the linear probabilistic quantum model may be viewed as giving rise to a system of systems (Jamshidi, 2009) each characterized by a linear probabilistic quantum system model. From the control problem point of view, the difficulty (degree of complexity) arises in as much as there is inherent uncertainty (multiple probable states) and each of the multiple system's control strategy (between stages 3* and 4 at the receiving end) cannot depend solely on its own on-board sensory information but also on the sensory information reaching its multiple actuators and controllers on telecommunication links from stage 3 at the sending end).

Accordingly, the main challenge in the design of controllers (appropriate Pauli gates) has been successfully met for the quantum system-of-systems for teleporting a qubit by developing a comprehensive transfer function model of multiple models analytically. Furthermore, it is at the higher end of complexity scale (Kitto, 2008) that the graph theoretic quantum system modelling might possibly hold even greater promise and potential for modelling extremely complex systems successfully in future.

5. CONCLUSIONS

Natural phenomenon has apparently no order and therefore it could be considered as having an order zero. Modern science tries to gain control over natural phenomena and therefore it is discovering order among unordered things, so it is an order of first degree that modern science provides to its trainees. Coming to systems science, it tries to consider order among ordered things, so here the order is of the second degree. In the quest for generalization, Howard et. al. at (2014) at University of Waterloo extended it further from qubits to qudits, in particular qutrits, i.e. order of degree or dimension three. They were motivated in realizing the advantages of quantum computing by maintaining coherence for long enough duration and they were trying to determine necessary and sufficient conditions for doing so. They have already succeeded in proving the necessary conditions, and are quite hopeful that they will be able to gain access to the sufficient conditions for maintaining coherence to realize the benefits of quantum computing. The University of Waterloo group might be said to have gone to an order three, (whereas systems science has an order of second degree).

We sense a great dilemma which faces scientists both in matters of small things as well as in matters of large things. Both the problems need resolution and are linked inextricably together. There are researchers on quantum and unified field theory and so on but they are not looking further beyond Planck's dimension in the small size. It is unscientific to stop there, the particles have grown so subtle that we have not devised physical instruments to measure them. So one should accept the kind of instruments which exist as we perceive those subtle particles. The dilemma is that 10^{-35} metre and beyond, the scientists are not able to measure smaller than 10^{-35} metre Planck's length.

Similarly, on the large side, scientists are not able to consider more than 10^{10} light years, so they do not know what exists in space beyond 10^{10} light years. So they are limited deliberately on these counts, whereas mathematics which is part of science, shows that particles are there which are subtler, subtler and subtlest ones. They move to infinity, they are most subtle, they become very small or subtle when we are close to zero, infinity is the macrocosm problem. Scientists can neither access infinity, nor zero, but none would say mathematics is not part of science.

To make the scientific community see what the reality is, the best way forward seems to make them realize that their own mathematics shows that we have to tackle a problem with zero and infinity, since they are not admitting zero point loops. Sen (2015) recently mentioned that they are limited to one-point loops of strings, because they are unique, but he mentioned in the same breath, string theory has landscapes which spoil the unitary conception and that by giving example of water, ice and steam, the three phases of water themselves present problems which scientists have not been able to resolve. This shows that they are proving to be inadequate with their kind of instrumentation. We should in fact try to detect those subtler particles than Planck's constant and long distances beyond 10^{10} light years. This is the crux of this chapter and we submit this inference based on modelling theory of mathematics, logic and induction.

References

Dogra S., Arvind, Dorai K., Implementation of the quantum Fourier transform on a hybrid qubit-qutrit NMR quantum emulator, IISER Mohali, arXiv:1503.06624 [quant-ph], March 2015.

Greenberger D.M., Horne M.A., Zeilinger A. (1989), *Bell's theorem, Quantum Theory, and Conceptions of the Universe*, pp. 73-76, Kluwer Academics, Dordrecht, The Netherlands (1989).

Howard M., Wallman J., Veitch V., Emerson J., "Contextuality supplies the 'magic' for quantum computation", Nature, Vol. 510, pp. 351-355, June 19, 2014.

Jamshidi Mo (Ed)., Systems of System Engineering, Principles and Applications, CRC Press, Taylor & Francis Group, New York, 2009.

Koenig, H.E., Tokad, Y. and Kesavan, H.K., Analysis of Discrete Physical Systems, McGraw-Hill, New York, 1967.

Kitto K., "High end Complexity", International Journal of General Systems, Vol. 37, No. 6, Dec. 2008, 689-714.

Satsangi P.S. (2006a), "Linear Graph Theory for Modelling a Variety of Systems", Int. Conf. on Differential Geometry and Topology in the Perspective of Modern Trends (DGTPMT – 2006), Dayalbagh Educational Institute, Dayalbagh, Agra, February 2006.

Satsangi P.S. (2006b), "Generalizing Physical Systems Through Applied Systems Research from "Real" Physical Systems through "Conceptual" Socio-Economic-Environmental Systems to "Complete" (Physical-Mental-Spiritual) Creational Systems", International Journal of General Systems, Vol. 35, No. 2, 2006, pp. 127-167.

Satsangi P.S. (2009), "Linear Graph Theoretic General Systems Paradigm – a learning system modelling methodology", Editorial Review, Literary Paritantra (Systems) – An International Journal on Literature and Theory, Vol. 1, Nos. 1 & 2 , Spring 2009.

Satsangi P.S. (2016), Modelling microtubules in the brain as *n*-qudit quantum Hopfield network and beyond, Vision Talk delivered at Integrated East-West Forum at The Science of Consciousness Conference (TSC 2016), April 25, 2016, Tucson, Arizona, USA.

Savage G. J. and Kesavan H. K. (1977), "A graph-theoretic approach to field problems," Int. Conf. on Numerical Methods, 1977.

Savage, G.; Madan, V.; Kesavan (1980), H., The magnetic field problem: A graph-theoretic model, IEEE Transactions on Magnetics, Volume 16, Issue 4, Jul 1980, pp. 579–585.

Sen Ashoke, String Theory and Cosmology: Tying the Two Ends, Harish-Chandra Research Institute, Allahabad, Diamond Jubilee Lecture delivered at Dayalbagh Educational Institute, Agra, October 2015.

Seshu, S. and Reed, M.B., Linear Graph Theory and Electrical Networks (Addison-Wesley, Reading, Mass.)., 1961.

Srivastava D.P., Sahni V., Satsangi P.S., (2011) "Graph-theoretic quantum system modelling for information/computation processing circuits", International Journal of General Systems, Taylor and Francis, UK, Vol. 40, No. 8, November 2011, pp. 777–804, ISSN No. 0308-1079.

Srivastava D.P., Sahni V., Satsangi P.S. (2014) "Graph Theoretic Quantum System Modelling for Neuronal Microtubles as Hierarchical Clustered Quantum Hopfield Networks", International Journal of General Systems, Taylor & Francis, UK, Vol. 43, No. 6, August 2014, pp. 633-648, ISSN No. 0308-1079.

Srivastava D.P. (2013), " Graph Theoretic Quantum Field / System Modelling For Quantum Information / Computation Circuits And Algorithms", Ph.D. Thesis, Dayalbagh Educational Institute, Dayalbagh, Agra, India, 2013.

Srivastava D.P., Sahni V., Satsangi P.S., (2016), "Modelling microtubules in the brain as n-qudit quantum Hopfield network and beyond", International Journal of General Systems, Vol. 45. No. 1, February 2016, pp. 41-54, DOI: 10.1080/03081079.2015.1076405, ISSN No. 0308-1079.

Wilmott C., On Swapping the states of two qudits, arXiv:1101.4159, January 2011.

Appendices

Appendix 1

काल नगर मानो देहैं उजाड़ी

(As if the Merciful Lord would devastate the Region of *Kala* or Evil)

Excerpts from the Historic Panel Discussion with leading scientists on 'Consciousness : Integrating Eastern and Western Perspectives' at the Integrated East-West Forum of 'The Science of Consciousness' (TSC 2016) Conference, Tucson, Arizona, USA April 25, 2016

Revered Prof. Satsangi : Prof. Gennaro had been promoting Higher Order Thought (HOT) Theory but when he applies infinite "regression" to it, he fights shy of it and does not want to pursue it to its logical abstraction, which would take him to the primary source of consciousness or primary source of thought which would explain everything. So why is it so, why do you feel shy of mathematical abstraction, logic and induction principles, which point the way to an ultimate primary source of consciousness.

Prof. Rocco Gennaro : Good question. I suppose one of the reasons is, we are not convinced that if something can be mathematically modeled, that it is something which reflects in reality.

Revered Prof. Satsangi : Isn't mathematics part of modern science, do you exclude mathematics from modern science?

Prof. Rocco Gennaro : Modern science can certainly construct various models but there can also be many mathematical models which are inconsistent with each other.

Revered Prof. Satsangi : Point out the inconsistency. We in our paper have shown that through mathematical abstraction, you can reach the primary source of thought or consciousness or whatever designation you wish to give, that explains everything. Nobody has come up yet with pointing out any flaw in that reasoning. Why is this so? Why are you fighting shy of the mathematical logical induction which lead you to the ultimate source, ultimate answers which you are seeking.

Prof. Rocco Gennaro : I am not sure what Higher Order Thought theory leads to mathematically, some might think it might lead to regression analysis, but the Higher Order Thought Theory really has to do with what makes you stay conscious at the moment.

Revered Prof. Satsangi : Precisely that, when infinite "regression" leads you to the primary source, why don't you pursue that.

Prof. Rocco Gennaro : I might pursue it, there is a point where you get abstraction, second level up, described earlier, that maybe, there are other levels of consciousness beyond that, for example, infinity . .

Revered Prof. Satsangi : What is beyond infinity?

Prof. Rocco Gennaro : Can we experience infinity? You might say yes. Can you experience infinity in a finite period of time? I am not sure.

Revered Prof. Satsangi : Sure. Sure. You can.

Prof. Rocco Gennaro : I am not sure.

Revered Prof. Satsangi : Never tried.

Prof. Rocco Gennaro : The relationship between mathematics and logic is very important obviously and can be applied to Higher Order Thought Model, but I am not sure it forces us to some beginning stage or something.

Prof. Stuart Hameroff : I just read a review of a book by Max Tegmark, 'Our Mathematical Universe', where he essentially tries to say that everything is mathematics, The criticism of that book is, that as Rocco said, that not all mathematics is relevant, not all mathematics describes the universe and the other is that mathematics, at least according to Penrose, is description of underlying geometry and the universe has an intrinsic structure that we don't really understand yet, that is a geometry, that gives rise to mathematics, physical constants and consciousness somehow, and the fine-tuning principle, entropic principles, question of why the universe is perfectly tuned to life and consciousness. There are basically two answers to that and one is that we have to live in a universe which is just perfect, and there are infinite number of universes according to multiple-worlds hypothesis and we are in the one that can support consciousness. That doesn't seem right to me, that there are all these other universes that are useless and we are in the one. It seems more likely to me as if the universe itself evolved to optimize consciousness and that consciousness has physical constants, that are intrinsic to the geometry of the universe, that helped evolve the universe and that consciousness is really steering the universe. It is behind the progressive evolution of the universe.

Revered Prof. Satsangi : We subscribe fully to the space-time geometry and we are explaining things precisely through space-time geometry and the field theory, quantum field theory, I have said there is something like Hilbert space but of a much larger dimension. You are using those principles, but when it tends to infinity, you do not want to grapple with that problem.

Prof. Stuart Hameroff : I did not catch all of that, but if you talk of infinity, there is a problem, even if you believe as Penrose does, the Big Bang was preceded by another eon and there is a sequence of big bangs, and each time, the physical constants mutate and evolve like an organism.

Revered Prof. Satsangi : He is perfectly right. He is perfectly right.

Prof. Staurt Hameroff : I am glad we agree on that.

Revered Prof. Satsangi : It is because of lack of mathematical preparation and application of logic and induction in the right way, you don't want to pursue that primary source of consciousness or primary source of thought or primary source of life, whatever you call it.

Prof. Stuart Hameroff : There is still the question whether it starts in infinite past or goes to infinite future.

Revered Prof. Satsangi : Now, you don't want to approach zero also. That is the whole difficulty, when it comes to finer particles, you are shy of going to zero and when it comes to bigger and bigger distances, you are shy of approaching infinity. What kind of scientific people does this world have, who denounce mathematics and the logical induction, that shows the way to reach zero as well as infinity.

Mr Prem Prashant : Prof. Stuart Hameroff – Prof. Barrell in his lecture today mentioned objectively observed subjective space as one of the components for integrating eastern and western perspectives and this is the problem area which needs a little bit of elaboration, how do you objectively observe a subjective space. The concept and the understanding of infinity can come only from subjective space and this subjective space, how can it be investigated in an objective manner. Prof. Barrell.

Prof. James Barrell : The Higher States of Consciousness, as I mentioned today, the difference between a kind of awareness in the moment and what we are experiencing, an embodied presence, once we get to higher states of consciousness, and those higher states were no longer localized, consciousness is no longer localized, and we are noticing our experiences and I have experienced that non-localized state, and many of you may have experienced those non-localized states, we may go in and out of it every once in a while, we may relive those higher states, there is no individual observer necessary, there is just an awareness. But the idea is that if you experience higher states of consciousness, you can live to those states, there is no observer, you can go on.

Revered Prof. Satsangi : Prof. Anirban Bandyopadhyay also mentions his problem of triplets. That arises because he wants to approach zero on one side and infinity on the other, besides whatever object you have in this world, you call it objective theory, it can only be approached by approaching zero on one side and infinity on the other, that is why you have triplets.

Prof. Anirban Bandyopadhyay : Actually, I wanted to make this response to Stuart also, that in the history of quantum theory in 1920s and 1930s, there were situations whenever we encounter singularity, we do renormalization by brute force, we jump the singularity point but if you take clocking cycle after clocking cycle after clocking cycle, we go to what is total time, infinity. So we had historically this kind of situation, and what we did to solve the problem, we did renormalization. Feynman himself said it is a hooky-pooky action. Nobody liked it but we solved it. I think that a time would come in history when we would look back at that problem and get inside that singularity and see how far we can go, so the point of zero, everywhere from the zero, there is an infinite point and it is well known. You see the Feynman diagram, you will see there is a fractal point, path inside path inside path, you just calculate it, you will reach infinity everywhere. You just take out Google search and put renormalization, you will find fractal paths, they can't solve it, so what they do is forcibly jump, as if whatever be the value, it is equal to one. Just to match the data, that is why I said nested time cycle, so that enter inside the singularity, go to some depth and get some data out, in any fractal system, you always reach infinity. So, there is matter and wave interaction. We are talking about great things like consciousness and other things, simple photon interaction, you cannot explain without imagination, by brute force, considering that there is no singularity.

Mr Prem Prashant : And if you look at the Fibonacci numbers and the Fibonacci curve which is prevalent all over nature, it combines zero and infinity which brings zero and infinity together in the fractal world. That is what fractal world is.

Prof. Anirban Bandyopadhyay : And not only Fibonacci, if you think of pi, if you think of e, e is an infinite series, pi is an infinite series, take the square of it, e squared plus pi squared, and we tested it to 15 digits, now we are going higher and higher orders, you perfectly derive pi. Infinity does not mean that it cannot give you perfect 2.00000 . . . , so that integer you are seeing could arise from a completely undefined space. Why don't you try, there are so many students, take a calculator or write a program and check it, infinite series which never ever can give you a perfect integer. You will get a perfect integer with this relationship. There are ample examples of universal constants wherefrom infinite series, you can reach to an absolute integer.

Prof. James Barrell : One of the questions I have is how does one experience infinity, we are talking about being outside of time and one of the ways of being outside of time is to remove conceptualizations of this world in which we are living, we get a whole different kind of time and space and the important question consciousness has to do with is what do you mean by time.

Revered Prof. Satsangi : Transcendental meditation and ultra-transcendental meditation are the answers.

Prof. Stuart Hameroff : I might comment that how do we experience infinity is one thing, how do we experience anything, what is consciousness, even if it is looking at your cell phone or feel anything, consciousness is a problem and normal consciousness and enlightened states and experiencing things like infinity are additional problems. But, we have not gone past the first problem yet. Regarding singularity, I read an article recently someone sent to me, they were trying to explain Hawking radiation, that inside of black hole was actually a quantum superposition, perhaps something like bosons, and it collapsed and what came out as Hawking radiation, and this person who sent me the article, said would not Penrose and you therefore have to say that black hole is conscious, that there is subjective reduction and expecting me to deny it and we have also said neutron star with large scale superpositions could have some sort of consciousness, maybe cognitive and meaningful, but experiential. I guess it is a question to physicists, would consciousness in black hole solve problems of infinity and normalization.

Mr Prem Prashant : It does not solve the problem. The information content inside black hole is proportional to the area and not the volume of the black hole which means that the information inside the black hole is two-dimensional and the real world we see is three-dimensional one, and gives an impression that everything we see in the real world is a projection, it is a three-dimensional hologram projection of information which is contained on the surface of the black hole, which is two dimensional. There is a theory which says that the entire universe is a closed system, it is a black hole and the entire information is contained in it, but it is digitalized information which is projected as a hologram and gives the impression of a real universe.

Revered Prof. Satsangi : I do not subscribe to this view. Infinite dimensional consciousness is what we should pursue.

Prof. Stuart Hameroff : We may have islands of consciousness.

Revered Prof. Satsangi : Prof. Kak, why don't you come in?

Prof. Subhash Kak : Let me wear my computer scientist hat, the artificial intelligence perspective of all of this is that why worry about internal states, just look at behaviour. If you are only looking at behaviour, then one could talk about unanimity on what is happening and therefore people who are doing AI (artificial intelligence), their hope is that the world will be dealing with AI machines and humans would not be needed anymore, and that may not be very far off, we are very close to that singularity. From an operational point of view, can we think of situations where we are not different, if not from machines of now, machines of the future. But having said this, let me try to find some common ground. You know if you look at neuroscience, we are a machine, if you look at physics, you cannot flout laws of nature, we must be machine like. If on the other hand, you look at Indian approaches to reality, where you start off with consciousness as a ground, there also it is acknowledged by people within the tradition that you cannot find any traces of consciousness, if you look for it within materiality.

Revered Prof. Satsangi : But why not practice the right meditation practice?

Prof. Subhash Kak : No, no, I agree. Prof. Satsangi, I totally agree with you. I was just looking at it as an outsider when people are debating and to that extent, there is this common ground we have not been able to find, so the question is ultimately to find proof within oneself, or as I have tried to do for the past many years, are there traces of the working of the freedom, ultimately consciousness is the freedom, are there traces of the workings of this freedom which cannot be captured by laws as we know, social, political, economic, physical, biological, which would give us proof of the kind that people may find credible, that indeed this means that there is more to reality than materiality. So, there is a lot of common ground, we cannot find it, but on the other hand there is possibility, that one can establish it, and if we can establish it, it will be a major achievement.

Revered Prof. Satsangi : Let me comment, I briefly touched on it in my talk; we can show you, we can demonstrate, such social measures as CSR, that is Corporate Social Responsibility, that index is higher for those who practice meditation rather than the ones who do not practice meditation.

Prof. Subhash Kak : I think that is a great point. That is a point Prof. Barrell also made that there are correlates and computer scientists are saying that if we can find out where is the activity inside the brain, you do fMRI or whatever, possibly you can read people's thoughts and you can do other things, and therefore you are taking a subjective feeling and finding an objective correlate and that could be helpful. We don't know where all that might go and certainly that is where science is going.

Revered Prof. Satsangi : You are on the right approach.

Appendix 2

"I shall be with one and all and they shall be looked after with more and more Grace"

Divine Promise of Param Purush Puran Dhani Huzur Soamiji Maharaj fully redeemed during unique events unparalleled in Satsang history from Basant 2016 to Holi 2016 and whirlwind world tour on Mission Science of Consciousness

It should be humbling for us, and awe-inspiring, to realize that the Divine Promise of Param Purush Puran Dhani Huzur Soamiji Maharaj, Radhasoami Sahab, revealed in His parting Instructions will always hold true and even truer, "Let no Satsangi, whether a householder or a Sadhu, feel distracted. I shall be with one and all and they shall be looked after with more and more Grace." The sole objective of this compilation is to preserve the cherished memories of the Infinite Blessings showered on Satsangis from all over the world in observing how complete Surrender and Obedience to the Will of Huzur Radhasoami Dayal is achieved. The twist and turn of events played out during a unique period in Satsang history from end-2015 to early-2016, provided such Blessings of the Lord which would otherwise not be accumulated even in several eons and cycles of birth and rebirth. This is an extended report of the Holi 2016 celebrations at Dayalbagh, which has not been attempted so far and may also dispel misconceptions, if any, among a miniscule section of people about this extraordinary phase in Satsang history during which all Satsangis were not just soaked, but drenched in the Infinite Grace and Mercy of Huzur Radhasoami Dayal.

The golden words of Param Guru Huzur Sarkar Sahab ring very true at the onset of this compilation, "Huzur Radhasoami Dayal is omnipotent. He has the power to ordain as He pleases. It is not at all difficult for Him to rejuvenate His constitution. But apparently it is not possible to understand His *Mauj*. It is in His hands alone to change the *Mauj* or not. We people are helpless in the matter." A pertinent point to start this account would be the morning Satsang on February 5, where Gracious Huzur declared in the open Satsang that His health was not fully well, and therefore His movements had become slow and consequently, it delayed Him frequently, but treatment was in progress for it. He advised everyone to stick to the path of duty (करनी) and carry out whatever duties had been allotted to them in a regulated manner. The path taken out by *mauj* also referred to the path of duty (करनी). This discourse has already been published in Dayalbagh Herald. The regular routine of Gracious Huzur, which is extremely hectic and would leave even the best of young men gasping for breath had started slowing down from around the Birthday of Param Guru Huzur Mehtaji Maharaj in December 2015 and continued to slow down further during Bhandara of Param Guru Huzur Sahabji Maharaj and Basant in February 2016. Gracious Huzur started taking very meagre quantities or portions of food served, reducing further and further even the tiny amounts He normally partakes. Gracious Huzur paid regular visits after morning fields to the physiotherapy unit of Saran Ashram Hospital.

It subsequently emerged that a former colleague of Gracious Huzur, who had been in regular touch through email and had also visited DEI some time back, had expressed a keen desire to get initiated and had also enrolled as a *jigyasu* at one of the Branch Satsangs and had been attending Satsang off and on for almost an year. Gracious Huzur had been so kind and merciful to Him that He used to give Chyavan Prash from His Own personal stock, when the colleague used to visit Dayalbagh and request for Chyavan Prash during meetings at the fields. Infinite Reservoir and Ocean of Mercy that He is, Gracious Huzur advised His colleague to apply for formal initiation during the coming zonal Bhandara, rather than continue as a *jigyasu* for the customary three years in such cases. In end-November 2015, the colleague wrote to Gracious Huzur by email that his movements had become slow due to knee and back problems, and he wished to defer admission into Radhasoami Faith due to extremes of weather. Gracious Huzur got a reply sent to him in early December by email that, "It is best to follow the prompts of your conscience." Subsequently, Gracious Huzur mentioned to some persons that Param Guru Huzur Sahabji Maharaj had departed from His physical frame for showing similar soft corner for a non-Satsangi. No one then dreamt the import of these remarks made in January-February 2016. The incident referred to by Gracious Huzur pertained to December 1920, around Timarni, between Pantalai and Harda when Param Guru Huzur Sahabji Maharaj departed from His physical frame and it had turned almost to dust. But in obedience to the *Mauj* of Radhasoami Dayal, Param Guru Huzur Sahabji Maharaj had to return to His Body again and finding the body in a decayed condition, He took 18 hours to be Himself again. Param Guru Huzur Sahabji Maharaj has explained about His illness in His own golden words (Souvenir, Chapter V, Para 89), "The Satguru is granted extraordinary powers over the Forces of Nature. He can, if He so wills, break the laws of nature, but He has to pay for it. Of course, He willingly submits to the penalty for such transgression. In the case of

Satsangis, such acts of His receive the approval of the Supreme Being, but in the case of non-Satsangis, the punishment has to be undergone." Param Guru Huzur Sahabji Maharaj had saved the life of His family doctor, a non-Satsangi, on repeated prayers by members of His family. The Laws of Nature being inviolable, He had to suffer the penalty, 'Life for Life', and had to depart from His physical frame and to reappear in it after some time. This was the reason of His temporary departure from the world.

Bhandara of Param Guru Huzur Sahabji Maharaj was celebrated at Dayalbagh on February 7. On February 8 evening, Gracious Huzur instructed that various items meant for His attention like programme card for zonal Satsang, homoeopathic medicine and research paper review be first symbolically offered to Param Guru Huzur Dr. Lal Sahab on the *singhasan* in Satsang. Mohalla visits on February 9 and 10 were also conducted but continued till quite late in the evening. One of the Branch Secretaries was also called on February 9 morning and instructed to follow due procedures and guidelines in recommending initiation forms. Basant celebrations were organized like every year during the Basant week. Gracious Huzur was pleased to continue this phase of slow movements for the whole of February and early-March.

The birthday of Gracious Huzur on March 9 was celebrated on similar lines as Birthday of Param Guru Huzur Mehtaji Maharaj by distributing Prasad in the morning Satsang and fields.

On March 10 evening, on the eve of His departure to Delhi for passport formalities in connection with planned visit to TSC 2016 (The Science of Consciousness) Conference at Arizona USA, Gracious Huzur summoned those connected with the TSC conference organization and told them that prospects for His foreign visit seemed to be positive at the moment and after celebrating His birthday on the lines (तर्ज) of Birthday of Param Guru Huzur Mehtaji Maharaj, His health seemed to have reached a turning point. It might be mentioned that during a visit to birth place of Param Guru Huzur Mehtaji Maharaj at Batala during Satsang tour in summer 2015, Gracious Huzur had mentioned that 130th Birthday of Param Guru Huzur Mehtaji Maharaj in December 2015 can be celebrated and a workshop had been organized at DEI close to that date to mark the momentous occasion, with participation of academicians from IIT Roorkee (formerly Thomason College of Civil Engineering and later, University of Roorkee), the alma mater of Huzur Mehtaji Maharaj. Gracious Huzur also mentioned that if He did not go abroad this time, He would not ever undertake a foreign trip afterwards. Gracious Huzur then came to DEI Quantum-Nano Centre around 8.30

pm and delivered a Vision Talk in video-conferenced mode to DEI-ICT Centre, Soami Nagar, New Delhi.

On March 11, after morning Satsang and PT, Gracious Huzur left for Delhi and the Regional Passport Office, Ghaziabad was also visited for completing the necessary formalities for issue of passport. Through Supreme Grace and Mercy of Huzur Radhasoami Dayal, Gracious Huzur and Rani Sahiba were issued passports the same day. Gracious Huzur and party returned to Dayalbagh on March 12 morning.

On March 13, invitations were received for Gracious Huzur from Prof. Stuart Hameroff, Chairman and Chief Organizer of the TSC series of conferences at University of Arizona, USA; Prof Peter Roe, University of Waterloo, Ontario, Canada as well as Kiel University, Germany. Gracious Huzur replied to all of them by email on March 14 that He holds the necessary documents (passport issued on behalf of Central Government of India) for the purpose. A small committee was constituted by Gracious Huzur to plan the foreign visit and its logistics.

On March 15, a tentative schedule was presented by the Committee for a three week tour from end-April to early-May for Approval of Gracious Huzur. Gracious Huzur issued the following order on March 16 :

March 16, 2016

ORDER

Dear Brothers and Sisters of Continents of North America (USA and Canada, spanning 3000 miles from the East Coast to the West Coast), Europe (UK and continental Europe) and Asia (from the Middle-East to the Far-East),

Satsang and Seva should be sincerely performed with the feeling of *Deenta* and one should strive to attain *Sharan* of Huzur Radhasoami Dayal as Graciously Advised by Param Guru Huzur Dr. Lal Sahab.

2. For the first three years before grant of first initiation, it is advised that one should sincerely and regularly perform Satsang and *Seva*. First initiation may be subsequently granted. The second initiation may also be granted after six years of *Sumiran* and *Dhyan*.

3. It is important to involve Satsangis of nearby areas in *Seva* and organization of Satsang activities in a feeling

of Brotherhood and Sisterhood to attain maximum benefit. The benefit accruing from such activities is a gift from the Supreme Lord, Huzur Radhasoami Dayal, and one should have full and complete Faith in *sarv samarthta* of Huzur Radhasoami Dayal.

It is with this objective that Satsang activities be planned in Continents of North America (USA and Canada, spanning 3000 miles from the East Coast to the West Coast), Europe (UK and continental Europe) and Asia (from the Middle-East to the Far-East). It is important that Satsang properties acquired or constructed through contributions of Satsangi brothers and sisters be given precedence for Satsang activities including stay arrangements during Satsang tours. Modern ICT techniques should be utilized to ensure maximum participation of Satsangi brothers and sisters in surrounding areas.

Hearty Radhasoami.

(Prem Saran Satsangi)

This order was emailed to organizers of the foreign trip spread all over the world, along with a tentative itinerary.

On March 17, visa applications were prepared by the Committee for Schengen and British visas for Gracious Huzur, Respected Rani Sahiba and accompanying tour party members and appointments were fixed in Delhi by Dr. Anoop Srivastava for the next day.

On the morning of March 18, matters came to a head and were precipitated by the evening. Gracious Huzur was to leave for Delhi to apply for Schengen and British visas, but He arrived in the morning Satsang without any luggage as is usual in Satsang tours and outstation trips, and did not get down from the Scorpio parked in the portico of Satsang Hall. He expressed annoyance with the affairs of Dayalbagh to members of the Dayalbagh administration and despite repeated pleas made by all, refused to get down from the vehicle. All Satsangis present were stunned by the Instructions that after cremation, His Holy Ashes should be interred in Pawan Smrityalaya. The morning Satsang was held in a sombre mood and Gracious Huzur remained in the Scorpio and after that, the vehicle headed to the *kothi* in Prem Nagar. Gracious Huzur kept on sitting in the Scorpio and told everyone to perform their *karni* (duty) and refused to step down despite repeated pleas by one and all. After mutual consultation, it was decided by those around that since the day's duty and schedule involved a visit to Delhi, it should be continued with. Gracious Huzur and party reached residence of Dr. Anoop Srivastava at Pandara Road, New Delhi in the morning itself, but Gracious Huzur still refused to get down and told everyone to do whatever they wanted. He was helped by members of the Holy family to come down from the vehicle, but He started withdrawing Himself internally, so much so that He had to be almost carried inside the house. A pall of gloom started to descend on those assembled outside on witnessing this scene. A few doctors were summoned and some medical equipment was arranged, but the situation continued to be critical. The evening Satsang was held in the room itself, by members of the Holy family and a few other Satsangis present. His legs, knees, hands and arms indicated that His spirit was withdrawing from the body. Matters became extremely critical in the night.

On March 19 morning, Gracious Huzur went around the residence of Dr. Anoop Srivastava all by Himself and all of a sudden, came out from the front entrance and sat in the Scorpio all alone, much to the utter bewilderment, disbelief, as well as sense of relief and joy of all Satsangis gathered outside. The doctors around requested that a visit to hospital for CT Scan was advisable. Gracious Huzur said that CT scan is done for those who had to recover. The members of the party decided that it would be best to proceed to Dayalbagh. The party reached Dayalbagh on March 19 afternoon and one and all in Dayalbagh were relieved to have the Darshan of Gracious Huzur, who walked inside the *kothi* from the Scorpio Himself, but all were fully aware of the incidents of March 18. Gracious Huzur came out soon after from the *kothi* and headed to His office, where He told the officers of Radhasoami Satsang Sabha that He was handing over all administrative powers to them. Gracious Huzur then returned to the *kothi* and asked those around why were they not heading for the crematorium. Paras 80 to 85 from Souvenir, Chapter V, referring to the Timarni events of Param Guru Huzur Sahabji Maharaj were read out, as per instructions of Gracious Huzur to read them in the same spirit as in the time of Huzur Sahabji Maharaj, and the following lines were recited several times by members of the Holy family and few others :

चादर झीनी मोहि दीनी कि न दीनी।
हे नाथ! चादर झीनी मोहि दीनी कि न दीनी।

i.e. O Lord! Have You granted to me or not this physical covering, i.e. the body, complex and subtle as it is!

The recitation continued in different pitches for some time, so high that people from the neighbouring houses assembled outside. All of a sudden, Gracious Huzur, who had been silent all along, much to the joy of those assembled inside, in a soft tone, spoke the golden word "दीनी" (Granted). A wave of joy and relief spread all around and those assembled inside the room loudly said, "Radhasoami". It was announced to the anxious Satsangis who had assembled outside the *kothi* that *Mauj* (Will of the Lord) has now changed. चादर दीनी है। (The covering has been granted!) and a wave of jubilation and exultation spread all around Dayalbagh. Gracious Huzur mentioned that the decision to stay on with us was not due to any of our prayers, but will be decided by our seven Revered Leaders. Immediately afterwards, Gracious Huzur walked out of the *kothi* and sat in the Scorpio and headed for evening Satsang to the delight of all.

On March 20 morning, after arrival in morning Satsang, He was pleased to call a few Satsangi brothers and sisters in the Satsang Hall portico. In the fields, function of Music Training School was held and field interviews were conducted in a very fast mode. In the evening, Gracious Huzur was pleased to Bless members of the Holy family and few others gathered around at the *kothi* by giving an opportunity to offer obeisances at the Holy Feet of Huzur Radhasoami Dayal.

On March 21 morning, Gracious Huzur came out of the *kothi* at 4.00 am and expressed His displeasure to those running here and there. He clearly told them that whatever is to be obtained can be obtained from the Holy Feet of Huzur Radhasoami Dayal (जो कुछ मिलना है, यहाँ है). Para 88 from Souvenir, Chapter V pertaining to Param Guru Huzur Sahabji Maharaj going around Dayalbagh, two days after arrival from Timarni and making enquiries about the identity of long-familiar buildings and mentioning "My memory has become poor" was read out in Hindi. Gracious Huzur then went to the fields near *nahar* and worked for some time. Gracious Huzur then came near DEI Ex-Students Association Canteen and got down from the Scorpio and slowly walked around various buildings and drew some lines in the sand, like Param Guru Huzur Sahabji Maharaj had sketched an 'E' at the time of foundation laying ceremony of REI Building, which is in close vicinity. At the *kothi*, Gracious Huzur mentioned that those around may dust His bedsheet, if they so desired. It is worth recalling that Param Guru Huzur Sahabji Maharaj, after resuming His physical frame near Timarni, had similarly remarked in His characteristic humorous way when His bed-sheet was being dusted, "Why do you throw all that away? It is the dust of my body". After evening Satsang, a visit to Delhi was planned for the next day to fulfil the Schengen and British visa application formalities, which could not be fulfilled during the earlier visit on March 18.

On March 22 morning, Gracious Huzur visited Delhi and fulfilled the formalities for Schengen and British visa applications for Himself and Respected Rani Sahiba. There was some mistake inadvertently committed by those around at Delhi and Gracious Huzur started withdrawing again, but they profusely apologized and Gracious Huzur was pleased to return to Dayalbagh.

March 23 was the all-important Holi day, which has been celebrated for several years as the birthday of Gracious Huzur also. The whole congregation assembled for the morning Satsang, at the usual time and waited for arrival of Gracious Huzur and the celebrations were also being telecast all over the world. Gracious Huzur arrived for the morning Satsang around 8.15 am. On the way to Satsang, He mentioned that no one should follow Him and He entered Satsang Hall by loudly saying 'Radhasoami'. After morning Satsang was over, the prayer *He Dayal Sad Kripal* was recited 2-3 times after which Gracious Huzur got up from the *singhasan* and climbed the stairs to the *Swarup* of Param Guru Huzur Dr. Lal Sahab. He then prostrated Himself before the resplendent *Swarup* of Param Guru Huzur Dr. Lal Sahab and offered His obeisances, and then all of a sudden, to the sudden disbelief of all, lay down on the *singhasan* and said 'Radhasoami' before the *swarups* of our seven Revered Leaders. The chants of 'Radhasoami' started all over in Satsang Hall and a wave of panic and fear gripped one and all. Everybody was alarmed at first and feared the worst may happen. However, the Hand of protection of Huzur Radhasoami Dayal was fully visible and guided and comforted all Satsangi brothers and sisters in this difficult time. The import of the Advice of Gracious Huzur given during frequency measurement experiments in meditation sessions in Satsang Hall on an earlier occasion, 'To avoid "interference", no person may be present behind or near Singhasan in any future experiment', became apparent and came to the rescue. This Advice was used to keep all those suggesting various measures to be undertaken in this unprecedented situation, at a safe distance. Gracious Huzur remained in this position on the *singhasan* and made no movement. His entire body lay flat without any movement, but there was a halo about His face. Nobody dared disturb Him and many hours passed in this condition, while chants of 'Radhasoami' filled the atmosphere. A miniscule section of misguided people gave up hope and thought it was only a matter of a few hours more. Paths were recited continuously by gents and ladies path parties. After twelve hours, around 8.30 pm, President Sabha mustered the courage to ask Gracious Huzur if He would like to go to the *kothi*, to which Gracious Huzur replied, "जी हाँ" (Yes indeed). A stretcher was brought and Gracious Huzur was taken on the stretcher to the waiting SNC ambulance outside. A pall of gloom descended on all Satsangis.

On March 24 morning, Gracious Huzur did not come out of the *kothi* for fields or morning Satsang. The Message of our seven Revered Leaders to Gracious Huzur on March 23 after Holi Satsang was read out in English as well as Hindi at the *kothi*. Gracious Huzur immediately rushed to the front entrance of the *kothi* and sat in the Scorpio and came to Satsang Hall, where the message reproduced below was read out three times each in English and Hindi.

"Message of Param Purush Puran Dhani Huzur Soamiji Maharaj, Param Guru Huzur Maharaj, Param Guru Maharaj Sahab, Param Guru Huzur Sarkar Sahab, Param Guru Huzur Sahabji Maharaj, Param Guru Huzur Mehtaji Maharaj and Param Guru Huzur Dr. Lal Sahab to Param Guru Huzur Prof. Satsangi Sahab on 23.3.2016 after Holi Satsang

We are now in the hundredth year of the foundation of education in Dayalbagh and are embarking on a unique period similar to the latter phase of the regime of Sir Sahabji Maharaj extending for nearly two decades, with unparalleled progress and development on all sides including the establishment of Intermediate Classes, Technical College and Leather Working School, expansion of Model Industries, Dayalbagh Dairy, Saran Ashram Hospital, Banks and League of Service. In this phase, the institutions already established continued to grow and develop as years passed. Several exhibitions were organized and speeches were delivered all over the country including Ajmer, Amritsar, Allahabad, Ambala, Bahawalpur, Benares, Bombay, Bareilly, Cawnpore, Gorakhpur, Jaipur, Lahore, Karachi, Ludhiana, Moradabad, Patna, Tirunelveli and Roorkee. The high points of the second phase were the Jubilee celebrations for the 20th year of the regime of Sahabji Maharaj, agreement with Beas Satsang, Convocation Address delivered at Agra University, All India Scout Mela organized at Dayalbagh and conferment of Knighthood on Sir Sahabji Maharaj by the British Government. This era also witnessed a host of visitors and nationalists including Viceroy of India and authors like Paul Brunton and Major Yeats-Brown. Sir Sahabji Maharaj wrote numerous articles published in the leading newspapers of the day.

At this point, it is instructive to note that the foundation of Dayalbagh and education in Dayalbagh was laid with a humble prayer by its Founder, which follows in His own golden words :

"Lord, we are totally ignorant! We have neither name, nor

fame, nor have we the finances. We are destitutes and paupers. You had ordered me to go ahead and had also said that You would be here, Pray now come to our rescue!" Huzur Sarkar Sahab appeared instantly and explained the plan of the REI building, where education in Dayalbagh started.

Sir Sahabji Maharaj also conveyed the Message of Huzur Radhasoami Dayal,

"If Radhasoami Dayal had so ordained that, like other incarnations and adepts, His stay in this world should be for a short period only, there would have been no necessity for elaborate or permanent arrangements of any kind for Him and He would have managed somehow or other to carry out His mission and receded from this plane after revealing His message and teachings to the world. But the situation happens to be quite different... (i.e.) .. to make arrangements on a permanent and extensive scale in Satsang. It may, however, be borne in mind that the aim and object of all these arrangements shall always be that the message of Radhasoami Dayal may reach the ears of all humanity with facility and that the largest number of people may have the opportunity of profiting by His teachings."

We are extremely fortunate to embark on this phase of increased development and expansion in all spheres and are poised to make rapid strides in leaps and bounds."

On returning to the *kothi*, Gracious Huzur Instructed that His cremation may be performed, while He bent on the wooden table. The path "मोहि मिला सुहाग गुरु का" recited at cremations in Dayalbagh was recited by those present followed by "तेरे चरनों में". It was announced that the first phase of the regime of Gracious Huzur comes to an end with this symbolic cremation. The path "सजनवा जाय छिपे कौनी ओर" recited during the interim periods in Dayalbagh Satsang was recited twice. Gracious Huzur then told all members of the Holy family to rush out and sit in the Scorpio and fast rounds of Dayalbagh colony were taken, symbolizing the fast-paced development and progress that has dawned on the Satsang community in the second phase. Gracious Huzur also sat in the driver's seat of the Scorpio signifying that He is Himself steering the ship of the Satsang community in this phase. During this time, a few misguided members had talked in hushed tones that Gracious Huzur had become physically weak and could not climb the stairs of the Singhasan.

On March 25, Gracious Huzur reached Satsang Hall at 2.30 am and in the pitch darkness, climbed the iron stairs of the solar panels installed on the southern side near Pawan Smrityalaya and then further moved across the iron structures supporting the panels, navigating a very precarious and dangerous climb overlooking the PT field, that not even the young would attempt, even in broad daylight. In fact, the lock at the upper end of the flight of stairs had not been opened for many years and had to be broken since nobody had climbed that high, while Gracious Huzur stood on top of flight of stairs. This gave a befitting answer to all those who had misled themselves of the powers of the Supreme Being Radhasoami Dayal, encouraging us to achieve higher and higher, in the fastest possible time. Gracious Huzur then entered the Satsang Hall from the gents side and exited from the ladies side several times, and instructed the ever-increasing congregation to run faster and faster and always stay ahead. This golden opportunity was provided to brothers, sisters and children who had come from all over the world for Holi. After repeating this flurry of activity a few times, morning Satsang was held. Gracious Huzur then called the doctors who had advised a CT Scan be conducted on Him and ordered that they will now proceed to AIIMS, New Delhi. The CT Scan was done at AIIMS and as expected, everything came out as normal as it should be. Both the to and fro trips were so fast, that by 11 a.m., Gracious Huzur was back in Dayalbagh and headed to His office. In the evening Satsang, He gave some instructions to officers of Sabha regarding conforming to the Will of Huzur Radhasoami Dayal and was pleased to take a few sips of water at the *kothi*, to the relief of all.

Since Bhandara week was going on in Dayalbagh, updesh interviews were pending. To the surprise of all, 250 updesh interviews were conducted in the fields on March 26 morning and Meeting of Radhasoami Satsang Sabha was also held in the fields.

March 27 was the day of auspicious Bhandara of Param Guru Huzur Mehtaji Maharaj. After the morning Arti, Gracious Huzur reached the fields near Tannery and instructed that path recitation may be arranged in the fields by members of all Holy families. After path recitation by Holy families was arranged impromptu, Gracious Huzur met a delegation from Soami Bagh and also expressed a desire to Sabha officers to visit Peepal Mandi in due course to offer obeisances at the Holy Samadh of Param Guru Huzur Maharaj. During the Bhandara in the afternoon, sale of Holy books was held very fast and Gracious Huzur proceeded to *katai* (harvesting in the fields) directly in the afternoon.

On March 28, after morning Satsang and PT, there were 450 updesh interviews in the fields. In the afternoon, Gracious Huzur walked from His office and went around the offices of the Radhasoami Satsang Sabha and various Societies till Model Industries Gate. He then went around the mohallas of Dayalbagh in the Scorpio and made all members of the congregation run in front, enthusing gents, ladies and children with a spirit of going faster and faster in this new phase of Grace and Mercy. This golden opportunity provided earlier to pilgrims who had come for Holi, was also availed by all Satsangi brothers, sisters and children who had come for the Bhandara. The slogan repeated several times by Gracious Huzur was, "आगे चलना है।" (We have to move ahead). He also made some Satsangi brothers sit in the front as well as hang from the sides of the Scorpio enthusing them with a new vigour. Gracious Huzur walked around Satsang Hall and Swet Nagar barefooted and then headed straight for the fields near the Rifle Range, where harvesting of *jaw* had been lagging since several days. The entire stretch of *jaw* was harvested by a large number of brothers and sisters who had gathered, while Gracious Huzur walked barefooted around the fields, round and round, several times. The office-bearers of the Radhasoami Satsang Sabha, DEI University and several others apologized for all their mistakes from time to time and also promised to mend their ways. Gracious Huzur set the target of two days for harvesting *jaw* and then proceed to harvesting of wheat.

On March 29, after morning Satsang, Gracious Huzur headed for the fields and rode in several cars belonging to field and security volunteers around the fields and encouraged Satsangi brothers and sisters to proceed ahead with harvesting work faster and faster, in the shortest possible span of time. The slogan He gave all Satsangis was, "राधास्वामी गुरु सर्व समरथ" (Radhasoami Guru is All Powerful) which was announced several times on the Public Address system also as well as from the moving vehicle by volunteers. In the afternoon, the marathon runs in Dayalbagh mohallas by gents, ladies and students of all ages were repeated. In the night, rounds of Dayalbagh colony were taken at very high speed with several brothers sitting in front of the Scorpio as well as hanging outside. Gracious Huzur ensured that nobody stayed behind.

On March 30, Gracious Huzur reached morning Satsang at 1.30 am and then proceeded to finish the harvesting of 15 acres of *jaw* as well as some wheat fields. Breakfast was served in the fields itself from the various canteens of Dayalbagh, as well as flavoured milk of Dayalbagh Dairy prepared by DEI volunteers. The Instructions from Gracious Huzur to all concerned were "एक बार जो कह दिया वह final है, उसके बाद कुछ नहीं पूछना है।" (Whatever has been said once or the first time is final, act on it and fulfil it without any ifs and buts or seeking out clarifications.) He also discouraged the habit of passing the buck by telling those managing affairs not to take names of each other (किसी और का नाम नहीं लेना है). He also mentioned that by approaching Him twice, thrice, again and again for the same matter, we diminish the blessings and benefit to be derived by half, one-third, and so on. While returning from fields, Gracious Huzur was pleased to mention that we are celebrating the birthday of Param Guru Huzur Mehtaji Maharaj while celebrating His Bhandara. He also mentioned that Bhandara of Param Guru Huzur Sarkar Sahab is also close by. He then repeated the daily schedule or *dincharya* of Param Guru Huzur Mehtaji Maharaj by going to Satsang Hall for morning Satsang followed by PT, then visiting Bhandar Ghar, fields, office and then evening Satsang. He also mentioned that turning point in His health had come by celebrating the birthday and following the *dincharya* of Param Guru Huzur Mehtaji Maharaj. A few misguided brothers used to question the *sarv samarthta* of Param Guru Huzur Mehtaji Maharaj as He required assistance for His personal hygiene and had to be carried to Satsang, without realizing that He had the power to ordain as He pleased. It was not at all difficult for Him to rejuvenate His constitution, but apparently it is not possible to understand the *Mauj* of Saints. Simulation on physical plane of some exercises pertaining to higher regions were performed in the *kothi* and Gracious Huzur was pleased to bless a few Satsangi brothers by taking their assistance for putting on new clothes after several days.

On March 31, Gracious Huzur reached morning Satsang at 1.30 am and then went to the fields and a record 64 acres of wheat were harvested. Gracious Huzur frequently went around in the Scorpio all over the fields where gents, ladies as well as students were harvesting and motivated them. Rounds were taken of Dayalbagh colony with loud announcements to encourage residents as well as pilgrims in Sadans to go to the fields and it was announced that all those who go to the fields today would attain salvation. Large number of men, women and children from the colony joined for work in the fields around 9 am. He then proceeded to the Satsang Hall and conducted a simulation of the forthcoming TSC 2016 (The Science of Consciousness) Conference Panel Discussion and referred to Prof. Stuart Hameroff and Prof. John Hagelin. The turning point in health of Gracious Huzur by following *dincharya* of Param Guru Huzur Mehtaji Maharaj for one day was announced to update the members of the Satsang congregation and they were swept with a feeling of delight. Gracious Huzur took off His *kurta* and sat in the Scorpio outside in *banian* in a scene reminiscent of the times of Param Guru Huzur Mehtaji Maharaj, while evening Satsang continued.

On April 1, massive harvesting operations were undertaken and the previous day's record was also exceeded by harvesting 70 acres in a single day. Gracious Huzur went around the fields in the Scorpio throughout the day without any rest or break. He also visited DEI Central Office and senior administrative officers escorted Him to the fields. Prof. S.S. Prabhu, IIIT Bangalore was visiting DEI for Valedictory Function of Summer School in Science for High School Students. During one of the field rounds, Gracious Huzur came to DEI Quantum-Nano Centre towards the end of the Valedictory function and met Prof. Prabhu in the driveway. He again headed for the fields and supervised harvesting operations till late in the night.

On April 2, Gracious Huzur arrived in the fields for wheat harvesting and for the third successive day, previous day's record acreage was further exceeded by finishing 74 acres in a single day. Through Supreme Grace and Mercy of Huzur Radhasoami Dayal, the long waiting times for an American visa interview appearing on website since many days suddenly reduced to a single day at 4.45 am and Dr. Anoop Srivastava scheduled the biometric appointment for April 3 evening and US embassy interview on April 4 morning for Gracious Huzur and Respected Rani Sahiba from the fields itself. Gracious Huzur and Rani Sahiba had already been issued British and Schengen visas by this time. Gracious Huzur supervised the harvesting operations by repeated rounds and still found out time to view video recording of TSC 2015 Vision Talk delivered at Helsinki in June 2015. Gracious Huzur expressed displeasure during visit to evening fields that harvesting target had not been achieved till then. He summoned various officials from Dayalbagh administration, Regional associations, DEI University and then sat down for harvesting Himself, till late in the night. He also discussed arrangements at Beas Satsang and visit by their Leader in March 2011.

On April 3, Gracious Huzur called the financial authorities of Dayalbagh to the fields and discussed how He could contribute His entire savings of Rs. 15 lakhs to Dayalbagh societies. Gracious Huzur left Dayalbagh around 1.30 pm for US Visa Offsite Facilitation Centre, Nehru Place, New Delhi and gave His fingerprints for US visa along with Respected Rani Sahiba. In the meantime, at Dayalbagh, harvesting of wheat continued without any break since the morning from Radha Bagh to Poiya Ghat till 2 am in the early hours of April 4, and harvesting of the entire wheat crop for the season was completed.

On April 4 morning, immediately after morning Satsang at Karol Bagh, Gracious Huzur reached the US Embassy at 6.35 am for appointment scheduled at 8 am. Through Supreme Grace and Mercy of

Huzur Radhasoami Dayal, all security protocols and procedures at US Embassy smoothly proceeded and US visa was approved for Gracious Huzur and Respected Rani Sahiba.

On April 4, Gracious Huzur returned to Dayalbagh around 10.45 am and took a round of the fields soon after and supervised the bundling and loading operations for the wheat crop harvested till the wee hours that day. He went to the fields again after evening Satsang and stayed there from 6 pm to 10 pm. He then returned to the fields at 2 am and stayed there till 8 am, by which time, all standing crops, including *jaw*, *chana*, *masoor* and mustard were harvested, thus concluding the harvesting season.

On April 5 morning, Gracious Huzur signed the authority letter to collect His passport from the US embassy and also signed His Canadian visa application sitting in the Scorpio in the portico of Satsang Hall. He gave a cheque of over Rs. 2 lacs to the organizers of TSC 2016 from His personal funds to cover His travel. Gracious Huzur was pleased to Bless 'Mission Radhasoami' by twice signing SSI Newsletter 'Paritantrika' which spelled out the Vision of our 'Mission Consciousness', in the golden words of Param Guru Huzur Sahabji Maharaj:

> "हमारे चले जाने के बाद सतसंग की ज्योति जो प्रज्वलित की गई है उसका प्रकाश हर जगह इस तरह से फैलाओ कि जिससे मनुष्य मात्र को तुम्हारी पवित्र सेवाओं का ज्ञान हो और जिससे तुम्हारे परम पिता की जो अपने धाम में विराजमान हैं महिमा और यश समस्त संसार में फैल जाए।"

> (English Translation)
> "May the radiance of Satsang (Meditation through "Surat-Shabda Yoga" of the Eastern Spiritual Philosophy of Saints) which has been kindled, be spread all over, after we have left, so that Mankind may know about your holy services and the magnificence and glory of our Supreme Father, resplendent in His Abode, spread all over the cosmic Universe."

On April 6 morning, news came in that German visa had been denied for some members of the DEI delegation. Gracious Huzur instructed that our contacts at Kiel University be told in no uncertain terms, that this was the final reference to them and there would be no further reference after this. At around 8 am, concerned individuals were informed over phone from Scorpio while on round of fields near Punjabi Farm that the foreign visit programme had been cancelled and Gracious Huzur will stay put in Dayalbagh. Gracious Huzur's and Rani Sahiba's passports were collected from Nehru Place, New Delhi, of course with US visas affixed on them, and brought back to Dayalbagh. A fire broke out in the Dairy compound due to suspected short circuit and a portion of the wheat crop stored there in front of the Jubilee Gate was damaged. Gracious Huzur stood there for several hours and personally supervised the cleanup operations. The concerned persons apologized to Gracious Huzur for the mishap. Gracious Huzur's passport was presented back to Him in the fields and He was pleased to remark, "आगे की करनी कीजिए ।" (Proceed to perform further duties without any delay).

On April 7 morning, Gracious Huzur came to the fields and Instructed all concerned that He had made two firm convictions (दृढ़ निश्चय). The first was that all wheat will be threshed today (the planned target of Agriculture Department was for a few days). The second was that He will not travel to Arizona. email was immediately sent to all concerned with the foreign visit organization, but it is the miracle of Huzur Radhasoami Dayal that the typist made a typographical error and sent out the email, "It is the firm conviction (*dridh nischay*) of Gracious Huzur that He will travel for the TSC 2016 Arizona conference" which is what the *Mauj* of Gracious Huzur ultimately was. Ten threshers were hired from nearby farmers as well as Satsangi brothers to supplement the five threshers of Agriculture Department and threshing work continued without interruption the whole day. Dairy farm looked like a *mela* with ladies also fully participating in supplying bundles till 6 pm and gents stayed awake the whole night operating threshers in groups of Punjab and Haryana regions as well as local Agra Branches and Dayalbagh residents. While threshing was going on in the Dairy compound, Gracious Huzur enquired repeatedly from the *kothi* about the progress. He stayed in the *kothi* and the manglacharan "परम पुरुष पूरन धनी" was recited several times with the first few lines slightly modified as "परम पुरुष पूरन धनी, प्रोफेसर प्रेम सरन सतसंगी". The lines "चेतो मेरे प्यारे तेरे भले की कहूँ, वक़्त गुरु की मान तेरे भले की कहूँ" were also recited several times. It was also discussed among those present that a king cannot pose as a commoner because regal splendour and aura cannot remain hidden. Similarly, a servant cannot pose as a king, since a servant always remains a servant in body and mind, irrespective of what he may pose, while a king always remains a king with unsurpassed dignity and majestic bearing. A servant cannot masquerade as a king and a king cannot stay disguised as a commoner for long. Gracious Huzur advised everybody to be "राधास्वामी में लीन" (engrossed and wrapped in Radhasoami) with their families. Through Supreme Grace and Mercy of Huzur Radhasoami Dayal, what appeared to be an impossible task in the morning with mountains of wheat crop lying all around, was finished in the wee hours before morning Satsang the next day and all that remained were sacks of grain and mountains of *bhoosa*.

On April 8 morning, updesh interviews in the fields were halted in between since the persons authorized to initiate were not available and one of them had gone out of station also. Gracious Huzur took a round of the Dairy compound and Dayalbagh in the Scorpio. He again took a round at around 3.30 pm and due to constant preoccupation with work and no breaks, He changed His clothes in the Scorpio itself. In the evening Satsang, Radhasoami was continuously recited by all present from 6.30 pm to 8.00 pm.

On April 9 morning, Gracious Huzur sat in the Scorpio while regular morning Satsang was going on and then came out and stood for several hours till 10.00 am, while Radhasoami was recited by everyone in Satsang Hall. He then drove back to the *kothi* while gents, ladies, students and children from the permitted zones of Punjab and Haryana also got golden opportunity, similar to that provided to Satsangis during Holi and Bhandara of Param Guru Huzur Mehtaji Maharaj in end-March, to run in front of the Scorpio in marathon style. A volunteer who had used the word रुकना (to stop) in an announcement was corrected that this word is not in the dictionary of Satsang. It was announced that portals for first initiation are wide open today and we can also be rather liberal in granting first initiation like Soami Bagh and Beas to increase numbers. Legal advisers were consulted for filing a petition in the courts that Radhasoami name is superior to Manuwaad since Radhasoami name gives access to Nirmal Chetan Desh, or highest region of Pure Spirituality while Manuwaad gives access only till Para-Brahma. We have got several witnesses over 90 years in our community who have taken initiation in the time of Param Guru Huzur Sahabji Maharaj, and have given written testimony of this fact. After evening Satsang, Gracious Huzur visited Quantum-Nano Centre and viewed a few presentations as a rehearsal for the upcoming TSC 2016 conference. He was pleased to mention that He will present a preamble in His Vision Talk at the TSC 2016 conference.

April 10 was the auspicious Bhandara day. After morning Arti, field work and Bhandara, Gracious Huzur viewed video-recording of TSC Panel Discussion. In the night, He very kindly accorded permission to Dr. Anoop Srivastava for submitting His Canadian visa application.

On April 11, instructions to prepone Zonal Satsang and Bhent were given and Prasad was given in Zonal Satsang to students under 15 years along with their parents. Hints were given about Satsang tour to Punjab and a visit to Holy Samadh of Param Guru Huzur Maharaj at Peepal Mandi. Gracious Huzur was pleased to mention that, "Huzur Radhasoami Dayal will not relinquish me and I will not relinquish Huzur Radhasoami Dayal". During the field interviews that day, He had also accepted invitation from Satsangis of Sri Lanka to visit their country and remarked that first visit outside India will be to Sri Lanka.

On April 12, invitation card for TSC pre-event rehearsal at DEI on April 15 was presented to Gracious Huzur after fields. The Monday Prasad was presented before Gracious Huzur outside His Office.

April 13 was a very significant day and also marks a turning point. Gracious Huzur got officials of Radhasoami Satsang Sabha contacted telephonically whether it was appropriate (उचित) for Him to come to Satsang. He arrived in Satsang but sat in the Sabha Members' block in the front and summoned Sabha officials in the fields and Instructed them to convene a general meeting of Satsangis using modern ICT protocols to seek their consensus. He also visited the garden of Quantum-Nano Centre and took a round of Sabha departments like Control Room, CCTV Monitoring Centre, PV Primary School, Dayalbagh Press, Netra Kendra, Nagar Panchayat, Dayal Nagar, Saran Ashram Hospital, Radha Nagar as well as DEI University. Gracious Huzur checked whether the log books and other papers were up to date at several places and also marked the attendance of volunteers and reporting staff. He remarked that in Satsang, there is evolution with sustained hard work (सख़्त मेहनत) rather than revolution, which would result in utter failure collapsing like a pack of cards. Gracious Huzur also took round of Dayalbagh colonies and mentioned that He was particularly upset that though there was no reduction in the quantum of work Param Guru Huzur Mehtaji Maharaj continued to do till the end, some misguided person had made adverse remarks about His working after Centenary Celebrations of Radhasoami Satsang in 1961. Gracious Huzur delivered a discourse in evening Satsang on the *Mauj* of Huzur Radhasoami Dayal which has already been published in Dayalbagh Herald, mentioning that it is only Divine Will which prevails on Him like a magic wand.

On April 14, Gracious Huzur delivered a discourse in evening Satsang that He has no hesitation in telling the world that He has learnt scientific techniques from the west and is now applying them to study the philosophy and meditation practices of the East in the TSC Vision Talk at the pre-event rehearsal scheduled for the next day. Western scientists should not shy away from applying their own techniques to study of eastern philosophy.

On April 15, Dr. Thubten Samphel, Director, Tibet Policy Institute, Dharamshala who was the Key Note Speaker at TSC pre-event rehearsal at DEI that day, visited the morning fields and offered his respects in Tibetan tradition by bowing and presenting a white *khata* (Tibetan ceremonial scarf) to Gracious Huzur. Gracious Huzur warmly welcomed him to Dayalbagh. Dr. Samphel kindly accepted to undergo 15-channel MEG testing at Quantum-Nano Centre, DEI while performing Buddhist meditation. Gracious Huzur delivered the Vision Talk at TSC 2016 pre-event rehearsal at Quantum-Nano Centre which left everyone spellbound and gave an indication of the nature of things to come. He also delivered remarks in the Panel Discussion on zero and infinity which have already been published in Dayalbagh Herald. He also complimented a young student presenter who had quoted Param Guru Maharaj Sahab's Bachans which brought out His forthright nature when He had rebuked members of the Central Administrative Council to remind them about the paramount authority of the Sant Satguru.

On April 16, Gracious Huzur sat in His office for a long time. He did not look at any files or papers, and instead contemplated with the photograph of Param Guru Huzur Dr. Lal Sahab in front of Him.

Sunday, April 17, was a historic day as general meeting of Satsangis was convened in modern ICT mode with all branches in the e-Satsang cascade also connected. It is important to note that Param Guru Huzur Sahabji Maharaj and Param Guru Huzur Mehtaji Maharaj had also convened such public meetings and removed numerous misgivings and doubts among Satsangis. When these meeting dispersed, all doubts of Satsangis had been removed. Before the meeting on April 17 started, Gracious Huzur signed papers which had been duly vetted by legal advisors, donating His entire personal savings of Rs. 15 lacs to Alumni Association of Dayalbagh Educational Institutions (AADEIs). After the introduction and presentations by Sabha officials, Murar declaration issued from the Holy Land of Murar in 2010 during sesquicentenary celebrations of Radhasoami Faith, calling for brotherly relations and affectionate behaviour among the followers of all sects of Radhasoami Faith was read out on the Directions of Gracious Huzur. Gracious Huzur mentioned that He had taken note of the wishes of Satsangis regarding the forthcoming world tour on 'Mission Science of Consciousness', but He will act according to the *Mauj* of Huzur Radhasoami Dayal. After the meeting, Gracious Huzur went back to the fields. From the fields, He went straight to His office and asked for files and papers to be put up. On the file regarding three proposed Satsang Tours to (i) Punjab and Haryana, (ii) Himachal Pradesh and (iii) South and East India, Gracious Huzur wrote the Instructions that they depend on the Will of Huzur Radhasoami Dayal. Before evening Satsang, Gracious Huzur went to Pawan Smrityalaya and offered obeisances to Param Purush Puran Dhani Huzur Soamiji Maharaj.

On April 18 morning, Gracious Huzur desired to proceed to Peepal Mandi to the Holy Samadh of Param Guru Huzur Maharaj immediately after morning Satsang and PT, but was told by one of the officials that there is still some time. Gracious Huzur referred to the Bachan of Param Guru Maharaj Sahab regarding the paramount authority of Sant Satguru. He then visited the Jamuna Pump House and Pump House of Sewage Treatment Plant (STP), which has been set up under an agreement with the Government that while Dayalbagh has provided land at concessional rates for the STP plant, water to the tune of 16 million litres per day (mld) will be supplied to Dayalbagh free of cost, in perpetuity. As against this, only 3 mld of water was being received as per the log book and there were technical issues also with the pumps. Some officials and workers tried to argue and present things as normal and cited a few lame excuses. They were severely rebuked and reminded of the golden words of Param Guru Maharaj Sahab regarding the paramount authority of Sant Satguru. The operators of the pump apologized and told the truth about laxity in operation and maintenance of the pumps in front of Gracious Huzur. Gracious Huzur mentioned about the economical way of living taught by Param Guru Huzur Mehtaji Maharaj and got instructions conveyed to organizers of the foreign tour that He will present at the TSC 2016 conference through video-conferencing from Dayalbagh and not travel abroad.

Gracious Huzur then went to Holy Samadh of Param Guru Huzur Maharaj at Peepal Mandi and offered His obeisances and humble bhent at the Holy Samadh which also houses various articles used by Param Guru Huzur Maharaj like bed, palanquin and *kharaun*. Gracious Huzur also briefly met Revered Prof. Agam Prasad Mathur (Dadaji Maharaj), leader of the Radhasoami Satsang at Peepal Mandi and told him that He had come as per Orders of Param Purush Puran Dhani Soamiji Maharaj. Revered Prof. Mathur garlanded Gracious Huzur. At the insistence of Revered Prof. Mathur, Gracious Huzur momentarily sat down, but got up immediately. Gracious Huzur then returned to Pawan Smrityalaya, only to find it locked. He then proceeded to the *kothi* for a brief while and without getting down from the Scorpio, told officials of Sabha and others to get ready to proceed to New Delhi. Gracious Huzur and party proceeded to the residence of Dr. Anoop Srivastava at Pandara Road, New Delhi and after a brief halt of ten minutes, returned to Dayalbagh and proceeded to Satsang. On the way back, instructions had been conveyed to screen the video-recording of Vision Talk delivered at

TSC 2016 pre-event rehearsal at DEI on April 15 and also arrange for distribution of Monday *chana* prasad in Satsang Hall, Dayalbagh. Both these activities were carried out immediately after coming to Satsang Hall from Delhi. After this afternoon Satsang, transcript of the Vision Talk delivered on April 15 was presented to Gracious Huzur by the conference organizer. Gracious Huzur corrected it in a few minutes and got it returned through email. After evening Satsang, He asked the organizer of TSC 2016 about his departure schedule for the conference abroad (गए नहीं). Gracious Huzur called Sabha officials and told them to finalize the proposed tour to Punjab and Haryana in the night.

On April 19, after morning Satsang and PT, Gracious Huzur and party left for tour of Punjab and Haryana till April 22. Detailed account of this has already been published in Dayalbagh Herald.

Soon after coming back to Dayalbagh on April 22, Gracious Huzur went to the STP pump house and expressed displeasure that no efforts had been made to increase the capacity of water being pumped, despite it being the backbone of agriculture in Dayalbagh. He remarked that Satsangis in branches outside were far more sincere, but some people in Dayalbagh had become complacent and started adopting corrupt practices. Senior officials were summoned and similar instructions were given to Sabha administration in the office too. Gracious Huzur said that He would be leaving on the foreign trip soon, but would ensure that things are set right in the meantime and the capacity increased to around 9-10 mld through proper maintenance and supervision in the ensuing days.

On April 23 morning, Gracious Huzur left for Delhi and undertook the visit to various foreign countries crossing the Pacific and Atlantic Oceans showering Grace and Mercy on *jivas* all over the world from April 24 - May 2, detailed description of which has already been published in Dayalbagh Herald.

On arrival at Dayalbagh on May 2, Gracious Huzur went to the DEI Quantum-Nano Centre within a few hours and participated in the DEI-Kiel Workshop held at Kiel University, Germany through video-conferencing. The workshop was attended by Gracious Huzur on May 3 also. Subsequently, the other two national tours proposed by Sabha officials, to Himachal Pradesh and the historic tour commemorating the hundredth year of first visit of Param Guru Huzur Sahabji Maharaj to South India in 1916, were also undertaken in May-June 2016, with the latter also including a visit to Sri Lanka flying over the Indian Ocean, fulfilling all instructions according to the Will of Huzur Radhasoami

Dayal. Detailed account of these tours has been published separately in Dayalbagh Herald.

This account will be incomplete without mentioning that when the colleague of Gracious Huzur who had withdrawn his initiation application in November-end 2015 visited DEI for an academic workshop in July 2016 soon after this twist and turn of events, Gracious Huzur was extremely kind and courteous to him. Gracious Huzur not only attended the workshop session addressed by His colleague, but also praised him. Next day, in the morning fields, Gracious Huzur very kindly asked His colleague to join Him for a bottle of flavoured milk of Dayalbagh Dairy prepared by DEI volunteers. The colleague happily sipped away and chatted for a long time unaware of the *leela* (cosmic dance) of the Supreme Lord. While lesser mortals with human failings were filled with feelings of revulsion and disgust, it is only the Supreme Lord who can manifest this extraordinary spirit of magnanimity and forgiveness in such cosmic proportions.

Infinite Blessings have been showered on all of us by offering obeisances to Param Purush Puran Dhani Soamiji Maharaj at Pawan Smrityalaya, Param Guru Huzur Maharaj at Holy Samadh at Peepal Mandi, Param Guru Maharaj Sahab at Holy Samadh at Samiabagh (Banaras) and Param Guru Huzur Sarkar Sahab at Holy Samadh at 'Radhasoami Vihar' at Murar, all within this short span of two months. We are now in the hundredth year of the foundation of education in Dayalbagh and have embarked on a unique period similar to the latter phase of the regime of the Founder of Dayalbagh, Sir Sahabji Maharaj extending for nearly two decades, with unparalleled progress and development on all sides. We are extremely fortunate to embark on this phase of increased development and expansion in all spheres and are rushing forward with rapid strides in leaps and bounds. The Master has now switched to a schedule which even the strongest of us in the pink of health cannot even remotely hope to match. The opportunities granted to Satsangis from all over the world in marathon runs with Huzur Radhasoami Dayal have put the community in overdrive and all obstacles have been removed in accelerating the progress full throttle in top gear, faster and even faster, to higher and even loftier goals, in the shortest possible span of time. In His Divine Mercy, He takes the burden of *karmas* of His sinful and erring children on His shoulders day and night and cushions them from any suffering. He is now himself in the driver's seat and the mantra for exponential growth on the trail blazing path is *karni*, keeping to the path of duty. We are all wise enough to be fully aware of our duties and responsibilities. It devolves on all of us to follow the right path and proceed faster and faster on it. The Master has now switched to a much faster *yana* or vehicle of salvation in the second phase and has blessed the coffers of the community by donating His entire personal savings of the first phase to Mission Science of Consciousness. There is no reason for any of us to hold back our own progress or that of our community. This is the time to gird up our loins and charge headlong into Satsang activities without thinking, dithering or delaying any further.

During this unique period, the pure in heart had glimpses of all the seven colours of the spectrum in a single white light (Divine Personality) - The extraordinary spirituality and saintliness of Soamiji Maharaj; Ideal *sewak* (disciple) like Huzur Maharaj; Tall and strong with boundless courage like Maharaj Sahab; Refined tastes with emphasis on *karni* (duty) like Sarkar Sahab; Regal splendour of Huzur Sahabji Maharaj; Engineer and *fakir* like Huzur Mehtaji Maharaj and Teacher perfect with compassion personified like Huzur Dr. Lal Sahab. Blessed are the pure in heart : for they shall see God. May the Supreme Father have mercy.

In the era of Huzur Sahabji Maharaj, it was said

क्या हुस्न था कि आँख ने देखा हज़ार बार।
फिर भी नज़र को हसरते दीदार रह गई ।।

(What a beauty, charm and grace it was!
The eye beheld it thousands of times!
Even so, the eyes still yearn for a glimpse of it!)

Today, in a similar era, we can say

वो हुस्न आज भी बरकरार है ।
कारवाँ–ए–सतसंग मिशन राधास्वामी को तैयार है ।।

(That majestic grandeur still continues to charm us
The caravan of Satsang is ready for 'Mission Radhasoami')